Learning With Escape Rooms in Higher Education Online Environments

Alexandra Santamaría Urbieta
Universidad Internacional de La Rioja, Spain

Elena Alcalde Peñalver
Universidad de Alcalá, Spain

IGI Global
PUBLISHER of TIMELY KNOWLEDGE

A volume in the Advances in Educational Technologies and Instructional Design (AETID) Book Series

Published in the United States of America by
IGI Global
Information Science Reference (an imprint of IGI Global)
701 E. Chocolate Avenue
Hershey PA, USA 17033
Tel: 717-533-8845
Fax: 717-533-8661
E-mail: cust@igi-global.com
Web site: http://www.igi-global.com

Library of Congress Cataloging-in-Publication Data

Names: Santamaría Urbieta, Alexandra, 1985- editor. | Alcalde Penalver, Elena, 1988- editor.
Title: Learning with escape rooms in higher education online environments / Alexandra Santamaría Urbiet and Elena Alcalde Peñalver, Editor.
Description: Hershey, PA : Information Science Reference, [2023] | Includes bibliographical references and index. | Summary: "Today's students are digital natives (Prensky, 2001) and require new and innovative methodologies. Gisbert & Esteve (2011) describe this generation as having a marked digital literacy and a constant need to be connected. Moreover, they stand out for having grown up with technology, feeling comfortable with multi-tasking, relying on graphics for communication, as well as thriving on instant gratifications and rewards (Akçayır, Dündar, & Akçayır, 2016). Consequently, teachers or "digital immigrants", as Prensky (2001: 1) refers to those educators who "were not born into the digital world" but have adopted and use many of the aspects of new technology, need to offer state-of-the-art approaches that catch their attention and relate to their every-day lives. Gamification is one of these emerging trends that shows no signs of stopping (Kapp, 2012) and, although mainly used in business contexts, "the penetration of the gamification trend in educational settings seems to be still climbing up to the top" (Dicheva et al., 2016: 2). Teachers, professors and educational professionals, in general, have the opportunity of creating new, challenging, significant, and interactive learning experiences for today's students. Boredom, lack of attention and loss of interest contribute "usually adversely towards student engagement, learning and overall performance across a diverse range of settings including universities" (Sharp et al., 2017: 2). An escape room is a real-life team-based puzzle game where people are locked in a room and solve puzzles together to get out (Chen, 2015). Some common elements of this game are that it is team-based, has a clear objective, and is themed under a story. As stated by York and William (2018) in the case of other learning games, some benefits of the escape room applied to a classroom are that it provides learners with shared-goal orientation because, instead of making players compete, it reduces their cognitive load and promotes interaction in a social and collaborative learning environment. Moreover, it is a social experience that provides students with meaningful interaction. This publication will present a list of escape rooms for higher education, covering different topics and fields, and suggested online environments. Considering the difficulty of teachers bringing innovative methodologies to online education, this book will present a list of different escape rooms so that other teachers around the world can replicate them"-- Provided by publisher.
Identifiers: LCCN 2022039886 (print) | LCCN 2022039887 (ebook) | ISBN 9781668460818 (hardcover) | ISBN 9781668460856 (paperback) | ISBN 9781668460825 (ebook)
Subjects: LCSH: Education, Higher--Computer-assisted instruction. | Escape room games. | Group work in education. | Teaching--Aids and devices.
Classification: LCC LB2395.7 .L45 2023 (print) | LCC LB2395.7 (ebook) | DDC 378.1/7344678--dc23/eng/20220902
LC record available at https://lccn.loc.gov/2022039886
LC ebook record available at https://lccn.loc.gov/2022039887

This book is published in the IGI Global book series Advances in Educational Technologies and Instructional Design (AETID) (ISSN: 2326-8905; eISSN: 2326-8913)

British Cataloguing in Publication Data
A Cataloguing in Publication record for this book is available from the British Library.

For electronic access to this publication, please contact: eresources@igi-global.com.

Advances in Educational Technologies and Instructional Design (AETID) Book Series

Lawrence A. Tomei
Robert Morris University, USA

ISSN:2326-8905
EISSN:2326-8913

Mission

Education has undergone, and continues to undergo, immense changes in the way it is enacted and distributed to both child and adult learners. In modern education, the traditional classroom learning experience has evolved to include technological resources and to provide online classroom opportunities to students of all ages regardless of their geographical locations. From distance education, Massive-Open-Online-Courses (MOOCs), and electronic tablets in the classroom, technology is now an integral part of learning and is also affecting the way educators communicate information to students.

The **Advances in Educational Technologies & Instructional Design (AETID) Book Series** explores new research and theories for facilitating learning and improving educational performance utilizing technological processes and resources. The series examines technologies that can be integrated into K-12 classrooms to improve skills and learning abilities in all subjects including STEM education and language learning. Additionally, it studies the emergence of fully online classrooms for young and adult learners alike, and the communication and accountability challenges that can arise. Trending topics that are covered include adaptive learning, game-based learning, virtual school environments, and social media effects. School administrators, educators, academicians, researchers, and students will find this series to be an excellent resource for the effective design and implementation of learning technologies in their classes.

Coverage

- Game-Based Learning
- Web 2.0 and Education
- Instructional Design Models
- Curriculum Development
- Virtual School Environments
- Educational Telecommunications
- E-Learning
- Digital Divide in Education
- Higher Education Technologies
- Social Media Effects on Education

IGI Global is currently accepting manuscripts for publication within this series. To submit a proposal for a volume in this series, please contact our Acquisition Editors at Acquisitions@igi-global.com or visit: http://www.igi-global.com/publish/.

The Advances in Educational Technologies and Instructional Design (AETID) Book Series (ISSN 2326-8905) is published by IGI Global, 701 E. Chocolate Avenue, Hershey, PA 17033-1240, USA, www.igi-global.com. This series is composed of titles available for purchase individually; each title is edited to be contextually exclusive from any other title within the series. For pricing and ordering information please visit http://www.igi-global.com/book-series/advances-educational-technologies-instructional-design/73678. Postmaster: Send all address changes to above address.

Titles in this Series

For a list of additional titles in this series, please visit: www.igi-global.com/book-series/advances-educational-technologies-instructional-design/73678

Handbook of Research on Facilitating Collaborative Learning Through Digital Content and Learning Technologies
Jared Keengwe (University of North Dakota, USA)
Information Science Reference • © 2023 • 495pp • H/C (ISBN: 9781668457092) • US $270.00

Handbook of Research on Advancing Teaching and Teacher Education in the Context of a Virtual Age
Aaron Samuel Zimmerman (Texas Tech University, USA)
Information Science Reference • © 2023 • 412pp • H/C (ISBN: 9781668484074) • US $270.00

Handbook of Research on Interdisciplinary Preparation for Equitable Special Education
Dena D. Slanda (University of Central Florida, USA) and Lindsey Pike (University of Central Florida, USA)
Information Science Reference • © 2023 • 657pp • H/C (ISBN: 9781668464380) • US $270.00

Shaping the Future of Online Learning Education in the Metaverse
Gürhan Durak (Balıkesir University, Turkey) and Serkan Cankaya (Izmir Democracy University, Turkey)
Information Science Reference • © 2023 • 350pp • H/C (ISBN: 9781668465134) • US $215.00

Digitalization, New Media, and Education for Sustainable Development
Lars Keller (University of Innsbruck, Austria) Gerd Michelsen (Leuphana University, Germany) Martin Dür (University of Innsbruck, Austria) Syamsul Bachri (Universitas Negeri Malang, Indonesia) and Michaela Zint (University of Michigan, USA)
Information Science Reference • © 2023 • 335pp • H/C (ISBN: 9781799850335) • US $225.00

Assessment Methods and Success Factors for Digital Education and New Media
Francisco Vicente Cipolla Ficarra (Latin Association of Human-Computer Interaction, Spain & International Association of Interactive Communication, Italy)
Information Science Reference • © 2023 • 411pp • H/C (ISBN: 9781799887218) • US $215.00

Shaping Online Spaces Through Online Humanities Curricula
Julie Tatlock (Mount Mary University, USA)
Information Science Reference • © 2023 • 290pp • H/C (ISBN: 9781668440551) • US $215.00

Cases on Effective Universal Design for Learning Implementation Across Schools
Frederic Fovet (Royal Roads University, Canada)
Information Science Reference • © 2023 • 300pp • H/C (ISBN: 9781668447505) • US $215.00

IGI Global
PUBLISHER of TIMELY KNOWLEDGE

701 East Chocolate Avenue, Hershey, PA 17033, USA
Tel: 717-533-8845 x100 • Fax: 717-533-8661
E-Mail: cust@igi-global.com • www.igi-global.com

Editorial Advisory Board

Table of Contents

Detailed Table of Contents

This chapter provides a detailed presentation of a virtual escape room implemented in the teaching and learning of psychodiagnostics and displays the students and lecturers' first experiences with its use. The activity was offered to 500 students of a compulsory first-year course of an MSc in General Health Psychology program. Ninety-four students entered the escape room, and 39 students completed the activity. All students reported that they enjoyed the escape room, and half of them reported learning and extending their knowledge as the main reason for carrying out the activity. Importantly, the activity increased the students' self-confidence towards the diagnosis establishment. The lecturers described the activity as a useful tool for enhancing the teaching and learning process in an innovative, intuitive, and motivating way. Thus, this virtual escape room seems to be a feasible and useful tool for lecturers that look for ways to enrich their teaching practice and to achieve a deep learning of the diagnostic procedures for their students.

The general objective of this research is to analyze the perception that undergraduate and graduate students have about the use of escape rooms in the subjects of Economic History and International Economic Environment taught in a degree and a post-degree at two online universities. As specific objectives, this study evaluates, on the one hand, the degree of dynamism, commitment, and involvement of students in the virtual classroom because of the use of escape rooms and, on the other, the impact on their academic performance. This work applies the experimental method from two randomly generated samples in each of the two subjects considered for this analysis. The data to carry out this analysis will be obtained from an ad hoc questionnaire to collect, among other aspects, the perceptions about the impact of the experience. The information generated will be treated with non-parametric inference tools.

The development of research competence in teacher training is essential to improve educational quality. For this reason, it is necessary that educational processes proposed at university adapt to current demands, incorporating gamification procedures and new technologies as teaching-learning tools. The objective of this chapter was to analyze the application of an educational escape room for the development of research competence in students of the Primary Education Degree. The results of this study showed that the application of the virtual escape room allowed the development of positive attitudes towards research, as well as the strengthening of some of skills and concepts acquired. In the same way, the importance of the university professor as a guide and counselor of educational processes planned in the Primary Education Degree was highlighted. The use of the virtual escape room emerges as a mechanism for the research competence development in higher education.

In recent years, there has been a dramatic rise of the use of escape rooms in education. It is a creative form of a gamified learning experience that proves to be effective especially in higher education and online learning environments. This research describes a breakout learning experience, framed in an online master's degree of educational innovation for professional educators. It was designed as a final review of the main theoretical concepts from the course, fostering students' self-assessment. In addition, this experience would pose an example of an active methodology activity that may serve as an inspiration for the students' own teaching practice, presenting them with a student-centered strategy that can provide an innovative dynamic in their classes.

Educational innovation methods are of vital importance for the competency-based learning process. This escape room has been designed for a quantitative subject in social science degrees taught at an online university. Quantitative subjects, such as statistics, present for these students certain difficulties due to their great theoretical-practical load. The design of the escape room uses a popular legend as the basis of the storytelling, structured in a video presentation and four missions. Each mission is related to a unit of the syllabus and has been developed according to continuous evaluation and as a revision element for the exam. The introduction of this resource has shown very positive results, increasing the success rate of students, with a very high net promoter index and very positive individualized comments from students.

This experience arises intending to increase the motivation of university students to contribute to devote more attention, time, and effort to the learning situations they experience. From this idea, the implementation of active methodologies aims to give students a leading role, providing them with new experiences that favour the understanding and consolidation of content and the development of skills and competencies in search of valuable and situated learning. Within these methodologies, the authors highlight some that resort to playful elements to improve the commitment to the different learning processes. This chapter presents perceptions and assessments of students after participating in a project to develop digital competencies based on gamification and having as the main element a hybrid escape room, with live and digital proposals set in the successful Spanish TV series "La Casa de Papel."

This chapter examines three educational escape rooms applied in engineering courses in the specific area of computer networks. This analysis includes background, design decisions, implementation details, and obtained results. The objective is to provide a quick overview of ideas for teachers who want to initiate the field. Preliminary results seem promising in terms of student engagement and motivation, which is particularly relevant in online environments. The current literature indicates a trend about educational escape rooms during the last years, which will likely increase, while future research should focus on tools and resources to implement them and collaboration among professors to perform extensive evaluations in terms of learning outcomes.

Educational escape rooms (EERs) engage learners, develop their collaboration skills, and help them apply content knowledge. While the health professions were quick to identify how EERs could be used to support their unique learning outcomes, basic science disciplines such as biology, chemistry, and physics have been slower to do so. This chapter is a step-by-step guide to help undergraduate science educators design EERs based on the tools that researchers use in their work (for example, models, datasets, 3D objects). Because many of these tools are freely accessible online, they lend themselves to be used in online EERs. The process described in this chapter is designed to be easy to implement. The online science EERs developed using these steps will immerse learners in role play as they use the tools of scientists in authentic ways.

Online higher education is in demand, so much so that even face-to-face higher education is applying digital technologies to achieve greater motivation in the classroom. However, this does not mean that online education has everything won; it must continue to innovate in its methodologies to motivate students. The authors offer a proposal for the implementation of an educational escape room as a way to achieve greater motivation in the learning process through a playful experience. Although its use in educational contexts is increasingly common, until now it has not been applied in areas related to the study of consumer behavior. Thus, an explorative, innovative, and didactic escape room is provided based on consumer behavior subject. Several learning activities are employed, and guidelines for assessing and measuring learning are proposed. It is expected that this chapter will serve as a basis for those professionals interested in applying this methodology.

International education has been and continues to be a significant contributor to most developed economies despite COVID-19 preventing student mobility and severely impacting the way curricula were taught. Innovations in international recruitment and curricula were essential to ensure students had a legitimate taste of university life and to engage in internationalization activities. In this chapter, the authors present an escape room based on the United Nations Sustainable Development Goals, which were used for both academic sessions and as part of the business management undergraduate curriculum as an internationalization at home activity. The authors provide a guide of how to develop the escape room online and present tips for best practice.

This chapter explores the theoretical underpinnings, advantages, and potential limitations of employing a game-informed educational escape room in an online learning environment. Drawing on the wealth of literature published thus far on the virtues of such active methodologies for second language learning pedagogical contexts, the author explores its viability for a transnational education context. A Sino-British transnational education partnership was chosen as the didactic setting in which the proposal is grounded with a specific focus on a preparatory ESAP pre-sessional course prior to the commencement of the cohort's final and postgraduate year at the partner institution. The details of the learning design have been provided together with a final critical discussion that aims to inspire like-minded teaching practitioners to adapt and reflect on what has been written and experiment in their own classrooms.

Preface

Learning With Escape Rooms in Higher Education Online Environments is a must-read book on higher education in the twenty-first century, in a world where technological innovations and the consequences of the COVID-19 pandemic have severely affected class dynamics and that of the processes of teaching and learning.

This volume is a compilation of contributions meant to explore the perfect tandem created between Information and Communication Technologies, gamification, and education. Digital gamification or based-education information and communication technologies and by extension digital escape rooms are here presented as an important breakthrough to solve quandaries in education such as demotivation, poor results, and high attrition rates.

One of the difficulties that a teacher finds in the classroom is to keep the attention and curiosity of the students for the subject. Considering that the students of today resemble less and less those of the past decades, innovation in educational approaches and methodologies, such as experiential learning, are gaining ground progressively to the more traditional ones. Escape rooms have been enjoying success lately in all educational levels, mostly because these are based on the development of mental abilities to solve enigmas and problems so that students put creativity and critical thinking into play. These games originally come from adventure games and the Real Escape Game created in Japan in 2007. Later, escape room experiences spread very quickly and in 2015 these were already known throughout the world.

Many educators are already working on its implementation in the classroom with very remarkable benefits for both students and teachers. From an early age, children learn by playing naturally, so introducing the game in the classroom increases children's willingness to learn and makes them to be actively involved in the process. Usually, teachers find difficult to dive in, partly because of the great array of alternatives that exist nowadays. In order not to get lost in these endless possibilities, the ultimate goal of all these teaching experiences must be taken into account: an improvement of students' learning process. Besides, educators are expected to develop a series of skills when committed to bring escape rooms to the classroom (physical or virtual), such as a digital competence, an appropriate organizational capacity, a good resource management, and a great dose of imagination and creativity, since it is essential to design the game with a well-defined orientation towards students' acquisition and consolidation of theoretical and practical contents.

The main purpose of an educational escape room is the creation of a didactic situation in which a group of learners will be given a certain time to solve an enigma or problem through a set of clues related to the contents of a particular course. In this way, a series of cognitive mechanisms are activated that enhance the abilities of the players. The game has a story or narrative, which has to do with how the escape room is contextualised. The objective is to exit the room and for this the players must use their intellectual, creative, and deductive reasoning capacities. As the reader will see in the chapters that conform this volume, educational escape rooms can also be implemented virtually which helps to bridge the gap between traditional methodologies and the emergence and establishment of new technologies in the daily work of educators in the classroom.

One of the first advantages of gamification in general and of escape rooms in particular is that it helps to break the often-heavy daily routine in the classroom. When educators fall into predictable lesson structure and contents, not only do the students get uninterested but so do the teachers, even though educators are aware of the importance of active methodologies. Thus, combining an escape room with other educational techniques and tools can be a very rewarding and successful strategy for educators because students acquire or develop the ability to improve their reflective process in the situation to be resolved. Besides, students have to bring into play their personal communication skills and their ability to work in a team, being the latter very remarkable in that students can discover new facets of their classmates. And finally, students will become more motivated towards the learning process. In this sense, this volume aims to show that using this tool to learn in some areas generates an increase in the motivation of students of all educational levels in their learning process. The game stimulates students, since by agreeing to the rules of the game and by scaling levels after solving each challenge, they are rewarded accordingly. For these reasons, escape rooms are a quite flexible tool that can be implemented in large and smaller groups of students as well as in a presence-based or virtual classroom.

Learning With Escape Room in Higher Education Online Environments is formed by 14 chapters written by experts in this type of gamified experiences implemented in graduate and postgraduate courses from different parts of the world: the University of Alcalá (Spain), the Anglia Ruskin University (United Kingdom), the University of British Columbia (Canada), the University of Castilla–La Mancha (Spain), the Coventry University London (United Kingdom), the University of Dundee (United Kingdom) and the Universidad Internacional de La Rioja (Spain). These chapters study the application and impact of this type of gamified activities in the fields of Business, Economics, Education, Engineering, Natural Sciences, Physical Activity, Psychology and Statistics enforce the findings of research on the effectiveness of educational rooms.

Chapter 1 provides a detailed presentation of a virtual escape room implemented in the teaching and learning of Psychodiagnostics and displays the students and lecturers' first experiences with its use. The activity was offered to 500 students of a compulsory first-year course of an MSc in General Health Psychology program. Ninety-four students entered the escape room, and thirty-nine students completed the activity. All students reported that they enjoyed the escape room, and half of them reported learning and extending their knowledge as the main reason for carrying out the activity. Importantly, the activity increased the students' self-confidence towards the diagnosis establishment. The lecturers described the activity as a useful tool for enhancing the teaching and learning process in an innovative, intuitive, and motivating way. Thus, this virtual escape room seems to be a feasible and useful tool for lecturers that look for ways to enrich their teaching practice and to achieve a deep learning of the diagnostic procedures for their students.

The general objective of Chapter 2's research is to analyze the perception that undergraduate and graduate students have about the use of escape rooms in the subjects of Economic History and International Economic Environment, taught in a degree and a post-degree at two online universities. As specific objectives, this study evaluates, on the one hand, the degree of dynamism, commitment, and involvement of students in the virtual classroom because of the use of escape rooms and, on the other, the impact on their academic performance. This work applies the experimental method from two randomly generated samples in each of the two subjects considered for this analysis. The data to carry out this analysis will be obtained from an ad hoc questionnaire to collect, among other aspects, the perceptions about the impact of the experience. The information generated will be treated with non-parametric inference tools.

Students often show negative attitudes and emotions towards the study of science. It is important to design learning situations that achieve positive emotions among students, since it has been shown that these favour the learning process. The aim of the study in Chapter 3 was to implement a virtual escape room in the subject of Knowledge of Natural Sciences in the Degree of Primary Education at the Universidad Internacional de La Rioja (UNIR), in an entirely online environment, and to analyse the self-perceived emotions of the students and the degree of satisfaction with the learning experience. The results show that the experience has a positive impact on learning, the emotions experienced and the satisfaction of the students. It is concluded that virtual escape rooms are presented as a way of approaching learning through different creative challenges, which allow for the creation of a positive emotional environment in which the teaching and learning process is more attractive.

For a society in progress and constant development is essential and faced with the changes experienced in society (pandemics, wars) as well as in education (lack of motivation of students, increase in dropouts and poor results in studies) the educational system suggests the need for change, proposing the use of more innovative and active methodologies that give the student a leading role and make them the protagonists of the teaching-learning process. Chapter 4 presents an activity with escape room developed with students of the Master's Degree in Special Education that aims to facilitate the learning of practical cases on the subject of Developmental Disorders.

The objective of Chapter 5 is to present an innovative escape room proposal designed and implemented in the subject of Teaching innovation and initiation to educational research of the Master's Degree in Secondary Teacher Training at the Universidad Internacional de la Rioja (UNIR) in Spain with a double final: work on the skills covered in the subject and learn innovation by innovating. On the one hand, the escape room project will present the academic context and the proposal structure (narrative, content worked on, missions and rewards, ICT tools used). On the other hand, an analysis of the impact that this experience has had on the motivation and satisfaction of the students will be carried out and on their improvement in the acquisition of the skills taught in the subject. The instrument used to carry out this analysis will be a questionnaire. The results show an improvement in student motivation with the escape room application in the classroom.

The development of research competence in teacher training is essential to improve educational quality. For this reason, it is necessary that educational processes proposed at university adapt to current demands, incorporating gamification procedures and new technologies as teaching-learning tools. The objective of Chapter 6 was to analyze the application of an educational escape room for the development of research competence in students of the Primary Education Degree. The results of this study showed that the application of the virtual escape room allowed the development of positive attitudes towards research, as well as the strengthening of some of skills and concepts acquired. In the same way, the importance of the university professor as a guide and counselor of educational processes planned in Primary Education Degree was highlighted. The use of the virtual escape room emerges as a mechanism for the research competence development in higher education.

In recent years, there has been a dramatic rise of the use of escape rooms in education. It is a creative form of a gamified learning experience, which proves to be effective especially in higher education and online learning environments. The Chapter 7 research describes a breakout learning experience, framed in an online Master's degree of Educational Innovation for professional educators. It was designed as a final review of the main theoretical concepts from the course, fostering students' self-assessment. In addition, this experience would pose an example of an active methodology activity that may serve as an inspiration for the students' own teaching practice, presenting them with a student-centered strategy that can provide an innovative dynamic in their classes.

Chapter 8 focuses on educational innovation methods are of vital importance for the competency-based learning process. This escape room has been designed for a quantitative subject in social science degrees taught at an online university. Quantitative subjects, such as statistics, present for these students certain difficulties due to their great theoretical-practical load. The design of the escape room uses a popular legend as the basis of the storytelling, structured in a video presentation and four missions. Each mission is related to a unit of the syllabus and has been developed according to continuous evaluation and as a revision element for the exam. The introduction of this resource has shown very positive results, increasing the success rate of students, with a very high net promoter index and very positive individualized comments from students.

This experience arises intending to increase the motivation of university students to contribute to devote more attention, time and effort to the learning situations they experience. From this idea, the implementation of active methodologies aims to give students a leading role, providing them with new experiences that favour the understanding and consolidation of content and the development of skills and competencies in search of valuable and situated learning. Within these methodologies, we highlight some that resort to playful elements to improve the commitment to the different learning processes. Chapter 9 presents perceptions and assessments of students after participating in a project to develop digital competencies based on gamification and having as the main element a hybrid escape room, with live and digital proposals set in the successful Spanish TV series "La Casa de Papel".

Chapter 10 examines three educational escape rooms applied in engineering courses in the specific area of computer networks. This analysis includes background, design decisions, implementation details and obtained results. The objective is to provide a quick overview of ideas for teachers that want to initiate in the field. Preliminary results seem promising in terms of student engagement and motivation, which is particularly relevant in online environments. The current literature indicates a trend about educational escape rooms during the last years, which will likely increase, while future research should focus on tools and resources to implement them, and collaboration among professors to perform extensive evaluations in terms of learning outcomes.

Educational escape rooms (EERs) engage learners, develop their collaboration skills, and helps them apply content knowledge. While the health professions were quick to identify how EERs could be used to support their unique learning outcomes, basic science disciplines such as biology, chemistry, physics, and mathematics have been slower to do so. Chapter 11 is a step-by-step guide to help undergraduate science educators design EERs based on the tools that researchers use in their work (for example, models, datasets, 3D objects). Because many these tools are freely accessible online, they lend themselves to be used in online EERs. The process described in this chapter is designed to be easy to implement. The online science EERs developed using these steps will immerse learners in role play as they use the tools of scientists in authentic ways.

Online higher education is in demand, so much so that even face-to-face higher education is applying digital technologies to achieve greater motivation in the classroom. However, this does not mean that online education has everything won, but it must continue to innovate in its methodologies to motivate students. The authors offer a proposal for the implementation of an educational escape room as a way to achieve greater motivation in the learning process through a playful experience. Although its use in educational contexts is increasingly common, until now it has not been applied in areas related to the study of consumer behavior. Thus, an explorative, innovative and didactic escape room is provided based on consumer behavior subject. Several learning activities are employed, and guidelines for assessing and measuring learning are proposed. It is expected that Chapter 12 will serve as a basis for those professionals interested in applying this methodology.

International education has been and continues to be a significant contributor to most developed economies despite COVID-19 preventing student mobility and severely impacting the way curricula were taught. Innovations in international recruitment and curricula were essential to ensure students had a legitimate taster of university life and to engage in internationalization activities. In Chapter 13, the authors present an escape room based on the United Nations Sustainable Development Goals which was used for both academic taster sessions and as part of the Business Management Undergraduate curriculum as an internationalization at home activity. The authors provide a guide of how to develop the escape room online and present tips for best practice.

Chapter 14 explores the theoretical underpinnings, advantages, and potential limitations of employing a game-informed educational escape room in an online learning environment. Drawing on the wealth of literature published thus far on the virtues of such active methodologies for second language learning pedagogical contexts, the author explores its viability for a transnational education context. A Sino-British transnational education partnership was chosen as the didactic setting in which the proposal is grounded with a specific focus on a preparatory ESAP pre-sessional course prior to the commencement of the cohort's final and postgraduate year at the partner institution. The details of the learning design have been provided together with a final critical discussion which aims to inspire like-minded teaching practitioners to adapt and reflect on what has been written, and experiment in their own classrooms.

Verónica Membrive
Universidad de Almeira, Spain

Madalina Armie
Universidad de Almeira, Spain

Verónica Membrive *studied English and earned a Master's Degree in English Studies in 2011. She completed her Ph.D. at the University of Almería (2017) on Irish travel writers in Spain during the twentieth-century. She has delivered papers on Walter Starkie, Kate O'Brien and Pearse Hutchison and their travels in Spain. She is currently teaching English at the University of Almería. Her field of research is Irish Literature, with a special focus on the relationships between Ireland and Spain. She has been awarded the International George Campbell Award for her research on Hiberno-Spanish cultural relations (University of Málaga, 2018).*

Madalina Armie *earned a Master's Degree in English language and literature (2014) from the University of Almería. She completed her PhD on the contemporary Irish short story at the turn of the twenty-first century at the University of Almería (2019), for which she obtained the EIDUAL Dissertation Award 2019 for Best Doctoral Dissertation (2021) and the honorary second prize for the Best Doctoral Dissertation in Studies for Equality and the Fight against Gender Violence of the University of Almeria (2022). Her current areas of research include the contemporary Irish short story and Irish women's writing. She has published articles and reviews in international journals, such as Irish Studies Review, Estudios Irlandeses, Review of Irish*

Studies in Europe (RISE) and Studi Irlandesi. Armie is the author of the monograph The Irish Short Story at the Turn of the Twenty-first Century: Tradition, Society and Modernity and one of the editors of Trauma, Memory and Silence of the Irish Woman in Contemporary Literature Wounds of the Body and the Soul published both by Routledge. She is currently teaching at the University of Almeria, Spain.

Chapter 1
The Use of an Online Escape Room in Psychodiagnostics:
An Exploratory Project With Postgraduate Psychology Students

Eleni Petkari
https://orcid.org/0000-0002-9261-6253
Universidad Internacional de La Rioja, Spain

Ana Calvo
Department of Personality, Assesment, and Clinical Psychology, School of Psychology, Universidad Complutense de Madrid, Spain

ABSTRACT

This chapter provides a detailed presentation of a virtual escape room implemented in the teaching and learning of psychodiagnostics and displays the students and lecturers' first experiences with its use. The activity was offered to 500 students of a compulsory first-year course of an MSc in General Health Psychology program. Ninety-four students entered the escape room, and 39 students completed the activity. All students reported that they enjoyed the escape room, and half of them reported learning and extending their knowledge as the main reason for carrying out the activity. Importantly, the activity increased the students' self-confidence towards the diagnosis establishment. The lecturers described the activity as a useful tool for enhancing the teaching and learning process in an innovative, intuitive, and motivating way. Thus, this virtual escape room seems to be a feasible and useful tool for lecturers that look for ways to enrich their teaching practice and to achieve a deep learning of the diagnostic procedures for their students.

INTRODUCTION

One of the most essential components of the curriculum of postgraduate psychology programs is the teaching and learning of diagnostic procedures. Students face the challenge of understanding the theory

DOI: 10.4018/978-1-6684-6081-8.ch001

and prospective application of available manualized guides, which are quite complex and heavy in content. This chapter aims to describe the application of a virtual escape room in the teaching and learning of psychodiagnostics as an attempt to address this challenge. A step-by-step guide is provided on how to implement this novel approach in a virtual environment. After offering detailed explanations of its components and their connection to learning outcomes, the chapter presents a preliminary examination of the escape room application by analyzing students' and lecturers' experiences and aims to explore its feasibility and applicability in the context of a postgraduate psychology program.

BACKGROUND

The Educational Context of Teaching Psychodiagnostics

Clinical and health practice in psychology involves the process of evaluating the patients' clinical manifestations, and depending on the professionals' competencies, establishing diagnoses (Sánchez et al., 2017). The so-called psychodiagnostic process is a core feature of the curriculum of postgraduate programs in clinical and general health psychology around the globe and aims at linking theory to the clinical practice of future mental health professionals. The diagnosis establishment is primarily based on the Diagnostic and Statistical Manual of Mental Disorders (DSM-5; APA, 2013), which is a globally used handbook that includes criteria for determining the presence of most mental disorders. Though it has been criticized for not being able to fully represent the patient's experience, it is suggested that the DSM-5 boosts a critical evaluation of the symptoms' manifestation (Fluyau, 2018). Although it is an advantageous tool, this manual is dense and full of long lists and complex terminology, making the teaching and learning process tedious for mental health trainees, who typically skim through the pages superficially (Jibson & Seyfried, 2017). Additionally, since the DSM-5 defines diagnoses through a list of descriptive symptoms in diagnostic categories (Berrios, 2012), one criticism is that the subjective experience of the patients is missing in the diagnostic process (Etxeandia-Prandera et al., 2021). Thus, students usually only reach a shallow level of learning through memorizing the manual's content, overlooking the patient's perspective, and remaining far from achieving practice-based and meaningful learning. In fact, the APA panel on the DSM-5 celebrated on May 18-22, 2013, recommended the promotion of a holistic view of the person, together with diagnosis, to make its instruction more meaningful for future mental health professionals (Summers & Kreider, 2014). Therefore, there is a clear need for creating a path that mitigates the complexity of diagnostics and accounts for the distance between theory and practice, aiming at deep learning of the diagnostic procedures and psychopathology (Anderson & Krathwohl, 2001).

Innovative Methods for Teaching Psychodiagnostics

Following the proposal of the Lancet commission on the education of health professionals (Frenk et al., 2010), academic institutions should take advantage of new technologies for developing professional competencies, instead of adhering to traditional instruction methods that are based on pure information transmission. According to Frenk et al. "more than ever, these institutions have the duty of teaching students how to think creatively to master large flows of information in the search for solutions" (2010, p. 1951). Thus, incorporating diagnosis and psychopathology assessment into the curriculum in an interactive and novel way seems to be the way forward (Kupfer, 2014).

For instance, the technique of having students match case study scenarios with DSM criteria was previously used as a means of going beyond the passive learning mode and getting students actively involved in the learning process (First et al., 2019). The implementation of film-based projects depicting case studies has also shown to improve attitudes towards the learning of complex content (Wedding & Niemec, 2014). Also, evidence from neuropsychological studies proposes that as movies combine image and sound stimuli, they promote deep learning through the establishment of key neural channels (Darbyshire & Baker, 2012). Another innovative method includes the use of puzzles, crosswords, and word search to teach psychopathology in a playful and innovative way (Souza et al., 2021). These authors suggest that such tools allow for a relaxed learning process through creative failure, where the students have the opportunity to learn through their incorrect answers. Overall, the ludic component of such educational practices seems to create a positive environment and increase students' motivation (Monteiro et al., 2020). Leisure activities take part of everyday life, thus using playful materials seems to instigate a natural process of learning (Daltro & Bueno, 2010).

Escape Rooms as an Innovative Teaching Method

The gamification of the teaching and learning process is widely implemented across educational settings, aiming at increasing the students' motivation and achieving substantial learning (Kalogiannakis et al., 2021). A type of game commonly used is the "escape room" (Wiemker, 2015), a typically "live-action team-based game", where participants are required to solve a series of puzzles, quizzes, or riddles, to manage "escaping" a room, finding a murderer, or combating a virus. The educational model of escape rooms, in contrast to the purely leisure-oriented escape rooms, has well-defined learning goals and is designed for a specific target group of students or trainees (Veldkamp et al., 2020). This game-like format invites students to engage in the learning process in an original and interactive way, introducing them to a state of "flow" (Csíkszentmihályi, 2020). The flow is the ultimate stage of creativity, reached through two pathways: 1) by paying full attention to the game and thus achieving meaningful processing of the information, and 2) by becoming fully engaged with the activities, making students contemplate the difficulties as challenges. Though the use of escape rooms in educational contexts has undergone considerable growth in recent years, one meta-analysis suggests that up to 2019 there were only seven published studies describing the application of escape rooms in an online environment (Fotaris & Mastoras, 2019). The same authors point out the need for incorporating a debriefing stage in the game, where students have the opportunity to reflect on the content included in the escape room and their mistakes, and thus achieve deeper levels of learning.

Use of Escape Rooms with Students of Health Professions

Although the escape rooms have been widely used in the medical and nursing training field (Veldkamp et al., 2020), with clear benefits related to connecting theory to clinical practice (Rodríguez-Ferrer, et al., 2022; San Martin et al., 2020), their application in the field of psychology and diagnostics to date is scarce. A recent study implemented two face-to-face escape rooms with undergraduate psychology students for courses related to general psychology and research methods, reporting measurable benefits evidenced by the exam performance. Specifically, the students performed better in the exam sections related to the contents included in the escape room, and they also reported increased levels of intrinsic motivation towards the subject (LaPaglia, 2020). Only one study to date has investigated the application of an escape room on psychopathology-related topics, and this study targeted undergraduate psychology students (Medina & Martín, 2022). This escape room was delivered in a face-to-face group format and students reported being satisfied with their learning, the teaching process, and the overall experience with the escape room. Although it seems to have benefited the students' learning process, the setting of the escape room was a psychiatric hospital, where students had to solve case studies to convince the teachers that they were mental health professionals and not cohabitants of a patient who had escaped. Such rationales should be strictly avoided in educational practice, as students may reproduce the negative mindsets observed onto their teachers through the hidden curriculum (Holmes et al., 2015) and thus increase their stigmatized attitudes towards people with mental illness. It is important to train future mental health professionals not only on how to apply theoretical knowledge to their practice through psychodiagnostics but also on how to apply soft skills related to empathy, understanding and acceptance of other people's suffering (Teding van Berkhout & Malouff, 2016).

To the knowledge of the authors, there are no further escape room implementations in the field of psychology and/or psychodiagnostics, and there are no reported experiences with online environments. Of note, attempts to apply such novel methods in the teaching and learning process should be rigorously evaluated, to develop evidence-based research that can help to shape best practices and guide the training of future mental health professionals.

Exploring the Implementation of an Online Escape Room in Teaching Psychodiagnostics

Considering the above, this project aims to a) explore the feasibility and acceptability of an online escape room as a tool for learning diagnostic-related procedures; b) to explore whether the activity increases the confidence and decreases the levels of perceived difficulty when establishing a mental disorder diagnosis; and c) to examine the stakeholders' (students and lecturers) views and satisfaction with the activity, as well as to gather their proposals for reshaping and expanding it further. As this is an exploratory project, there are no established hypotheses. However, the authors expected that student participants would provide positive feedback on their experience with the activity and would increase their confidence in establishing diagnoses and decrease their perception of difficulty concerning the diagnostics procedure.

METHODOLOGY

Population and Participants that Entered the Escape Room

The activity was offered to 500 students of a compulsory first-year course on Assessment and Psychodiagnostics, which forms part of the MSc in General Health Psychology program at the Universidad Internacional de La Rioja (a Spanish online university). A total of 94 students entered the escape room, and 39 students completed the activity.

Focus Groups Participants

The participants of the post-escape focus group were five lecturers and one student, all female identifying. Three of them were lecturers of the Assessment and Psychodiagnostics course, and the remaining two psychology lecturers taught other courses. All five lecturers had both teaching and clinical experience as general health psychologists.

Instruments

The Online Escape Room

The escape room was created in an online escape room platform called genial.ly, which students access through a link. The online escape room is designed to be solved in an asynchronous and independent mode at the students' own pace. Therefore, its format deviates from the original escape room set-up, as it is tailor-made to the students' profile (typically professionals attending an online postgraduate course, with barely any compulsory class attendance). Also, following previous recommendations (Fotaris & Mastoras, 2019), the online escape room involves several debriefing activities so the students may develop a self-directed learning experience. There is no final prize for the students. The overall activity duration is approximately 1.5 hours.

The Setting and the Story

This online escape room uses a sequential puzzle format. Students are situated in a library and must solve four missions to achieve the password that opens the Big Book of Diagnostics Figure 7 shows the first slide of the escape room. An introductory video presents the story and the game characters, who consist of avatars representing four General Health psychologists who have recently graduated. These avatars guide students through solving their missions, asking for the students' help to understand what is going on with their patients. When the students are successful in doing so, the avatars provide students with some of the letters of the secret password that solves the escape room (Figure 8). At the end of the experience, students need to put the letters in the right order for creating the password, which is "empathy". This word is chosen as the password to convey the message that empathy is essential in guiding the practice of future mental health professionals.

The Missions

Students are asked to help their avatar colleagues with three fictional case studies of patients that fulfill the DSM-5 criteria for major depressive disorder, schizophrenia, and bipolar disorder I. Patients express subjective complaints corresponding to their mental illness condition. The fourth mission is about understanding the diagnostic establishment steps while focusing on general key aspects of the diagnostic procedure.

The Puzzles

Each case study is presented in different formats and students must solve several puzzles consisting of symptom naming; understanding disorder characteristics in terms of duration, functioning, subjective experience, and symptom composition; matching criteria with their clinical representation; and matching symptoms with potential diagnostic entities (see Figure 9). At the end or throughout the mission, each avatar provides students with explanations of the right and wrong answers (see Figure 10) using short tutorials, DSM-5 material, and external links.

The Bloom's taxonomy framework (Anderson & Krathwohl, 2001) was used to organize the teaching objectives and align them with the learning outcomes that each activity aimed to achieve. See Table 1 for a detailed explanation of the four missions and their puzzles and activities, as well as their corresponding teaching/learning alignment based on Bloom's taxonomy.

Instructions

Before entering the escape room, students are instructed on how to navigate through its pages and missions. They are informed that they can go back to the initial mission page and read the case again or start the mission all over. Further, they can save the game at any stage and get back to where they left it later. However, they cannot pass from one mission to the next without solving the previous mission, as each are password protected and can open only with the provided key letters (see Figure 11).

Connection with Theory, Tools, and Materials

Students are expected to actively look up information on how to solve the cases, using the internet to access DSM-related material in the university's virtual library and the material from the Assessment and Psychodiagnostics course. Also, students are expected to visit the external links provided in the escape room after the puzzles are solved to develop a more comprehensive view of the right answers.

Some of the tools used to create the materials for this escape room were:

- iMovie to create the video displaying the setting and explaining the escape room
- Avatarmaker.com to create the avatars of the four psychologists
- Smallpdf.com to encrypt a .pdf file that included the case study for the second mission
    - The password to open the file is provided at the end of the first mission and consists of the same letters provided as part of the final password.
- Makebadg.es to create the badges that appear at the end of each mission and include the password letters
- Blabberize.com to make one of the avatars speak and guide the students through their missions
- Certify'em for Google Forms to create certificates of achievement offered to students when they solve all four missions

Questionnaires

The pre-escape room questionnaire (A) includes questions on gender, age, years of professional experience as a psychologist, aspects related to the level of perceived confidence and difficulty for establishing a diagnosis and aspects related to the Assessment and Psychodiagnostics course content.

The post-escape room questionnaire (B) includes the same questions on the level of perceived confidence and the level of difficulty for establishing a diagnosis, as well as questions on aspects related to the experience with the escape room and proposals for improvement. This second part of the questionnaire was adapted from a previously validated instrument created for similar purposes (see Peñalver & Urbieta,

2020). Questions related to group aspects of the original instrument were dropped, as the escape room used in the present project was held individually. See Appendix 1 for both questionnaires.

Focus Group

The online focus groups aimed at extracting key concepts for modifying the current escape room and guiding the design of future activities. Thus, the focus group topic guide included questions on technical aspects during the escape room navigation, the content of the case studies, questions and debriefing and proposals for expanding the activity with more content. See Appendix 2 for a detailed list of the topics discussed.

Procedure

Upon receiving approval by the Universidad Internacional de La Rioja Research Ethics Committee, students were offered the escape room activity as a complementary task for their Assessment and Psychodiagnostics course, after covering learning material on psychosis, mood, and bipolar disorders. The activity was available after the students received conventional sessions on this content, as it is suggested that the implementation of the escape room after instruction is more effective compared to when it is offered before they are familiarized with the content (Buchner et al., 2022). Five lecturers explained the activity to their groups of students and showed the escape room's introductory slide during one of their routine virtual classes. Students could access the activity through the course's page on the course's online learning platform, where they could also find detailed instructions for its completion. Students who decided to enter the escape room signed a document of informed consent and completed questionnaire A. The link to the escape room was open from May to July 2022. Students were instructed to complete the activity at their own pace and then complete questionnaire B. Confidentiality and anonymity were assured at all stages, as students were asked to create a six-digit individual pin code that was used for identification purposes during the completion of both questionnaires. Using the pin code served a two-fold purpose: 1) students could contact the researchers and ask for their pin code-related data to be withdrawn, and 2) the researchers were able to match the pre-post questionnaire answers by pin code. In a separate question, students were also asked to provide their emails in the event that they wished to be contacted for research purposes in the future.

One week after closing the escape room link, lecturers and students were invited to an exploratory online focus group aimed at sharing their experiences with the activity and collecting recommendations for expanding the activity further. Two researchers (AC and EP) moderated the focus group, which lasted about 95 minutes. At the culmination of the focus group, participants were thanked and debriefed.

Analyses

Descriptive statistics (mean, standard deviations, and frequencies) were used to examine the sample characteristics and the students' experience and satisfaction with the escape room. Differences between people who completed the escape room and those that started but did not finish the activity were examined through the use of chi-square for comparing across genders and professional experience, and through the use of independent samples t-test for comparing across age, self-confidence for diagnosis establishment and perceived difficulty of differential diagnosis. Differences in the latter before and after completing the activity for students who finished the escape room were checked through a Wilcoxon sign rank test. Qualitative input collected through the open-ended question regarding experiences and proposed changes to the escape room was grouped into categories based on the input affinity and presented in percentages. The focus group analysis was based on group data and aimed to identify key aspects shared by the participants. Results are presented through broad content categories.

RESULTS

Sample Description Escape Room

A total of N = 94 participants entered the escape room, though some participants entered the escape room but did not complete it (*n* = 55). Most of the participants were women (90.4%), between ages 22 to 54 (*M= 37.3; SD* = 9.3). The majority of participants reported no previous professional experience (56.4%), whereas only 5.7% had more than five years of experience. Participants who completed the escape room did not differ from those who did not in terms of age, gender, or professional experience (see Table 2 for details).

Participants' Perceptions of the Escape Room

Results of the participants' perceptions of several aspects of the activity are presented in Table 4 and divided into the following three areas: 1) motivation for entering the escape room, 2) navigation in the escape room, and 3) aspects related to course perception and learning. Two-thirds of the sample reported that this was their first time entering an escape room, and half of the students reported *learning and extending their knowledge* as the main reason for completing the activity. All students reported that they enjoyed the escape room experience. *Focusing on the key aspects for establishing a diagnosis* and *for carrying out the differential diagnosis* were considered the most important characteristics, whereas the *step-by-step procedure for diagnosis establishment* was considered the least important. Almost all students expressed they would be interested in participating in a similar escape room in the future. When it comes to their learning appraisal, almost all students expressed the need to have *more information on differential diagnosis, at least for some of the diagnostic categories.* Students perceived that the escape room had a high contribution to their learning and course content assimilation. Most of them reported that the escape room increased their motivation for adopting an active approach to diagnostics-related information seeking.

Figures 1-6 show the overall students' appraisal of the escape room and its contribution to learning. As observed, most of the students considered that the escape room and the included activities were *easy*, in addition to being *fun*. When it comes to their learning, the majority considered that the activity helped them develop new skills and learn more than with traditional teaching-learning methods. Finally, *fun, interesting, original,* and *motivating* were the aspects that best described the escape room, based on the students' appraisal.

Change in Self-Confidence and Difficulty Perception

Students who completed the activity ($n = 39$) reported a mean of 2.97 ($SD = .743$) in self-confidence for establishing diagnostics when entering the escape room and a mean of 3.59 ($SD = .595$) after completing the activity. The Wilcoxon sign rank test findings revealed that there were statistically significant differences ($Z = -4.233$; $p < .001$) between responses before and after the activity, with students reporting more self-confidence for establishing a diagnosis after the escape room completion.

On the other hand, the perceived difficulty for performing differential diagnosis was $M = 3.15$ ($SD = .709$) before entering the escape room and $M = 3.05$ ($SD = .759$) after completing the escape room. Findings of the Wilcoxon sign test revealed no significant differences between the two time points ($Z = -.720$; $p = .472$).

Proposals for Changes

When students were asked to propose changes to the escape room, 61.5% reported that they would not change anything, 28.2% proposed extending the activity with more cases and 10.3% proposed changes related to technical or content issues, such as the possibility of moving backwards during the activity or to modify the last activity by replacing the torch with another modality.

Sample Description Focus Groups

The focus group participants' characteristics can be seen in Table 3. The lecturers' mean age was 37.4 years (SD=4.7). They had a mean of 9.6 years of professional experience ($SD = 6.9$) and a mean of 8.2 years ($SD = 5.5$) as lecturers. The one student involved in the focus group was 31 years old with no previous clinical experience.

Focus Groups Findings

Technical Issues

All focus group participants mentioned the need to add a backwards button in the escape room, as well as to add reminders of the key letter after each mission; they proposed these technical issues as potential difficulties faced by students who did not complete the activity. They also proposed that, perhaps by shortening the activity, the students would be able to complete it in one attempt instead of saving the game and completing it later, which may affect their motivation. On the other hand, focus group participants found the instructions to be well-defined and appropriate for guiding the game.

Activity Content

All focus group participants welcomed the activity as a useful tool for enhancing the teaching and learning process in an innovative, intuitive, and motivating way. The lecturers considered the case studies to be adequate in terms of difficulty, whereas the student that took part in the focus group mentioned that she perceived them as difficult. However, the student mentioned that this provided them with a valuable opportunity to actively seek information, revise the course's material and increase their understanding of the diagnostic process. All focus group participants noted the connection between theory and practice achieved through the missions. They found the debriefing useful and particularly appraised the external links for further information. However, they proposed the use of formal and organizational webpages instead of dissemination blogs to align the activity with the postgraduate's general standpoint for evidence-based practice implementation.

Proposed Future Changes

All participants highlighted the need to include clinical cases that present comorbidity or more complex characteristics, as well as cases that incite reflection on the limits between normal and pathological. In terms of diagnoses, all participants agreed on the need to expand the escape room with cases related to personality disorders and eating and anxiety disorders, as well as to further expand the content on the psychosis-related cases. Also, participants proposed the first-person format for presenting cases, with patients telling their stories and psychologists performing a complete evaluation of their characteristics, as well as the use of different age-range cases to better reflect the psychologist's routine practice.

DISCUSSION

This is the first implementation of an online escape room for the teaching and learning of psychodiagnostics. Based on the quantitative and qualitative preliminary findings of the students' questionnaires and the focus group input, the escape room seems to have achieved its initial purpose as an original tool aimed to offer an attractive teaching and learning alternative for the psychodiagnostics course. As suggested by the findings, students have embraced the activity and reported positive experiences during their navigation to the escape room. Importantly, they have also considered that the activity has contributed to their learning and further understanding of diagnostic procedures. The significant increase in the students' self-confidence with establishing a diagnosis after completing the escape room is encouraging and invites for a more systematic implementation of the activity. In this sense, the focus group input, and the students' proposals for ways to go forward have provided valuable feedback for planning next steps.

FUTURE RESEARCH DIRECTIONS

Though the implementation of the escape rooms in the educational contexts has been conceived as a face-to-face group activity, the present attempt supports that even when the escape room is designed for virtual contexts and implemented as an individual activity, it may have a valuable contribution to the students' learning. Future endeavors should include the design of broader escape rooms involving all the course's material, with case studies that reflect the clinical routine practice. This way, they may provide an excellent tool for both revising the heavy course content and for establishing a connection between theory and practice for future mental health professionals. Also, future research should focus on a more exhaustive exploration of what works and why during the escape room implementations, also examining their application with undergraduate students. This may be achieved through targeting wider student populations, through implementing more detailed surveys and focus groups that involve a wider representation of stakeholders (i.e., more students and program academic directors).

CONCLUSION

The current study shows how the use of a virtual escape room can enhance the process of teaching and learning psychodiagnostics. The virtual escape room is a valuable tool for lecturers that look for ways to reach students' needs and unleash their potential when it comes to understanding diagnostic procedures and applying their theoretical knowledge. The students' feedback on the usefulness of the virtual escape room application is more than encouraging for continuing to explore the usability of this tool and for systematizing its use to increase future professionals' confidence towards their practice.

REFERENCES

American Psychiatric Association. (2013). *Diagnostic and statistical manual of mental disorders* (5th ed.). APA.

Anderson, L. W., & Krathwohl, D. R. (2001). *A taxonomy for learning, teaching, and assessing: A revision of Bloom's taxonomy of educational objectives*. Longman.

Berrios, G. E. (2012). Descriptive psychopathology: Historical and conceptual aspects. *Revista Latinoamericana de Psicopatologia Fundamental, 15*, 171–196. doi:10.1590/S1415-47142012000100012

Buchner, J., Rüter, M., & Kerres, M. (2022). Learning with a digital escape room game: Before or after instruction? *Research and Practice in Technology Enhanced Learning, 17*(1), 1–16. doi:10.118641039-022-00187-x PMID:35310067

Csíkszentmihályi, M. (2020). *Finding flow: The psychology of engagement with everyday life*. Hachette.

Daltro, M. R., & Bueno, G. (2010). Ludicidade e narrativa: Estratégias de humanização na graduação médica [Ludicity and narrative: humanization strategies in medical graduation]. *Revista Brasileira de Educação Médica, 34*(4), 497–505. doi:10.1590/S0100-55022010000400004

Darbyshire, D., & Baker, P. (2012). A systematic review and thematic analysis of cinema in medical education. *Medical Humanities, 38*(1), 28–33. doi:10.1136/medhum-2011-010026 PMID:22282424

Etxeandia-Pradera, J. I., Martinez-Uribe, D., Bellver-Pradas, F., Gonzalez-Piqueras, J. C., Nacher, J., & Aguilar, E. J. (2021). Training Psychiatry Residents in Descriptive Psychopathology: A Systematic Review. *Psychopathology, 54*(1), 1–17. doi:10.1159/000512791 PMID:33611314

First, M. B., Erlich, M. D., Adler, D. A., Leong, S., Dixon, L. B., Oslin, D. W., Goldman, B., Koh, S., Levine, B., Berlant, J. L., & Siris, S. G. (2019). How the DSM is used in clinical practice. *The Journal of Nervous and Mental Disease, 207*(3), 157–161. doi:10.1097/NMD.0000000000000953 PMID:30768542

Fluyau, D. (2018). Integrating DSM/ICD, research domain criteria, and descriptive psychopathology in teaching and practice of psychiatry. *Frontiers in Psychiatry, 9*, 484. doi:10.3389/fpsyt.2018.00484 PMID:30344498

Fotaris, P., & Mastoras, T. (2019, October). Escape rooms for learning: A systematic review. In *Proceedings of the European Conference on Games Based Learning* (pp. 235-243). Academic Press.

Frenk, J., Chen, L., Bhutta, Z. A., Cohen, J., Crisp, N., Evans, T., Fineberg, H., Garcia, P., Ke, Y., Kelley, P., Kistnasamy, B., Meleis, A., Naylor, D., Pablos-Mendez, A., Reddy, S., Scrimshaw, S., Sepulveda, J., Serwadda, D., & Zurayk, H. (2010). Health professionals for a new century: Transforming education to strengthen health systems in an interdependent world. *Lancet*, *376*(9756), 1923–1958. doi:10.1016/S0140-6736(10)61854-5 PMID:21112623

Holmes, C. L., Harris, I. B., Schwartz, A. J., & Regehr, G. (2015). Harnessing the hidden curriculum: A four-step approach to developing and reinforcing reflective competencies in medical clinical clerkship. *Advances in Health Sciences Education: Theory and Practice*, *20*(5), 1355–1370. doi:10.100710459-014-9558-9 PMID:25319835

Jibson, M. D., & Seyfried, L. S. (2017). DSM-5 Teaching Materials: A Critical Review. *Academic Psychiatry*, *41*(1), 138–144. doi:10.100740596-016-0614-z PMID:27752943

Kalogiannakis, M., Papadakis, S., & Zourmpakis, A. I. (2021). Gamification in science education. A systematic review of the literature. *Education Sciences*, *11*(1), 22. doi:10.3390/educsci11010022

Kupfer, D. (2014). DSM-5: New opportunities and challenges for teaching and training. *Academic Psychiatry*, *38*(1), 58–60. doi:10.100740596-013-0002-x PMID:24488597

LaPaglia, J. A. (2020). Escape the evil professor! Escape room review activity. *Teaching of Psychology*, *47*(2), 141–146. doi:10.1177/0098628320901383

Medina, V. L., & Martín, H. V. (2022). Analysis of the validity of a psychopathology escape room in high education. In *16th International Technology, Education and Development Conference Proceedings* (pp. 6536-6536). IATED.

Monteiro, B. M. M., Ono, B. H. V. S., Silva, E. D. S. M., & Souza, J. C. (2020). Acrostics and Crosswords as Advance Organizers to Meaningful Learning in Medical Education. *Creative Education*, *11*(8), 1213–1222. doi:10.4236/ce.2020.118090

Peñalver, E. A., & Urbieta, A. S. (2020). Enhancing medical translation skills through a gamified experience. Failure or success? *Panace*, *21*(51), 4–12.

Rodríguez-Ferrer, J. M., Manzano-León, A., Cangas, A. J., Aguilar-Parra, J. M., Fernández-Jiménez, C., Fernández-Campoy, J. M., Luque de la Rosa, A., & Martínez-Martínez, A. M. (2022). Acquisition of Learning and Empathy Towards Patients in Nursing Students Through Online Escape Room: An Exploratory Qualitative Study. *Psychology Research and Behavior Management*, *15*, 103–110. doi:10.2147/PRBM.S344815 PMID:35046736

San Martin, L., Walsh, H., Santerre, M., Fortkiewicz, J., & Nicholson, L. (2021). Creation of a "Patient" hospital escape room experience to reduce harm and improve quality of care. *Journal of Nursing Care Quality*, *36*(1), 38–42. doi:10.1097/NCQ.0000000000000485 PMID:32282503

Sánchez, T., Barbeito, S., Becerra-García, J. A., & Calvo, A. (2017). Progress of Health Psychology regulation: A comparison between countries. *Acta Medica International*, *4*(1), 46–50. doi:10.5530/ami.2017.4.9

Summers, R. F., & Kreider, T. R. (2014). DSM-5: A teachable moment. *Academic Psychiatry*, *38*(1), 55–57. doi:10.100740596-013-0009-3 PMID:24419821

Teding van Berkhout, E., & Malouff, J. M. (2016). The efficacy of empathy training: A meta-analysis of randomized controlled trials. *Journal of Counseling Psychology*, *63*(1), 32–41. doi:10.1037/cou0000093 PMID:26191979

Veldkamp, A., van de Grint, L., Knippels, M. C. P., & van Joolingen, W. R. (2020). Escape education: A systematic review on escape rooms in education. *Educational Research Review*, *31*, 100364. doi:10.1016/j.edurev.2020.100364

Wedding, D., Boyd, M. A., & Niemiec, R. M. (2014). *Movies and mental illness: Using films to understand psychopathology*. Hogrefe Publishing.

Wiemker, M., Elumir, E., & Clare, A. (2015). Escape room games. *Game Based Learning, 55*, 55-75.

KEY TERMS AND DEFINITIONS

Avatars: A virtual identity representing a role or a person in a video game or other online activity.

Bipolar Disorder: A mental disorder characterized by periods of elevated mood and self-esteem, interchanged with periods of low mood and hopelessness, that significantly disturb the person's life.

Bloom's Taxonomy: A framework used to align teaching strategies with learning goals.

Diagnostic and Statistical Manual of Mental Disorders (DSM-5): A manualized guide for establishing mental health diagnoses.

Differential Diagnosis: A procedure through which the mental health professional needs to decide what is the best diagnosis that describes the person's symptoms and difficulties.

Major Depressive Disorder: A mental disorder characterized by low mood, loss of interest in everyday activities, lack of pleasure experience and lack of self-care, affecting the person's everyday functioning.

Psychodiagnostics: The operational procedures of understanding and establishing a mental health diagnosis.

Schizophrenia: A severe mental disorder characterized by hallucinations, delusions, and disorganized thoughts and behaviors, causing severe disturbance to the person's everyday life and functioning.

APPENDIX A

Tables and Figures

Table 1. Learning outcomes to be achieved through the escape room based on Bloom's Taxonomy

Missions	Puzzles and content	Learning Outcomes
Mission 1: Psychologist Avatar Estela explains a case study of a patient with depression. Students are asked to answer questions based on the case study's characteristics. At the end, they are given the first two letters of the final password in the form of a badge.	-Quiz with four multiple choice questions, each with three possible answers. -Explanations for each quiz solution highlighting key aspects of the case. -Mini tutorial on how to determine whether a subjective/objective manifestation is considered psychopathological (i.e. weight loss, lack of interest in relationships). -External link to the DSM-5 major depressive disorder criteria and connection with the case study characteristics.	● *Identify* the two key symptoms of depression according to the DSM-5 ● *Understand* that a single symptom or manifestation is not enough for reaching conclusions related to psychopathology ● *Relate* a symptom to several potential diagnoses ● *Compare* the characteristics of different diagnostic entities that share common symptoms with depression ● *Generate* a diagnostic hypothesis based on the above
Mission 2: Psychologist Avatar Ruben leads students to an encrypted pdf that opens with the letters provided by Estela and exposes a case study of a patient with schizophrenia. Students are first asked to match the DSM-5 criteria with the patient's manifestations and then answer questions based on the case characteristics. At the end, Ruben provides them with the last letter of the password in the form of a badge.	-Activity connecting the patient's symptoms with their DSM 5 denomination. -Quiz with five questions, each with a true/false response format. -Detailed explanations after each quiz solution highlighting key aspects of the case. -External links to a) the DSM-5 symptoms of schizoaffective and delusional disorder, and b) evidence on the potential relationships between substance abuse and psychoses.	● *Classify* the case characteristics based on the DSM 5 ● *Contrast* the symptoms of schizophrenia with those of delusional disorder ● *Understand* the differences between schizophrenia and schizoaffective disorder ● *Differentiate* schizophrenia from drug-induced psychosis
Mission 3: Psychologist Avatar Mercedes exposes a case study of a patient with bipolar disorder I orally and in written form. Again, students must use the letter provided by Ruben to make Mercedes speak out. Students are asked to answer a series of questions guided by Mercedes through several options. The fifth and sixth letters of the password are provided when the case is solved in the form of a badge. Sound effects are used throughout this mission.	-Quiz with five multiple choice questions, each with four potential answers. -Detailed explanations on the DSM-5 criteria for bipolar disorder and differential diagnosis between bipolar I and II, psychotic and mood disorders. -External link with an explanatory video on how patients experience an episode of mania.	● *Listen* to relevant content and *distinguish* key aspects of the case ● *Examine* the characteristics of a person with bipolar disorder I ● *Differentiate* between bipolar I and II ● *Contrast* this case with those presented in missions 1 and 2 ● *Conclude* on what makes them different in terms of diagnoses
Mission 4: Psychologist Avatar Alberto provides the key aspects of the diagnostic process step by step. To meet him, students must use the fifth and the sixth letter of the password. Alberto lends his torch to students and asks them to look for the sequential steps of the diagnostic process in a blue screen using the torch's light. Finally, students are provided with the third and fourth letter of the password in the form of a badge.	-An activity with a torch that pretends to establish an order for the diagnostic process highlighting the aspects of functionality, severity, temporality, organic syndromes, and differential diagnosis. -A series of key questions are proposed for guiding the clinical reasoning process of diagnosis establishment. -Detailed explanations on how to address each step.	● *Organize* the diagnostic process ● *Reflect* on the importance of each step ● *Check* its application to the three case studies presented in the previous missions ● *Establish* priorities based on the patient's subjective experience ● *Synthesize* the information of the four missions
End of the escape room.	-Students are provided with the opportunity to obtain a certificate with their name acknowledging their participation. -A key message regarding their future practice is presented at the end.	● *Recognize* their personal achievement ● *Reflect* on the use and usefulness of psychodiagnostics

Table 2. Sociodemographic characteristics of the escape room participants (N = 94)

Participants	Entered the escape room but not completed it n = 55	Completed the escape room n = 39	Differences between groups
Age (*M, SD*)	37.18 (10.30)	37.64 (8.50)	t = .233 p=.817
Gender (Female%)	89.1%	92.3%	χ^2 = .273 p=.602
Professional experience			χ^2 = 4.971 p=.174
None	60%	51.3%	
Less than one year	14.5%	7.7%	
One to five years	21.8%	30.8%	
More than five years	1.8%	10.3%	
Perceived confidence for diagnosis establishment (*M, SD*)	2.89 (.685)	2.97 (.743)	t = .562 p=.576
Perceived difficulty of differential diagnosis (*M, SD*)	3.18 (.611)	3.15 (.709)	t = -.205 p=.838

Table 3. Characteristics of the focus groups participants

Participant	Age	Academic experience in years	Clinical experience in years
Lecturer 1	38	6	13
Lecturer 2	33	5	3
Lecturer 3	45	18	20
External Evaluator 1	34	4	5
External Evaluator 2	37	7	7
Student	31	-	0

Table 4. Participants' experiences and perceptions of the escape room

Areas		Percentage
Motivation for entering the escape room		
Previous experience with an escape room	None	69.2%
Reasons for entering the escape room	Learning and extending knowledge	51.1%
	Learning through leisure activities	18.1%
	Interest/Curiosity	22.8%
	Lecturer's recommendation	6.5%
Navigation in the escape room		
Percentage of students who enjoyed the experience		100%
Most important aspect highlighted	Focus on the key aspects for the diagnosis establishment	33.3%
	Carry out a differential diagnosis	33.3%
Less important aspect highlighted	Consider the diagnostic process step by step	56.4%
Activity enjoyed the most	Second mission (schizophrenia)	25.6%
	Third mission (bipolar disorder)	25.6%
Activity enjoyed the least	Fourth mission (Step by step diagnosis establishment)	46.2%
Keen on participating in an escape room with similar characteristics		97.4%
Aspects related to course perception and learning		
Opinion on whether the course content should focus more on differential diagnoses	No, there is enough information	6.4%
	Yes, more time should be spent to analyze differential diagnoses	42.6%
	Perhaps for some diagnostic categories	51.1%
Contribution of the escape room to learning	Yes	94.9%
Contribution of the escape room to the course take in knowledge	Yes	94.9%
Motivation through the escape room for active search on diagnostics-related content	Yes	89.7%

Figure 1. The escape room was difficult

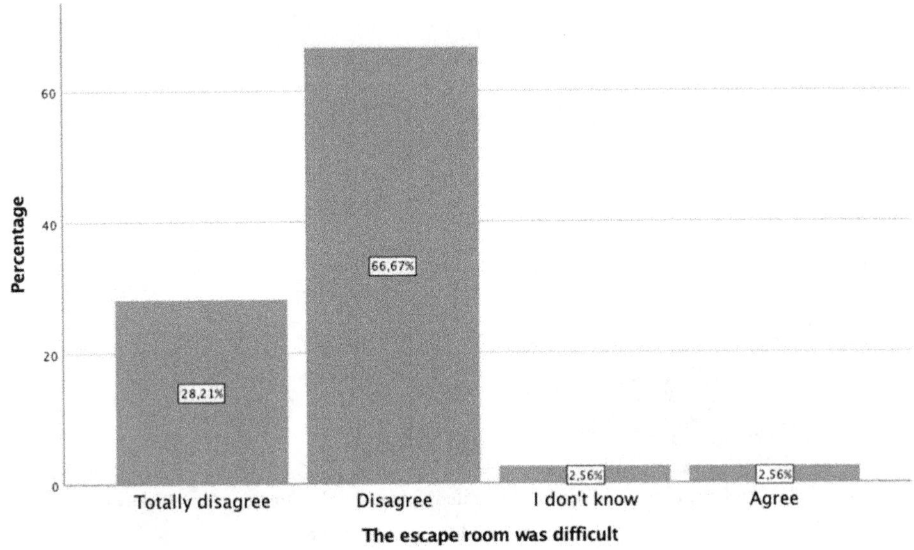

Figure 2. The escape room was fun

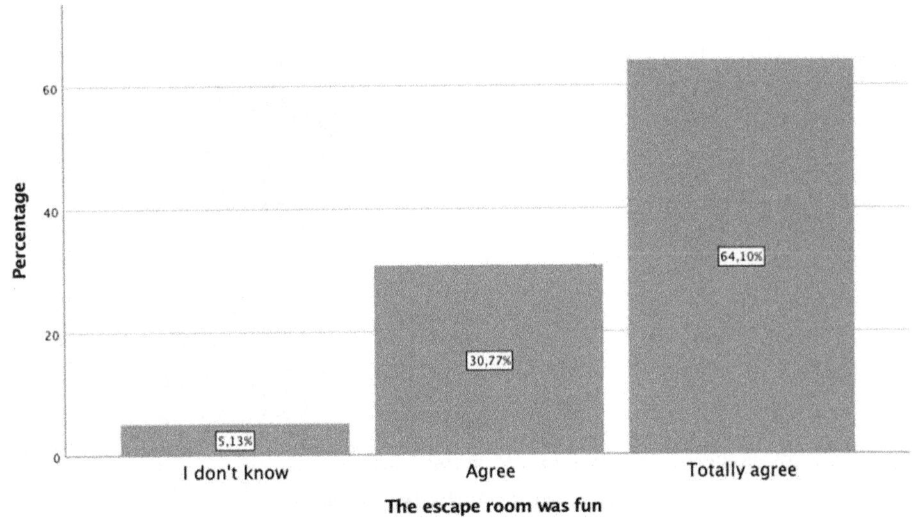

Figure 3. The activities were difficult

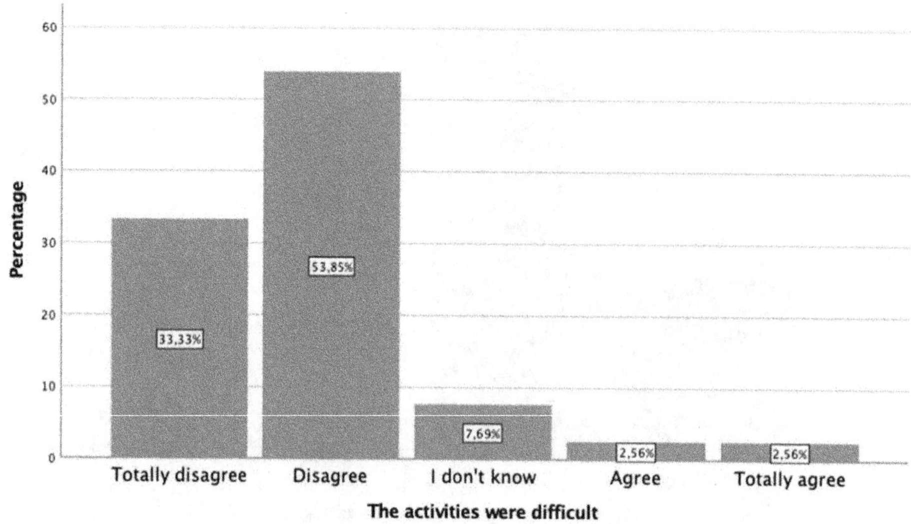

Figure 4. The escape room helped me develop new skills

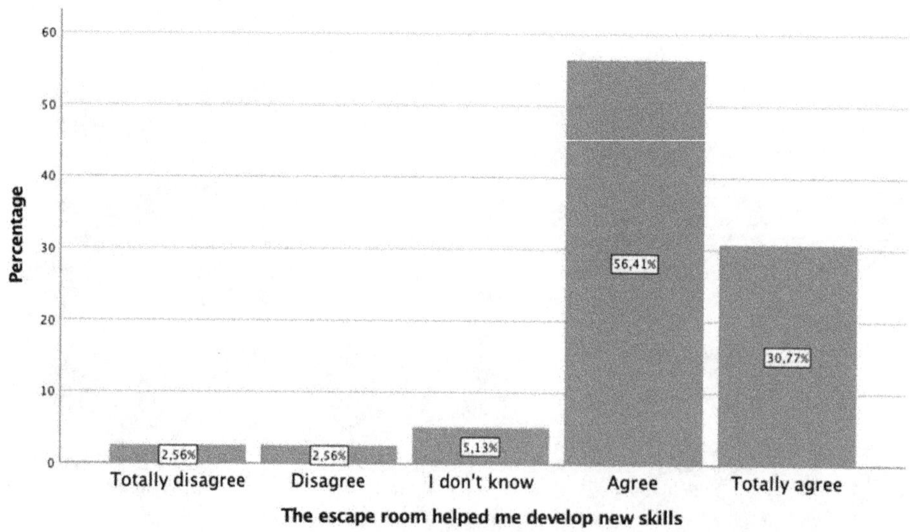

Figure 5. This method helped me learn more than with traditional methods

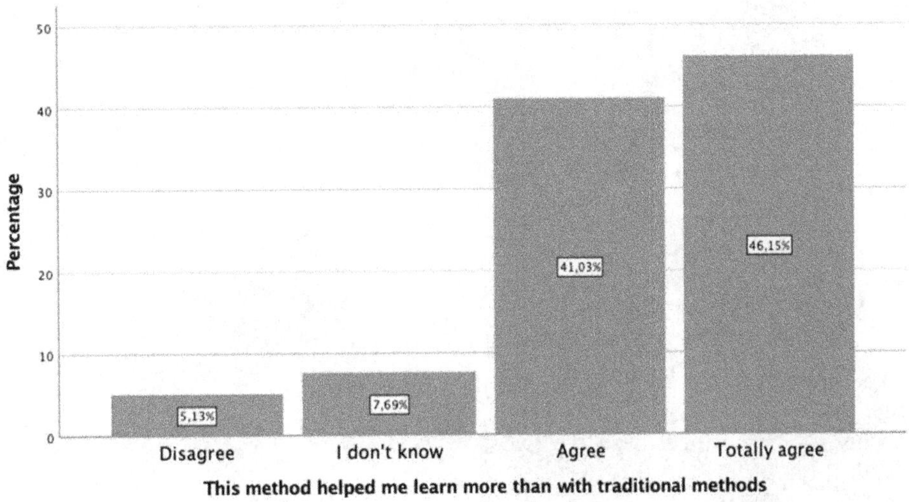

Figure 6. Overall appraisal of the escape room

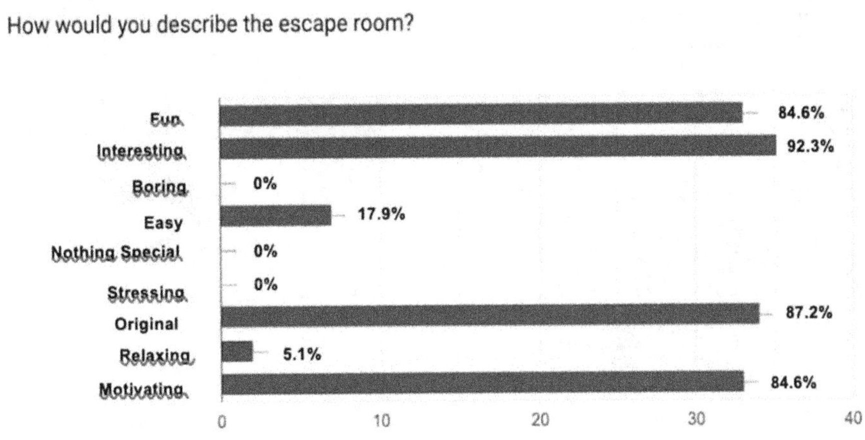

Figure 7. The first slide displayed in the escape room
Note 1 "Attention! The password for opening the Big Book against the wrong diagnosis has gone missing. Click on the envelope to know more" (translation from the original text)

Figure 8. Providing the letters at the end of a mission
Note 2. "Thank you for helping me, my dear colleague! You can click on the circle to get the first two letters of the PASSWORD that opens the Big Book" (translation from the original text)

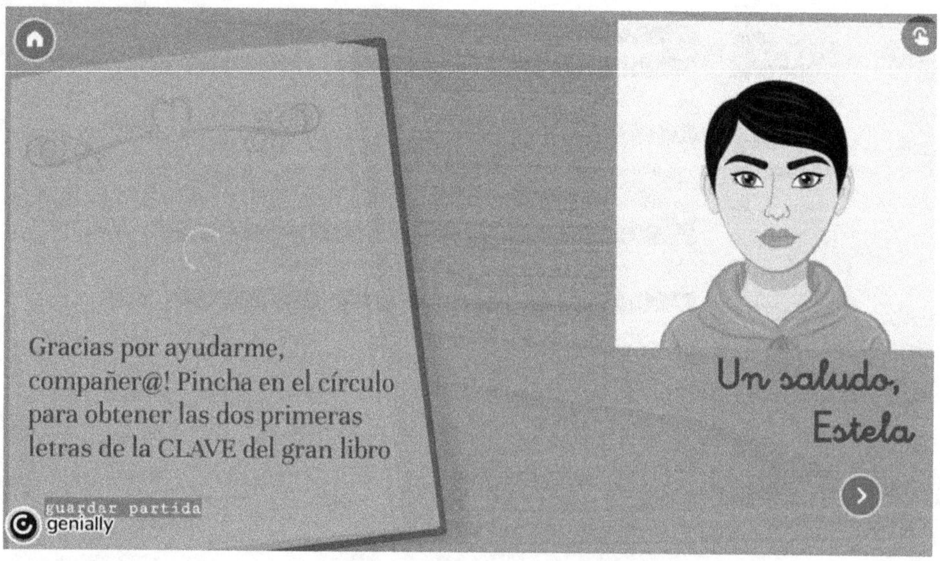

Figure 9. Example of quiz

Note 3. "Our patient, B., suffers: Bipolar Disorder II, Bipolar Disorder I, Major Depressive Disorder, Schizophrenia" (translation from the original text)

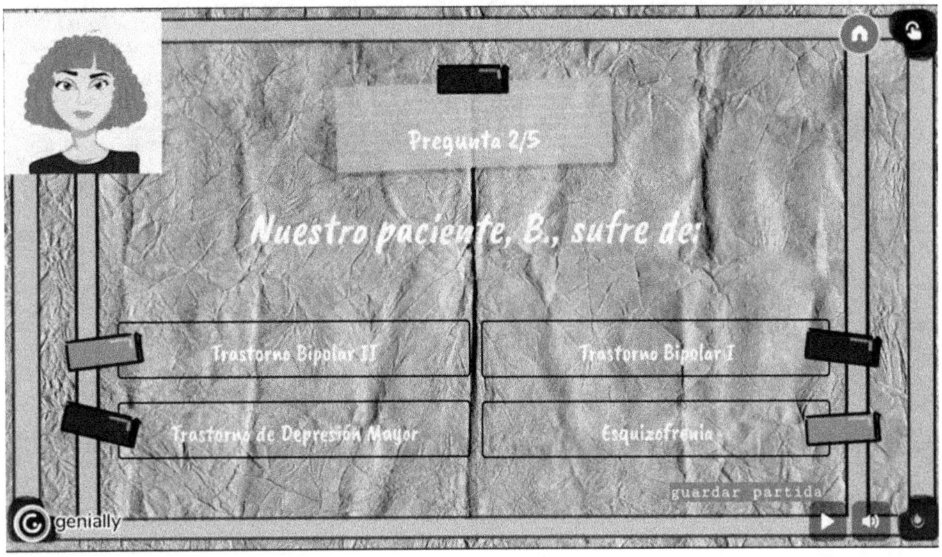

Figure 10. Debriefing-Explanations of right and wrong answers

Note 4. "Exactly, N., suffers from: 1. Two positive symptoms (persecutory delusions and auditory hallucinations), 2. Disorganized language (neologism: constructing words that make sense only to the person but not to others), and 3. a negative symptom (anhedonia)" (translation from the original text)

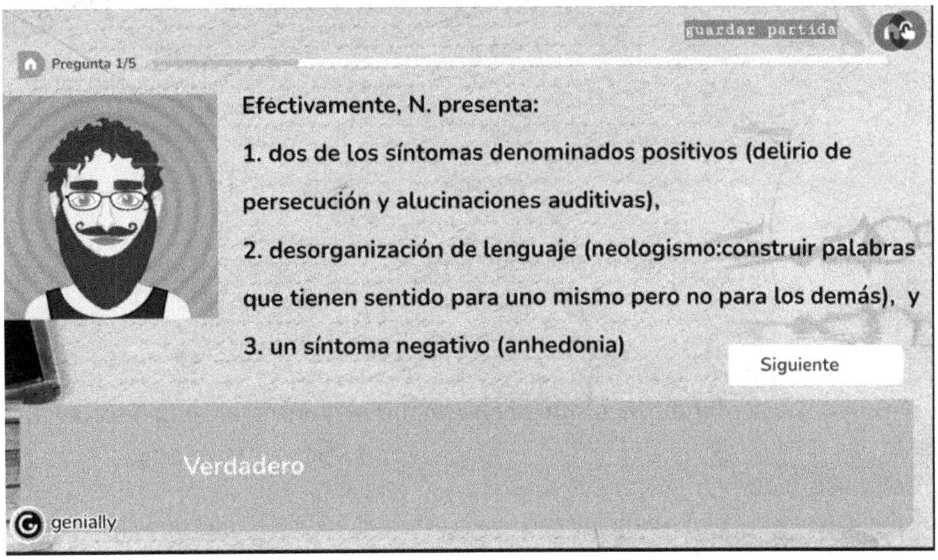

Figure 11. Missions display
Note 5. "Complete-Complete-Help Mercedes-Closed" (translation from the original text)

APPENDIX B

Questionnaire A: Pre-escape room

1. Create your personal pin code using your name initials and four digits (eg: * FJSR1602)
2. What is your age?
3. What is your gender
   Female
   Male
   Other
   Prefer not to say
4. Time of professional experience as a psychologist
5. How confident do you feel for establishing a mental health diagnosis?
   1 2 3 4 5
   Not at all Very confident
6. What is your difficulty for distinguishing between different mental health disorders
   1 2 3 4 5
   None Extremely high
7. Do you think the course of Assessment and Diagnostics should focus more on differential diagnoses?
8. Why did you decide to enter the escape room?
   No, there is enough information
   Perhaps for some diagnostics
   Yes, more time should be spent to analyze differential diagnoses

Questionnaire B: Post-escape room

1. What is your PIN?
2. How confident do you feel for establishing a mental health diagnosis?
   1 2 3 4 5
   Not at all Very confident
3. What is your difficulty for distinguishing between different mental health disorders
   1 2 3 4 5
   None Extremely high
4. Did you take part in an escape room before?
   Yes
   No
5. Did you enjoy the escape room
   Yes
   No
6. In your opinion, what was the MOST important aspect of the Escape room?
   Connect the patients' symptoms with the DSM-5 criteria for each disorder
   Carry out a differential diagnosis
   Consider the diagnostic process step by step
   Focus on the key aspects for the diagnosis establishment
7. In your opinion, what was the LEAST important aspect of the Escape room?
   Connect the patients' symptoms with the DSM-5 criteria for each disorder
   Carry out a differential diagnosis
   Consider the diagnostic process step by step
   Focus on the key aspects for the diagnosis establishment
8. Do you think that the Escape Room activity has contributed to your LEARNING of diagnostic processes?
   Yes
   No
   Perhaps
9. Do you think that the Escape Room activity has helped you to TAKE IN THE KNOWLEDGE gained through the contents of the Assessment and Psychodiagnostics course?
   Yes
   No
   Perhaps
10. Do you consider that the Escape Room activity has motivated you to perform an active search on diagnostic procedures?
    Yes
    No
    Perhaps
11. What was the activity that you enjoyed THE MOST?
12. What was the activity that you enjoyed THE LEAST?

13. Would you be willing to take part in an escape room of this type?
    Yes
    No
    Perhaps
14. Would you change anything in the escape room? If yes, what would that be?
15. How would you describe the escape room? Mark all that is true
    Entertaining
    Interesting
    Boring
    Easy
    Nothing special
    Stressing
    Original
    Relaxing
    Motivating
16. Choose the answer that best expresses your opinion:

	Totally disagree	Disagree	I don't know	Agree	Totally agree
The escape room was very difficult					
The escape room was fun					
The activities were difficult					
The escape room helped me develop new skills					
This method helped me learn more than traditional methods do					

APPENDIX C

Focus Group Topic Guide

Experience with Navigation in the Escape Room
What is your perception of the escape room's difficulty?
Were the instructions enough to guide you through the escape?
Would you change anything in terms of appearance, surface, buttons, etc.?
What do you think of the activity's duration?
Experience with the Escape Room Content
What do you think of the case studies? Were they representative enough?
What do you think of the case studies' difficulty?
What do you think of the questions for understanding the case?
What do you think of the debriefing information?
Proposals and Recommendations for the Future

What would you like to see in a future escape room? (i.e. comorbidity, severity…)
What are the diagnoses that you feel are more complex to teach?
How do you think those could be included in a future escape room?

Chapter 2
Invigorating Virtual Classrooms in Degree and Post-Degree Studies of Economics With Escape Rooms

Marta Magadán-Díaz
https://orcid.org/0000-0003-3178-3215
Universidad Internacional de La Rioja, Spain

Jesús I. Rivas-García
Universidad Internacional de La Rioja, Spain

ABSTRACT

The general objective of this research is to analyze the perception that undergraduate and graduate students have about the use of escape rooms in the subjects of Economic History and International Economic Environment taught in a degree and a post-degree at two online universities. As specific objectives, this study evaluates, on the one hand, the degree of dynamism, commitment, and involvement of students in the virtual classroom because of the use of escape rooms and, on the other, the impact on their academic performance. This work applies the experimental method from two randomly generated samples in each of the two subjects considered for this analysis. The data to carry out this analysis will be obtained from an ad hoc questionnaire to collect, among other aspects, the perceptions about the impact of the experience. The information generated will be treated with non-parametric inference tools.

INTRODUCTION

The widespread use of mobile technology in the classroom has created new opportunities for teachers to adopt digital gamification (Magadán & Rivas, 2022a; Saleem et al., 2021). The use of games in educational contexts has a great reception by teachers because it intensifies the concentration of students,

DOI: 10.4018/978-1-6684-6081-8.ch002

motivates them, involves them, and improves not only the learning experience but also grades (I. García, 2019; Licorish et al., 2018; Magadán & Rivas, 2022a; Robson et al., 2015).

Getting started in postgraduate courses in the area of Economics can be a complex process for university students, mainly because it involves developing different skills and competencies related to abstract thinking, analytical skills, case study, or calculation skills, among others. However, using escape rooms as virtual classroom gamification tools can ease and simplify this learning process.

From an educational perspective, educational escape rooms -due to their link with gamified structures- are tools belonging to the gamification methodology (Makri et al., 2021). Gamification in education gained popularity in the early 2010s (Kapp, 2012). It is a learning strategy that, by incorporating a ludic or game vision, increases the student's commitment to achieving better academic results (Dichev & Dicheva, 2017; Magadán & Rivas, 2022b; Sánchez et al., 2020), allowing them to develop curricular, cognitive and social skills (Manzano et al., 2021). The central idea of gamification leads to the logic that the motivational force of games can be transferred to educational contexts (Makri et al., 2021), requiring the student to have a proactive attitude to build their learning process (Parra et al., 2020). The inclusion of playful activities in the classroom improves participation, cooperation, creativity, and learning outcomes (Magadán & Rivas, 2021; Parra et al., 2020; Santamaría & Alcalde, 2019; Zhang et al., 2019). Its origin is playful and can be set in 2007 in Japan, although it has a rapid acceptance, first in Asia and then throughout Europe (Borrego et al., 2017).

Borrowing elements from role-playing games, scavenger hunts, movies, and TV shows, an escape room is a live-action game where players uncover clues, solve puzzles, and complete tasks within a limited time (Nicholson, 2018). Players may be called upon to solve a crime, save a fictional character, or find something. From a pedagogical point of view, the socio-constructivist approach (Vygotsky, 1978) is the base for escape rooms. Students build their knowledge through lived experiences in real-time, advancing through various challenges along the route map drawn in the escape room and facing a wide variety of problems of varying complexity until they reach the goal that can, in some cases, involve obtaining a previously established reward as an additional element of motivation.

The escape rooms must have a narrative that helps the participants understand their mission within it and generate concern and interest in the game (Connelly et al., 2018). When they rely on film references (series or movies), it is crucial to generate the same sensations and emotions that their protagonists' experience and, at the same time, recreate and respect the original plots, which contributes to increasing the credibility and sense of immersion of the students. in experience (Navarro & Pérez, 2022). This type of approach increases motivation and generates a higher student's commitment to learning (Borrego et al., 2017; Morell et al., 2020), facilitating the assimilation of specific content in an active way (Navarro & Pérez, 2022; Parra et al., 2020).

However, due to its emerging nature, the scientific literature on educational experiences supported by escape rooms in higher education in economics is not abundant. However, there are good practices developed in other academic disciplines, such as Medicine, Pharmacy, or Biology (Alonso & Schroeder, 2020; Baker et al., 2020; Hawkins et al., 2020; Morell et al., 2020), or subjects of Science, Technology, Engineering and Mathematics, known by the acronym STEM (Borrego et al., 2017; Fuentes et al., 2020; López et al., 2019; Piñero, 2020), language teaching (Santamaría & Alcalde, 2019), subjects related to the environment and tourism studies (Ouariachi & Van Dam, 2022; Ouariachi & Wim, 2020; Pakhalov & Rozhkova, 2020), among others. Finally, there are few implementations of escape rooms in business education (Martina & Göksen, 2020).

The general objective of this study is to analyze the perception that undergraduate and graduate students have about the use of escape rooms in the subjects of Economic History and International Economic Environment, taught in undergraduate and postgraduate courses in two Spanish online universities. As specific objectives, this study evaluates, on the one hand, the degree of dynamism, commitment, and involvement of students in the virtual classroom due to the use of escape rooms and, on the other, the impact on their academic performance. To this end, the present study adresses the following research questions:

RQ1. How do students perceive the use of escape rooms in the virtual classroom?

RQ2. Does the use of escape rooms impact the learning performance of students?

A digital escape room set in the series "The Ministry of Time" has been designed and implemented to address the general objective and the research questions. This work tries to cover the existing gap in studies on the use of escape rooms in subjects of Economy.

BACKGROUND

The escape room offers active and interactive apprenticeship to students (Adams et al., 2018), enhancing the learning experience (Franco & DeLuca, 2019). It provides a dynamic educational environment that improves knowledge retention and reinforces learning. Also, it increases the understanding of the concepts taught in the classroom (Jambhekar et al., 2019), motivation, and the willingness to learn (Borrego et al., 2017; López et al., 2019), encouraging students to study (de la Flor et al., 2020; Gómez et al., 2019). Its use increases the students' ability to think critically, delegate tasks, and work as a team (Brown et al., 2019; Clauson et al., 2019; Garwood, 2020; Morell et al., 2020). In addition, it allows students to apply their knowledge innovatively (Craig et al., 2019; Garwood, 2020; Makri et al., 2021; Wise et al., 2018). Students consider that its use in the classroom is relevant and helpful for learning, revision, and application of knowledge, motivation and collaboration, a better understanding of new concepts, and, therefore, laying the foundations for deep learning (Aubeux et al., 2020; Baker et al., 2020).

The escape room experience is fun and motivating and helps improve learning, communication, and cooperation (Santamaría & Alcalde, 2019; Veach, 2019). Academic literature found statistically significant differences between genders since men show a higher positive emotional assessment of the game than women (Gutiérrez et al., 2020). Women show a more outstanding commitment to the activity, while men showed more stress caused by the time limit to solve problems (P. A. García et al., 2020).

In terms of experience, students with previous experience in performing escape rooms are more likely to be successful in the game (Caldas et al., 2019), while students with no experience had more problems understanding the puzzles and resources (Clauson et al., 2019).

Students perceive the physical escape room as more intriguing and pleasant than the virtual one. In the first case, the experience is more immersive, fostering greater competition among the participants due to communication between them (Ang et al., 2020). The escape room can be a powerful tool to facilitate the socialization of new students (it works as an icebreaker) and provides possibilities for study orientation and collaborative skills development (Nybo et al., 2020). Through gamification, students can implement various skills included in the study plans (González et al., 2021).

Despite the possible benefits that an escape room can bring to the teaching-learning process, there is also a negative tendency to use games in a formal educational context: mainly due to the possible inconveniences such as increased demotivation, the difficulty of the game, or excessive consumption of design and implementation time, among others (P. A. García et al., 2020).

CONTEXTUALIZATION

The great challenge in designing an escape room is that planning, and preparation require considerable time to devise and interconnect the tests involved (Brown et al., 2019; Gómez et al., 2019). The virtual room of escape room must be as realistic as possible to create a familiar environment for the player (Béguin et al., 2019). Regarding the itinerary, it is better to take a linear approach, that is, the puzzles follow a predetermined order so that, in this way, the responsible teacher or game director (game master) can supervise and control the progress of the participating teams (Nicholson, 2018). The escape rooms must be contextualized in a suggestive theme since the narrative is essential to understand their objectives and generate concern and interest in the game (Connelly et al., 2018). Finally, academic literature emphasizes that, for teachers, it is also an intellectual challenge to create puzzles to address the learning objectives, using previously acquired knowledge to solve problems (Cain, 2019; Jambhekar et al., 2019).

The experiences addressed in this research were part of Economic History subjects, of the Degree in Business Administration and International Economic Environment, of the master's degree in Foreign Trade Management and Internationalization of Companies. This research created the escape room titled 'The Ministry of Time: Save Bretton Woods', taking advantage of the popularity of the television series 'The Ministry of Time' in Spain.

METHODOLOGY

This work has used the experimental method to answer the research questions raised. This methodology has been and is widely applied in research related to teaching and learning in very diverse areas of knowledge (Friedman & Sunder, 1994; Guimarães & Lima, 2021; Kagel & Roth, 2020; Kusainov et al., 2021; Levchyk et al., 2021; Mateu, 2021). The experimental method is suitable for identifying causal relationships (Friedman & Sunder, 1994; Kagel & Roth, 2020) and evaluating -thanks to the possibility of control- the impact of the use of audiovisual resources in the classroom (independent variable) on learning performance (dependent variable). Another advantage is replicability: the experiments can be reproduced as many times as required to confirm or refute the evidence of the results obtained, which provides transparency to the research process (Kagel & Roth, 2020; Rogers & Revesz, 2020).

Like any research method, the experimental methodology has disadvantages related to control problems of the variables investigated, the non-representativeness of the selected samples, or the non-comparability of the established groups, among others (Friedman & Sunder, 1994; Rogers & Revesz, 2020; Ross & Morrison, 2013). These disadvantages are part of the method limitations that researchers tried to control to minimize their effects on the experimental process conducted (Rogers & Revesz, 2020).

The experimental sessions took place at the end of the first and second semesters of the 21-22 academic year, respectively, on the subjects of the International Economic Environment and Economic History. The learning platforms for the academic subjects were CANVAS, for International Economic Environment, and MOODLE, for Economic History. The virtual classroom for contact with the students was Adobe Connect, and the online tool used for the design and execution of the escape room was Genially

Table 1. Number of students enrolled and selected

Subject: Economic History		
Students enrolled	25	
Randomly generated samples without repetition	M_{11} (Intervention group)	M_{12} (Control group)
Students in each sample	20	20
Subject: International Economic Environment		
Students enrolled	84	
Randomly generated samples without repetition	M_{21} (Intervention group)	M_{22} (Control group)
Students in each sample	20	20

Source: own elaboration.

(Genial.ly). The questionnaire linked to the escape room to assess the students' perceptions was Google Forms, and Quizizz was the tool to design the learning control test to assess academic performance.

The number of students enrolled in the course was 25 in Economic History and 84 in International Economic Environment. The procedure for selecting intervention and control samples in each subject was as follows: the names of the students were ordered alphabetically by the first surname in a list and, from a simple function in Excel that generates random numbers (=RANDOM. BETWEEN (a; b)), and researchers obtained two samples of students for each subject, the control sample, and the intervention sample, getting as many random numbers as were necessary through the F9 key.

Table 1 shows the number of students enrolled in both subjects and the randomly selected ones for each sample.

The students of the respective intervention groups, M11, and M21, were contacted through the Moodle and Canvas platforms, respectively, so that they would carry out the escape room entitled "The Ministry of Time: Save Bretton Woods". The students in the intervention groups used an average of 20 minutes to complete it. Researchers introduced within the escape room design itself a questionnaire designed with Google Forms to obtain their impressions of the experience. In the M11 sample, 59% of the participants were women, and the mean age was 27.5 years, while in the M21, 63% of the participants were women, and the mean age was 29.6 years. The students in the control groups were not notified of their participation in the experiment until the end to avoid changes in their behavior if they were aware of monitoring their results through the knowledge control test developed in Quizizz.

Table 2 shows the main information about the escape room designed and used in this research:

After the escape room and the completion of the survey, before obtaining a reward (knowing one of the questions from the final exam), they were given a gamified control test through Quizizz to evaluate their learning performance. The test consisted of a battery of 10 multiple choice questions, with four possible alternatives, of which only one option was correct. The maximum time for carrying out the control test was 20 minutes since the researchers limited the time per answer to 2 minutes. Figure 1 shows the experimental process carried out on each of the subjects:

This study applied the Mann-Whitney non-parametric inference contrast before analyzing the results from the control test. In this way, it was possible to verify whether there were significant differences

Table 2. Data about the escape room used

Title	The Ministry of Time: Save Bretton Woods
Author	Dra. Marta Magadán-Díaz
Tester	Dr. Jesús I. Rivas-García
Public access link	https://view.genial.ly/62054ed05ef0f90018c5ecde/interactive-content-escape-room-salva-el-bretton-woods
Slides	63
Videos	2
Built-in tools	Google forms: https://docs.google.com/forms/d/e/1FAIpQLSdn12q-SMOTxbxN1rlo r1r1RrU3q4UeUnNWs0-zpD-lHBgH0g/viewform

Source: own elaboration

between the samples belonging to the intervention groups and the control groups to reinforce the results obtained in each academic subject.

RESULTS AND ANALYSIS

This study adresses the following research questions: a) How do students perceive the use of escape rooms in the virtual classroom?; and b) Does the use of escape rooms impact the learning performance of students?

Students' Perceptions on the use of Escape Rooms in the Virtual Classroom

This research collected the students' perceptions from the intervention groups regarding the performance of the escape room through the questionnaire designed in Google Forms (see link in Table 2).

Figure 1. Experimental process. Source: own elaboration

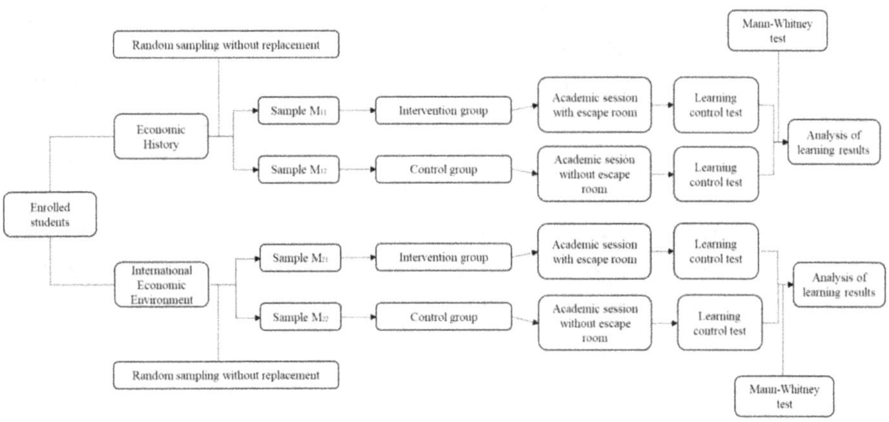

Figure 2. What adjectives best describe, in your opinion, this activity? Source: own elaboration.

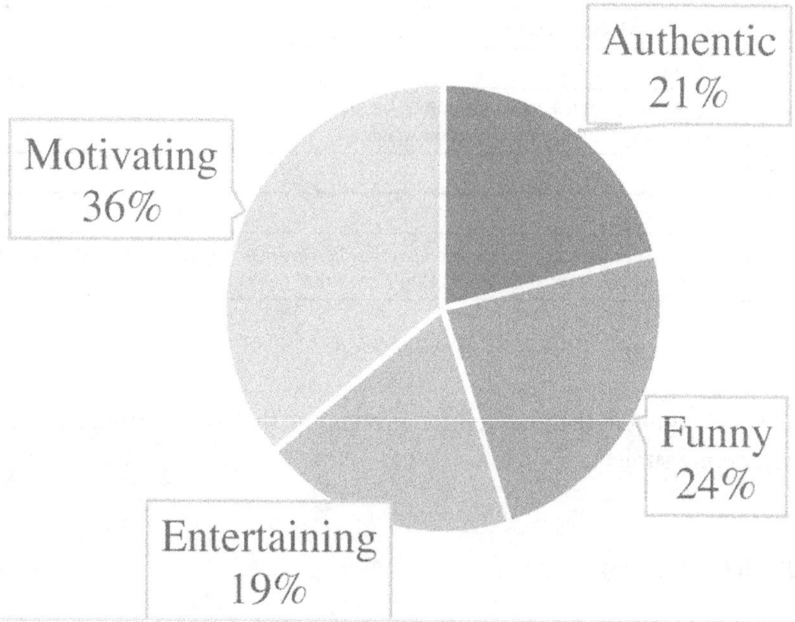

When asked to define their experience with certain adjectives, the students of the intervention group in the Economic History subject found the escape room motivating, fun, authentic, and entertaining (see Figure 2).

In the International Economic Environment subject, the same expressions also prevailed to assess the escape room but were hierarchized differently: authentic, motivating, funny, and entertaining (see Figure 3).

As can be seen, motivation and authenticity are among the qualities that have attracted the most attention, respectively, among the students of each of the intervention groups, which confirms the importance that, when designing an escape room, these factors must keep in mind to motivate, amuse and entertain students (Navarro & Pérez, 2022).

Figure 4 shows the results obtained from the questionnaire given to the students of the intervention group in Economic History on the motivating effect of the escape room.

Figure 5 shows the results obtained from the questionnaire given to the students of the intervention group in the International Economic Environment on the motivating effect of the escape room.

As can be seen, the students stated -in both cases- that they felt very motivated, both in the execution of the escape room and in the development of the subject, reaching a high degree of satisfaction and fulfilling their expectations about the tool, which confirms the findings of academic literature (Aubeux et al., 2020; Baker et al., 2020; Borrego et al., 2017; I. García, 2019; Licorish et al., 2018; López et al., 2019; Magadán & Rivas, 2022a; Robson et al., 2015).

Figure 3. What adjectives best describe, in your opinion, this activity? Source: own elaboration.

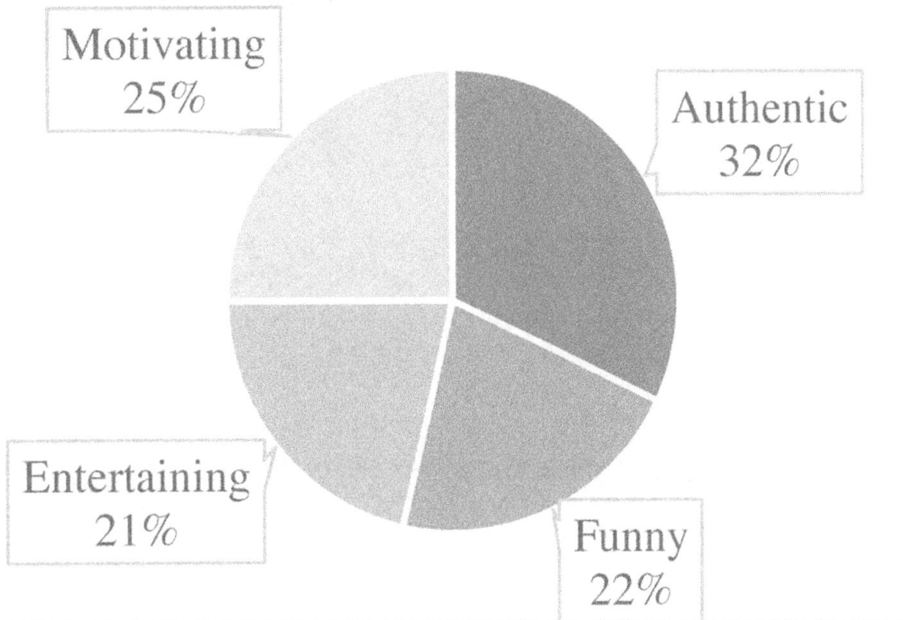

Escape Room Impact on Students' Learning Performance

Figure 6 shows the results obtained from the questionnaire given to the students of the intervention group in Economic History on the impact of the escape room on the learning process.

Figure 7 shows the results obtained from the questionnaire given to the students of the intervention group in the International Economic Environment about the impact of the escape room on the learning process.

The students from the intervention groups of both subjects consider that the didactic use of the escape room makes them active and not passive agents of their own learning process (Parra et al., 2020), positively assimilating a playful method of accessing knowledge that is perfectly applicable in the context of higher education, which confirms the findings of the academic literature (Adams et al., 2018; Dichev & Dicheva, 2017; Franco & DeLuca, 2019; Magadán & Rivas, 2021; Parra et al., 2020; Sánchez et al., 2020; Santamaría & Alcalde, 2019; Veach, 2019; Zhang et al., 2019).

Figure 8 shows the results obtained from the questionnaire given to the students of the intervention group in Economic History about their evaluation of the experience with the escape room.

Figure 9 shows the results obtained from the questionnaire given to the students of the intervention group in the International Economic Environment about their evaluation of the experience with the escape room.

The results obtained show the students from the intervention groups of both subjects perceive that the escape room has enabled them to reinforce their knowledge and detect those aspects they should prepare for better. Also, they pointed out that the difficulty level of the game was adequate, according to the findings of the academic literature (Craig et al., 2019; Garwood, 2020; Jambhekar et al., 2019;

Figure 4. Dimension 1. Motivation. Source: own elaboration.

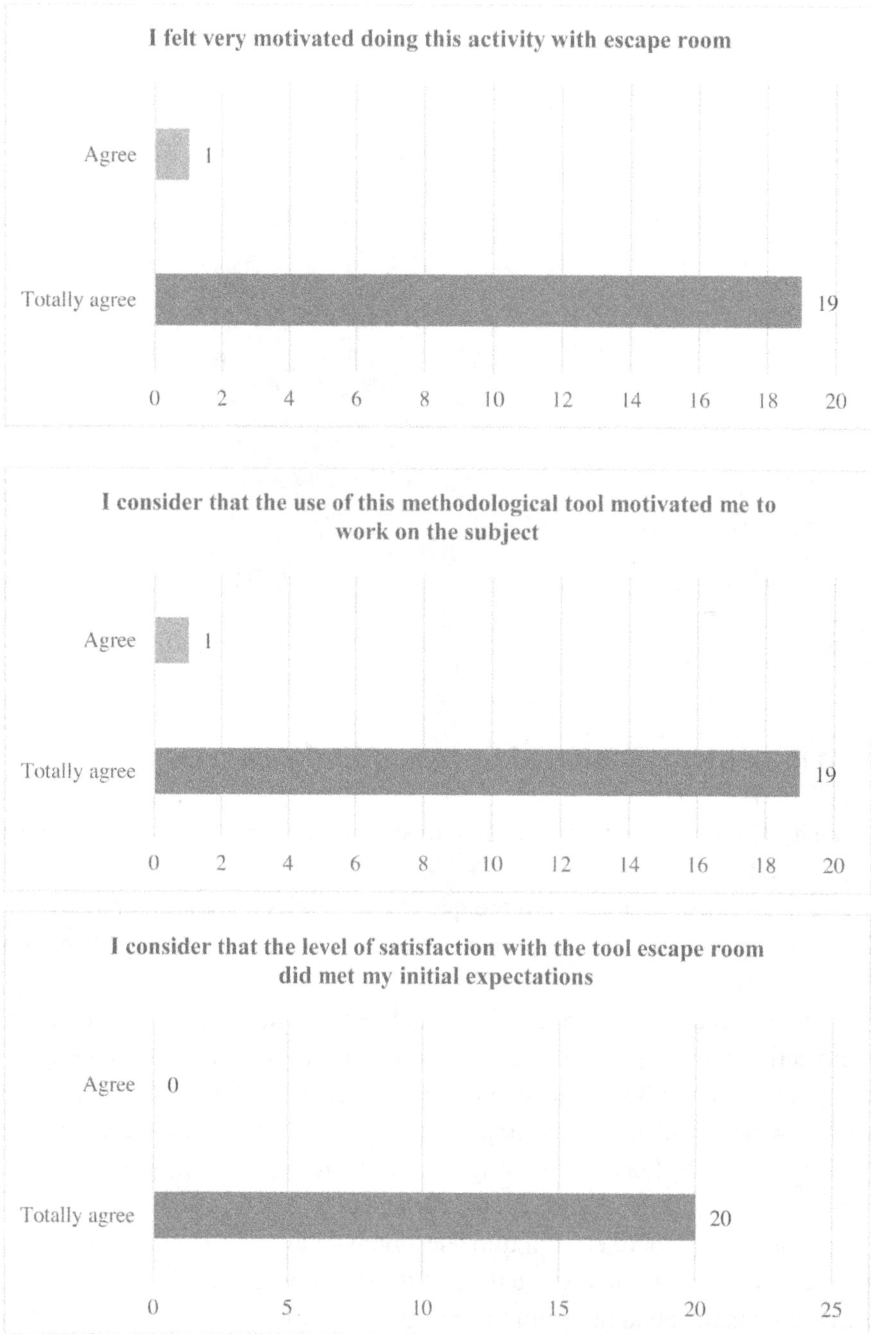

Makri et al., 2021; Wise et al., 2018). Furthermore, the students not only think that the tool is useful (Aubeux et al., 2020; Baker et al., 2020) but would like to do more similar activities.

Table 3 shows the literal expressions used by the students of the intervention groups in Economic History and International Economic Environment to explain why they liked participating in the escape room.

Figure 5. Dimension 1. Motivation. Source: own elaboration.

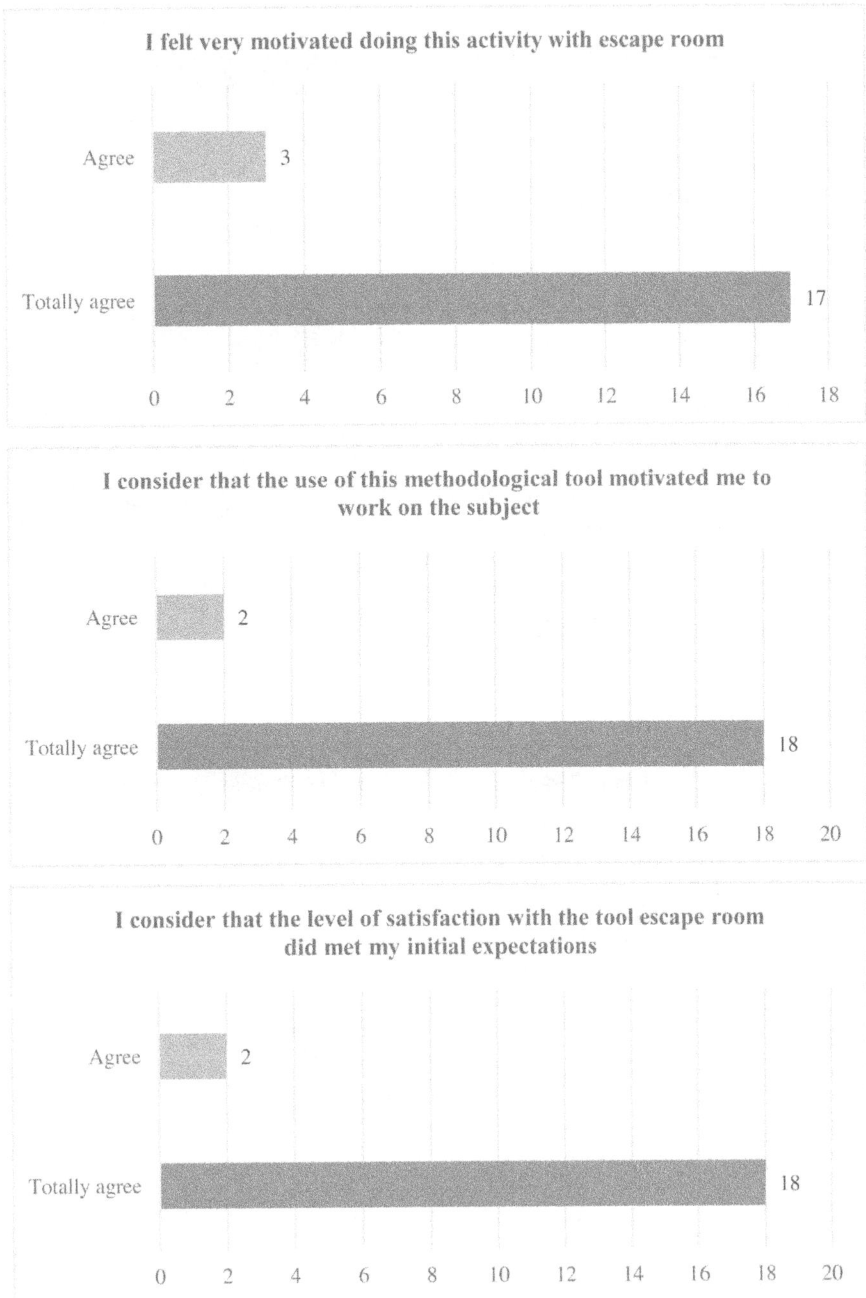

As can be seen, most responses confirm and underline the novelty and innovation of learning through the escape room and its dynamic and playful nature (Borrego et al., 2017).

Table 4 shows the literal expressions used by the students of the intervention groups in Economic History and International Economic Environment to point out what they liked the most about the escape room experience.

Figure 6. Dimension 2. Learning. Source: own elaboration.

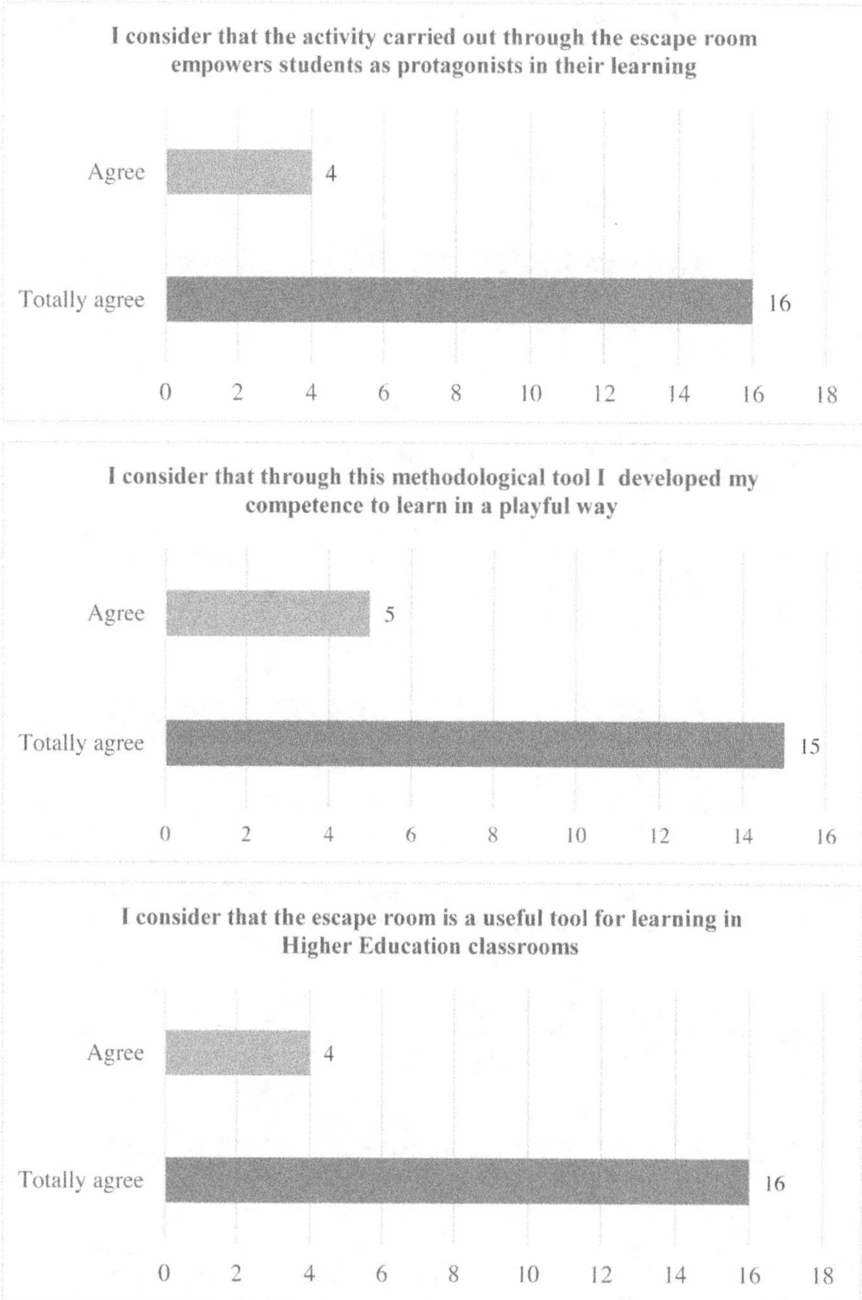

As seen, the aspects pointed out as elements that have most attracted them are very diverse but summarized in the idea that they find it a suggestive, attractive, practical, and fun way of learning that rewards them for their effort (de la Flor et al., 2020; Gómez et al., 2019).

Figure 7. Dimension 2. Learning. Source: own elaboration.

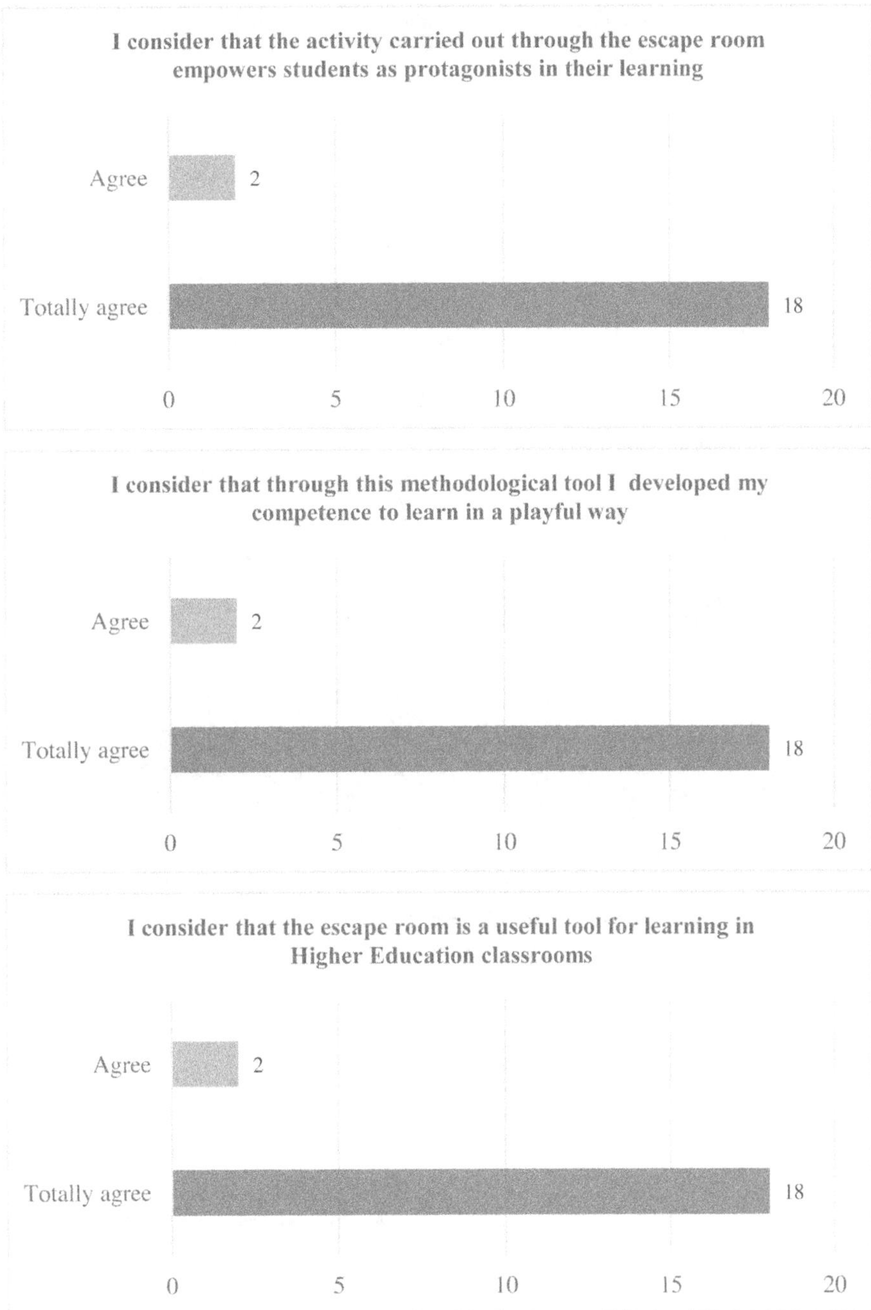

Table 5 shows the literal expressions used by the students of the intervention groups in Economic History and International Economic Environment to indicate what resources they used to carry out the escape room.

Basically, the most used resources were class notes and content (Aubeux et al., 2020; Baker et al., 2020; de la Flor et al., 2020; Gómez et al., 2019).

Figure 8. Dimension 3. Evaluation. Source: own elaboration.

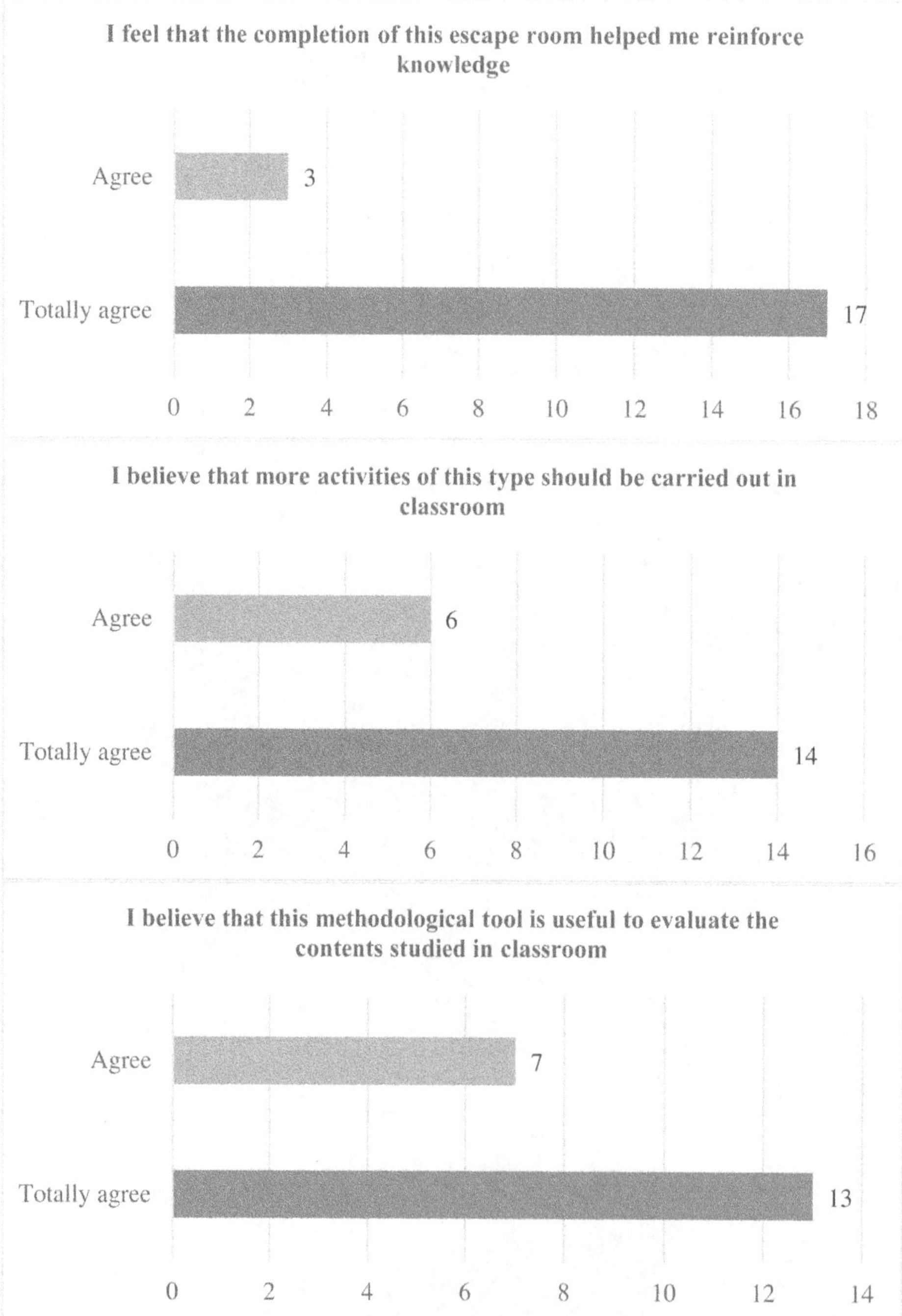

Finally, Table 6 shows the literal expressions used by the students of the intervention groups in Economic History and International Economic Environment to express their general opinions about the escape room carried out.

Figure 9. Dimension 3. Evaluation. Source: own elaboration.

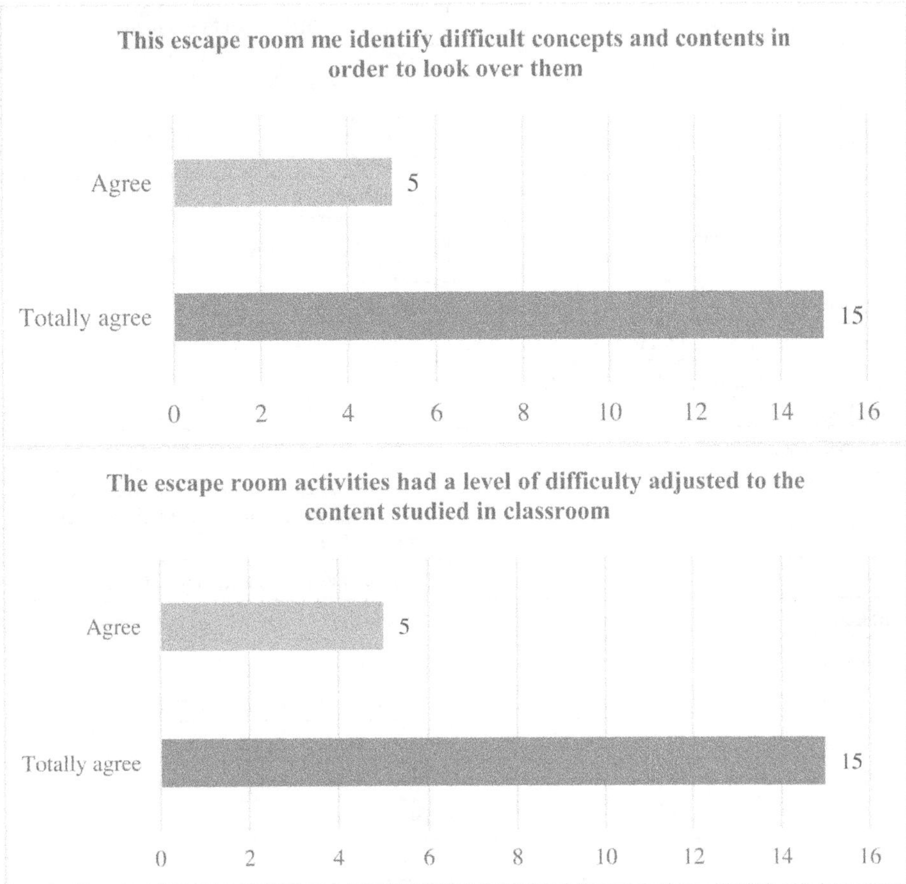

The students' evaluations were positive and enthusiastic, pointing out that the escape room was a great way to learn (de la Flor et al., 2020; Gómez et al., 2019).

This research used the Mann-Whitney non-parametric inference test (see Table 7) to reinforce the results obtained.

As shown in Table 7, the Mann-Whitney test confirms the alternative hypothesis, revealing significant differences in the learning control test between the intervention and control samples of each academic subject analyzed. Therefore, such differences come from the differentiated treatment in the intervention groups compared to the control groups.

CONCLUSIONS

As stated at the beginning of this research, the general objective was to determine if the use of escape rooms improved the performance of undergraduate and graduate students, considering respectively two subjects, Economic History and International Economic Environment.

The first research question posed in this study was to determine the students' perception of escape rooms. The second research question was whether the escape rooms impacted the students' learning

Table 3. Why did you like to participate in this escape room?

Economic History	International Economic Environment
"It's a game, but at the same time, you learn and share your previous knowledge."	"It's a new way of learning."
"Because it's very instructive and enjoyable."	"It's a very dynamic and entertaining way to retain specific information."
"Exciting learning method."	"It's funny."
"It made me strengthen my knowledge and trust more in my abilities."	"I've reviewed concepts and learned in a 100% didactic way."
"I strengthened my knowledge."	"Very interactive."
"It's very interactive and helps us learn dynamically."	"It's very didactic and, at the same time, helps me study."
"It's very dynamic. It seeks to remember what has been learned and makes it interesting to investigate."	"Because it's dynamic and different."
"Because I've reviewed concepts and learned in a 100% didactic way."	"Fascinating interaction that enriches knowledge."
"An interactive and different experience."	"It's dynamic, different, and fresh content, and I am a big fan of the Ministry of Time."
"Good learning method."	"Learning by doing this kind of game is very interesting."
"Original and different."	"Because it helps me study and it's funny."
"Great learning strategy."	"It's funny and enriching."
"I was delighted to pass the tests of the game."	"It's innovative and a funny way to learn."
"It seems to be a playful and very visual activity to fix ideas."	"Because it helps me study and it's fun."
"It has helped me easily and enjoyably review concepts and ideas."	"It's enjoyable learning in this way."
"Funny."	"Didactic."
"Interesting."	"It is a good and attractive way to teach and fix knowledge."
"It's a new way of learning."	"It's pretty practical and visual."
"It's dynamic and different."	"It makes learning more dynamic."
"I find it very entertaining."	"It's something innovative that I'm not used to."

Source: own elaboration.

performance. A digital escape room set in the series "The Ministry of Time" was designed and applied to address the general objective and the research questions formulated above.

Concerning the first research question of this work, after completing the questionnaire linked to the escape room and designed in Google Forms, this study identified those recurring words and expressions revealing a positive perception of the use of the escape room in the classroom. The surveyed students valued that this didactic tool encouraged their participation and interaction in the virtual classroom, increased their motivation, and facilitated their learning in a pleasant and funny way.

Regarding the second research question, the first result is that the intervention groups of both subjects obtained better scores in the gamified test with Quizizz compared to the control groups. The Mann-Whitney non-parametric inference test confirmed the robustness of these results. This research concluded that the escape room positively impacted the students' learning performance, no matter if their educational level was undergraduate or graduate: their perceptions were the same.

Table 4. What do you like the most about the escape room?

Economic History	International Economic Environment
"The character's role and game."	"The way of learning."
"The interactivity."	"The design and variety of issues and questions posed."
"The simplicity with which it can be done."	"The link with the subject."
"Put into practice what has been learned.	"The way it all intertwines."
The clues."	"The intrigue and immersion."
"The fact of putting myself in the skin of the protagonist."	"I really liked the theme of solving the case."
"I liked the graphic design, the idea, and the activity."	"It's useful for learning and studying."
"I really liked the theme."	"The Interaction and logic applied to its development."
"A friendly way to learn."	"I liked that the escape room was based on the Ministry of Time."
"The implication and the relationship with the subject."	"The information, visualization, and reward get"
"The format."	"I liked it all."
"The reward."	"The missions."
"The intrigue."	"It was funny."
"The story that is told."	"The dynamics and interface."
"The tests one is facing."	"The interactivity."
"The connection with the challenges posed."	"You learn while playing."
"The original way of approaching a historical subject."	"The game put me in the character's shoes."
"I liked everything in general."	"The reward."
"I liked the escape room was based on The Ministry of Time, and the images."	"I liked a lot looking for the codes."
"I liked to become the protagonist of the story."	"A funny way to learn."

Source: own elaboration.

The findings obtained in this study may be of interest to other fields of knowledge where the design and application of escape rooms have not yet been sufficiently developed due to the uncertainty about its impact on academic performance or its positive assessment by students.

This research has, among others, the following limitations: a) the results put the focus on a profile of undergraduate and postgraduate students from specific subjects; b) only two samples are analyzed, instead to design more complex experimental treatments; c) this study used only one escape room.

Future lines of research should focus on overcoming the above limitations, expanding subjects and samples, and combining a mixed methodology of the QUAN®qual type, that is, a sequential analysis scheme centered on the quantitative perspective to guide qualitative work.

Although this work has significant contributions, the results are subject to the limitations of an experimental study. In future research, it would be interesting to use more than one escape room and contrast the results from the students' perceptions of different subjects, degrees, and academic levels to properly assess the value of this educational tool.

Table 5. What resources have you used to play the escape room?

Economic History	International Economic Environment
"The class notes."	"The reading of documents got from the platform."
"The escape room clues."	"Those from the escape room and the external resources that were requested. For example, Amazon to find the ISBN."
"Class documents."	"What I learned in class."
"The study material."	"Some specific Internet searches."
"My class notes, my phone's camera to remember the clues, and Amazon."	"Class documents."
"Internet search."	"The class notes."
"The material from the platform."	"Internet search."
"Some specific Internet searches."	"I used the contents seen in class."
"Only Amazon to search the ISBN of one of the tests."	"I followed the clues."
"Class themes and videos."	"The class notes."
"Classes and notes."	"Follow the escape room clues."
"Knowledge acquired in classes."	"Follow the clues."
"The subject content."	"The notes and PPTs."
"Internet searches."	"The notes and Internet."
"The contents seen in classes."	"The class notes."
"The notes and PPTs."	"Class sessions and documents from the platform."
"The viewing of the corresponding class."	"My class notes and Internet."
"The PPTs of the themes."	"Class notes and the escape room clues."
"The notes and Internet."	"Only my class notes."
"Following the tracks and study material on the platform."	"The notes and game clues."

Source: own elaboration.

Table 6. Write your general opinion about the escape room "The Ministry of Time: Save Bretton Woods."

Economic History	International Economic Environment
"Funny."	"Very funny, since it makes you feel part of the event, and one gets more involved."
"Different from what we usually do in class."	"Very entertaining and mysterious at the same time in terms of deciphering the case."
"I liked that the game implemented the topics seen in class."	"Very good and practical."
"It has been a fantastic tool."	"Very interesting."
"It is very entertaining, and you learn more."	"Cool."
"Enriching and entertaining."	"It helped me reinforce what I learned in class."
"A good learning technique."	"It is a helpful tool to strengthen my "knowledge and improve my learning."
"Very original."	"It helped me reinforce my knowledge."
"I enjoyed it, and it was a way to remember what I saw in class. I loved! Thanks for the experience." "Motivational."	"It was a refreshing and intriguing activity."
"It has been well. It was entertaining."	"It is a tool that helps me improve in learning."
"Interesting."	"It helped me study."
"I loved it because it helped me to remember what I learned."	"The environment formed to carry out the activity invites the participants to be much more attentive to develop it."
"Very good and practical."	"It is a fun way to learn."
"Super entertaining and a great way to present what you have learned."	"Very useful for the exam."
"Very interesting."	"It is very entertaining, and you learn more."
"Very entertaining."	"It was an exciting activity with the "information about the classes we had previously seen."
"It was an excellent tool for having fun learning."	"Very dynamic and fun."
"It helps highlight study areas I need to review on."	"It is a great way to attract attention and interest in the subject."
"It is helpful to remind the concepts seen in classrooms."	"Entertaining."
"Excellent activity."	"It is a practical tool to clarify concepts."

Source: own elaboration.

Table 7. Mann-Whitney test

Sample	Sample size	Value of U for each sample	Critical value of U	Result	Hypothesis
M_{11}	20	67	$U_{20,20} = 88$ (α=0.001)	$U_{20,20} > U_{M11}$	H_1 is accepted, and H_0 is rejected.
M_{12}	20	245.5			
M_{21}	20	52		$U_{20,20} > U_{M21}$	H_1 is accepted, and H_0 is rejected.
M_{22}	20	328.5			

Source: own elaboration.

REFERENCES

Adams, V., Burger, S., Crawford, K., & Setter, R. (2018). Can you escape? Creating an escape room to facilitate active learning. *Journal for Nurses in Professional Development, 34*(2), 1–5. doi:10.1097/NND.0000000000000433 PMID:29481471

Alonso, G., & Schroeder, K. T. (2020). Applying active learning in a virtual classroom such as a molecular biology escape room. *Biochemistry and Molecular Biology Education, 48*(5), 514–515. doi:10.1002/bmb.21429 PMID:32812701

Ang, J. W. J., Ng, Y. N. A., & Liew, R. S. (2020). Physical and digital educational escape room for teaching chemical bonding. *Journal of Chemical Education, 97*(9), 2849–2856. doi:10.1021/acs.jchemed.0c00612

Aubeux, D., Blanchflower, N., Bray, E., Clouet, R., Remaud, M., Badran, Z., Prud'homme, T., & Gaudin, A. (2020). Educational gaming for dental students: Design and assessment of a pilot endodontic-themed escape game. *European Journal of Dental Education, 24*(3), 449–457. doi:10.1111/eje.12521 PMID:32142189

Baker, C., Crabtree, G., & Anderson, K. (2020). Student pharmacist perceptions of learning after strengths-based leadership skills lab and escape room in pharmacy practice skills laboratory. *Currents in Pharmacy Teaching & Learning, 12*(6), 724–727. doi:10.1016/j.cptl.2020.01.021 PMID:32482276

Béguin, E., Besnard, S., Cros, A., Joannes, B., Leclerc-Istria, O., Noel, A., Roels, N., Taleb, F., Thong-phan, J., Alata, E., & Nicomette, V. (2019). Computer-security-oriented escape room. *IEEE Security and Privacy, 17*(4), 78–83. doi:10.1109/MSEC.2019.2912700

Borrego, C., Fernández, C., Blanes, I., & Robles, S. (2017). Room escape at class: Escape games activities to facilitate the motivation and learning in computer science. *Journal of Technology and Science Education, 7*(2), 162–171. doi:10.3926/jotse.247

Brown, N., Darby, W., & Coronel, H. (2019). An escape room as a simulation teaching strategy. *Clinical Simulation in Nursing, 30*, 1–6. doi:10.1016/j.ecns.2019.02.002

Cain, J. (2019). Exploratory implementation of a blended format escape room in a large enrollment pharmacy management class. *Currents in Pharmacy Teaching & Learning, 11*(1), 44–50. doi:10.1016/j.cptl.2018.09.010 PMID:30527875

Caldas, L., Eukel, H., Matulewicz, A., Fernández, E., & Donohoe, K. (2019). Applying educational gaming success to a nonsterile compounding escape room. *Currents in Pharmacy Teaching & Learning, 11*(10), 1049–1054. doi:10.1016/j.cptl.2019.06.012 PMID:31685175

Clauson, A., Hahn, L., Frame, T., Hagan, A., Bynum, L. A., Thompson, M., & Kiningham, K. (2019). An innovative escape room activity to assess student readiness for advanced pharmacy practice experiences (APPEs). *Currents in Pharmacy Teaching & Learning, 11*(7), 723–728. doi:10.1016/j.cptl.2019.03.011 PMID:31227096

Connelly, L., Burbach, B., Kennedy, C., & Walters, L. (2018). Escape room recruitment event: Description and lessons learned. *The Journal of Nursing Education, 57*(3), 184–187. doi:10.3928/01484834-20180221-12 PMID:29505080

Craig, C., Ngondo, P., Devling, M., & Scharlach, J. (2019). Escaping the routine: Unlocking group intervention. *Communication Teacher*, *34*(1), 14–18. doi:10.1080/17404622.2019.1593475

de la Flor, D., Calles, J. A., Espada, J. J., & Rodríguez, R. (2020). Application of escape lab-room to heat transfer evaluation for chemical engineers. *Education for Chemical Engineers*, *33*, 9–16. doi:10.1016/j.ece.2020.06.002

Dichev, C., & Dicheva, D. (2017). Gamifying education: What is known, what is believed and what remains uncertain: A critical review. *International Journal of Educational Technology in Higher Education*, *14*(1), 9. doi:10.118641239-017-0042-5

Franco, P., & DeLuca, D. (2019). Learning through action: Creating and implementing a strategy game to foster innovative thinking in higher education. *Simulation & Gaming*, *50*(1), 23–43. doi:10.1177/1046878118820892

Friedman, D., & Sunder, S. (1994). *Experimental methods. Cambridge Books*. Cambridge Books. doi:10.1017/CBO9781139174176

Fuentes, A., Parra, M. E., López, J., & Segura, A. (2020). Learning mathematics with emerging methodologies—The escape room as a case study. *Mathematics*, *8*(9), 1586. doi:10.3390/math8091586

García, I. (2019). Escape room como propuesta de gamificación en educación [Escape room as a proposal for gamification in education]. *Revista Educativa Hekademos*, *27*, 71–79. https://hekademos.com/index.php/hekademos/article/view/17

García, P. A., González, V., & Serrano, J. L. (2020). La habitación de escape como estrategia en la resolución de problemas [The escape room as a problem solving strategy]. *REDU. Revista de Docencia Universitaria*, *18*(2), 97–114. doi:10.4995/redu.2020.13573

Garwood, J. (2020). Escape to learn! An innovative approach to engage students in learning. *The Journal of Nursing Education*, *59*(5), 278–282. doi:10.3928/01484834-20200422-08 PMID:32352543

Gómez, J. L., Gómez, J., Albedín, L., Correa, M., González, E., & Cañadas, G. A. (2019). The impact on nursing students'opinons and motivation of using a "Nursing Escape Room" as a teaching game: A descriptive study. *Nurse Education Today*, *72*, 73–76. doi:10.1016/j.nedt.2018.10.018 PMID:30453202

González, M., Rodríguez, A., & Padilla, M. T. (2021). La gamificación como estrategia metodológica en la Universidad. El caso de BugaMAP: percepciones y valoraciones de los estudiantes [Gamification as a methodological strategy in the University. The BugaMAP case: students' perceptions and assessments]. *Pixel-Bit. Revista De Medios Y Educación*, *63*, 293–324. doi:10.12795/pixelbit.90394

Guimarães, L., & Lima, R. da S. (2021). Active learning application in engineering education: Effect on student performance using repeated measures experimental design. *European Journal of Engineering Education*, *46*(5), 1–23. doi:10.1080/03043797.2021.1934406

Gutiérrez, L., Márquez, V., Román, P., Rodriguez, M., Ropero, C., & Molina, G. (2020). Escape rooms as a clinical evaluation method for nursing students. *Clinical Simulation in Nursing*, *40*, 73–80. doi:10.1016/j.ecns.2020.05.010

Hawkins, J., Wiles, L., Tremblay, B., & Thompson, B. (2020). Behind the scenes of an educational escape room. *The American Journal of Nursing, 120*(10), 50–56. doi:10.1097/01.NAJ.0000718636.68938.bb PMID:32976152

Jambhekar, K., Pahls, R., & Deloney, L. (2019). Benefits of an escape room as a novel educational activity for radiology residents. *Academic Radiology, 27*(2), 276–283. doi:10.1016/j.acra.2019.04.021 PMID:31160173

Kagel, J., & Roth, A. (2020). *The handbook of experimental economics* (Vol. 2). Princeton University Press.

Kapp, K. (2012). *The gamification of learning and instruction*. Pfeiffer.

Kusainov, A., Yessenova, K., Kassymova, R., Moldassan, K., & Sembayeva, A. (2021). Comparative analysis of the process of training education managers in educational institutions. *International Journal for Research in Vocational Education and Training, 8*(2), 186–207. doi:10.13152/IJRVET.8.2.3

Levchyk, I., Chaikovska, H., Yankovych, O., Kuzma, I., & Rozhko-Pavlyshyn, T. (2021). Formation of sustainable development competencies in primary school children. *Journal of Education Culture and Society, 12*(2), 341–360. doi:10.15503/jecs2021.2.341.360

Licorish, S. A., Owen, H. E., Daniel, B., & George, J. L. (2018). Students' perception of Kahoot!'s influence on teaching and learning. *Research and Practice in Technology Enhanced Learning, 13*(9), 1–23. doi:10.118641039-018-0078-8

López, S., Gordillo, A., Barra, E., & Quemada, J. (2019). Examining the use of an educational escape room for teaching programming in a higher education setting. *IEEE Access: Practical Innovations, Open Solutions, 7*, 31723–31737. doi:10.1109/ACCESS.2019.2902976

Magadán, M., & Rivas, J. (2021). El empleo de los recursos audiovisuales como herramienta de aprendizaje [The use of audiovisual resources as a learning tool]. *Techno Review. International Technology. Science and Society Review, 10*(2), 185–198. doi:10.37467/gkarevtechno.v10.3118

Magadán, M., & Rivas, J. I. (2022a). Gamificación del aula en la enseñanza superior online: El uso de Kahoot [Classroom gamification in online higher education: The use of Kahoot]. *Campus Virtuales, 11*(1), 137–152. doi:10.54988/cv.2022.1.978

Magadán, M., & Rivas, J. I. (2022b). Percepções dos alunos de pós-graduação em face da gamificação em sala de aula com Quizizz [Percepções dos alunos de pós-graduação em face da gamificação em sala de aula com Quizizz]. *Texto Livre, 15*, e36941. doi:10.35699/1983-3652.2022.36941

Makri, A., Vlachopoulos, D., & Martina, R. (2021). Digital escape rooms as innovative pedagogical tools in education: A systematic literature review. *Sustainability, 13*(8), 4587. doi:10.3390u13084587

Manzano, A., Camacho, P., Guerrero, M. Á., Guerrero, L., Aguilar, J. M., Trigueros, R., & Alias, A. (2021). Between level up and game over: A systematic literature review of gamification in education. *Sustainability, 13*(4), 2247. doi:10.3390u13042247

Martina, R., & Göksen, S. (2020). Developing educational escape rooms for experiential entrepreneurship education. *Entrepreneurship Education and Pedagogy, 16*, 495–527. doi:10.1177/2515127420969957

Mateu, G. (2021). Innovative education management: An empirical study. *TEC Empresarial, 15*(3), 2–17. doi:10.18845/te.v15i3.5760

Morell, B., Eukel, H., & Santurri, L. (2020). Soft skills and implications for future professional practice: Qualitative findings of a nursing education escape room. *Nurse Education Today, 93*, 104462. doi:10.1016/j.nedt.2020.104462 PMID:32791421

Navarro, C., & Pérez, I. J. (2022). El escape room como estrategia didáctica en el Máster de Profesorado [The escape room as a didactic strategy in the Master's Degree in Teachers]. *Retos, 44*, 221–231. https://dialnet.unirioja.es/servlet/articulo?codigo=8127983

Nicholson, S. (2018). Creating engaging escape rooms for the classroom. *Childhood Education, 94*(1), 44–49. doi:10.1080/00094056.2018.1420363

Nybo, S. E., Sahr, M., Young, M., Axford, K., Sohn, M., Lyons, M., & Klepser, M. (2020). Design of a large-scale escape room for first-year pharmacy student orientation. *Currents in Pharmacy Teaching & Learning, 12*(11), 1340–1347. doi:10.1016/j.cptl.2020.06.002 PMID:32867932

Ouariachi, T., & Van Dam, M. (2022). Educational innovation to address climate change issues: The emerging trend of (online) escape rooms. In *Handbook of Research on Using Disruptive Methodologies and Game-Based Learning to Foster Transversal Skills* (pp. 263–278). IGI Global. doi:10.4018/978-1-7998-8645-7.ch013

Ouariachi, T., & Wim, E. (2020). Escape rooms as tools for climate change education: An exploration of initiatives. *Environmental Education Research, 26*(8), 1193–1206. doi:10.1080/13504622.2020.1753659

Pakhalov, A., & Rozhkova, N. (2020). Escape rooms as tourist attractions: Enhancing visitors' experience through new technologies. *Journal of Tourism, Heritage & Services Marketing, 6*(2), 55–60. https://papers.ssrn.com/sol3/papers.cfm?abstract_id=3748091

Parra, M. E., Segura, A., Morales, M., & López, E. (2020). Relación de los factores asociados en el desarrollo de experiencias gamificadas [List of factors associated with the development of gamified experiences]. *Campus Virtuales, 9*(1), 113–123. http://www.uajournals.com/ojs/index.php/campusvirtuales/article/view/641

Piñero, J. C. (2020). Educational escape rooms as a tool for horizontal mathematization: Learning process evidence. *Education Sciences, 10*(9), 213. doi:10.3390/educsci10090213

Robson, K., Plangger, K., Kietzmann, J. H., McCarthy, I., & Pitt, L. (2015). Is it all a game? Understanding the principles of gamification. *Business Horizons, 58*(4), 411–420.

Rogers, J., & Revesz, A. (2020). *Experimental and quasi-experimental designs*. Routledge.

Ross, S., & Morrison, G. (2013). Experimental research methods. In *Handbook of research on educational communications and technology* (pp. 1007–1029). Routledge.

Saleem, A., Noori, N., & Ozdamli, F. (2021). Gamification applications in E-learning: A literature review. *Technology, Knowledge and Learning*, 1–21. doi:10.1007/s10758-020-09487-x

Sánchez, D. R., Langer, M., & Kaur, R. (2020). Gamification in the classroom: Examining the impact of gamified quizzes on student learning. *Computers & Education, 144*, 103666. doi:10.1016/j.compedu.2019.103666

Santamaría, A., & Alcalde, E. (2019). Escaping from the English classroom. Who will get out first? *Aloma: Revista de Psicologia. Ciències de l'Educació i de l'Esport Blanquerna, 37*(2), 88–92. doi:10.51698/aloma.2019.37.2.83-92

Veach, C. C. (2019). Breaking out to break through: Re-imagining first-year orientations. *RSR. Reference Services Review, 47*(4), 556–569. doi:10.1108/RSR-06-2019-0039

Vygotsky, L. S. (1978). *Mind in society: The development of higher psychological processes*. Harvard University Press.

Wise, H., Lowe, J., Hill, A., Barnett, L., & Barton, C. (2018). Escape the welcome cliché: Designing educational escape rooms to enhance students' learning experience. *Journal of Information Literacy, 12*(1), 86–96. doi:10.11645/12.1.2394

Zhang, X. C., Diemer, G., Lee, H., Jaffe, R., & Papanagnou, D. (2019). Finding the 'QR' to patient safety: Applying gamification to incorporate patient safety priorities through a simulated 'escape room' experience. *Cureus, 11*(2), e4014. doi:10.7759/cureus.4014 PMID:31007972

KEY TERMS AND DEFINITIONS

Active Methodology: Any interactive didactical process based on teacher-student, student-student and/or student-materials communication, upgrading the learning commitment of the latter and leading them to training satisfaction and intellectual enrichment.

Educational Game: A game or activity used as a teaching technique to encourage or stimulate some type of learning. Its goal is that students learn knowledge or skills in a playful environment.

Escape Room: An individual or team game based on solving a series of tests and finding objects with a previously set goal: escape from a room before the end of a specific time or obtain a key code to save or get out of a situation and win a reward, among other possibilities.

Game-Based Learning (GBL): The use of games as support tools for learning processes.

Gamification: The use of games or playing elements to strengthen or complement educational processes.

Motivation: A psychological component that drives, guides, sustains, supports, and shapes an individual's behavior.

Virtual Classroom: A digital environment in which the exchange of knowledge that makes learning possible, takes place.

Chapter 3
Future Teachers Seek to Avoid Climate Emergency With a Virtual Escape Room:
Can a Virtual Escape Room Generate Positive Emotions in Students?

Patricia de Paz Lugo
https://orcid.org/0000-0001-9217-0637
Universidad Internacional de La Rioja, Spain

Carmen Romero García
Universidad Internacional de La Rioja, Spain

Natalia Serrano Amarilla
https://orcid.org/0000-0002-8337-7211
Universidad Internacional de La Rioja, Spain

ABSTRACT

Students often show negative attitudes and emotions towards the study of science. It is important to design learning situations that achieve positive emotions among students, since it has been shown that these favour the learning process. The aim of this study was to implement a virtual escape room in the subject of Knowledge of Natural Sciences in the Degree of Primary Education at the Universidad Internacional de La Rioja (UNIR) in an entirely online environment and to analyse the self-perceived emotions of the students and the degree of satisfaction with the learning experience. The results show that the experience has a positive impact on learning, the emotions experienced, and the satisfaction of the students. It is concluded that virtual escape rooms are presented as a way of approaching learning through different creative challenges, which allow for the creation of a positive emotional environment in which the teaching and learning process is more attractive.

DOI: 10.4018/978-1-6684-6081-8.ch003

INTRODUCTION

The approach to science has as a drawback the great demotivation it generates in students, which comes from the use of complex scientific language and the abundance of abstract concepts (Yllana-Prieto et al., 2021). The use of a student-centered methodology, such as gamification, can offer a positive stimulus that motivates and therefore promotes meaningful learning in science (Klisch et al., 2012).

As part of their training, students of the Primary Education Degree must achieve sufficient scientific literacy in order to reach their teaching competence. For this reason, the subject of Knowledge of Natural Sciences is part of their curriculum. Teachers in training present low perceived self-efficacy in science teaching (they see themselves as poorly qualified to teach science) (Brígido and Borrachero, 2011). As students at an online university, such as UNIR (Universidad Internacional de La Rioja), they face the risk of feeling isolated and even unmotivated (Jeong et al., 2019). In addition, students are not obliged to attend classes since they can visualize the lectures online on deferred. Their participation as active subjects is therefore not ensured, which is one of the great problems of online education (Parra-González and Segura-Robles, 2019). This hinders the development of interpersonal skills (collaboration, communication, etc.), but also skills related to the scientific field, such as reasoning, argumentation, issuing hypotheses, critical thinking, information search, decision making, research, problem-solving, etc. (Pedrinaci et al., 2012). Likewise, the opportunity to teach science in a useful, meaningful, and contextualized way within the daily life of the student is lost. That is why, in the present work, an educational escape room has been designed and implemented in a virtual classroom, as a gamified strategy, on Ecology and the environmental consequences of human activity, with the objectives of:

1. To know the self-perceived emotions of the students, as well as their degree of satisfaction with the learning experience.
2. To assess the students' perception of the effect of the escape room on learning through variables such as motivation, creativity and critical thinking.
3. To raise awareness of human involvement in environmental pollution.

BACKGROUND

Emotions in STEM Education

Emotions have traditionally been the object of analysis in the educational field in order to study evaluation anxiety and performance, as well as the relationship between emotion and motivation with respect to academic success and failure (Pekrun, 2005). However, in the 21st century and with the growing interest in interpersonal skills and emotional competencies, this trend is changing, giving emotions a key role in the teaching-learning process (Barragán et al., 2007). Moreover, the development of positive emotions has a direct impact on motivation, which depends largely on the type of methodology used in the teaching-learning process (Moreno et al., 2019). In fact, methodologies that allow the learner to be an active subject generate more positive emotions than a transmission-reception approach (Jeong et al., 2019). Likewise, it cannot be ignored that "emotions influence not only motivation but also factors as important in education as attention, memory, decision making, social relations or creativity" (Guillen, 2017, p.44).

On the other hand, emotions are connected to the teaching and learning of specific knowledge (Garritz & Ortega-Villar, 2013). Thus, from early ages, a growing disinterest in science and specifically the expression of negative emotions (rejection and boredom) for STEM (Science, Technology, Engineering and Mathematics) disciplines has been observed (Miller et al., 2018; Yllana-Prieto et al., 2021,), which implies a decrease in the choice of this type of university careers in adulthood (Van Aalderen-Smeets & van der Molen, 2015). Vázquez & Manassero (2007) demonstrated how positive emotions play a key role in the teaching-learning process of STEM subjects by influencing the cognitive factor while making the process more attractive. Along the same lines, Mellado et al. (2014) state that "positive emotional states favor science learning and the engagement of students as active learners, while negative ones limit the ability to learn" (p.13).

The teaching-learning process of science has traditionally been characterized by an abstract transmission of concepts, which to a greater extent, has led to this rejection and disinterest in science (Vázquez & Manassero, 2007). It is important that, in order to increase motivation for science, it is taught from a science-technology-society-environment (STSE) approach, as intended with the promotion of the Sustainable Development Goals agreed in the 2030 Agenda, among which stand out responsible consumption, healthy living, peaceful conflict resolution, acceptance and management of uncertainty, respect for the environment among others (United Nations General Assembly, 2015). Likewise, to maintain interest and achieve the much desired meaningful learning, it is necessary to convey the usefulness and practicality of science in the student's daily life, encouraging the issuance of hypotheses, experimentation, as well as reasoning. In addition, the contents to be taught must be not only useful but also meaningful (based on the students' previous knowledge) and verifiable (through practical activities) (Pedrinaci et al., 2012).

Dropout rates in e-learning systems are influenced not only by the characteristics of the virtual environment but also by factors such as motivation and emotions (Rebollo et al., 2008). Initially, the didactic methods used in these systems promoted learners to observe and listen through online platforms, in a passive way, with little interaction (Phelps & Vlachopoulos, 2019). This led to negative feelings such as isolation, lack of autonomy and leadership and lower motivation (Jeong et al., 2019), even when the student does not have to move geographically to attend classes and therefore conflicts between work schedules and family commitments are avoided (Ludwing-Hardman & Dunlap, 2003). However, with the shift in the educational paradigm from a learning-centered to a student-centered education, this situation has been reversed. The handicaps of distance education programs have been reduced, by allowing the application of playful and cooperative strategies, and with flexibility and the use of novel ICT tools being attractive advantages for digital natives. In fact, in the specific case of STEM education and healthcare disciplines, with their interdisciplinary nature, digital technologies are gaining special relevance when dealing with highly abstract contents such as virtual reality, augmented reality, 360 videos, simulators, the use of QR codes, among others (Makri et al., 2021). On the other hand, it should not be forgotten that those students who take an active role in STEM courses obtain better grades than those who do not (Wiswall et al., 2014).

Gamification and Educational Escape Rooms

The use of active, student-centered methodologies has the advantage of increasing motivation, but also student performance, collaboration and satisfaction, especially in STEM subjects (Klisch et al., 2012), as well as the consolidation of long-term memory (Tokuhama, 2010). Among these methodologies, gamification stands out since it has acquired a fundamental role in motivating students in their learning process (Landers & Callan, 2011) and involving them in it (Kapp, 2012), thus favoring meaningful learning (Villalustre & del Moral, 2015).

According to Kapp (2012), gamification is the use of game mechanics and aesthetics to engage and motivate, promoting learning and problem-solving. The term was coined in 2002 (Marczewski, 2013) and was not used in educational contexts until 2010 (Deterding et al., 2011). Lately, it has been applied in different subjects at different educational levels, mainly in primary and secondary education and especially in face-to-face contexts, although this is changing rapidly in virtual environments.

We can find multiple benefits in the educational game, such as the creation of different learning rhythms and knowledge of the progress of the student body and the promotion of creativity and allowing error without connotations of a negative nature, among others (Pisabarro & Vivaracho, 2018). It should be remembered that when the student is intrinsically motivated, i.e. s/he gets pleasure from performing the task, s/he will devote more time to what interests him/her, resulting in a greater mastery of the content, feeling self-realised (Pérez et al., 2019). Gamification can increase this intrinsic motivation and therefore improve the self-regulation of students, since it arouses curiosity, thus increasing dopamine synthesis and consequently the activity of the hippocampus, facilitating meaningful learning (Gruber et al., 2016; Guillén, 2017). In addition, curiosity "activates emotional mechanisms of the student that will allow him to focus attention and thus learn" (Guillén, 2017, p. 68).

According to Sharp et al. (2017), "boredom, inattention, and loss of interest tend to contribute negatively to student engagement, learning, and overall performance in a wide range of settings, including universities" (p.2).

Game-based learning and gamification, as previously discussed, can positively impact student motivation and engagement and therefore learning. Specifically, escape rooms are one of the many teaching tools used to apply this active methodology.

The escape room phenomenon has a fairly short history. The first real escape room was developed in Kyoto in 2007 for teams of 5 to 6 players to escape from a single room (Nicholson, 2015). The phenomenon quickly spread around the world and is now known as a global entertainment phenomenon for both adults and children.

However, video games were already using escape games before real life versions existed (Miller, 2015). Therefore, we can say that virtual escape rooms predate analogue ones.

These escape rooms are defined as activities of a playful nature, where a group of people are locked in one or more rooms and have a time limit to escape by solving a series of enigmas (Nicholson, 2015; Eukel, et al., 2017; Zhang et al., 2017).

Although escape rooms were initially created for recreational aims, they are also used for educational purposes. They allow the development of skills such as teamwork and collaboration, information seeking, creativity, problem-solving, self-regulation, critical thinking, communication, and the ability to develop the digital competence under pressure (Bober, 2010; Shakeri et al., 2017; Veach, 2019).

In the formal educational context, references to the use of escape rooms at the university level abound (Fotaris & Mastoras, 2019). While it is true that publications on escape room experiences have increased in recent years, demonstrating their effectiveness in increasing student interest and motivation, especially in face-to-face contexts (Santamaría & Alcalde, 2019; Moreno et al., 2019; Sánchez-Martín et al., 2020; López-Pernas et al., 2019; Jiménez et al., 2020; García-Tudela et al., 2020), escape room experiences in virtual environments are still scarce. STEM and healthcare disciplines stand out as pioneers in the application of these digital escape rooms in their curricula. The development of digital resources has enabled virtual escape rooms to increasingly become a teaching strategy, thanks to increased cost-effectiveness, accessibility and ease of use (Ang et al., 2020). Thus, a digital escape room uses a combination of ICT resources that allow the simulation of a series of locks to be opened, puzzles to be solved in order to escape and reach a predetermined goal (Kroski, 2020).

The benefits of these digital escape rooms are no different from those of face-to-face escape rooms, as stated by Makri et al. (2021). Escape rooms also promote motivation and commitment in the learning process, as well as interpersonal skills such as communication, collaboration, problem-solving, creativity, digital competencies and affective skills. Regarding the development of affective skills, the studies are based on the opinions of students after the application of the digital escape room, who positively value this activity as fun, interesting, challenging and enjoyable. All these positive emotions are directly associated with intrinsic motivation (Glavas & Stascik, 2017). Moreover, Yllana-Prieto et al. (2021), following the implementation of a science-focused virtual escape room, observed a significant increase in the intensity of positive emotions felt by future teachers, specifically in emotions such as "joy", "satisfaction", and "fun". They also observed negative emotions associated with the online environment, such as "nervousness", "frustration", and "concern".

In order to achieve all of the above benefits, a number of factors must be taken into account when designing the escape room (Makir et al., 2021), such as:

1. the size of the team (being the standard between 3-6 students, to obtain greater participation) (Cain, 2019);
2. the time frame (usually ranging between 45-60 minutes),
3. the type of games, puzzles and structure (using resources such as augmented reality, mixed reality, QR codes, 3D simulation, videos, digital puzzles, crossword puzzles, hidden objects, cryptograms, etc.).

Furthermore, for learners to reach a state in which they are focused and engaged to perform to the best of their abilities, Nakamura & Csikszentmihaalyi (2002) propose that tasks should be clear and achievable with an ascending level of progress (increasingly difficult), learners must receive immediate feedback, experience autonomy and control of their actions, and activities must be engaging.

METHOD

In this research, a fundamentally quantitative methodology was used with a descriptive and transversal methodological design of a survey type in order to determine the students' perception of learning and emotions with respect to the gamification experience implemented. It was complemented with the use of qualitative techniques of content analysis to delve deeper into the students' perception of the satisfaction achieved. This design allows us to assess aspects related to content learning, emotions experienced and satisfaction in a learning experience based on an escape room.

Description of the Context and Participants

The sample used was non-probabilistic by convenience since the escape room was implemented in a subject in which the researchers taught. The resulting sample consisted of 32 students taking the subject Knowledge of the Sciences of Nature in the degree in Primary Education Teaching during the 2021/2022 academic year at the Universidad Internacional de La Rioja, which is completely online. 84.4% are women, and 15.6% are men, with an average age of 33.47 years. With regards to their experience in escape room, only 37.5% of the students recognize that they have participated in an Escape Room before.

Instrument

In order to collect information about the gamification experience based on an Escape Room, an ad hoc instrument was used, consisting of three dimensions. At the beginning of the questionnaire, a series of items are included to inquire about the socio-demographic characteristics of the sample. The first dimension is called *Learning* and is made up of 10 items selected from the instrument previously validated by Parra-González and Segura-Robles (2019) to determine the students' perception of motivation, fun, subject understanding and development of skills such as creativity, autonomy and critical thinking. In addition, two dimensions are included to assess the emotions experienced by students during the escape room: a dimension called *Emotional Wellbeing* consisting of 15 positive emotions and an *Emotional Distress* dimension consisting of 14 negative emotions, both selected from the instrument proposed by Rebollo et al. (2008). Each item was rated according to a Likert-type scale (1 - Strongly disagree, 2 - Disagree, 3 - Neither agree nor disagree, 4 - Agree, 5 - Strongly agree). Finally, in order to find out student satisfaction with the learning experience, it was included a closed-ended question with three options (I love it, I liked it, but less than I expected, and I did not like it). In addition, to evaluate satisfaction, an open-ended question was included so that students could indicate what they liked best and their general opinion of the Escape Room.

The reliability analysis of the instrument, carried out using *Cronbach's Alpha,* was 0.893, so the instrument was considered to have adequate reliability for the study.

The questionnaires were elaborated in *Google Forms* and shared with the students at the end of the online gamification experience.

Description of the Escape Room and its Challenges

The virtual escape room was designed with the Genially tool as a support, and it's named "Save yourself, planet".

The escape room follows a futuristic narrative set in the year 2050, as well as catastrophic, as it proposes a daunting future in which climate change has caused dramatic consequences: the natural resources of planet Earth are at their limit, the sea level has risen so much that some cities have disappeared, the increase in the average global temperature has caused the disappearance of many species of living beings, and natural disasters occur (hurricanes, strong winds, extreme snowfall).

In this hostile environment, a hurricane causes the destruction of part of the school, causing the students to be locked in. To get out, they will have to type in a password that they will obtain after overcoming a series of challenges related to the environment and sustainability.

Following an introductory motivational video, which explains the narrative, aesthetics and dynamics of the virtual escape room, students must overcome five digital challenges.

In the first one, they are asked to answer some questions in a Google form about the increase of the greenhouse effect and climate change after watching a short video of about 3 minutes. By correctly answering the questions in the quiz, they get the first digit of the password.

In the second challenge, they will have to use the Genially magnifying glass to find the correct word about microplastics, one of the main environmental problems of our time. To obtain the necessary information, they can first watch a short video of just over one minute embedded on the page.

The third challenge includes a case study to calculate the carbon footprint of a family of four. The case study provides information on monthly electricity consumption, the type of car they own and the number of kilometers they drive per month, as well as bus and train commutes. The embedded calculator will allow them to obtain the result of tons of carbon produced by this family during a month and learn which actions in our daily lives produce the most greenhouse effect gases.

In the next challenge, they will have to research the sixth mass extinction, the one we are currently in, and answer the questions of the "Do you want to be a millionaire?" quiz.

In the last challenge, an alphabet soup is presented in which they must find seven actions that could contribute to curbing global warming, such as reducing the consumption of red meat, using public transport or buying fewer clothes.

To obtain the last digit of the password and be able to open the digital padlock inserted in Genially, all participating students must answer the questionnaire about the learning experience and the emotions it has made them feel.

Procedure

The escape room has been carried out online synchronously on the Adobe Connect platform, which enables the teacher to play video and audio, share the blackboard and a notepad, exchange comments with students through an interactive chat function, as well as several files. In addition, the software allows splitting the class into independent breakout rooms that simulates the distribution into groups in a face-to-face class where each group works autonomously using all the functionalities of the platform.

The activity was carried out collaboratively in groups of 4 to 6 students, under the guidance of the teacher who gave feedback to each group during the activity.

Data Analysis

Descriptive statistics were calculated to determine the general characteristics of the selected sample and the mean scores of the dimensions and items under study. The data were organized, coded and analyzed using the SPSS 26.0 statistical package.

To carry out the qualitative analysis of the answers obtained in the open question about the students' opinion on the learning experience, a coding system was applied, establishing a system of categories according to the answers obtained. For this analysis, articles, prepositions, conjunctions and determiners were omitted. After reading all the answers, the following categories were established: collaborative work, challenges, fun, original and attractive, understanding concepts, dynamic, motivation, making more escape rooms, learning by playing, exciting and visual. Subsequently, a content analysis was performed using the Atlas.ti program. For this purpose, the comments made by the students were assigned to these categories. Finally, it is obtained a list with the number of times each category is repeated and all the phrases associated with each of them.

RESULTS

The analysis of the results shows that the mean of all the items obtained in the learning dimension was 4.41. Figure 1 shows the average of each of the items that define this dimension. All the items have a very favorable rating, with an average of over 3.88 (scale of 1 to 5). It is worth noting that the items with a higher average are "It motivated me" (M=4.72), "I had fun learning" (M=4.66), "It increased my creativity" (M=4.63) and "I would like to learn other content through the Escape Room" (M=4.59), with the lowest rated items being "I did not get stuck and it was not difficult to make progress" (M=3.88) and "It was a learning challenge" (M=3.97).

Figure 1. Mean (M) of the items of the learning dimension (scale 1 to 5). Source: Authors.

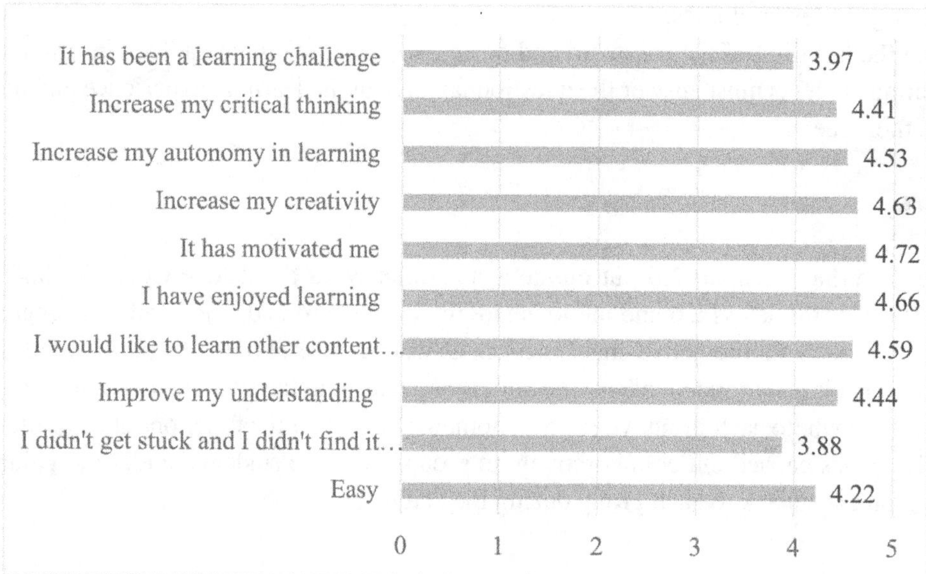

Figure 2 shows the mean obtained for each of the positive emotions experienced by the students during the escape room. These results indicate that the level of emotional well-being experienced by the participants during the Escape Room is much higher than the level of emotional discomfort (Figure 2). The students indicated that they mainly felt optimistic and confident (M=4.44 in both), enthusiastic (M=4.41), happy (M=4.38) and stimulated (M=4.32), satisfied and attracted (M=4.22 in both) by and during the learning experience. The least experienced emotion, relief, obtained an average of 3.56 (scale of 1 to 5).

On the other hand, negative emotions have also been analysed in detail (Figure 3), obtaining very low results in all of them. All emotions obtained an average figure below 1.53 (scale of 1 to 5). Specifically, students indicated that they had hardly ever experienced sadness or loneliness (A=1.19 in both), mistrust (A=1.22), or anger (A=1.23). The negative emotions that reached the highest levels, although still low, were insecurity (A=1.53), tension-concern or frustration (A=1.52 in both) and stress-fatigue (A=1.44).

Figure 2. Mean of positive emotions (scale 1 to 5). Source: Authors.

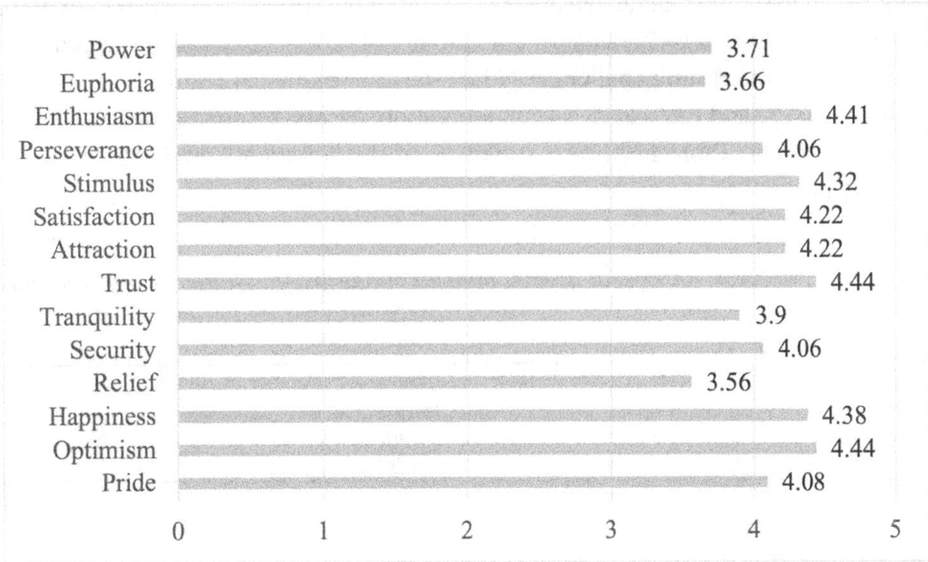

Figure 3. Mean of negative emotions (scale 1 to 5). Source: Authors.

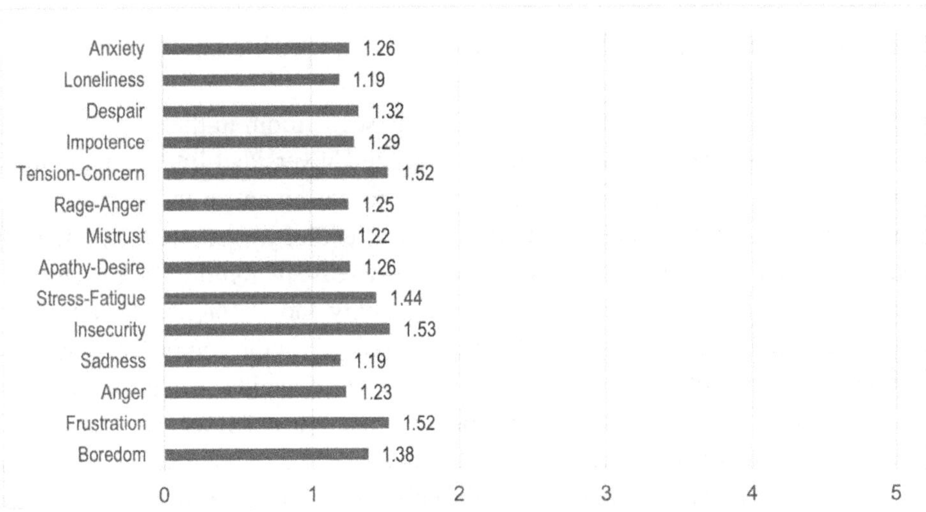

We considered the mean of all positive emotions (M=4.11) as a measure of emotional well-being and the mean of negative emotions (M=1.33) as a measure of emotional distress. The results indicate that the level of emotional well-being experienced by the participants while performing the escape room is much higher than the level of emotional distress.

In terms of satisfaction, 87.5% of the students loved participating in the Escape Room, 9.4% liked it, although less than expected, and 3.1% did not like it.

In order to go deeper into the students' satisfaction with the learning experience based on the escape room, a qualitative analysis of students' answers to the open question asking them to express their general opinion of the escape room is carried out. The number of times each category appears is as follows: collaborative work (11), interesting challenges (11), fun (10), original and attractive (7), understanding concepts (7), dynamic (5) and motivating (4), making more escape rooms (2), learning by playing (2), exciting (2) and visual (1). Table 1 shows a summary of the comments made by the students for the most repeated categories.

Table 1. Qualitative analysis. Representative comments made by the students and the most repeated categories.

Categories	Comment
Collaborative work	*I enjoyed working in a group interacting with my colleagues to solve the challenges.*
Challenges	*Variety of very interesting activities to obtain information and learn more about a topic*
Fun	*It is an entertaining and fun way to find out more about what we are studying.*

Finally, it should be noted that at the end of the session in which the escape room was carried out, the students expressed some suggestions for improvement, such as using a countdown in the challenges to increase tension and including a note in the calculator challenge indicating that the "more information" section should be read.

SOLUTIONS AND RECOMMENDATIONS

The results of this research show that the use of a virtual escape room in the subject of Knowledge of Natural Sciences of the Degree in Primary Education at the Universidad Internacional de La Rioja in an entirely online environment produces a perception of improvement in the learning process of the students, future teachers of primary education, in the area of ecology, sustainability and environment.

Fundamentally, the learning experience has managed to increase their motivation to study the contents of the subject, has increased their perception of their creativity and autonomy, as well as the development of their critical thinking. It also increases their understanding of the contents and motivates them to learn others through this type of playful activities. These results coincide with those obtained by Makri et al. (2021), who stated that online escape rooms bring as many benefits as face-to-face ones in terms of motivation and improvement of learning, and with those stated by Shakeri et al. (2017), in terms of improving the development of critical thinking and the ability to collaborate and communicate. Likewise, students state that they have fun while learning, as Glavas and Stascik had already reported in their 2017 study of virtual escape rooms. Among active methodologies, Game-Based Learning and Gamification are increasingly gaining relevance, which have demonstrated broad benefits for learning in general and for STEAM learning in particular, such as increasing students' creativity, as well as their intrinsic motivation for learning (Pisabarro & Vivaracho, 2018), involving students in their learning (Landers & Callan, 2011), and favouring meaningful learning (Kapp, 2012; Villalustre & del Moral, 2015).

Regarding the emotions experienced by the students participating in the virtual escape room, it can be affirmed that this activity fundamentally promotes positive emotions, with the perception of emotional well-being being much higher than the level of emotional discomfort perceived by the participants. Among the main positive emotions experienced by the students when participating in the virtual escape room were enthusiasm, optimism, joy, confidence, stimulation, satisfaction, security, pride and attraction. Similarly, several studies have shown that online escape rooms promote positive emotions, mainly joy, satisfaction and fun (Glavas & Stascik, 2017; Yllana-Prieto et al., 2021). Some studies point out that virtual escape rooms also promote negative emotions, such as nervousness, worry or frustration among students (Yllana-Prieto et al., 2021). However, the results of our study show that students report that they have hardly felt any negative emotions during the escape room, although those that have reached higher levels have been worry and frustration, coinciding with those detected in previous studies by other authors (Yllana-Prieto et al., 2021). The use of active methodologies promotes positive emotions (Jeong et al., 2019), increases motivation, collaboration, student satisfaction, and long-term memory consolidation (Tokuhama, 2010), which therefore increases their academic performance, especially in STEM subjects (Klish et al., 2012; Vázquez & Manassero, 2007).

With respect to satisfaction with the learning experience based on the virtual escape room, it is verified how collaborative work is the item best valued by students, as previous research has already pointed out (Makri et al., 2021; Shakeri et al., 2017), closely followed by the interest in challenges and fun, a fact that reaffirms the work of Glavas and Stascik (2017).

These results confirm that virtual escape rooms, as occurs with face-to-face ones, promote positive emotions and affective and social skills that result in an increase in student motivation towards the study of the content and, consequently, in improved learning (Guillén, 2017; Makri et al., 2021; Vázquez & Manassero, 2007).

However, research in the field of educational escape rooms is still at a preliminary stage, and the emphasis has been on exploring what an escape room is and how to apply it for educational purposes (Taraldsen et al., 2020). The review articles developed to date on educational escape rooms show that the research on the topic focuses on developing an escape room and collecting feedback and responses from participants after trying it out in class, while, in general, little attention is paid to the research design and methods used to collect and analyse the data (Taraldsen et al., 2020).

FUTURE RESEARCH DIRECTIONS

Several articles agree that more research is needed on the effects of escape rooms in education (Baker et al., 2020; Liu et al., 2020) through the application of more complex research designs and data collection and analysis (Taraldsen et al., 2020). For example, including longitudinal studies that track students who have used escape rooms as long-term teaching resources and studies that focus on student teachers' beliefs with regard to the use of escape rooms as tools for future education.

Teachers manifest low perceived self-efficacy in science teaching (Brígido & Borrachero, 2011); being essential to implement active methodologies in the teaching of subjects dedicated to the scientific training of future teachers, with the aim of promoting positive emotions that favour intrinsic motivation and improve teachers' learning outcomes, avoiding the promotion of negative attitudes towards sciences (Vázquez & Manassero, 2007).

However, several studies have analysed how general constraints can influence the escape room experience, for example, the issue of time. In some types of escape rooms, time is extremely important, especially when the narrative involves saving lives (Novak et al., 2019), as is the case in "Save Yourself,

Planet". In other contexts, for instance, if the goal is to collect samples from a crime scene to analyse them later in the laboratory, time is not so important (Ferreiro-González et al., 2019).

In view of the results obtained, we propose to continue implementing this virtual escape room, incorporating the appropriate improvements, such as the inclusion of a countdown and facilitating access to additional information in the challenge of calculating the carbon footprint, with future promotions of students of the Degree in Primary Education Teacher at the Universidad Internacional de La Rioja. In this way, one of the limitations of the study could be solved, which is the sample size. Therefore, it would be important to repeat this study with a larger number of students in this subject, as well as in other STEAM subjects, to corroborate the results presented and establish correlations between the positive and negative emotions shown by students when participating in the learning experience and their academic performance in the subject.

Likewise, we intend to evaluate the effectiveness of this virtual escape room in classroom environments and at different educational levels. Several studies have shown that we are in a crisis of science education, as many high school students feel negative emotions toward the study of science (Miller et al., 2018; Yllana-Prieto et al., 2021) and do not choose scientific university careers (Van Aalderen-Smeets & van der Molen, 2015). The use of virtual escape rooms in the Biology and Geology class in secondary education could contribute to reversing this situation, so we intend to continue investigating the scope of this gamified activity in the secondary classroom and assessing its effect on students' motivation and interest in the study of science.

CONCLUSION

It is concluded that the learning experience through the virtual escape room "Save yourself planet" has a positive impact on the satisfaction, motivation and learning of students, who have been involved and enjoyed the experience while deepening their knowledge of key aspects of the subject. Student satisfaction is high, highlighting mainly the collaborative work, interesting challenges and fun. Regarding the perception of the effect of the escape room on student learning, students consider that it increases their motivation, creativity, and critical thinking. It is verified that positive emotions have been generated among the participating students, as opposed to negative ones. Among the main emotions perceived by the students during the virtual escape room were enthusiasm, confidence, optimism and joy. At the same time, we have managed to raise awareness among students regarding the involvement of human beings in environmental problems and the possible measures we should take to minimize this climate emergency.

REFERENCES

Ang, J. W. J., Ng, Y. N. A., & Liew, R. S. (2020). Physical and Digital Educational Escape Room for Teaching Chemical Bonding. *Journal of Chemical Education*, *97*(9), 2849–2856. doi:10.1021/acs.jchemed.0c00612

Asamblea General de las Naciones Unidas. (2015). *Resolución Aprobada por la Asamblea General el 25 de septiembre de 2015* [Resolution Adopted by the General Assembly on September 25, 2015]. https://www.senado.gob.mx/comisiones/fomento_economico/eventos/docs/resolucion_080916.pdf

Baker, C. M., Crabtree, G., & Anderson, K. (2020). Student pharmacist perceptions of learning after strengths-based leadership skills lab and escape room in pharmacy practice skills laboratory. *Currents in Pharmacy Teaching and Learning, 12,* 724-727.

Barragán, R., Buzón, O., & García Pérez, R. (2007). Diagnóstico y evaluación de aprendizajes universitarios con e-portafolios: regulación de aprendizajes Blended-Learning y nuevos roles del alumnado [Diagnosis and evaluation of university learning with e-portfolios: regulation of Blended-Learning learning and new student roles]. In F. Etxeberría, L. Sarasola, J. F. Lukas, J. Etxeberría, & A. Martxueta (Coords.), *Actas del XIII Congreso Nacional de Modelos de Investigación Educativa, AIDIPE.* San Sebastián.

Bober, M. (2010). *Games-based experiences for learning*. Manchester Metropolitan University.

Brígido, M., & Borrachero, A. B. (2011). Relación entre autoconcepto, autoeficacia y autorregulación en ciencias de futuros maestros de primaria [Relationship between self-concept, self-efficacy and self-regulation in science of future primary school teachers]. *INFAD Revista de Psicología, 1*(2), 107–113.

Cain, J. (2019). Exploratory implementation of a blended format escape room in a large enrollment pharmacy management class. *Currents in Pharmacy Teaching & Learning, 11*(1), 44–50. doi:10.1016/j.cptl.2018.09.010 PMID:30527875

Deterding, S., Dixon, D., Khaled, R., & Nacke, L. (2011). Gamification: Towards a definition. *Proceedings of the 2011 Annual Conference Extended Abstracts on Human Factors in Computing Systems.* http://gamification-research.org/wp-content/uploads/2011/04/02-Deterding-Khaled-Nacke-Dixon.pdf

Eukel, H. N., Frenzel, J. E., & Cernusca, D. (2017). Educational Gaming for Pharmacy Students-Design and Evaluation of a Diabetes-themed Escape Room. *American Journal of Pharmaceutical Education, 81*(7), 6265. doi:10.5688/ajpe8176265 PMID:29109566

Ferreiro-González, M., Amores-Arrocha, A., Espada-Bellido, E., Aliaño-González, M. J., Vázquez-Espinosa, M., González-de-Peredo, A. V., Sancho-Galán, P., Álvarez-Saura, J. Á., Barbero, G. F., & Cejudo-Bastante, C. (2019). Escape Classroom: Can you solve a crime using the analytical process? *Journal of Chemical Education, 96*(2), 267–273. doi:10.1021/acs.jchemed.8b00601

Fotaris, P., & Mastoras, T. (2019). Escape rooms for learning: a systematic review. *Proceedings of the 13th European Conference on Games Based Learning ECGBL 2019*, 9.

García-Tudela, P. A., Solano-Fernández, I. M., & Sánchez-Vera, M. M. (2020). Análisis de una Escape Room Educativa en clase de matemáticas en educación primaria [Analysis of an Educational Escape Room in mathematics class in primary education]. *REDIMAT – Journal for Research in Mathematics Education, 9*(3), 273–297. doi:10.17583/redimat.2020.4437

Garritz, A., & Ortega-Villar, N. A. (2013). El aspecto afectivo en la enseñanza universitaria. Cómo cinco profesores enseñan el enlace químico en la materia condensada [The affective aspect in university education. How five professors teach chemical bonding in condensed matter]. In V. Mellado, L. J. Blanco, A. B. Borrachero, & J. A. Cárdenas (Eds.), *Las emociones en la enseñanza y el aprendizaje de las ciencias y las matemáticas* (Vol. 2, pp. 277–304). UEX-DEPROFE.

Glavas, A., & Stascik, A. (2017). Enhancing positive attitude towards mathematics through introducing Escape Room games. In *Mathematics Education as a Science and a Profession* (pp. 281–294). Element.

Gruber, M. J., Ritchey, M., Wang, S. F., Doss, M. K., & Ranganath, C. (2016). Post-learning Hippocampal Dynamics Promote Preferential Retention of Rewarding Events. *Neuron, 89*(5), 1110–1120. doi:10.1016/j.neuron.2016.01.017 PMID:26875624

Guillén, J. C. (2017). *Neuroeducación en el aula: de la teoría a la práctica* [Neuroeducation in the classroom: from theory to practice]. CreateSpace.

Jeong, J. S., González-Gómez, D., Gallego-Picó, A., & Bravo, J. C. (2019). Effects of active learning methodologies on the students' emotions, self-efficacy beliefs and learning outcomes in a science distance learning course. *JOTSE: Journal of Technology and Science Education, 9*(2), 217–227. doi:10.3926/jotse.530

Jiménez, C., Arís, N., Magreñán Ruiz, A. A., & Orcos, L. (2020). Digital escape room, using Genial.Ly and a breakout to learn Algebra at Secondary Education Level in Spain. *Education in Science, 10*(10), 271. doi:10.3390/educsci10100271

Kapp, K. (2012). *The gamification of learning and instruction: Game-based methods and strategies for training and education*. John Wiley & Sons.

Klisch, Y., Miller, L. M., Wang, S., & Epstein, J. (2012). The impact of a science education game on students' learning and perception of inhalants as body pollutants. *Journal of Science Education and Technology, 21*(2), 295–303. doi:10.100710956-011-9319-y PMID:23926416

Kroski, E. (2020). What Is a Digital Breakout Game? *Library Technology Reports, 56*, 5–7.

Landers, R. N., & Callan, R. C. (2011). Casual social games as serious games: The psychology of gamification in undergraduate education and employee training. In M. Ma & A. Oikonomou (Eds.), Serious games and edutainment applications (pp. 399-423). Springer.

Liu, C., Patel, R., Ogunjinmi, B., Briffa, C., Allain-Chapman, M., Coffey, J., … Shelmerdine, S. C. (2020). Feasibility of paediatric radiology escape room for undergraduate education. *Insights Imagine,* 11.

López-Pernas, S., Gordillo, A., Barra, E., & Quemada, J. (2019). Analyzing learning effectiveness and students' perception of an educational escape room in a Programming Course in Higher Education. *IEEE Access: Practical Innovations, Open Solutions, 7*, 184221–184234. doi:10.1109/ACCESS.2019.2960312

Ludwing-Hardman, S., & Dunlap, J. C. (2003). Learner support services for online students: Scaffolding for success. *International Review of Research in Open and Distance Learning, 4*(1), 1–8.

Makri, A., Vlachopoulos, D., & Martina, R. A. (2021). Digital Escape Rooms as Innovative Pedagogical Tools in Education: A Systematic Literature Review. *Sustainability, 13*(8), 4587. doi:10.3390u13084587

Marczewki, A. (2013). *Game Mechanics in Gamification.* Gamified UK. https://www.gamified.uk/2013/01/14/game-mechanics-in-gamification

Mellado, V., Borrachero, A. B., Brígido, M., Melo, L. V., Dávila, M. A., Cañada, F., Conde, M. C., Costillo, E., Esteban, R., Martínez, G., Ruiz, C., Sánchez, J., Garritz, A., Mellado, L., Vázquez, B., Jiménez, R., & Bermejo, M. L. (2014). Las emociones en la enseñanza de las ciencias [Emotions in science teaching]. *Enseñanza de las Ciencias, 32*(3), 11–36. doi:10.5565/rev/ensciencias.1478

Miller, K., Sonnert, G., & Sadler, P. (2018). The influence of students' participation in STEM competitions on their interest in STEM careers. *International Journal of Science Education, 8*(2), 95–114. doi:10.1080/21548455.2017.1397298

Miller, S. (2015). *The art of the escape room.* Retrieved from https://www.newsweek.com/2015/05/01/art-escape-room-323150.html

Moreno Fuentes, E., Perales Molada, R., & Hidalgo Navarrete, J. (2019). Estudio cualitativo sobre el uso de la gamificación en la Educación Superior para promover la motivación del alumnado [Qualitative study on the use of gamification in Higher Education to promote student motivation]. *Aula de Encuentro, 21*(2), 5–26. doi:10.17561/ae.v21.n2.1

Nakamura, J., & Csikszentmihalyi, M. (2002). The concept of flow. In C. R. Snyder & S. J. Lopez (Eds.), *Handbook of Positive Psychology* (pp. 89–105). Oxford University Press.

Nicholson, S. (2015). *Peeking Behind the Locked Door: A Survey of Escape Room Facilities.* White Paper. Available at Http://Scottnicholson.Com/Pubs/Erfacwhite.Pdf

Novak, J., Lozos, J. C., & Spear, S. E. (2019). Development of an interactive escape room intervention to educate college students about earthquake preparedness. *Nature Hazards Review, 20*(1).

Parra-González, M. E., & Segura-Robles, A. (2019). Traducción y validación de la escala de evaluación de experiencias gamificadas (GAMEX) [Translation and validation of the gamified experiences evaluation scale (GAMEX)]. *Bordón. Revista de Pedagogía, 71*(4), 87–89. doi:10.13042/Bordon.2019.70783

Pedrinaci, E., Caamaño, A., Cañal, P., & de Pro, A. (2012). *11 ideas clave: El desarrollo de la competencia científica* [11 key ideas: The development of scientific competence]. Grao.

Pekrun, R. (2005). Progress and open problems in educational emotion research. *Learning and Instruction, 15*(5), 497–506. doi:10.1016/j.learninstruc.2005.07.014

Pérez Vázquez, E., Gilabert Cerdá, A., & Lledó Carreres, A. (2019). Gamificación en la educación universitaria: El uso del *escape room* como estrategia de aprendizaje [Gamification in university education: The use of the *escape room* as a learning strategy]. In R. Roig-Vila (Ed.), *Investigación e innovación en la educación superior. Nuevos contextos, nuevas ideas* (pp. 660–668). Octaedro.

Phelps, A., & Vlachopoulos, D. (2019). Successful transition to synchronous learning environments in distance education: A research on entry-level synchronous facilitator competencies. *Education and Information Technologies, 25*(3), 1511–1527. doi:10.100710639-019-09989-x

Pisabarro, A. M., & Vivaracho, C. E. (2018). Gamificación en el aula: Gincana de programación [Gamification in the classroom: programming gymkhana]. *ReVisión: Revista de Investigación en Docencia Universitaria de la Informática, 11*(1), 85–93.

Rebollo Catalán, M. Á., García Pérez, R., Barragán Sánchez, R., Buzón García, O., & Vega Caro, L. (2008). Las emociones en el aprendizaje online [Emotions in online learning]. *RELIEVE-Revista Electrónica de Investigación y Evaluación Educativa, 14*(1). https://www.uv.es/RELIEVE/v14n1/RELIEVEv14n1_2.htm

Sánchez-Martín, J., Corrales-Serrano, M., Luque-Sendra, A., & Zamora-Polo, F. (2020). Exit for success. Gamifying science and technology for university students using escape-room. A preliminary approach. *Heliyon, 6*(7), e04340. doi:10.1016/j.heliyon.2020.e04340 PMID:32671257

Santamaría, A., & Alcalde, E. (2019). Escaping from the English classroom. Who will get out first? Aloma: *Revista de Psicología. Ciències de l'Educació i de l'Esport, 37*(2), 83–92. doi:10.51698/aloma.2019.37.2.83-92

Shakeri, H., Singhal, S., Pan, R., Neustaedter, C., & Tang, A. (2017). Escaping together: the design and evaluation of a distributed real-life escape room. In *Proceedings of the Annual Symposium on Computer-Human Interaction in Play*. ACM. 10.1145/3116595.3116601

Sharp, J. G., Hemmings, B., Kay, R., Murphy, B., & Elliott, S. (2016). Academic boredom among students in higher education: A mixed-methods exploration of characteristics, contributors and consequences. *Journal of Further and Higher Education, 41*(5), 657–677. doi:10.1080/0309877X.2016.1159292

Taraldsen, L. H., Haara, F. O., Lysne, M. S., Jensen, P. R., & Jenssen, E. S. (2020). A review on use of escape rooms in education – touching the void. *Education Inquiry, 13*(2), 169–184. doi:10.1080/20004508.2020.1860284

Tokuhama, T. (2010). *The new science of teaching and learning: using the best of mind, and education science in the classroom*. Columbia University Teachers College Press.

Van Aalderen-Smeets, S. I., & van der Molen, J. H. W. (2015). Improving primary teacher attitudes toward science by attitude-focused professional development. *Journal of Research in Science Teaching, 52*(5), 710–734. doi:10.1002/tea.21218

Vázquez, A., & Manassero, M. A. (2007). En defensa de las actitudes y emociones en la educación científica (I): Evidencias y argumentos generales [In defense of attitudes and emotions in science education (I): Evidence and general arguments]. *Revista Eureka sobre Enseñanza y Divulgación de las Ciencias, 4*(2), 247-271. http://hdl.handle.net/10498/16108

Veach, C. C. (2019). Breaking out to break through: Re-imagining first-year orientations. *RSR. Reference Services Review, 47*(4), 556–569. doi:10.1108/RSR-06-2019-0039

Villalustre, L., & del Moral, M. E. (2015). Gamificación: estrategia para optimizar el proceso de aprendizaje y la adquisición de competencias en contextos universitarios [Gamification: strategy to optimize the learning process and the acquisition of skills in university contexts]. *Digital Education Review, 27,* 13-31. https://revistes.ub.edu/index.php/der/article/view/11591

Wiswall, M., Stiefel, L., Schwartz, A. E., & Boccardo, J. (2014). Does attending a STEM high school improve student performance? Evidence from New York City. *Economics of Education Review*, *40*, 93–105. doi:10.1016/j.econedurev.2014.01.005

Yllana-Prieto, F., Jeong, J., & González-Gómez, D. (2021). Analysis of Pre-Service Teachers' emotions during a STEM online Escape Room. *Proceedings of SOCIOINT 2021 8th International Conference on Education and Education of Social Sciences.* 10.46529ocioint.202155

Zhang, F., Doroudian, A., Kaufman, D., Hausknecht, S., Jeremic, J., & Owens, H. (2017). Employing a user-centered design process to create a multiplayer online escape game for older adults. *Proceedings of the Annual Symposium on Computer-Human Interaction in Play*, 296–307. 10.1007/978-3-319-58536-9_24

KEY TERMS AND DEFINITIONS

Carbon Footprint: Volume of greenhouse gases produced by human activity.

Climate Change: A change in the temperature and weather patterns of planet Earth caused by an increase in the greenhouse effect.

Creativity: Ability to create new ideas or original solutions.

Critical Thinking: Ability to question statements that are often taken as true.

Emotions: Psychological and physiological reactions produced in response to a stimulus.

Greenhouse Effect: A natural phenomenon that helps maintain a temperature suitable for life on Earth. The problem is that this effect is increasing due to the increase in the production of greenhouse gases by human action.

Greenhouse Gases: Gases that absorb and emit infrared radiation and contribute to the greenhouse effect. The main greenhouse gases are carbon dioxide, methane, water vapor, nitrous oxide and ozone.

Interpersonal Skills: Skills that enable us to establish positive relationships with others.

Microplastics: Particles smaller than 5 mm in size resulting from the degradation of plastic waste.

Motivation: A state that initiates or maintains a person's behavior toward the achievement of a particular goal or end.

Satisfaction: A feeling of well-being felt when a purpose has been achieved, or a need has been met.

Sixth Mass Extinction: Process of species extinction in which we find ourselves today due to human action.

STEAM: Science, technology, engineering, arts, and mathematics.

Universidad Internacional de La Rioja: Private Spanish distance learning university.

Chapter 4
Escape Room as a Tool for the Study of Special Needs in University Education

Blanca Tejero
Universidad Internacional de La Rioja, Spain

Jessica Ortega-Barón
Universidad Internacional de La Rioja, Spain

Blanca Betes
Universidad Internacional de La Rioja, Spain

ABSTRACT

For a society where progress and constant development are essential and that faced with the changes experienced in society (pandemics, wars) as well as in education (lack of motivation of students, increase in dropouts, and poor results in studies), the educational system suggests the need for change, proposing the use of more innovative and active methodologies that give the student a leading role and make them the protagonists of the teaching-learning process. This chapter presents an activity with escape room developed with students of the Master's Degree in Special Education that aims to facilitate the learning of practical cases on the subject of developmental disorders.

INTRODUCTION

In recent years, teaching innovation has experienced a great boost and acceleration at different educational levels. One of the reasons that has favored this impulse is the events experienced during the health crisis that we have been suffering in recent years. At the beginning of the pandemic, education had to quickly adapt to the circumstances and change traditional teaching methods for other new online ones that were adjusted to the situation that was being suffered (Scavarda, Dias, Reis, Silveira, & Santos, 2021; Tejedor 2021). Another of the factors that has propitiated this great impulse has been the technological change

DOI: 10.4018/978-1-6684-6081-8.ch004

that it has produced in recent tears and of which we are participants. The use of technology enhances and helps the development of learning.

As Jenaro, Flores, Poy, González and Martínez (2013) state, in university teaching on many occasions, some strategies are abused, specifically exhibitions or master classes, debates, seminars, group work and the like. To correct this trend, before the start of the pandemic, the education system was trying to turn around by proposing new approaches to the skills and objectives that students must achieve (Tejedor, 2021). These new approaches should focus on "students acquiring skills and competencies during their studies that they can apply later in their personal and professional lives, for example, leadership skills, cooperation and teamwork, as opposed to memorization and repetition" (Area Moreira, 2008, p. 66-79). With the implementation of innovative methodologies in the classroom, we also want to facilitate student learning by proposing to relate motivation, learning and fun. To achieve these objectives, the new teaching methods raise the need to change the positions held by teachers and students in traditional methods. Teachers will not have to be the only protagonists in the teaching-learning process, but students have to become more involved and have a greater protagonism and a more active role in teaching (Strachan & Liyanage, 2015). The question that most professionals ask themselves is how can these goals be achieved?

To achieve these objectives, the new teaching methods, gamification, is proposed as a tool to arouse the interest and curiosity of students, attract their attention, improve their motivation, as well as facilitate their learning (Dicheva, Dichev, Agre, & Angelova, 2015). With gamification, it is intended that learning be different since it suggests that starting from a more motivating position, skills such as teamwork can be worked on, difficult to work with other methodologies, which will be required later from the students in the professional world.

Following this line, one of the alternative strategies to traditional teaching that can be applied in online higher education are the so-called Escape Rooms. The Escape Room is a dynamic and fun experience, born in the environment of online video games, which has reached the educational world, and due to its characteristics. it is making a niche in the world of education (Santamaría Urbieta & Alcalde Peñalver, 2019). Currently, the Escape Room is beginning to be used as new teaching dynamics that can motivate students more, promoting greater and better learning, and it can also be used to evaluate students' knowledge, as well as their abilities to work in teams and be competitive.

Believing in the educational potential of the application of Escape Rooms in online university classrooms, the objectives of this article are:

- To increase students' participation.
- To intensify the motivation of students towards learning the subject of General Developmental Disorders.
- To promote student learning of the practical part of the subject of General Developmental Disorders.
- To promote the development of student skills and competencies by using the escape room as a learning tool.

To achieve this objective, the theme and the tests to be passed in the Escape Room must be related to the curricular contents of the subjects covered in the Master's Degree in Special Education.

BACKGROUND

Online University

In recent years, there has been a transition from an industrial society into a more innovative society, characterized by rapid changes in technology, globality and the implementation of digital culture. University teaching has had to confront, assume and adapt to new educational challenges. These changes have led to a reflection on what adjustments have to be produced in teaching and learning in order to meet and respond to the needs posed by students of the 21st century (Kirschner & Erkens, 2013). Universities consider educational models focused on the integral training of their students using the best internship and educational methodologies. Its objective is that students finish their training with a high level of knowledge of the content taught, as well as with the acquisition of valuable professional and personal skills. In order to respond to these needs and, at the same time aided by existing technological advances, new models are proposed for training, e-learning (online modality) or b-learning (blended modality), in Higher Education. The educational system has had to make a great effort in order to adapt to these new training models, assuming a great challenge for educational centers and for all the components of the community.

The new model of online education or distance education is adaptable and can be used at different levels of studies. Regarding university education in different universities multiple degrees are offered, thereby expanding the existing training offer in Spain by innovating the way of learning. The use of online teaching as an innovative way of learning is increasing due to the flexibility of the method, which makes it possible to reconcile studies with work, family life, geographical location and even the economic situation of the student.

Online education facilitates the acquisition of new knowledge and skills as well as reinforces the existing ones. As Choudhury and Pattnaik (2020) say, the advantages offered by online education flexibility, autonomy, saving time or making it compatible with other family and social duties, must be combined with the use of innovative methodologies and adequate strategies to overcome its weak points such as isolation and lack of teamwork.

Taking into account its great advantages, innovation processes related to the use of Information and Communication Technologies (ICT) in online university teaching are increasingly betting on these teaching and learning proposals that allow greater interactivity and collaboration among students. With the rapid development of ICT, a strong interest has emerged in the study of online collaborative learning or Computer Supported Collaborative Learning (CSCL), which refers to the learning process that is carried out by sharing objectives and tasks, with technologies as mediators of this process (Kirschner & Erkens, 2013). In this line, Barab, Michael, Thomas, and Merrill (2001) indicate that collaborative learning is a process of co-construction of meaning and insist that online environments help more participatory educational models and expand opportunities for learning, communication, and knowledge distribution.

Universities have made a great effort to include new technological advances in their classrooms, in their educational system, which has allowed greater flexibility in learning, thus covering the need for international integration, constant innovation, or adapting to the new demands. Using ICTs in learning means applying an innovative methodological approach, different from the one used up to know which meant the simple acquisition of content. Currently, technology has come to occupy a very prominent and important position in the teaching-learning center.

Among all the teaching innovations that have been implemented, one of the most used and that is making a name for itself is the use of games, 'gamification' or 'gamification' (Landers, 2014). By applying the game to the educational field, the classrooms can become an adventure setting and can be done online through the new training and technological models. If this modality is adopted, the students will participate from their homes or jobs as a member of a group that will fight to solve a problem related to the contents of the course. Through this experience, the weak points attributed to online training will be worked online as well as the acquisition or review of already acquired knowledge and personal and professional skills that are so important for a good development, both personal and professional.

Gamification

The inclusion and increase of information and communication technologies (ICT) mean that educational systems have to be in constant change and evolution. This requires educational centers to be "in a race in which the relevance of their work and the possibilities of development depending on their ability to evolve and find new forms, processes and structures to put knowledge at the service of society" (Arechavala & Sánchez, 2017, p. 22). The aforementioned boosts innovation in education and the application and implementation of methods other than the traditional ones (New Media Consortium, 2018). The changes that are being experienced are the result of the implementation of new methodologies that apply different and new technological resources, which has produced not only an increase in distance education but also an innovation in education (Romiszowski, 2003).

Gamification, both virtual and physical, is a teaching methodology that is in full swing and that is gaining more and more supporters and attention (Raitskaya & Tikhonova, 2019). Gamification consists of the use of game elements in a different context than the traditional one, it is a non-ludic context such as the educational one is, (Bodnar, Anastasio, Enszer, & Burkey., 2016; Huang, Hew, & Lo, 2018; Pérez-Manzano & Almela Baeza, 2018) with the aim of facilitating the learning of content and skills. Unlike traditional methods, it proposes a different way of learning through different challenges, which will make students more motivated in the learning process.

In the current context, the use of games in teaching offers great educational benefits. Some authors remark the benefit of transferring game elements and methodologies to the classroom, with the aim of promoting the complex content learning, present in the different curricular areas (Borrego, Fernández, Blanes & Robles, 2017; Ke, 2014; Pérez-Manzano & Almela - Baeza, 2018). Currently, there is an increase in the implementation of innovative methodologies in teaching and the game is one of the most used in the classroom due to its ability to enable learning in a more participatory way by students since it increases their motivation. (Jabbar & Felicia, 2015; Ke, 2014; Pérez-Manzano & Almela-Baeza, 2018). In addition, the use of the game in the classroom makes it possible to obtain immediate feedback on the student's satisfaction, the possibility of making reports on the development of the activity in its different phases, as well as the knowledge of the type of rewards that motivate the student to continue progressing in the activity (Bodnar et al., 2016). The bibliography already includes some experiences that have used gamification in the educational system such as Trivial, Kahoot or Socrative, for the learning of contents of certain parts of the curricular subjects (De Soto García, 2018; Del Moral, Guzmán Duque, & Fernández García,2018)). As the results obtained are very positive, its application has spread and is being put into practice in different sections of education, including university, and in different studies such as law, architecture, philosophy, etc. The success of gamification may lie in the fact that it converts tough and unmotivating experiences, such as the acquisition of certain curricular content, into a much more attractive and motivating experience that leads the student to become more involved in its learning, to have a greater desire to participate and collaborate in teamwork and to develop a greater effort in order to apply the knowledge acquired during the course (Bodnar et al., 2016; Revuelta 2015; Pisabarro & Vivaracho, 2018). In gamification, not only the most advantaged students may participate, but the group will integrate people with different levels, which allows everyone to participate and contribute, to a greater or lesser extent, to the resolution of the game and therefore to the learning, thus facilitating multidirectional communication in the team.

As one of the great challenges in teaching is to get the student motivated towards the acquisition of learning, after the results obtained with gamification, it can be stated that it could be a valid methodology to use in the classroom. According to some authors (Jabbar & Felicia, 2015; Huang et al., 2018) gamification, due to its characteristics, could make the student commit and participate more in their learning process, forgetting the more traditional role of a mere listener and adopting a more innovative role, that of becoming the center of learning (Konopka, Adaime, & Mosele, 2015).To achieve the engagement and motivation of the students, we must take into account two fundamental factors of gamification: the mechanics and the narrative. The mechanics are the rules in a game (Cortizo et al., 2011), and the narrative is the story, the plot line of the game that has to raise interest and attract the players so that their participation and involvement in the game is greater (Prieto, Díaz, Monserrat, & Reyes, 2014; Rodzuan, Ahmad, Ali, & Nordin, 2018).

According to Pérez-López, Rivera and Trigueros (2017), in order to have this type of more innovative methodology applied in the classroom, it is necessary to have a nice working atmosphere in the classroom, the experience must be focused on the game, and once the experience is over, a reflection and group evaluation among all those who have participated in the game should be carried out. Even when the atmosphere in the classroom was good at the beginning, gamification would contribute to increasing it because for the proper resolution of the game it is necessary that there is a connection between the members of the group who play the game. (Rodriguez & Santiago, 2015). In addition to learning content and increasing motivation with gamification, other benefits are also obtained, such as the learning of transversal skills (Menon and Romero 2020; Zamora-Polo, Luque-Sendra, et al., 2019) and increases problem-solving ability (Kapp, 2012)

The escape room is an example of gamified activity. The escape room is a game in which a number of people will have to cooperate and collaborate to be able to solve different challenges, enigmas and missions, which will allow them to complete the activity and solve the problem or be able to leave the aforementioned escape room (Borrego, Fernández, Blanes, & Tobles, 2016; Eukel, Frenzel, & Cernusca, 2017).

Escape Room

The results obtained from the different studies carried out on university students reveal the lack of motivation that students feel in the teaching-learning process. Given this lack of motivation of university students, it raised the need to make a change oriented towards the implementation of more active innovative methodologies, which allow the student to have a more active and leading role in their learning process. Game-based learning is included within the innovative methodologies since they put the student at the center of the learning process and not the teacher as traditional methodologies do, and this manages to achieve a better predisposition of students towards learning (Boyle et al., 2016; Tobias, Fletcher, Bediou, Wind, & Chen, 2014).

Within Game-Based Learning are the well-known escape rooms (Fotaris & Mastoras, 2019). An educational escape room is a playful activity in which students must overcome certain tests or challenges in a limited time and complete missions which will allow them to leave a room in which they are locked up by solving the posed problems that arise. The escape room is an educational strategy that promotes active learning, and that can be combined with other methodologies, or it can act alone.

The escape room has its origin in video games, later transforming into in vivo experiences. The tendency to apply this experience born outside the classroom to teaching is increasing, its characteristics allow it to be adjusted to different curricular areas and educational levels, adapting to the diversity of the students who participate in it (Lázaro, 2019).

As an educational strategy, its success is due to the fact that it produces and increases the intrinsic motivation of students (Teixes,2015, p- 17-26). During the development of the activity, the students do not feel that they are being evaluated and strengthening the contents and skills previously acquired, but rather that they think they are playing. In order to be successful, the escape room must have a seductive and attractive plot line that encourages students to solve the problem that they have been asked, this will arouse their curiosity, which will encourage the students to identify themselves with the role that has been assigned to them, and also to feel fully integrated into the game. which will encourage them to identify with the role that has been given to them and fully integrate into the game.

Due to the benefits obtained with the application of escape rooms, educational escape rooms are emerging in university education (Haake, 2019; Santos, Miguel, Queiruga -Dios, & Encinas, 2020). There are works that collect proposals for certain Escape Rooms in different disciplines such as education, nursing or architecture (Adams, Burger, Crawford, & Setter, 2018; Moreno-Fuentes, 2019; Onecha, Sanz, & López, 2019). However, in the educational sector and more specifically in the master's degree in Special Education, it is difficult to find any work related to the theme raised, hence the value that this article can have.

The results obtained after its implementation have been mostly positive since it was possible to increase the motivation of the students towards the study of the contents treated, they developed cooperative work between the members of the groups, it allowed them to develop key competences of the aforementioned study, and increased interaction and exchange of reflections and comments between students and teachers. However, the negative aspect might be that the number is scarce, the most notable being the increase in work for the teacher involved in the planning, creation, development and application of the escape room.

For the design of an educational escape room whose realization is going to be carried out in the online modality, a series of phases must be followed to ensure the success of the room (López-Pernas, Gordillo, Barra, & Quemada, 2020; Gómez,2020). First, in order to set the goals, it is necessary to know the needs presented by the group that is going to carry out the experience, its learning characteristics and its reality. After learning this data, the goal to be achieved and its completion will be posed, these goals must be feasible and measurable.

In a second phase, the plot line that will be the common thread throughout the entire escape room is proposed. This will be created and proposed by the professor according to the contents developed in the subject. The argument that is developed has to be attractive to the students so that it motivates them to participate in the game. The story has to make sense to them from the beginning and must not decay over time; that's why it has to be based on their tastes, language, it has to seem very close to the reality they live and in which they operate. The game has to be enriched with elements that challenge them and motivate them to continue playing but must always have a connection to the content they have studied in the subject. What it will really make the difference is how the story is presented, the context used and the elements to be used both in the development of the story and in the creation of challenges and missions.

Very important for the success of the escape room is to know and take into account different data in the development, such as the duration, where is it going to take place, who are the people that are going to participate and how many participants will form the groups, if it is voluntary or mandatory to pass the escape room subject. Designing an escape room for primary school is not the same as designing an escape room for university students or for an online postgraduate degree; this issue will be discussed in this article. With this analysis, we intend to develop a very personalized escape room for our students.

Once known the goals to be achieved, the plot line and other data such as those mentioned above, it is time in this fourth phase to design the challenges and missions that will have to be overcome to successfully complete the escape room. In the elaboration and design of the challenges and missions, must be taken into account the elements which are quite characteristic and appear in most of the escapes room (Wiemker, Elumir, & Clare,2015). Normally, the students have to find clues or lost objects that their location will allow them to overcome the established challenges and missions. The clues are usually shown in the shape of anagrams, pictograms, encrypted words that they will have to decipher. In all of them, the ability to observe, the expertise and the ability of the participants to find and relate the different clues that have been hidden around the room is tested, and for this, they will have to memorize the different clues that will pop up throughout the game. The different tests must have an order in which they have to be overcome, therefore.

In a fifth phase, the phases to be overcome must be built, as well as the clues that will help them to overcome the tests. It is necessary to anticipate and take into account the blocking that certain groups might go through when trying to solve certain tests or challenges, requiring additional help to be able to get over the block and continue with the game. To overcome this obstacle, you have to design some tracks that might help them. In addition to the design, it must be established how many complementary clues can be requested, when they can be given, and what the penalty will be after delivery.

In the last and seventh phase, the escape room will be tested. This process is essential for its success because if we start the experience and we have not tested it, we may find that a series of problems, which apparently didn´t exist, will come out or arise. They are solvable and yet in a previous test they would have been easily correctable. The appearance of these failures during the final design of the escape room can cause its failure or decrease its success.

In short, empirical studies show that the escape room is an appropriate tool to promote student learning and motivation. As teachers, our job is to be a mediator or guide that facilitates student learning and for this we are going to provide them with basic knowledge, as well as the most innovative tools and methodologies to increase their learning and motivation. The escape room is proposed, because we believe in the positive value that gamification has in learning to promote practical exercises that allow applying what is learned in the theoretical part of the subject.

MAIN FOCUS OF THE ARTICLE: ESCAPE ROOM ONLINE

In this section, a specific experience of an escape room will be proposed. This experience would be part of the subject Developmental Disorders of the Master's Degree in Special Education. Given the results obtained from the surveys carried out on students about their degree of satisfaction with both the Master's and the subject, a project designed under the ideologies of active methodologies and ICT is proposed.

The aim of this project is to improve the motivation of the students, as well as to facilitate and enrich the learning of a very important part of the subject, such as the practical cases since it is the point that worries most the students and that has obtained the worst score in the satisfaction survey.

In the master's degree in Special Education, the aim is to provide a holistic training that includes theoretical-practical learning through exposure and teaching of theoretical content and the practical part that consists of working on real cases. The case study has unquestionable advantages as a pedagogical method since it incorporates a diversity of skills in students that are not incorporated with the study of theoretical content. This is considered basic for the training of future professionals because it fosters the ability to solve problems through critical and reflective thinking and boosts the dialogue between professionals and students. The potential of the case study as an instrument for the training of students with similar experiences to those lived in the day to day of their profession makes us consider the need to develop new methods of more innovative case studies.

Method

Within the active methodologies, the Escape Room rooms are chosen to work on the practical cases of the Developmental Disorders subjects of the Master's in Special Education, considering it as a tool that the student may find more fun and therefore it could motivate them more. This would be translated into a greater involvement of the students and a greater acquisition of knowledge and skills that will give them a competitive advantage in the labor market. The final interest is to intensify the motivation, participation and learning of the students in the realization of practical cases. The realization and participation of the escape rooms will help students to detect and recognize the different developmental disorders early in order to plan and develop the appropriate intervention programs for the specific needs that these children present.

Along with the realization of different Escape Rooms throughout the programming of the subject, it is intended to review and strengthen the contents given in the theoretical part of the Master, assess the degree of skills and competences that students have for the resolution of practical cases that are risen to them, as well as the group cohesion existing between them. Students have to interact with each other and socialize by putting their knowledge at the service of other classmates, so that everyone contributes their qualities to the group seeking a common good.

Context

To carry out the escape room, groups will be formed, according to the number of students attending the course, not exceeding 8 participants per group. The groups will be formed in alphabetical order so that they are homogeneous in order not to facilitate discrimination and rivalry between the groups, but rather cohesion, participation and healthy competition.

This project will be carried out in an online university, concretely in the International University of la Rioja, as this is one of the conditions that the university requires students for their enrollment, that students have good digital knowledge and good technology management. To ensure success and reduce technical and computer problems, the escape room will be developed on the Adobe Connect platform, which is the same platform used to teach the classes.

The duration of the practice depends on the difficulty of the experience, the level of the students, the number of members of each group. Generally, it will be established as a general duration that each experience lasts two hours and takes place in a single session. To design these sessions, it would be convenient to take into account the period in which the theoretical knowledge will be taught, which is the basis and foundation of the practical part of the subject. These activities will be established at the end of each school term.

Application Used

The escape room design has been made with the Genially platform. This platform has been chosen because it is free and provides quick and easy handling, as well as many templates and resources created especially for education. It is a very intuitive tool which allows you to easily create interactive digital content. The results obtained by the teachers, the game director and the students will be very satisfactory.

Preparation of Instructions

At the beginning of the game, before entering the escape room, the game director or the teacher in charge of the subject will normally provide the participants with a series of fundamental instructions for the success of the game. To give the instructions, the game director can give them directly or can play the role of a character, which is related to the theme and plot line of the escape room. Characters or other elements are usually used to introduce the participants to what the game itself is and begin to create an expectant and fun atmosphere, completely different from the classroom, which will draw the attention of the students, motivate their participation and openness to the game. First, the game director welcomes the players, introduces himself and with a brief explanation explains who he is and what his role will be in the experience. He then explains to them the objective to be achieved by carrying out this activity, the theme on which the design is based, the plot line, and finally, he suggests the existence of some missions that students will have to accomplish in order to escape from the room and terminate the activity. Finally, he will explain to them that there are some challenges that they will have to overcome to fulfill the missions. The instructions will end by telling them that they will be able to ask for help, how they will ask for it, how many times and the price they will have to pay for it. By establishing rules, the activity is given a more serious and rigorous character, showing that it is an activity designed, devised and planned for the students who will carry it out.

The fulfillment of this activity is designed to comply with the practical part of the subject, which allows an expectant student to integrate into this dynamic as it is new, present-day, challenging and tests his/her skills, knowledge and both personal and professional skills. After the start, as they solve the challenges and missions, the students will gain confidence, and they will feel more attracted and challenged by the game, thereby increasing their concentration, participation and fun. The end of the game is usually very exciting for them since they receive immediate positive feedback when they can leave the room or solve the problem after completing all the missions and challenges that are included in the escape room.

Plot Thread

The escape room is titled "Zurban School", Figure 1. It is an ordinary concerted school located in the Northwest area of the Community of Madrid.

Figure 1. Title of the escape room
Source: (self-made, 2022)

Before starting the game and on a different page from the escape room one, the students will be explained what the escape room and the mission consist of, Figure 2. This week, although we are in January and the second term begins, they have received an application for admission from a new student. Juan is 12 years old, he is in 3rd ESO, and his academic record is not very good. He has been expelled from his last school for conduct and behavior problems, as well as for the bad relationships he had with his classmates and teachers. The Zurbano school is a very special school, it stands out for having a special consideration and dealing with "difficult and diversified students". When the game director, represented by her avatar, has given all the necessary instructions to understand and be able to develop the game properly, the mission entrusted to her is explained to them in order to end the meeting and be able to leave the game.

Once the instructions have been completed and the mission explained, the game starts, and students go to the room where their escape room. This morning, the faculty of the school have been summoned by the director to have a session, Figure 3, in order to study Juan's case and make a decision on whether or not to approve his admission to the school.

In this escape room, it is considered that the students who study the subject of Developmental Disorders and who are going to carry out this experience represent the different professionals who constitute the school faculty, teachers, director, psychologist, speech therapist or specialized personnel, Figure 4, and it is they who are going to have to solve the four missions proposed in the escape room, Figure 5.

Creation of Challenges and Missions

After the escape room presentation, we are now going to describe the missions, Figure 5, which the students will have to carry out in order to complete this experience.

Figure 2. The mission
Source: (self-made, 2022)

The argument of the missions is related to the matter that is taught in the subject of Developmental Disorders throughout the course. The correct completion of the four missions that conform the escape room will make it possible to achieve the objective that is set when performing in the escape room. The

Figure 3. The mission
Source: (self-made, 2022)

Figure 4. Teachers
Source: (self-made, 2022)

groups that participate have to solve the four missions to find out what is happening to Juan, what type of problem he has that affects him so much in the social relations that he establishes with his classmates and with the teachers and encourages him to present those behavioral problems due to which he was

Figure 5. Missions
Source: (self-made, 2022)

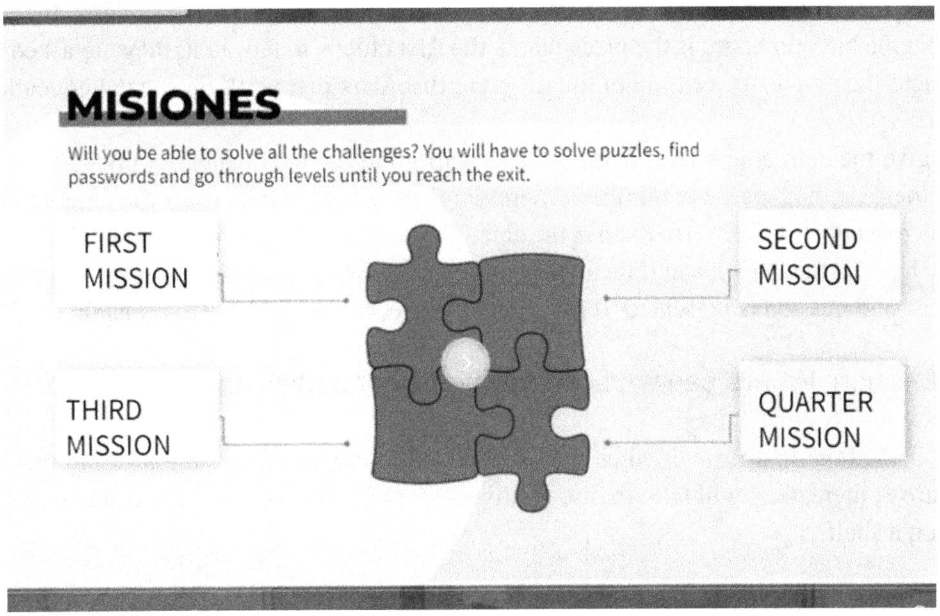

Figure 6. 1st Mission
Source: (self-made, 2022)

expelled from the previous school. Knowing the type of disorder in question, students will be able to propose the appropriate intervention for the needs that Juan has, so to try to reduce, diminish or eliminate those very disruptive behaviors that he currently presents.

First Mission: Look for the First Clue Where do you Leave the Important Notes?

In this first mission, Figure 6, the team will have to find the first clue that will allow them to carry out the challenge that they will have to overcome to move on to the second mission. First, the team has to discover that the bulletin board is the place where the first clue is found. In it, they are asked about "the manual where the diagnostic criteria of the different disorders that work on special educational needs appear".

If they give the correct answer, "DSM 5", they will go to the next panel, Figure 7, where they will check that there are no letters but numbers; therefore they will have to convert the letters into numbers using the pictograph that is given to them in the clue. The numbers obtained will have to be marked on the thread they have on that panel, and if the numbers they mark are correct, they will pass to the next panel where the second mission is presented. If they are not correct they will have to try again until they get it.

Second Mission: Where can we Look for the Second Mission?

The teams passed the first mission, then they will be led to a panel where the meeting room is shown again, Figure 8, there, they will have to discover the next clue. This second clue is found in a book that is located on a shelf.

Figure 7. 1st Challenge
Source: (self-made, 2022)

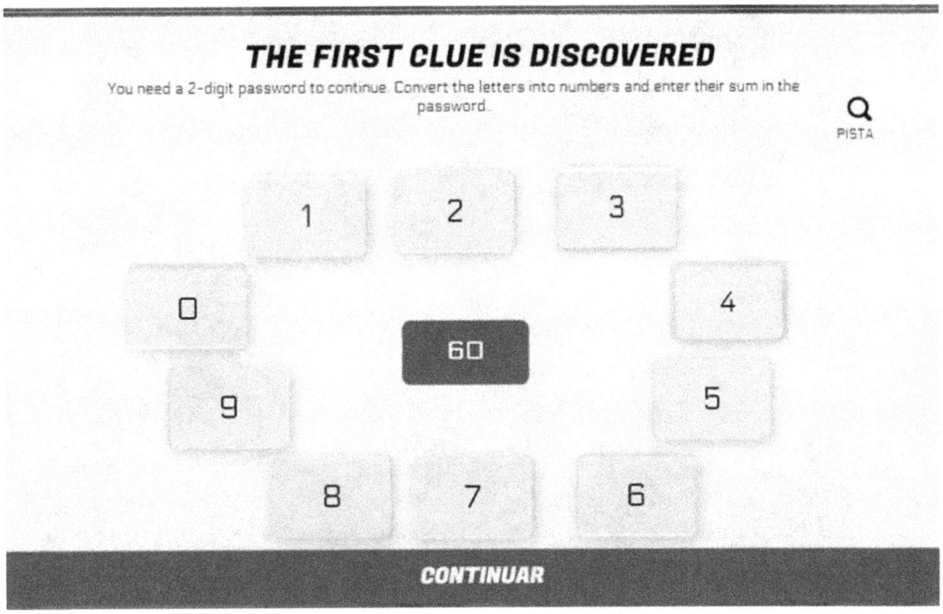

Figure 8. 2nd Missions
Source: (self-made, 2022)

The book collects very important information to know the possible disorder you have. This information was given by the parents in the interview with the director. Now, with the data they have, the

Figure 9. 2nd challenge
Source: (self-made, 2022)

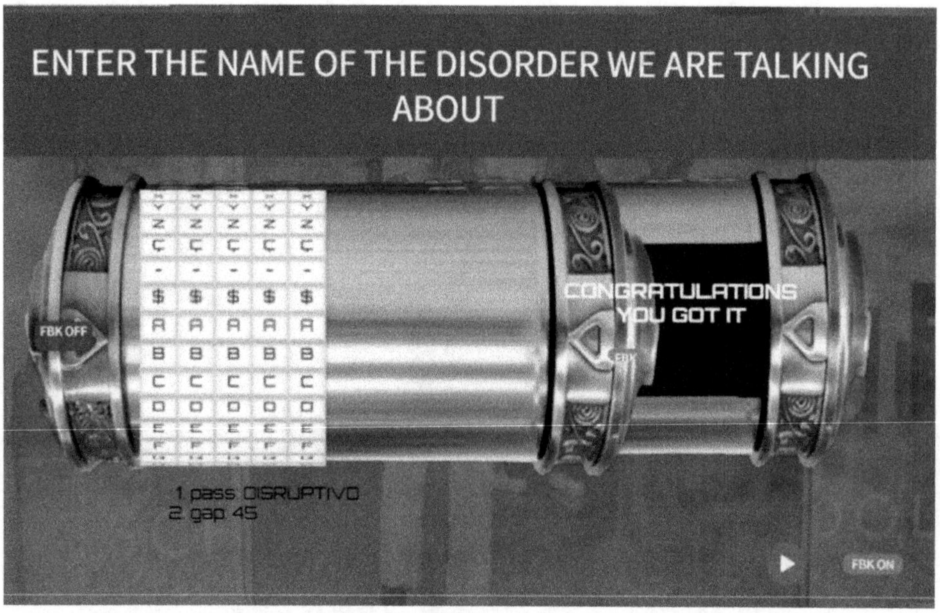

students have to know the name of the possible disorder that Juan suffers from, and they have to enter that name in a padlock to see if it is correct or not, Figure 9, if it is correct the padlock will open, and they can move on to the next mission.

Third Mission: Specify the Type of Disorder that Juan has

The students are already on the third mission. At this time, they know the type of disorder that Juan has, "Disruptive Disorder", but within that general category there are several possibilities of different disorders, so it is essential to know the specific type of disorder in order to plan the intervention. To discover the specific type of disorder, students will be provided with some essential clues since these characteristics are what allow us to differentiate this type of "Challenging Disruptive Disorder" from other Disruptive Disorders such as Intermittent, Antisocial or Conduct Disorder. To check if their diagnosis is really correct, they will have to type on the typewriter, Figure 10, the name of the type of disruptive disorder they think it is. If they type "Challenging" then they will get an alert telling them that they have succeeded, and they will move to the next panel.

Fourth Mission: Type of Intervention Proposed

They are already in the fourth and last mission, Figure 11, at this point the students know the type of disorder that Juan has, Defiant Disruptive Disorder, and now due to the knowledge acquired in the subject they should know the type of intervention that they would have to do to respond to the needs that Juan has. It's time to put that acquired knowledge to the test.

Figure 10. 3rd Challenge
Source: (self-made, 2022)

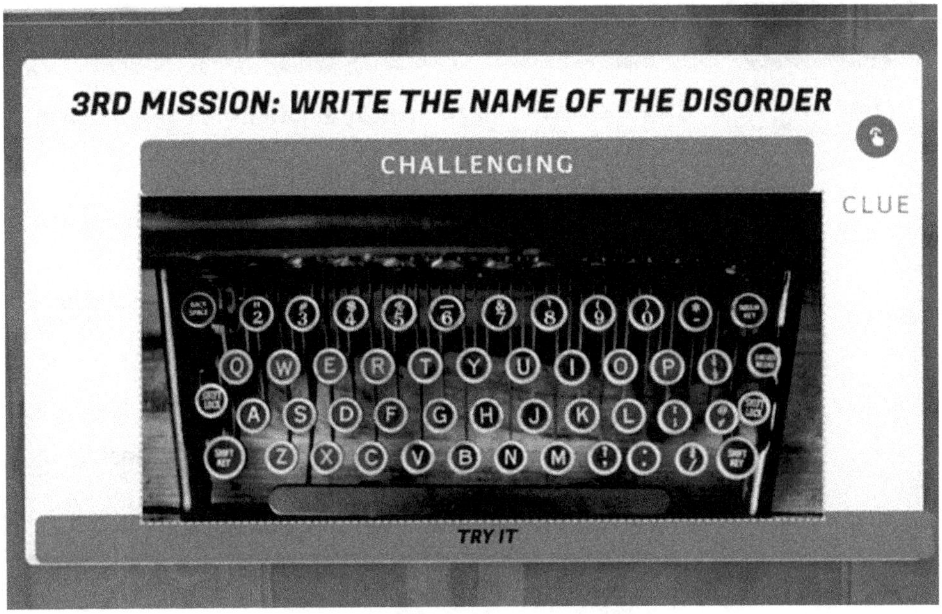

Figure 11. 4th Mission
Source: (self-made, 2022)

In this fourth and last mission, Figure 12, they will be asked to select 5 interventions that they could carry out to work on the deficits that Juan presents.

Figure 12. 4th track
Source: (self-made, 2022)

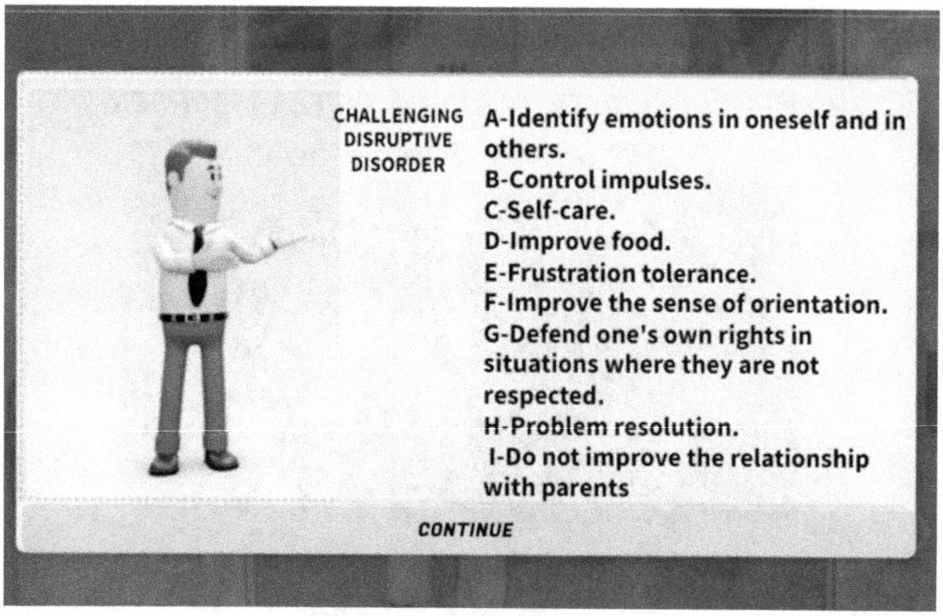

Once the interventions have been chosen, they have to transform the letters that designate each intervention into a number and the sum of all the numbers will be the number of the door they have to choose,

Figure 13. 4th Challenge
Source: (self-made, 2022)

Figure 14. End of the escape room
Source: (self-made, 2022)

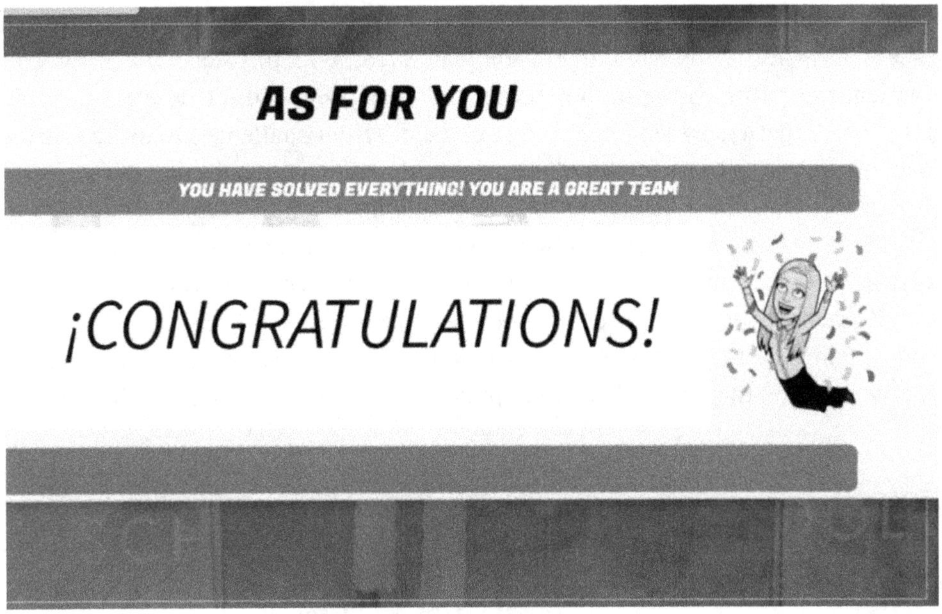

Figure 13, in order to finish and leave the escape room. The transformation from letters to numbers can be done by means of the pictopist that is in the clue that is given in that panel.

Finally, if the choice of the door is the right one, they will go to the next and last panel, Figure 14, where they are informed that they have already finished the escape room.

Evaluation of the Experience

In this experience, the evaluation to be carried out consists of several steps. An initial evaluation aims to assess the knowledge that students have about the escape room, as well as the motivation and needs that the student expresses about the realization of practical cases in the subject, and how he values the learning and practice of cases through the realization of escape room. A process evaluation will also be implemented through systematic observation throughout the duration of the escape room. This observation will be conducted by the game director and it is suggested to be performed through observation so as not to interrupt the progress of the activity and therefore contaminate the field of study. Lastly, a final evaluation will be carried out, it will consist of two parts, a first part in which a debate will be opened among all the groups, talking about what they thought of the experience and the development of the activity. After the group debate, another individual evaluation will be carried out where each student will have to answer a series of questions on different issues such as motivation, acquisition of skills and consolidation of content, as well as satisfaction with this type of methodology as a tool for learning.

The final individual evaluation will be accomplished through an anonymous survey that will be passed to the students. The survey form is developed in Google and in it, students are asked to honestly answer the items that are presented to them. Once the item-type questions are finished, a space is left for open questions where students can ponder and share on the positive and negative aspects that they think could be modified or eliminated in order to improve the online escape room they have done. As we are very interested in knowing how the students have experienced and perceived the experience, we are going to pass three scales that will help us collect this information. The first scale is called Gameful experience scale (GAMEX) (Eppmann, Bekk, & Klein, 2018), with this scale, it is intended to measure how the experience of participating in the escape room has been. This scale measures the emotional states that they have experienced while carrying out the different challenges to overcome the missions.

With a second scale, López-Pernas et al. (2019), we intend to measure the attitude of the students towards the escape room, their satisfaction after completing it and if they eventually would like to participate in another escape room again. Finally, with a third scale, according to Jambhekar, Pahls, & Deloney (2020), we want to measure the degree to which the activity has allowed putting into practice what has been learned throughout the contents of the subject.

The results obtained in the different past tests as well as the observation made will allow us to obtain very valuable information that will help us to improve and excell the designs of future escape rooms.

CONCLUSION

Finally, in this section, we are going to expose the main conclusions that we have drawn after developing a postgraduate escape room for online training. We consider that the reflections that we are going to present below, due to the scarce bibliography in online postgraduate courses in special education, can be useful for professionals who, like us, are interested in the implementation of new and more active methodologies for the dynamization of classes and subjects in online postgraduate training. These reflections will be of interest and the escape room can be an example for teachers who teach lessons at the online postgraduate university level and are interested in working on learning through gaming.

After completing the design of the escape room and testing its effectiveness with a small sample of students, one of the first conclusions obtained was that in order to ensure its effectiveness, before starting with the design, it is essential to determine the objectives to be pursued with its fullfilment as well as the context where it will be accomplished. It is primordial that the design of the escape room allows the students to concentrate only on carrying out the missions, that all the members of the groups need to coordinate and cooperate actively to achieve a common purpose such as overcoming challenges. Besides the tests that must be overcome and the missions that must be fulfilled, the escape room must allow them to experience a variety of positive emotional states, such as joy, satisfaction but at the same time a small part of negatives ones, such as frustration, stress or anxiety when they don´t manage to solve the tests within the desired time interval. Feeling these negative emotional states is not bad since one of the objectives that are proposed to achieve with the realization of the escape room is to exercise and control the different emotional states that arise in situations where decisions have to be made and problems solved. Fundamental for the escape room to meet this objective and be effective for learning is to control the degree of difficulty because if that difficulty is not adjusted to the students who will be taking part in it, the frustration or stress may be excessive for the majority of the groups and lead them to give up or not to do it in the estimated time.

As stated at the beginning of the article, the game, after the successes obtained, it is positioning itself in learning and education and after the experience of designing this activity, we are committed to opening a new dimension in the teaching and learning of online postgraduate courses by working on the practical cases of the Neuropsychological Intervention subject through escape rooms (Santamaría Urbieta

& Alcalde Peñalver, 2019). This proposal is based on the fact that through the escape rooms, students will be able to carry out different activities such as solving real cases, reviewing content, debates and decision-making that will help them train for their future professional activity. To achieve this goal, it is essential that the escape rooms are designed, taking into account very realistic academic topics that must be adjusted to the reality of their future professions.

When proposing the learning and teaching of a part of the subject through escape room, we consider that the interest and motivation of the students for the subject will increase as it is a novel teaching method and will promote a positive attitude and assessment of the effort made by both, the teacher and the university for the introduction of innovative methodologies in the master's degree (Dicheva et al., 2015). The design, performance and application of an escape room cause a considerable increase in the workload for the teacher, but this load will be compensated with the satisfaction obtained when the students successfully complete the activity, and after the closing debate it will be verified that it has been fulfilled the aforementioned objectives.

REFERENCES

Adams, V., Burger, S., Crawford, K., & Setter, R. (2018). Can you escape? Creating an escape room to facilitate active learning. *Journal for Nurses in Professional Development*, *34*(2), E1–E5. doi:10.1097/NND.0000000000000433 PMID:29481471

Area Moreira, M. (2008). La innovación pedagógica con TIC y el desarrollo de las competencias informacionales y digitales [Pedagogical innovation with ICT and the development of informational and digital competencies]. *Revista de Investigación en la Escuela*, *64*, 5–17.

Arechavala Vargas, R., & Sánchez Cervantes, C. F. (2017). Las universidades públicas mexicanas: Los retos de las transformaciones institucionales hacia la investigación y la transferencia de conocimiento [Mexican public universities: the challenges of institutional transformations towards research and knowledge transfer]. *Revista de la Educación Superior*, *46*(184), 21–37. doi:10.1016/j.resu.2017.09.001

Barab, S. A., Thomas, K., & Merrill, H. (2001). Online learning: From information dissemination to fostering collaboration. *Journal of Interactive Learning Research*, *12*(1), 105–143.

Bodnar, C. A., Anastasio, D., Enszer, J. A., & Burkey, D. D. (2016). Ingenieros en juego: Juegos como herramientas de enseñanza para estudiantes de ingeniería [Engineers at play: games as teaching tools for engineering students]. *Revista de Educación en Ingeniería*, *105*(1), 147–200.

Borrego, C., Fernández, C., Robles, S., & Blanes, I. (2016). Room escape en las aulas: Actividades de juegos de escape para facilitar la motivación y el aprendizaje de las ciencias de la computación [Room escape in the classroom: escape game activities to facilitate motivation and learning in computer science]. *Revista del Congrés Internacional de Docència Universitària i Innovació*, *3*, 1–7.

Boyle, E. A., Hainey, T., Connolly, T. M., Gray, G., Earp, J., Ott, M., Lim, T., Ninaus, M., Ribeiro, C., & Pereira, J. (2016). An update to the systematic literature review of empirical evidence of the impacts and outcomes of computer games and serious games. *Computers & Education*, *94*, 178–192. doi:10.1016/j.compedu.2015.11.003

Choudhury, S., & Pattnaik, S. (2019). Emerging themes in e-learning: A review from the stakeholder's perspective. *Computers & Education, 144*, 103657. doi:10.1016/j.compedu.2019.103657

Cortizo Pérez, J. C. C., Carrero García, F., Monsalve Piqueras, B., Velasco Collado, A., Díaz Del Dedo, L., & Pérez Martín, J. (2011). Gamificación y Docencia: Lo que la Universidad tiene que aprender de los Videojuegos [Gamification and Teaching: What the University has to learn from Video Games]. In Retos y oportunidades del desarrollo de los nuevos títulos en educación superior. VIII Jornadas Internacionales de Innovación Universitaria.

De Soto García, I. S. (2018). Herramientas de gamificación para el aprendizaje de ciencias de la tierra [Gamification tools for earth science learning]. *Edutec-e Revista Electrónica de Tecnología Educativa, 65*(65), 29–39. doi:10.21556/edutec.2018.65.1143

Del Moral, M. E., Guzmán Duque, A. P., & Fernández García, L. C. (2018). Game-Based Learning: Increasing the Logical-Mathematical, Naturalistic, and Linguistic Learning Levels of Primary School Students. *Journal of New Approaches in Educational Research, 7*(1), 31–39. doi:10.7821/naer.2018.1.248

Dicheva, D., Dichev, C., Agre, G., & Angelova, G. (2015). Gamification in education: A systematic mapping study. *Journal of Educational Technology & Society, 18*(3), 75–88.

Eppmann, R., Bekk, M., & Klein, K. (2018). Gameful experience in gamification: Construction and validation of a gameful experience scale. *Journal of Interactive Marketing, Elsevier, 43*, 98–115. doi:10.1016/j.intmar.2018.03.002

Eukel, H. N., Frenzel, J. E., & Cernusca, D. (2017). Educational gaming for pharmacy students–design and evaluation of a diabetes-themed escape room. *American Journal of Pharmaceutical Education, 81*(7), 6265. doi:10.5688/ajpe8176265 PMID:29109566

Fotaris, P., & Mastoras, T. (2019, October). Escape rooms for learning: A systematic review. In *Proceedings of the European Conference on Games Based Learning* (pp. 235-243). Academic Press.

Gómez, M. (2020). A COVID-19 intervention: Using digital escape rooms to provide professional development to alternative certification educators. *Journal of Technology and Teacher Education, 28*(2), 425–432.

Haake, S. (2019). Stealing the exams: using a narrative technique in designing an escape game in university context. In C. Busch (Ed.), *Proceedings of the European Conference on Games-Based Learening* (pp. 1004-1007). Academic Press.

Huang, B., Hew, K. F., & Lo, C. K. (2018). Investigating the efects of gamiication-enhanced lipped learning on undergraduate students' behavioral and cognitive engagement. *Interactive Learning Environments, 10*, 1–21.

Jabbar, A. I., & Felicia, P. (2015). Gameplay Engagement and Learning in Game-Based LearningA Systematic Review. *Review of Educational Research, 85*(4), 740–779. doi:10.3102/0034654315577210

Jambhekar, K., Pahls, R. P., & Deloney, L. A. (2020). Benefits of an escape room as a novel educational activity for radiology residents. *Academic Radiology, 27*(2), 276–283. doi:10.1016/j.acra.2019.04.021 PMID:31160173

Jenaro, C., Flores, N. E., Poy, R., González, F., & Martínez, E. (2013). Metodologías docentes en la educación superior. Percepciones del profesorado sobre su importancia y uso [Teaching methodologies in higher education. Faculty perceptions of their importance and use]. *Revista de Enseñanza Universitaria, 39*, 1–16.

Kapp, K. (2012). *The Gamification of Learning and Instruction: Game-Based Methods and Strategies for Training and Education*. John Wiley and Sons.

Ke, F. (2014). An implementation of design-based learning through creating educational computer games: A case study on mathematics learning during design and computing. *Computers & Education, 73*, 26–39. doi:10.1016/j.compedu.2013.12.010

Kirschner, P. A., & Erkens, G. (2013). Toward a framework for CSCL research. *Educational Psychologist, 48*(1), 1–8. doi:10.1080/00461520.2012.750227

Konopka, C., Adaime, M. B., & Mosele, P. H. (2015). Active Teaching and Learning Methodologies: Some Considerations. *Creative Education, 6*(14), 1536–1545. doi:10.4236/ce.2015.614154

Landers, R. N. (2014). Developing a theory of gamified learning: Linking serious games and gamification of learning. *Simulation & Gaming, 45*(6), 752–768. doi:10.1177/1046878114563660

Landers, R. N., Armstrong, M. B., & Collmus, A. B. (2017). How to use game elements to enhance learning: Applications of the theory of gamified learning. In *Serious games and edutainment applications* (pp. 457–483). Springer. doi:10.1007/978-3-319-51645-5_21

Lázaro, I. G. (2019). Escape Room como propuesta de gamificación en educación. *Revista Educativa Hekademos, 27*, 71–79.

López-Pernas, S., Gordillo, A., Barra, E., & Quemada, J. (2019). Examining the use of an educational escape room for teaching programming in a higher education setting. *IEEE Access: Practical Innovations, Open Solutions, 7*, 31723–31737. doi:10.1109/ACCESS.2019.2902976

Menon, D., & Romero, M. (2020). Game mechanics supporting a learning and playful experience in educational escape games. In *Global perspectives on gameful and playful teaching and learning* (pp. 143–162). IGI Global. doi:10.4018/978-1-7998-2015-4.ch007

Moral Pérez, M., Fernández García, L. C., & Guzmán Duque, A. P. (2016). Proyecto Game to Learn: aprendizaje basado en juegos para potenciar las inteligencias lógico-matemática, naturalista y lingüística en primaria [Game to Learn Project: game-based learning to enhance logical-mathematical, naturalistic and linguistic intelligences in primary school]. *Píxel-Bit. Revista de Medios y Educación, 49*, 177–193.

Moreno-Fuentes, E. (2019). El "Breakout EDU" como herramienta clave para la gamificación en la formación inicial de maestros/as [The "Breakout EDU" as a key tool for gamification in initial teacher training]. *Revista electrónica de tecnología educativa, 67*, 66-79.

New Media Consortium. (2018). *NMC Horizon Report - 2017 Higher Education Edition*. Retrieved from: http://cdn.nmc.org/media/2017-nmc-horizon-report-he-EN.pdf

Onecha, B., Sanz, J., & López, D. (2019). Los límites de la ludificación en la enseñanza de la arquitectura. La técnica del Escape Room [The limits of gamification in architecture education. The Escape Room technique]. *Journal of Interdisciplinary Studies in Architecture and Urbansim, 12*(12), 122–133. doi:10.26754/ojs_zarch/zarch.2019123549

Pérez-López, I. J., Rivera, C., & Trigueros, C. (2017). The Prophecy of the Chosen Ones": An Example of Gamification Applied to University Teaching. *Revista Internacional de Medicina y Ciencias de la Actividad Física y del Deporte, 17*(66), 243–260.

Pérez-Manzano, A., & Almela-Baeza, J. (2018). Gamificación transmedia para la divulgación científica y el fomento de vocaciones procientíficas en adolescentes [Transmedia gamification for the popularization of science and the promotion of pro-science vocations in adolescents]. *Comunicar, 26*(55), 93–103.

Pisabarro, A. M., & Vivaracho, C. E. (2018). Gamificación en el aula: Gincana de programación [Gamification in the classroom: programming gymkhana]. *ReVisión, 11*(1), 85–93.

Prieto, A., Díaz, D., Monserrat, J., & Reyes, E. (2014a). Experiencias de aplicación de estrategias de gamificación a entornos de aprendizaje universitario [Experiences in the application of gamification strategies to university learning environments]. *Revisión, 7*(2), 76–92.

Raitskaya, L., & Tikhonova, E. (2019). Habilidades y competencias en la educación superior y más allá. *Revista de Lengua y Educación, 5*(4), 4–8.

Revuelta, F. I. (2015). *Gamification to learning motivation*. Ponencia presentada en Conference Asia-Paciic Economic Cooperation - Observatory of Best Practices with ICT, Lima, Perú.

Rodríguez, F., & Santiago, R. (2015). *Cómo motivar a tu alumnado y mejorar el clima en el aula* [How to motivate your students and improve classroom climate]. Texto-Digital.

Rodzuan, A. R., Ahmad, A., Ali, N. M., & Nordin, A. I. (2018). Understanding Emotional Engagement Amongst Primary School Children for Designing Gamification in Learning. *Advanced Science Letters, 24*(3), 1599–1602. doi:10.1166/asl.2018.11117

Romiszowski, A. (2003). The future of E-learning as an educational innovation: Factors influencing project success and failure. *Revista Brasileira de Aprendizagem Aberta e a Distância, 2*(1), 1–14.

Sánchez Martin, J., Zamora Polo, F., Corrales Serrano, M., & Luque Sendra, A. (2017). Exit for success. Gamifying science and engineering university-level classes using escape-room pedagogy. *Heliyon*.

Santamaría Urbieta, A. & Alcalde Peñalver, E. (2019). Escaping from the English classroom. Who will get out first? *Aloma: Revista de psicologia, ciències de l'educació i de l'esport Blanquerna, 37*(2), 83-92.

Santos, M. J. Miguel, M. Queiruga-Dios, A., & Encinas, A. H. (2020). Looking for the antidote for contaminated water: learning through and escape game. *Advances in Intelligent System and Computing, 951*, 217-226.

Scavarda, A., Dias, A., Reis, A., Silveira, H., & Santos, I. (2021). A covid-19 pandemic sustainable educational innovation management proposal framework. *Sustainability, 13*(11), 6391. doi:10.3390u13116391

Strachan, R., & Liyanage, L. (2015). Active student engagement: The heart of effective learning. In Global Innovation of Teaching and Learning in Higher Education (pp. 255-274). Springer.

Teixes, F. (2015). *Gamificación: Fundamentos y aplicaciones* [Gamification: Fundamentals and applications]. UOC.

Tejedor, E. (2021). El impacto de las tecnologías en el mundo de la enseñanza [The impact of technologies on the world of education]. *Revista de Investigación e Innovación Educativa, 49*, 33–49.

Tobias, S., Fletcher, J. D., Bediou, B., Wind, A. P., & Chen, F. (2014). Aprendizaje multimedia con juegos de ordenador. In R.E. Mayer (Ed.), The Cambridge handbook of multimedia learning (pp.762–784). Cambridge University Press.

Wiemker, M., Elumir, E., & Clare, A. (2015). Escape room games, "Can you transform an unpleasant situation into a pleasant one? *Game Based Learning, 1*, 55–68.

Zamora, F., Luque, A., Sánchez, J., & Aguayo, F. (2019). Conceptual frameworkfor the use of building information modeling in engineering education. *International Journal of Engineering Education, 35*(3), 744–755.

KEY TERMS AND DEFINITIONS

Computer-Supported Collaborative Learning: It refers to the learning process that is carried out by sharing objectives and tasks, with technologies as mediators of this process.

Distance Training: It is a training in which, unlike the online modality, students do not need any device with an internet connection because the training center provides them with the paper materials or multimedia format.

Distributed Knowledge: It is all the knowledge that a community of agents possesses and might apply in solving a problem.

Escape Room: It is a game in which the participants are locked in a room, and in order to get out of it, they have to overcome some challenges that are presented to them to solve different missions that are related to the theme of the escape room. Once all the missions have been accomplished in the available time, the participants win the game, and they can leave the room.

Gamification: It is a tool of innovative methodologies that consists of the use of games in the educational field with the aim of facilitating learning.

Information and Communication Technologies (ICT): They are the set of resources, the different tools and technological programs that contribute to the processing and learning of educational information.

Innovative Methodologies: These are new educational teaching methodologies that place the student at the center of learning; they teach them and provide the tools to make their learning more active and meaningful.

Master's Degree in Special Education: This master's is a postgraduate training that trains different professionals to be able to work with people who have functional diversity and/or special needs in different inclusive environments.

Online Training: Online training is taught in a non-face-to-face way through a device with an Internet connection; this facilitates and allows students to carry out the aforementioned training from any place which has an Internet connection.

Chapter 5
Learning to Innovate by Innovating:
An Escape Room Experience in Training Future High School Teachers

Àngela Janer-Hidalgo
Universidad Internacional de la Rioja (UNIR), Spain

ABSTRACT

The objective of this work is to present an innovative escape room proposal designed and implemented in the subject of teaching innovation and initiation to educational research of the Master's Degree in Secondary Teacher Training at the Universidad Internacional de La Rioja (UNIR) in Spain with a double final: work on the skills covered in the subject and learn innovation by innovating. On the one hand, the escape room project will present the academic context and the proposal structure (narrative, content worked on, missions and rewards, ICT tools used). On the other hand, an analysis of the impact that this experience has had on the motivation and satisfaction of the students will be carried out and on their improvement in the acquisition of the skills taught in the subject. The instrument used to carry out this analysis will be a questionnaire. The results show an improvement in student motivation with the escape room application in the classroom.

INTRODUCTION

Innovation in education has been fundamental to educational improvement, facilitating development initiatives and projects that have achieved relevant, lasting, and meaningful changes in student learning (Castro, Gómez & Carranza, 2022; Selznick et al., 2022). There are numerous current instances of innovative experiences at all educational levels, from preschool through higher education. This paper will focus on the latter, higher education.

This paper describes the design, execution, and evaluation of an innovative gamification experience. It deals with an escape room experience in a course entitled *Innovation in Teaching and Introduction to*

DOI: 10.4018/978-1-6684-6081-8.ch005

Educational Research in the University Master's Program in Secondary Teacher Training of the Universidad Internacional de La Rioja (UNIR), Spain.

This university master's degree trains future teachers of compulsory secondary education. It is mandatory to train prospective teachers in innovative methodologies they can put into practice in their future classrooms.

The subject selected by the author to conduct the escape room, Innovation in Teaching, and Introduction to Educational Research, covers a series of aspects that must be considered when designing and analyzing innovation projects, including analyzing existing models and real innovative experiences as well as using the available tools and resources to carry them out. An expected outcome of the course is that students comprehend the role of research and innovation as fundamental elements in improving education and acquire the knowledge to analyze current innovation projects. It is also expected that students become acquainted with planning and executing their own projects.

The escape room teaches students about educational innovation. Students not only participate in a gamified experience but also reinforce concepts of innovation and go deeper into its intricacies.

The goal of the study is to measure the degree of motivation and satisfaction of students with the course whereby a gamified escape room experience. It is a proposal that is not only committed to teaching innovation but is also a way of rethinking teacher training so that they learn by doing and then transfer it to their future classrooms.

In the first section, the state of educational innovation, gamification, and the use of escape rooms in educational settings are presented.

In the second section, the methodology employed in the study, the sample of students who participated in it, and the implementation of the escape room are presented.

In the third point, the innovation proposal is presented, describing the academic context where it has been applied and the structure of the escape room (narrative, missions, rewards, content...).

In the fourth point, an analysis of the impact that this experience has had on the motivation and satisfaction of the students, as well as on their improvement in the learning process and acquisition of the skills dealt with in the subject, is presented. The main results of this analysis have been obtained from a semi-structured questionnaire made available to all the students who have participated in the escape room.

And finally, the main conclusions are detailed and possible future lines of research.

BACKGROUND

Nowadays, educational systems should have the huge responsibility to adapt themselves to the current needs of societies and to the socio-educational reality in which students are involved. The incorporation of competence approach in the European Higher Education Area (EHEA[1]) has been characterized by a paradigm shift in teaching. These new teaching and learning approaches are student-centered, giving them a more participatory and active role in the teaching and learning processes, considering continuous assessment as a training process and the use of information and communication technologies (ICT) (Salinas, 2004; Delgado & Oliver, 2006; López-Noguero, 2008; Serra-Olivares et al., 2018, García Lázaro, 2019).

In this scenario of new teaching and learning approaches, teachers' and institutions' responsibility for innovation and implementing emerging methodologies is essential to increase motivation, meaningful learning, and student commitment to their learning process. Integrative learning and innovation are theoretically and practically connected (Selznick et al., 2022).

For students to see the usefulness of what they are learning and transfer their learning to similar situations, training and learning processes must relate to reality, to whatever is happening in the world. (Ortiz-Colón, Jordán & Ágreda, 2018). Therefore, when selecting or designing innovative training-learning strategies, it is necessary to think about contextualized activities that deal with current problems and that favor the critical thinking of students.

Learning through practice and ongoing social interactions are essential (Hevia Artime & Fueyo Gutiérrez, 2018). This may look like providing spaces for students to learn in a more dynamic and participatory way, enabling them to exchange their experiences and know how to reflect critically on what they are learning. This approach stands in contrast to more traditional methodologies such as lectures, or solving problems where students have a more passive role as recipients of the content provided by the teacher and learning is only memorized.

Integrating practice in professional situations forces students to make decisions about the different possible approaches of theory, methodological variances, technological options, etc. On the other hand, they put in practice specific communication skills that take them away from a role of receiving information and being mere learners to get on the path of becoming professionals who must moderate, participate, and give feedback in a group setting (Hevia Artime & Fueyo Gutiérrez, 2018, p. 353).

Gamification: An Innovative Methodology

Gamification is an emerging and innovative methodology that fosters a more active role in students and generates more meaningful learning. Many authors agree that this methodology motivates students because it presents knowledge in an attractive way, develops problem-solving skills, and fosters teamwork. Gamification is a powerful methodological strategy for educators training students at any level in the education system (Borrego *et al.,* 2017; Ortiz-Colón, Jordán & Ágreda, 2018, Dreimane, 2019; García Lazaro, 2019).

Gamification is defined below, the main elements that compose it, as well as the advantages and disadvantages of its implementation in classrooms.

Definition and Characterization of Gamification

The term "gamification" was born in 2002 (Marczewski, 2012), but it was not implemented in classrooms until the second half of 2010 (Santamaria & Alcalde, 2020). Burke (2012) defined gamification as using game designs and techniques in non-game contexts to develop development skills and behaviors. The gamification methodology enables the transfer of games to educational-professional settings to improve students' outcomes, promote more meaningful learning and increase their motivation. It allows students to absorb knowledge, permits teachers to customize activities/content according to the needs of students, improves their skills, motivates them, and favors the acquisition of knowledge (Majuri, Koivisto, & Hamari, 2018; Dreimane, 2019; Gómez López et al., 2022).

Figure 1. Basics of gamification.
Source: Werbach & Hunter (2012, p. 78-80)

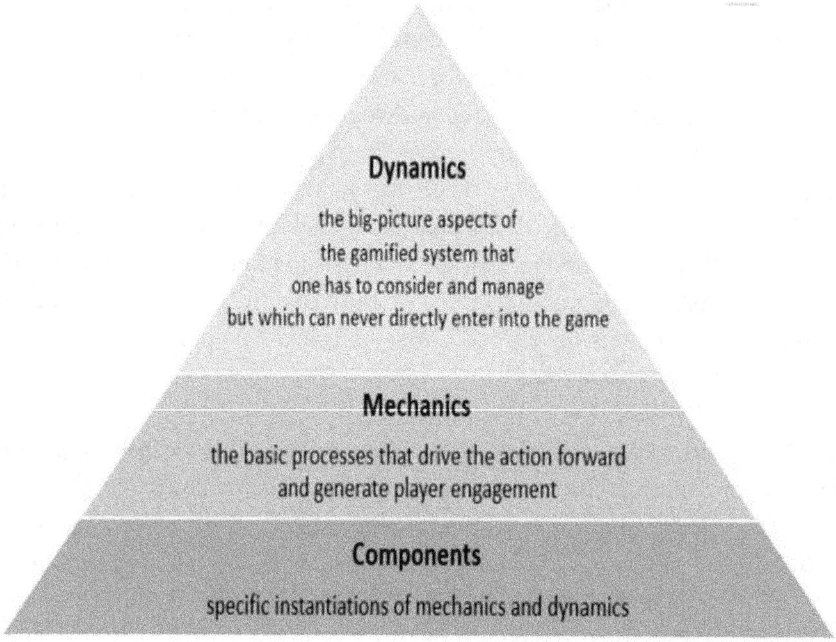

Main Elements of Gamification

According to Werbach and Hunter (2012), the foundational or main elements that make up gamification are dynamics, mechanics, and components. Dynamics are the concept, the leitmotif of the game. They are related to the motivations the game is intended to elicit. Mechanics are the processes that move the game forward: challenges, opportunities, competition, collaboration, rules, feedback, transitions, acquisition of resources, etc. Thirdly, components are specific implementations of dynamics and mechanics: avatars, insignias, points, collections, rankings, levels, and teams, among others. The interaction of these three elements results in a gamified activity (Ortiz-Colón, Jordán & Ágreda, 2018).

Gamification is used in education as a learning tool in different areas and subjects to foster collaborative behavior and attitudes and independent study (Ortiz-Colón, Jordán & Ágreda, 2018). In addition, gamified experiences include feedback, which is immediate and allows students to know the progress they are making, and rewards that motivate them to continue advancing (Sierra & Fernández-Sánchez, 2019). It is important for educators to connect the dynamic of the game with the content of the course and its learning objectives to select gamified activities that serve the needs and interests of students to boost their interest, participation, and motivation. (Oliva, 2016).

To meet learning objectives, the gamified activity is designed according to a series of aspects; it must have a systematic development process (Marne et al., 2012):

- *Pedagogical objective:* defines the purpose and the learning that is pursued.
- *Simulation:* for it to be a game, it must have well-defined rules and parameters.

- *Interaction with simulation:* promotes interaction with the players, in this case, the students, to encourage the learning process.
- *Problems and progression:* develop the methodological route that will be followed, along with its missions and learning challenges for fulfilling the pedagogical objective. In addition to defining the way, the feedback given to the player about his progress must be specified.
- *Decoration:* specifies the multimedia tools that will be used to attract the player's attention.
- *Condition of use:* Define who, when, where, and how the game will be played, that is, the rules of the game. Thus, a game can be virtual, asynchronous, group, or individual, among others, but must always comply with fulfilling its learning objective (Lozada & Betacur, 2015).

Teachers wishing to apply gamification in their classrooms will consider the elements described herein.

Advantages and Disadvantages of Using Gamification in Classrooms

The study conducted by Hanus & Fox (2015) proved that the use of innovative methodologies such as gamification results in an increased commitment of students to their learning process, which in turn increases their motivation and interest in the subject at hand.

Lee & Hammer (2011) emphasize three areas in which gamification can intervene positively: in the **cognitive dimension**, the game creates meaningful and contextualized experiences that allow the transfer of knowledge acquired in similar situations; in the **emotional dimension,** since the game stimulates emotions such as curiosity or frustration and gives students tools to overcome these situations and continue advancing in the game; and in the **social dimension**, since it facilitates collaborative work.

Implementing the gamification methodology in the classroom, however, also entails a series of obstacles that should be considered. According to Werbach and Hunter (2012), it is crucial to have a detailed plan of the entire game and its elements as defined in the previous section (dynamics, mechanics, and components). This will help minimize mistakes such as "pointification," giving points anywhere or everywhere without it making sense or having a learning objective, "exploitation ware," conducting activities that are not of interest to students, or "gaming the game," losing sight of the game's learning objective and its pedagogical objective (Borrás, 2015).

The advantages and disadvantages of gamification in classrooms are summarized in the table below.

In 2014, the Horizon report of the New Media Consortium affirms that gamification would experience an increase in the classroom, at any educational level, in the coming years, and this would favor the development of innovations in the educational field (Burke, 2012). There are universities that have successfully applied gamification techniques where an increase in student motivation and participation has been shown (Millán, 2017; Santamaria & Alcalde, 2019; Sierra & Fernández-Sánchez, 2019; Gómez López et. al, 2022).

Escape Rooms: A Gamification Proposal in Education

One of the innovative techniques included in gamification is the escape room.

An escape room is a puzzle game that resembles real-life situations in which people must collaborate to solve various puzzles, with a time limit, to get out of a room (Eukel et al., 2017; Santamaria & Alcalde, 2019).

Table 1. Advantages and disadvantages of gamification

Advantages	Disadvantages
• Promotes student interaction • Improves the teaching-learning process • Increases the attention, motivation, and involvement of students • Fosters active participation • Enables direct feedback for students; thus, they are constantly informed of their progress in the subject. They have the chance to correct their mistakes and be more aware of their learning • Facilitates problem-solving • Develops creativity • Teachers receive feedback on students' progress	• Potential for the game to cause distractions, and this leads to a waste of time/ loss of productivity • If gamification is not applied and supervised well, it can lead to excessive competitiveness. • Finding the balance between fun and educational • The possibility of creating a temporary motivation. If motivation is founded solely on achieving awards, it will be diminished when the newness wears off.

Source: (prepared by the author based on Lee & Hammer, 2011).

Escape rooms originated in Japan in 2007, but they quickly spread to different areas of Europe (Borrego et al., 2017). According to some authors, the escape room, as a learning strategy, promotes motivation and generates more outstanding student commitment to learning (Borrego et al., 2017; Eukel et al., 2017; Nebot and Campos, 2017; Ortiz-Colón, Jordán & Ágreda, 2018). Thus, applying this gamified experience in the classroom facilitates the assimilation of content in curricular areas, allowing participants to engage in their learning process actively. In the same way, it promotes creativity, imagination, logical thinking, and deductive reasoning (Kapp, 2012; Garcia Lázaro, 2019).

Educational escape rooms create a creative and dynamic learning environment that may be implemented at any educational level and in any subject. The teacher assumes the role of the game master and must establish the educational objectives set for the activity. Will be responsible for ensuring that the development of the escape room is dynamic, offering support and guidance at the time required so that the game does not block (Piñero, 2019).

The first step of this gamification model is to draw a detailed plan of the activity considering the students who will participate in it, including their stage of development, emotional development, and cognitive development. Subsequently, the learning objectives are defined. They will be useful for evaluating the educational experience upon its termination. The theme is also defined at this time (narrative or storyline, the story that will guide the escape room), as is the sequence of the challenges or mission's students must solve. Said missions must be related to the curricular content studied in the classroom. The rewards students will obtain throughout the escape room are also defined previously. Finally, feedback is provided by all students to ascertain their opinions about their experience and to solve whatever challenges they were unable to solve. (García Lazaro, 2019).

Here we present the design of an innovative proposal for a virtual escape room that aims, on the one hand, to apply innovative strategies within the classroom to make students the protagonists of their learning process and, on the other hand, to offer students innovative tools and strategies to transfer to future educational contexts. The purpose is to teach innovative techniques by implementing them to foster learning-to-learn competence[2] (Molins & Vidiella, 2018).

The escape room proposal described below is an innovative experience applied within higher education that aims to contribute to proving the potential of gamification in the classroom as it can develop cognitive, emotional, and social skills (Santamaria & Alcalde, 2020) and secure students' commitment to their learning process (Sierra & Fernández-Sánchez, 2019).

METHODOLOGY

This work constitutes an analysis of a first experience with the design and implementation of a virtual escape room in higher education. This innovative proposal was carried out in the first four-month term of the 2021-2022 academic year in the subject *Innovation in Teaching and Introduction to Educational Research*[3] of the University Master's Program in Secondary Teacher Training (Universidad Internacional de la Rioja, UNIR). A total of 20 students participated.

Once the escape room was designed and carried out in the classroom, a semi-structured questionnaire with open and closed questions was implemented to assess students' degree of motivation for this game (see annexes). The closed questions include elements related to the format and design of the escape room (narrative, diversity of missions, rewards, resources used, extra material on the subject) and about the improvements acquired in their learning process (meaningful learning development, relationship with the syllabus of the subject, improvement of skills, quality of the innovation proposal), their degree of motivation and degree of satisfaction. These closed questions have been analyzed quantitively. The indicators analyzed in this part of the questionnaire are described below.

The open questions analyzed qualitatively include assessments of the difficulties students experienced throughout the escape room, how the proposal helped them better understand the subject, and a final assessment of the experience of participating in the gamified activity.

The study was designed to contribute to research on the advantages of gamification in higher education, alluding to the need to present the content attractively and playfully.

At the beginning of the course, students were informed of the implementation of this innovation proposal, that their participation was voluntary and anonymous, and that the results gathered in the questionnaire would serve to improve the escape room and advance research on the pedagogical benefits of gamification in university courses.

The academic context wherein the escape room was carried out is described below. The design of the innovative proposal (design and implementation of the escape room) is also presented.

CREATION OF THE EDUCATIONAL ESCAPE ROOM

Academic Context

A virtual escape room proposal is presented in the *Teaching innovation and initiation to educational research* subject of the Online Master's Degree in Secondary Teacher Training at the Universidad Internacional de la Rioja (UNIR), Spain.

Students who pursue this degree acquire the necessary skills and competences to work as teachers in Compulsory Secondary Education, Baccalaureate, Professional Training, and Language Teaching (having completed this degree is a mandatory requirement to become a secondary teacher in Spain, as established by Organic Law 2 /2006, of May 3, Education).

The subject selected for conducting the escape room, *Teaching innovation and initiation to educational research*, is a course that shows students the role of innovation and projects to improve schools. The subject employs a practical approach intended to boost student participation, instructing them on the aspects to consider when designing or analyzing innovation projects, including analyzing the dif-

Table 2. Description of the quantitative indicators analyzed in the questionnaire.

EVALUATION INDICATORS	DESCRIPTION
Narrative (the story)	Story of the escape room
Initial video (Passport)	Using the *Flipgrip* application, students must record an introductory video explaining who they are, what expectations they have of the course and what they expect to learn.
Diversity of missions	Missions that must be successfully completed to exit the escape room
Resources used	Diversity of ICT resources and applications used throughout the escape room (*Flipgrip, Genially, QR*…).
Format and design	Design of the online escape room, the format and platforms used
Extra material on the subject	Resources and tools are offered throughout the escape room as rewards (innovation projects around the world, fun facts, videos, and interesting articles…).
Degree of motivation	Level of student motivation
Degree of satisfaction	Level of satisfaction with escape room participation
Meaningful learning development	The extent to which the escape room has favored the acquisition of learning that is more meaningful and permanent
Relationship with the syllabus of the subject	Degree of consistency and relation between the content of the escape room and the syllabus of the subject (refer to table 3, content).
Improvement of skills	How the escape room has contributed to improving the acquisition of competences outlined in the subject (refer to table 3, competences)
Quality of the innovation proposal (escape room)	Level of quality of the innovation proposal (final assessment of whether it was a good experience).

Source: (prepared by the author).

ferent models that exist and real innovative experiences. In performing said analyses, they have at their disposal a set of tools and resources (one of which is gamification.)

The table below (Table 3) lists the subject's content and competences.

In the training of future secondary education teachers, it is fundamental to carry out innovative proposals such as the one described herein, designed to elicit critical thinking, reflection, and commitment to improving teaching and learning processes.

The escape room covers all themes included in the subject (see Table 3). Every mission corresponds with one theme. The escape room experience lasts the entire length of the subject. Students begin with the first theme and conclude with the eighth.

The proposal offers insights into understanding gamification and innovative tools and strategies for students (future secondary education teachers) to transfer to the educational environment (Manzano León et al., 2022). Thus, the design of the experience aspires to fulfill the idea that "*Innovation is learned by innovating.*"

Through this proposal, students can gradually assimilate the contents while acquiring the skills of the subject (see Table 3). Furthermore, as students complete the missions, they receive feedback on their learning process, including the mistakes they made, the right answer, and where they can access the resources to improve the difficulties, they experienced…). This enables the opportunity to amend potential mistakes and redirect the learning process, both for students as well as for educators (Ricoy & Fernandez- Rodríguez, 2013).

Table 3. Contents and skills covered in the Teaching innovation and initiation to educational research course.

<table>
<tr><th>THEME</th><th>CONTENT</th><th>SPECIFIC COMPETENCES</th></tr>
<tr><td>1</td><td>Educational innovation and school improvement</td><td rowspan="8">CE22: Know and apply innovative teaching proposals in the field of the specialization studied.
CE23: Critically analyze the performance of teaching, good practices, and guidance using quality indicators.
CE24: Identify the problems related to teaching and learning the specialization subjects and propose alternatives and solutions.
CE25: Know and apply basic methodologies and techniques of educational research and evaluation and design and develop research, innovation, and evaluation projects.</td></tr>
<tr><td>2</td><td>Models and methodologies to generate educational innovation</td></tr>
<tr><td>3</td><td>Design of teaching innovation practices</td></tr>
<tr><td>4</td><td>The innovative use of resources and teaching aids for the classroom</td></tr>
<tr><td>5</td><td>Student-centered teaching-learning strategies</td></tr>
<tr><td>6</td><td>Evaluation as a resource for innovation and learning</td></tr>
<tr><td>7</td><td>From educational research to classroom research</td></tr>
<tr><td>8</td><td>Teacher self-assessment. Learn to innovate.</td></tr>
</table>

Source: (prepared by the author based on the syllabus of the Teaching innovation and initiation to educational research subject of the UNIR).

Description of the Innovation Proposal

The escape room, "*Discover to innovate: start your journey,*" was held virtually.

The learning objective of the escape room is to reinforce the content of the subject in a more dynamic and fun way to promote more meaningful learning, increase student motivation, and improve their learning outcomes.

Escape room participation enables students to deepen and better understand the content of the subject, review the most important concepts, and become acquainted with resources and tools related to educational innovation.

Is structured into eight missions related to the eight themes of the subject:

- Mission 1 – theme 1 (Educational innovation and school improvement).
- Mission 2 – theme 2 (Models and methodologies to generate educational innovation)
- Mission 3 – theme 3 (Design of teaching innovation practices)
- Mission 4 – theme 4 (The innovative use of resources and teaching aids for the classroom)
- Mission 5 – theme 5 (Student-centered teaching-learning strategies)
- Mission 6 – theme 6 (Evaluation as a resource for innovation and learning)
- Mission 7 – theme 7 (From educational research to classroom research)
- Mission 8 – theme 8 (Teacher self-assessment. Learn to innovate)

The teacher guides the story of the escape room, presenting the different missions to which the students must respond and unlock as the different contents of the subject are covered in class. The students access and solve the escape room, which allows them, on the one hand, to review and internalize the learning autonomously, and on the other hand, to share it and connect it with everything that is worked on in the course.

The escape room has been designed using the digital tool *Genially*. A variety of ICT resources have been employed in the preparation of the missions: *Flipgrip* for video production, *QR* scanners to access articles to be read by students, YouTube videos, quizz, collaborative murals…

Here are the main elements of the escape room:

Narrative

The narrative of the escape room is a journey around the world. Students discover that the planet is on the brink of destruction due to climate change. They must travel through different countries searching for a scientific formula necessary to produce new clean energy that is renewable and sustainable and will ultimately save the planet.

To discover this formula, they must solve a series of challenges by traveling around the world. Knowing each context's different environments and particularities gives them excellent knowledge to make the appropriate decisions and act.

This storyline was selected because the author considers it fundamental to deal with relevant contemporary issues such as climate change. Students participating in this escape room are future secondary education teachers. They will therefore need to guide their students and help them grow in awareness of the issues we face today, including fostering a critical spirit and commitment to their world. For this reason, the narrative of the escape room is related to an actual and polemic problem.

To undertake this trip (start the escape room), students must complete their passports (Figure 2). To do this, the students must access *Flipgrid*, an ICT tool that allows them to record videos. The objective of this challenge is that the students can introduce themselves to the rest of the class and talk about their educational experience and expectations for the subject, thus creating a space for group interaction and cohesion.

Missions

As stated in the previous section, there are eight missions related to the eight themes of the subject. Each of these missions takes place in a different country, and in each of these countries, if students complete the mission, they obtain a reward, one of the numbers of the scientific formula they are attempting to discover. Once they complete the eight missions, they will have the complete formula and discover the source of clean and renewable energy that will save the planet. If that is not the case, the planet will be destroyed.

Each mission is explained below:

- DESTINATION 1 (MISSION 1): complete a quiz about the most critical innovation concepts.
- DESTINATION 2 (MISSION 2): in the second mission, they must complete two challenges. The first is a game of matching correct concepts (they must classify the teaching innovation models according to their type and scope), and the second involves solving an image quiz (they must choose the correct image according to the concept of innovation that appears).
- DESTINATION 3 (MISSION 3): true or false statements about good teaching practices.
- DESTINATION 4 (MISSION 4): in this mission, they must complete two challenges. The first is a memory game related to virtual education. In the second, they must watch a video about the

Figure 2. Escape room passport.
Source: prepared by the author.

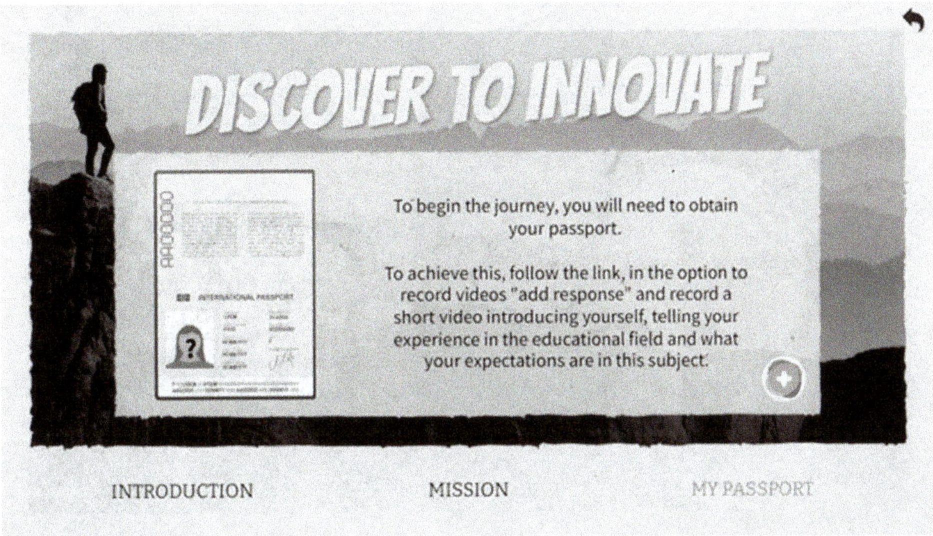

impact of the pandemic on education, especially in the use that has been made of digital resources and answer a quiz.

- DESTINATION 5 (MISSION 5): In mission 5, they must also complete two challenges. The first is the maze game: they must get out of a maze by making the right decisions on applying an innovative change in an educational center and the aspects that must be considered in its planning. The

Figure 3. Map of missions.
Source: prepared by the author

Figure 4. The final screen of the escape room: unlocking the keypad.
Source: prepared by the author

second challenge is the game of the double ICT, where they must find a partner for the digital resource. Once they have completed it, they have direct access to all the ICT resources in the game.

- DESTINATION 6 (MISSION 6): the game of correct sentences on innovative evaluation.
- DESTINATION 7 (MISSION 7): through a QR code, they must read a scientific article on educational research and answer a quiz.
- DESTINATION 8 (MISSION 8): in the last mission, students must complete two challenges. The first is a game entitled "What is different?" (They must know how to find the differences in a group of students to understand their specific needs). The second challenge is a memory game about different spaces to continue training as future teachers and develop professionally. Once completed, they have direct access to these continuous learning spaces.

When all the missions have been completed, students have in their possession all the numbers that make up the scientific formula and can unlock the keypad and save the planet from destruction.

Rewards

The rewards obtained throughout the escape room are more specific resources to be applied in educational contexts, curiosities and innovative experiences carried out all over the world, access to current and exciting ICT tools to implement in education, scientific articles on innovation, interaction spaces such as educational, social networks, virtual learning communities, etc.

Figure 5. Percentage of responses to the question "Has the Escape Room helped you to understand the subject better"?
Source: prepared by the author.

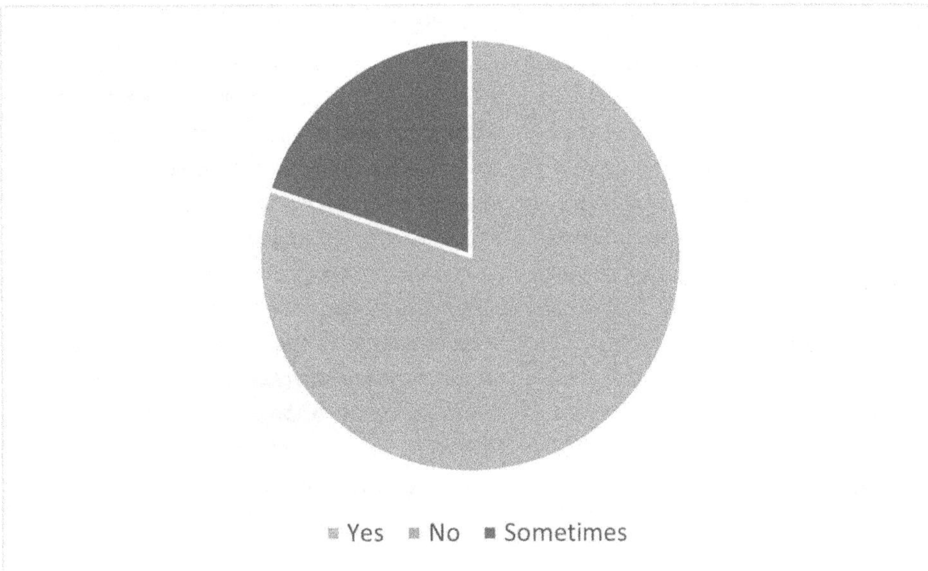

ANALYSIS OF THE QUESTIONNAIRE

This section presents the results gathered from the questionnaire (see annexes) carried out in the last phase of the escape room. The main results describe the impact this innovative proposal had on the students, their degree of motivation and satisfaction, and how the experience helped them better understand the subject.

These results will yield a better understanding of how the escape room worked to apply to other students and classes and will contribute more knowledge of educational research on gamification in higher education.

The quantitative data of the questionnaire's closed questions provide an overview of different aspects and indicators analyzed in the innovative proposal (see Table 2). These data have been contrasted, on the one hand, with the contributions made by the students throughout the subject. The innovation proposal has been implemented simultaneously in the different live virtual classes, so the teacher has guided and provided continuous feedback throughout the process. And, on the other hand, with the answers to the open questions of the questionnaire (see annexes).

There has been a very positive response to the introduction of this type of activity within a subject on teaching innovation because, on the one hand, content specific to the subject is worked on and, on the other hand, spaces and resources are offered to learn to innovate in the classroom (learning that will have to be transferred in a future educational context).

Most students have not had difficulties participating in the escape room; they consider it intuitive and easy to follow once the concepts are understood. The challenges that some have mentioned were related to technical failures that have been solved throughout the process.

Figure 6. Evaluation of the different indicators of the escape room.
Source: prepared by the author.

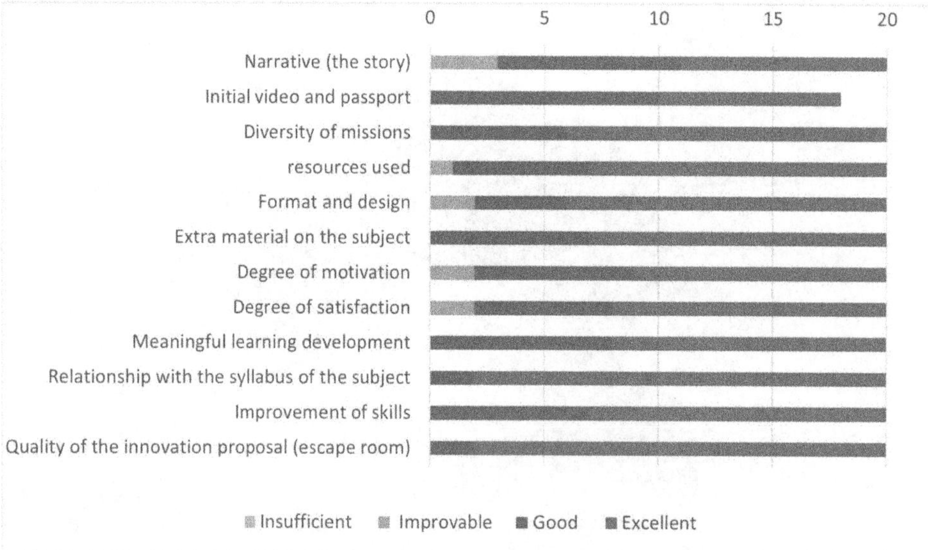

As seen in the following graph (Figure 6), in most of the analyzed indicators, there has been a positive response. Positive feedback has also been obtained on the structure and design of the escape room. However, some students point out that aspects can be improved, such as the narrative (the story of the escape room), the format and the general design, and the different resources used throughout the missions.

There is a good relationship between the entire escape room and the subject's different contents; 80% believe this relationship and cohesion are excellent, and 20% consider it good because a practical connection is established between the studied concepts in the various missions. They consider that, by participating in this gamified activity, the contents of the subject are reinforced entertainingly, and learning is more fun, dynamic, and attractive.

Regarding the innovative proposal's impact on improving students' learning processes and acquisition of skills, it is also observed that everyone believes it is good or excellent. The students remarked that the innovative proposal had reinforced their learning more visually and practically.

Participating in the escape room has helped them grasp the subject's concepts and clarify mental schemes about the most critical aspects of each topic, which have been contrasted and shared with the different activities carried out in the classroom.

In addition, it can also be seen in Figure 6 that all the students who have participated appreciate the extra material offered as a reward throughout the entire escape room (65% believe it is excellent and 35% good). It has provided them with additional and empirical information on the educational projects being carried out worldwide in innovation, which is motivating.

Students believe that the missions to complete throughout the escape room are dynamic, fun, and motivating because they use a diversity of tools (quizz, videos, QR scans, collaborative murals…) that help them better understand the content of the subject and promote more meaningful learning.

Their assessment of their degree of satisfaction and motivation is positive (more than half believe it is excellent). These data are contrasted with the contributions made throughout the subject and the open questions of the questionnaire. The feedback received from the students throughout the development of the subject has been very enriching. All missions of the escape room have a direct relationship with everything worked on in the online weekly classes. The students have valued very positively the continuous practicality and applicability of the learning and the opportunity to review it in a more dynamic way through the escape room.

In short, all the students who have participated rate the quality of the innovation proposal as very good. The students believe that it has helped them to reflect on the importance of innovation and, in the same way, internalize this concept to implement it in the future as teachers. It has been a very appropriate activity to strengthen the knowledge of the subject since the transferability of what has been learned throughout the entire teaching and learning process is very positive.

The main goal of this study was to measure the degree of motivation and satisfaction of students with the course through the execution of the escape room. The results prove a high degree of motivation and satisfaction and that the escape room has contributed to improving their learning in the subject. Students consider that it has been a very useful, motivating, and fun proposal that has given them innovative tools they can use in their professional future.

DISCUSSION AND CONCLUSION

Society is constantly changing, so the educational system must adapt accordingly (Millán, 2017). Economic, technological, climatological, cultural, political, and social changes and, in the face of these changes, educational institutions should not remain on the sidelines; they need to adapt to the socio-educational reality of the students (García Lázaro, 2019).

The constant need to update educational methods must be considered to improve the quality of education (Lozada & Betancur, 2016).

In this context, educational innovation has been fundamental in the most efficient educational improvements because it generates new ways of working, new teaching and learning approaches, and students play an active and leading part (Castro, Gómez-Guzmán & Carranza, 2022).

Educational Innovation Projects allow for initiatives that can bring about the deep and lasting changes that quality institutions pursue (Castro, Gómez-Guzmán & Carranza, 2022).

Educational innovation should not be a one-time activity, it is to be included in the educational curriculum, in all the subjects, and in the daily work of educators at all educational levels (López, 2019).

Proposals such as this, the use of an escape room, are focused on new teaching and learning models that break with traditional education (where students adopt a passive role) and result in scenarios that invite reflection, a critical spirit, and a commitment with society's problems and foster more meaningful learning.

Fostering more meaningful learning in the classroom through innovative proposals will help students develop the ability to adapt to different situations, make decisions in problematic situations, and possess the necessary tools to develop comprehensively (Youngerman & Culver, 2019; Selznick & McCarthy, 2020).

Higher education has the potential to offer flagship experiences through which knowledge is generated that is contextualized, meaningful, and actively supports open discovery (Selznick et al., 2022). University education should employ the most innovative methodologies that generate room for dialogue, collaborative work, and the acquisition of the necessary competences to succeed professionally. By utilizing the pedagogical potential of new technologies to offer quality and current teaching. This makes even more sense in undergraduate and graduate degrees in education, where a country's future teachers are trained.

Adequate teacher training in teaching innovation and the application of technology in the classroom is essential to ensure that future teachers can apply and transfer it in their classrooms. Prospective teachers need practical knowledge about innovative and/or technological resources to feel comfortable with future applications in their respective classrooms (Ortega-Ruipérez, 2018). It is important to continue building a culture of innovation within educational centers, where teachers have a proactive attitude, a special sensitivity in the entire academic community aimed at adapting to constant change, promoting creativity, and dialogue with a renovating future that ensures a permanent improvement in educational quality (López Martín, 2017).

All of which demands rethinking teacher training in the framework of understanding the curriculum as a stage for action and development of a proactive culture and special sensibility of the entire educational community toward the ongoing improvement of teaching quality which we have referred to as a culture of innovation. These educators are well-trained pedagogically, have the competences to prove their leadership in educational innovation initiatives, are concerned about constantly rethinking their own practice, open to collaborative work, not foreign to research on renewing methodologies, ready to foster creativity, are accomplices of the learning of their students, committed to professional retraining throughout their entire career, determined about participating in professional networks and communities, in sum, educators who are aware of the importance and essential nature of their pedagogical responsibility to win the future of education (López Martín, 2019, p.93).

This innovation proposal not only entails an experience with a gamified activity in higher education but also aims to be a start towards changing the training of future teachers, making it known that in the university environment, they can offer active learning spaces to achieve this transferability.

And it is in this context that studies are necessary that address the student learning process with the application of innovative methodologies such as gamification, especially with the use of the escape room in the university context (Eukel et al., 2017; De Soto García, 2018; Pérez-Manzano and Almela-Baeza, 2018; Sierra & Fernández, 2019).

Gamification is presented as an alternative to traditional classroom instruction and is increasingly used in higher education (Lozada & Betancur, 2016). Gamification offers the opportunity to work on two fundamental aspects of the teaching and learning processes: motivation and commitment (Lee & Hammer, 2011).

To achieve the success of innovative gamified proposals in the higher university context, a profound reflection on the objectives will be necessary to design and develop a contextualized and coherent activity. Any innovation proposal requires methodological planning, review, and continuous monitoring to measure the progress and improvement of students.

Escape rooms as gamified strategies can support university training because, as stated by Oliva (2016), it eliminates the uncertainty about What am I learning for? And What do I learn with? as well as the monotony of lectures. As proven by this experience, a gamified activity helps both teachers and students to ascertain the level of progress in personal learning and the amendment of mistakes. It fosters attention and involvement in the subject and favors the improvement of learning outcomes.

The utility provided by the gamification strategy applied to the university context contributes to the interest and commitment of students to learn. And all this takes on even more meaning if we train future teachers.

All the work presented here aims to disseminate an innovative proposal that can be replicated and improved in future courses but which, in turn, can be considered a good teaching practice based on the results obtained and the feedback from the student body. The main results indicate that the degree of motivation and satisfaction of students is very positive because not only have they learned the content of the subject throughout the escape room, but they have also discovered a variety of innovative tools they can transfer to their future classrooms when they become secondary education teachers.

In general terms, it is believed that these interventions should be constituted as current methodological lines since they allow a greater transferability of knowledge and much more meaningful learning connected to reality.

With the progress of university education in the EHEA, the teaching and evaluation systems should evolve toward less traditional methodological lines and more toward innovative experiences that promote inclusive learning (Castañeda-Vázquez et al., 2019).

Innovation is a fundamental element in transforming and improving education.

FUTURE RESEARCH POSSIBILITIES

With the analysis of this first innovation proposal, it is important to note that:

- Education has the responsibility of adapting to the new needs of society, so it is essential to continue researching those innovative methodologies that allow greater contextualization and adaptation to the singularities of the student body and the context itself.
- Considering that gamification is a new topic, and it is beginning to generate more interest in Higher Education, it is essential to share good practices with the entire educational community to continue progressing in this cutting-edge field.
- Educational gamification is a teaching and learning methodology that should be an indispensable part of the pedagogical training of future teachers. It motivates students by attractively presenting knowledge, achieving commitment, and developing collaboration, empathy, and problem-solving skills (Dreimane, 2019, García Lázaro, 2019).
- Gamification is a fundamental methodological strategy in the future since its role of creating commitment will facilitate the sharing and development of new ideas, favoring innovations in the classroom beyond novel experiments (Ortiz-Colón, Jordán & Ágreda, 2018).
- We must bet on innovative methodologies or tools, such as the Escape Room, which reinforces the competence of "learning to learn" and favors the transfer of learning in real life.
- The application of an escape room as a gamification tool allows students to gradually assimilate the subject's contents while acquiring the subject's skills. In addition, they receive continuous feedback on their learning process, which will enable them to rectify possible errors and redirect the learning process, both for students and teachers (Ricoy & Fernandez-Rodriguez, 2013).
- It is important to rethink the training of future teachers so that they are committed to their work and are in a continuous search for methodological innovation. For this reason, it is necessary to de-

velop proposals such as the one presented here, a practical and contextualized proposal. LEARN INNOVATION BY INNOVATING.

REFERENCES

Borrás, O. (2015). *Fundamentos de la Gamificación* [Fundamentals of Gamification]. Gabinete de Tele-Educación. Universidad Politécnica de Madrid.

Borrego, C., Fernández, C., Blanes, I., & Robles, S. (2017). Room escape at class: Escape games activities to facilitate the motivation and learning in computer science. *JOTSE: Journal of Technology and Science Education, 7*(2), 162–171. doi:10.3926/jotse.247

Burke, B. (2012). *Gamification 2020: What is the future of gamification?* Gartnet.

Castañeda-Vázquez, C., Espejo-Garcés, T., Zurita-Ortega, F., & Fernández-Revelles, A. (2019). La formación de los futuros docentes a través de la gamificación, tic y evaluación continua [The training of future teachers through gamification, ICT and continuous evaluation]. *SPORT TK-Revista EuroAmericana de Ciencias del Deporte, 8*(2), 55–63. doi:10.6018portk.391751

Castro, P., Gómez Guzmán, P., & Carranza, S. (2022). Investigación e Innovación en la Consolidación de una Disciplina Educativa [Research and Innovation in the Consolidation of an Educational Discipline]. *REICE. Revista Electrónica Iberoamericana sobre Calidad, Eficacia y Cambio en Educación, 20*(1), 5–20. doi:10.15366/reice2022.20.1.001

De Soto García, I. S. (2018). Herramientas de gamificación para el aprendizaje de ciencias de la tierra [Gamification tools for learning earth sciences]. *EDUTEC: Revista Electrónica de Tecnología Educativa, 65*(65), 29–39. doi:10.21556/edutec.2018.65.1143

Delgado, A. M., & Oliver, R. (2006). La evaluación continua en un nuevo escenario docente. *Revista de Universidad Y Sociedad Del Conocimiento, 3*(1), 1–13.

Dreimane, S. (2019). Gamification for education: Review of current publications. In L. Daniela (Ed.), *Didactics of smart pedagogy* (pp. 453–464). Springer. doi:10.1007/978-3-030-01551-0_23

Eukel, H. N., Frenzel, J. E., & Cernusca, D. (2017). Educational Gaming for Pharmacy Students Design and Evaluation of a Diabetes hemed Escape room. *American Journal of Pharmaceutical Education, 81*(7), 62–65.

García Lazaro, I. (2019). Escape room como propuesta de gamificación en educación [Escape room as a gamification proposal in education]. *Revista Educativa Hekademos, 27*, 71–79.

Gómez López, M, Manzano Sánchez, D, Sánchez, B.J., & Valero, A. (2022). The War of the Atlethes: una propuesta de gamificación aplicada a la docencia universitaria para favorecer los valores educativos y la responsabilidad. *Espiral. Cuadernos del profesorado, 15*(30), 38-50.

Hanus, M. D., & Fox, J. (2015). Assessing the effects of gamification in the classroom: A longitudinal study on intrinsic motivation, social comparison, satisfaction, effort, and academic performance. *Computers & Education, 80*, 152–161. doi:10.1016/j.compedu.2014.08.019

Hevia Artime, I., & Fueyo Gutiérrez, A. (2018). Aprendizaje situado en el diseño de entornos virtuales de aprendizaje: Una experiencia de aprendizaje entre pares en una comunidad de pràctica [Learning situated in the design of virtual learning environments: a peer-to-peer learning experience in a community of practice]. *Revista Aula Abierta, 47*(3), 347–354. doi:10.17811/rifie.47.3.2018.347-354

Kapp, K. M. (2012). *The gamification of learning and instruction: game-based methods and strategies for training and education*. John Wiley & Sons.

Lee, J., & Hammer, J. (2011). Gamification in Education: What, How, Why Brother? *Academic Exchange Quarterly, 15*(2), 1–5.

Ley Orgánica 2/2006, de 3 de mayo (BOE del 4 de mayo), de educación (LOE).

López Martín, R. (2019). La Innovación docente en la formación del profesorado. Principios y directrices de futuro [Teaching innovation in teacher training. Principles and guidelines for the future]. *Crónica, Revista científico profesional de la pedagogía y psicopedagogia, 4,* 83-94.

López-Noguero, F. (2008). Hacia un espacio europeo de aprendizaje para toda la vida. Evolución y desarrollo de la Educación Permanente en la Unión Europea [Towards a European area of lifelong learning. Evolution and development of lifelong learning in the European Union]. *Pedagogía social. Revista interuniversitaria, 15*, 123-135.

Lozada, C., & Betancur, S. (2016). La gamificación en la educación superior: Una revisión sistemática [Gamification in higher education: a systematic review]. *Revista Ingenierías Universidad de Medellín, 16*(31), 97–124. doi:10.22395/rium.v16n31a5

Majuri, J., Koivisto, J., & Hamari, J. (2018). Gamification of education and learning: A review of empirical literature. *Proceedings of the 2nd international GamiFIN Conference, CEUR-WS.*

Manzano León, A., Aguilar Parra, J. M., Fernández, J. M., Trigueros Ramos, R., Martínez Martínez, A. M., & Rodríguez Ferrer, J. M. (2022). Play and learn: Influence of gamification and game-based learning in the reading processes of secondary school students. *Revista de Psicodidáctica, 27*(1), 38–46.

Marczewski, A. (2012). *Gamification: A Simple Introduction*. Lulu.

Marne, J., Wisdom, B., Kim-Bang, H., & Labat, J-M. (2012). *The six facets of serious game design: a methodology enhanced by our design pattern library*. Paper presented in 21st Century Learning for 21st Century Skills, Saarbrücken, Germany.

Millán, M. (2017). La gamificación en la evaluación continua de los procesos de enseñanza-aprendizaje en la educación superior. Una aportación basada en la evidencia en el ámbito de las Ciencias Sociales [Gamification in the continuous evaluation of teaching-learning processes in higher education. An evidence-based contribution in the field of Social Sciences]. In J. Ruiz-Palmero, J. Sánchez-Rodríguez, & E. Sánchez-Rivas (Eds.), *Innovación docente y uso de las TIC en educación* (p. 114). UMA Editorial.

Molins, L. L., & Vidiella, M. C. P. (2018). La competencia de aprender a aprender en el marco de la educación superior [The competence to learn to learn within the framework of higher education]. *Revista Iberoamericana de Educación, 78*(2), 59–76. doi:10.35362/rie7823183

Oliva, H.A. (2016). La gamificación como estrategia metodológica en el contexto educativo universitario [Gamification as a methodological strategy in the university educational context]. *Realidad y reflexión, 44*, 30-47.

Ortega-Ruipérez, B. (2018). Directrices pedagógicas para la docencia de innovación y TIC en la formación de futuros docentes [Pedagogical guidelines for teaching innovation and ICT in the training of future teachers]. In R. Roig-Vila (Ed.), *El compromiso académico y social a través de la investigación e innovación educativas en la Enseñanza Superior* (pp. 345–355). Octaedro.

Ortiz-Colón, A. M., Jordán, J., & Ágreda, M. (2018). Gamificación en educación: Una panorámica sobre el estado de la cuestión [Gamification in education: an overview of the state of the art]. *Educação e Pesquisa, 44*(1). Advance online publication. doi:10.15901678-4634201844173773

Pérez-Manzano, A., & Almela-Baeza, J. (2018). Gamification and Transmedia for Scientific Promotion and for Encouraging Scientific Careers in Adolescents. *Comunicar: Media Education Research Journal, 26*(55), 93–103. doi:10.3916/C55-2018-09

Piñero Charlo, J.C. (2019). Análisis sistemático del uso de salas de escape educativas: estado del arte y perspectivas de futuro [Gamification in education: an overview of the state of the art]. *Espacios, 40*(44).

Recommendation of the European Parliament and of the Council of 18 December 2006 on Key Competences for Lifelong Learning (2006/962/EC). Retrieved from https://eur-lex.europa.eu/eli/reco/2006/962/oj

Ricoy, M.C. & Fernandez-Rodriguez, J. (2013). La percepcion que tienen los estudiantes universitarios sobre la evaluacion: un estudio de caso [College students' perception of assessment: a case study]. *Educación XX1, 16*(2), 321-342.

Salinas, J. (2004). Innovación docente y uso de las TIC en la enseñanza universitaria [College students' perception of assessment: a case study]. *Revista Universidad y Sociedad Del Conocimiento, 1*(1), 1–16.

Santamaría, A. & Alcalde, E. (2019). Escaping from the English classroom. Who will get out first? *Revista de psicologia, ciències de l'educació i de l'esport, 37*(2), 83-92.

Santamaría Urbieta, A., & Alcalde Peñalver, E. (2020). Una experiencia universitaria de gamificación en línea o en el aula presencial: ¿es este recurso de aprendizaje posible en ambos entornos? [A gamification university experience online or in the face-to-face classroom: is this learning resource possible in both environments?]. *Revista Brasileira de Lingüística Aplicada, 20*(4).

Selznick, B., & McCarthy, S. (2020). Toward a theory of social innovation for higher education. In A. J. Fulford (Ed.), Philosophy and Theory in Higher Education (pp. 49–69). Peter Lang. doi:10.3726/PTIHE032020.0004

Selznick, B. S., Dahl, L. S., Youngerman, E., & Mayhew, M. J. (2022). Equitably Linking Integrative Learning and Students' Innovation Capacities. *Innovative Higher Education, 47*(1), 1–21. doi:10.100710755-021-09570-w PMID:34334931

Serra-olivares, J., Garcia-rubio, J., Madrona, P. G., Cejudo, C., & Gonzalez, S. (2018). Estilos de aprendizaje y evaluacion formativa: Estudio con universitarios de Educacion Fisica chilenos [Learning styles and formative assessment: Study with Chilean Physical Education university students]. *SPORT TK-Revista EuroAmericana de Ciencias Del Deporte, 7*(1), 129–137. doi:10.6018/321991

Sierra, M. C., & Fernández-Sánchez, M. R. (2019). Gamificando el aula universitaria. Análisis de una experiencia de Escape Room en educación superior [Gamifying the university classroom. Analysis of an Escape Room experience in higher education]. *Revista de Estudios y Experiencias en Educación, 18*(36), 105–115. doi:10.21703/rexe.20191836sierra15

Universidad Internacional de la Rioja. (2021-2022). *Innovación docente e Iniciación a la Investigación Educativa* [Teaching Innovation and Initiation to Educational Research] [Course program]. Author.

Werbach, K., & Hunter, D. (2012). *For the win: How game thin-king can revolutionize your business.* Wharton Digital Press.

Youngerman, E., & Culver, K. C. (2019). Problem-based learning (pbl): Real-world applications to foster (inter)disciplinary learning and integration. In T. Trolian & E. Jach (Eds.), *New Directions for Higher Education* (pp. 23–32). Wiley. doi:10.1002/he.20342

ENDNOTES

1. The European Higher Education Area (EHEA) is a group of 48 countries that cooperate to achieve comparable and compatible higher education systems throughout Europe. Member countries of the EHEA follow the directives of the so-called Bologna Process to achieve these goals.
2. The competence "*Learning to learn*" was defined as "the ability to pursue and persist in learning, to organize one's own learning, including through effective management of time and information, both individually and in groups. his competence includes awareness of one's learning process and needs, identifying available opportunities, and the ability to overcome obstacles in order to learn successfully. This competence means gaining, processing and assimilating new knowledge and skills as well as seeking and making use of guidance" (European Parliament, 2006, p.16).
3. The following section, entitled *Academic Context*, provides a detailed explanation of the content of the subject.

APPENDIX A

An Evaluation Questionnaire Passed to the Students

1. 1. Have you participated in the subject's Escape Room?
    - Yes, I have done everything
    - Yes, but I haven't done all the missions
    - No, it seems too long
    - No, due to lack of time
    - No, because it doesn't motivate me
2. Has doing the Escape Room helped you better understand the subject?
    - Yes
    - No
    - Sometimes
3. Why do you think it has helped you? In what way?
4. Have you had difficulty following the Escape Room? Which? (If you have not done everything, specify which mission you have stayed on and the reason)

Table 4. Evaluation of the indicators of the escape room.

	Insufficient	Improvable	Good	Excellent
Narrative (the story)				
Initial video (Passport)				
Diversity of missions				
Resources used				
Format and design				
Extra material on the subject				
Degree of motivation				
Degree of satisfaction				
Meaningful learning development				
Relationship with the syllabus of the subject				
Improvement of skills				
Quality of the innovation proposal (escape room)				

Source: (prepared by the author).

5. Evaluate the following indicators on the use of the Escape Room in this subject:
6. Final evaluation or other comments you want to add about the Escape Room.
7. Do you consent to use this data for research purposes?

Chapter 6
Research Competence Development in Higher Education Through a Virtual Educational Escape Room

María Isabel Gómez-Núñez
Universidad Internacional de La Rioja, Spain

María Ángeles Cano-Muñoz
Universidad Internacional de La Rioja, Spain

Juan Antonio Gómez-Núñez
Universidad de Castilla-La Mancha, Spain

ABSTRACT

The development of research competence in teacher training is essential to improve educational quality. For this reason, it is necessary that educational processes proposed at university adapt to current demands, incorporating gamification procedures and new technologies as teaching-learning tools. The objective of this chapter was to analyze the application of an educational escape room for the development of research competence in students of the Primary Education Degree. The results of this study showed that the application of the virtual escape room allowed the development of positive attitudes towards research, as well as the strengthening of some of skills and concepts acquired. In the same way, the importance of the university professor as a guide and counselor of educational processes planned in the Primary Education Degree was highlighted. The use of the virtual escape room emerges as a mechanism for the research competence development in higher education.

INTRODUCTION

The development of scientific thought is one of the fundamental areas of teacher training during educa-

DOI: 10.4018/978-1-6684-6081-8.ch006

tion at university stage. Prospective Primary School teachers or any other specialist within Educational Sciences are required to acquire concepts, skills and develop attitudes related to research competence in educational contexts, such as the basic knowledge of science and research methodology, the understanding and application of the investigative process, the analysis and interpretation of results and possibilities of disseminating the research carried out (Salmento et al., 2021). Research competence in education emerges, therefore, as one of the main components of the aforementioned scientific thought (Murtonen & Salmento, 2019).

In the case of Spain, the current Spanish Organic Law 3/2020, of December 29, which modifies the Organic Law 2/2006, of May 3, of Education (LOMLOE), in Article 2, Section 2, points out the importance of public authorities paying preferential attention to the qualification and training of teachers, to their teamwork, to research and innovation to achieve educational renewal, as factors that would promote the improvement of the teaching quality. Similarly, Article 102, Section 2, determines the use of Information and Communication Technologies (ICT), as well as digital and foreign language training for all teachers.

These statements mean new challenges for current Spanish universities, which must encourage potential teachers to acquire the necessary tools to respond effectively to today's society demands. In this sense, competence in educational research stands out as one of the professional identity and teaching function essential components (Martín-Gómez et al., 2022; Toquero, 2021).

RESEARCH COMPETENCE IN TEACHER PROFESSIONAL DEVELOPMENT

Research competence integrates a set of concepts, skills, attitudes and learning strategies (know how to learn) aimed at the implementation of the different tasks that make up a research process. That is to say, research competence includes basic professional and scientific knowledge, pedagogical attitudes and values, research skills and learning techniques (i.e., searching and selection of information, needs detection and problems specification, setting of objectives, information collection and analysis procedures or presentation and interpretation of results). Other tasks that would compose this competence would be the ability to work in a team, make reports, be creative in solving educational problems and have adequate communication skills (Böttcher & Thiel, 2018; Gómez-Núñez et al., 2020; Sabariego et al., 2020; Syzdykbayeva et al., 2015). Teachers show their investigative aptitude by searching for new solutions to the detected difficulties, analysing, synthesising and knowing the proposed actions, by significantly reflecting on the carried out studies, adjusting their investigative processes, using and disseminating their studies, improving their professional skills and being creative in innovative processes that are implemented within school contexts (Balloo, 2019; Dzyubenko et al., 2021).

In this sense, it is important to emphasize that teacher training, from the university stage, is based on educational research, so as to enable the professional development of teachers committed to their work, as well as reflective and critical teachers who are capable of developing knowledge from and about their own practical experiences (Freixa, 2017; Zabalza, 2012). However, qualitative studies such as the one by Toquero (2021) point out some difficulties detected by teachers in relation to the development of their research competence: problems in searching for information (references location, databases access), in the synthesis of scientific literature and in the detection of gaps in existing knowledge, lack of skills for the construction of the theoretical framework (i.e., sections specification, topics), as well as doubts in the application of the scientific methodology and its evaluation. These problems raise the need for university professors to reformulate their methodological principles and pedagogical practices, in order to adapt to the new demands of teaching profession. Therefore, the application of research-based learning within different subjects that make up the study plans is proposed (Brew & Saunders, 2020). The students of the Degrees in Early Childhood and Primary Education must be actively involved in educational processes based on research, so as to favor the transfer of reflections and research competence both in the academic field, and in their future work within real educational contexts (Afdal & Spernes, 2018; Willegems et al., 2017).

THE DEVELOPMENT OF RESEARCH COMPETENCE IN INITIAL DISTANCE TEACHER TRAINING: ACTIVE LEARNING AND GAMIFICATION

The approach of remote or online teaching-learning processes is one of the challenges that higher education faces. This educational modality, also called e-learning (for a review, see Basak et al., 2018), is essential to reinforce professional skills and higher-order cognitive processes to face the challenges of today's society (Wang et al. al., 2022). The new pedagogical models, integrated into the information and knowledge society, must incorporate ICT, also called "Learning and Knowledge Technologies" (LKT; Archer et al., 2019), as necessary tools for adaptation to current social and educational demands (Vidal-Esteve et al., 2019).

From this reality, a relatively recent term has emerged: Gamification, which has a growing presence in education world for digital learning spaces creation. Authors agree that gamification consists of applying game dynamics, mechanics and components in contexts that are not properly playful, with the purpose of transmitting a message or content, influencing behavior and/or generating certain attitudes in those who play it, through a playful experience that encourages motivation, involvement and fun (Deterding et al., 2011; Landers, 2014; Llorens-Largo et al., 2016). The benefits of gamification as a learning strategy have been widely studied, highlighting the promotion of active cognitive processes as the main reason for its use, due to the commitment it generates in students to the teaching-learning process (García-Lázaro, 2019; Werbach & Hunter, 2020).

The term "escape room" applied in education, is a relatively recent idea, although its origin for recreational purposes dates back to 2007 in Japan. Despite the variations, this game can adopt, escape rooms have a series of common characteristics: a thematic environment that follows a narrative line, puzzles with different degrees of difficulty (generally in increasing order), a limited time for their resolution (which entails adequate time management), the need to cooperate with the rest of the team members to solve the challenges, clues to interpret and analyze, a main challenge accompanied by some secondary challenge and the use of symbols which require coding (Nicholson, 2015; Wiemker et al., 2015). The key to the educational escape room is found in the Flow Theory, which highlights the need to find a balance between the demand level of the proposed challenges and the use of the skills required by the participants to overcome them, which favors attention, motivation and, in short, that the game can be a way to achieve significant learning (Aguilera et al., 2014; Grande-de-Prado, 2019; Lozano-López & Lázaro, 2019).

In the university environment and, more specifically, in research carried out in studies related to Educational Sciences, escape room experiences show signs of their positive assessment for the training of students in skills related to critical and lateral thinking, attention to detail and problem solving (Romero et al., 2019), especially related to the research competence on which this work focuses. In addition, escape room experiences stimulate cooperation learning and communication skills, promoting collaborative work

(Bilbao et al., 2022), as well as the development of creativity, increased motivation, interest, participation and personal commitment in the classroom or lesson dynamics (Agreda et al., 2019; Pérez et al., 2019; Sierra & Fernández-Sánchez, 2019). Along with these benefits, these experiences allow teachers, in their initial training process, to experientially learn new teaching and teamwork methodologies that, in the future, they can put into practice with their students (López-Secanell & Ortega-Torres, 2020). All this reinforces the pedagogical potential of the study presented below.

OUR STUDY: NEEDS ANALYSIS

Research competence development in initial teacher training emerges as one of the fundamental requirements for improving educational quality (Gómez-Nuñez & Cano-Muñoz, 2022; Toquero, 2021). The expansion of Sars-Cov2 (the virus that causes COVID-19) accelerated the process of including new technologies within higher education, showing the difficulties of said transition, such as the lack of teachers involvement, the lack of teachers and students knowledge in educational digital platforms and resources, or the necessary methodological adaptation to the new demands (Torres-Martín et al., 2021). The scope of educational objectives and competencies, as well as the construction of significant learning by the students, require the analysis of the models and theories about learning, the assessment of applied teaching methods and the evaluation of technological tools included (Dabbagh, 2005). In this sense, Bloom's Taxonomy (1956), which was revised by Krathwohl and Anderson (2009) to introduce not only the types of knowledge or cognitive skills, but also the learning processes to its reach, offers a basis to rethink of the teaching-learning processes in university online training. In that regard, the importance of learning from mistakes, teaching divided into small steps, the rewards definition for the adequacy of activities, the use of oral presentations, visual resources, learning based on problem solving, the group discussion promotion through virtual forums or game-based learning, constitute educational standards that should be followed in e-learning environments, so that students achieve the objectives and competencies determined in study plans (Barari et al. al., 2020). In this sense, the virtual educational escape room comes as one of the main methodological tools in the post-COVID digital era, as long as this situation has led to progress in the digital transformation of our environment and in the demand for digital skills in the future professionals (Salvador-Gómez et al., 2022).

The evidence extracted from university teaching is added to this scientific justification. The satisfaction surveys completed by the students about the subject on which this study is based, during the 2020/2021 academic year, revealed deficiencies in different areas: the density of the syllabus, the excess of theory and the insufficiency of practical experiences that allow the application of concepts and procedures studied. In the same way, the evaluations carried out by the teaching staff revealed lack of persistence, interest and motivation of the students, an aspect that was reflected in the low quality of the continuous evaluation activities delivered, in the low active participation in virtual classes and in the decrease in attendance at said sessions. These aspects, along with the repetition of the same format of practical experiences in class and outside of it, were also decisive for teaching quality and motivation. For all these reasons, it was necessary to transform the teaching-learning procedures applied, in order to optimize the adaptation to the distance learning modality, to the needs of the students and to those perceived by the teachers.

The objective of this study was to analyze the application of an educational escape room for the development of research competence in students of the Primary Education Degree. This main objective was specified in the following specific objectives:

- Examine the research competence degree perceived by the students after completing the educational escape room.
- Know the students assessment about the development of the escape room as a learning mechanism within *Theory and Practice of Educational Research* subject.
- Identify possible needs or difficulties during the implementation of educational escape room.

METHOD

This innovation proposal was developed in *Theory and Practice of Educational Research* subject in the first year of the Primary Education Degree in a private Spanish university, with an online teaching modality. The educational escape room was presented virtually so that the students could develop it individually. The application of the innovation proposal took place in three different sixty-minute revision sessions of the subject. In this way, it was intended to facilitate the participation of students in a synchronous way. Likewise, based on the distance learning modality, the possibility of participation was offered to students who viewed the recorded sessions.

A mixed research approach was used, assuming the complementarity between cognitivist and positivist paradigms. On the one hand, from a qualitative approach, a descriptive case study was developed (Merriam, 1988), which allowed the proposed innovation to be characterized and understood in depth. On the other hand, from a quantitative approach, a cross-sectional descriptive design was applied (Gómez-Núñez et al., 2020), which made it possible to determine the research competence degree perceived by the students themselves at the end of their involvement in the escape room.

Participants

This innovation proposal is aimed at first-year students of the Primary Education Degree in a private Spanish university, chosen through intentional non-probabilistic sampling. In this way, the participants were selected on purpose, according to the criteria of accessibility to the study sample. In addition, the participants had to meet the criteria of being enrolled in the subject of *Theory and Practice of Educational Research* in the Primary Education Degree. This type of sampling is suitable when the representativeness of the sample is not a relevant factor in the research (Gómez-Núñez et al., 2020). In this case, it was only intended to analyse the development of the escape room in a specific group as a pilot study, without extrapolate these results to reference population. The final sample consisted of 22 participants (72.72% female, 27.28% male) aged between 18 and 22 years ($M = 20.53$, $SD = 1.74$).

Techniques and Instruments

The innovation proposal assessment was carried out through the following data collection techniques and instruments:

- Participant observation of the experience during class time, analysis of doubts in the discussion forum created in Teams Microsoft platform and complimentary use of a field diary (teacher's notebook) where difficulties, questions, dilemmas or relevant aspects were noted down.
- *Ad hoc* questionnaire for the self-perceived research competence assessment. This instrument allowed the analysis of the research competence degree perceived by the students themselves. This measurement tool was made up of ten items that had to be assessed using a ten-point interval scale, in which 1 was the lowest score and 10 was the highest score. In addition, this questionnaire included an additional open question so that the participants could make a constructive review of the practical experience developed and its assessment within the scope of the study subject. The internal consistency index (Cronbach's Alpha) for the questionnaire (taking into account only the ten items assessed using the aforementioned interval scale) was .82, considered satisfactory (George & Mallery, 2003).

Procedure

The phases for the development of the educational escape room as an innovation experience are specified below:

Phase One: Needs Diagnosis

The low results in the satisfaction surveys of the Primary Education Degree students in the subject of *Theory and Practice of Educational Research* during 2020/2021 academic year showed failures in the methodological approach in virtual sessions. In this sense, the students considered the sessions excessively difficult and theoretical. Moreover, they informed of an excessive use of Power Point as a basic resource in the development of the sessions, lack of practical activities that were motivating and too many tasks related to the exam exercises. In addition, the scores for the practical exam activities were relatively low, ranging from pass to good marks (scores between 5 to 6.9). Likewise, the dialogue held with the new students for 2021/2022 academic year during the presentation session allowed the knowledge of their first demands, opinions, uncertainties and needs. For this reason, a change in the methodological procedures was proposed that would be applied, on a pilot basis, in three review sessions of the aforementioned subject. This transformation consisted of the planning and implementation of an educational and virtual escape room that would enable students to review, in an interactive and dynamic way, the concepts, skills and attitudes studied in the key ideas of the syllabus.

Phase Two: Teacher Training

The teacher of *Theory and Practice of Educational Research* subject enrolled and took the course "Initiation to escape room design for online educational environments", promoted by the reference university. Teacher professional development is essential to adapt the methodological approaches that transform the teaching processes. The final work of the aforementioned training course consisted of the creation of a virtual escape room applicable to one of the subjects assigned to the teacher in question. From this approach derived the planning and real application of the escape room entitled "The Illusionist of Time". The argument of this escape room focuses on the temporary change that the participants of this activity have suffered. Thus, we are located in a Primary School in which the participants in the escape room are active teachers. Exhausted by the multitude of daily tasks, they fall asleep in school library. However, when they wake up, they discover that an evil witch, "The Illusionist of Time", has cast a spell to transport them to a different time period. That is, although they remain within the same school, they have gone back in time. The objective of the game will be to escape and return to the current moment. To do this, participants must solve four educational research challenges and complete a questionnaire, which will allow them to obtain the key that will open "The secret box of time". There, they will find their rewards: a) a key to escape from their old school and return to the present; b) a diploma as an educational research expert. In the drawing up of this escape room, a large part of the tools offered in the course proposed by the university were used: Canva and Flexclip for the creation of videos, Pixels for the use of free memes and videos, Yerai.com website for writing letters, generators of QR codes, PowerPoint for clues offered during the development of the challenges, Google Forms for making questionnaires together with the Cerify'em application, Genial.ly for carrying out activities, challenges or loks, and the Wix platform for drawing up the complete web page containing the escape room.

Phase Three: Educational Process Planning

At this stage, the teaching-learning process was organized with the inclusion of the educational escape room. This proposal was developed in three sixty-minute review sessions on *Theory and Practice of Educational Research* subject within the first year of the Primary Education Degree, as mentioned above. The planning was flexible in order to adapt the methodological approach to the needs of students and to the changing environment circumstances. In this sense, students' suggestions were addressed and the doubts expressed throughout the sessions were resolved. In addition, the time offered to solve each challenge was extended based on the achievements of the students, and reflection was made about the difficulties found after each challenge carried out. The participation was individual. Likewise, as it is an online teaching modality with non-compulsory attendance at virtual sessions, students were also offered the possibility of participating asynchronously. In this sense, with the purpose of resolving all the doubts that arose, a discussion forum was opened on the Teams platform. In this space, the participating students could ask questions, difficulties and offer suggestions, which were recorded in the teacher's diary.

Phase Four: Escape Room Application and Data Collection

This intervention development had a double objective within the reference subject: a) reinforce the learning acquired linked to the initial stages of the research process; b) develop the research competence of the students of the Primary Education Degree. The phases that constituted the educational process are specified below:

- Review session 1: "The Illusionist of Time". In this first session, the escape room is presented, the video with the initial instructions is displayed and the first challenge is carried out. It consists of solving a quiz with questions about the initial subject contents. Three answers are offered for each question, with only one true option. The correct resolution of this activity allows obtaining the first part of the code for opening "The secret box of time".
- Review session 2: "Touring our school". Attending to the syllabus key ideas development, access is given to the second and third challenges. In the second challenge, students strengthen the recognition and study of the problem and objective of different investigations through the analysis

of empirical scientific articles. To do this, a maze made through a presentation of the Genial.ly platform is used. The correct resolution of this second challenge makes it possible to obtain the second part of the code to open "The secret box of time". In the third task, a scoring questionnaire is carried out using the Google Forms application and Certify'em. The correct resolution of this challenge allows students to obtain a certificate and the third part of the code of "The secret box of time".

- Review session 3: "Descriptive statistics". In order to reinforce the exercises related to the univariate descriptive statistics, the search for the correct result for different problems is proposed (activity made with Genial.ly). The correct resolution of the exercise offers the fourth part of the code of "The secret box of time". After solving this fourth challenge, students must complete a questionnaire to analyse their own research competence. This instrument was created using the Google Forms application and is included on the escape room website. Completing this questionnaire offers the last part of the code that makes up the key to open "The secret box of time". In this way, the participants obtain the key to escape and return to their school in the present.

Phase Five: Evaluation and Interpretation of the Results

This phase happened simultaneously with the escape room application, through observation and recorded notes in the teacher's diary. Thus, problems, doubts and suggestions made by the students during the course of the escape room are addressed. Subsequently, the results extracted from the questionnaire (items and open questions) were analysed and interpreted.

Data Analysis

Descriptive statistical analysis was carried out for the scores given by the students to the items of the self-perceived research competence evaluation questionnaire. The statistics examined were mean, standard deviation, frequencies and percentages.

The internal consistency analysis of the instrument was carried out with Cronbach's Alpha coefficient. George and Mallery (2003) make the following recommendations for the evaluation of the index obtained: less than 0.5 would be considered unacceptable, between 0.5 and 0.6 poor, between 0.6 and 0.7 questionable, between 0.7 and 0.8 acceptable, between 0.8 and 0.9 good and values equal to or greater than 0.9 would be considered excellent.

All statistical analyzes were performed with the statistical package SPSS 24.

In the case of the notes collected in the teacher's diary (derived from the observations made in virtual sessions and in the discussion forum in the Teams platform) and the answers to open question contained in the ad hoc questionnaire, a qualitative content analysis was developed. The qualitative data analysis process consisted of three main phases (Rodríguez et al., 1999): a) Data reduction; b) Data disposition and transformation; c) Obtaining and verifying conclusions. In the data reduction phase, the analysis units were separated according to thematic criteria, they were coded, synthesised and grouped, giving rise to the categories and subcategories of analysis. In the data disposition and transformation phase, the categories were explained including the pertinent examples of analysis units. Finally, in the obtaining and verifying conclusions phase, the results obtained were interpreted taking into account theoretical framework. Obtaining qualitative data through different instruments (field diary and open question of the ad hoc questionnaire) allowed triangulating the information and obtaining a broader and more comprehensive vision of the development of the escape room. This made it possible to improve the educational experience in the future.

Table 1. Descriptive analysis of participants' responses: mean and standard deviation.

Questionnaire items	M	DT
I understand the main characteristics of educational research (paradigms, approaches, process, etc.).	7.58	1.26
I am able to analyze an educational research article according to the following basic elements: problem and objectives definition, method or design identification, proposal of limitations and/or modifications.	7.83	1.28
I am able to develop an univariate descriptive statistics process (mean, variance, etc.) and to interpret the results obtained.	9.33	.62
I am able to propose, in a coherent way, a research design based on the following basic elements: problem statement and specification of the researched questions, objectives formulation (general and specific), researched justification, method or design, sampling and information collection techniques or instruments.	7.17	.80
I think that I would be able to develop a basic research and innovation process in a real educational context, taking into account the ethical aspects that guide the process.	7.75	1.09
I am able to write an academic paper related to educational research through adequate writing (correct vocabulary, APA regulations, etc.) and a content logical structure.	8.08	1.04
I think that educational research is essential for my professional development as a teacher.	9.08	1.19
I think that educational research is essential for the improvement of teaching-learning processes.	9.75	.83
My motivation towards educational research is increased thanks to practical tasks and gamification activities (games, escape rooms, etc.).	9.50	.96
The knowledge and use of ICT (Information and Communication Technologies) are essential resources for current educational research development.	9.42	.76

RESULTS

Quantitative Data Analysis: Results of the Descriptive Study

Table 1 shows the findings referring to the mean and dispersion of the scores for each of the items of the research competence questionnaire self-perception.

Participants gave the highest scores (^{3} 9) to the most attitudinal and motivational aspects, such as the positive assessment of the importance of educational research for the improvement of teaching-learning processes, the increase in student motivation towards investigative tasks thanks to gamification activities such as the escape room, the relevance of ICT for current educational research development or the significance of educational research for the teacher professional development. In the case of the skills perceived by the students, only the development of univariate statistical processes obtained a score higher than 9. On the contrary, knowledge and skills related to the understanding of the characteristics of educational research, analysis of scientific articles, the approach of a coherent research design and implementation of a research process in a real educational context or writing of academic papers obtained scores below 9 points, with an average of 7.17-8.08.

Table 2 shows the results of the descriptive analysis of frequencies and percentages of scores given by the students for each of the questionnaire items.

Table 2. Descriptive analysis of the frequencies and percentages of responses about self-perceived research competence.

Questionnaire Items	1	2	3	4	5	6	7	8	9	10
I understand the main characteristics of educational research (paradigms, approaches, process, etc.).	0	0	0	0	2 (8.3)	2 (8.3)	6 (25)	10 (41.7)	2 (8.3)	2 (8.3)
I am able to analyze an educational research article according to the following basic elements: problem and objectives definition, method or design identification, proposal of limitations and/ or modifications.	0	0	0	0	0	4 (16.7)	6 (25)	8 (33.3)	2 (8.3)	4 (16.7)
I am able to develop a univariate descriptive statistics process (mean, variance, etc.) and to interpret the results obtained.	0	0	0	0	0	0	0	2 (8.3)	12 (50)	10 (41.7)
I am able to propose, in a coherent way, a research design based on the following basic elements: problem statement and specification of the research questions, objectives formulation (general and specific), research justification, method or design, sampling and information collection techniques or instruments.	0	0	0	0	0	6 (25)	8 (33.3)	10 (41.7)	0	0
I think that I would be able to develop a basic research and innovation process in a real educational context, taking into account the ethical aspects that guide the process.	0	0	0	0	0	4 (16.7)	4 (16.7)	12 (50)	2 (8.3)	2 (8.3)
I am able to write an academic paper related to educational research through adequate writing (correct vocabulary, APA regulations, etc.) and a content logical structure.	0	0	0	0	0	2 (8.3)	4 (16.7)	10 (41.7)	6 (25)	2 (8.3)
I think that educational research is essential for my professional development as a teacher.	0	0	0	0	0	0	4 (16.7)	4 (16.7)	2 (8.3)	14 (58.3)
I think that educational research is essential for the improvement of teaching-learning processes.	0	0	0	0	0	0	2 (8.3)	0	0	22 (91.7)
My motivation towards educational research is increased thanks to practical tasks and gamification activities (games, escape rooms, etc.).	0	0	0	0	0	0	2 (8.3)	2 (8.3)	2 (8.3)	18 (75)
The knowledge and use of ICT (Information and Communication Technologies) are essential resources for current educational research development.	0	0	0	0	0	0	0	4 (16.7)	6 (25)	14 (58.3)

The scores between 1 and 4 were not selected by any of the study simple components. It indicated that all the participants evaluated their own research competence in a positive way (with scores higher than 5). With results that are consistent with those shown in Table 1, the best-valued items alluded to the importance of educational research for teachers' professional development and the improvement of educational quality. Those results also showed the usefulness of gamification activities such as the escape room as a motivational factor, the relevance of knowledge and use of ICT in inquiry processes or the ability to develop univariate statistical procedures. In these cases, more than half of the sample selected scores that ranged between 9 and 10. On the contrary, the elements that showed the lowest scores were

Table 3. General and specific categories

General categories	
1. Escape room assessment	2. Subject assessment
Specific categories	
1.1. Escape room positive aspects	2.1. Teaching-learning process quality
1.2. Escape room difficulties	2.2. Teaching-learning process needs

related to the understanding of research processes characteristics, analysis of scientific articles, research design approach and its application to real contexts or writing of academic papers. The items that defined these competency elements were the only ones that received lower scores from some participants, which ranged between 5 and 6.

Qualitative Data Analysis: The Voices of the Students

The content analysis of the information collected led to the creation of a category system shown in Table 3:

Escape Room Assessment

In this general category, all those units of meaning that made reference to the assessments made by the students about the proposed escape room were grouped. This general category integrated two specific categories: positive aspects and difficulties.

Under the denomination of *escape room positive aspects*, textual segments focused their attention on benefits and efficiency of the escape room for the consolidation of concepts, procedures and attitudes towards the subject, as well as in relation to the development of the own motivation and competence in educational research were integrated, as showed below:

"The escape rooms are very good, it helps motivation, review and internalization of the contents, since it requires action." (Participant 002)

"I have made this escape room without studying, just with what I have learned in the lessons and the only thing I have seen that I have to review is the types of design and some theory, but everything else is acquired, so I'm calm and ready for the exam." (Participant 017)

Regarding the specific category *escape room difficulties*, different problems detected by the students in the escape room development were grouped. Below, some textual segments that exemplify these elements are showed:

"(…) I consider that it is an insufficient self-assessment practice. The only problem I have found is in the second challenge; I did not understand how to relate the letters to obtain the code." (Participant 008)

"In challenge four I found the way the game is built very stimulating, specifically the use of the flashlight makes it more interesting and fun. On the contrary, it has not been as easy for me to detect the operation of the maze and the mechanics as in the other three challenges." (Participant 022)

These findings showed the effectiveness of the escape room for the consolidation of the key ideas of the subject and for the increase of students' motivation towards it and, in general, towards educational research. In the same way, this activity allowed participants to detect which competency areas (concepts, skills or attitudes) they should reinforce. On the contrary, the difficulty of the second challenge stands out, even comparing it with the rest of the challenges. In addition, some evaluations indicated that, despite the usefulness of this escape room, it is still insufficient as a practice for developing and reinforcing one's own research competence.

Subject Assessment

This general category includes two specific categories focused on the quality of teaching-learning process proposed in the discipline of *Theory and Practice of Educational Research*, as well as the needs detected throughout its development.

The first specific category was *teaching-learning process quality*, which grouped meaning units focused on positive assessments that students made about the educational process development proposed in the subject:

"At first I thought it was one of the most difficult subjects and, moreover, I had not heard of it before. Little by little I have been changing my mind because thanks to the teacher for her dedication and involvement, documents that she has posted, interactive games, etc., I have been motivating myself much more about the subject despite its small difficulties." (Participant 003)

"The subject seemed a bit hard at first, but as the classes went by and we started with statistics and practicing the exercises together in class, I finally liked it, and the truth is that I didn't expect it." (Participant 011)

"For me, the key to learning is having a good teaching guide who makes you enjoy the trip, who knows how to explain each of the details of the landscape, so that you want to go back into those places and discover them in more depth. I have not only learned educational research, I have learned how to motivate the student, how to make the difficult easy (...)." (Participant 024)

The second specific category was *teaching-learning process needs*, which included textual segments about difficulties, shortcomings and improvement proposals for the subject:

"Finally, I would like to state that I am very interested in learning about these gamified learning mechanics because I think they are a way to motivate and engage students to get involved in learning with more complicated content." (Participant 008)

"As constructive criticism, I could comment that the notes are very dense." (Participant 015)

"The subject includes a lot of topics and it is difficult, it requires more time than the others." (Participant 020)

The information offered by participants showed the relevance of planning dynamic, interactive teaching-learning processes that do not focus only on the theoretical explanation of the content. Likewise, these students positively value the resources uploaded to virtual campus, such as documents for resolving doubts, review activities, use of ICT and, above all, teaching involvement in the subject. The importance of closeness, trust, transmitted tranquility and accompaniment or guidance throughout the development of the educational process is reinforced. In the case of needs, the syllabus density, the difficulty of the key ideas and the importance of including gamified or interactive activities to optimize the motivation, learning and skills development of students are informed.

DISCUSSION

The exposed results allowed for analysing the application of the educational escape room for the development of research competence in students of Primary Education Degree, as well as the specific aims derived from it.

In relation to the first objective, the degree of research competence perceived by the students after completing the educational escape room "The Illusionist of Time" was examined. Taking into account the definition of the analysed construct, students' self-perception of the concepts, skills, attitudes and motivation towards educational research was assessed (Böttcher & Thiel, 2018; Gómez-Núñez et al., 2020; Sabariego et al., 2020; Syzdykbayeva et al., 2015). In this sense, the findings showed the importance given to educational research for teaching-learning processes improvement and teacher professional development, as well as the training acquired for univariate descriptive statistical procedures application. These data coincide with what was established by authors such as Freixa (2017) and Zabalza (2012), who underlined the need to favor the professional development of teachers who are committed to their work, thoughtful, critical and capable of generating knowledge through their own educational research. In the same way, participants referred to an increase in their motivation thanks to gamified activities such as escape rooms, as well as the relevance of ICT within current educational research as resources for learning and knowledge. These results reinforce the current importance of e-learning as an educational modality within higher education (Basak et al., 2020; Wang et al., 2022) and, therefore, of ICT incorporation, transformed into LKT, as essential resources for meaningful learning development and adaptation to the new students' demands (Archer et al., 2019; Vidal-Esteve et al., 2019). In this sense, a virtual escape room comes as a playful activity that increases students' motivation and interest (Agreda et al., 2019; Pérez et al., 2019; Sierra & Fernández-Sánchez, 2019).

On the other hand, elements related to research competence that obtained the lowest scores were linked to the understanding of educational research characteristics, analysis of scientific articles, approach to a coherent research design, research process implementation in a real educational context or writing of academic papers. These shortcomings coincided with some difficulties exposed in previous studies (Toquero, 2021), which reinforces the need to improve the adaptation of the methodology and resources to students' needs in higher education (Torres-Martín et al., 2021). Research-based learning (Brew & Saunders, 2020) and the application of innovative methodological approaches, such as those related to gamification in the classroom (or in virtual lessons) (Aguilera et al., 2014; Werbach & Hunter, 2020) emerge as proposals to improve academic quality in initial teacher training.

Regarding the second specific objective, students assessment of escape room development as a learning mechanism within the *Theory and Practice of Educational Research* subject was analysed, which was in line with what was previously stated. That is, the analysis carried out by the students shows a change in the assessment of the mentioned area of study. At the beginning of *Theory and Practice of Educational Research* discipline, the students complained about the little use of knowledge related to research for their academic and professional future. In addition, the most of contents were problematic for them, without critically analysing what concepts they had to reinforce or the great commitment that an educational research process requires. However, according to participants' perceptions, the practice of the escape room allowed consolidation of the subject key ideas, increased their motivation towards it and towards educational research and, in addition, made it possible to detect areas of competence or knowledge that they had to reinforce. The students increased their participation in the class sessions, raised a greater number of doubts, improved the quality of the research approaches carried out and it was increased their interest in educational research through the search of scientific studies in data bases or virtual libraries. These findings coincided with what was exposed in works such as Romero et al. (2019), who highlighted the importance of escape room experiences for the development of skills related to problem solving, critical review or attention to detail. In the same way, the escape room effectiveness is reinforced to increase the motivation, commitment and interest of the students towards what is studied and the dynamics that occur within the classrooms or lessons (Agreda et al., 2019; Pérez et al., 2019; Sierra & Fernández-Sánchez, 2019). This would, in turn, allow teachers in training to learn new teaching methodologies in an active, experiential way that, in the future, can be put into practice with their own students (López-Secanell & Ortega-Torres, 2020).

To these results is added the students' positive evaluation of methodological change proposed in subject development in which this innovation proposal is focused. The effectiveness of dynamic, interactive teaching-learning processes that do not focus only on the magisterial presentation of the content is highlighted. These assessments show the importance of learning through play and the challenges raised by escape rooms (Agreda et al., 2019; López-Secanell & Ortega-Torres, 2020; Pérez et al., 2019; Sierra & Fernández-Sánchez, 2019), and the need of using active and participatory learning as the most optimal mechanism for the research competence development (Gómez-Núñez & Cano-Muñoz, 2020). In addition, students valued the resources offered throughout the subject development, the doubts resolution in sessions and through open discussion forums, the uses of ICT as LKT and the teacher's involvement in the entire educational process, attending to its role of support and guidance. The digital competence development of future teachers can only be achieved through the immersion of students in this type of tools (Vidal-Esteve et al., 2019; Wang et al., 2022). It strengthens the importance of rethinking educational processes in university online training, attending to the changes of a more technological society and following approaches that are not only focused on the content to be acquired, but also on the ways of contacting students, teaching and learning (Krathwohl & Anderson, 2009).

Finally, the third objective focused on the identification of possible needs during the implementation of the educational escape room. The study sample highlighted the difficulty of some of the challenges included in the escape room, as well as its insufficiency as reinforcement practice for the research competence evaluation through the practical final exam of the subject. In the same way, the study discipline density, the complexity of the key ideas and the importance of including gamified or interactive activities throughout the course were underlined. These proposals coincided with what was established in the review by Barari et al. (2020), in which the importance of learning based on problem solving, promotion of interaction and significant learning through ICT tools and planning of teaching processes divided into different phases, was emphasized, with activities that adapt to students learning styles and needs. In this sense, the escape rooms emerge as didactic procedures that would allow the approach of new forms of teaching and learning, which involve students in new experiences that increase their creativity, motivation and interest in the study content in general (García- Lázaro, 2019; Grande-de-Prado, 2019; Lozano-López & Lázaro, 2019), and towards subjects related to educational research in particular (Cano-Muñoz & Gómez-Núñez, 2020).

Learning to think scientifically, to research in education and to extrapolate what has been learned to different academic and work contexts in which a teacher develops his professional practice is essential for teachers' professional development (Balloo, 2019; Dzyubenko et al., 2021; Martín -Gómez et al., 2022; Salmento et al., 2021; Toquero, 2021). To this end, as demonstrated in this study, didactic procedures linked to gamification, such as the educational and virtual escape room, come as innovation proposals capable of improving the students' research competence. Furthermore, these experiences increase students' motivation and interest in complex subjects included in Primary Education Degree study plans, such as those linked to educational research.

LIMITATIONS AND FUTURE RESEARCH DIRECTIONS

Despite the importance of the findings obtained, they must be evaluated taking into account several limitations that must be resolved in future lines of research. In the first place, we are faced with a pilot experience of a voluntary nature, in which not all the students of *Theory and Practice of Educational Research* subject participated. In addition, we started from an individual work modality, which did not allow a joint resolution of the challenges. For future applications, it is recommended to review the planning of educational escape room, encouraging the students' cooperative work in solving the activities proposed both inside and outside of virtual lessons. Secondly, the level of research competence self-perceived by the students before the start of the escape room was not taken into account. In future works, a measurement should be carried out prior to application of the escape room, in order to analyse the possible changes in research competence reported by the students. Finally, following the approach of needs detected by the sample, it is advisable to expand the escape room, creating a methodological approach that enables the introduction of gamification in all sessions that make up the subject.

CONCLUSION: PRACTICE IMPLICATIONS

The practical experience presented in this research shows that there is another way of teaching within the university context. The application of gamification through the development of virtual escape room points out the importance of using the game as a teaching and learning mechanism. The results of this study show the improvement of the research competence of the students of the Degree in Primary Education in aspects as essential as the identification of problems and research objectives, the application of univariate descriptive statistical analysis, the decision-making regarding the best research method or design to respond to a problem or the consolidation of concepts related to educational research. In addition, the students' comments and the teacher's observations allowed us to analyse the importance given to research and how positive attitudes were developed in this knowledge field. In conclusion, the research about the proposed innovation entailed the following practical implications:

- Increase in the research skills of first-year students of Primary Education Degree.
- Reinforcement of the theoretical-practical knowledge of *Theory and Practice of Educational Research* subject.
- Increased student motivation towards practical experiences linked to educational research.
- Optimization of the academic results of the students of the first year of Primary Education Degree with respect to *Theory and Practice of Educational Research* subject.
- Promotion of student creativity in terms of the development and application of educational innovations in their future teaching career. In this sense, it is necessary to highlight the importance of teachers knowing and participating in gamification experiences developed online. The pandemic caused by the expansion of Sars-Cov2 showed the existing digital divide and the lack of training in new technologies of primary teachers. Although the teaching modality in Primary Education is

face-to-face, it is also necessary for future teachers to know gamification mechanisms that can be applied with students who cannot attend face-to-face (i.e., illness or hospitalization) or to improve the adaptation of educational process to today's digital society.

Researching about teaching practice itself in university contexts emerges as a basic mechanism to detect shortcomings, improve proposed actions, foster critical review, optimize professional skills and increase creativity in innovative processes planned and applied (Flecha & Molina, 2015; Gómez-Núñez & Cano-Muñoz, 2020; Páez-Martínez, 2020; Zabalza, 2016).

REFERENCES

Afdal, H. W., & Spernes, K. (2018). Designing and redesigning research-based teacher education. *Teaching and Teacher Education*, *74*, 215–228. doi:10.1016/j.tate.2018.05.011

Agreda, M., Ortiz, A. M., Tallón, S., & López, J. (2019). Escape rooms: actividades gamificadas para la formación de profesionales educativos [Escape rooms: gamified activities for the training of educational professionals]. In E. Sánchez-Rivas, J. Ruiz-Palmero, & E. Sánchez-Vega (Coords.), *Innovación y tecnología en contextos educativos* (pp. 399-409). UMA editorial.

Aguilera, A., Fúquene, C. A., & Ríos, W. F. (2014). Aprende jugando: El uso de técnicas de gamificación en entornos de aprendizaje. *IM-Pertinente*, *2*(1), 125–143.

Balloo, K. (2019). Students' difficulties during research methods training acting as potential barriers to their development of scientific thinking. In M. Murtonen & K. Balloo (Eds.), *Redefining scientific thinking for higher education* (pp. 107–137). Palgrave Macmillan. doi:10.1007/978-3-030-24215-2_5

Barari, N., RezaeiZadeh, M., Khorasani, A., & Alami, F. (2022, October 3). Designing and validating educational standards for E-teaching in virtual learning environments (VLEs), based on revised bloom's taxonomy. *Interactive Learning Environments*, *30*(9), 1640–1652. Advance online publication. doi:10.1080/10494820.2020.1739078

Basak, S. K., Wotto, M., & Belanger, P. (2018). E-learning, M-learning and D-learning: Conceptual definition and comparative analysis. *E-Learning and Digital Media*, *15*(4), 191–216. doi:10.1177/2042753018785180

Bilbao, N., Romero, A., Portillo, J., & López, A. (2022). Escape room digital para el desarrollo del aprendizaje cooperativo en educación superior [Digital escape room for the development of cooperative learning in higher education]. *Education in the Knowledge Society*, *23*. Advance online publication. doi:10.14201/eks27126

Bloom, B. S. (1956). *Taxonomy of educational objectives: The classification of educational goals. Book 1. Cognitive domain*. Longman.

Böttcher, F., & Thiel, F. (2018). Evaluating research-oriented teaching: A new instrument to assess university students' research competences. *Higher Education*, *75*(1), 91–110. doi:10.100710734-017-0128-y

Brew, A., & Saunders, C. (2020). Making sense of research-based learning in teacher education. *Teaching and Teacher Education*, *87*, 102935. doi:10.1016/j.tate.2019.102935

Cano-Muñoz, M. Á., & Gómez-Núñez, M. I. (2020). Aprendizaje basado en el juego en la educación superior: análisis de una experiencia de escape room [Play-based learning in higher education: analysis of an escape room experience]. In E. López-Meneses, D. Cobos-Sanchiz, L. Molina-García, A. Jaén-Martínez, & A. H. Martín-Padilla (Eds.), *Claves para la innovación pedagógica ante lo nuevos retos. Respuestas en la vanguardia de la práctica educativa* (pp. 2731–2739). Octaedro.

Dabbagh, N. (2005). Scaffolding: An important teacher competency in online learning. *TechTrends, 47*(2), 39–44. doi:10.1007/BF02763424

Deterding, S., Khaled, R., Nacke, L., & Dixon, D. (2011). *Gamification: Toward a definition. In 29th Annual CHI Conference on Human Factors in Computing Systems*. ACM Press. https://bityl.co/3ify

Dzyubenko, S. V., Sergeyeva, M. G., & Samokhin, I. S. (2021). Improvement of Research Competencies of School Teachers in Context of Modernization of National Education. *Nauchnyi Dialog*, (2), 303–321. doi:10.24224/2227-1295-2018-2-303-321

Flecha, R., & Molina, S. (2015). Actuaciones educativas de éxito como base de una política educativa basada en evidencias [Successful educational actions as the basis of an evidence-based educational policy]. *Avances en Supervisión Educativa, 32*, 1–18. doi:10.23824/ase.v0i23.23

Freixa, M. (2017). *Professorat novell: Copetències docents a l'inici de l'exercici professional* [Novice teaching staff: Teaching skills at the beginning of the professional practice]. Agencia per la Qualitat del Sistema Universitari de Catalunya.

García-Lázaro, I. (2019). Escape room como propuesta de gamificación en educación [Escape room as a gamification proposal in education]. *Revista Educativa Hekademos*, (27), 71-79. https://hekademos.com/index.php/hekademos/article/view/17/7

George, D., & Mallery, P. (2003). *SPSS for Windows step by step: A simple guide and reference. 11.0 update* (4th ed.). Allyn & Bacon.

Gómez-Núñez, M. I., & Cano-Muñoz, M. Á. (2020). El desarrollo de la competencia investigadora: Experiencia online en orientación educativa [The development of research competence: Online experience in educational guidance]. *Revista Educativa Hekademos*, (29), 32-42. https://hekademos.com/index.php/hekademos/article/view/23

Gómez-Núñez, M. I., Cano-Muñoz, M. Á., & Torregrosa, M. S. (2020). *Manual para investigar en educación. Guía para orientadores y docentes indagadores* [Manual for research in education. Guide for counselors and teachers inquirers]. Narcea.

Grande-de-Prado, M. (2019). Escape room: mapeo sistemático de literatura científica educativa en español [Manual for research in education. Guide for counselors and teachers inquirers]. In S. Alonso, J. M. Romero, C. Rodríguez-Jiménez, & J. M. Sola (Eds.), *Investigación, Innovación docente y TIC. Nuevos horizontes educativos* (pp. 117–128). Dykinson.

Krathwohl, D. R., & Anderson, L. W. (2009). *A taxonomy for learning, teaching, and assessing: A revision of Bloom's taxonomy of educational objectives*. Longman.

Landers, R. N. (2014). Developing a theory of gamified learning. *Simulation & Gaming*, *45*(6), 752–768. doi:10.1177/1046878114563660

Llorens-Largo, F., Gallego-Durán, F. J., Villagrá-Arnedo, C. J., Compañ-Rosique, P., Satorre-Cuerda, R., & Molina-Carmona, R. (2016). Gamificación del Proceso de Aprendizaje: Lecciones Aprendidas [Manual for research in education. Guide for counselors and teachers inquirers]. *VAEP-RITA*, *4*(1), 25–32.

López-Secanell, I., & Ortega-Torres, E. (2020). Escape room educativa: Concepción de los futuros maestros de Educación Secundaria en especialidad de Educación Física y Tecnología sobre la experiencia de diseñar y participar en una escape room educativa [Educational escape room: conception of future teachers of Secondary Education in specialty of Physical Education and Technology on the experience of designing and participating in an educational escape room]. *Didacticae*, (8), 1–17. doi:10.1344/did.2020.8.176-192

Lozano-López, C. M., & Lázaro, M. N. (2019). Escape FolRoom: Propuesta de juego integrada en clase de Formación y Orientación Laboral [Escape FolRoom: Proposal of integrated game in class of Training and Career Orientation]. *International Journal of Nursing Education*, (4), 91–105. doi:10.24310/IJNE2.2.2019.7453

Martín-Gómez, P., García Rodríguez, M. L., & Mena Marcos, J. J. (2022). El prácticum en el grado de maestro/a de educación infantil: Análisis de diarios docentes [The practicum in the degree of teacher of early childhood education: Analysis of teaching diaries]. *Revista Complutense De Educación*, *33*(1), 131–140. doi:10.5209/rced.73838

Merrian, S. B. (1988). *Case study research in education*. San Francisco, CA: Jossey Bass.Murtonen, M., & Salmento, H. (2019). Broadening the Theory of Scientific Thinking for Higher Education. In M. Murtonen & K. Balloo (Eds.), *Redefining scientific thinking for higher education* (pp. 3–29). Palgrave Macmillan.

Nicholson, S. (2015). *Peeking behind the locked door: A survey of Escape room facilities*. https://goo.gl/1eaC7G

Pérez, E., Gilabert, A., & Lledó, A. (2019). Gamificación en la educación universitaria: El uso del escape room como estrategia de aprendizaje [Gamification in university education: The use of the escape room as a learning strategy]. In R. Roig-Vila (Ed.), *Investigación e innovación en la Enseñanza Superior. Nuevos contextos, nuevas ideas* (pp. 660–668). Octaedro.

Rodríguez, G., Gil, J., & García, E. (1999). *Metodología de la investigación cualitativa* [Qualitative research methodology]. Aljibe.

Romero, A., López, A., Tejada, E., & Bilbao, N. (2019). Calidad tecnopedagógica del escape room en educación superior [Techno-pedagogical quality of the escape room in higher education]. In E. Sánchez-Rivas, J. Ruiz-Palmero, & E. Sánchez-Vega (Coords.), *Innovación y tecnología en contextos educativos* (pp. 389-398). UMA editorial.

Sabariego, M., Cano, A. B., Gross, B., & Piqué, B. (2020). Competencia investigadora e investigación formativa en la formación inicial del docente [Research competence and formative research in initial teacher training]. *Contextos Educativos. Review of Education*, (26), 239–259. doi:10.18172/con.4326

Salinas, M. I. (2011). *Entornos virtuales de aprendizaje en la escuela: tipos, modelo didáctico y rol del docente* [Virtual learning environments at school: types, didactic model and role of the teacher]. Universidad Católica de Argentina.

Salmento, H., Murtonen, M., & Kiley, M. (2021). Understanding Teacher Education Students' Research Competence Through Their Conceptions of Theory. *Frontiers in Education, 6*, 763803. doi:10.3389/feduc.2021.763803

Salvador-Gómez, A., Escrig-Tena, A. B., Beltrán-Martín, I., & García-Juan, B. (2022). El escape room virtual: herramienta docente universitaria para el desarrollo de competencias transversales y para la retención del conocimiento [The virtual escape room: university teaching tool for the development of transversal competences and for the retention of knowledge]. *Tecnología. Ciência & Educação (Bauru), 21*, 7–48. doi:10.51302/tce.2022.664

Sierra, M. C., & Fernández-Sánchez, M. R. (2019). Gamificando el aula universitaria. Análisis de una experiencia de Escape Room en educación superior [The virtual escape room: university teaching tool for the development of transversal competences and for the retention of knowledge]. *Revista de Estudios y Experiencias en Educación, 18*(36), 105–115. doi:10.21703/rexe.20191836sierra15

Syzdykbayeva, A. D., Bainazarova, T. B., & Aitzhanova, E. N. (2015). Formation of research competence of the future elementary school teachers-in the process of professional training. *International Education Studies, 8*(4), 200–209. doi:10.5539/ies.v8n4p200

Torres Martín, C., Acal, C., El Homrani, M., & Mingorance Estrada, Á. C. (2021). Impact on the virtual learning environment due to COVID-19. *Sustainability, 13*(2), 582. doi:10.3390u13020582

Vidal-Esteve, M. I., Vega-Navarro, A., & López-Gómez, S. (2019). Uso de materiales didácticos digitales en las aulas de Primaria [Use of digital teaching materials in Primary classrooms]. *Campus Virtuales, 8*(2), 103-119. http://www.uajournals.com/campusvirtuales/journal/15/8.pdf

Wang, V., Hitch, L., & Torrisi-Steele, G. (2022). Active learning online: Necessity, faculty role, and a concept model for course design. *International Journal of Online Pedagogy and Course Design, 12*(1), 1–13. doi:10.4018/IJOPCD.2022010105

Werbach, K., & Hunter, D. (2020). *For the win, revised and updated edition: The power of gamification and game thinking in business, education, government, and social impact*. Wharton School Press. doi:10.2307/j.ctv2hdrfsm

Wiemker, M., Elumir, E., & Clare, A. (2015). Escape room Games. "Can you transform an unpleasant situation into a pleasant one?" *Game Based Learning, 55*.

Willegems, V., Consuegra, E., Struyven, K., & Engels, N. (2017). Teachers and preservice teachers as partners in collaborative teacher research: A systematic literature review. *Teaching and Teacher Education, 64*, 230-245. doi:10.1016/j.tate.2017.02.014

Zabalza, M. Á. (2012). Las competencias en la formación del profesorado: De la teoría a las propuestas prácticas [Competences in teacher training: From theory to practical proposals]. *Tendencias Pedagógicas*, (20), 5-32. https://dialnet.unirioja.es/servlet/articulo?codigo=4105027

Zabalza, M. Á. (2016). Ser profesor universitario hoy [Being a university professor today]. *La Cuestión Universitaria*, (5), 68-80. http://polired.upm.es/index.php/lacuestionuniversitaria/article/view/3338/3403

KEY TERMS AND DEFINITIONS

Descriptive Case Study: Research design that provides an in-depth understanding of a program or an innovation. This design has a illustrative character, so it is not based on previous hypotheses or universal theories.

Distance Teaching: Educational modality that takes place virtually or online, through Information and Communication Technologies (ICT), apps and platforms linked to the Internet.

Learning and Knowledge Technologies (LKT): Learning tools which can be applied in educational contexts, that is, ICT have been renamed LKT in reference to the use that students make of this resource to progress in their learning

Primary Education Degree: University career with a duration of four years, which allows the academic and professional development of teachers for children from 6 to 12 years old (Primary Education).

Research Competence: Set of knowledge, skills, attitudes and learning strategies that allow developing of efficient and effective research processes in different educational or scientific fields.

Research Skills: Ability or set of abilities allow research process development (i.e. search for information, data analysis, coherent writing, etc.). Skill should not be confused with competence. The term "competence" is broader and would include the concept of ability or skill.

Spanish Organic Law: Regulation elaborated by the Spanish government of compliance in all the regions or provinces of this country. These regulations are usually adapted (within certain limits) to meet the needs and demands of different educational contexts.

Chapter 7

Lost in the Island:
A Gamified Experience for Professional Educator Training

Eva Garcia-Beltran
https://orcid.org/0000-0002-9922-1334
Universidad Internacional de La Rioja, Spain

ABSTRACT

In recent years, there has been a dramatic rise of the use of escape rooms in education. It is a creative form of a gamified learning experience that proves to be effective especially in higher education and online learning environments. This research describes a breakout learning experience, framed in an online master's degree of educational innovation for professional educators. It was designed as a final review of the main theoretical concepts from the course, fostering students' self-assessment. In addition, this experience would pose an example of an active methodology activity that may serve as an inspiration for the students' own teaching practice, presenting them with a student-centered strategy that can provide an innovative dynamic in their classes.

INTRODUCTION

The rise of the use of escape rooms in education is indisputable, especially in the last decade. Although there is a great range of contributions about gamification in educational contexts, both from defenders and from detractors, the scientific community is still divided (Onecha-Pérez, Sanz-Prat & López-Valdés, 2019).

Recently, the educational escape room is gaining prominence in higher education (Eukel & Morrell, 2021). It is a methodological strategy that usually involves a challenge in which students must complete missions, find clues or solve puzzles that lead to a key or a code that is needed to open a lock to leave the room in the game takes place. From this initial approach, other modalities have been developed, such as digital escape rooms (Neumann, Alvarado-Albertorio & Ramírez-Salgado, 2021), or clue games in

DOI: 10.4018/978-1-6684-6081-8.ch007

which the objective is not to escape from a physical room, but to solve a mystery, escape from danger or simply win the game (Macías-Guillén, et al., 2021).

Probably there is still a resistance coming from the most traditional academic sectors to accept a connection between games and learning, not recognizing game-based learning with sufficient rigor when it comes to achieving the learning objectives (Bellotti et al., 2013). In fact, popular opinion and classical literature often suggest that it is one thing to play and quite another to learn, that they should be kept apart as if enjoying were to corrupt the learning process with opposite values to those of rigor, fairness, and discipline. Traditional methodology puts the emphasis on effort as the key of meaningful learning, but fails to take into account that an adequate level of motivation can lead the individual to develop the same effort but without the feeling of suffering that seems irremediably linked to it, following the 'Flow theory' of Csíkszentmihályi (1975) within the current of positive psychology. Flow is the state in which the person is absorbed in an activity that completely attracts their attention, fully enjoying it and almost losing track of time, with actions and thoughts perfectly aligned.

It seems as if learning is not carried out through effort and even including a certain amount of suffering, it will not be of sufficient quality.

However, teachers today perceive very different realities in their classes. They discover how a glimpse of fun manages to fully change the mood of a group of students and makes them receptive to new experiences and learning. The game allows you to safely experiment, exploring options and consequences, and join forces in a collaborative effort to achieve a common goal. The game transports us to other moments in history, simulates social interaction and fosters the study of other cultures, perspectives and experiences (Cortizo et al., 2011).

The game facilitates the connection with reality, simulating contexts that seem authentic such as environmental disaster zones that allow learning about natural sciences, foreign countries in order to practice languages, or experiment with real texts to improve literacy. As long as the game is well designed, it offers enormous potential to teach complex thinking skills such as creativity and innovation, critical thinking and problem solving, among others. (Murphree &Vafa, 2010).

It is certainly challenging to assess the effectiveness of gamified experiences in supporting long-term skill acquisition and practice. Evaluation itself is a complex process, when it comes to other types of interventions and educational programs, so evaluating a gamified activity, with its own factors and contexts, can become even more so. Despite these challenges, in the last decade, research into gamification in learning has blossomed exponentially.

We have also seen a huge increase in the creation and use of learning games in classrooms and informal education settings, as well as a growth in the number of websites, apps and other media dedicated to education. Today, a multitude of platforms, tools and systems that facilitate the creation of gamified experiences in an accessible and open way is available for everyone, and of course, for educators.

But gamification is not only present in education. In fact, it started to be part of daily like in other areas such as marketing or banking (Sierra Daza & Fernández-Sánchez, 2019).

However, despite this wide range of available resources, scientific research and reliable conclusions are still scarce. Most of the published investigations are case studies and are usually focused on escape rooms in the digital field, which are undoubtedly interesting as they offer inspiration and contrasted results in terms of the opinions coming from the students who have participated. However, often the conclusions may not be easily extrapolated without a broader theoretical basis, and also because educational interventions are complex open situations, greatly dependent on the context in which they take place, so that the transfer of knowledge in this area must always be accompanied by a particular implementation in a new environment.

In this chapter, a breakout learning experience is described. It was introduced with a dual purpose. First, as it was designed as a review of the main theoretical concepts from the course, it tried to help students self-assess their own knowledge, so they can focus and review properly for the exam. But, in addition to that, this experience would be an example of applying an active methodology activity that may serve as an inspiration for their teaching practice, presenting them with a student-centered strategy that can provide an innovative dynamic in their classes.

Also, as in any gamified learning experience, there was an aim of increasing the students' engagement, by providing a motivating and challenging learning experience, and thus contributing to generating more significant learning.

BACKGROUND

Both gamification and game-based learning represent an opportunity to introduce experiential and inquiry-based learning, as constructivism theory proposes (Rouse, 2017). Specifically, and according to Grande de Prado, García Martín, Baelo and Abella García (2020), educational escape rooms are a type of game-based learning experience in which narrative plays such a relevant role. The story provides the context for the different tests the students must pass, and it helps to make sense within the whole experience. As stated by Negre i Walczak (2017), within the educational escape rooms, there is a subcategory called 'breakout', in which the narrative story does not involve the action of *escaping* from a closed place, but rather managing to open a box that is secured with a padlock. The challenge is to open that padlock, which will generally be protected with a code, for which it will be necessary to pass a certain number of tests, enigmas, or questions.

This type of game-based learning has many different applications. Although it tends to have a greater presence in the primary and secondary education stages (Grande de Prado, García Martín, Baelo & Abella García, 2020), a growing presence of these initiatives is observed in the higher education stage. Specifically, it is relatively frequently applied to the context of programming education, as shown in the works by López-Pernas, Gordillo, Barra and Quemada (2019a; 2019b), and Borrego, Fernández, Blanes and Robles (2017), as well as in language teaching, as evidenced by the works of Santamaría and Alcalde (2019), and Moreno (2019).

As this educational resource has become more popular, teachers are designing their own experiences and sharing them on platforms such as Breakout EDU, which has more than 40,000 members (Sanchez & Plumettaz-Sieber, 2018). The inspiration for these activities is very varied and includes video games, movies or television series (Franco & DeLuca, 2019). These teachers, in their role as instructional designers, share a common goal of energizing their students' learning environment. And, according to results, they are clearly rewarded by their students, who appreciate the variety of tests and problem-solving challenges they are presented with, and they must work them out relying on their own intuition, knowledge and skills, and often collaborating with their peers (Veldkamp et al., 2020).

Nevertheless, this methodology faces several limitations. One is the budgetary restriction, as funds are usually limited in education. Also, there are often difficulties in putting it into practice in face-to-face classes. The challenges imposed by the COVID-19 pandemic have given a boost to online and hybrid teaching, although often as an emergency measure without sufficient preparation. The hybrid dimension of teaching opens new possibilities for instructional design and fosters the use of innovative solutions in educational settings (Veldkamp et al., 2020).

What is Important in a Learning Game?

Educational games are characterized by having a set of learning objectives, and obviously this is not present in a traditional game. They are not intended to entertain users, and this has a significant impact on their design. In a traditional game, one of the key questions is whether it is fun; however, in an educational game, although fun also plays a very important role, it is much more relevant if it is able to maintain the necessary motivation in the learners (players) to achieve the learning objectives. A fun educational game will manage to keep the user's attention, who will play voluntarily and for a longer time, which will allow a longer exposure to the educational material that is presented (Becker & Parker, 2014).

Designing educational playful experiences requires incorporating learning objectives, and this can be difficult. These learning goals should be part of what the user must experience, consider, practice and reflect on within the experience. Both the learning objectives and the goals of the game must be aligned, so that the playful experience is successful in terms of accomplishing curriculum's learning outcomes, and at the same time maintaining the game's motivation and fun. This can be challenging, but when the process of learning and acquiring skills is designed in a way that is fun in itself, it can be done (Koster, 2005).

When it comes to gamified experiences in the classroom, several options are available: the teacher may use a ready-made experience and try to adapt it to the specific situation. In these cases, the gaming experience itself will possibly have a higher quality since it will have been conceived and developed by a professional. The professional game designer knows how to design the gameplay and the different elements of the game, such as game mechanics, navigation, interaction, and levels, and how to make it all come together for a fun and interesting experience for the player (Iuppa & Borst, 2010).

However, when this strategy is chosen, the match with the specific learning objectives may fail, since a pre-designed tool is being used and it has been adapted to a situation for which it has not been specially designed. To try to avoid this problem, many teachers decide to design an *ad-hoc* gamified experience themselves for their learning objectives, although in this case, the designer will be a teacher instead of a professional game designer. Also, teachers tend to think this process is long and laborious, as they lack preparation and tools.

Educators and professional game designers build and develop their goals differently. The educator, or instructional designer, aims to develop a game that helps students achieve learning objectives. They have the expertise to choose and plan which content and learning activities will best support the different learning processes that traditionally lead students to achieve learning goals (Laerke Weitze, 2014).

In contrast, the professional game designer has a different viewpoint that involves at least two design disciplines: game design and software design (i.e., programming knowledge, computer algorithm design, and simulation design) and despite the plentifulness of software design models (Budgen, 2003), there are far fewer models for game design. Salen and Zimmerman's (2004) game rules and Fullerton's game design workshop (2008) address the game design process, but do not include a concise design model. According to Fullerton (2008), games are formal systems that include a variety of elements, including but not limited to: goals, procedures, rules, resources, limits, conflicts, and dramatic elements. As Laerke Weitze (2014) points out, where the teacher traditionally focuses on learning, the game designer focuses on how to build an interesting and coherent experience. The resulting game must be a balance between the goals of these two perspectives.

'Genially' is an accessible and open tool for all types of publics that helps teachers' lack of designing skills, both in terms of graphics and software development. It provides editable templates and a good number of tools for designing interactive experiences, requiring less effort than the final result suggest. Teachers can develop playful experiences such as digital escape rooms, using all their subject knowledge as well as the students' profiles and needs for whom the experience will be intended. Thus, they can create good playful experiences that fully adapt their group-class's circumstances, without many of the technical deficiencies as newbie designers.

Evaluation Through Gamification

Whenever learning objectives are mentioned, it is essential to verify its achievement, or in other words, to undertake an evaluation in terms of the learning results. Each learning objective must be able to be measured and evaluated (Hirumi et al., 2010). Therefore, how the learning objectives are implemented in the game should lead to an efficient and useful learning evaluation: to what extent the gamified experience has helped students in their learning process (Institute of Play, 2014).

In this specific experience, as it is designed to be carried out autonomously and asynchronously, the student is expected to conduct their self-assessment, so that they can assess whether they already learned the concepts correctly or, on the contrary, they find areas in which they must place a greater attention.

As Pérez-López and García Rivera (2017) point out, often with the concept of self-assessment, students need to get rid of some ideas that they have had to learn throughout their student career, in what these authors call 'poisonous pedagogy' (p.125). Sometimes, they just see evaluation as an audit that threatens punishment, instead of seeing it as an opportunity that empowers them to be the only owners of their learning, from a place of self-criticism and reflection.

The main objective of this article is to show a real experience carried out in the context of online higher education, which was designed with a twofold objective: first, it was intended to use the gamification experience as a self-assessment tool so that students could assess their own level at the end of the subject and before facing the final exam. As pointed out by Bellotti et al. (2013), one of the main contributions of serious games is that, in addition to increasing student motivation and engagement, they can serve as a valid and rigorous evaluation tool.

Secondly, and given the profile of the Master's students, which will be explored later, this experience aims to serve as an example of design within the framework of the Active Teaching-Learning Methodologies subject, showing the possibilities of various digital tools. for the creation of educational content.

THE LEARNING EXPERIENCE

Context

'Lost in the island', which is the title of the experience presented in this article, has been designed as a final review for the subject 'Active Teaching-Learning Methodologies', which belongs to the Master's degree in Educational Innovation. The topics covered in this subject are cooperative learning, project-based learning, challenge-based learning, gamification and innovative evaluation. Both the subject, as well as the Master's degree as a whole, have a focus on practice, with a methodology based on solving challenges cooperatively. Active methodologies are not only a curricular content of the study but are very present to students to encourage their learning by doing.

Also, it has to be pointed out that this Master's degree takes place entirely within an online environment. That means there is a large part of the teaching-learning process which happens asynchronously. This has a significant impact not only on the learning rhythm of the group, but also on the kind of mentorship the teacher must provide to their students, as well as the need to provide additional support to those who decide to carry out the activity asynchronously.

This degree's students are education professionals, mainly teachers from different educational stages, including other non-formal education professionals (such as teaching staff in military schools, cultural organizations, etc.) as well as members of managerial teams. Students come from Spain and from different Latin American countries, mainly Colombia and Ecuador.

Specifically, the sample of students with whom this experience has been carried out consists of 43 students, of which 60.5% came from Ecuador (26 of them), 30.2% from Colombia (13), 7% from the Dominican Republic (3) and 2.3% from Peru (1 student). 30 students responded to the satisfaction survey, which represents 69.7% of the total.

All these students are professionally linked to education: 62.8% of them are teachers with more than 5 years of experience, and 27.9% are less-experienced teachers. 9.3% of them are non-teaching professionals, such as researchers, content developers or academic directors.

Regarding their previous experience with active teaching-learning methodologies, which is the specific subject in which this learning experience is framed, only 4.7% reported extensive experience in its application at the beginning of the course, 51.2% of them claimed to have some experience with them. 27.9% said they knew them but without having worked directly with them, while 20.9% admitted not knowing anything about them.

Among those who claim to have worked with active methodologies, the most used are cooperative learning (used by 91.9%), project-based learning (31.8%) and, more rarely, gamification (22.7%).

Their main motivation for taking this Master's degree is their interest in increasing their innovative teaching skills, either by using new methodologies, the introduction of technological tools in their lessons or by acquiring a new vision in the leadership of his educational institution.

The Breakout

'Lost in the island' is an educational breakout which is set right after a plane crash, taking after a well-known series from a few years ago. The starting assumption is that the protagonist is a teacher who accompanies his group on their end of studies trip, in which they suffer a plane crash, being abandoned on a desert island.

The first thing that the students find at the beginning of the experience is a one-minute video that tries to set the scene for the challenge they must solve. The video, like all the contents of the escape room, was originally created by the teacher. Afterwards, the students are presented with the main challenge: trying to escape from the deserted island where their plane crashed. To do this, they will try to use a mobile phone that looks operational which has been found among the crash wreckage. The students must turn on the mobile to ask for help, and they need the four digits of the PIN code. The challenge is formed by four test stations, and in each of them they will find some tests they will have to solve correctly to

Figure 1. Breakout presentation
Source: Screenshot from the breakout

obtain a PIN digit. Completing all four successfully, they will have the complete PIN code to turn on the mobile phone, so they can ask for help to escape the island.

All missions include questions and tests from the subject syllabus, and they have been designed in different formats. The questions are multiple choice questions designed interactively, so immediate feedback is provided: the student can select a different option if their original choice is not correct. This allows taking part in the experience both synchronously as well as asynchronously.

Figure 2. Mission presentation
Source: Screenshot from the breakout

Figure 3. Missions map
Source: Screenshot from the breakout

The first mission lies in correctly answering five questions aimed to differentiate between challenge-based learning and project-based learning. For each of the statements, the students are requested to determine which category (or categories) suits best. If the answer is correct, then the student moves on to the next question. If it is incorrect, they have the opportunity to try again. Once the mission is accomplished, the students receive the first digit of the PIN code (which they must write down) and return to the mission's map.

Figure 4. First mission: among the wreckage
Source: Screenshot from the breakout

Figure 5. Second mission: the monster in the forest
Source: Screenshot from the breakout

In the next mission, the students must go through the forest to answer three questions about the gamified teaching methodology. Two options are presented to the students and similarly to the previous mission, they have the opportunity for a second try in case the answer is not correct. When all the questions are completed, the second digit of the PIN code is provided, and they return to the missions map.

The third mission takes place in the jungle and deals with cooperative learning. The students are requested to match the name of three strategies within this methodology with their correct definition. There is a time limitation of 3 minutes to complete the mission; then, the solution is displayed so the students can check the correctness of their answers. Automatically, the third digit of the PIN code is provided, and they return to the mission's map.

The last mission takes place in one of the famous Dharma stations which were introduced by the previously mentioned "Lost" TV show. The students will have to face a test inspired by the famous TV quiz show 'Alphabetical', with relevant terms and vocabulary from the subject. For each of the letters of the alphabet they have to respond with a term that begins or contains the indicated letter, and two options are displayed. If the correct answer is selected then they move on to the next letter. If not, the game marks it and they are given a second opportunity.

The author considered to include a "Help" button as many of the students would complete the escape room asynchronously. However, the idea was finally rejected since all the missions enable the option of having as many attempts as needed to find out the correct answer. Even if the students fail a question, the activity is designed to provide feedback and allow them to solve it correctly. Eventually all the students should be able to conclude the escape-room with no additional support from the teacher.

Students know that there is an interesting final reward that increases their extrinsic motivation, although they do not know exactly what it is. It was decided not to reveal it so that there would be more intrigue to discover it. The reward is a real question to be included in the examination, which the students value very positively and helps them reducing the level of anxiety the exam generates, and it is delivered after successfully opening the lock,

Figure 6. Third mission: the jungle
Source: Screenshot from the breakout

Figure 7. Fourth mission: 'Alphabet'
Source: Screenshot from the breakout

The complete breakout can be accessed through this URL: https://tinyurl.com/escapelaisla

Table 1. Questions in the survey and their type

Question	Type
Did you carry out the activity synchronously (during the online session) or asynchronously (after the session finished)?	Close-ended
Have you ever participated in an educational breakout or escape room, in a virtual or face-to-face class?	Close-ended
Did you like participating in this breakout?	Close-ended
What did you like most about the breakout?	Open
What resources have you used to breakout?	Open
What adjectives best describe, in your opinion, this activity?	Close-ended
Give your opinion on the following statements	Likert scale
Write your general opinion about the breakout	Open

Source: Own elaboration

THE QUESTIONNAIRE

At the end of the learning experiences, students were asked to fill in a satisfaction survey, which was designed in Google Forms.

The instrument had a total of 9 questions; 4 of them where close-ended questions, in order to find out if they have carried out the activity synchronously (during the online session) or asynchronously (after the session finished) and also whether it was the first time they faced a learning experience like this.

The first question about their overall satisfaction was also close-ended, as well as a question suggesting some adjectives to describe the experience.

The questionnaire also included a question with a Likert scale with 5 response options (Disagree, Slightly agree, Agree, Neither agree nor disagree, Strongly agree) and 5 open questions to find out their opinion about the learning experience, which elements they liked best, what kind of resources they needed what aspects they would improve and their overall impression.

RESULTS

30 students out of 43 responded the anonymous questionnaire provided after the breakout. Results are very eloquent in terms of the students' engagement achieved in this kind of learning experience.

The excellent results of the satisfaction survey show how pleased the sample of students were with the experience. For most students (26 of them) it was the first time they faced a gamified experience of this format, which undoubtedly contributes to their satisfaction through the surprise factor it exerts on them. This, undoubtedly, contributes to increase the positive impact. It can be deduced a regular use of this type of methodology may be perceived as a routine, reducing the interest and motivation.

When asked whether they liked the activity all of them unanimously answered that they did. Among the reasons they gave to justify their answers, they highlighted the possibility of reviewing concepts in a dynamic way, the motivation they got from the story and the proposed challenges, as well as the opportunity to experience themselves a learning challenge that can serve as an example for their own

Figure 8. Have you ever participated in an educational breakout or escape room, in a virtual or face-to-face class?
Source: Own elaboration based on the questionnaire results.

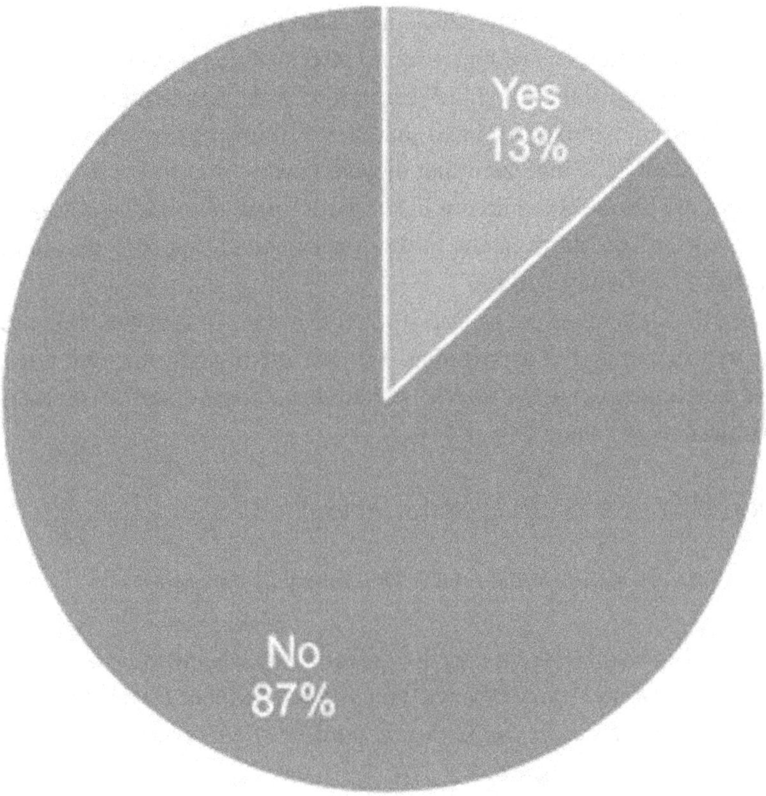

designing as teachers, as they can dare to use these interactive tools, and develop their own innovative content to enrich their lessons.

Regarding the perception of fun provided by the activity, 86.7% of the students (26) strongly agreed with the phrase 'It was fun to participate', and the remaining 13.3% (4) affirm simply agree.

Regarding the difficulty the participants have perceived in the educational experience, there are three questions that explore this aspect. On the one hand, the phrase "The game was too difficult", 18 of the students (60%) who responded to the survey indicated that they do not agree at all with the statement, while 20% showed little agreement. agreement. However, there were three participants who answered that they agreed, so it is necessary to consider that although it is not a majority opinion, 10% of the students who answered had a feeling of difficulty when facing the tests contained in the breakout.

Also finding out about the perceived difficulty level, 'I got stuck more than once and it was hard to move forward", with which 70% of those surveyed (21) indicated they did not agree at all and 10% somewhat agree. Finally, regarding the difficulty perception, the statement 'The breakout was too confusing' was proposed. All the students disagreed with it.

In terms of the usefulness students perceive, it is observed that the students consider the activity has helped them revise the important concepts facilitating their learning. Additionally, they express it has supported their ability to self-assess their level of knowledge on the subject.

When it comes to the statement 'This game has helped me review the concepts of the subject', 80% (24) strongly agreed, while 6 participants (20%) indicated they did not agree at all. This polarization of opinions regarding this question is striking, with no intermediate options.

Attending to the statement 'I think I could learn more about active methodologies through activities like this', 86.7% of the participants (26) stated that they strongly agree, while 6.7% said that they agree. On the other hand, another 6.7% indicated that they somewhat disagree with this statement.

Lastly, in terms of the phrase 'I would not like to participate in more activities like this and it did not helped me at all', 96.7% of the participants in the survey stated that they do not agree at all, and only one person answered they slightly agreed.

In general terms, the students express a very positive impression of the educational experience, and they highlight how entertaining the activity has been for them when reviewing the most relevant concepts. The idea of including a gamified activity to help the students' self-assessment process made a lot of sense in this subject, as the students point out:

'It gives us the possibility to clarify and improve learning'

'Very entertaining and very hand in hand with the identity of the student'

'I liked the way they designed it, it is an excellent resource to review topics. I really liked participating in this game, since it was very entertaining and educational. I found it very fun and interesting, I would like them to apply this type of tool in all classes as reinforcement. Thank you, it was great.'

'It was fun and refreshing. It helped me self-assess my knowledge'

'I did not think that this type of dynamic activities could be carried out through technological tools.'

'I have discovered a new tool and strategy of learning and teaching to learn.'

'It seems very appropriate to the subject we are learning.'

'It is good to know other alternatives and in this case the use of active methodologies is being applied, the use of technological tools, and the review is very successful.'

As mentioned before, one of the main objectives of this experience was offering inspiring examples for students so they dare to venture themselves into designing these learning experiences. Many of them also point out the relevance it has for them as teachers, since they want to be able to create similar content for their own classes. This also emphasizes the goal to inspire these educators to include what they have learned into their own classrooms.

'I have found it to be a very attractive method of evaluation, effective and I am really going to imitate it, and try something similar to be able to evaluate in my subject.'

Figure 9. Students' overall opinion word cloud
Source: Own elaboration through Jason Davies® word cloud generator.

'Finally I would like to thank you for sharing this very well designed example to exemplify the class.'

'I loved this experience. I find several uses for it: to review the topics of the subject and as an inspiration to use genially to create these learning experiences, since I limit myself to using it a lot to make presentations. It has given me light on all the tools that can be used with this tool. Thank you!'

'As I mentioned before, it's excellent. It is more I would like to learn to create a lot of content of this type.'

'Very interesting, I would like to learn how to apply it.'

'I loved the idea of the escape room in Genially, it was very creative and above all it is a very useful tool to review the concepts. It also inspires me to use this tool to create escape rooms for my classes.'

'I loved it, it generated a number of ideas that I can apply in my class I'm dying to try it and learn how to handle it.'

Students' overall impression is displayed in Figure 9, a word cloud created with their answers to this open question, originally in Spanish and not translated to keep their own words.

When answering the question about when they carried out the activity, most of the students said they carried out the activity asynchronously (25 of them) compared to 5 who carried it out during the class. This is something very common in the context of online teaching, which in fact encourages that a large part of the student's learning takes place asynchronously, since this also stimulates their autonomy and self-regulation.

Figure 10. Did you carry out the activity synchronously (during the online session) or asynchronously (after the session finished)?
Source: Own elaboration based on the questionnaire results.

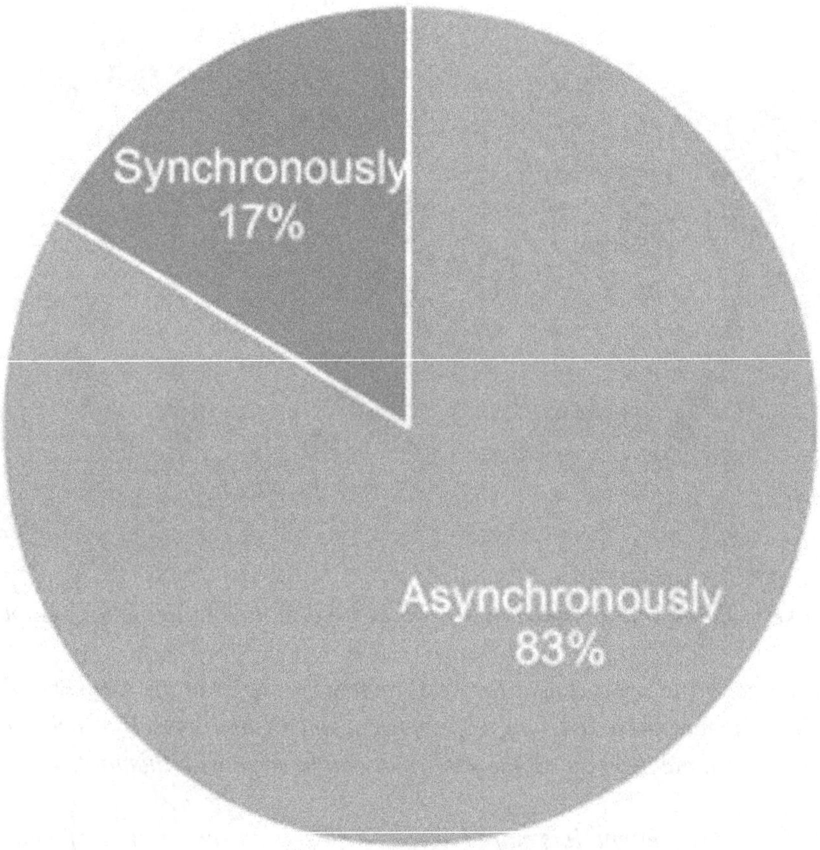

Students were given a list of adjectives to choose from to describe the experience. They could choose more than option, as well as adding other adjectives of their choice. The results are displayed in Figure 11.

DISCUSSION AND CONCLUSIONS

Undeniably, students receive enthusiastically this type of educational experiences because they take them out of the routine they are used to. Most educational systems are close to teacher-centered methodologies instead of student-centered, maybe because of overcrowded classrooms or escaping the dedication that an innovative teaching approach requires.

The European Higher Education Area is committed to active learning systems as a strategy to face the new socio-educational realities that students must face (Grande de Prado, García Martín, Baelo and Abella García, 2020).

Figure 11. Adjectives the students choose to describe the experience
Source: Own elaboration based on the questionnaire results.

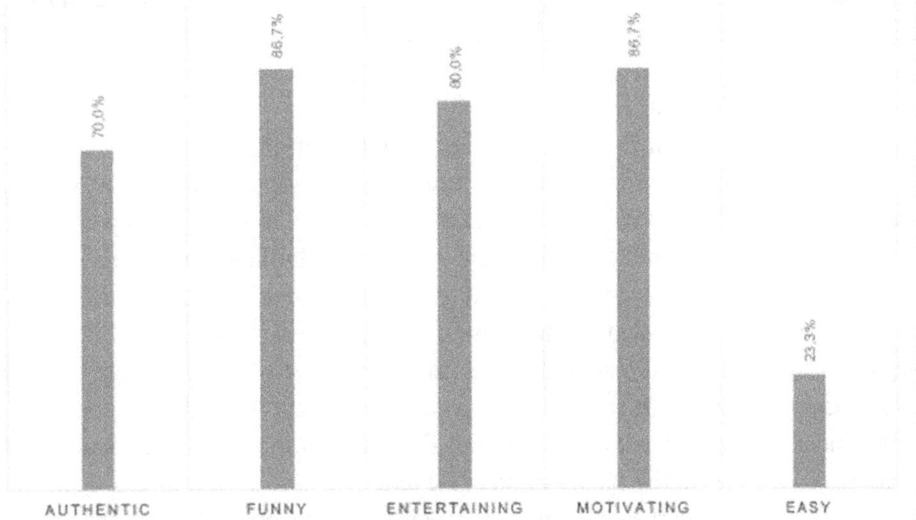

The application of active methodologies is especially relevant in the online teaching environment, where working on student motivation and engagement is indeed necessary. Information and Communication Technologies contribute to learning in a collaborative and creative way (Fernández and Valverde, 2014; Sierra-Daza and Fernández-Sánchez, 2017). Specifically, mobile learning implies a mode of e-learning or learning methodology mediated by devices such as mobile phones or tablets (Cruz and López, 2007; Fu and Hwang, 2018; Moreno-Martínez, Leiva and Matas, 2016). As Cruz and López (2007) state, mobile learning 'is a technological model, where the use of mobile devices is based on a previous instructional design, which must clearly define why, what for and how it will be used. this type of wireless technology'(p. 7).

Due to its potential in terms of didactics, active methodologies (and especially gamification) foster adaptation to different learning rhythms, by admitting mistakes, facilitating instant feedback and promoting creativity, which is confirmed by the results obtained in this learning experience. Similarly, gamification increases student engagement, as well as the amplification of knowledge provided by the socialization of learning (O'Donovan, Gain & Marais, 2013; Villagrasa & Durán, 2013).

Higher education can really benefit from active methodologies, and this is indeed confirmed by research, as most of the studies focus on gamification experiences in the field of higher education, representing 46% of primary research (De Sousa Borges, Durelli, Reis & Isotani, 2014).

After the process that reformed university teachings within the European Higher Education Area (EHEA), a new structure and curricular organization was created with the ECTS credits (European Credit Transfer and Accumulation System). It means highlighting the student's learning not online inside the classroom, but also outside it, and for this it is essential to encourage their autonomy and self-regulation (Rayón Rumayor, de las Heras Cuenca & Muñoz Martínez, 2011). This viewpoint is also paramount in the online learning environment.

Analyzing the cloud of words obtained from the general opinions about the activity (about which the last question of the questionnaire aims to investigate), it is remarkable the feeling of gratitude expressed by the students, since they value the dedication to develop this initiative. In addition, being teachers these Master's students, they are much more sensitive to the fact that teaching through active methodologies (in which the student has a leading role) requires a much greater effort and dedication from the teacher than delivering masterclasses. The preparation of teaching materials requires creativity, resources and skills in the field of instructional design, which undoubtedly exceed the mere expert exposition of the topics contained in the curriculum.

Attending to the prospective of this line of research and given the fact this is the first escape room designed by the author after receiving specialized training, it may be improved and evolved according to the feedback received from the students who take part on it. The learning experience could be expanded by including more tests, and could even be enriched with other educational resources, such as more videos, more interactive tests and a longer duration. Quite possibly an experience with all these elements would favor the achievement of the 'flow state' by the students.

The described experience was designed to be carried out individually though, as pointed out by Rouse (2017), learning based on this methodology can extensively benefit by means of a cooperative learning environment, so next experiences should be designed taking this into account, so that students can collaborate in order to solve the puzzles and achieve a much more meaningful learning together.

In addition, it should be remarked that the very positive results obtained, and the satisfaction of the students has inspired the direction of the Master's degree in Educational Innovation to implement a the same methodology in the rest of the subjects, including an escape room to carry out a general review of the concepts at the end of each of them. Teachers from the other subjects are expected to design the learning experience, with the help of the Master's degree leadership, as they probably won't be familiar with this technique. So this initiative has paved the way to follow a new methodology in the study, as it is its aim is to bring educational innovation not only in the contents, but also in the methods developed inside of the classrooms.

REFERENCES

Becker, K., & Parker, J. (2014). An Overview of Game Design Techniques. In K. Schrier (Ed.), *Learning, education and games. Volume one: Curricular and design considerations* (pp. 179–198). Carnegie Mellon University.

Bellotti, F., Kapralos, B., Lee, K., Moreno-Ger, P., & Berta, R. (2013). Assessment in and of serious games: An overview. *Advances in Human-Computer Interaction, 2013*, 2013. doi:10.1155/2013/136864

Borrego, C., Fernández, C., Blanes, I., & Robles, S. (2017). Room escape at class: Escape games activities to facilitate the motivation and learning in computer science. *JOTSE, 7*(2), 162–171. doi:10.3926/jotse.247

Budgen, D. (2003). *Software design* (2nd ed.). Addison-Wesley.

Cruz, R. & López, G. (2007). Una visión general del m-learning y su proceso de adopción en el esquema educativo [An overview of m-learning and its adoption process in the educational scheme]. *2º Coloquio Internacional: Tendencias Actuales de Cómputo e Informática en México.*

Csikszentmihalyi, M. (1975). *Beyond boredom and anxiety*. Jossey-Bass.

De Sousa Borges, S., Durelli, V. H., Reis, H. M., & Isotani, S. (2014). A systematic mapping on gamification applied to education. *Proceedings of the 29th annual ACM symposium on applied computing*, 216-222. 10.1145/2554850.2554956

Eukel, H., & Morrell, B. (2021). Ensuring educational escape-room success: The process of designing, piloting, evaluating, redesigning, and re-evaluating educational escape rooms. *Simulation & Gaming*, *52*(1), 18–23. doi:10.1177/1046878120953453

Fernández, M. R., & Valverde, J. (2014). A Community of Practice: An Intervention Model based on Computer Supported Collaborative Learning. *Comunicar: Media Education Research Journal*, *21*(42), 97–105. doi:10.3916/C42-2014-09

Franco, P. F., & DeLuca, D. A. (2019). Learning through action: Creating and implementing a strategy game to foster innovative thinking in higher education. *Simulation & Gaming*, *50*(1), 23–43. doi:10.1177/1046878118820892

Fu, Q. K., & Hwang, G. J. (2018). Trends in mobile technology-supported collaborative learning: A systematic review of journal publications from 2007 to 2016. *Computers & Education*, *119*, 129–143. doi:10.1016/j.compedu.2018.01.004

Fullerton, T. (2008). *Game design workshop: A playcentric approach to creating innovative games*. Morgan Kaufman. doi:10.1201/b13172

Grande-de-Prado, M., García-Martín, S., Baelo, R., & Abella-García, V. (2020). Edu-Escape Rooms. *Encyclopedia*, *1*(1), 12–19. doi:10.3390/encyclopedia1010004

Hirumi, A., Appelman, B., Rieber, L., & Eck, R. V. (2010). Preparing Instructional Designers for Game-Based Learning: Part 1. *TechTrends*, *54*(3).

Institute of Play. (2014). *Q Design pack, Games and Learning*. http://www.instituteofplay.org/work/projects/q-design-packs/q-games-and-learning-design-pack/

Iuppa, N., & Borst, T. (2010). *End-to-end Game Development: Creating Independent Serious Games and simulations from start to finish*. Elsevier, Focal Press.

Koster, R. (2005). *A Theory of Fun for Game Design*. Paraglyph Press.

Laerke Weitze, C. (2014). Developing Goals and Objectives for Gameplay and Learning. In K. Schrier (Ed.), *Learning, education and games. Volume one: Curricular and design considerations*. Carnegie Mellon University.

López-Pernas, S., Gordillo, A., Barra, E., & Quemada, J. (2019a). Analyzing learning effectiveness and students' perceptions of an educational escape room in a programming course in higher education. *IEEE Access: Practical Innovations, Open Solutions*, *7*, 184221–184234. doi:10.1109/ACCESS.2019.2960312

López-Pernas, S., Gordillo, A., Barra, E., & Quemada, J. (2019b). Examining the use of an educational escape room for teaching programming in a higher education setting. *IEEE Access: Practical Innovations, Open Solutions*, *7*, 31723–31737. doi:10.1109/ACCESS.2019.2902976

Macías-Guillén, A., Díez, R. M., Serrano-Luján, L., & Borrás-Gené, O. (2021). Educational Hall Escape: Increasing Motivation and Raising Emotions in Higher Education Students. *Education Sciences, 11*(9), 527. doi:10.3390/educsci11090527

Moreno, E. (2019). El "Breakout EDU" como herramienta clave para la gamificación en la formación inicial de maestros/as [The "Breakout EDU" as a key tool for gamification in the initial training of teachers]. *EDUTEC. Revista electrónica de tecnología educativa*, (67), 66-79.

Moreno-Martínez, N., Leiva, J. J., & Matas, A. (2016). Mobile learning, Gamificación y Realidad Aumentada para la enseñanza-aprendizaje de idiomas [Mobile learning, Gamification and Augmented Reality for language teaching-learning]. *International Journal of Educational Research and Innovation, 6*, 16–34.

Murphree, C., & Vafa, S. S. (2020). Use of escape rooms in education. In *Society for Information Technology & Teacher Education International Conference*. Association for the Advancement of Computing in Education (AACE).

Negre i Walczak, C. (2017). 'BreakoutEdu', microgamificación y aprendizaje significativo ['BreakoutEdu', microgamification and meaningful learning]. *Educaweb*. https://www.educaweb.com/noticia/2017/07/26/breakoutedu-microgamificacion-aprendizaje-significativo-15068/

Neumann, K. L., Alvarado-Albertorio, F., & Ramírez-Salgado, A. (2020). Online approaches for implementing a digital escape room with preservice teachers. *Journal of Technology and Teacher Education, 28*(2), 415–424.

O'Donovan, S., Gain, J., & Marais, P. (2013). A case study in the gamification of a university-level games development course. *Proceedings of the South African Institute for Computer Scientists and Information Technologists Conference*, 242-251. 10.1145/2513456.2513469

Onecha-Pérez, B., Sanz-Prat, J., & López-Valdés, D. (2019). Los límites de la ludificación en la enseñanza de la arquitectura. La técnica del Escape Room [The limits of gamification in the teaching of architecture. The Escape Room technique]. *ZARCH: Journal of Interdisciplinary Studies in Architecture and Urbanism*, (12), 122-133.

Pérez-López, I., & García Rivera, E. (2017). Formar docentes, formar personas: Análisis de los aprendizajes logrados por estudiantes universitarios desde una experiencia de [Train teachers, train people: analysis of the learning achieved by university students from an experience of]. *Signo y Pensamiento, 70*(36), 112–129. doi:10.11144/Javeriana.syp36-70.fdfp

Rayón Rumayor, L., de las Heras Cuenca, A. M., & Muñoz Martínez, Y. (2011). La creación y gestión del conocimiento en la enseñanza superior: La autonomía, autorregulación y cooperación en el aprendizaje [Train teachers, train people: analysis of the learning achieved by university students from an experience of]. *Revista Iberoamericana de Educación Superior*, *2*(4), 103–122.

Rouse, W. (2017). Lessons learned while escaping from a zombie: Designing a Breakout EDU game. *The History Teacher, 50*(4), 553–564.

Salen, K., & Zimmerman, E. (2004). *Rules of play: Game design fundamentals*. MIT Press.

Sanchez, E., & Plumettaz-Sieber, M. (2018). Teaching and learning with escape games from debriefing to institutionalization of knowledge. In *International conference on games and learning alliance*. Springer.

Santamaría, A. & Alcalde, E. (2019). Escaping from the English classroom. Who will get out first? *Aloma: revista de psicologia, ciències de l'educació i de l'esport Blanquerna, 37*(2), 83-92.

Sierra Daza, M. C., & Fernández-Sánchez, M. R. (2019). Gamificando el aula universitaria. Análisis de una experiencia de Escape Room en educación superior [Train teachers, train people: analysis of the learning achieved by university students from an experience of]. *Revista de estudios y experiencias en educación, 18*(36), 105-115.

Veldkamp, A., Daemen, J., Teekens, S., Koelewijn, S., Knippels, M. C. P., & Van Joolingen, W. R. (2020). Escape boxes: Bringing escape room experience into the classroom. *British Journal of Educational Technology, 51*(4), 1220–1239. doi:10.1111/bjet.12935

Villagrasa, S., & Duran, J. (2013). Gamification for learning 3D computer graphics arts. *Proceedings of the First International Conference on technological ecosystem for enhancing multiculturality*, 429-433. 10.1145/2536536.2536602

KEY TERMS AND DEFINITIONS

Active Methodologies: A methodology formed by a set of pedagogical strategies that force students to play an active role in their learning process during classroom activities.

Breakout: A break from a restraining condition or situation, such as an escape from prison, not necessarily physical lockdown.

Escape Room: A room in which people are locked playing a game which requires them to solve a series of puzzles with a time limit in order to find the key to unlock the room.

Gamification: The application of typical elements of game playing (e.g., point scoring, competition with others, rules) to other areas of activity, such as education.

Innovation: The action or process of making changes in something established, especially by introducing new methods, ideas, or products.

Learning Experience: Any interaction, course, program, in which learning occurs, regardless of where it takes place.

Online Education: A type of education which is delivered and administered using the internet.

Self-Assessment: The assessment or evaluation of oneself or one's actions, attitudes, or performance.

Chapter 8
Maruxaina:
The Sea Nymph Who Will Be Judged

Beatriz Lopez- Bermudez
Universidad Internacional de La Rioja, Spain

Lara Mata Martinez
Universidad Internacional de La Rioja, Spain

ABSTRACT

Educational innovation methods are of vital importance for the competency-based learning process. This escape room has been designed for a quantitative subject in social science degrees taught at an online university. Quantitative subjects, such as statistics, present for these students certain difficulties due to their great theoretical-practical load. The design of the escape room uses a popular legend as the basis of the storytelling, structured in a video presentation and four missions. Each mission is related to a unit of the syllabus and has been developed according to continuous evaluation and as a revision element for the exam. The introduction of this resource has shown very positive results, increasing the success rate of students, with a very high net promoter index and very positive individualized comments from students.

INTRODUCTION

The students of social sciences and especially in economics and business studies show great motivation in subjects with content on business strategy and fundamentals of economics. However, quantitative subjects generate great concern and fear in these students. In addition, as it is an online university in the first class of statistics, we asked students the feelings they have about this subject with one word, and 80% answered: "worried". Also, we have realized in more than four years of teaching statistics that students need to be guided and motivated in each class. Besides, it's easier for us (professors) to follow the acquisition of knowledge if we continuously monitored the acquisition of the contents throughout the whole course.

For this reason, this 2021-2022 academic year we have introduced gamified resources as a methodology to improve the skills education process. In the previous course, competitive quizzes have been

DOI: 10.4018/978-1-6684-6081-8.ch008

introduced through online tests in live sessions as a pilot test. These quizzes have generated very positive results among the students. Paniagua and Istance (2018) has identified gamification as a method of innovation that can be introduced in various sectors, among which we highlight education. Therefore, with this process, we intend to motivate students with a dynamic resource that helps them review theoretical concepts. For the correct use and resolution of the gamification, we will use different software resources, such as Genially (2022), Google Forms (2022) all of them have free access, although premium accounts are required for some specific details.

The strategy of gamification proposed is focused on the review sessions planned on the subject of Statistics in three degrees: Marketing, Finance and Accounting, and Business at the Universidad Internacional de la Rioja. We have a two-phase implementation schedule program. The first phase is designed synchronously to facilitate the monitoring of the students' evolution and increase motivation. Then, we open the possibility of an asynchronous way posted on the forum of Statistics. The asynchronous path was done with a previous breakout, but only a few students have done it. The limited success of this previous breakout was due to the fact that the whole exercise was proposed the week previous to the exam. This escape room takes up what was learned in the previous pilot and improves the presentation, missions, and implementation of it.

The main objective is to see if the online escape room has a direct impact on greater motivation, less fear, and, therefore, greater acquisition of concepts and practical development of the subject. For this purpose, a popular legend is used as the main story through which four missions have been structured to match with the review sessions of the subject. The story is about a sea nymph living on the coast of northwestern Spain, in a town of sailors. The population is divided between whether the nymph is kind, warning the sailors of rough seas and therefore alerting them, or mean, causing them to be shipwrecked. Therefore, the population needs a neutral soul that drinks the concoction to be able to judge and solve the problem. The student will have to sentence the nymph by drinking a concoction that it will be prepared with the rewards (ingredients) of each mission.

To evaluate the escape room, we will be used different KPIs. The first one will be to compare the grades of students from the previous year in the same subject in the same degree. The second indicator will be obtained by using the statistics of visualization of each breakout compared to the students that took the exam. Finally, the third indicator will be collected with a survey, asking students their feedback on satisfaction and improvements. Different strategies have been developed depending on the degree we are introducing the escape room. The results do not show relevant differences in the two strategies, but it can be affirmed that the students have used it as a revision resource. In the first strategy, the students have been presented with the resource in May, while in the second it has been presented in June. However, the high point of the escape room query was in the last week of June, coinciding with the week before the exam. The main results of the escape room show a high success among students.

Thus, this chapter is structured in four parts, this introduction, the second part a development of the literature on gamification using new technologies as an innovative element in higher education; the third part develops the escape room with a detailed explanation; the fourth, develops and points out the timing and, finally, the results, conclusions, and bibliographical references are presented.

BACKGROUND

Gamification can be designed as the application of digital game elements in non-game contexts to motivate the behavior used (Educause, 2011; Bai et al. 2020). Huotari and Hamari (2012) highlight the role of gamification in invoking the same psychological experiences generally as games. Gamification has emerged across industries and disciplines as a way to engage users in non-game contexts using techniques derived from video game design. There are multiple literature reviews on gamification in different sectors, but in this case, we will focus on the education sector. Not surprisingly, gamification has been extensively addressed and implemented in this field, where supporting and retaining engagement is a constant challenge. Gamification in education and learning most often uses possibilities that signal achievement and progress (Huang et al., 2020), while social and immersion-oriented possibilities are much less common. Several researchers identified that gamification has the potential to have a positive impact on user performance, productivity, and engagement (Simoes et al., 2013). By implementing the gamification method, students will learn from academic materials with the use of game elements and will adapt to different learning styles (Arockiyasamy, Surendheran & Bullard, 2016; McGrath & Bayerlein, 2013). Thus, since the implementation in Europe of the European Higher Education Space, which is characterized by a great weight in education in competencies and innovation, gamification is a key resource. It manages, from a dynamic perspective, to transmit the theory of a higher education subject from a perspective of applied and developed skills by the students.

Although there is a lot of research on gamification, there is a lack of studies that show the assessment of the adequacy of such interventions with this type of tools and classroom strategies for the acquisition of Social Science content (Gómez-Trigueros, 2019). The implementation of gamified strategies in the classroom requires, as it has already been pointed out, systematization of the process in order for the methodology to achieve its intended objectives (Gómez-Trigueros, 2019). Also, when designing a gamification process it is necessary to consider different aspects such as quests, badges and awards, points and experience, leader boards, collaboration, levels, avatars, timed activity, storytelling, responsive feedback, competition, adaptivity, and non-linear navigation (Huang et al., 2020). Video games applied to formal educational settings hypothetically aim to engage students in deeper learning processes and experiences, optimistically leading to better student learning outcomes (Majuri et al., 2018). In other words, it is necessary to introduce the concepts of the subject in terms of content, time, etc. and, at the same time, it is essential to identify common elements of gamification. Among the common elements of the game, it is necessary to highlight badges, challenges, classification/ranking, levels/unlocking, history, points, progress bar, or avatars (Giannetto et al., 2013; Huang & Hwe, 2018; Richter et al., 2015; Sailer et al., 2017). However, not all gamification design elements have the same effect on student learning outcomes (Huang et al. 2020). The gamified learning environment allows feedback to be presented uniquely, as feedback can be carefully coordinated with the narrative and goals of the task.

In this escape room, we use two of the most relevant and valued resources by the students. First, quests, missions, or modules, are resources to organize the game into significant parts so that users clearly understand how to complete each task. In this case, the gamified educational environment is made up of multiple units, which can be called quests, missions, tasks or modules, etc. They are structured in sequence or a non-linear approach. Completion of these units meets the desired learning objectives. And, narrative or storytelling, quests, missions, or modules all involve some form of narrative structure, a clear goal, and are often part of a larger progression model. Narrative refers to the way events unfold as the user plays through the gamified system. A gamified environment begins with an authentic context for a series of missions, tasks, or modules. It can be fleshed out with a narrative before the user progresses to a new mission, task, or module (Huang et al, 2020). Care to consider gamification design elements beyond "chunk" such as collaboration and quests/missions/modules when designing/implementing gamification learning environments.

Today's students are digital natives (Prensky, 2001) and require new and innovative methodologies. Sanchez-Caballé et al. (2020) describe this generation as having a marked digital literacy and a constant need to be connected. Through technological advances that enable more digitized learning environments, as well as the use of, for example, the technical possibilities developed around video games to create immersive and engaging learning experiences, the trend of gamification of education and learning has been on the rise.

Gamification in the present study is the application of the characteristics of video games applied to formal educational environments. Educational settings are hypothesized to engage students in deeper learning processes and experiences, optimistically leading to better student learning outcomes (Cózar-Gutiérrez y Sáez-López, 2016). While this is not an entirely new concept in education, the advent of modern information and communication technologies (eg smartphones) has propelled the concept into reality in many different types of educational settings. Landers' (2014) theory of gamified learning to frame the research problem account for important educational variables and operationalize gamification according to theory and practice. Preparing students for learning a new culture imposed by our virtual era (Adell & Castañeda, 2012) is a challenge for educators and it forces us to rethink the goals of education (Mishra et al. 2020).

There are gamification processes where the results have not been as good as expected since they were treated as ordinary technology users. However, in this escape room, the barrier of the classic is broken since it is online delivery. In addition, different resources are used, such as Excel, Forms, and Genially, which enhance the student's sense of innovation and manage to apply and develop specific and generic skills in their learning. The implementation of gamification elements on the website would increase user motivation and enhance engagement during the learning process, as well as allow users to use the website for a long-term period.

THE ESCAPE ROOM

The Escape Room by Missions

This escape room is inspired by a popular legend, based on the existence of a sea nymph who lives on an island on the coast of northern Galicia (Spain). The myth said that some days this mermaid is shown as a beautiful creature, with long blonde hair, and on other days she looks like an ugly witch with sunken eyes that seems to catch you with her fingers. Because of this, the villagers are divided among those who believe that she has good behavior, and she warns of the storms and dangers of the sea. But some assure that her intention is sinister, that she is envious of the wives of the sailors. Every year, on the second Saturday of August the locals go out to capture her, bring her to land, and carry out a trial to decide if during that year she has been guilty or guiltless. If it has been good, it will be danced with until dawn and if it has been bad, it will be burnt.

The assembly of the escape room is in the Genially software, it organizes as a presentation of 51 slides. In addition, Excel and Forms resources are used for some of the tests and as support to perform

Figure 1. Missions of the escape room

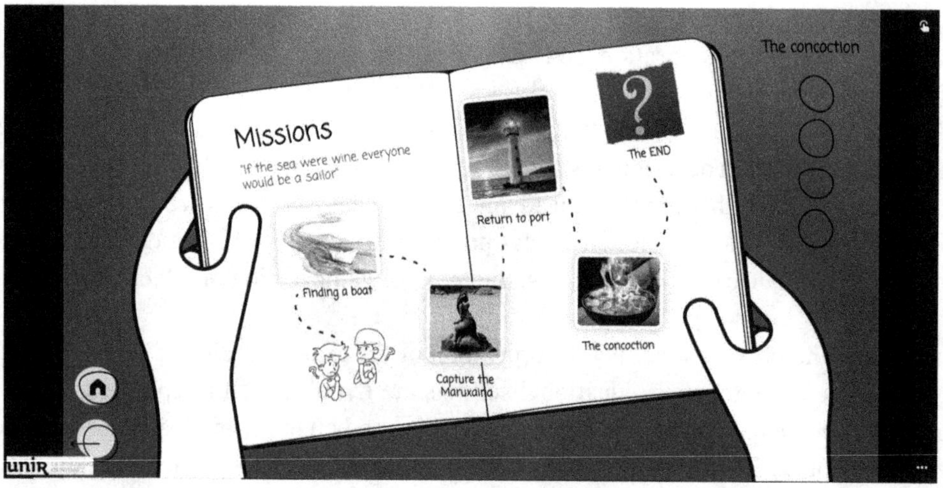

the mathematical calculations. We guarantee in this way that the students are able to develop the concepts in a practical way and they do not advance without achieving the correct results, as many of the missions have codes to be able to advance.

Based on the myth the escape room is created and structured in four missions (Figure 1). The first mission is called "finding a boat"; the second mission is to "capture the Maruxaina"; the third mission is to "return to port" and, finally, the fourth mission is to drink "the concoction". On each mission, the students will obtain an ingredient to prepare the final concoction that they have to mix and drink.

The structure of the escape room is aligned with the syllabus of the subject of Statistics. This subject is divided into 7 units; thus, the first mission corresponds to the first two units about types of variables and descriptive statistics; the second mission with unit three, that is, on the linear regression; mission three with unit four which compiles analyzes and indicators of temporary variables, and finally mission four corresponds to the last units because they are very interrelated with the evaluation and correct graphical representations according to the type of variable and creation of dashboards.

Before starting the missions, the students have a video with a short explanation of the legend to attract them to start the escape room.

Mission One: Finding a Boat

Finding a boat is the first mission that consists of carrying out the "fisherman's net" test. Once the students completed the mission they will obtain the first ingredient of the concoction, the bottle with crystal liquid.

The fisherman's net (Figure 2) presents different letters on its knots. The first step is to download an Excel file, which includes 3 tabs with three-variable frequency distribution tables so that students can carry out the analysis that has been explained in the first two units of the statistics syllabus. One of the variables is qualitative, the other in intervals, and the last one quantitative without intervals, to cover the different types explained.

This mission requires the teacher to guide the students, that is, the best way to solve this first mission is synchronous. In this way, the escape room is presented to all the teachers which will motivate them to start practicing the first mission. The first step is to download the data in Excel. Next, students should

Figure 2. Fisherman's net

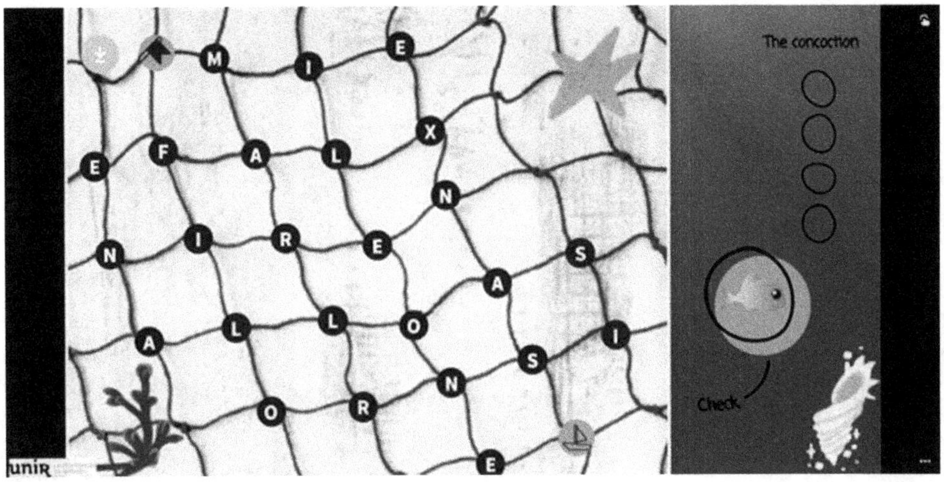

focus on the knots with letters, in each one, there is a question. To know the correct answer the student should assess the value in the Excel file and then search for the answer in the knots(letters) connected with the letter there are answering. Each question appears in blue, and each answer appears in green. When the student found the correct answer in green, they have the next question to advance in blue in the same box.

For example, the first question (Flag bottom) "What is the proportion of Faroese-flagged boats?" has the correct answer in node "F" with the value of "0.0095". This result leads the students to another question "What is the value of mode in relation to the boats' flags?" (Figure 3). To answer the 9 questions proposed across the net, the students will review the following calculations: understand the cumulative absolute frequency; median; mean and median with a variable in intervals; typical deviation; quartiles; and Fisher's skewness coefficient.

It is important to remark that students must write down on a piece of paper the letters on the knots that are solving the fisherman's net. The final code "FARILLONS" will be used to check if the students have correctly solved the questions. If it is correct the check box leads students to the reward, the crystal liquid for the concoction.

Mission Two: Capture the Maruxaina

Mission two is one of the most difficult from the story and statistics concepts perspective. Therefore, this mission will be solved in a group session. The class will be divided into three groups, and each of them will select one of the three types of fish. Each fish leads the students to a personalized slide with data and questions (Figure 4). The first part of this mission can be done synchronously or asynchronously. However, to complete this mission, students must communicate with each other, and therefore, synchronous completion is recommended. This mission uses the concepts of unit three of the statistical syllabus such as linear regression estimation, covariance, coefficient of determination, and coefficient of correlation.

As an example, we have a group that has chosen the manta ray, so they will move to their specific questions (Figure 5). The first step will be to download the data in Excel, and the second is to open the questionnaire. To complete the mission students should assess concepts such as the covariance, the

Figure 3. Example of the questions and answers on the Fisherman's net

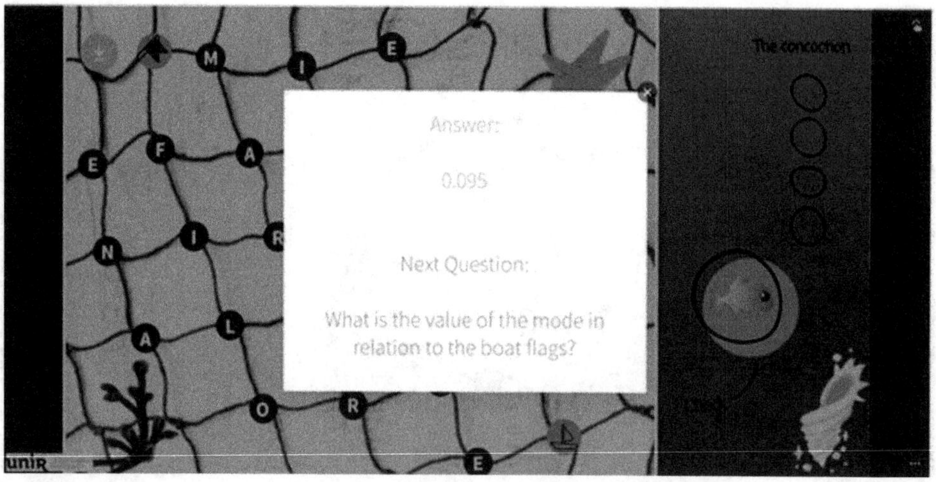

mean, the correlation relation, and the linear regression. Thus, the data provides ten values of dimension (variable X) and weight (variable Y) of the ray fish variety. To obtain the code that unlocks the next part of the mission, the first value of each question (form) must be registered.

When the students advance to the next screen, they believe that they will obtain the next ingredient, but Figure 6 appears. This part requires all three class groups to communicate and share their results. To solve this question each group would assess the coefficient of determination of the linear regression. If students don't want to communicate to their colleagues, they would solve the questions about the three types of fish. Once the students solve this last question the reward appears, in this case, the second ingredient for the concoction is citrus.

Figure 4. Choose your team to capture the Maruxaina

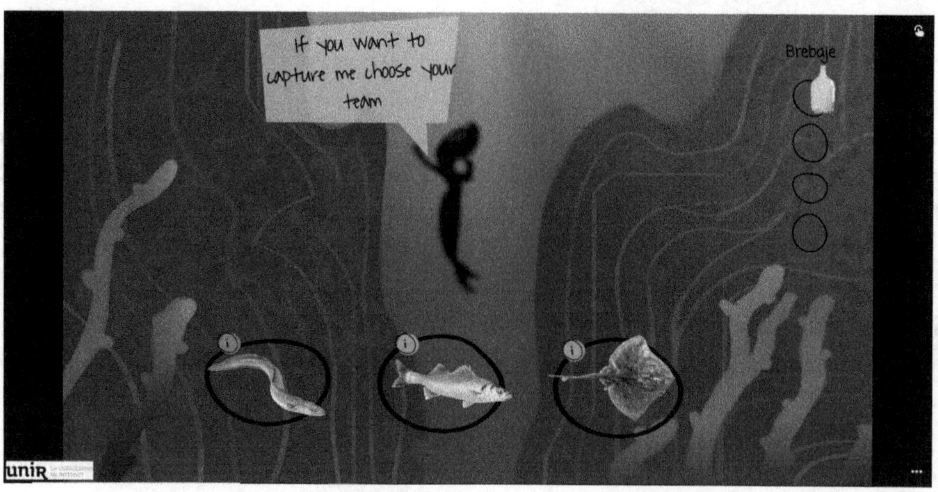

Figure 5. Manta ray group quiz

Mission Three: Return to Port

Return to port is the third mission, where the students are on a boat and each correct question brings the boat closer to land (Figure 7). There are ten questions about unit four of the syllabus. So, questions are related to temporal analysis, variation rates, index number analysis, and real versus nominal prices. Before starting the questions, the data are provided in an Excel file with the values of the period, prices of two species of fish, and the general prices index. Each question has three possible options. If the answer is wrong students can go back to that question again, and if the answer is correct, they will progress to the next one. Once the ten questions are correct, students will be rewarded with the third ingredient to prepare the concoction, coffee.

This type of mission can be raised asynchronously or synchronously. On the other hand, for future applications and improvements, a timer and a competition-type scheme can be included with the use of

Figure 6. The second part of the capture of the Maruxaina

Figure 7. Start if return to the port mission

resources such as Quizizz (2022). Synchronous competitions have been used in online sessions outside of this escape room, and the results are very satisfactory as it significantly increases student motivation.

Mission Four: The Concoction

The concoction mission is divided into three parts. In the first one, there are four multiple choice questions. If students complete the questions correctly, they will be rewarded with the fourth ingredient, sugar. Then, to mix the ingredients students should solve a crossword, and finally, they will debate about a dashboard to mix and drink the concoction.

This mission has been structured according to the main objectives of the units of the subject. The three objectives are: to evaluate the adequacy of the graphical representations, to identify each of them by name, and to be able to evaluate a dashboard (variables, graphics, content, etc.)

In the first four questions, the students should evaluate the graphical representations, whether they are correct or not, and what errors are identified. Questions have four possible answers, with only one correct. These four questions are related two by two, that is, each pair of questions is made on the same graphic representation. Firstly, the students have to evaluate if it is correct and then identify errors regarding the adequacy of the graph, variables, and data.

The next phase is the crossword (Figure 8) where students will put on the boxes the name of the graphics. It is about identifying the name of the graphs and, if it is done synchronously in a session, students are asked to identify the types of variables that could be used in each of them. In the crossword you can see squares of different colors, these letters will form the key to advancing to the last phase of the mission. This is an example of the use of codes to control that students do not skip parts of the mission and that it is a scheduled review of concepts.

This code unlocks the last part of the mission that presents a dashboard and questions about it (Figure 9). Each question has its answer on a later screen, that is, in this part, answers are not thought to be true or false because needs a further explanation with the answer.

This part of the escape room is the most complex to do asynchronously, so a discussion during the session is highly valuable. Each question can have more than one correct solution, and for this reason, it

Figure 8. The crossword

is important to listen to all the ideas of the students. It is important to emphasize that students must have an answer in the escape room that guides them a posteriori and that manages to synthesize the key points of the correct answer. For this reason, there are two screens, the first has the questions with a dashboard to analyze, and then, a specific one where each question has an answer appears with general lines.

Once the fourth mission is finished, students will advance to "the end" part of the map (Figure 10). In this part, students found a congratulated message and a survey to give their feedback about the escape room. During the whole escape room, in the rewards slides, we use images as gifts. And in the final slide, there is a song to cheer up students, in particular these elements help to connect with younger generations.

In addition, we take advantage of the last part of the mission to remind students that this tool is key to reviewing the subject for the final exam. Thus, the key points of the program are found in the resources, and the Excel program, employed during the escape room can be used to solve the exam. Finally, the escape room improvement questionnaire is included to obtain anonymous feedback from the students.

Figure 9. The debate about the dashboard

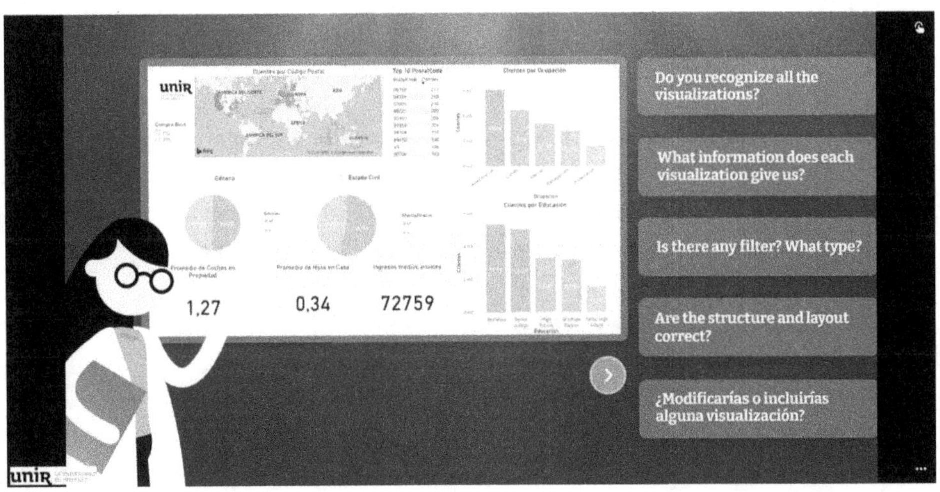

Figure 10. Final slide with congratulations

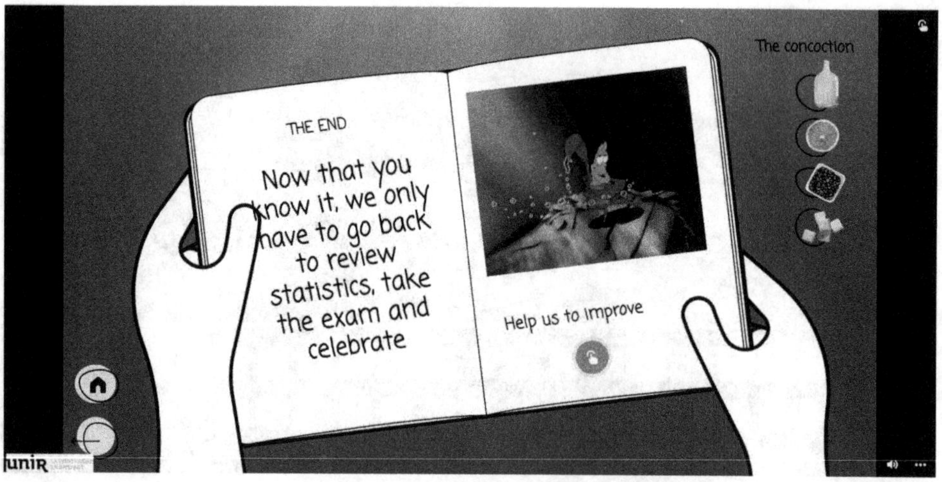

Timing

The escape room has been developed for the subject of Statistics for the degrees of Marketing, Business Administration and Management (Business), and Finance and Accounting (Accounting). Two different strategies have been applied to introduce the escape room.

During the 15 weeks of the teaching course, there are 5 review sessions used for the students to reinforce the theoretical concepts. The first strategy was to introduce the escape room from the first review session in the sixth week. The first strategy was employed in Marketing and Accounting. In contrast, the escape room was presented to the students in the last 4 weeks of the course in the Business Degree.

Hence, the first strategy request to open just one mission at a time and block the following ones, because not all the topics have been taught, so we managed to guide the students in the review. In the Business degree, the escape room was completely open from the day we published the resource. In this case, it is used as a global review, and it is explained that each mission works with different units and the student, although they must do it in order, can choose to alternate the missions. In addition, it is important to highlight that the escape room is part of the methodology developed in Statistics. The entire course is structured around 40% continuous assessment and 60% final exam. The test of each unit and three activities take part in the continuous evaluation. The continuous assessment is designed to complete within 11 weeks.

Then from 12 to 15 weeks, the focus is on review sessions with the escape room. The structure of the escape room is related to the exam, this means that the escape room has four missions related to the same units as the four exercises of the examen. This helps students to review statistics and at the same time feel more comfortable when they face the exam because the type of questions and exercises are similar.

RESULTS AND FUTURE RESEARCH DIRECTIONS

To assess the effectiveness of the escape room we have used different parameters (Table 1). First, is the success rate which is calculated as the number of students who passed the exam among the students who

Table 1. KPIs results for evaluation

Degree		Business	Accounting	Marketing
Success rate	2021-2022	75,8%	94,6%	75,8%
	2020-2021	73%	92%	70%
Visualizations stats the week before the exam		159	74	68
Visualizations stats after the exam		292	125	106
How many missions do you complete? (answer all)		87,5%	70,30	62%
How do you rate the experience of using this resource? (Being 1 = very bad and 5 = very good)		4,58	4,95	4,88
Do you consider that the use of this type of interactive resources can contribute to improve learning in subjects of a quantitative nature? (Being 1 = nothing and 5 = a lot)		4,87	4,95	4,88
Net promoter index		87,5	92,31%	100%

took it. Second, we have the visualization values of the escape room in each of the degrees and, finally, a survey to compile students' feedback.

The results of the success rate will be compared with that of previous years. On the other hand, the survey has a total of five short questions. In the first question, students must answer how many missions they have completed in the escape room. In the second question, they are asked to rate between 1 and 5 how they value the escape room experience (1 is the lowest score and 5 is the highest). The third question with values between 1 and 5 asks them to assess the use of this type of resource to favor the learning process of quantitative subjects. The fourth question is to generate the net promoter index and therefore if they would recommend this type of resource to future partners. The net promoter index measures the likelihood of the students of Statistic to promote the subject through new students. To obtain the net promoter index, students were asked to rate between 0 and 10, the values 9 and 10 are taken as promoters, the values 7 and 8 passive, and from 0 to 6 detractors. Finally, the last question is open so they can comment on how they would improve the escape room.

In the Business Degree, 95 students took the examen, and 72 passed it, so, the success rate was 75,8%. The success rate has improved in comparison with previous years. We should exclude the second term of 2019-2020, because of the compulsory lockdown due to COVID-19 pandemic. During the 2020-2021 course the success rate was 73%, 2019-2020 was 81,1% and 2018-2019 was 69.2%.

Also, the visualizations of the escape room were 292 by the end of the course, considering 95 students took it. We must remember that in the Business Degree we present the escape room since week eleven, this first week the visits were 62 and before the exam week, the visualizations were 159. It seems that the students have used the resource to review on more than one occasion. Other explanation implies the student has not solved the escape room at once, he entered on different occasions to solve each of the missions.

The student feedback collects by the survey shows that 87,5% of students complete the whole escape room. To the question about how the students rate the experience of using this resource? from 1 to 5, the average was 4,58. And, for the question about if they consider the utilization of escape rooms to improve learning from 1 to 5, the average was 4,87. Finally, we assess the net promoter index which was 87,5%.

In the Accounting degree, 35 students pass the examen from a total of 37 who have taken it. The success rate is 94,6%. Students with a Accounting degree are known for achieving a high success rate, but the record has been reached this year. In the 2020-2021 year the rate was 92%, in 2019-2020 was 93%; and, 91% in 2018-2019.

Regarding visualizations, the first part of the escape room, when they only have access to the first mission has 22 visualizations that value increases to 74 until the week before the exam. Also, we want to highlight that class attendance in these weeks has been low, around 10 students on average. The escape room closes with a total of 125 visualizations once the exam has passed. This value practically reaches the students presented for the exam (37) for the four missions, a total of 148 hypothetical visualizations. In the direct feedback survey, results show that 70,30% completed the escape room. To the questions about how the students rate the experience and if the escape room improves their learning process the average results for each question was the same 4,95. And, finally, Accounting students are also promoters with a value of 92,31% for the net promoter index.

In the Marketing Degree, 66 students took the examen, and 50 passed it, so the success rate was 75,8%. The evolution of the success rate in this degree is not questionable. During the lockdown (2019-2020) the rate was 90%, but during 2020-2021 the rate barely reaches 70%, and in 2018-2019 the rate was 72.3%. The perception is that marketing students are more motivated by these methodologies applied to quantitative subjects.

The visualizations results show a pattern like the Accounting students, the first mission has only 15 visualizations. The week before the examen the amount increases to 68 and, finally the escape closes with 106 visualizations. If we join these data with the answers to the survey we will see that only 62% of the students that answer the survey have completed the escape room. The average value of respondents to how the students rate the experience of using this resource was 4,88. There is no doubt about if they would recommend the escape room as an improvement to their learning process because the average is 5 (the maximum value). Also, the net promoter index was 100%, which means all the students give a promoter value.

Finally, in the open answer (Table 2) included in the survey the students suggest introducing a quest related to competing against the clock; and introducing a more detailed explanation about the first mission. It is necessary to point out that all of the answers highlight the escape room is a very helpful and high-quality resource for studying a difficult subject such as Statistics as a social science student.

CONCLUSION

The learning process has been modified in the last decades from the pure acquisition of concepts to the current one based on competencies. The skills that higher education students acquire, develop and subsequently apply have been designed from the European Higher Education framework.

In this case, we selected the subject of Statistics from an online university. It is important to emphasize that quantitative subjects for students of social sciences have the greatest difficulty for them in the degree. Also, marks arise that low scores are usually achieved in this type of subject in average terms. These results are the cause of the fear of this type of subject, the loss of motivation, and the difficulty in enjoyably reviewing the concepts. Therefore, the aim was to develop a resource that would motivate and engage the student in the subject in a dynamic way.

Table 2. KPIs results for evaluation

Useful and great to review concepts	"I found it very useful!"
	"It seemed to me that everything was great, very helpful to practice with the theory of the syllabus."
	"I thought it was great"
	"The idea is brilliant. Thank you very much for the effort."
	"I loved it, it seems super didactic and helps to review the subject as a whole. Thanks for the initiative!!!"
	"I think it's a fantastic material to prepare the subject, congratulations!!!"
	"The activity is hard work, it helps in a didactic way to understand the concepts and remember them through the missions"
	"I loved. With this, I reviewed all the concepts of statistics, and it has helped me prepare for the exam. I feel really prepared."
Future improvements	"Some quick visualization tests or detection of some quick data to compete against the clock"
	"I would look for a method to lock the spreadsheets in such a way that the modifications made by a student cannot be saved in the system."
	"To introduce a part with the solution and all steps to know where we have make a mistake"

Before introducing this resource, in the previous course, we carried out some other test-type competitions. In these live online sessions, we observed that the students competed, engaged, and were motivated to review the concepts to have good results in these sessions. Therefore, in the 2021-2022 academic year we decided to implement an escape room, a much more developed resource for the entire subject of Statistics.

The escape room follows the structure of the Statistics syllabus, it has been planned according to continuous assessment and as a review for the final exam. Thus, it has been implemented in three degrees with two different strategies. On the one hand, Accounting and Marketing, have been introduced since the first review session, therefore, the missions are opened one by one in the corresponding review sessions. While in the Business degree the resource has been opened in the last four weeks of the course, therefore, the entire escape room is opened from the first review session (week 6).

The escape room has four missions, the first mission, finding a boat, is related to unit one with descriptive statistics and classification of variables; the second mission, capture the Maruxaina, develops the concepts of units two and three about the linear regression; mission three, return to port, work with the concepts of temporal analysis; and the last mission uses the concepts of units five to eight about graphic representations and dashboards. This last mission seems not compensated with the previous ones, but the last topics are so related that it doesn't make sense to separate them.

The academic team has taken various gamification courses and has been introducing small resources for some time. In order to fully develop the escape room, a review of the academic literature has been carried out. In that process, it has been detected that certain elements motivate students more, such as missions, good storytelling, and progress blocked by codes. For this reason, we have taken a popular legend about a sea nymph, which has been structured in four missions and with advances through codes that must be obtained by correctly performing the calculations.

Undoubtedly, one of the most important phases of the escape room is its development, but it is necessary to keep in mind how its introduction in the learning process will be evaluated. For this reason, different KPIs have been used to able to have references. Firstly, the success rate is used (the percentage of students who have passed among those who have taken the exam), secondly, the number of views which we extract from the Genially stats; and, thirdly, the values that we extract from the student satisfaction survey. This satisfaction survey includes questions about how many missions have been completed, how satisfied they are, the net promoter index, and an open question for students to give their opinion anonymously about the resource.

Regarding the timing of the resource, it should be emphasized that it could be carried out synchronously or asynchronously. The students need a brief explanation such as initial guidance to understand and start the escape room. In the live sessions, we have experienced less participation than as usual and since not all the students have the same rhythm, we recommend the asynchronous form. The optimum would be to carry out mission two in the live session because it requests working in a team group, therefore, a workshop could be held and prior inform in advance to students so that they could review before the session and can extract the maximum performance.

The two implementation strategies carried out have shown that the resource has been used mainly in the last few weeks, as a resource for dynamic review of the subject, for this reason, we believe that for future practices it should be carried out as in the case of the Business Degree from week 11 of course. Although presenting it in week 6 can indeed motivate the student not to abandon the subject.

Concerning the success rates, it is worth mentioning that in the three degrees they have improved with this resource, and the net promoter index of the resource has been identified as a promoter in all three degrees with values of 87.5% in Business, 92.3% in accounting and 100% in marketing. In addition, the students in the comments have valued the effort of the teachers when preparing the resource, they have expressed that it has been a key to review the subject and they have proposed possible improvements.

Finally, as future lines of improvement, time-limited tests could be included, or competitive quizzes where students see their position within the total classroom in each mission. In addition, more missions could be generated, but we could not extend to more than 5 because the course is organized as a four-month subject. Considering the implementing strategies, we believe that the most successful one has been that of the Business Degree since the resource has been used more at the end of the course as an element of review and preparation for the exam.

ACKNOWLEDGMENT

We would like to express our gratitude to Alexandra Santamaria Urbieta and Elena Alcalde Peñalver to enhance gamification in higher education.

This research received no specific grant from any funding agency in the public, commercial, or not-for-profit sectors.

REFERENCES

Arockiyasamy, G., Surendheran, K., & Bullard, S. K. (2016). The influence of playing video games on academic performance among graduates of Karunya University. *Journal of Advances in Humanities and Social Sciences*, *2*(3), 119–132.

Bai, S., Hew, K. F., & Huang, B. (2020). Does gamification improve student learning outcome? Evidence from a meta-analysis and synthesis of qualitative data in educational contexts. *Educational Research Review, 30*, 100322. doi:10.1016/j.edurev.2020.100322

Cózar-Gutiérrez, R., & Sáez-López, J. M. (2016). Game-based learning and gamification in initial teacher training in the social sciences: An experiment with MinecraftEdu. *International Journal of Educational Technology in Higher Education, 13*(1), 1–11. doi:10.118641239-016-0003-4

Educause. (2011). *7 things you should know about gamification*. Retrieved from http://www.educause.edu/library/resources/7-things-you-should-know-about-gamification

Esteve, F., Adell, J., & Gisbert, M. (2014). Diseño de un entorno 3D para el desarrollo de la competencia digital docente en estudiantes universitarios: usabilidad, adecuación y percepción de utilidad [Design of a 3D environment for the development of digital teaching competence in university students: usability, adequacy and perception of utility]. *Revista Latinoameericana de Tecnología Educativa, 13*(2), 35–47.

Genially. (2022). https://genial.ly/es/

Giannetto, D., Chao, J., & Fontana, A. (2013). Gamification in a social learning environment. *Issues in Informing Science and Information Technology, 10*, 195–207. doi:10.28945/1806

Gómez-Trigueros, I. (2019). Methodologies Gamified as Didactic Resources for Social Sciences. *International Journal of Emerging Technologies in Learning, 14*(23), 193–207. doi:10.3991/ijet.v14i23.10794

Google Forms. (2022). https://docs.google.com/forms

Huang, B., & Hew, K. F. (2018). Implementing a theory-driven gamification model in higher education flipped courses: Effects on out-of-class activity completion and quality of artifacts. *Computers & Education, 125*, 254–272. doi:10.1016/j.compedu.2018.06.018

Huang, R., Ritzhaupt, A. D., Sommer, M., Zhu, J., Stephen, A., Valle, N., Hampton, J., & Li, J. (2020). The impact of gamification in educational settings on student learning outcomes: A meta-analysis. *Educational Technology Research and Development, 68*(4), 1875–1901. doi:10.100711423-020-09807-z

Huotari, K., & Hamari, J. (2012, October). Defining gamification: a service marketing perspective. In *Proceeding of the 16th international academic MindTrek conference* (pp. 17-22). 10.1145/2393132.2393137

Landers, R. N. (2014). Developing a theory of gamified learning: Linking serious games and gamification of learning. *Simulation & Gaming, 45*(6), 752–768. doi:10.1177/1046878114563660

Majuri, J., Koivisto, J., & Hamari, J. (2018). Gamification of education and learning: A review of empirical literature. In *Proceedings of the 2nd international GamiFIN conference, GamiFIN 2018*. CEUR-WS.

McGrath, N., & Bayerlein, L. (2013). Engaging online students through the gamification of learning materials: The present and the future. In *ASCILITE-Australian Society for Computers in Learning in Tertiary Education Annual Conference* (pp. 573–577). ASCILITE.

Paniagua, A., & Istance, D. (2018). *Teachers as designers of learning environments. In Educational Research and Innovation*. OECD. doi:10.1787/9789264085374-en

Prensky, M. (2001). *Digital game-based learning*. McGraw-Hill.

Quizizz. (2022). https://quizizz.com/

Richter, G., Raban, D. R., & Rafaeli, S. (2015). Studying gamification: The effect of rewards and incentives on motivation. In T. Reiners & L. C. Wood (Eds.), *Gamification in education and business* (pp. 21–46). Springer International Publishing. doi:10.1007/978-3-319-10208-5_2

Sailer, M., Hense, J. U., Mayr, S. K., & Mandl, H. (2017). How gamification motivates: An experimental study of the effects of specific game design elements on psychological need satisfaction. *Computers in Human Behavior*, *69*, 371–380. doi:10.1016/j.chb.2016.12.033

Sánchez-Caballé, A., Gisbert Cervera, M., & Esteve-Mon, F. M. (2020). The digital competence of university students: A systematic literature review. *Revista de Psicologia. Ciències de l'Educació i de l'Esport*, *38*(1), 63–74.

Simões, J., Redondo, R. D., & Vilas, A. F. (2013). A social gamification framework for a k-6 learning platform. *Computers in Human Behavior*, *29*(2), 345–353. doi:10.1016/j.chb.2012.06.007

KEY TERMS AND DEFINITIONS

Concoction: It is a mixture of spirituous liquid, citrus, coffee beans that is drunk at popular parties in Galicia (Spain).

Dashboard: Is a type of graphical user interface which often provides at-a-glance views of key performance indicators (KPIs) relevant to a particular objective or business process.

Farillons: Rocky islands near the coast of northern Galicia where the Maruxaina lives.

Fisherman's Net: It is a series of threads, woven and tied to a top rope or floats and a bottom rope of weights, which is used to catch fish.

Key Code: Is a set of numbers or letters necessary to advance in the different quests.

Maruxaina: It is a sea nymph that lives on the rocky islands near the north coast of Galicia (Spain).

Net Promoter Index: Is a numerical value that reports on the level of satisfaction of the respondents and tells you how likely they are to promote the resource.

Chapter 9
An Interactive Escape Room That Increases the Digital Skills of the Physical Activity and Sport Science Students

Pablo Sotoca Orgaz
https://orcid.org/0000-0001-5032-0131
University of Alcalá, Spain

Marta Arévalo Baeza
https://orcid.org/0000-0002-1942-9128
University of Alcalá, Spain

Alexandra Santamaría Urbieta
https://orcid.org/0000-0003-0935-0616
Universidad Internacional de La Rioja, Spain

ABSTRACT

This experience arises intending to increase the motivation of university students to contribute to devote more attention, time, and effort to the learning situations they experience. From this idea, the implementation of active methodologies aims to give students a leading role, providing them with new experiences that favour the understanding and consolidation of content and the development of skills and competencies in search of valuable and situated learning. Within these methodologies, the authors highlight some that resort to playful elements to improve the commitment to the different learning processes. This chapter presents perceptions and assessments of students after participating in a project to develop digital competencies based on gamification and having as the main element a hybrid escape room, with live and digital proposals set in the successful Spanish TV series "La Casa de Papel."

DOI: 10.4018/978-1-6684-6081-8.ch009

INTRODUCTION

There is a growing interest in improving success and performance rates in digital literacy skills at the university level. Due to the progressive use of portable devices and accessibility to the Internet, this dizzying technological advance has led to a significant burden of technological mediation in the teaching and learning processes at the university (Adell et al., 2018). However, incorporating devices and connections in academic spaces does not guarantee the development of digital competencies. In this context, the challenge is to ensure that students take advantage, on the one hand of the professional potential offered by digital tools and, on the other, that the usefulness of these resources allows them to be used as a tool to support their academic activities. Undoubtedly, this technological use is modifying the educational conception of decades ago, being able to carry out accessible and personalized learning, either formally or informally, with the development of digital tools and resources generated expressly for the educational environment (Álvarez et al., 2016). For this, university students need to have the digital skills that allow them to efficiently use the resources of a technological nature available to them. In addition, for developing digital skills in university classrooms, the best methodological strategies must be created, which must start from previous training and knowledge on the part of teachers who decide to implement it in the classroom (Pico, 2013). For the tasks that teachers propose, we can find some strategies that increase the levels of intrinsic motivation. Many of them are emerging methodologies that resort to game systems in contexts that are not playful in the first instance. There is no doubt that play is a social process that helps motivation and encourages learning to be generated. Proof of this is both the number of studies we find in different stages and the educational levels (Sainz et al., 2019).

This chapter shares a learning proposal on digital competencies, understood as skills, knowledge and critical attitudes in Information and Communication Technologies (from now on, ICT) through playful and active methodologies. This educational experience starts from an immersive gamification called "The Paperless House" and is framed in the teaching innovation project of the University of Alcalá in the 2018/2019 academic year. The innovation project had as its main component a digital Escape Room (also known by many authors as digital BreakOut) that was set in a spin-off of the successful TV series "Money Heist" (in Spanish "La Casa de Papel", making a play on words indicating that it was a digital experience). After the 15-week immersion, the participants answered a questionnaire to assess their perception and commitment to the training process they had experienced.

BACKGROUND

The Bologna Declaration and the creation of the European Higher Education Area (EHEA) have led to a conceptual, methodological, and structural redefinition of the university environment (Fernández et al., 2018). In this sense, one of the fundamental changes lies in the pedagogical renewal (De Miguel, 2006), focusing its interest on the use of active methodologies that allow students to "actively seek meaning to the object of learning" (Ruiz-Martín, 2020, p.55). Some of the allies that favour this transformation are ICT because they multiply the possibilities of incorporating emerging methodological proposals (Fernández & Valverde, 2014; Sierra-Daza & Fernández-Sánchez, 2017).

However, in addition to how teachers integrate these types of resources into their teaching design, the correct or incorrect use of these will depend on the individual (Area, 2010; Marqués, 2012). For this reason, some authors highlight the relevance of focusing on multimodal literacy in today's information society due to the influence of massive information which can be accessed through digital devices (Castillo et al., 2015). It is paramount to encourage young people to review how they use digital environments and, above all, to accompany them in the professional use required in the university environment. This formative challenge requires the best strategies that encourage the involvement of students in developing digital skills. Gamification is a successful methodological framework for motivating university students in the classroom that sometimes resorts to technology for its development. In addition to gamification, other elements such as escape rooms have proven to be powerful tools for developing competencies, mainly transversal or soft skills (Sánchez-Martín et al., 2020).

Currently, more and more teachers have decided to incorporate digital games and other ludic strategies in the classroom through active methodologies such as game-based learning (Pacheco & Causado, 2018). These resources improve cognitive processes for learning (Boyle et al., 2016; Tobias et al., 2014), in addition to increasing the benefits of digital literacy (Area, 2015; Marín et al., 2020). As highlighted by numerous studies, the use of digital games allows the development of so-called 21st-century skills (Jenkins et al., 2006), among which the digital competence of individuals stands out (Gros, 2009). At the same time, it is a playful proposal that can cover curricular content, without focusing expressly on the achievement of academic knowledge (Garmen et al., 2018), in addition to being a motivating proposal for students (Etxebarria, 2009) that can favour inclusion in the classroom (Garmen et al., 2016; Marín et al., 2012).

However, just as we find studies with commercial video games in the educational field (Castillo et al., 2015; Gros, 2008), nowadays, the creative potential of the teacher has been put into value through the creation of playful digital proposals. These are thanks to the new incorporation of freely available software, platforms, and applications that allow the generation of puzzles in a virtual environment (Clarke et al., 2017; Nicholson, 2018; Negre & Carrión, 2020). Among these resources, the so-called escape games stand out. The escape room in its digital version is an adaptation of the live proposal in which different riddles or puzzles must be solved in a given time frame through the collaboration of players who share a common goal to leave a room in the shortest possible time (Hayden et al., 2020; Nicholson, 2018; Zhang et al., 2018). This practice, increasingly widespread in the different educational stages, generates some controversy when it comes to cataloguing it with some specific nomenclature within the playful pedagogies in which concepts such as gamification, game-based learning, or serious games converge (Negre & Carrión, 2020).

The present experience is gamification, understood as using playful elements in non-game contexts (Deterding, 2011). Gamification is intended to create a system with game elements and non-game elements without the students having the feeling that they are playing a game. The objectives, together with all game and non-game elements, are independent of each other, forming a whole (Labrador, 2020). Furthermore, it is characterized by the search to increase students' motivation, interest, and involvement in the teaching and learning processes (Hanus & Fox, 2015; Kapp, 2012; Zichermann & Cunningham, 2011).

Moreover, following the line of numerous authors (Abt, 1987; Göbel et al., 2010; Slussareff et al., 2016), digital escape rooms are part of a growing number of "serious games" that are explicitly created for learning in the classroom. For this reason, these resources must be previously contextualized by each teacher and serve as a trigger in the students' learning process. In addition, this digital game system could have characteristics and elements like those of many current video games. If the digital game arises from modifying an existing video game and is considered as such, it could be implemented through a game-based learning methodological strategy (Fotaris & Mastoras, 2019). As seen in Figure 1, gamification, game-based learning, and serious gaming are not incompatible, but they are not synonymous either.

Figure 1. Relationship of concepts in the designed project
Source: Adapted from Labrador (2020)

As it happens in this experience, the digital escape room can be used as a trigger of motivation within gamification processes (Pérez-López, 2020; Sotoca, 2020), either in its digital or analogue version.

Moreover, throughout the gamified intervention, storytelling was emphasized for the sole purpose of making the experience more immersive, as well as a way of demonstrating another way of provoking skill development and exemplifying the application of knowledge in a more attractive way (Boal & Schultz, 2007; Santamaría Urbieta & Alcalde Peñalver, 2021). As Flanagan (2015) points out, storytelling in the educational field favours sharing ideas and experiences and bringing out emotions. Thanks to the contextualization of the concepts, this technique allows creative and innovative learning, showing very positive results when evaluating the concepts understood and facilitating their understanding by students (Ramos-Villagrasa et al., 2019).

The assessment of the success of these methodological frameworks is related to the involvement, commitment, and perseverance promoted to perform the designed tasks. Moreover, from these behaviours of adherence to the proposed challenges, the sense of the intervention's success is in the learning achieved on the digital competencies worked on. In short, the motivation to be promoted in this escape room is the one that refers to "the mechanisms that make us do and desire to do certain things" (Jiménez, 2017, p. 23) as it allows to design dynamic, novel, and attractive environments, which can increase motivation (Martín-González et al., 2021).

Interactive Escape Room: *La Casa Sin Papel*

The experience described below was part of the call for Teaching Innovation Projects (PID) for the 2018-2019 academic year of the University of Alcalá (Madrid, Spain). The committee approved it with the identification number UAH/EV1018. These projects aim to provide a framework for participation aimed at teachers who wish to implement innovative actions in their subjects.

Context

This educational innovation proposal was developed in the Degree of Physical Activity and Sport Sciences of the University of Alcalá (Madrid, Spain), specifically in the "Technology and Physical Activity" subject. During the academic year, 73 first-year students participated, divided into three groups. The teaching period lasted 15 weeks, with a total of two weekly classes of one and a half hours each.

Project Proposal and Evaluation Method

The project aimed to design an educational experience in digital competencies through an escape room strategy using technological resources. The aim was to evaluate different aspects of the proposed escape room, which includes assessing participant's level of motivation and commitment to the proposal, as well as judging the training potential of this emerging recreational methodology in the university environment.

For this purpose, an ad hoc questionnaire was designed and answered anonymously by 63 students, 15 women, and 48 men. These figures correspond to 86.3% of the total students who participated (73 students), which provides the reliability of the sample concerning the population.

The students' learning objectives concerning digital competencies were:

1. To acquire digital competencies using ICT and Learning and Knowledge Technologies (LKT), which will be relevant in their professional future.
2. To use the Internet as a source of lifelong learning and a space for communication, professional relationship, or collaborative networking.
3. To generate critical reflections on the impact of technology on current and future society, starting from different prisms such as marketing, body image, gender, or the relevance of the body and movement in social networks.
4. To encourage autonomy and tolerance to uncertainty, while considering the different learning rhythms through problem-solving.
5. To encourage creativity by designing new digital proposals embodied in different formats.

Proposal Development

To describe this innovation proposal, we have adapted and used as a reference some of the pieces of the "Tangram of gamification" by Sotoca and Pérez-López (2019). This guide aims to help teachers to generate gamification proposals. On this occasion, we recurred to an engaging narrative, a premiere or starting point, an experience or adventure, some allies for motivation, and a grand finale. This way, it is possible to identify how the experience has been developed throughout each of the weeks based on the designed elements. The particular format intended for the interactive escape room revolves around other elements such as the setting, the narrative, or the game dynamics generated through different mechanics throughout the training.

The Narrative

The Spanish series *La Casa de Papel* (Money Heist) was reborn on the Netflix platform with record audience figures on the international scene (Neira et al., 2021). The plot tells the story of a person who calls himself The Professor, a thinking mind who recruits a band of robbers to commit the biggest heist of the century, robbing the Spanish Mint. After several months of preparation, they had only 11 days to pull off the big heist successfully.

This series has an International Emmy Award and has expanded its story through different formats, media, products, and cultural languages, thanks to its powerful transmedia narrative (Guerrero, 2016).

The narrative of the series became a motivating trigger because, when this escape room was to be launched with students, the 3rd season was about to premiere, a reason of interest for the students enrolled in the subject "Technology and Physical Activity" of the degree in Physical Activity and Sport Sciences at the University of Alcalá. To understand the narrative of the spin-off created, we include a summary from the final chronicle of the experience (Sotoca, 2019) that aims to collect the fictional immersion that is the basis of this proposal:

The music plays, and the members of the New Resistance pack up to return to their lives. These hackers, who pretend not to generate suspicion in their environment, have been chosen by the Professor. This distorted voice represents a privileged mind that planned the biggest heist ever seen in Spain, assaulting the Spanish Mint. His new mission leads him to decrypt one last safe, the enigmatic Digital Safe No. 13 that had been left unopened.

This interactive escape room is based on decrypting the precious Safe. However, getting there is a challenge materialized in the need to open 12 previous safes located on a Genially platform. This challenge made the work of the participants difficult. On some occasions, they had to overcome real tests through different metacognitive, physical, and creative challenges in the field of training, physical exercise, leisure and free time, sports management, or physical education.

Several groups were able to reach the precious loot inside by managing to decipher all the passwords that allowed access to the final safe. Some arrived too late, and others were left along the way. Fact or fiction? All we know is that while some are still asking questions, others are dancing to the rhythm of the song Bella Ciao.

The Premiere

On the first day of class, the students enter the room to find only a pen drive on the computer with a message of instructions to follow on the screen. A message from a distorted voice, which calls itself The Professor, guides the students to a place in the Faculty of Medicine and Health Sciences (University of Alcalá), where they find Vancouver and Bremen, the teachers of the subject, who are the first two members of the New Resistance. The adventure of learning through the resolution of the boxes, which involves accepting this formative challenge, is briefly explained. After the group discusses the pros and cons of accepting such a challenge, several of them raise their voices saying that, although the path may seem complex, it may be worth it to participate in a great challenge. They are intrigued to know what is in the 13th box! Everything is ready (see Figure 2), and the group is divided into small teams named after cities. All they need to do now is to wait for the Professor's orders. He will communicate soon with the whole group. For the moment, they just look each other in the eyes and wonder why they have been chosen.

*Figure 2. Digital Escape Room design and access**
Source: own elaboration.

The groups of students choose these names, looking for name of a city in the world, emulating those of the characters in the fictional series. This is how Antananarivo, Jakarta, Honolulu, Houston, Lima, Havana, Cancun, Dublin, Dakar, Fallujah, Cairo, Toulouse, Chernobyl, Milan, Rome, Athens, Istanbul and Salsipuedes were recruited. The choice of these names was carried out by the groups of students. They are names of cities in the world, emulating those of the characters in the fictional series. A total of 18 hacker gangs composed of the student teams would seek to decrypt the prized Safe Number 13 (see Figure 3).

The Adventure: A Unique Experience

The plot generated in each of the sessions, as well as the subject contents that were addressed, are perfectly synchronized with the different digital safes that they will progressively have to open (see Table 1). In some hybrid tests (i.e., both analogue and digital), the Professor's messages and the collaboration of Vancouver and Bremen as subject teachers made it easier to know what they had to do at each moment to decrypt the following safes.

Figure 3. Avatars of some components of the New Resistance
Source: own elaboration.

Below is an example of a digital safe with its respective evidence and instruction to get the following code. The password to access the digital safe number 7 was 2272, and the result came out of the following riddle:

What is the body mass index (BMI) of a person who weighs 72,000 grams and is 178 centimeters tall?
What is the body mass index (BMI) of a person who weighs 72,000 grams and is 178 centimeters tall?
The password consists of 4 digits (including the whole number and the first two decimal places without rounding).

Once the students solved the riddle, inside safe number 7, they could find the following message:

Someone is trying to access our data. We are suffering an attack on our system! You will have to solve the three spreadsheets included in the Help section. Don't forget to use the data in the attached files!

In the "Physical condition" file, students had to add up all the averages, subtract the highest, multiply it by the lowest and, through the conditional, add up those people who would pass the test. Students had to add this result to the total number that comes from adding up all the auto summaries obtained from the "Medal display" file. The result will allow them to open the next safe. Students were reminded that they should not forget the graphs to prevent enemies from accessing their information.

As evidence to block the attack (nº7): Send Excel files with correct results.

The following is an example of a hybrid safe with the essential use of technological devices.

Example of a hybrid mission (nº4):

Table 1. Safes that made up the Digital Escape Room: plot, modality and applications used

Safe	Chapter/Narrative	Modality	Subject's content
No. 1	The New Resistance	Digital	Presentation • Name and avatar • Social Networks – #LaCasaSinPapel
No. 2	(Disc)connected	Digital	Disconnection from the network • Critical thinking • Text-image interaction – Canva, Photokit, etc.
No. 3	Cargo van	Digital	Management of audiovisual content • Use of Wix, Genially, BookCreator, WordPress, Blogger, Tumblr, etc.
No. 4	Hostage on the run	Hybrid	Sports training • Use of GPS and mobile applications (Strava, Runtastic, Endomondo, etc.) • Video editing (Media maker, Sony Vegas, iMovie, etc.
No. 5	Security cameras	Hybrid	Sports training • Use of applications and software for sports gesture analysis and video editing. • Kinovea, Coach Eye, etc. • Video editing
No. 6	The Professor's call	Digital	Podcast on Physical Education • Audio editing – Audacity • Audio management platforms: Anchord, iVoox, SoundCloud
No. 7	Calculus problems	Digital	Sports management • Data management - Excel
No. 8	Gambling your life	Digital	Physical exercise and health • Design and image treatment with Canva, Photoshop, Desygner, etc.
No. 9	Challenged	Digital	Physical education • Analysis of profiles on social networks such as Twitter, Instagram, etc.
No. 10	Tokyo (collaboration in person with the expert Mª José Camacho)	Hybrid	Cyberactivism, physical exercise and health • Critical analysis and representation through image, irony and memes.
No. 11	Mapping the plan	Digital	Project planning • Applications to manage and plan personal tasks (Trello, Google Calendar, etc.). • Text documents (Word, Docs, etc.) for developing a project on mobile applications.
No. 12	Berlin (virtual collaboration with the expert Isaac Pérez)	Digital	Event management and marketing • Mobilization through social networks in an interuniversity event through Twitter. Connecting students of the Degree in Physical Activity and Sports Sciences from the University of Alcalá (Madrid, Spain) and the University of Granada (Granada, Spain).
No. 13	Safe No. 13	Hybrid	Cooperative work • Cooperative and analogical Escape Room in the Computer Classroom. • Resolution of the digital Escape Room.

Source: own elaboration

One of our hostages has escaped, and we have to follow him. We are lucky that he is a sedentary person and running alongside him is something that is not very complex. Let's follow him all the way! To do this, you must choose a sedentary person in your environment and run with him for 30 minutes at least twice. When you do so, use one of the proposed applications. Plan the route and generate a drawing through the streets of your city in the shape of a safe.

Students will have 45 minutes to download a GPS application and test its operation. In teams, they will have to perform a small test around the University Campus that lasts exactly 15 minutes to learn the ins and outs of the app. The first three teams will have an extra clue for the opening of the safe number five. The kilometers traveled during that time, the intensity, and the originality of the drawing will be considered. The evidence students will have to gather in hybrid mission number four are the following: the edited video where they must appear with their hostage showing, at different points of the route, the GPS mobile application that will control their route and activity. The minimum time must be in accordance with the World Health Organization (2020).

The Allies

Online ICT and LKT

The digital platform Genially[1] is the interactive online software chosen to create the different safes with their respective passwords (Figure 4). To move forward in the escape room, each group has to decipher them, which were enabled (visualized) according to the speed of each of the groups over the weeks (Figure 6). When a box was enabled, this indicated that a team was trying to decipher it, something that could not be done by those who were still in one of the previous safes or if they had missed the time. This online material was only accessible in the computer room during class hours.

Similarly, multiple mobile applications related to the field of physical activity and sport were also used as a transition between the different safes, allowing them to interact with the faculty's environment to acquire clues that would enable them to decipher the password to the next online safe. This analogue-digital hybrid promoted movement in consideration of the number of hours students could remain seated in front of the computer screen, creating active breaks that lifted the students out of their chairs. Some of the applications used addressed content such as generating pairings in sports tournaments (My Tournaments), analyzing the start and finish line in athletics races (Track Starter and Photo Finish), and creating knots (Knots 3D) or using tactical boards for different sports, among others.

Other Motivation Boosters

Throughout the term, several elements were used to ensure that the motivation of members of the group remained high. In the beginning, a costume was used, which was very well received by some students who even made T-shirts with their names and the logo created for the experience (see Figure 5).

The Icing on the Cake

An event announced through the social network Twitter, using the hashtag #LaEFvaEnSerie, became the prelude to the opening of the safe number 13. Without a doubt, it was a moment of celebration at the possibility of reaching the coveted box. The members of the New Resistance had the support of students from the University of Granada to mobilize numerous primary and secondary physical education teachers who debated, based on four chapters, about the future of this subject. The debate lasted two hours and

Figure 4. Genially design with the use of password and hide page options
Source: own elaboration

had the participation of many referents of the field who were critical of the state of physical education in our country, Spain (see Image 5).

The opening of safe No.13 was done through a live Escape Room where, with a countdown of 60 minutes, they had to cooperate to open the last box, with its different types of locks and elements such as a cryptex, QR codes, riddles, or messages with invisible ink. Once the last box was opened, they were able to decipher the password that would open Safe No.13, the last escape game where there were phone calls from the Professor that allowed them to get closer to the final objective.

A badge with a text message reminded them that, despite being accustomed to lectures at the university level where repetition and memorization sometimes seem to be the only way to acquire knowledge, other methodologies can generate learning that is remembered over time. All the participants decided to challenge the system and take a step forward to demonstrate that their involvement could generate new forms of knowledge. There is no better way to experience a different kind of learning, with its successes and mistakes, than to live it in the first person (see Figure 6).

SOLUTIONS AND RECOMMENDATIONS

After the experience, information was collected from only 63 of the 73 participants through a questionnaire generated ad hoc (Appendix 1). If we look at the first questions that address the use of gamification in the classroom, it is observed that 97% had not participated in an experience of these characteristics during their educational stage. As for the general self-perception about the learning acquired thanks to this methodology, the results are positive, with 7 out of 10 students considering that it is a methodology with which they have acquired relevant knowledge in a playful, motivating, and useful way. More than 85% of the sample believes that gamification can be an appropriate methodology for developing this subject, and only 10% do not consider it appropriate in the university environment. In this line, 53 of the 63 respondents "agree" or "totally agree" that this methodology gives the student greater in the learning process, compared to other methodologies more commonly used in the university setting. This data reinforces the idea that students should make decisions within the teaching and learning process

Figure 5. Marketing campaign and event #LaEFvaenSerie
Source: https://twitter.com/PabloSotoca/status/1123285948551389186?s=20&t=oQ-TuHlhN9-lhMFYLYmR5Q (Sotoca, 2019); https://twitter.com/RedPajaritos/status/1123297647094267905?s=20&t=oQ-TuHlhN9-lhMFYLYmR5Q (Varys, 2019)

Figure 6. Moments of the experience and student material
Source: own elaboration

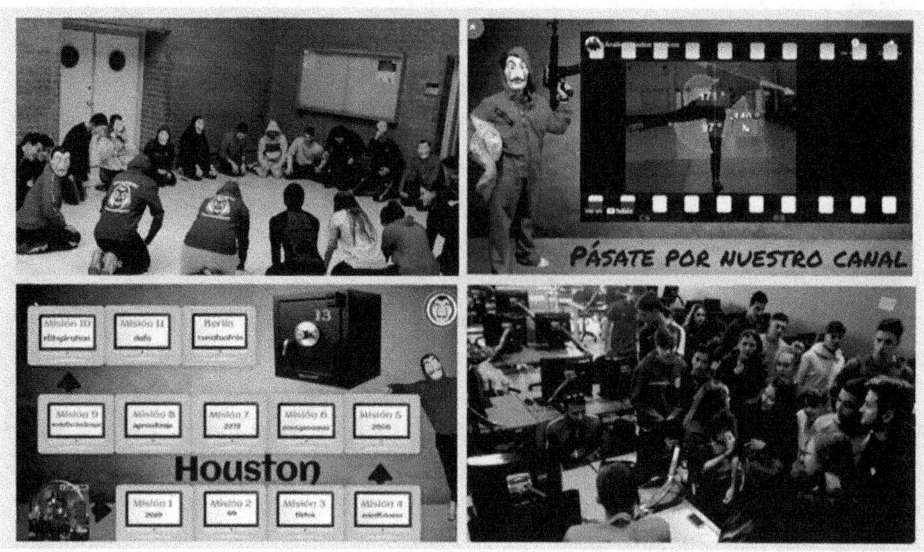

for the acquisition of different competencies (Fernández et al., 2018; Fernández, 2009) allowing them to increase their motivation and commitment to learning in the university stage, whenever they wish to do so (Simões et al., 2013).

Regarding the design of the experience, the most attractive and motivating innovation element implemented is the uncertainty and surprise generated before entering the classroom before the new challenges (79%). In this sense, as Ruíz-Martín (2020) warns, the role of emotions moderated in the learning process is being studied, specifically concerning curiosity and surprise. According to Ruíz-Martin, events that occur with a certain dose, provoked by curiosity or interest, increase the capacity to commit to the task of learning and remembering what has been addressed. Curiosity should lead the person to pay attention and explore the new things they perceive. In the case of surprise, it refers to those things that are out of the routine, such as when the teaching is presented through escape challenges. The motivation generated from creating learning situations that arouse curiosity and surprise should enhance performance in the proposed teaching tasks that would lead to the development of digital skills in this case. The motivation that is of interest in university learning is that which induces the student to make more effort and devote more time and attention to the learning object (Ruíz-Martín, 2020).

The second most motivating element is using an interactive system of safes in the form of a Digital Escape Room or BreakOut, which has supported a large part of the proposal (69%). In this sense, the objective of an Escape Room is to open a locked box with padlocks using the codes obtained, solving problems, tests, or enigmas (Sánchez-Rodríguez et al., 2019), allowing to achieve metacognitive, physical, and creative challenges. That is why, when asked about which elements of the tasks were most motivating, working in groups (64%) stood out in first place, followed by the challenges that provided clues to decipher the passwords of the following boxes and that invited action and movement (58%).

In educational terms, the challenge presented by this project was not only the technological domain but to know and explore possible didactic uses for learning (Granados, 2014). This way, ICTs become Technologies for Learning and Knowledge (TAC) to enhance teaching and learning processes (Granados, 2014; Lozano, 2011; Quintero, 2021). In this sense, the participating students emphasize the importance of having a personal web space where they can generate their own content (49%). Although in the beginning, only in-person escape rooms were carried out, since the COVID-19 pandemic, digital versions have been promoted (Cadieux et al., 2020). These seek to open boxes that are not hidden but must be opened after deciphering locks, riddles, and digital passwords, a modality known as virtual BreakOut or digital escape room (Cadieux et al., 2020; Makri et al., 2021).

Although teachers' assessment was positive, teachers do not "generate" learning; they can only provide the appropriate circumstances for it to occur and encourage students to engage in actions that will lead them to achieve it. In this regard, the questionnaire also included a self-evaluation that focused on the subject's acquisition of knowledge and digital competencies in the context of physical activity and sport throughout the four months. All students reported feeling that they have acquired knowledge and improved their technological skills. However, 46% thought they had improved quite a lot, 36% stated that they had increased their technological expertise, and 9% reported that they had increased their technological skills. In this sense, Ruíz-Martín (2020) warns that teaching occurs when the teacher provides the conditions and facilitates the experiences for student learning, always in relation to specific objectives.

Concerning the narrative, on a Likert scale of one to five, more than 90% believe that their level of participation, commitment, and dedication to the subject was rated at four or higher. In addition, about 70% of the sample considered that they were unaware of the final grade at any time because they were immersed in the experience, something they valued positively. This result indicates that intrinsic motivation prevailed over extrinsic motivation in a high percentage of the class (Ryan & Deci, 2000). It is possible that resorting to adapted fiction could generate intrinsic motivation in the students (Sotoca & Pérez-López, 2020). Video platforms are here to stay and have become high-impact audiovisual distributors, causing the production and co-production of highly relevant serialized fiction (Calderón, 2020). Undoubtedly, these entertainment companies have transformed our cultural industry and lifestyle. As revealed by different studies, one of the leading entertainment preferences of the audience is fiction series (Calderón, 2020; Pérez-López, 2019), as they turn their contents into a source of inspiration to generate pedagogical proposals (Blanco, 2020).

In the open-ended question asked ("Write your general opinion about the activity. How you felt, if you liked it, if you didn't and if there were anything you would change"), some criticisms also appear regarding the complexity of some tasks and the overall workload. Although to a greater extent, the responses rated the experience as very positive. As Ruiz-Martín (2020) warns, it is not only that didactic activities can be exciting for learning to be effective, but rather it is a matter of creating learning situations that consider the socioemotional dimension. In this sense, and after categorizing various types of responses on qualifiers given to the training experience, terms such as "incredible", "different", "original", "innovative", "novel", or "fun" are repeated. Similarly, there are comments that value teachers' intervention in the gamification process where words such as "enthusiasm" or "involvement" stand out.

In the design of an educational escape room, regardless of the type of modality, the most important thing is to know what knowledge we want to transmit, why we want to do it with this methodology and what skills and competencies we want to develop. Subsequently, importance should be given to the choice of the theme and narrative (Nicholson, 2015), considering it a key element, as it also occurs in gamification processes (Pérez-López, 2020). Possible examples of themes or settings include a saga of fiction novels, a successful thriller movie, a place such as an auditorium, the library, the laboratory, or an ancient era setting, etc. Once the narrative has been selected, with its consequent aesthetics, the challenges and tests must be selected and designed. The selection will depend on the previously chosen objectives and the experience of the designer, as well as the expertise of the students. The proposed difficulty should be a challenge for the participants, considering the Flow Theory (Csikszentmihalyi, 2011) so that the students do not get bored while performing the task, and conversely, do not give up due to difficulty level.

Learning situations should be designed and implemented with the necessary material, spatial, temporal, and human resources. Although face-to-face experiences may provide benefits (Yañez-Flores, et al., 2022), they may not always be possible due to the resources they demand. Therefore, partial or total virtualization may be an appropriate way of working (Yañez-Flores, et al., 2022), especially if what is being proposed as objectives is the specific development of digital competencies.

For this reason, the possibility to create ludic material through online resources is exposed through the Genially platform. This allows embedding numerous possibilities such as interactive links, videos, text, and elements in JavaScript language or Scorm format that could facilitate the creation of an online meta-game (game over game). This would enable the transformation of this hybrid (digital and analogue) experience into a fully online digital resource that could occupy one or several sessions, depending on the complexity of the game designers. This new resource could be enhanced by attending to the RAMP model (Marczewski, 2018), where the Relationships, Autonomy, and Mastery of the participants are determined, as well as the Purpose intended to be generated by the game designer. The connection between participants could be made through platforms such as Discord or Team Speak live communication. The design of the escape can determine the players' autonomy in the power of decisions according to the digital challenges. Similarly, the complexity will depend on the knowledge and skills of the students, being able to use a time bomb (application of regressive time) to make the process more difficult. Finally, the purpose will depend on the teacher's interest according to the students' demands or the needs of the proposal.

CONCLUSION

The reflections, results, and considerations addressed in this chapter on the gamified methodological framework, centered on a digital escape room, supports that this type of training practice can be carried out in the university environment. In the first place, its implementation will be effective if it considers the theoretical foundations of these playful methodological strategies and the efficient use of ICT and TAC so that they are truly allied resources. Secondly, it should be kept in mind how relevant it is for educational success that the contextualization of the intervention design should be based on the situation in which the proposal will be developed. Thirdly, the motivation that this type of didactic framework can achieve is a factor that intensifies learning, translated into dedication, commitment, and dedication to the tasks designed by teachers.

Finally, we must include evaluations of the interventions we design and apply in university classrooms in face-to-face or digital formats. Analyzing students' performance in terms of acquisition of knowledge and motivation is particularly important. As for future work, it would be interesting to apply and analyze the experience in other university degrees or studies where results can be compared with control groups where the same objectives and contents are worked on, but without these gamified frameworks. In short, this proposal has achieved the students' learning objectives. Still, studies are undoubtedly needed to discover the key aspects of these types of methodological strategies and possible revisions of the hybrid interventions.

ACKNOWLEDGMENT

Thank you to Carlos Mínguez, Physical Education teacher and director of the podcast *No Es Gimnasia,* for lending his voice and making the calls on behalf of The Professor. Also, many thanks to University teachers María José Camacho and Isaac Pérez for participating in the plot as Tokyo and Berlin. Likewise, thank you to the students of the latter for participating and promoting the debate through social networks.

REFERENCES

Abt, C. C. (1987). *Serious Games*. University Press of America.

Adell, J., Castañeda, L., & Esteve, F. (2018). ¿Hacia la Ubersidad? Conflictos y contradicciones de la universidad digital [Towards Ubersity? Conflicts and contradictions of the digital university]. *RIED-Revista Iberoamericana De Educación a Distancia, 21*(2), 51–68. doi:10.5944/ried.21.2.20669

Álvarez, E., Bellezza, A., & Caggiano, V. (2016). Realidad aumentada: innovación en educación [Augmented reality: innovation in education]. *Didasc@alia: Didáctica y educación, 7*(1), 195–212. https://dialnet.unirioja.es/descarga/articulo/6568046.pdf

Area, M. (2010). ¿Por qué formar en competencias informacionales y digitales en la educación superior? En Competencias informacionales y digitales en educación superior [Why train in informational and digital skills in higher education? In Informational and digital competences in higher education]. Revista de Universidad y Sociedad del Conocimiento, 7(2).

Area, M. (2015). La alfabetización digital y la formación de la ciudadanía del siglo XXI [Digital literacy and the formation of citizenship of the XXI century]. *Revista Integra Educativa, 7*(3), 21-33. http://www.scielo.org.bo/scielo.php?script=sci_arttext&pid=S1997-40432014000300002

Blanco, M. (2020). La pedagogía en el aula en la era Nétflix: Explicar contenidos a través de la cartelera de las plataformas digitales [Pedagogy in the classroom in the Nétflix era: Explaining content through the billboard of digital platforms]. In Innovación Docente e Investigación en Educación y Ciencias Sociales. Avanzando en el proceso de enseñanza-aprendizaje. Academic Press.

Boal, K. B., & Schultz, P. L. (2007). Storytelling, time, and evolution: The role of strategic leadership in complex adaptive systems. *The Leadership Quarterly, 18*(4), 411–428. doi:10.1016/j.leaqua.2007.04.008

Boyle, E. A., Hainey, T., Connolly, T. M., Gray, G., Earp, J., Ott, M., Lim, T., Ninaus, M., Ribeiro, C., & Pereira, J. (2016). An update to the systematic literature review of empirical evidence of the impacts and outcomes of computer games and serious games. *Computers & Education, 94*, 178–192. doi:10.1016/j.compedu.2015.11.003

Cadieux, M., Campos-Zamora, M., Zagury-Orly, I., & Dzara, K. (2020). Journal Club Using Virtual Breakout Rooms: Interactive Continuing Education with No Learner Preparation During COVID-19. *The Journal of Continuing Education in the Health Professions, 40*(4), 217–219. doi:10.1097/CEH.0000000000000321

Calderón, M.E. (2020). SVOD: El nuevo campo de batalla por las audiencias [SVOD: The new battleground for audiences]. *Ctrl: Control & Strategias, 676*, 65-67.

Castillo, H., Herrero, D., Checa, M., & Monjelat, N. (2015). Desarrollo de competencias a través de los videojuegos deportivos: alfabetización digital e identidad [Skills development through sports video games: digital literacy and identity]. *Revista de Educación a Distancia*, (33). https://revistas.um.es/red/article/view/233111

Clarke, S. J., Peel, D. J., Arnab, S., Morini, L., Keegan, H., & Wood, O. (2017). EscapED: A Framework for Creating Educational Escape Rooms and Interactive Games for Higher/Further Education. *Int. J. Serious Games, 4*(3), 73–86. doi:10.17083/ijsg.v4i3.180

Csikszentmihalyi, M. (2011). *Flow*. Ed. Kairós.

De Miguel, M. (Coord.). (2006). Metodologías de enseñanza y aprendizaje para el desarrollo de competencias [Teaching and learning methodologies for the development of competences]. Alianza Ediorial.

Deterding, S. (2011). Situated motivational affordances of game elements: a conceptual model. In *Gamification: Using Game Design Elements in Non-GamingContexts, a Workshop at CHI* (pp. 1–4). ACM.

Etxeberria, F. (2008). Videojuegos consumo y educación [Video games, consumption and education]. In Videojuegos: una herramienta educativa del "homo digitalis." Universidad de Salamanca.

Fernández, A. (2009). *Metodologías activas para la formación en competencias* [Active methodologies for competency training]. Universidad Politécnica de Valencia.

Fernández, M., Pascual, H. M., & Romero, M. A. (2018). Características del alumnado de los grados de Magisterio en las nuevas metodologías del EEES [Characteristics of the students of the degrees of Teaching in the new methodologies of the EHEA]. In C. Monge & P. Gómez (Eds.), *Innovando la docencia desde la formación del profesorado* (pp. 87–107). Editorial Síntesis.

Fernández, M. R., & Valverde, J. (2014). A Community of Practice: An Intervention Model based on Computer Supported Collaborative Learning. *Comunicar*, *42*(42), 97–105. doi:10.3916/C42-2014-09

Flanagan, S. (2015). How does storytelling within higher education contribute to the learning experience of early years students? *Journal of Practice Teaching & Learning*, *13*(2-3), 146–168. doi:10.1921/jpts.v13i2-3.822

Fotaris, P., & Mastoras, T. (2019). *Escape rooms for learning: A systematic review. In Proceedings of the 13th European Conference on Games Based Learning, Dinamarca*. Universidad de Dinamarca del Sur. https://bit.ly/3c4q09v

Garmen, P., Rodríguez, C., García, T., García, P., & Suárez, N. (2018). El potencial de los videojuegos para intervenir con dificultades de aprendizaje [The potential of video games to intervene with learning difficulties]. *Novatica*. https://www.novatica.es/el-potencial-de-los-videojuegos-para-intervenir-con-dificultades-de-aprendizaje

Göbel, S., Hardy, S., & Wendel, V. (2010). Serious Games for Health – Personalized Exergames. In *18th ACM International Conference on Multimedia* (pp. 1663–1666). 10.1145/1873951.1874316

Granados, J., López, R., Avello, R., Luna, D., Luna, E., & Luna, W. (2014). Las tecnologías de la información y las comunicaciones, las del aprendizaje y del conocimiento y las tecnologías para el empoderamiento y la participación como instrumentos de apoyo al docente de la universidad del siglo XXI [Information and communication technologies, learning and knowledge technologies and technologies for empowerment and participation as instruments to support the teacher of the university of the XXI century]. *Medisur*, *12*, 289-294. https://medisur.sld.cu/index.php/medisur/article/view/2751

Gros, B. (2008). *Videojuegos y aprendizaje* [Video games and learning]. Graó.

Gros, B. (2009). Certezas e interrogantes acerca del uso de los videojuegos para el aprendizaje. *Comunicación (Cartago)*, *7*(1), 251–264. https://idus.us.es/handle/11441/58304

Guerrero, M. (2016). *Historias más allá de lo filmado fan fiction y narrativa transmedia en series de televisión* [Stories beyond the filmed fan fiction and transmedia narrative in television series]. Universidad Popeu Fabra.

Hanus, M. D., & Fox, J. (2015). Assessing the effects of gamification in the classroom: A longitudinal study on intrinsic motivation, social comparison, satisfaction, effort, and academic performance. *Computers & Education, 80*, 152–161. doi:10.1016/j.compedu.2014.08.019

Hayden, L., Olav, F., Skjerdal, M., Reitan, P., & Jenssen, S. (2022). A review on the use of escape rooms in education – touching the void. *Education Inquiry, 13*(2), 169–184. doi:10.1080/20004508.2020.1860284

Jenkins, H., Purushotma, R., Clinton, K., Weigel, M., & Robinson, A. (2006). *Confronting the challenges of participatory culture: Media education for the 2º Century*. The MacArthur Foundation.

Jiménez, L. (2017). *El poder y la ciencia de la motivación* [The power and science of motivation]. Autoedición.

Kapp, K. M. (2012). *The Gamification of Learning and Instruction: Game-based Methods and Strategies for Training and Education*. John Wiley & Sons.

Labrador, E. (2020). *Gamificación, juegos serios y ABJ* [Gamification, serious games and BPA]. Retrieved April 10, 2022, from http://emil-lab.eu/gamificacion-serious-games-y-abj

Lozano, R. (2011). De las TIC a las TAC: Tecnologías del aprendizaje y del conocimiento [From ICT to TAC: learning and knowledge technologies]. *Anuario ThinkEPI, 5*, 44–47.

Makri, A., Vlachopoulos, D., & Martina, R. A. (2021). Digital escape rooms as innovative pedagogical tools in education: A systematic literature review. *Sustainability, 13*(8), 4587. doi:10.3390u13084587

Marczewski, A. (2018). *Gamification. Even ninja monkeys like to play*. Unicorn Edition.

Marín, V., Morales, M., & Reche, E. (2020). Aprendizaje con videojuegos con realidad aumentada en educación primaria [Learning with video games with augmented reality in primary education]. *Revista de Ciencias Sociales, 26*(2), 94-112.

Marín, V., & Ramírez, A. (2012). Posibilidades educativas de los videojuegos y juegos digitales en educación inclusiva [Educational possibilities of video games and digital games in inclusive education]. In V. Marín (Coord.), Los videojuegos y los juegos digitales como materiales educativos (pp. 165-191). Síntesis.

Martín-González, E., Godoy-Giménez, M., Fernández-Martín, P., León, J., González-Rodríguez, A., Mora, S., Sánchez-Kuhn, A., Carmona, I., García-Pérez, Á., Flores Cubos, P., Estévez, A. F., & Moreno, M. (2021). Escape room as a tool to improve the motivation and commitment of students. *Actas 15th International Technology, Education and Development Conference INTED2021*, 5868-5873. 10.21125/inted.2021.1180

Negre, C., & Carrion, S. (2020). *Desafío en el aula: Manual práctico para llevar los juegos de escape educativos al aula* [Classroom Challenge: A practical manual for bringing educational escape games into the classroom]. Paidós Eduación.

Neira, E., Clares, J., & Sánchez, J. (2021). New audience dimensions in streaming platforms the second life of Money Heist on Netflix as a case study. *El Profesional de la Información, 30*(1), e300113. doi:10.3145/epi.2021.ene.13

Nicholson, S. (2015). *Peeking Behind the Locked Door: A Survey of Escape Room Facilities.* https://scottnicholson.com/pubs/erfacwhite.pdf

Nicholson, S. (2018). Creating engaging escape rooms for the classroom. *Childhood Education, 94*(1), 44–49. doi:10.1080/00094056.2018.1420363

Pacheco, M., & Causado, R. (2018). El aprendizaje basado en videojuegos y la gamificación como Estrategias para construir y vivir la convivencia escolar [Classroom Challenge: A practical manual for bringing educational escape games into the classroom]. *Revista CEDOTIC, 3*(1), 59-80. http://investigaciones.uniatlantico.edu.co/revistas/index.php/CEDOTIC/article/view/1971

Pérez-López, I. J. (2020). *De las 7 Bolas de Dragón a los 7 reinos de Poniente: viajando por la ficción para transformar la realidad* [From the 7 Dragon Balls to the 7 kingdoms of Westeros: traveling through fiction to transform reality]. CopiDeporte.

Pico, S. (2013). Formación TIC del profesorado para garantizar el éxito en la integración de la tecnología [ICT teacher training to ensure success in technology integration]. *Ítaca:Revista de Filologia, 4*(4), 65–80. doi:10.14198/ITACA2013.4.03

Prat, Q., Camerino, O., & Coiduras, J. L. (2013). Introducción de las TIC en educación física. Estudio descriptivo sobre la situación actual [Introduction of ICT in physical education. Descriptive study on the current situation]. *Apunts. Educación Física y Deportes, 113*, 37-44. .(2013/3).113.03 doi:10.5672/apunts.20140983.es

Quintero, L. E. (2021). *EXPANDEF. La Educación Fïsica y las tecnologías de la información y la comunicación (TIC)* [EXPANDEF. Physical education and information and communication technologies (ICT)]. Autopublicación en Amazon Fullfilment.

Ramos-Villagrasa, P. J., Fernández-Campo, A., Oliván, B., Fernández del Río, E., Berges, A., Hernández, S., Huarte, S., & Martín-Peña, J. (2019). Storytelling: Una metodología de aprendizaje activo para la enseñanza de la psicología social en la educación superior [Storytelling: An active learning methodology for teaching social psychology in higher education]. *Suma Psicologica, 16*(1), 11–19. doi:10.18774/0719-448x.2019.16.349

Ruiz, R., & Tesouro, M. (2013). Beneficios e inconvenientes de las nuevas tecnologías en el aprendizaje del alumno. Propuestas formativas para alumnos, profesores y padres [How do we learn? A scientific approach to learning and teaching]. *Revista Educación y futuro digital, 5,* 17-25. https://redined.mecd.gob.es/xmlui/bitstream/handle/11162/118963/EYFD_72.pdf

Ruíz-Martín, H. (2020). *¿Cómo aprendemos? Una aproximación científica al aprendizaje y la enseñanza* [How do we learn? A scientific approach to learning and teaching]. Graó editorial.

Ryan, R. M., & Deci, E. L. (2000). Self-determination theory and the facilitation of intrinsic motivation, social development, and well-being. *The American Psychologist, 55*(1), 68–78. doi:10.1037/0003-066X.55.1.68 PMID:11392867

Sainz, B., de la Torre, I., López, M., Aguiar, J., & de Castro, C. (2019). Aplicación plural de herramientas para gamificar. Análisis y comparativa [Plural application of tools to gamify. Analysis and comparison]. *V Congreso de Innovación Educativa y de Docencia en Red*, 991. http://ocs.editorial.upv.es/index.php/INRED/INRED2019/paper/viewFile/10467/4798

Sánchez-Martín, J., Corrales-Serrano, M., Luque-Sendra, A., & Zamora-Polo, F. (2020). Exit for success. Gamifying science and technology for university students using escape-room. A preliminary approach. *Heliyon*, *6*(7), 1–11. doi:10.1016/j.heliyon.2020.e04340 PMID:32671257

Sánchez-Rodríguez, J., Ruiz Palmero, J., Sánchez Rivas, E., & Sánchez Vega, E. (2019). *Escape room y breakout. Aproximación bliométrica en bases de datos* [Escape room and breakout. Bibliometric approach in databases]. Universidad de Málaga. https://riuma.uma.es/xmlui/bitstream/handle/10630/19157/EscapeRoom_BreakOut.pdf?sequence=1&isAllowed=y

Santamaría Urbieta, A., & Alcalde Peñalver, E. (2021). Multimodal Discourse in Digital Storytelling: An Assessment Tool Proposal. *Computer Assisted Language Learning Electronic Journal*, *22*(2), 14-25. http://callej.org/journal/22-2/Urbieta-Penalver2021.pdf

Sierra-Daza, M. C., & Fernández-Sánchez, M. R. (2019). Gamificando el aula universitaria. Análisis de una experiencia de Escape Room en educación superior [Gamifying the university classroom. Analysis of an Escape Room experience in higher education]. *Revista de Estudios y Experiencias en Educación*, *18*(36), 105–115. doi:10.21703/rexe.20191836sierra15

Simões, J., Díaz-Redondo, R., & Fernández-Vilas, A. (2013). A social gamification framework for a K-6 learning platform. *Computers in Human Behavior*, *29*(2), 345–353. doi:10.1016/j.chb.2012.06.007

Slussareff, M., Braad, E., Wilkinson, P., & Strååt, B. (2016). Games for learning. In R. Dörner, S. Göbel, M. Kickmeier-Rust, M. Masuch, & K. Zweig (Eds.), *Entertainment computing and serious games.* (pp. 189-211). Springer. http://link.springer.com/chapter/10.1007%2F978-3-319-46152-6_9

Sotoca, P. [@PabloSotoca]. (2019, Apr. 30). *Capítulo 1. Terminó la espera. Arranca la nueva temporada de #LaEFvaEnSerie* [Chapter 1. The wait is over. The new season of #LaEFvaEnSerie begins] [Tweet]. Twitter. https://twitter.com/PabloSotoca/status/1123285948551389186?s=20&t=oQ-TuHlhN9-lhMFYLYmR5Q

Sotoca, P. (2020). Rally Edukar: Una propuesta de gamificación que promueve el empoderamiento de la mujer en el deporte [Edukar Rally: A gamification proposal that promotes the empowerment of women in sport]. *EmasF. Revista digital de Educación Física, 65*, 16-31.

Sotoca, P., & Pérez-López, I. (2019). Gamificación educativa: kit de montaje basico [Educational gamification: basic assembly kit]. In Didáctica de la Educación Física en Educación Infantil y Primaria (pp. 393-406). Universidad Internacional de la Rioja.

Tobias, S., Fletcher, J. D., & Wind, A. P. (2014). Game-Based Learning. In J. M. Spector, M. D. Merril, J. Elen, & M. J. Bishop (Eds.), *Handbook of Research on Educational Communications and Technology* (pp. 485–503). Springer. doi:10.1007/978-1-4614-3185-5_38

Varys, L. [@RedPajaritos]. (2019, Apr. 30). *Continuamos con el segundo capítulo de esta apasionante temporada... Espero que sigáis con este mismo entusiasmo e ilusión #LaEFvaEnSerie* [We continue with the second chapter of this exciting season... I hope you continue with this same enthusiasm and enthusiasm #LaEFvaEnSerie] [Tweet]. Twitter. https://twitter.com/RedPajaritos/status/1123297647094267905?s=20&t=oQ-TuHlhN9-lhMFYLYmR5Q

World Health Organization. (2020). *Physical activity. Key facts.* Retrieved April 16, 2022, from https://www.who.int/en/news-room/fact-sheets/detail/physical-activity

Yañez-Florez, S. M., Hernández-Cueto, J. L., Salinas-Aguirre, M., & Moncada-Rodriguez, G. R. (2022). The university perception of the teaching learning process: Online education vs fase-to-face education. *Journal of Teaching and Educational Research*, *8*(21), 12–19. doi:10.35429/JTER.2022.21.8.12.19

Zhang, X. C., Hyunjoo, L., Rodriguez, C., Rudner, J., Chan, T., & Papagnou, D. (2018). Trapped as a group, escape as a team: Applying Gamification to incorporate team-building skills through an "Escape Room" experience. *Cureus Journal of Medical Science*, *10*(3), 50–62. doi:10.7759/cureus.2256 PMID:29725559

Zichermann, G., & Cunningham, C. (2011). *Gamification by design: Implementing game mechanics in web and mobile apps*. O'Reilly Media, Inc.

KEY TERMS AND DEFINITIONS

Bella Ciao: One of the representative songs of the Original Soundtrack of the series "La Casa de Papel". The symbol of the people's revolution is the same that the hackers were looking for in this experience.

Break Out: Playful experience that focuses on solving riddles and metacognitive tests to open a series of locks that close a box, trying to open it before the time limit. Some authors speak of digital BreakOut and digital Escape Rooms interchangeably in their digital versions, something that does not occur in its analogue version.

Escape Room: Playful experience that occurs within a physical space where metacognitive tests must be solved to leave the room in a limited time. Some authors speak of BreakOut and digital Escape Room interchangeably in its digital version, something that does not occur in its analogue version. In the virtual world, it can be similar to graphic adventure video games, provided that the plot arises in a room and there is a certain time to get out of it. However, new educational trends resemble the resolution of digital puzzles that allow the opening of digital locks through passwords in a limited time.

Hackear: It is an online tool of Spanish origin that allows generating visual and interactive content easily and quickly.

***La Casa Sin Papel*:** Name adapted from the original title of the international television series "Money Heist". Despite the English translation, in Spanish, this fictional story is known as *La Casa de Papel.*

Professor: In the series, he is the person in charge of plotting the plan to pull off the big heist. In the project, he was represented by a voice that contacted the students by text, audio or telephone.

Serious Games: Any system that is a game and whose primary purpose is not fun, although it should always be implied. They have been designed for a specific purpose and are designed specifically for that purpose.

Spin-Off: In the audiovisual world, works that arise from other existing works that focus on including more details or aspects different from the original are considered.

ENDNOTES

* The password is the surname of the founder of the first INEF (National Institute for Physical Education) in Spain.

1 Genially (https://app.genial.ly/dashboard)

APPENDIX A

Questionnaire

1. Have you participated in a gamification project before?
   a. Yes
   b. No
2. Through gamification:
   a. you learn more and in a more relevant and playful way than with other methodologies.
   b. you learn the same as using other methodologies but in a more relevant and playful way.
   c. you learn the same as using other methodologies but investing more time and work.
   d. you learn less than with other methodologies.
3. Gamification seems to me... (select one option by value: Strongly Disagree - Disagree - Agree - Strongly Agree)
   a. a suitable methodology for learning the use of ICT.
   b. that it is suitable for teaching at the university level.
   c. that achieves a protagonism of the student that is not achieved with other teaching methodologies
   d. that it is more motivating.
4. What innovation techniques have been most attractive and motivating to you? Select those you want (more than one answer is possible).
   a. Global safe system
   b. Brief use of apps to get the codes
   c. Use of Twitter and Instagram
   d. Uncertainty and surprises when arriving at class
   e. Connecting with the teacher in Tokyo and Berlin
   f. Work in groups of three through cities
   g. Progress bar system
   h. Contain all evidence of learning (assignments) on a website
   i. Extra boxes
   j. Other:
5. What elements have motivated you the most in your experience in the course? Select those you want (more than one answer is possible)
   a. Challenges completed by group
   b. Challenges completed individually
   c. Activities performed in the classroom
   d. Out-of-classroom practical activities
6. Evaluate the teacher's participation in this teaching and learning process (write about knowledge, accessibility, motivation, and general opinion).
7. Evaluation of the subject: (Select one option per value: Strongly Disagree - Disagree - Agree - Strongly Agree)

a. Assessment methods are appropriate for the level of education (university) and the type of content.
b. Subject assignments are adequate to assess the student's performance in the subject.
c. The final grade of the activities has remained in the background, and the intrinsic motivation has prevailed when carrying out the tasks.
d. The balance between group and individual tasks has been appropriate.
e. The workload outside of the classroom is appropriate for the educational level (and the content).

8. What aspects of the course did you find most relevant and enriching?
9. Your acquisition of knowledge and skills in ICT and physical activity:
   a. It has not increased
   b. It has somehow increased
   c. It has increased significantly
   d. It has increased incredibly
   e. It has increased dramatically
10. Your level of participation, commitment and dedication to the course has been, generally speaking… Linker scale (minimum) 1-5 (maximum)
11. Write your general opinion about the activity. How you felt, if you liked it, if you didn't and if there were anything you would change.

Chapter 10
Three Practical Examples of Educational Escape Rooms in ICT Engineering Courses

Elisa Rojas
Universidad de Alcalá, Spain

ABSTRACT

This chapter examines three educational escape rooms applied in engineering courses in the specific area of computer networks. This analysis includes background, design decisions, implementation details, and obtained results. The objective is to provide a quick overview of ideas for teachers who want to initiate the field. Preliminary results seem promising in terms of student engagement and motivation, which is particularly relevant in online environments. The current literature indicates a trend about educational escape rooms during the last years, which will likely increase, while future research should focus on tools and resources to implement them and collaboration among professors to perform extensive evaluations in terms of learning outcomes.

INTRODUCTION

Engineering degrees in higher education require a profound knowledge in basic sciences (such as mathematics and physics), but they also rely on very practical learning. In the end, engineers will work with daily problems and challenges, and their main objective is to solve them applying ideas and tools.

In the specific field of Information and Communications Technology (ICT), these tools and practical environments change every day. Although engineering foundations still remain the same, the speed of technological advances is very high; hence, professors need to catch up with industry requirements and trends, and to update the content of their courses every academic year. At the same time, this reality affects the methodology leveraged for teaching engineering, since traditional passive master classes tend to be inefficient to cover the syllabus, and that is why engineering courses usually implement active learning methods, in the form of practical laboratories, for students to test and develop their own knowledge (Balamuralithara & Woods, 2009).

DOI: 10.4018/978-1-6684-6081-8.ch010

Recently, other active learning methods, such as flipped classroom or gamification have been implemented in engineering courses in the ICT field of the Universidad de Alcala (UAH) (Estriegana et al., 2019), obtaining good results not only quantitatively as part of their final grades, but also when checking motivation and participation of students. In this regard, some professors of the ICT field in UAH wondered whether using escape rooms, as a complementary activity to these active learning methods, could eventually strengthen, even more, the good results obtained. The reason to do so is that escape rooms are indeed very similar to practical situations in engineering workplaces: a problem or a solution for a client needs to be found, and the engineers need to use any tools or resource available, together with their knowledge, to accomplish it (Gordillo et al., 2020).

The main objective of this chapter is to describe the design and implementation of three practical examples of escape rooms in computer science and telecommunication engineering courses in UAH. In particular, the courses belong to the field of computer networks. Our intention is to provide the foundational ideas, the design decisions, the resources needed to implement them and the obtained results, also taking into consideration changes and evolutions of it, as well as advantages and disadvantages.

The remainder of this chapter is organized as follows: In the next section, the chapter reviews related work in the field of escape rooms in engineering. Afterwards, the three examples of escape rooms are described, each of them providing background, design decisions, implementations and results. This is followed with a section discussing the previous results, summarizing them, and providing general recommendations. Finally, the author provides future research directions and concludes the chapter.

Related Work

Recent works have applied escape rooms in diverse engineering courses. If checked in chronological order, the first one is from Borrego et al. (2017), who presented an escape room designed to increase motivation of students in courses of the second year of the degree. To this purpose, they leveraged typical material from the field (e.g., latptop), and not so common too (e.g., walkie talkie), to implement several riddles related to computer networks.

Regarding escape rooms for first-year students, Walsh & Spence (2018) prepared one to improve basic research skills of first-year students. Participants were voluntary and the library staff also participated in the design, obtaining good feedback from all. Davis & Lee (2019) also focused on first-year students, but in this case on an introductory course for engineering. They designed puzzles and escape rooms, and surveyed more than 200 unique students before, during and after the end of the semester. The average result obtained was 8.2 out of 10 on enjoyment, and 7.3 on aesthetics.

On more advanced engineering topics, Ross & Bell (2019) designed escape rooms activities using a hardware decoder box, once again focused on engagement of students, which was achieved according to their evaluation. Lopez-Pernas et al. (2019) prepared an educational escape room in a programming course, comprehensively analyzing the applied methodology, results and lessons learned. In this regard, they concluded that working in pairs was best for programming purposes, puzzles should be carefully ordered (so that students do not miss any step), and some kind of monitoring activity should be included to provide hints to students when needed and facilitate the game flow. They also highlighted the importance of defining the learning objectives and evaluation. Heckelman & Bucholz (2020) implemented an escape room in Matlab (a common tool for engineering degrees among others), and provided the developed code in an open GitHub repository. Otemaier et al. (2020) prepared an escape room tested with 53 undergraduate students about mathematical logic, obtaining good feedback and proving escape rooms could not only be applied for soft skills, but also for technical or hard skills.

In the specific field of security, Beguin et al. (2019) prepared an escape room focused on computer security, with positive feedback. It is remarkable how they also emphasized the need for a game master to monitor the execution of the escape room, by checking no technical difficulties appear and players stick to the game. Seebauer et al. (2020) provided a preliminary idea for an escape room about cryptography. Löffler et al. (2021) demonstrated that a physical escape room about cybersecurity can be transformed into a virtual one, keeping player immersion.

In relation with industrial and electronic engineering, Valero Cerda (2019) reviewed and provided a detailed implementation of the first escape room designed for a robot academy, created by diverse international students from Europe. Tejado et al. (2021) implemented an escape room for "Industrial Process Control", a fourth-year optional course, demonstrating high potential to support learning in engineering.

Focusing on engagement, Sanchez-Martinez et al. (2020) analyzed diverse escape rooms applied in the fields of both engineering and education and the results were analogous in terms of opinion about the implemented activities. Ross & Bennett (2020) analyzed multiple escape rooms for engineering students proving that engagement is a cornerstone of educational escape rooms.

About distance learning, Gordillo et al. (2020) evaluated learning effectiveness of online educational escape rooms in software engineering, which was positively assessed, together with motivation, once again. They highlighted the power of escape rooms to provide a good feeling of immersion, almost the same to face-to-face escape rooms, and the need for software tools specifically designed to create education escape rooms.

Finally, Ross & de Souza-Daw (2021) prepared diverse puzzles and escape rooms with a different approach to the ones previously mentioned, as in this case all of them were first checked by experts in the telecommunications engineering field (and not by students). The authors examined this preliminary evaluation to improve them before actually proceeding with the implementation with students in engineering courses. They also obtained additional feedback, for instance, about enjoyment.

Among all analyzed works, most of them highlighted engagement as one key advantage. Many of them suggested extensions and improvements as future work, as the majority only provided one year of testing. It is also pertinent to mention that some of them emphasized the need of a game master to keep the player flow. Finally, only a few implemented the escape rooms in online or virtual mode.

ESCAPE ROOM 1: MYSTERY AND PADLOCKS IN A NETWORK MANAGEMENT COURSE

Background and Motivation

The first escape room was designed for the "computer networks management" courses from two types of ICT engineering degrees in UAH: computer science and telecommunication. These courses belong to the first semester of the fourth year of their respective degrees, which are taught to around 60 to 70 students in total. Although the courses globally differ in content, they share some of their sessions, and this was leveraged to have a bigger group of students to test the developed escape room.

The reason to choose these courses, among others in which the author was participating as well, was the need for an update on the content of the course after the author taught it during her first year at university. More specifically, the methodology of the courses was excessively classic, while the content was intended for hands-on work. Therefore, the commitment of students was not as good as it could be.

Additionally, three additional factors triggered the creation of the escape room:

- **Degree year:** These courses are taught during the fourth year of both degrees, which is the last one. Additionally, one of them is an elective or optional course (in fact, both of them were so at the beginning, but one of them shifted to mandatory after a degree plan update). As last-year courses, they are very focused on industry needs and practical work, as the theoretical foundations are provided during the first two years. In this regard, students are looking for active learning. Therefore, although practical sessions already accomplish this criterion, a change in the methodology towards active theory sessions would be aligned with the need of students.
- **Number of students:** The number of students was around 20 to 25 in each course, with a total of 40 to 50 in total, which later on shifted to around 60 to 70 students (after the change in the plan mentioned before). The number of students per group was slightly high for the implementation of the escape room but, at the same time, it could provide additional insights and analysis from a wider range of students after the implementation of the use case. Therefore, the number of students represented a good trade-off.
- **Coordination and professors:** The number of professors to teach the theory part of the course was two and, at the same time, both coordinated together the subject. This facilitated the actual implementation of the escape room following the guidelines of the course and the general administrative rules of the degree planification.

Design Decisions

The design decisions were driven by the three factors mentioned in the previous section. First of all, as a last-year course, it should be a hands-on escape room implemented in a theory class, which could let students apply knowledge from that session, while having fun. Additionally, it should not overlap with any of the already existing content from the practical laboratory sessions.

Secondly, considering the number of students, the escape room was designed for groups of around 10 students (which would be translated into two or three groups, based on a typical amount of 25 students per course). The duration was defined of around one hour (i.e., the duration of one session), and the execution could be performed face-to-face, online, or in a hybrid mode (online together with face-to-face). The main difference is that the first allowed the inclusion of actual physical lockers and other resources in the classroom, while in the second those resources are substituted for virtual equivalent ones.

The third design decision was based on the third factor, which was indeed an opportunity rather than a constraint. The professor selected this course among others because they could implement creative ideas for the escape room as course coordinator. In this sense, the theme selected was "mystery" and the implementation should have diverse paths to achieve the goal (or at least some parts of it). This could facilitate that each group of students could work either in smaller groups in parallel or all together, adjusted to their own pace and strategy.

Finally, aesthetics and atmosphere were considered crucial to increase students' engagement and motivation. In this regard, and considering the selected theme of the escape room, although ICT elements would be driving the escape room, additional physical resources like padlocks or hidden messages should be incorporated as well. Additionally, to foster reasoning and strategic thinking, some role elements

Figure 1. Screenshot of the index webpage of the first escape room

could also be introduced, following the idea of card games like "Les Loups-garous de Thiercelieux" (Ulloa & Barrantes, 2008).

Implementation and Resources Needed

The implementation of this escape room was planned as a long-term idea, in which the escape room could evolve and be modified in the upcoming years. For this reason, the foundation was a web-based design based on HTML5 and deployed on GitHub (which lets users hosts personal webpages for free based on a specific URL). This web-based framework consisted of a set of puzzles, which would be accessed not necessarily in order, and diverse hidden webpages that should be discovered by students after solving each of the different puzzles, following the defined theme.

GitHub webpages are hosted in open repositories and code can be checked by any user, and that is why the complete framework was created with around 10 valid pages and more than 50 "dumb" pages (containing nonsense or even misleading information). As students of this escape rooms were engineers, the objective was to avoid, as much as possible, that they "hacked" the game and won without following its rules. To start the escape room, all students started from the same webpage, which was accessed by students from a QR. That index page is illustrated in Figure 1.

Additionally, a couple of different padlocks were introduced in the escape room as illustrated in Figure 2, which would be hidden inside the classroom as part of the puzzles. Some messages in paper were also included, such as hints, random messages (with no particular meaning) and role-playing call-outs (for the strategic side of the escape room).

The development difficulty could be considered "medium", as it required some knowledge to develop HTML code, and quite some time to write it and deploy it, after diverse tests (with laptop and

Figure 2. Padlocks leveraged for the first escape room

smartphone devices). The rest of items of the escape room did not require much effort in comparison with the previous parts.

As for the years of implementation, the escape room was designed in 2017/2018 and implemented to be tested for the very first time in 2018/2019. To complete the tests with additional students, the escape room was also evaluated during 2019/2020 and 2020/2021. Although it was still leveraged for the courses in 2021/2022 and it is planned for upcoming years, these academic years were not evaluated in detail because novel sessions were included in the course and the results could then change based on this new context.

Finally, it is important to highlight that, although this escape room was originally designed to be implemented in face-to-face classes, the shift to online classes was rather easy by simply converting the physical elements into virtual ones. In fact, this happened during academic year 2020/2021, as courses were all online after the COVID-19 pandemic situation started.

Gameplay Details

As an example of a gameplay, this escape room is usually implemented in one hour. As the course sessions are two-hour length, the students are usually kindly asked to go outside the class during the break after one hour of class. The professor would then close the room and prepare all padlocks, hidden in the class, together with some hints printed in paper and a big QR projected on the class screen. After the break, students go back to class, and they would only see an intriguing QR. Most of students naturally scan the QR and are brought to the main webpage, as illustrated in Figure 1. This website has different

Figure 3. Example of puzzle in Escape Room 1

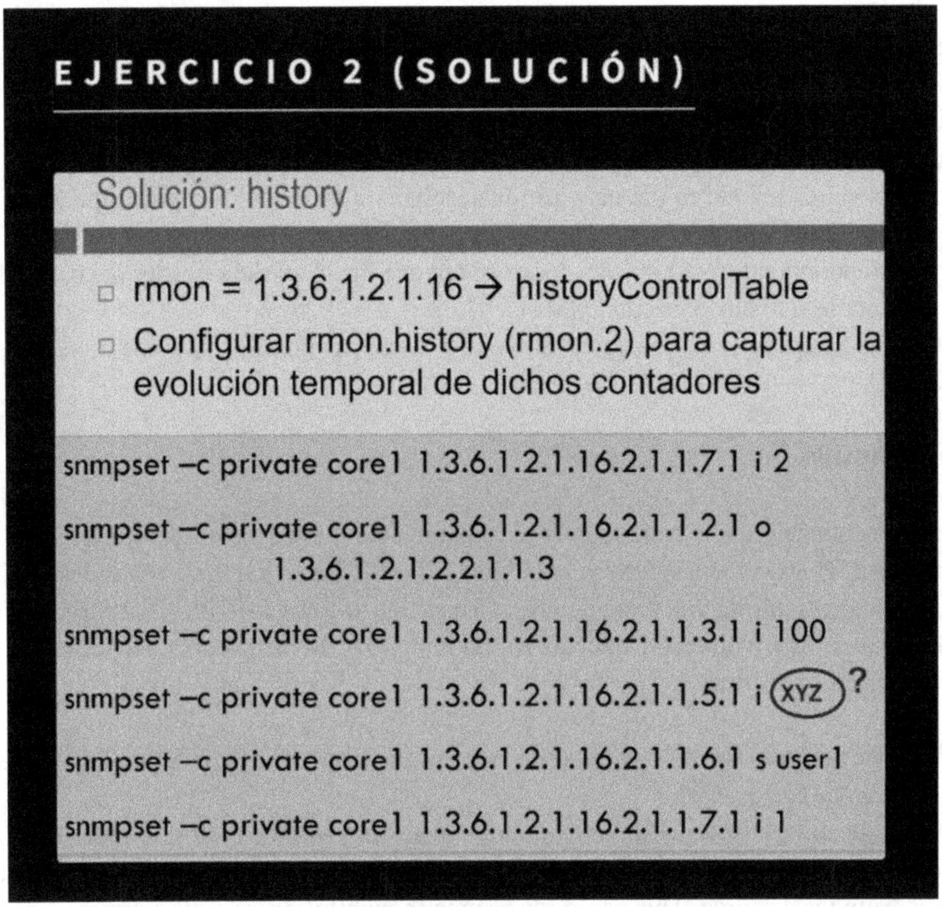

sections that, when clicked, present diverse information, including slides from class, exercises or hints about the game like "Please try to visit the alternative URL, substituting XYZ by these numbers".

After this initial launch, there are several exercises about the session (Remote MONitoring framework, RMON), which is presented in a theoretical way first and the student need to practice now during the escape room. An example of exercise is depicted in Figure 3. The students need to solve a problem and three digits (represented by the letters XYZ) are unknown. At this point, the students already know that XYZ, when used in the alternative URL, will redirect them to other websites where they can found additional quizzes and hints.

In this regard, students need to correctly solve the puzzles to be correctly redirected to other webpages and continue the game. At some point, the webpages directly provide codes for the padlocks, which would finalize the gameplay.

During the gameplay, hints are also hidden in these websites, as well as in printed form inside the class, so that they students can keep the game flow at all times. Furthermore, the professor can also intervene during the session, providing additional hints, if the students are stuck at some point.

As it can be observed, puzzles are generic enough to be exchanged by any other type of problem from any other course. As far as the students obtain chains of three numbers (XYZ) from the puzzles, these could be used in URLs containing additional websites and puzzles, and this can be extended as needed by the implemented activity.

In summary, the main challenges of this educational escape room are:

- Exploring the main website and all websites linked to the first one in a hierarchical way.
- Exploring the class for hints and additional resources, as well as the padlocks to be unlocked.
- Solving exercises related to the network management course and recognize the XYZ pattern to look for additional websites.
- Filtering important information from non-relevant one (many of the websites are basically "spam", which do not lead to any particular place).
- Working in groups to rapidly explore as many websites as possible (if done alone, this could be too slow).

Obtained Results

As previously mentioned, this escape room was implemented during the academic year 2018/2019 for the very first time. However, during the year before, 2017/2018, a quick survey was designed to obtain feedback from students during that year already, as a baseline to compare with. That survey was intended to be brief so that, even if voluntary, students would reply to it. In fact, it only had three questions that could be rated from 1 to 5 stars:

- **Usefulness:** Students should rate the usefulness of the course for their future jobs, based on their own experience and opinion.
- **Interest (absolute):** Students should rate how interesting was the course in their opinion.
- **Interest (relative):** Students should rate how interesting was the course if compared to other courses from their degree. This could raise some thoughtful differences from the previous question because opinions are always subjective, but they might be more valuable if applied in a relative way.
- **Comments:** Open section for the students to provide any type of feedback about the course.

However, it is important to highlight that this survey was not designed specifically for the escape room, but for a set of new sessions implemented following active learning methodologies. At the same time, only around half of the theory sessions were updated, which is around one quarter of the whole course. Therefore, the effect of the escape room might not be so evident overall.

As it can be observed in Figure 4, during four years usefulness remained around the same value (in this case, around a result of 4 stars), while the interest about the courses changed. The difference between 2017/2018 and 2018/2019 is particularly remarkable because, while usefulness remained exactly the same (around 4), the interest in the courses drastically increased (from 3 to almost 5 stars). Additionally, in the comments section, students highlighted one of the most engaging sessions of the course was the one devoted to the escape room. These results partially demonstrate the motivation level of students from 2017/2018, in which active learning methodologies were not implemented, to 2018/2019, when they were implemented for the first time.

However, values from years 2019/2020 and 2020/2021 are not so remarkable (although interest level is still higher than in 2017/2018), and this might be due to several reasons. First of all, in 2019/2020 one

Figure 4. Average evaluation of courses during four academic years

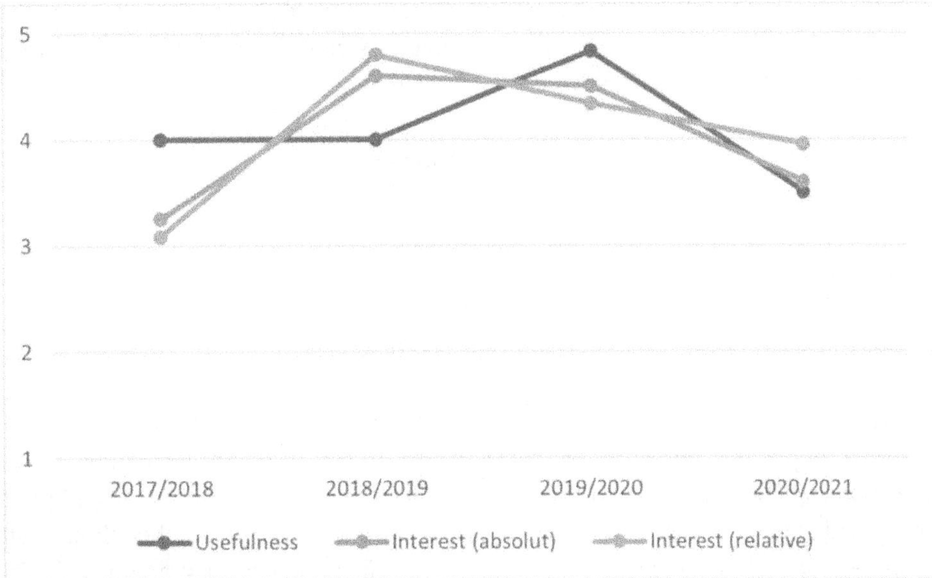

of the courses became mandatory (and it was optional before) and, furthermore, that academic year the laboratory sessions were partially updated. Mandatory courses are likely to generate less interest than optional ones, as the latter are specifically selected by students; while the update of the laboratories could explain why the usefulness boosted up to almost an average of 5 stars. Secondly, in 2020/2021 the number of students from the mandatory course increased, representing more than two thirds of the total students (instead of around one half of it), which could affect the results even in more percentage and, additionally, the course was developed online due to the COVID-19 pandemic, which also raised differences in comparison to face-to-face courses. For this reason, this evaluation was discontinued after 2020/2021, because it was considered that results were not so meaningful anymore (because of several changes every academic year).

Apart from this survey, additional results were collected in terms of final grades and professor's evaluation by students. The former one slightly increased, but not enough to be consider a meaningful result, while the second one improved by more than 5%, and once again many positive comments about the escape room were provided in it as well. In this regard, the main conclusion is that escape rooms serve to enhance motivation, hence demonstrating the results found in the literature.

ESCAPE ROOM 2: FOLLOWING THE "AMONG US" TREND IN A NETWORK MANAGEMENT COURSE

Background and Motivation

The second escape room was also implemented in the same engineering courses of the first one, based on two main reasons: (i) the good results obtained in terms of students' engagement, and (ii) the need to update course sessions to virtual mode due to the COVID-19 pandemic scenario. Differently from the first escape room, this second escape room was not motivated by un update on the course methodology but, instead, by an unforeseen change in the lesson delivery method.

The selected session for this escape room was particularly challenging for a shift to virtual environments, because students had to first go out of the classroom and look for a set of hints and then, once back in the classroom, solve a set of practical exercises. As the dynamics of the session had some similarities with an escape room, when converted to an online version, upgrading it to a virtual escape room seemed to make sense.

Design Decisions

In this case, the design decisions were driven by two factors:

- **Lack of time for the update:** During the first year of the COVID-19 pandemic, regulations were updated very frequently. Therefore, there was some uncertainty about the method to teach lessons, as at the end of 2020 the situation had improved, but it was still bad, so the discussion about face-to-face, hybrid or strictly virtual mode for teaching was constant during the whole academic year. Once this session was specifically set to online mode, just a few weeks remained for it to happen, and more session needed to be updated too, so the time to modify it was scarce. As a consequence, the resulting escape room should be simple enough to be implemented without major issues.
- **Online teaching platform:** The platform leveraged for online teaching, which was Blackboard Collaborate, was crucial to design this escape room, because its available functionalities would define the possibilities to implement the educational escape room.

In the case of atmosphere design, the "Among Us" videogame was considered because it was a clear trend for young people at the end of 2020, as many people started to play it (and even to stream it) during COVID-19's lockdowns. In fact, diverse teachers started to use it as a theme in their lessons (Gracey, 2021). Therefore, the aesthetics of this videogame were leveraged to capture students' attention.

Implementation and Resources Needed

The implementation followed the dynamics of "Among Us", in which a set of tasks need to be done around a scenario with different rooms. The team wins if all tasks are finished. However, inside the team, there is a small set of intruders who will fight against this finalization, hampering the execution of tasks and even "killing" some of the people. While the intruders know the identity of each other, the rest of people do not, so they will have to fight to perform all tasks even if obstructed by the intruder players.

For this reason, the first step was to implement a set of tasks, as images (originally created by the professor, to avoid any copyright concerns), with the aesthetics of the game. These images would be projected in diverse rooms created in the online teaching platform, that is, Blackboard Collaborate. Students could change from one room to other upon request. As for the assignment of roles, these were provided via a confidential note through the same platform, prior to the beginning of the escape room. Additionally, players would be grouped in different teams of four or five people each, so that the first one to accomplish all tasks would win. The reason to create these groups was to avoid that some students did not work to solve the puzzles at all, because this could potentially happen in big classes (one of them had more than 50 students).

The development difficulty could be considered "low", as the only thing needed was to convert some wording of exercises in shorter ones integrated in images. The key aspect was to reduce the wording as much as possible, so that they could fit in these images. Therefore, the puzzles were not only about solving the exercise, but also about understanding what task or exercise was requested by each image and why.

Gameplay Details

In the case of this second escape room, the gameplay consists of decoding a message codified in BER (Basic Encoding Rules). The session starts with a theoretical introduction, and, after a break, the students are invited to join an online teaching platform (Blackboard Collaborate, in this case) that is divided into several rooms. Each room contains a piece of the message that can be individually decoded, but that has no specific meaning alone. It is up to students to recognize that the different rooms contain pieces of the message and that all together would solve the puzzle.

For example, the string that follows represents one of these messages coded in BER:

30 82 00 32 02 01 00 04 06 70 75 62 6C 69 63 A2 82 00 23 02 04 59 57 65 EF 02 01 00 02 01 00 30 82 00 13 30 82 00 0F 06 08 2B 06 01 02 01 04 09 00 41 03 01 92 7C

As it can be observed, it looks like an encrypted piece of information. If each room contains a part of this string, students can decode it and, in cooperation with the rest of the team, compose the complete message. The professor is in charge of acknowledging the correct solution of the problem.

Moreover, as previously mentioned, different roles are assigned to students. Some of them are "standard" roles, which only need to decode the message, while other are "intruders" that need to sabotage the decoding of the message, by providing incorrect solutions or discussing aspect when solving it in groups, for example. This latter role can also "kill" (that is, exclude from the game) specific players by voting in secret every certain time defined by the professor (this voting action can be implemented via any online polling tool, and in our case we implemented it via Microsoft Forms). This type of role should not be too evident or, otherwise, it will be recognized and excluded from the game too. The objective of including diverse roles was to slightly hinder the evolution of the problem and, also, to include small challenges and doubts when decoding, which can be interesting to improve the learning outcomes of students.

Once again, these puzzles are based on simple exercises, which can be substituted by others from different courses, but students are in charge of looking for the objective, asking themselves questions about the meaning of those strings and their relationship with the course contents.

In summary, the main challenges of this educational escape room are:

- Exploring the different rooms in the online platform.
- Acknowledging they contain strings of coded information.
- If "standard" role:
    - Applying their knowledge to decode the different strings in each room.
    - Working together to combine all decoded information together (moreover, if decoded separately, the decoded message can be merged later on more effectively).
    - Discovering the coded message
- If "intruder" role:
    - Applying their knowledge to decode the different strings in each room in a wrong way, without being too evident.
    - Generating doubts about the solution of the different coded strings.

  - Getting to know other "intruders" too, so that they can sabotage whole pieces of information (e.g., if they all are in charge of one room, they can definitely provide a wrong decoding to tamper the overall solution, which could be one potential game strategy).

Obtained Results

This escape room was only implemented during the academic year 2020/2021. As it was highly dependent on the platform leverage for virtual classes, once face-to-face sessions were recovered, the session was recovered as it was previously implemented.

Therefore, no particular emphasis was made to evaluate it, as it was always thought as something temporary. However, considering results from the official survey from UAH that all students filled for professors, once the course finalizes, the qualitative evaluation seemed quite similar to the obtained for the first implemented escape room. In general, students liked the atmosphere, they felt intrigued by the tasks and engaged by the session. They also agreed they learnt a lot from that session. Nevertheless, as negative aspects, they highlighted that the session flow was slightly slow due to the virtual implementation of rooms. More specifically, the professor could not monitor and check the progress of all students at a glance (because of the limitations of the online teaching platform), which hindered the evolution of the escape room. Additionally, switching from one room to another required around 10 seconds, which might seem not too long to wait, but it severely interrupted the game flow in their opinion, especially when having to move very quickly among rooms to finalize the escape room as soon as possible.

ESCAPE ROOM 3: USING THE UNREAL ENGINE IN AN INTEGRATED SCENARIO FOR SEVERAL NETWORK ARCHITECTURE COURSES

Background and Motivation

The third escape room was thought as a proof of concept more than an actual implementation. The main idea was to evaluate to what extent preparing an integrated escape room for two courses would be challenging and valuable.

These two courses cover the "network architecture" topic and they are taught in the two semesters of the second year of the same two types of ICT engineering degrees from UAH than in the previous escape rooms. Contrary to the courses mentioned in the previous two escape rooms, these could be considered basic knowledge, as they are mandatory for all students, and they also represent the first subjects about computer networks in their respective degrees. The number of students varies from year to year, but it is always higher than 200 per academic year. As a consequence, the number of professors is high as well, and usually around 10.

Design Decisions

For this third escape room, the design decisions depended on the following factors:

- **Basic courses about computer networks:** As these two courses are basic and mandatory, it is particularly important that they motivate students as, later on, these students will select their optional courses based on their previous experience with the courses of the different specialization fields. This is important to benefit professors and research groups in the field. Therefore, an educational escape room was a good candidate to engage students and increase their motivation.

- **Big courses:** As previously mentioned, these courses have around 200 students per academic year, with different profiles. Moreover, around 10 professors teach in each of them (different in each course), also with different teaching styles. For this reason, the general methodology is still rather traditional and modifying sessions is usually performed slowly and through small changes, because it involves many different opinions. Therefore, to avoid any potential issues or conflicts, the escape room should be designed for a session out of the general schedule and should be optional for the students.
- **Learning outcomes:** The general opinion of professors about the learning degree of students is not outstanding for these two courses. This is particularly critical, because subsequent courses in the field require some foundations to be properly understood. Thus, a potential method to acknowledge the level of students could be an integrated escape room to gather all the knowledge from these courses in a single and final "test" to check the student's learning outcomes, which could also be implemented partially or in an incremental way to check their knowledge during the courses.
- **Aim high:** While the previous escape rooms were designed in a very practical manner, focusing on immediate results during the academic year they were implemented in, this escape room did not have any particular time constraint. Accordingly, the objective was to examine to what extent a complex and comprehensive escape room could be implemented and was worth the effort to do so.

Finally, regarding atmosphere, the theme was "science fiction", the duration was between 30 and 60 minutes, and the escape room was designed to be solved individually or in very small groups (two or three students at most).

Implementation and Resources Needed

Considering the expected complexity of the escape room, it was not developed by the course professor, but by one engineering student instead, as part of her final degree thesis (in Spanish, Trabajo Fin de Grado, TFG). To maximize possibilities of interaction and aesthetics, the escape room prototype was implemented as a customized videogame using Unreal Engine, a popular engine to develop videogames in the industry. It is important to highlight that, even if Unreal Engine is used by videogame companies, the software is completely free for non-commercial purposes and tutorials are available to learn how to use it. The TFG student had previously studied on the topic and framework, so she had enough expertise to code an escape room from scratch based on the requirements previously mentioned. For this reason, the implementation difficulty could be considered "high" this time.

The escape room driving story was about an engineer whose spaceship is damaged. In order to recover the control over it, being able to turn motors on again, the engineer needs to be able to convey the configuration information from a very old server in the ship (configured as a backup server) to the main server. However, even before that, the engineer needs to search for energy sources to be able to start that old server. This energy sources are collected by looking for energy spheres, as illustrated in the screenshot in Figure 5.

Figure 5. Screenshot of the videogame showing an energy sphere

Once ready, the information can be conveyed to the main control server following the principles of classical protocols from computer network architecture, namely: link layer (Ethernet, WiFi,…), network layer (IP), transport layer (TCP, UDP) and application layer (HTTP, FTP,…). In the particular case of the programmed videogame, the control panel was implemented as a command line interface, as depicted in Figure 6. This panel was developed as a configurable interface, similar to the one of a Linux-based server, in which users would set up diverse parameters. Additionally, one of the commands started the engine if everything was correctly configured. To accomplish this task, the old server would show some preliminary information once started with the energy spheres, so that students could know how to continue configuring the communication between both servers.

This educational escape room had additional videogame-based details, such as ambient music or even a so-called "pause" menu, which appeared when the users needed to stop the game for a while. This menu is illustrated in Figure 7. On the left side, it contains a set of hints with the quests to be accomplished, as a guideline; while on the right side, the player can exit or resume the game, for instance.

Although the proof of concept of this videogame-based escape room was successfully developed, additional details about the coding will not be disclosed in this chapter as they remain as technical content and are considered out of the scope of this chapter. However, the thesis of Mayoral Marín (2021) is available in open access format online, in Spanish, in case of interest.

Gameplay Details

The gameplay of this escape room follows a first-person shooter game environment and students need to explore the whole game to look for hints and one main puzzle, which is the one illustrated in Figure 6, as a command line prompt. In this case, the puzzle is basically based on a Cisco's PacketTracer lab practice, but instead of directly using the prompt in a computer, students will need to insert the commands as a player.

Figure 6. Screenshot of the videogame showing the control panel

Sample commands would look like, for instance:

>ip dest 192.168.101.1

Additionally, if students write a "?" in the command line prompt, hints will be provided, so the puzzle to be solved is relatively straightforward.

Differently from the two previous escape rooms, the quizzes in this case are not generic enough to be substituted by other ones, as they should follow a similar topic in the field of the course.

In summary, the main challenges of this educational escape room are:

Figure 7. Screenshot of the videogame showing the "pause" menu

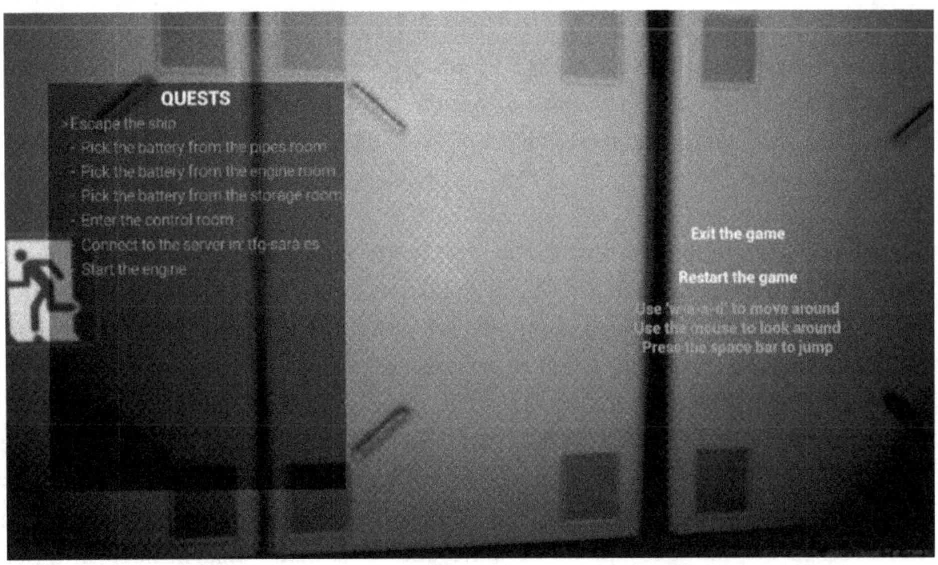

- Exploring the different areas of the game.
- Collecting energy sources to activate the command line prompt or screen.
- Acknowledging that commands can be written in that screen and those commands are related with the theoretical part of the class.
- Acknowledging that some special commands can provide hints.
- Introducing the requested information step by step, with diverse commands that should be introduced with a particular order.
- Starting the engine once all correct commands have been introduced.

Obtained Results

The escape room was finalized in 2021, so it would have been possible to test it with students during academic year 2021/2022. However, there were two main reasons why it was not finally implemented with them:

- First of all, the escape room implementation was finalized, but the overall impression is that story and content should still be improved to make it more challenging and engaging. So far, the puzzle developed in the proof of concept was easy, because the focus was on the videogame development, in a comprehensive manner, and not exclusively on its storyline.
- Secondly, the escape room was designed by a professor that eventually did not teach many classes of those two courses during 2021/2022, so it could not finally be tested with students.

Therefore, the qualitative result of this proof-of-concept escape room is that the experience could be really immersive and engaging for students. However, the software required a non-negligible effort for development and maintenance, particularly to keep students motivated year after year without losing the effect of a first-time play.

DISCUSSION AND RECOMMENDATIONS

In the previous sections, three different escape rooms have been described and analyzed. In order to have a short guideline of them, Table 1 summarizes their key parameters and aspects, as a reference. As it can be observed, each educational escape room was prepared based on a different motivation and background, which yielded diverse results. From all of them, only the first one is currently still being implemented in class.

It is important to highlight that the first escape room was the one implemented a higher number of academic years. This could be due to its simplicity, with a medium difficulty of implementation (developing the website and including physical components). Additionally, the number of students involved the escape room is relatively high, and it can be easily reused for other courses, as the puzzles can be substituted by other ones, as far as the logic of the URL generation is maintained. Moreover, this escape room can be implemented in online, hybrid or face-to-face mode, which increases its potential applications.

On the other hand, the second and third escape rooms represent the simplest and the most complex escape rooms, respectively, which might fall too short or excessively ambitious. The author believes this is the main reason why both escape rooms have been eventually discontinued in time. However, the second escape room could still be leveraged for online environments, and it is versatile enough to be modified to include different puzzles every year, in an easy way. However, while the theme for this second escape room was based on a temporary trend, which is also limited in implementation due to copyright concerns, so the topic of the escape room should be eventually updated to a different one.

Therefore, the overall conclusion could be that sometimes "simple" does not necessarily means "worse" during the development of education escape rooms. As far as puzzles and atmospheres are aligned with the rest of the course, escape rooms could serve as an efficient method to engage students in their learning. In general, the author acknowledges this is the most important outcome of all implemented escape rooms: enhanced student motivation.

Table 1. Qualitative comparative of the three escape rooms

	Motivation	Theme and Platform	Years	Students	Difficulty	Continued?
Escape Room 1	Student engagement and effective learning	Mystery / Web-based	2018/2019, 2019/2020, 2020/2021, 2021/2022	~230 (60 per year aprox.)	Medium	Yes
Escape Room 2	Shift from face-to-face to online classes	Among Us / Blackboard Collaborate	2020/2021	~70	Low	No
Escape Room 3	Proof-of-concept for a comprehensive escape room	Science fiction / Unreal Engine	None	None	High	No

Regarding lessons learned, the author would like to highlight the following ones:

- **Students' enthusiasm:** The general enthusiasm of students in this type of activities is usually high, independently of the topic or the design. This might be due to the unique nature of the activity. That is, implementing an escape room is singular enough to engage students, but this could eventually lose effectiveness if applied in many different courses.
- **Evaluation:** Although it is relatively simple to measure motivation of students, evaluating results and learning outcomes might not be trivial (particularly if the number of students per year is small and, hence, not statistically meaningful). Therefore, so far, the author considers engagement is a proven quality of escape rooms, but additional studies need to be performed to evaluate other metrics.
- **Coordination with other professors:** In courses comprised of more students, evaluation could be easier. However, at the same time, more students are usually translated into more professors involved in the course, which could hinder coordination and implementation. Therefore, it is quite important to select the appropriate courses; ideally, a set of around 20 to 30 students and two or three professors would be preferable.
- **Technology:** Technological tools are a cornerstone of educational escape rooms, especially if implemented online. When designing new escape rooms, professors should not be afraid of looking for new tools and using them. When a tool partially or completely suits an escape room design,

it greatly facilitates implementation, even if the tools need first to be studied by the professor to be used. In this regard, some type of repository with tools would simplify the process.

- **Year after year:** One of the biggest challenges, based on the previous learned lessons and the author's opinion, is to keep the escape room as special as the first time it was implemented. For example, for the first described escape room, the professor that implemented it always hesitated whether the students would know about it and about its solution. This did not happen the first time, but it could be a potential problem for the following years, particularly if some of the students would not pass the course and had to repeat it. For this reason, course selection is also relevant. Additionally, if the design involves a solution, or a story, that can be changed when needed in an easy way, it could avoid this type of issues.

Finally, the author would like to provide the following general recommendations for those people interested in the implementation of educational escape rooms in their classes, although many of them are closely related:

- **Inspiration:** As in other methodologies, to motivate students, first the professor needs to be motivated as well. Therefore, the first step should always be obtaining inspiration from other escape rooms the professor liked and, at the same time, the more escape rooms are tested, the bigger will be the sources for inspiration.
- **Creativity:** Once the inspiration has set a path, creativity is inherent to the design of escape rooms. Professors should feel free to include any creative ideas to their educational escape rooms. In case of doubt, new ideas should always be included for fun and novelty (that is, trying to keep the surprise factor alive, as previously mentioned, even if thought as risky).
- **Timing:** Many professors ask for the perfect timing to include an educational escape room in their classes, but the truth is that there is no perfect timing. Therefore, this should not constrain the implementation of educational escape rooms, either, particularly if it is gradually applied and updated.
- **Complexity:** In relation with the previous aspect, it is better to start with an escape room easy to develop, which will eventually evolve to something more complex, than trying to reach perfection in the design. Complexity does not define success, as it can be observed in the evaluation of the three escape rooms of this chapter.
- **Tools:** Researching related works to gather tools and resources is also important. If implemented in virtual mode, the author recommends free online tools like Genially, RPG Playground or Gather town. However, in general, trying new tools for fun will serve for inspiration as well.

FUTURE RESEARCH DIRECTIONS

First of all, considering the literature review, it can be observed that this methodology is novel and most of works belong to the last three years. Furthermore, the expertise provided by the three educational escape rooms before in this chapter shows that the main advantage is the increase of students' motivation. Therefore, there could be a trend in the upcoming years, particularly in virtual environments in which engagement should be particularly strengthened.

In this regard, a future research direction could be related with the implementation of tools and resources, as previously mentioned. For example, metaverse environments for online teaching could facilitate the implementation of virtual escape rooms, while creating an immersive experience, without the need to code a videogame from scratch, as in the case of the third escape room.

For example, the e-CLOSE project (funded by the Erasmus+ programme of the European Commission, grant number 2020-1-PL01-KA226-HE-096239) is currently researching in these topics, to increase motivation of students in online environments, and it has developed a database of tools and tested a metaverse platform called WBS LearnSpace 3D, although there are other alternatives in this regard. Figure 8 depicts a screenshot of this platform being used for presentations of the final project of a course, performed by students, in UAH.

Figure 8. Screenshot of WBS LearnSpace 3D being used in a project presentation from students

There is also a need for more comprehensive evaluations in the field. Communities around the topic of educational escape rooms could possibly facilitate sharing experiences, and the evaluation of larger audiences by testing the same escape room for different groups of students belonging to different institutions.

Finally, future research could also focus on the evaluation of escape rooms in comparison with other methodologies, and also combined with them, taking into account the percentage of active learning applied during an academic year and how this affects overall students' results.

CONCLUSION

During this chapter, three educational escape rooms have been described and analyzed. These escape rooms were applied to courses from the area of computer networks that belong to engineering degrees of the ICT field in UAH. One of them was implemented for several academic years and it is still ongoing as one of the course sessions. The main conclusion is that educational escape rooms increase students' engagement among other benefits. However, additional evaluation in terms of learning outcomes, for example, is required to demonstrate which environments could actually benefit from educational escape rooms.

ACKNOWLEDGMENT

The author would like to thank Sara Mayoral Marín for the development of the proof-of-concept of the escape room based on Unreal Engine. This research received no specific grant from any funding agency in the public, commercial, or not-for-profit sectors, but it was supported by the teaching innovation project UAH/EV1115 of Universidad de Alcala.

REFERENCES

Balamuralithara, B., & Woods, P. C. (2009). Virtual laboratories in engineering education: The simulation lab and remote lab. *Computer Applications in Engineering Education*, *17*(1), 108–118. doi:10.1002/cae.20186

Beguin, E., Besnard, S., Cros, A., Joannes, B., Leclerc-Istria, O., Noel, A., Roels, N., Taleb, F., Thongphan, J., Alata, E., & Nicomette, V. (2019). Computer-security-oriented escape room. *IEEE Security and Privacy*, *17*(4), 78–83. doi:10.1109/MSEC.2019.2912700

Borrego, C., Fernández, C., Blanes, I., & Robles, S. (2017). Room escape at class: Escape games activities to facilitate the motivation and learning in computer science. *JOTSE*, *7*(2), 162–171. doi:10.3926/jotse.247

Davis, D., & Lee, J. G. (2019, June). Building escape rooms to increase student engagement in first-year engineering classes. *2019 ASEE Annual Conference & Exposition*. 10.18260/1-2--32486

de la Flor, D., Calles, J. A., Espada, J. J., & Rodríguez, R. (2020). Application of escape lab-room to heat transfer evaluation for chemical engineers. *Education for Chemical Engineers*, *33*, 9–16. doi:10.1016/j.ece.2020.06.002

Estriegana, R., Medina-Merodio, J. A., & Barchino, R. (2019). Analysis of competence acquisition in a flipped classroom approach. *Computer Applications in Engineering Education*, *27*(1), 49–64. doi:10.1002/cae.22056

Gordillo, A., López-Fernández, D., López-Pernas, S., & Quemada, J. (2020). Evaluating an educational escape room conducted remotely for teaching software engineering. *IEEE Access: Practical Innovations, Open Solutions*, *8*, 225032–225051. doi:10.1109/ACCESS.2020.3044380

Gracey, L. (2021). *Taking Among Us! to School.* Retrieved August 3, 2022, from https://blog.tcea.org/taking-among-us-to-school/

Heckelman, L. N., & Bucholz, E. K. (2020, June). Designing a MATLAB-based Escape Room. *2020 ASEE Virtual Annual Conference Content Access*. 10.18260/1-2--34402

Löffler, E., Schneider, B., Zanwar, T., & Asprion, P. M. (2021). Cysecescape 2.0—A virtual escape room to raise cybersecurity awareness. *International Journal of Serious Games*, *8*(1), 59–70. doi:10.17083/ijsg.v8i1.413

López-Pernas, S., Gordillo, A., Barra, E., & Quemada, J. (2019). Examining the use of an educational escape room for teaching programming in a higher education setting. *IEEE Access: Practical Innovations, Open Solutions*, *7*, 31723–31737. doi:10.1109/ACCESS.2019.2902976

Mayoral Marín, S. (2021). *Desarrollo e investigación de aplicaciones software formativas en enseñanza superior con el motor gráfico Unreal Engine*. Academic Press.

Otemaier, K. R., Zanese, P. G., Grein, E. E., & Bosso, N. S. (2020). Educational escape room for teaching Mathematical Logic in computer courses. *SBC—Proceedings of the SBGames,* 7-10.

Ross, R., & Bell, C. (2019, August). Turning the classroom into an escape room with decoder hardware to increase student engagement. In *2019 IEEE Conference on Games (CoG)* (pp. 1-4). IEEE. 10.1109/CIG.2019.8848020

Ross, R., & Bennett, S. (2020). *Increasing engagement with engineering escape rooms*. IEEE Transactions on Games.

Ross, R., & de Souza-Daw, A. (2021, April). Educational Escape Rooms as an Active Learning Tool for Teaching Telecommunications Engineering. In Telecom (Vol. 2, No. 2, pp. 155-166). MDPI. doi:10.3390/telecom2020010

Sánchez-Martín, J., Corrales-Serrano, M., Luque-Sendra, A., & Zamora-Polo, F. (2020). Exit for success. Gamifying science and technology for university students using escape-room. A preliminary approach. *Heliyon*, *6*(7), e04340. doi:10.1016/j.heliyon.2020.e04340 PMID:32671257

Seebauer, S., Jahn, S., & Mottok, J. (2020, April). Learning from escape rooms? A study design concept measuring the effect of a cryptography educational escape room. In *2020 IEEE Global Engineering Education Conference (EDUCON)* (pp. 1684-1685). IEEE. 10.1109/EDUCON45650.2020.9125333

Tejado, I., Pérez, E., Traver, J. E., Nuevo-Gallardo, C., Rodríguez, P., & Vinagre, B. M. (2021). Design of an Escape Room to Support Learning of Industrial Process Control in Engineering Degrees. In *INTED2021 Proceedings* (pp. 2171-2180). IATED. 10.21125/inted.2021.0471

Ulloa, R., & Barrantes, E. G. (2008). *Construyendo un escenario para la simulación de ataques en sistemas de agentes* [Building a scenario for the simulation of attacks on agent systems]. Jornadas Chilenas de Computación.

Valero Cerdá, J. I. (2019). *Escape Room for Robotics Academy* [Doctoral dissertation]. Universitat Politècnica de València.

Walsh, B., & Spence, M. (2018). Leveraging escape room popularity to provide first-year students with an introduction to engineering information. *Proceedings of the Canadian Engineering Education Association (CEEA)*. 10.24908/pceea.v0i0.13054

KEY TERMS AND DEFINITIONS

Active Learning: Active learning could be considered a technique or methodology in education whose purpose is to actively involve students in their learning process, and with a particular focus on in-class learning.

Computer Networks: The field of computer networks (sometimes also known as "telematics") is a part of telecommunication engineering focused on services and protocols needed to facilitate communication among computers. This field includes topics like packet routing across Internet or even network security aspects.

Flipped Classroom: Flipped classroom is one type of active learning methodology that consists of flipping the traditional timing for in-class and out-of-class activities. More specifically, instead of "passive" classes by professors that are later on practiced and studied by students at home, the idea is that students prepare the theoretical material in advance and use in-class time for practicing it.

Gamification: Gamification can refer to multiple aspects but, in the specific field of education it is a technique that mimics experiences from playing games (like scoreboards, badges, game dynamics, etc.) to implement them during class. The objective is to increase students' engagement.

Information and Communications Technology (ICT): The ICT term could be considered an extension of Information Technology (IT), with emphasis on communications (or telecommunications). Therefore, ICT involves any technological aspect in relation with information and communication.

Metaverse: A metaverse could be defined as a virtual world that simulates real environments with a particular focus on user immersion. Metaverses are usually created with virtual reality and/or augmented reality components.

Online/Virtual Teaching: Any type of teaching in which students and professor are not all physically present in the same location, or face-to-face. At the same time, online teaching can be synchronous (if when classes occur, professor and students are connected at the same time in an online session) or asynchronous (for example, if the professor records the classes and students watch them at their own pace). Additionally, hybrid modes of teaching (both online and face-to-face) could be implemented as well.

Unreal Engine: 3D computer graphics game engine developed by the company Epic Games and one of the most popularly leveraged by industry nowadays.

Chapter 11
Creating Online Educational Escape Rooms for Undergraduate Learners in the Natural Sciences:
Integrating Authentic Scientific Tools

Annie Prud'homme-Généreux
University of British Columbia, Canada

ABSTRACT

Educational escape rooms (EERs) engage learners, develop their collaboration skills, and help them apply content knowledge. While the health professions were quick to identify how EERs could be used to support their unique learning outcomes, basic science disciplines such as biology, chemistry, and physics have been slower to do so. This chapter is a step-by-step guide to help undergraduate science educators design EERs based on the tools that researchers use in their work (for example, models, datasets, 3D objects). Because many of these tools are freely accessible online, they lend themselves to be used in online EERs. The process described in this chapter is designed to be easy to implement. The online science EERs developed using these steps will immerse learners in role play as they use the tools of scientists in authentic ways.

INTRODUCTION

Escape rooms are "live action team-based games where players discover clues, solve puzzles, accomplish tasks in one or more rooms in order to accomplish a specific goal (usually escaping the room) in a limited amount of time" (Nicholson, 2016, p. 1). They are called escape room, ingress room, or breakout box (Fletcher, 2019; O'Brien & Pitera, 2019; Veldkamp, Daemen, et al., 2020), depending on whether players are attempting to escape a room or break into a box.

DOI: 10.4018/978-1-6684-6081-8.ch011

Educators were quick to spot the educational potentials of this game format. With small adaptations, it provides an engaging context for students to learn. Today a search of academic databases for "escape room" and "education" yields hundreds of results. Educational escape rooms (EERs) have been reported in nearly every discipline. In the sciences, they are used to teach discipline-specific content, to train learners in science communication (Wilkinson & Little, 2021), grant writing (Oestreich et al., 2021), and engage in journal clubs (Foulds & Forbes, 2021).

Systematic reviews have concluded that EERS are an effective way to engage learners (Fotaris & Mastoras, 2019; Makri et al., 2021; Ouariachi & Wim, 2020; Taraldsen et al., 2022; Veldkamp, van de Grint, et al., 2020). They also report content learning gains, which researchers attribute to an increased motivation to learn. Studies report that EERs promote communication and collaboration skills, that they help learners value teamwork, and that they promote an increased sense of belonging. Critical thinking, problem solving, and creativity are also reported outcomes.

Discipline-Specific Affordances of EERs

Allied health professions (e.g., medicine and nursing) are the disciplines that have most embraced escape rooms into their educational practices. The momentum has helped these educators recognize the unique opportunities that escape rooms can bring to training in their profession.

For example, health professionals often work in multidisciplinary teams (e.g., a nurse, a physician, and a pharmacist) where professionals collaborate to care for a patient. Health professionals see escape rooms as a tool to facilitate the development of interprofessional communication and collaboration skills (Dittman et al., 2021; Friedrich et al., 2020; Kutzin, 2019; Moore & Campbell, 2020, 2021).

Many health disciplines use simulations that immerse learners in scenarios like the ones they will encounter in their work practice. This role play helps students recognize when knowledge is relevant and convert theoretical to applied skills. However, these clinical simulations can be unengaging and do not provide opportunities to learn through mistakes. Drawing from those elements of EERs, several health profession educators have created hybrid games that combine simulations with escape rooms (Anderson et al., 2021; Mystakidis et al., 2019; Ross et al., 2021).

Thus, health professionals have recognized the ways in which EERs can meet their unique training needs: to foster interprofessional communication and collaboration and to immerse learners in real-world scenarios where they learn through errors and feedback.

Unique Affordance of Science EERs

What are the Unique Affordances of EERs in Science Training?

Inspired by health educators' focus on discipline-specific applications of EERs, this chapter identifies how online EERs can foster the development of skills unique to scientists – scientific thinking and the use of scientific tools. This opportunity has not been tapped into by most science EERs, probably because they were designed for in-person classes. Online EERs can make use of the online scientific tools that scientists use every day. The EER provides the context for a role play where students recognize when to use scientific tools and demonstrate their proficiency in using them to solve problems.

This chapter proposes strategies for designing EERs for undergraduate science courses. It focuses on the design of puzzles where students practice the skills of scientists. This responds to Lathwesen and

Belova (2021)'s review findings that called for more support of science educators in developing EERs. What follows are suggestions for developing puzzles, with resources and examples, to guide science educators in constructing online EERs that help learners become scientists.

BACKGROUND

This chapter assumes that the reader is familiar with the design of online escape rooms so that it may focus on advanced puzzle design that is specific to the practice of science. However, recognizing that some readers may be new to EER design, the first sections provide a primer with resources to learn about EER design. This is followed by sections describing the design of puzzles that capitalize on the unique affordances of the online environment to help students practice the skills of being scientists.

Overview of EER Design and Development Process

Learning to design an escape room begins with experiencing as many as possible. Table 1 provides a list of articles that describe science EERs.

Table 1. Examples of Science EERs. These articles provide access to their escape room materials often through supplementary materials or as URLs in the article.

Discipline	In-Person	Online
Biology	Brady and Andersen (2021); Boysen-Osborn et al. (2018)	Heim et al. (2022)
Chemistry	Avargil et al. (2021); Bezard et al. (2020); Clapson et al. (2019); Dietrich (2018); Elford et al. (2021); Gilbert et al. (2020); Musgrove et al. (2021); Nephew and Sunasee (2021); Peleg et al. (2019); Rivera-Trigueros et al. (2022a); Vergne et al. (2019); Yayon et al. (2019)	Ang et al. (2020); Cai (2022); de Souza and Kasseboehmer (2021); Estudante and Dietrich (2020); Monnot et al. (2020); Rahim (2022); Vergne et al. (2020)
Physics	Vörös and Sárközi (2017); Wimpfheimer (2020)	Rivera-Trigueros et al. (2022b)

Many resources can guide educators in the creation of EERs (Casler, 2022; Davis et al., 2022; Earle, 2022; Eukel & Morrell, 2021; Knoll & Brickmann, 2018; Ross et al., 2022). Nicholson and Cable (2020) wrote a comprehensive book on the design of EERs. On his website, Nicholson provides access to his articles on this topic (Nicholson, n.d.).

A handful of models exist to guide the design of EERs. These include Nicholson's (2015a) RECIPE framework, the COMET framework (Dittman et al., 2022), the escapED framework (Clarke S., 2016; Clarke et al., 2017), the STAR model (Botturi & Babazadeh, 2020), and the SEGAM model (Guigon et al., 2018).

Although models vary, the core steps in the design of an EER are similar. An overview is diagrammed in Figure 1. The process begins by articulating the learning objectives for the activity. This is followed by identifying a suitable storyline to provide context for the puzzles and to give players a sense of purpose and a goal. Then, the designer must decide on the structure of the EER. Options for EER structures are

Figure 1. Overview of the Educational Escape Room Design and Development Process. The steps for creating an EER are outlined in a sequential fashion in this diagram. The creation of puzzles is an iterative process that requires the designer to go through a series of sub-steps for each puzzle.

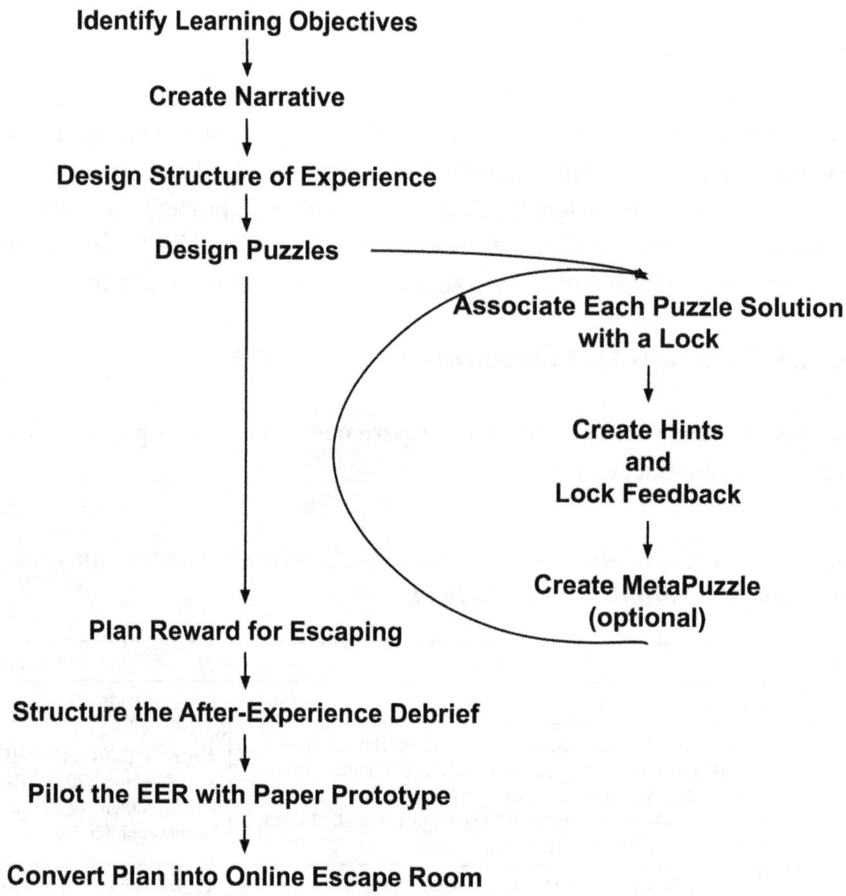

shown in Figure 2. Designers must also determine the number of puzzles to include, whether the experience is to be done alone or in groups, and whether it is a timed experience.

The next step is to develop each puzzle, making sure to link each one to the narrative and to the learning objectives. As part of this process, the designer should consider the clues that will be given to students to help them tackle each puzzle, the optional hints to help those who struggle, and the feedback provided when students think they have a solution.

The EER design should include a post-experience reflection. This is where EER players turn back into students and connect what they did with past and future learning (Botturi & Babazadeh, 2020; Nicholson, 2012; Sawyer *et al.*, 2016; Veldkamp, van de Grint, et al., 2020).

Once game development is done, it is time to pilot the game with target users. This can be done in a low-tech fashion, printing each puzzle on paper (and using sketches instead of polished products), and observing how players go through the game. This provides feedback to improve the EER design.

Figure 2. Options for Organizing Puzzles in an EER. In a sequential structure, players have access to one puzzle at the start of the experience. Solving it unlocks the next puzzle, which unlocks the next, and so on, until players escape the room. In an open structure, players have access to all puzzles from the beginning and they can complete them in any order. Each time they unlock one, they are rewarded with a clue. Combining these clues allows players to unlock the final lock, called the "meta-puzzle." The path-based and the pyramid structures are a combination of the sequential and the open structures. According to Veldkamp, van de Grint, et al. (2020), all EERs in health fields use the sequential design, while science EERs vary, with examples of sequential, open, and path-based design identified by the review. Figure adapted from Nicholson (2015b).

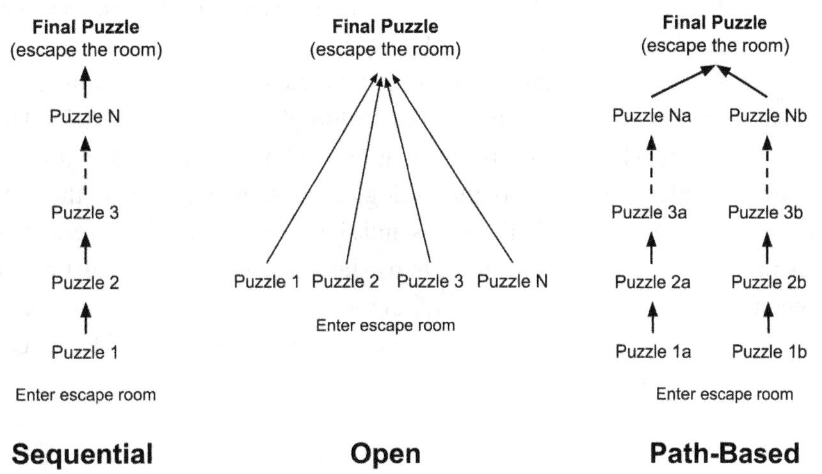

Once everything is complete, it is time to use digital platforms to create the online EER. While many tools can be used, most EERs simulate the physical escape room environment by using Google Slides to create an image of a room with invisible hotpots that students must find and that link to resources, clues, locks, and puzzles. Google Forms is used to create locks with feedback and to provide hints when needed. The best way to learn to use these tools to create an EER is to watch step-by-step video tutorials (EZ EdTech!, 2020; Holzweiss, 2021; Skeptical Educator; 2020).

Narrative Settings for Science EERs

Players in all escape games have the same goal: to escape a locked room or to break into one. The narrative gives players a sense of why they are trying to do this, who they are in the story, where they are, and when it is taking place. It is critical for role play and immersion.

Nearly all health profession EERs use clinical cases as the premise for their EER narrative. It introduces learners to environments where their discipline is practiced. Science EERs do not capitalize on this opportunity; rather, they tend to use fictional scenarios, like a mad scientist who threatens national security (de la Flor et al., 2020; Watermeier & Salzameda, 2019) or being unjustly accused of a crime (Sabitzer et al., 2021).

Taking a page from the health discipline, science EERs should endeavor to set the narrative in environments that capture the experience of being a practicing scientist. For example, the escape room could take place in a research laboratory where researchers conduct their work. It could surround the submission or adjudication of a research grant, the approval of a proposal by a research ethics board, the presentation of findings at a scientific conference, or the writing of a peer-reviewed article. Using these settings exposes students to environments common to scientific practice.

One popular approach for teaching science uses case studies (Allen & Tanner, 2003; Herreid, 2007). Cases are stories used for pedagogical purpose, usually combining an authentic story of discovery with a set of discussion questions to achieve a learning objective. The *National Center for Case Study Teaching in Science* hosts the largest collection of peer reviewed science cases. Recently transferred to the website of the *National Science Teaching Association* (n.d.), these nearly 1,000 cases could easily be adapted into an EER narrative. The opportunity to use case stories as inspiration for escape room narratives has also been noted by Casler (2022) and Grupel et al. (2022).

For example, a real-world inspired case follows the medical mystery of a woman who was informed by her physician that her genetics did not match her children's (Hutchison, 2007). This case could be converted into an EER by introducing the specter that the children will be taken away from the mother unless she can provide evidence that she is the biological mother. She enlists the help of a scientific expert (the students) to analyze her medical records and speak on her behalf in a court of law. The medical information is provided in a piecemeal fashion, as she undergoes testing (just as the information is provided in a piecemeal fashion in the case study; these constitute individual puzzles). Students must "unlock" each medical file mystery to provide a coherent defense in court. The clock is ticking – the legal proceedings are taking place in an hour!

PUZZLES FOR THE NATURAL SCIENCES

Puzzles: General Guidelines

Wiemker et al. (2015) describe an escape room as "just a series of puzzles." These puzzles are held together and given context through a narrative. Puzzles, in turn, are just a problem to solve. This may ease the mind of educators who worry that they are not game designer. Educators come up with problems for their students all the time through problem sets and quiz questions.

Unlike classroom problems, the solution to every puzzle in an EER is a code to open a lock. The way to align a puzzle solution with a code will depend on the nature of the puzzle. If it is a scavenger hunt, then details about the found object (the number of items, its location, its properties, etc.) can generate a code. Alternatively, providing multiple choice options for the puzzle solution and asking students to select the right one can yield a code.

There are a few rules to observe when creating puzzles.

1. **Clues direct players to a puzzle.** An EER is filled with what, at first sight, appear to be disparate pieces of information: a note from a character, a plane ticket, links to resources or a tool, a file in an odd format, etc. These are clues. Unlike a classroom problem set, the instructions are scattered around the escape room and players must find and reconstitute the instructions as part of the game.
2. **Each puzzle should have only one solution.** A problem that can have multiple right answers is not suited to become a puzzle unless the instructions constrict the responses to only one.

3. **Solutions yield more clues.** Once players solve a puzzle, there should be some sort of information disclosed that helps players progress to the next stage of the game. Typically, this is a code to open a lock or access to another room where they find clues to access the next puzzle.
4. **Add hints.** Hints help players when they are stuck. They direct them to new avenues of thinking to solve the puzzle. Including hints is optional.
5. **Add feedback.** Feedback is critical in learning through failure, and it is especially important in opening a lock. Players should know whether they were successful in solving a puzzle. If unsuccessful, the lock should make that clear and it may also provide feedback in the form of a hint.
6. **Puzzles should be integrated into the narrative.** Puzzles should make sense in the context of the narrative. As Nicholson and Cable (2020) point out, there are few examples where solving a crossword puzzle would make sense in the context of a story and its role play (p. 65).

Nicholson and Cable (2020) recognize seven types of puzzles, but it is perhaps sufficient for the design of science EERs to consider that there are only two. Some test students' knowledge and understanding. Such puzzles can help students review a unit's content and provide feedback on how well it was learned. However, it does not engage students in the types of activities that mirror what scientists do. The other type asks students to demonstrate their ability to use scientific tools. Students must apply scientific know-how in new contexts. These types of puzzles help students practice authentic scientific skills. The next sections provide resources and suggestions for developing each type of puzzle, with a focus on the latter.

Puzzles That Test Understanding

Most science EERs use puzzles that test students' understanding (Prud'homme-Généreux, in preparation). Their prevalence is likely due to the ease of creating them. Educators can take existing quiz questions and convert them into puzzles. All that is required is knowledge of common puzzle types and how to make them (Ellsworth-Lyman, 2021; Jackson & Drake, 2019; Morris, 2020; Selinker & Snyder, 2018). The most challenging aspect of designing such puzzles comes in integrating them into the narrative; there should be a reason for the players to engage in these activities in the context of the story. This section will provide examples of strategies for converting quiz questions into puzzles.

Berthod et al. (2020) provide examples of using answers to a multiple-choice quiz to yield a code. Here, the multiple-choice quiz is itself the puzzle. The response options for each question are associated with a letter or number. Several such questions yields a partial solution to the lock (for example, one digit of a four-digit code).

Quiz questions should not limit themselves to typical multiple-choice formats. For example, students may have to order steps of the scientific method, or the steps for sterilizing equipment in a microbiology laboratory. Each step is provided as a sketch with a letter next to it. By putting the steps in the correct sequence, the students reveal a code to open a lock.

Quiz questions that ask students to match related concepts can be converted into puzzles using one of the following two strategies. Berthod et al. (2020) ask students to match related concepts by drawing a line between them, and in the process, students trace Roman numerals that is the solution to the puzzle (Figure 3). Alternatively, the lines traced between related concepts might intersect with letters filling the space between the concepts, which, when read top to bottom, spell out a code (Figure 4). Both puzzle types could be implemented online using Google Slides.

Figure 3. Concept Matching to Generate a Code – Option 1. Students connect the dots between concepts listed at the top and bottom based on a prompt. The traced lines create a Roman number: XVI. This code could be interpreted as 1-0-5-1 (X = 10, V = 5, and I = 1) or 1-6 (XVI = 16). Through trial and error and feedback from the locks, students infer how to transfer the solution to this puzzle into a code to open a lock. Figure adapted from Berthod et al. (2020).

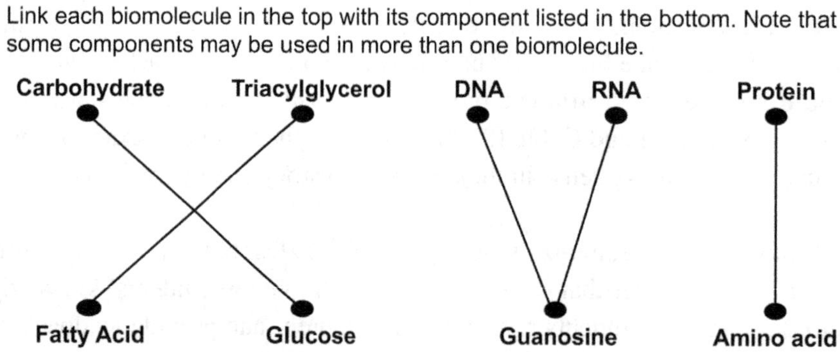

Fill-in-the-blank quiz questions can be easily converted into puzzles. Here, some of the letters of the words to be filled-in have a dot below them (or some other differentiator) suggesting that these letters are special. Students must fill-in-the-blanks correctly, and then determine that if they combine the letters with the dots below them, they can spell out a solution that provides a code to open a lock. Selinker & Snyder's book *Puzzlecraft* (2018) contains many additional ideas for the creation of word puzzles, from crosswords to scramblegories.

In a cloud wall puzzle, players find a series of letters arranged in a circle (Figure 5). The players also find a series of numbers. It is a cypher. To interpret it, players must recognize that the numbers correspond to the letters, counting from the one atop the circle (which is numbered 1) and going in a clockwise direction. Converting the numbers into letters yields a sentence that is a clue to the code.

The types of puzzles described in this section represent a form of gamified testing. They engage students in activities typical of classroom environments and can help students review content. However, they do not replicate the activities of scientists. The next sections suggest EER puzzles that challenge students to recognize when to use the tools of scientists, demonstrate that they can use them effectively to solve problems, and in so doing, practice being scientists.

Puzzles Where Players Apply What They Know

Puzzles where students role play being a scientist and where they must use the tools of scientists to solve puzzles engage students in activities that tap into higher levels of Bloom's taxonomy (Bloom, 1956). Unlike gamified multiple-choice quizzes, these activities are specific to science training. The EER role play provides context for using the tools, so students learn when to use them.

Few science EERs integrate these types of activities. Perhaps this is because most science EERs are physical, and it would be challenging to integrate online tools. Thus, the following puzzles make use of the unique affordances of the online medium of the EERs. The next sections will provide many

Figure 4. Concept Matching to Generate a Code – Option 2. Students draw a line between concepts on the left and right. In between the two columns are letters. Once students correctly connect concepts, they find that there are letters at the intersections of some of the lines. When read top to bottom, these letters reveal a code. Here, the code is M-A-R-S. Figure adapted from Selinker & Snyder (2018, p. 17).

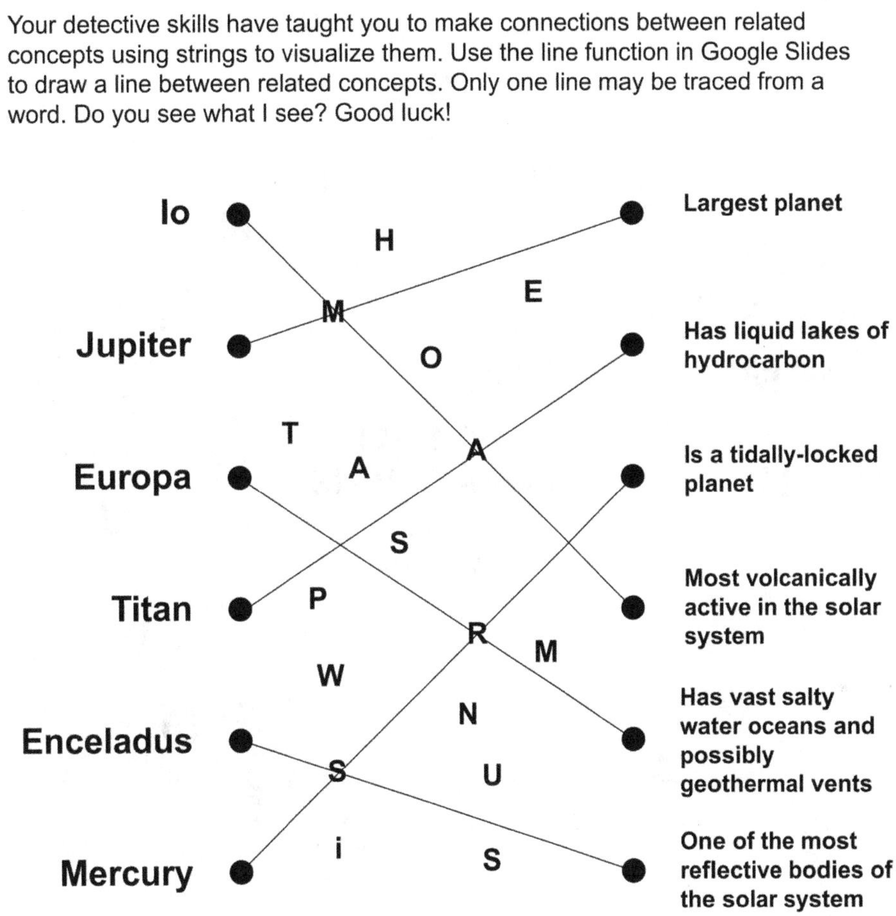

examples, to help science educators envision ways in which they might integrate these types of online tools and turn them into puzzles for an online EER for science learning.

Searching Databases Used by Scientists

The first strategy is to create puzzles that ask students to use online resources that scientists use every day. The most obvious ones are search engines that allow scientists to explore the primary literature in their field. Databases such as Pubmed, Medline, or Web of Science can be used. Students are given instructions to search for a particular article or set of articles. Perhaps the clues suggest the number of a record in the database (like a PMID). Perhaps the clues provide information about the name of an author and the journal in which their article is published, and the students must use their search skills to

Figure 5. Cloud Wall. The sequence of numbers corresponds to the position of the letters, counted from the top and going in a clockwise direction. Thus, 1-5-10-11 corresponds to 1=B, 5=A, 10=S, and 11=E, or the word "base." Solving for each number, students reveal the message "base unique to RNA." Using their knowledge of molecular biology, they deduce that uracil or U is the solution to this puzzle. Figure adapted from Selinker & Snyder (2018, p. 215).

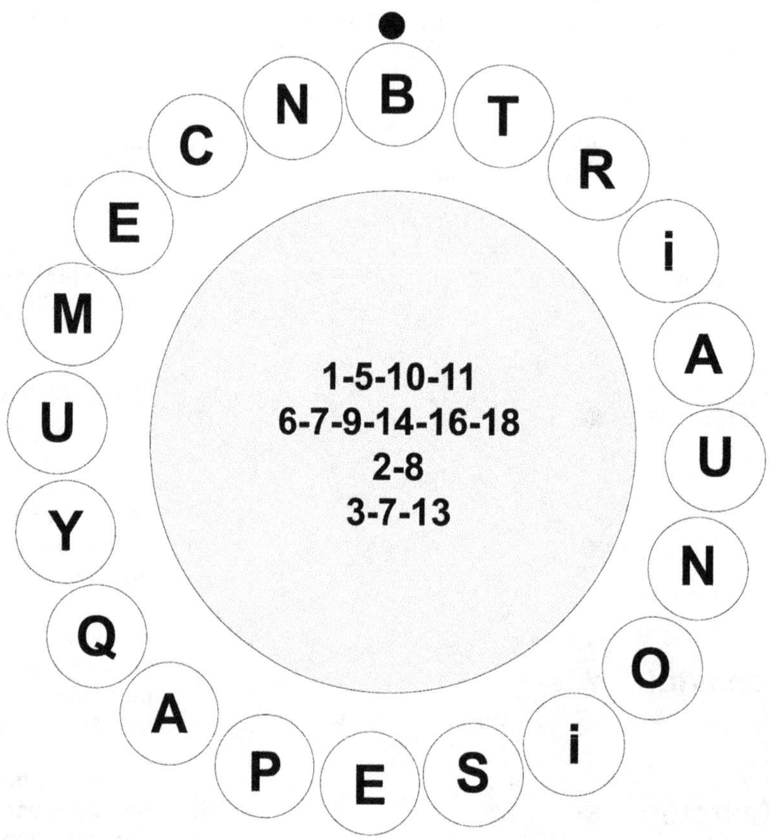

locate this source. The clues should also suggest what data to extract from the source once it is found. This could include the number of the record in the database (like the PMID), or one of the keywords associated with an article, or the ORCID of one of the authors (their unique author number), or the city where the first author's institution is located, or the number of the figure that demonstrates something that the students are seeking as part of the escape narrative. The data that the students extract from the article or search query should only be available to those who successfully execute the search and find the intended record(s). In this way, the escape room becomes a treasure hunt where players practice their skills of using search engines that are consulted by scientists.

Analyzing Online Datasets

With the rise of Big Data and with increased calls for transparency, many scientists make their research data openly available online. In addition, many public agencies make their data available so that researchers can mine them as they seek to answer research questions. These datasets represent an opportunity to practice data analysis using authentic data and for students to practice the scientific skills of data analysis, interpretation, and evaluation.

There are many sources of open data available online. Here are just a few:

- Biology
  - The genetic information for all genomes sequenced by public organizations is available on the National Center for Biotechnology Information website (NCBI., n.d.).
  - The World Health Organization and the American Center for Disease Control monitor the spread of several infectious diseases (CDC., n.d.; WHO., n.d.).
- Physics
  - The world's largest particle accelerator, CERN, makes the data from the collision of protons available online (CERN, n.d.).
- Interdisciplinary
  - The journal PLOS requires that its authors make their dataset publicly available, and it hosts many of them on its website (PLOS, n.d.).
  - The United States Geological Survey hosts datasets on natural hazards (USGS., n.d.), the National Aeronautics and Space Administration makes its observations of the Earth available on the EarthData website (NASA, n.d.). And, the National Oceanic and Atmospheric Administration has data about the climate, oceans, and meteorology (NOAA, n.d.).

With access to these datasets, students can download and manipulate the data using tools like Excel or R, like scientists do. If extracting datasets from their source, cleaning them, and sifting through their entirety is too advanced for students (or too times taking for the time devoted to the EER), the educator can extract the data and place a portion of it in a shareable spreadsheet file as a clue. This "pre-digested" dataset can be customized to the students' level of skills in data analysis.

If learning to use a spreadsheet or other software to analyze data is not part of a course's learning outcomes, there are simplified data exploration and visualization tools that can help. One is the HHMI BioInteractive Data Explorer tool that allows users to import their own dataset, or to work from one of several supplied with the tool (HHMI, n.d.). This online tool is a good way to introduce the concept of data analysis without getting bogged down in the intricacies of using a specific software package.

To use datasets and their analysis in an EER, it helps to think of the puzzle as a treasure hunt. The clues may direct students to a dataset and direct them to conduct specific analyses. Perhaps students must order the data in a specific way, or identify a specific record, or graph the data and extract information about the figure (like the slope or the coefficient of correlation between two variables). The specific question will depend on the level of skills of the students and the learning outcomes. Only those students who successfully execute the instructions will find the solution.

Using the Online Analysis Tools that Researchers Use

Researchers use a range of online freely accessible tools to manipulate and analyze data as part of their work. In molecular biology, many of the bioinformatics tools are available on the NCBI, Expasy, and EMBL-EBI websites (EMBL-EBI, n.d.; NCBI, n.d.; Swiss Institute of Bioinformatics, n.d.). These tools allow researchers to compare gene sequences, translate nucleic acid into amino acid sequences, predict a protein's transmembrane topology, and visualize evolutionary trees based on protein sequences. Other disciplines have similarly available tools.

There are two suggested ways to use these research tools in puzzles. The first follows the patterns presented thus far: the puzzle is a treasure hunt. The clues direct students to a familiar tool and include input data – perhaps a gene sequence. It directs students to use the tool, or alternatively, it may ask students to select the appropriate tool given the goals of the analysis (if recognizing when to use such a tool is a learning objective). The clues provide information about how to manipulate the data and what to extract.

For example, the clue may direct students to identify the one letter code for the amino acids encoded by nucleotide triplets beginning at the DNA sequence position 156, 188, and 1,980. Or, it might ask them to find the position of the first histidine in the encoded protein sequence – that position number is the solution to the puzzle. Or, it may give students a protein's amino acid sequence and direct them to use Phobius to determine how many times the protein is predicted to traverse the cell membrane. These puzzles allow students to practice using the tools of researchers. Only those students that correctly use the tool can obtain the output code.

If students have never used a tool before, the escape room can be designed to teach students to use it. This idea is inspired by the digital escape room *Smash with GSuite* (Smash with GSuite, n.d.). This free online escape room teaches users about the capabilities of GSuite tools (apps such as Google Docs and Google Sheets). The clues for each puzzle include a starting document, hints about the software to use, and instructions about how to manipulate the starting document. In following the instructions, players learn to use the features of the software. For example, in following instructions, students learn how to hide columns and rows in a spreadsheet. Following specific instructions reveals information in one cell, which contains the solution (code) for the puzzle.

A similar guided experience could be embedded in a narrative where a scientist is detained at an undisclosed location by a group that wants to release an infectious virus (the kidnapped researcher is an expert on this virus). Locked in a prison, the scientist managed to keep her phone and is guiding her novice lab assistant (the students) to continue her work using bioinformatics tools. She explains what to do in a step-by-step fashion but is worried that her captors will intercept her messages, so she splits them into clues. In following her directions, the apprentice can obtain the sought-after information – the amino acid that controls a virus's entry into the cell. They can convey this information to government officials and spoil the antagonists' plot. In going through the direction, the students are introduced to the tools and learn to use them for the first time.

Manipulating Objects in Three Dimensions

Many science disciplines study subjects that are too small or too large to view with the naked eye (e.g., molecules and astronomical objects). Free online tools help scientists visualize them in three-dimension (3D) and manipulate them to develop and test hypotheses. For example, chemists and molecular biologists use web tools such as MolView, PubChem 3D Viewer, RasMol, and the PDB's Mol 3D Viewer to

Figure 6. Example of a 3D Scavenger Hunt. A region of the E. coli protein enolase (PDB DOI: 10.2210/pdb1E9I/pdb) is viewed using the RCSB PDB 3D View tool. Students must identify the amino acid that hydrogen bonds with tyrosine 302. Using clues, student obtain the structure file for the correct protein, select a suitable 3D viewer, navigate to the target amino acid, and look for hydrogen bonding interactions. The figure shows the target tyrosine with its hexagonal ring in the middle of the image. The tool reveals that histidine 274 bonds to this amino acid. The solution for this puzzle is HIS274.

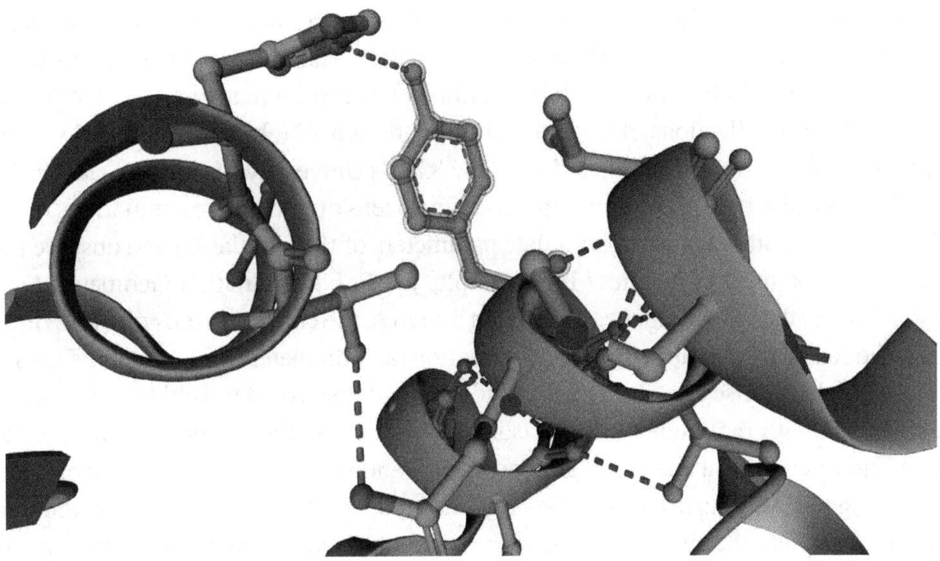

visualize the 3D structure of atoms and molecules (Bergwerf, 2015; Bernstein, n.d.; NCBI, n.d.; RCSB Protein Data Bank, n.d.). These visualization tools give users the ability to manipulate the structures, rotate them, zoom in or out, and highlight certain features like sulfur bridges between amino acids or hydrogen bonds between nucleobases. Researchers use these tools to visualize a structure and predict, for example, where a drug might interact with it.

Learning to use these "tools of the trade" is an important step in becoming a scientist. Students can practice manipulating 3D objects as part of an EER. For example, clues lead students to open a file containing information about a protein's 3D structure and are told to begin their journey at the N-terminus. They should follow the peptide bonds until they encounter the first di-sulfide bond and then hop to the peptide sequence joined at that site. From there, they can inspect the surrounding amino acids for the nearest charged amino acid and enter its three-letter code into the lock. Such an activity allows students to practice operating in the 3D environment to manipulate molecules and to interpret the images they see using their knowledge of biochemistry. The 3D scavenger hunt gives them purpose in inspecting the 3D object, to locate a target. A simpler example of a puzzle that requires the manipulation of a 3D protein is shown in Figure 6.

Using Online Simulations and Models

Simulations and models are digital recreations of natural phenomenon where users can modify parameters and observe their impact on the state of the system. By modifying the parameters, users gain a deeper understanding or how each variable impacts the system. In complex models, the tool is used to predict the impact of modifying some of the parameters – for example, what will happen to ocean acidification if the level of greenhouse gases increases to a threshold level. Simulations and models guide the work of many scientists.

Several free online science simulations were developed to help students gain a deeper understanding of natural phenomenon. They are visual, easy to manipulate, and easy to understand. An astronomy-specific simulation tool is Stellarium, which is an online planetarium that simulates the sky (Zotti et al., 2021). Two of the largest collections of educational simulations are Nobel Laureate Carl Wieman's PhET website (University of Colorado Boulder, n.d.) and the King's University Centre for Data Visualization in Science (The King's University, n.d.). Both sites contain dozens of interactive simulations in a wide range of scientific disciplines. Students can manipulate parameters of the simulation and observe their effects.

How might these be used as puzzles? For example, the PhET simulation Geometric Optics allows students to manipulate the rays of light coming from a source, the characteristics of a lens through which the rays pass (the radius of curvature, index of refraction, and diameter), and to see the resulting image produced by that light. To use this in a puzzle, students could be asked to find the parameters that will generate a reflection with particular characteristics. To determine this, students will need to play with the simulator, and through trial and error, gain an understanding of how each parameter affects the image. Remembering that all puzzles must have only one solution, designers should ensure that only one set of parameters can yield the target outcome in the reflection. Once students identify it, the parameters they used to obtain it become the solution, which can be used as a code to open a lock and progress to the next step.

Completing a Virtual or Remote Laboratory

Virtual laboratories are digital interactives that simulate the steps of conducting an experiment in a laboratory or in the field. Often, the experiments and data are authentic. For example, students may view pictures of fish taken by the scientists who originally conducted the experiment and they must measure the ratio of each fish's dorsal fin length to body length using digital tools provided in the virtual lab (HHMI, n.d.).

Some organizations have compiled links to free virtual laboratories from every scientific discipline into collections. These include the open textbook *Virtual Lab and Science Resource Directory* (Cheveldave, 2020) and the Arthur Lakes Library of the Colorado School of Mines website (Arthur Lakes Library, n.d.).

These are several ways to use virtual laboratories in a puzzle. The puzzle could be a riddle that asks students to be observant of the digital lab environment and to answer a question about it (for example, the name of a tool or equipment that can be seen on the lab bench). It could be a question that asks students to sequence the steps to be performed in this experiment, and that requires students to have completed and understood the virtual laboratory activity to answer it. The puzzle and its solution may also be information that can be extracted from the results of the experiment, something like the slope of the curve generated from the data.

In addition to virtual laboratories, remote laboratories allow students to control real scientific equipment at a distance. The equipment collects data and sends it to the student in real-time. Most involve students controlling purpose-build equipment in their own institution as part of their curriculum (Bhute et al., 2021; Van den Beemt et al., 2022). Engaging students in this activity as part of a puzzle could infuse an element of authenticity. The ways to connect this activity with the EER are identical to the suggestions presented above for virtual laboratories.

Using Online Educational Activities or Learning Objects

Online educational activities and learning objects are not tools that scientists use. However, they guide students to develop their scientific thinking skills. Some examples from the HHMI BioInteractive website (HHMI, n.d.) include:

- **Evaluating Science in the News,** which introduces students to criteria for evaluating scientific information. In a puzzle, students could be asked to apply the test to assess an article's reliability. In doing so they generate a code consisting of True or False for each criterion.
- **How Science Works** is an interactive tool that asks students to annotate a map of the scientific process as they dissect an example of a scientific investigation. In identifying which steps were met for a particular experiment, students could generate a code consisting of the first letter of each step.
- **Model Builder** allows students to create scientific models as concept maps. An automatic evaluation tool provides feedback, letting students know when their diagram matches the models that the educator input as the solution. In a puzzle, students could create a model. If they get it right, the tool provides feedback, in the form of a code to open a lock. Alternatively, perhaps a clue directed students to make the model and then count the number of out-going connections from one concept. This number is part of a code to open a lock.

Other online educational tools are available. One of the largest repositories is the Multimedia Education Resource for Learning and Online Teaching (MERLOT, n.d.). Another is CourseSource, a growing collection of evidence-based resources developed by educators for the teaching and learning of biology and physics (CourseSource, n.d.).

Participating in an Online Citizen Science Project

Citizen science projects are crowd-sourced research projects, typically led by scientists, that solicit the public's assistance in gathering data or in analyzing it. There is an increasing number of citizen science projects online. For example, the game Foldit is an online videogame that asks participants to fold proteins in three-dimensional space as perfectly as possible (UW Center for Game Science and Institute for Protein Design, 2017). The game embeds known rules of molecular and chemical interactions to give points for each attempt. Solutions that yield the most points are reviewed by researchers. This strategy has resulted in the publication of new protein structures.

The Zooniverse is a hub for online citizen science projects (Welcome to Zooniverse, n.d.). Visitors to the site can select a discipline and browse available citizen science projects from around the world.

Many astronomy projects invite the public to review vast amounts of telescopes data and to classify it based on a fit to certain patterns. This work helps researchers conduct their analysis of massive datasets.

It may be a bit more challenging to integrate an online citizen science activity into a puzzle because if students participate in a citizen science project, they will analyze different data than their peers. In other words, it may be hard to find one solution. However, the structure of the citizen science project and its methodology will not vary between students, and this can be used as solutions. For example, students could be asked to categorize a set of 20 galaxy images based on their shape. Once they have accomplished this task, they may answer questions about the distinction between the three galaxy types. Students must have tacit experience of the analysis to be able to answer the puzzle questions.

Using Mobile Learning with Geotagged Activities

The final idea is to make use of mobile learning, and specifically of geotagged applications (Forkosh Baruch & Meishar Tal, 2019). Haake (2019) and Fletcher (2019) describe examples of geotagged activities as part of an escape room. This can be done by using game platforms that allow users to create geotagged treasure hunts (sometimes called geocaching) (Barak & Ziv, 2013). The apps require users to bring their mobile device to a physical location. Once the app detects that the device's location (its GPS coordinates) matches a site, it releases information such as a clue. This could be helpful if educators want students to explore the campus to find concrete examples of a theoretical concept.

For example, students may be given a riddle or clues about a specific tree species that may only be found at one location on campus (in a biology course), or a site known to exhibit specific echo properties (in a course on sound mechanics). When the student correctly interprets the riddle and travels to that location, the app unlocks the next clue.

A way to integrate real-world visits into an EER that requires no additional software is to ask for information that can only be observed by traveling to a location. In the example of the trees provided above, students may be asked how many trees of this species are found at that site or the color of a nearby sign. Answering these questions is a solution to the puzzle.

FUTURE RESEARCH DIRECTIONS

As a closing remark, it is worth considering the adage that the best way to learn something is to teach it. Several educators have assigned the creation of EERs to their students (Bakkum et al., 2021; Botturi & Babazadeh, 2021; Davis & Lee, 2019; Heim et al., 2022; Pfeifer et al., 2021; Vicari, 2020). Heim et al. (2022) provides links to an example of a student-designed online escape room in ecology. These renewable assignments are not merely submitted for a grade (i.e., they are not disposable assignments) and will be used after submission, increasing motivation.

CONCLUSION

This chapter provides instructions for creating online EER for undergraduate science students that capitalizes on the use of free online tools that scientists use in their daily work. Embedding these tools in puzzles – often by creating treasure hunts – gives students practice in using these scientific tools in authentic, goal-oriented contexts. It is hoped that by following these steps, educators will find an easy recipe for creating EERs that engage learners while practicing to use scientific tools. Like the health practitioners who have adapted EERs to meet their unique educational needs, the online EERs that use scientific tools in puzzles could help to meet the unique needs of undergraduate science education.

REFERENCES

Allen, D., & Tanner, K. (2003). Approaches to cell biology teaching: Learning content in context—problem-based learning. *Cell Biology Education*, *2*(2), 73–81. doi:10.1187/cbe.03-04-0019 PMID:12888838

Anderson, M., Lioce, L., & Robertson, J., Lopreiato, J., & Díaz, D. (2021). Toward defining healthcare simulation escape rooms. *Simulation & Gaming*, *52*(1), 7–17. doi:10.1177/1046878120958745

Ang, J. W. J., Ng, Y. N. A., & Liew, R. S. (2020). Physical and digital educational escape room for teaching chemical bonding. *Journal of Chemical Education*, *97*(9), 2849–2856. doi:10.1021/acs.jchemed.0c00612

Arthur Lakes Library. (n.d.). *Open Educational Resources*. Colorado School of Mines. https://libguides.mines.edu/oer/simulationslabs

Avargil, S., Shwartz, G., & Zemel, Y. (2021). Educational escape room: Break Dalton's code and escape. *Journal of Chemical Education*, *98*(7), 2313–2322. doi:10.1021/acs.jchemed.1c00110

Bakkum, M. J., Richir, M. C., Sultan, R., de la Court, J. R., Lambooij, A. C., van Agtmael, M. A., & Tichelaar, J. (2021). Can students create their own educational escape room?: Lessons learned from the opioid crisis escape room. *Medical Science Educator*, *31*(6), 1739–1745. doi:10.100740670-021-01425-5 PMID:34950526

Barak, M., & Ziv, S. (2013). Wandering: A Web-based platform for the creation of location-based interactive learning objects. *Computers & Education*, *62*, 159–170. doi:10.1016/j.compedu.2012.10.015

Bergwerf, H. (2015). *MolView*. https://molview.org/

Bernstein, H. J. (n.d.). *RasMol and OpenRasMol*. Molecular Graphics Visualisation Tool. http://www.openrasmol.org/

Berthod, F., Bouchoud, L., Grossrieder, F., Falaschi, L., Senhaji, S., & Bonnabry, P. (2020). Learning good manufacturing practices in an escape room: Validation of a new pedagogical tool. *Journal of Oncology Pharmacy Practice*, *26*(4), 853–860. doi:10.1177/1078155219875504 PMID:31566110

Bezard, L., Debacq, M., & Rosso, A. (2020). The carnivorous yoghurts: A "serious" escape game for stirring labs. *Education for Chemical Engineers*, *33*, 1–8. doi:10.1016/j.ece.2020.06.001

Bhute, V. J., Inguva, P., Shah, U., & Brechtelsbauer, C. (2021). Transforming traditional teaching laboratories for effective remote delivery—A review. *Education for Chemical Engineers*, *35*, 96–104. doi:10.1016/j.ece.2021.01.008

Bloom, B. S. (1956). *Taxonomy of Educational Objectives: The Classification of Educational Goals* (1st ed.). Longman Group.

Botturi, L., & Babazadeh, M. (2020). Designing educational escape rooms: Validating the Star Model. *International Journal of Serious Games*, *7*(3), 41–57. doi:10.17083/ijsg.v7i3.367

Botturi, L., & Babazadeh, M. (2021). Fighting viruses though escape room design with students. *Proceedings of the European Conference on Games Based Learning*, 108-116. 10.34190/GBL.21.037

Boysen-Osborn, M., Paradise, S., & Suchard, J. (2018). The toxiscape hunt: An escape room-scavenger hunt for toxicology education. *Journal of Education and Teaching in Emergency Medicine*, *3*(1), 9–19. doi:10.5070/M531037616

Brady, S. C., & Andersen, E. C. (2021). An escape-room inspired game for genetics review. *Journal of Biological Education*, *55*(4), 406–417. doi:10.1080/00219266.2019.1703784

Cai, S. (2022). Harry Potter themed digital escape room for addressing misconceptions in stoichiometry. *Journal of Chemical Education*, *99*(7), 2747–2753. doi:10.1021/acs.jchemed.2c00178

Casler, K. (2022). Escape Passive Learning: 10 steps to Building an Escape Room. *The Journal for Nurse Practitioners*, *18*(5), 569–574. doi:10.1016/j.nurpra.2022.01.020

CDC. (n.d.). *Data*. https://data.cdc.gov/browse

CERN. (n.d.). *OpenDataCERN*. http://opendata.cern.ch/

Cheveldave, A. (Ed.). (2020). *Virtual Lab and Science Resource Directory*. BCcampus. https://opentextbc.ca/virtualscienceresources/

Clapson, M. L., Gilbert, B., Mozol, V. J., Schechtel, S., Tran, J., & White, S. (2019). ChemEscape: Educational battle box puzzle activities for engaging outreach and active learning in general chemistry. *Journal of Chemical Education*, *97*(1), 125–131. doi:10.1021/acs.jchemed.9b00612

Clarke, S. A. S., Keegan, H., Morini, L., & Wood, O. (2016). EscapED: Adapting Live-Action, Interactive Games to Support Higher Education Teaching and Learning Practices. In Games and Learning Alliance. GALA 2016. Lecture Notes in Computer Science (Vol. 10056). Springer. doi:10.1007/978-3-319-50182-6_13

Clarke, S. J., Peel, D. J., Arnab, S., Morini, L., Keegan, H., & Wood, O. (2017). EscapED: A Framework for Creating Educational Escape Rooms and Interactive Games to For Higher/Further Education. *International Journal of Serious Games*, *4*(3), 76-86. doi:10.17083/ijsg.v4i3.180

CourseSource. (n.d.). Evidence-based Teaching Resources for Undergraduate Biology and Physics. Qubes. https://qubeshub.org/community/groups/coursesource

Davis, D., & Lee, J. G. (2019). Building Escape Rooms to Increase Student Engagement in First-Year Engineering Classes. *2019 ASEE Annual Conference & Exposition*, Tampa, FL. 10.18260/1-2--32486

Davis, K., Lo, H.-y., Lichliter, R., Wallin, K., Elegores, G., Jacobson, S., & Doughty, C. (2022). Twelve tips for creating an escape room activity for medical education. *Medical Teacher*, *44*(4), 366–371. doi: 10.1080/0142159X.2021.1909715 PMID:33872114 de la Flor, D., Calles, J. A., Espada, J. J., & Rodríguez, R. (2020). Application of escape lab-room to heat transfer evaluation for chemical engineers. *Education for Chemical Engineers, 33*, 9–16. doi:10.1016/j.ece.2020.06.002

de Souza, R. T. M. P., & Kasseboehmer, A. C. (2021). The thalidomide mystery: A digital escape room using Genially and WhatsApp for high school students. *Journal of Chemical Education, 99*(2), 1132–1139. doi:10.1021/acs.jchemed.1c00955

Dietrich, N. (2018). Escape classroom: The Leblanc process - An educational "escape game". *Journal of Chemical Education, 95*(6), 996–999. doi:10.1021/acs.jchemed.7b00690

Dittman, J. M., Amendola, M. F., Ramraj, R., Haynes, S., & Lange, P. (2022). The COMET framework: A novel approach to design an escape room workshop for interprofessional objectives. *Journal of Interprofessional Care, 36*(1), 161–164. doi:10.1080/13561820.2020.1870442 PMID:33588677

Dittman, J. M., Maiden, K., Matulewicz, A. T., Beaird, G., Lockeman, K., & Dow, A. (2021). A flexible customizable virtual escape room approach for interprofessional learners. *Journal of Interprofessional Education & Practice, 24*, 100455. doi:10.1016/j.xjep.2021.100455

Earle, A. J. (2022). A How to Guide and Template for Designing a Puzzle Based Escape Room Game. *CourseSource, 9*. doi:10.24918/cs.2022.8

Elford, D., Lancaster, S. J., & Jones, G. A. (2021). Stereoisomers, not stereo enigmas: A stereochemistry escape activity incorporating augmented and immersive virtual reality. *Journal of Chemical Education, 98*(5), 1691–1704. doi:10.1021/acs.jchemed.0c01283

Ellsworth-Lyman, P. (2021). *The Do-It-Yourself Escape Room Book*. Skyhorse Publishing.

EMBL-EBI. (n.d.). *EMBL-EBI Services*. https://www.ebi.ac.uk/Tools

Estudante, A., & Dietrich, N. (2020). Using augmented reality to stimulate students and diffuse escape game activities to larger audiences. *Journal of Chemical Education, 97*(5), 1368–1374. doi:10.1021/acs.jchemed.9b00933

Eukel, H., & Morrell, B. (2021). Ensuring Educational Escape-Room Success: The Process of Designing, Piloting, Evaluating, Redesigning, and Re-Evaluating Educational Escape Rooms. *Simulation & Gaming, 52*(1), 18–23. doi:10.1177/1046878120953453

EZ EdTech! (2020). *Everything You Need to Know to Make a DIGITAL ESCAPE THE ROOM! Step by Step Tutorial.* YouTube. https://youtu.be/RT7sSLKvtxs

Fletcher, G. (2019). Ingress Rooms: Sustainable and Scalable Games for Learning. *Proceedings of the European Conference on Games Based Learning*, 227-234. 10.34190/GBL.19.166

Forkosh Baruch, A., & Meishar Tal, H. (2019). Strategies for Developing Mobile Location-Based Learning Activities by Teachers. In Mobile Technologies in Educational Organizations (pp. 85-95). IGI Global. doi:10.4018/978-1-5225-8106-2.ch005

Fotaris, P., & Mastoras, T. (2019, October). Escape rooms for learning: A systematic review. In *Proceedings of the European Conference on Games Based Learning* (pp. 235-243).

Foulds, J. L., & Forbes, K. L. (2021). Escaping the Routine Journal Club, Virtually. *Medical Education, 55*(5), 635–635. doi:10.1111/medu.14482

Friedrich, C., Teaford, H., Taubenheim, A., & Sick, B. (2020). Interprofessional health care escape room for advanced learners. *The Journal of Nursing Education, 59*(1), 46–50. doi:10.3928/01484834-20191223-11 PMID:31945176

Gilbert, B. C. T., Clapson, M. L., & Musgrove, A. (2020). ChemEscape, Polymer Chemistry: Solving Interactive Puzzles Featuring Scaffolded Learning to Promote Student Understanding of Polymers and Structure–Property Relationships. *Journal of Chemical Education, 97*(11), 4055–4062. doi:10.1021/acs.jchemed.0c00863

Grupel, D., Wennstroem, E., & Moran-Gilad, J. (2022). Escape room—The next generation of problem-based learning? *Clinical Microbiology and Infection, 28*(6), 768–770. doi:10.1016/j.cmi.2022.03.017 PMID:35339676

Guigon, G., Humeau, J., & Vermeulen, M. (2018, March). A model to design learning escape games: SEGAM. In 10th International Conference on Computer Supported Education (pp. 191-197). SCITE-PRESS-Science and Technology Publications.

Haake, S. (2019, October). Stealing the Exams: Using Narrative Techniques in Designing an Escape Game in University Context. In European Conference on Games Based Learning (pp. 1004-1007). Academic Conferences International Limited.

Heckelman, L. N., & Bucholz, E. K. (2020). Designing a MATLAB-based escape room. *2020 ASEE Virtual Annual Conference Content Access*. https://peer.asee.org/34402 doi: 10.18260/1-2--34402.

Heim, A. B., Duke, J., & Holt, E. A. (2022). Design, discover, and decipher: Student-developed escape rooms in the virtual ecology classroom. *Journal of Microbiology & Biology Education, 23*(1), 15–22. Advance online publication. doi:10.1128/jmbe.00015-22

Herreid, C. F. (2007). *Start with a Story: The Case Study Method of Teaching College Science*. NSTA press.

HHMI. (n.d.). *BioInteractive*. https://www.biointeractive.org/

Holzweiss, P. (2021). *How To Create a Virtual Escape Room*. YouTube. https://youtu.be/NXvLgLLzXCE

Hutchison, J. (2007). Giving birth to someone else's children? A case of disputed maternity. *Journal of College Science Teaching, 37*(1), 25–29.

Jackson, C., & Drake, P. (2019). *101 Puzzles for Low Cost Escape Rooms*. Moosehead Publishing.

Knoll, M., & Brickmann, M. (2018). Concept for a generic serious Escape Game for virtual and physical teams. In Edulearn 18. 10th International Conference on Education and New Learning Technology:(Palma, 2nd-4th of July, 2018). Conference proceedings (pp. 10022-10026). IATED Academy.

Kutzin, J. M. (2019). Escape the room: Innovative approaches to interprofessional education. *The Journal of Nursing Education, 58*(8), 474–480.

Lathwesen, C., & Belova, N. (2021). Escape rooms in STEM teaching and learning—Prospective field or declining trend? A Literature Review. *Education Sciences*, *11*(6), 308–308. doi:10.3390/educsci11060308

Makri, A., Vlachopoulos, D., & Martina, R. A. (2021). Digital escape rooms as innovative pedagogical tools in education: A systematic literature review. *Sustainability*, *13*(8), 4587. doi:10.3390u13084587

MERLOT. (n.d.). https://merlot.org

Monnot, M., Laborie, S., Hébrard, G., & Dietrich, N. (2020). New approaches to adapt escape game activities to large audience in chemical engineering: Numeric supports and students' participation. *Education for Chemical Engineers*, *32*, 50–58. doi:10.1016/j.ece.2020.05.007

Moore, L., & Campbell, N. (2020). Effectiveness of an escape room for interprofessional learning. *Medical Education*, *54*(11), 1047–1048. doi:10.1111/medu.14327 PMID:32885479

Moore, L., & Campbell, N. (2021). Effectiveness of an escape room for undergraduate interprofessional learning: A mixed methods single group pre-post evaluation. *BMC Medical Education*, *21*(1), 1–8. doi:10.118612909-021-02666-z PMID:33879150

Morris, J. (2020). *Escape Rooms in Education: A Practical Guide*. Amazon Publication.

Musgrove, H. B., Ward, W. M., & Hiatt, L. A. (2021). Escape from Quant Lab: Using Lab Skill Progression and a Final Project to Engage Students. *Journal of Chemical Education*, *98*(7), 2307–2312. doi:10.1021/acs.jchemed.1c00026

Mystakidis, S., Cachafeiro, E., & Hatzilygeroudis, I. (2019, July). Enter the serious E-scape room: A cost-effective serious game model for deep and meaningful E-learning. In 2019 10th International Conference on Information, Intelligence, Systems and Applications (IISA) (pp. 1-6). IEEE.

NASA. (n.d.). *EarthData: Open Access for Open Science*. https://www.earthdata.nasa.gov/learn/find-data

National Science Teaching Association. (n.d.). *NCCSTS Case Collection*. https://www.nsta.org/case-studies

NCBI. (n.d.). *All Resources - Tools*. https://www.ncbi.nlm.nih.gov/guide/all/

Nephew, S., & Sunasee, R. (2021). An Engaging and Fun Breakout Activity for Educators and Students about Laboratory Safety. *Journal of Chemical Education*, *98*(1), 186–190. doi:10.1021/acs.jchemed.0c01109

Nicholson, S. (2012, March). Completing the experience: Debriefing in experiential educational games. In *Proceedings of the 3rd international conference on society and information technologies* (pp. 117-121).

Nicholson, S. (2015a). A RECIPE for Meaningful Gamification. In T. Reiners & L. C. Wood (Eds.), *Gamification in Education and Business* (pp. 1–20). Springer International Publishing. doi:10.1007/978-3-319-10208-5_1

Nicholson, S. (2015b). *Peeking behind the locked door: A survey of escape room facilities*. https://scottnicholson.com/pubs/erfacwhite.pdf

Nicholson, S. (2016). *The State of Escape: Escape Room Design and Facilities Meaningful Play*. https://scottnicholson.com/pubs/stateofescape.pdf

Nicholson, S. (n.d.). *Scott Nicholson Website*. https://scottnicholson.com/

Nicholson, S., & Cable, L. (2020). Unlocking the potential of puzzle-based learning: Designing escape rooms and games for the classroom. *Sage (Atlanta, Ga.)*.

NOAA. (n.d.). *National Centers for Environmental Information*. https://www.ncei.noaa.gov/

O'Brien, K., & Pitera, J. (2019). Gamifying instruction and engaging students with Breakout EDU. *Journal of Educational Technology Systems*, *48*(2), 192–212. doi:10.1177/0047239519877165

Oestreich, J. H., Hunt, B., & Cain, J. (2021). Grant deadline: An escape room to simulate grant submissions. *Currents in Pharmacy Teaching & Learning*, *13*(7), 848–854. doi:10.1016/j.cptl.2021.03.013 PMID:34074517

Ouariachi, T., & Wim, E. J. L. (2020). Escape rooms as tools for climate change education: An exploration of initiatives. *Environmental Education Research*, *26*(8), 1193–1206. doi:10.1080/13504622.2020.1753659

Peleg, R., Yayon, M., Katchevich, D., Moria-Shipony, M., & Blonder, R. (2019). A lab-based chemical escape room: Educational, mobile, and fun! *Journal of Chemical Education*, *96*(5), 955–960. doi:10.1021/acs.jchemed.8b00406

Pfeifer, M., Völker, B., Böttcher, S., Köhler, S., & Scholl, P. M. (2021, March). Teaching Embedded Systems by Constructing an Escape Room. In *Proceedings of the 52nd ACM Technical Symposium on Computer Science Education* (pp. 1103-1109).

PLOS. (n.d.). *Open Data*. https://plos.org/open-science/open-data/

Rahim, A. S. A. (2022). Mirror mirror on the wall: Escape a remote virtual stereochemistry lab together. *Journal of Chemical Education*, *99*(5), 2160–2167. doi:10.1021/acs.jchemed.2c00050

RCSB Protein Data Bank. (n.d.). *Mol* 3D Viewer*. https://www.rcsb.org/3d-view

Rivera-Trigueros, I., López-Alcarria, A., Ruiz-Padillo, D.-P., Olvera-Lobo, M. D., & Gutiérrez-Pérez, J. (2022a). Design and Implementation of an Escape Room About the Discovery of the Periodic Table. In *Handbook of Research on Using Disruptive Methodologies and Game-Based Learning to Foster Transversal Skills* (pp. 397–422). IGI Global. doi:10.4018/978-1-7998-8645-7

Rivera-Trigueros, I., López-Alcarria, A., Ruiz-Padillo, D.-P., Olvera-Lobo, M. D., & Gutiérrez-Pérez, J. (2022b). A Digital Escape Rooms for Learning General Physics in HEIs: Building the Universe in Five Rooms. In Handbook of Research on Using Disruptive Methodologies and Game-Based Learning to Foster Transversal Skills (pp. 376-396). IGI Global. doi:10.4018/978-1-7998-8645-7.ch019

Ross, J. M., Wright, L., & Arikawa, A. Y. (2021). Adapting a classroom simulation experience to an online escape room in nutrition education. *Online Learning*, *25*(1), 238–244. doi:10.24059/olj.v25i1.2469

Ross, R., Hall, R., & Ross, S. L. (2022). Converting Course Material to Educational Escape Room Formats. In O. Bernardes, V. Amorim, & A. Carrizo (Eds.), *Handbook of Research on the Influence and Effectiveness of Gamification in Education* (pp. 164–188). IGI Global. doi:10.4018/978-1-6684-4287-6.ch009

Sabitzer, B., Groher, I., Hörmann, C., & Hofer, A. (2021). Toward the implementation of escape room games in an educational context. *Proceedings of the European Conference on Games Based Learning*, 925-928. 10.34190/GBL.21.125

Sawyer, T., Eppich, W., Brett-Fleegler, M., Grant, V., & Cheng, A. (2016). More than one way to debrief: A critical review of healthcare simulation debriefing methods. *Journal of the Society for Medical Simulation*, *11*(3), 209–217. doi:10.1097/SIH.0000000000000148 PMID:27254527

Selinker, M., & Snyder, T. (2018). *Puzzlecraft: How to Make Every Kind of Puzzle* (F. Heany, Ed.). Lone Shark Games.

Skeptical Educator. (2020). *Digital Escape Room Playlist.* YouTube. https://www.youtube.com/c/TheSkepticalEducator

Smash with GSuite. (n.d.). *BreakoutEDU*. https://sites.google.com/genoaschools.com/breakoutedu/play-here

Swiss Institute of Bioinformatics. (n.d.). *Expasy: Swiss BioInformatics Resource Portal.* https://www.expasy.org/

Taraldsen, L. H., Haara, F. O., Lysne, M. S., Jensen, P. R., & Jenssen, E. S. (2022). A review on use of escape rooms in education – touching the void. *Education Inquiry*, *13*(2), 169–184. doi:10.1080/20004508.2020.1860284

The King's University. (n.d.). *Centre for Visualization in Science.* https://www.kcvs.ca/

University of Colorado Boulder. (n.d.). *Simulation by PhET Interactive Simulations.* https://phet.colorado.edu/

USGS. (n.d.). *Science Data Catalog*. https://data.usgs.gov/datacatalog/

UW Center for Game Science and Institute for Protein Design. (2017). *Foldit Beta. Solve Puzzles for Science*. https://fold.it/

Van den Beemt, A., Groothuijsen, S., Ozkan, L., & Hendrix, W. (2022). Remote labs in higher engineering education: Engaging students with active learning pedagogy. *Journal of Computing in Higher Education*. Advance online publication. doi:10.100712528-022-09331-4 PMID:35974997

Veldkamp, A., Daemen, J., Teekens, S., Koelewijn, S., Knippels, M. C. P. J., & Joolingen, W. R. (2020). Escape boxes: Bringing escape room experience into the classroom. *British Journal of Educational Technology*, *51*(4), 1220–1239. doi:10.1111/bjet.12935

Veldkamp, A., van de Grint, L., Knippels, M.-C. P. J., & van Joolingen, W. R. (2020). Escape education: A systematic review on escape rooms in education. *Educational Research Review*, *31*, 100364. doi:10.1016/j.edurev.2020.100364

Vergne, M. J., Simmons, J. D., & Bowen, R. S. (2019). Escape the Lab: An Interactive Escape-Room Game as a Laboratory Experiment. *Journal of Chemical Education*, *96*(5), 985–991. doi:10.1021/acs.jchemed.8b01023

Vergne, M. J., Smith, J. D., & Bowen, R. S. (2020). Escape the (remote) classroom: An online escape room for remote learning. *Journal of Chemical Education, 97*(9), 2845–2848. doi:10.1021/acs.jchemed.0c00449

Vicari, C. (2020). Escape the Planet: Empowering Student Designers to Create a Science-Based Escape Room with Augmented Reality. *International Journal of Designs for Learning, 11*(2), 80–95. doi:10.14434/ijdl.v11i2.24110

Vörös, A. I. V., & Sárközi, Z. (2017, December). Physics escape room as an educational tool. In AIP Conference Proceedings (Vol. 1916, No. 1, p. 050002). AIP Publishing LLC. doi:10.1063/1.5017455

Watermeier, D., & Salzameda, B. (2019). Escaping boredom in first semester general chemistry. *Journal of Chemical Education, 96*(5), 961–964. doi:10.1021/acs.jchemed.8b00831

Welcome to Zooniverse. (n.d.). https://www.zooniverse.org/

WHO. (n.d.). *Global Health Observatory Data Repository*. https://apps.who.int/gho/data/node.home

Wiemker, M., Elumir, E., & Clare, A. (2015). Escape room games. *Game Based Learning, 55*, 55–75.

Wilkinson, C., & Little, H. (2021). "We had to be very clear that they weren't going to try to break into any of the cases": What potential do 'escape rooms' offer as a science communication technique? *Journal of Science Communication, 20*(1), C07. doi:10.22323/2.20010307

Wimpfheimer, T. (2020). A physical chemistry escape room laboratory: Is Schrödinger's Cat dead and/or alive? *Journal of Laboratory Chemical Education, 8*(1), 1–5. doi:10.5923/j.jlce.20200801.01

Yayon, M., Rap, S., Adler, V., Haimovich, I., Levy, H., & Blonder, R. (2019). Do-it-yourself: Creating and implementing a periodic table of the elements chemical escape room. *Journal of Chemical Education, 97*(1), 132–136. doi:10.1021/acs.jchemed.9b00660

Zotti, G., Hoffmann, S. M., Wolf, A., Chéreau, F., & Chéreau, G. (2021). The simulated sky: Stellarium for cultural astronomy research. *Journal of Skyscape Archaeology, 6*(2), 221–258. doi:10.1558/jsa.17822

KEY TERMS AND DEFINITIONS

Allied Health Professions: Careers that tend to human patients to maintain and improve health, such as physicians, nurses, and pharmacists.

Clue: Piece of instruction to solving a puzzle. A clue may also provide information about how to convert a puzzle solution into a code to open a lock (for example, the order of digits obtained from several puzzles that must be combined to open a lock).

Designer: The educator who creates, plans, implements, and assigns an EER to learners as part of a formal or informal activity in an instructional program.

Educational Escape Room (EER): An escape room designed to achieve a learning objective.

Escape Room: A series of puzzles tied together through a role-playing narrative.

Hint: Information that may be divulged to players in an escape room to help them solve a puzzle.

Lock: A mechanism that prevents progression through the escape room until a correct code is entered. Usually, the code is the solution to a puzzle or several puzzles.

Narrative: A story that provides the setting (who, what, where, when) and the goal (why) of an escape room. It also gives a role for the players to take on in the game.

Natural Sciences: Basic (non-applied) sciences such as biology, chemistry, and physics. May also include multidisciplinary disciplines such as biochemistry and astronomy.

Players: Undergraduate students who engage in an EER.

Puzzle: A problem that must be resolved to progress in the escape room experience.

Solution: The one correct interpretation of a puzzle. Usually, it is the code to open a lock.

Chapter 12
Unlocking Knowledge Through Escape Rooms in Online Higher Education:
Proposal for Learning About Consumer Behavior

Irene Aliagas
https://orcid.org/0000-0002-2848-329X
Universidad Internacional de La Rioja, Spain

Marta Retamosa
https://orcid.org/0000-0001-9984-7639
Universidad de Castilla-La Mancha, Spain

ABSTRACT

Online higher education is in demand, so much so that even face-to-face higher education is applying digital technologies to achieve greater motivation in the classroom. However, this does not mean that online education has everything won; it must continue to innovate in its methodologies to motivate students. The authors offer a proposal for the implementation of an educational escape room as a way to achieve greater motivation in the learning process through a playful experience. Although its use in educational contexts is increasingly common, until now it has not been applied in areas related to the study of consumer behavior. Thus, an explorative, innovative, and didactic escape room is provided based on consumer behavior subject. Several learning activities are employed, and guidelines for assessing and measuring learning are proposed. It is expected that this chapter will serve as a basis for those professionals interested in applying this methodology.

DOI: 10.4018/978-1-6684-6081-8.ch012

INTRODUCTION

It is becoming increasingly difficult to motivate students through traditional teaching methods, such as lectures, videos or tutorials. The problem with this type of didactic methods is that students are passive learners because there is hardly any interactivity with them (Phelps & Vlachopoulos, 2019). As a result, teachers are seeking to innovate their teaching practices in an attempt to engage students in their subjects and get them to learn (Navarro-Mateos & Pérez-López, 2022). As a potential solution, game-based learning has received increased attention from the education sector, as well as from academia and industry. It promises new opportunities to foster skills and increase knowledge by breaking out from the traditional classroom (Putz et al., 2020; Warmelink et al., 2017).

In recent years, escape rooms have been created not only for recreational purposes, but also as proposals for educational innovation. Thus, educational escape rooms (EERs) can be defined as a game with an educational learning purpose in which students have to discover clues, solve puzzles and complete riddles in one or more rooms, in order to achieve an objective (usually escape from the room) in a limited time. EERs are problem-based and time-constrained pedagogical activities that require participants to be active and collaborative in order to promote their learning (Veldkamp et al., 2020). Hence, they are used as an attempt to increase student motivation and engagement, by having fun and enjoying the experience.

In today's educational landscape, EERs scenarios are promising trends which can be implemented into many academic disciplines in higher education, such as English language learning (Santamaría & Alcalde, 2019), healthcare (Darby et al., 2020), mathematics (Fuentes-Cabrera et al., 2020), computer science (López-Pernas et al., 2019), or chemical engineering (De la Flor et al., 2020), among others.

Since EERs are considered to be an innovative and gamification-based educational methodologies, they should be designed with great consideration and follow the proper pedagogical theories to encourage the achievement of further learning (López-Pernas et al., 2019). In fact, not only academic achievement is achieved, but EERs also allow the development of competencies such as communication skills during the game and creative thinking (Fotaris & Mastoras, 2019).

Even though many studies have been conducted applying EERs into the physical classroom, studies carried out in an online classroom are scarcely to be found. Moreover, no scientific research has been conducted to explore the application and effects of a digital EER in online higher education on the subject of consumer behavior. This subject is included in the syllabus of several subjects, such as marketing or psychology, but this article focuses on the syllabus of the Master's Degree in Neuromarketing at the Universidad Internacional de La Rioja (UNIR). Its relevance lies in the fact that the main profiles in this field tend to come from social sciences, so they have limited knowledge of how the nervous system works and, in particular, the brain, which is the subject of interest. Thus, the content related to more psychological and cerebral aspects tends to be arduous and perhaps fails to sufficiently stimulate students' interest and motivation.

Therefore, the objective of this chapter is to provide a detailed proposal on the implementation of an EER in an online higher education environment. It is hoped that it will help students to consolidate the knowledge acquired in the subject of consumer behavior, as well as serve as a basis for other teachers to implement this methodology in their classrooms. To achieve this goal, it is explained how the current educational landscape requires active learning methodologies, then the role of gamification in education is highlighted, and finally the potential of educational escape rooms is discussed. Afterwards, a practical proposal that can be implemented in a real scenario is established.

BACKGROUND

Finding Motivation in Class Through Gaming

Today's students are 'digital natives', so they think and process information differently, challenging their teachers to keep them motivated and engaged through conventional learning (Fotaris & Mastoras, 2019). Therefore, teachers face the challenge of using multiple teaching strategies to engage students, where a good learning process can stimulate and motivate them. Nowadays, traditional learning methods are not considered to achieve these objectives. They focus on the figure of the teacher, with unidirectional communication and greater boredom and dissatisfaction with learning, which leads to poorer performance by students. Against this backdrop, the learning process in higher education has been undergoing changes in recent years. In contrast to the traditional teacher-centered model, new knowledge acquisition methodologies have emerged that can lead to greater student motivation and engagement by giving them a more active role in their learning (Chi & Wylie, 2014; Ferrer-Sargues et al., 2021).

In this relatively new educational context, the prevailing factor is game-based learning. Learning is sought through a playful experience in order to motivate students, since the aspect of playing a game leads to a better attitude towards this type of methodologies. In fact, game-based problems and challenges stimulate learning as there is immersion in the game (Hamari et al., 2016), going in line with the flow theory developed by psychologist Muhály Csikszentmihályi (1990). This points out that the mind enters a state where everything flows and it is easier to advance in the game if one manages to be involved in a fun activity and where there is a balance between personal skills, previous knowledge, and the acquisition of new ones, while being challenged. Thus, the interest in advancing in the game, acquiring a leading role and making decisions, will imply an active participation by the student, developing their skills, abilities and knowledge.

Results from previous experiments conducted in secondary and higher education settings showed that students who were subjected to learning with video games reported significant improvements in subject comprehension, diligence and motivation (Fotaris et al., 2016). It is important to keep in mind that it is not easy to address the problem of motivation in academia due to the multiple factors, patterns and models that address it (Aguiar-Castillo et al., 2021).

One of the increasingly popular educational methods is gamification, specifically, educational escape rooms. This has been reflected in several meta-analyses on the positive effects of gamification on both student learning (assessed through participation, attendance, test scores, and quality of work) and motivation to learn through game dynamics (Clark et al., 2016; Lister, 2015).

Gamification in the Educational Context

Gamification is a strategic tool that has been widely used in recent years in the educational context. As its name suggests, it consists of using dynamics or game elements in non-playful environments to make them more fun and increase students' motivation and engagement with the learning process (Aguiar-Castillo et al., 2021). Thus, learning becomes a more engaging, fun and productive experience (Barber, 2018). Specifically, gamification bases its method on a reward system that helps students to improve their attitude and predisposition towards teaching, leading to an increase in performance and dedication to the subject (Fuentes-Cabrera et al., 2020).

With its use in online higher education, the aim is to achieve greater motivation and engagement with course content by making the task more enjoyable (Aguiar-Castillo et al., 2021). In fact, there are authors who claim that gamification is increasingly used in online higher education, although not so much in face-to-face education (Deterning et al., 2011). That is why it can be said that the number of innovative practices based on gamification and applied to higher education has been growing in recent years. Moreover, the application of gamification to each of the fields of knowledge is being progressive and there are still many application possibilities to be explored. This is the case of Naik's (2017) research that talks about the use of games, simulation and escape room concepts in higher education to teach subjects such as mathematics. Also, the study by Eukel et al. (2017) employs gamification by proposing a game for pharmacy students to improve their knowledge of diabetes management. Del Castillo (2022) and Magadán and García (2022), use Kahoot as a gamification strategy when recalling subject concepts in a fun and entertaining way. In these cases, a positive impact on motivation, engagement and classroom dynamization was obtained.

Therefore, the use of game dynamics favors the active participation of students in class, increasing their motivation and helping them, for example, to overcome the fear of making mistakes by participating more in class (Zarzycka-Piskorz, 2016). Thus, gamified practices, although they are not games, are created to take advantage of human psychology in the same way that games do (Aguiar-Castillo et al., 2021). Thus, gamification would be a more rewarding and effective option than conventional motivation and loyalty techniques because, in the game, motivation is implicit (Werbach & Hunter, 2020).

Educational Escape Rooms as Playful Learning Environments

Escape rooms are nowadays a widespread leisure activity. Since their emergence in Japan in 2007, and until today, there are around 18,604 escape room games around the world (World of Escapes, 2022). That is why educators and researchers have begun to integrate this type of resource in their programs using them for training purposes, both in schools and universities, as well as in face-to-face or online environments (González-Norniella et al., 2018).

Although it is still a very small field, there is an increasing amount of literature about EERs. Most of the studies found are focused on teaching educational content, although some of them are also focused on promoting soft skills, such as cooperation or leadership (Fotaris & Mastoras, 2019, Veldkamp et al., 2020). In addition, EERs can be applied at different stages of the learning process, so the level of knowledge required will vary. Some are intended to introduce students to the subject matter, so no prior knowledge is necessary. Others pursue the objective of reinforcing the contents learned during the course, evaluating the knowledge acquired at the end of the semester, or even implementing it as a course exam (Boctor, 2013; López-Pernas et al., 2019; Veldkamp et al., 2020). EERs also vary with respect to the type of knowledge they are intended to teach. There are those focused on the acquisition of mathematical knowledge (Fuentes-Cabrera et al., 2020), learning English (Santamaría & Alcalde, 2019), knowing how to act when faced with a pharmaceutical problem (Eukel et al., 2017) or how to proceed in cardiac rehab (Ferrer-Sargues et al., 2021).

There are EERs that do not have a theme, but directly present the learning activities. However, this is not common, narratives are often used because they place students in the game to fulfill a specific role (Nicholson, 2015). Thus, storytelling becomes an essential element to make the experience immersive and get students to reach the flow state (Wiemker et al., 2015). Using a consistent theme means that there is a coherent story line that interrelates the themes and educational challenges, carrying out the proposed activities not because they are imposed, but because they help to solve the story (Nicholson, 2015). The themes that can be found are diverse, it all depends on the imagination of whoever develops the EER. The most common ones tend to be about science, space, environment or even a classroom.

As escape games entail the creation and learning of mental schemas about the dynamics of the game, the educational area takes advantage of this exciting interactive experience to achieve educational knowledge learning. Therefore, and with educational and research interests, the following section presents the exploitation of the EER within the educational field.

MAIN FOCUS OF THE CHAPTER: THE EDUCATIONAL ESCAPE ROOM PROPOSAL

Objective

This proposal aims to provide guidance for the development and implementation of an educational escape room as an activity to review the main concepts of the subject of consumer behavior and motivate students. Specifically, the two specific objectives to be achieved are:

1. To provide students with basic knowledge about the relationship between the human brain and decision making in the fields of marketing and organizations.
2. To bring students closer to the neuroscientific fundamentals and the assimilation of concepts, terminology and analysis techniques in a simple and practical way.

Academic Context

This teaching proposal is addressed to the subject of Consumer behavior within the Master in Neuromarketing of the Universidad Internacional de La Rioja (Spain).

Regarding the educational center, the Universidad Internacional de la Rioja is a private and online school for higher education. It comprises several faculties and it is in continuous search of learning innovation. Although it is known that some professors in the education faculty have developed some escape rooms for its students, none is known in the marketing area.

In particular, we focus on Neuromarketing master's degree because most of the profiles have a business administration, marketing or commercial orientation. However, neuromarketing is a combination of neuroscience and marketing, so it is needed to know at least basic concepts about how the brain works, being the main objective of the chosen subject matter. The subject of Consumer behavior is compulsory for these profiles that have no knowledge of neuroscience, being taught just before the first four-month period of the master's degree. Specifically, it is based on detailing the fusion between consumer behavior and neuromarketing and this is why this proposal can be innovative and pioneering in this context.

To assess whether they have acquired this fundamental neural and psychological knowledge, and to successfully complete the subject, an EER is proposed at the end of the course.

Figure 1. Visualization of the four educational challenges room
Source: Own work

Participants

A convenience sample will be chosen. The inclusion criterion will be to be enrolled in the subject on which the escape game is focused. Prior to data collection, students will be informed of the nature of the study, collecting their first and last names in order to be able to monitor their learning in the escape room sessions.

Design

The EER will be planned as a "special activity" for the last class of the course, being carried out two weeks before the end of the subject and the beginning of the main degree. Students were required to solve four challenges related to the four lessons of the subject (see Figure 1). This way, the escape room is planned to refresh the contents taught and to assess the knowledge acquired. In the days prior to its realization, students would be encouraged to review the documentation and contents of the subject; but only on the day of the escape room they would be informed of the event.

Since it was applied in a virtual classroom, the following considerations were taken into account:

- The activity was carried out individually.
- During the escape room, students will be connected to the subject classroom through Adobe Connect.
- The escape room will have a countdown of one hour.

- All challenges will be carried out digitally and will be completed in order.
- For each challenge there is a single solution and a reward for overcoming it.
- After completing each challenge, they will have to return to the website to fill out a Google Forms form. Knowledge will be tested by 2-5 questions and a code will be obtained in return.

Before starting the game, the professor, acting as the game master, will explain what an EER is and why it is applied in the subject. Then, she will explain the rules to solve it and the materials needed. She will guide students when needed, providing hints when necessary and solving complications during the games. Next, the narrative situation in which the game is framed will be presented in order to contextualize them and create a suitable atmosphere.

Students will have to work individually and manage to overcome the challenges. Once the students enter the room, a countdown will appear and they will have to complete all the missions to escape. Each game challenge has four rooms with a different scenario to give meaning to the escape room theme (Veldkamp et al., 2020):

- **Pre-game room:** it is used to introduce the plot of the mission, the escape room and the game mode, such as rules, materials, clues or questions from the students.
- **Playroom:** this is the center of the educational experience, as the pupils are the protagonists of the story and will have to overcome educational tasks.
- **Control room:** this is the point of contact between teacher and learners and provides support if necessary. Monitoring the process requires communication channels with the people in the room, such as cameras and microphones. Thus, the Adobe Connect platform will be used for synchronous implementation and the Google Jamboard platform will be used for asynchronous implementation.
- **Debriefing room:** this last space has the purpose of understanding what has happened in the room and bringing together what has been learned. Here the teacher and students can make an objective evaluation of the process.

An example of the different rooms used in the EER can be seen in Figure 2. Genially platform was used as a design application for the escape rooms, since it does not require previous design knowledge, is quite intuitive and it provides customized interactive content for educators.

Narrative

The overall theme of the educational escape room is behavioral science. It is chosen given its relation to the master's degree the students will be taking. A hacker has taken control of the building's entire system, so the students' mission is to regain control of it and the company's documents, eventually discovering the hacker's identity.

The activity begins by placing the students as part of the staff of the best neurotechnology laboratory, Neurotech, which aims to understand consumer behavior. One day they receive an urgent call from their department head because all the system has been hacked. A hacker has stolen all the files and hacked the entire computer system, so they will have to figure out how to get them back and how to regain control of the building. What they don't expect is for the hacker to open their eyes to realize that the bad guys are actually their bosses. They will have one hour to achieve the activity and defeat the hacker. If they

Figure 2. Examples of the different escape rooms used
Source: Own work on Genially platform

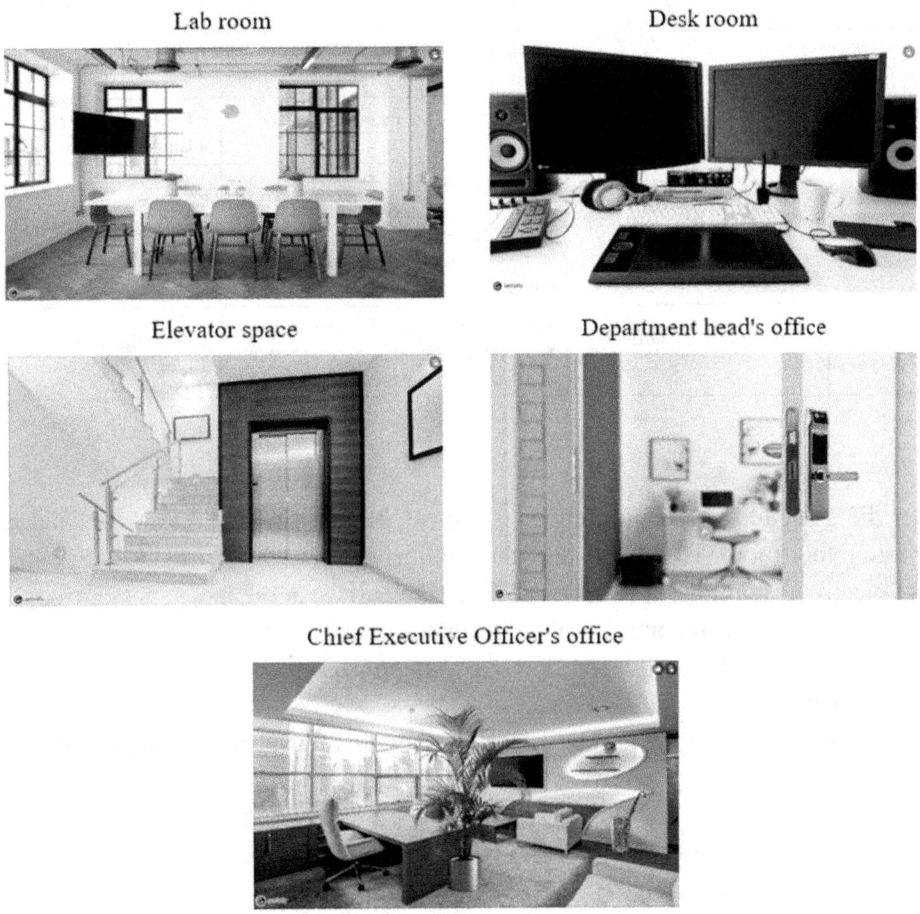

fail, the hacker will make the documents public, the company will be ruined and the reputation of the students will be affected forever.

Procedure

Six parts or mini escape rooms constituted the EER. The first and last challenges do not have an educational objective; their purpose is to immerse the student in the narrative. Then, Table 1 provides an overview of all the challenges of the educational game activity, indicating at each step of the process: 1) the objectives of the game, 2) the demonstration of educational knowledge, and 3) the specific tasks to be completed. The six parts of the escape game are described in detail below.

Step 1: Introduction

The purpose is to introduce the students to the escape room and to learn the dynamics of the game (rules, materials, clues, questions, etc.). Although there is no educational objective, they will have to create their own mental schemes about the functioning of the game and the plot.

Table 1. Summary of the proposed educational escape room challenges

Game challenge	Gaming objective	Educational skill demonstration	Tasks
1	Gain access to the hacker's account.	Brain structures and function knowledge.	Interactive questionnaire.
2	Retrieve workers' documents.	Knowledge of the main devices and ethical issues.	• Crossword puzzle. • Unlocking boxes.
3	Retrieve the department head's documents.	Being able to differentiate when each of the two systems proposed by Kahneman acts (fast versus slow), as well as other factors that influence the consumer's purchasing decision.	• Link concepts with their meaning. • Fill in the blanks.
4	Retrieve the Chief Executive Officer's documents.	To know the theory of the triune brain and the functioning of the components of the neuroleadership model.	• Solve the boxes. • Link concepts with their meaning.

Source: Own work

They start the game at the reception of the company building where they work, and are asked to come to the laboratory room. To achieve this, they will have to interact with different buttons in order to recover the electronic control of the building. Once they arrive at the lab, a message pops up on their computer: the hacker has taken control of their computers and, therefore, their contents. Students will have to recover the stolen information and find out who the hacker is.

Step 2: First challenge

Students must gain access to the hacker's account to begin recovering the documents.

- **Rooms**:
  - Pre-game room: Laboratory room.
  - Playroom: Desk room.
  - Debriefing room: Desk room.
- **Task instructions**: Identify each brain structure according to its location or function.
  1. When you look at another person head-on, their right cerebral hemisphere is in front of your left cerebral hemisphere, and their left cerebral hemisphere is in front of your right cerebral hemisphere. True or false? / Correct answer: True.
  2. The cerebral lobe that processes sensory information coming from all parts of the body through tactile stimuli is:
     a. Frontal lobe.
     b. Parietal lobe. / Correct answer.
     c. Temporal lobe.
     d. Occipital lobe.
  3. The brain lobe that is primarily associated with the processing of auditory stimuli is:
     a. Frontal lobe.
     b. Parietal lobe.
     c. Temporal lobe. / Correct answer.
     d. Occipital lobe.

4. The brain lobe that is responsible for processing more complex cognitive functions, such as reasoning and planning, is:
    a. Frontal lobe. / Correct answer.
    b. Parietal lobe.
    c. Temporal lobe.
    d. Occipital lobe.
5. The cerebral lobe whose main function is to process all visual information is:
    a. Frontal lobe.
    b. Parietal lobe.
    c. Temporal lobe.
    d. Occipital lobe. / Correct answer.

- **Game reward:** get the hacker's username and password.
- **Mission feedback:** "Congratulations! You have managed to outwit the hacker and get back into the system".
- **Learning assessment:** Students enter the data into the computer and, in order to prevent the hacker from regaining control, they program the best computer shields by answering two questions:
    - How many brain lobes can the brain be divided into? / Correct answer: 4.
    - How many cerebral hemispheres are there? / Correct answer: 2.
- **Game master reward:** They receive a badge with the numbers "47.48138955".

Step 3: Second challenge
Students must retrieve documents from all employees of the same rank.

- **Rooms**:
    - Pre-game room: Laboratory room.
    - Playroom: Desk room.
    - Debriefing room: Backup copy of the recovered documents.
- **Instructions for the first task:** Solve the crossword puzzle with the acronyms of the most used devices in neuromarketing to analyze consumer behavior. Use the clues to solve the crossword. Tap on a word and write the answer.
    1. It measures the electrical activity of the brain through sensors located on the scalp. Correct answer: EEG.
    2. It captures fixations in an area of interest. / Correct answer: ET.
    3. It records the galvanic response of the skin. / Correct answer: GSR.
    4. It assesses the implicit association between concepts and attributes. / Correct answer: TAI.
    5. It scans micro expressions (minimal facial movements). / Correct answer: FACS.
    6. It examines metabolic activity of the brain. / Correct answer: FMRI.

- **Reward for the first task**: They have their own username and password to access the documents.
- **Instructions for the second task:** Restore the facial coding systems of the building to be able to enter and exit freely through the rest of the office rooms, by clicking on each lock to open them.
    - Padlock 1: What is the name of the consent given to participants so that they have information about the experiment and their rights? / Correct answer: Informed consent.

Figure 3. Crossword puzzle of the second challenge
Source: Own work on Wordwall platform

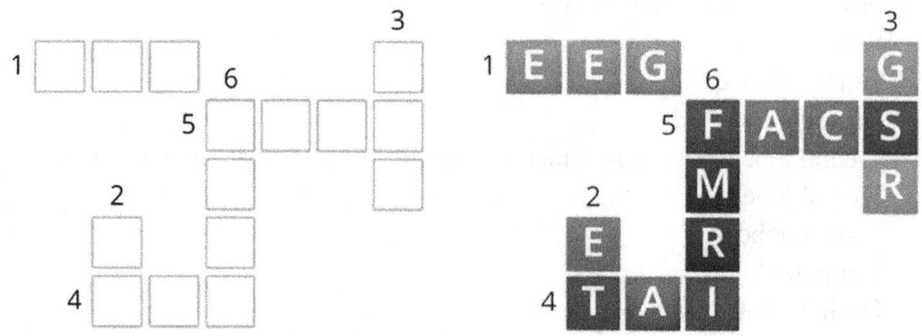

- ◦ Padlock 2: Neuromarketing does not need to be complemented by other types of techniques, such as quantitative or qualitative techniques. True or false? / Correct answer: False.
  - ◦ Padlock 3: The NMSBA code of ethics has been developed specifically for the field of neuromarketing. True or False? / Correct answer: True.
  - ◦ Padlock 4: Privacy, transparency and honesty are three principles that should guide neuromarketing studies. True or False? / Correct answer: True.
  - ◦ Padlock 5: The neuromarketing researcher is any person or organization that conducts or acts as a neuromarketing consultant in a research project. True or False? / Correct answer: True.
- **Reward for the second task:** The encryption systems are restored.
- **Mission feedback:** "You have managed to recover your documents and those of your colleagues! It has come to your attention that both the email and the password that the hacker has put in your user seem to indicate that there is something you don't know."
- **Learning assessment:** To make a backup copy of the recovered documents and passwords, they must answer two questions:
  - ◦ What device allows attentional measures to be obtained? / Correct answer: ET.
  - ◦ What device allows skin conductance measurement to be obtained? / Correct answer: GSR.
  - ◦ What device can measure cognitive load? / Correct answer: EEG.
  - ◦ What ethical principles should be kept in mind in research where neuromarketing techniques are applied? / Correct answer: Transparency, privacy and integrity.
- **Game master reward:** A badge with the numbers "19.14609412691246" is sent to the students.

Step 4: Third challenge
Students must retrieve documents from their department head.

- **Rooms:**
  - ◦ Pre-game room: Elevator space.
  - ◦ Playroom: Department head's office.
  - ◦ Debriefing room: Desk room.
- **Instructions for the first task:** Identify each action with the two systems proposed by Kahneman (fast versus slow). Drag and drop each item into its correct group.

1. Weigh whether to choose one brand or another. / Correct answer: 2.
2. Detect that one object is farther away than another. / Correct answer: 1.
3. Look for your house keys because you can't remember where you put them. / Correct answer: 2.
4. Show a disgusted face when tasting sour orange juice. / Correct answer: 1.
5. Buy a particular brand based on past experiences. / Correct answer: 1.
6. Park in a very narrow parking space. / Correct answer: 2.

- **Reward for the first task**: The computer scientist has been recovering the passwords of the company's bosses and the department head's password is "InvesT34n3uro".
- **Instructions for the second task:** Fill in the blanks so that the sentences about the main factors influencing the purchase decision process are correct.

There are (four) main factors that influence the purchase decision making process. First, (cultural) factors are capable of modifying perception, memory and (thinking). Secondly, (social) factors, such as family, reference and belonging groups, (roles) or status. Thirdly, (personal) factors refer to age, occupation, economic situation, lifestyle, self-concept or (personality). Finally, (psychological) factors include consumers' perceptions, motivations, beliefs, attitudes and learning, which is key to understanding why consumers behave as they do. These include Maslow (1943), who proposed a hierarchy of human needs that is still valid today: (physiological), security, (affiliation), recognition and (self-fulfillment). / Correct answers are shown in parentheses .

- **Reward for the second task:** They obtain the user to access the department head's documents, which is "J3faD3sLEAL".
- **Mission feedback:** "You have managed to recover your department head's documents! However, you have detected several files with strange and encrypted names, and that makes you suspicious. You decide to keep a copy of everything without her noticing. Later you will investigate what is really going on...".
- **Learning assessment:** To make a backup copy of the documents, students must answer two questions:
    - How many systems of thought did Daniel Kahneman propose? / Correct answer: 2.
    - What four factors are there that influence decision making? / Correct answer: Cultural, social, personal, and psychological.
- **Game master reward:** They will receive a badge with the word "Budapest" on it.

Step 5: Four challenge
Students must retrieve documents from the CEO of the company.

- **Rooms**:
    - Pre-game room: Department head's office.
    - Playroom: Chief Executive Officer's office.
    - Debriefing room: Desk room.
- **Instructions for the first task:** Solve the contents of each box according to the three brains theory. Touch each box one by one to open them and reveal the contents inside.
    - Box 1: The brain structures associated with the reptilian system are:

        a. Cerebellum, spinal cord and basal ganglia. / Correct answer.
        b. Thalamus, hypothalamus and amygdala.
        c. Corpus callosum, cerebral hemispheres and cerebral lobes.
    - Box 2: The brain structures associated with the limbic system are:
        a. Cerebellum, spinal cord and basal ganglia.
        b. Thalamus, hypothalamus and amygdala. / Correct answer.
        c. Corpus callosum, cerebral hemispheres and cerebral lobes.
    - Box 3: The brain structures associated with the rational system are:
        a. Cerebellum, spinal cord and basal ganglia.
        b. Thalamus, hypothalamus and amygdala.
        c. Corpus callosum, cerebral hemispheres and cerebral lobes. / Correct answer.
    - Box 4: Who establishes the triune brain theory:
        a. Paul McLean. / Correct answer.
        b. Daniel Kahneman.
        c. Nestor Braidot.
    - Box 5: The order of evolution of "the three brains" was:
        a. Limbic, rational, reptilian.
        b. Reptilian, rational, limbic.
        c. Reptilian, limbic, rational. / Correct answer.
- **Reward for the first task:** The IT guy gives you access to the CEO's computer password: "S3cRt".
- **Instructions for the second task:** Solve the correspondences in the STATUS model of neuro-leadership. Drag and drop each word next to its definition.
    - Accurate predictions about the future. / Correct answer: Certainty.
    - Control over one's own behavior and events that arise in the workplace. / Correct answer: Autonomy.
    - Sense of fair exchange. / Correct answer: Fairness.
    - Sense of importance, worth and dignity. / Correct answer: Status.
    - Feeling that there is a bond established with another person or with the company. / Correct answer: Relationship.
- **Reward for the second task:** the IT guy gives you access to the CEO's user: "CEO3stAFa".
- **Mission feedback:** "You have managed to recover the CEO's documents! However, you no longer harbor any doubts. The documents belonging to the highest ranks of the company are mysterious, so you decide to keep a copy of everything you have found to focus on solving the case".
- **Learning assessment:** To make a backup copy of the documents, students must answer these two questions:
    - According to the triune brain theory, what three brains are there? Indicate them in order of evolution. / Correct answer: Reptilian, limbic and rational.
    - What does the acronym SCARF stand for in English? / Correct answer: Status, certainty, autonomy, relatedness, and fairness.
- **Game master reward:** They will receive a badge with the word "Locate".

Step 6: Ending

Students have to find out who the hacker is. To do this, they must locate the address provided to them when completing the missions (i.e., badge data). Inside the game, they return to their desk, enter the data and discover that "Anonymous" was behind the hack. Their company has committed ethical, legal and moral infractions, they will have to decide whether to ally with Anonymous to combat this type of actions, or continue with the company, which will reward them monetarily for their silence.

Evaluation Methodology

The aim of this chapter is to present an alternative and attractive way to analyze the effectiveness of learning about consumer behavior through an EER. To this end, students' perceptions of the activity were obtained by applying the following two instruments:

1. **A pre-test and a post-test with educational questions to measure students' assimilation of knowledge.** Following the guidelines established by López-Pernas et al. (2019), in order to accurately measure the learning effectiveness of the EER, a pre-test will be conducted at the end of the teaching of all lessons, and a post-test after finishing each step of the EER. Both will contain the same ten questions on contents seen during the course, whose level of difficulty will be the same as the knowledge required to pass the EER tests. They can be consulted in the learning assessment sections of each step of the EER. The correct answers will not be revealed in the pre-test so that they do not learn them and can influence the post-test. The time limit to solve each test will be 10 minutes. Regarding correctness, 1 point will be awarded for each question answered correctly and 1/(N-1) will be subtracted for each answer answered incorrectly. Blank answers will not be penalized, so the maximum score will be 10 and the minimum 0.
2. **A survey to collect their perception and motivation about the EER.** To assess whether students find it beneficial to perform activities of this type, so that they serve as reinforcement of the material learned and help them when taking the exam in the future, the eight questions of Boctor (2013) will be adapted to the present EER. The responses to these questions will be assessed on a 5-point Likert-type scale, ranging from 1 = strongly disagree to 5 = strongly agree, being the following items:
    a. I felt this learning activity was beneficial.
    b. I enjoyed playing this game.
    c. I feel this activity will help me to answer test questions better.
    d. I learned new information related to consumer behavior.
    e. In the future, I want to use games like this to review material learned in class.
    f. This game helped me review neural bases for decision-making.
    g. I did not enjoy this escape game.
    h. I did not find this game beneficial to learning.

In addition, sociodemographic (e.g., sex and age), escape rooms experience, enjoyment playing escape rooms and perceived difficulty of the subject will be obtained. Escape rooms experience will be measured by asking for the number of escape rooms they have completed. The level of enjoyment of playing escape rooms, and the perceived difficulty of the subject, will be reached using a 5-point Likert scale, 1 = nothing at all to 5 = very much.

Data Analysis

It is recommended that the information collected be analyzed in the following order and with the specified statistical tests.

1. **Sociodemographic data, experience and enjoyment of escape rooms, and perceived difficulty of the subject:** The measures to be obtained will be percentages, means and standard deviations.
2. **Learning effectiveness data:** By means of a related samples t-test, the answers given in the pre-test and post-test will be compared. Thus, it will be possible to obtain the mean score obtained in both and check if there is a statistically significant difference between the two, which may indicate a difference in learning thanks to the EER. In addition, bivariate Pearson correlations will be calculated between gender, age, experience and enjoyment of escape rooms, difficulty of the subject, and pre-test and post-test learning. This will serve to contrast if some of these variables influence others and help to a greater or lesser learning through educational escape rooms.
3. **Students' perception and motivation data:** The reliability of the implemented scale and correlations between items will be calculated.

SOLUTIONS AND RECOMMENDATIONS

Throughout this chapter, the advantages of EERs for achieving greater learner motivation and higher learning rates have been discussed in depth. However, there are several considerations, recommendations and potential challenges to deliberate in the development of an EER. Regarding the considerations to be taken into account when developing and executing an online EER, the following can be distinguished:

- **Learning activities design:** It is recommended to use existing didactic templates for the design of learning activities, such as: BreakoutEDU (www.breakoutedu.com), Wordwall (www.wordwall.net) or Genially (www.genial.ly).
- **Time invested:** The time invested to devise, design and test the EER varies depending on the skills of the person designing it. However, the time cost to design it would be equivalent to the cost of preparing the syllabus to be taught and, moreover, the EER could also be reused in different courses. Platforms that contain ready-made EERs can be searched for and used (e.g., Genially), as they will require less time investment than if they have to be designed from scratch.
- **Playtime:** The time available in the classroom for the EER should be taken into account. In general, the duration is usually around 60 minutes so that there are no adverse effects, such as fatigue or boredom (Veldkamp et al., 2020).
- **Team size:** When an EER is carried out in groups, it is important to identify the right number of people to carry out the activity. The more people, the more participation is reduced. Typically, the range is between 3 and 6 people (Veldkamp et al., 2020). In online higher education, a problem to take into account is that not all students always attend class, so if the EER is not conducted during the scheduled class hours, it may not get the necessary sample of students willing to carry it out on their own, so the results obtained on whether the tool manages to be effective in learning cannot be generalized either.

- **Challenges and activities:** They should be embedded in the narrative so that students feel there is a purpose for their actions. In this way, performing the tasks will have an impact on the development of the game, but also on students' learning or knowledge reinforcement (Nicholson, 2015).
- **Hints:** They can be provided at the elapse of a specific time, when requested by learners or as an achievement after the resolution of a task. There can be a limited or unlimited number of hints (Eukel et al., 2017; Wiemker et al., 2015).
- **Rewards:** Sometimes the rewards are intrinsic, such as motivation for overcoming a challenge, but sometimes extra recognition is received, such as a hint for the next challenge or a final exam question (López- Pernas et al., 2019).

FUTURE RESEARCH DIRECTIONS

This chapter is only a proposal and has not been tested yet, but it is expected to serve as a basis for other professionals interested in EERs.

For further research, we propose to maintain the emphasis on the gamification of activities related to brain content, given that it is usually the most difficult to learn.

We encourage other professionals to use EERs in other classes in order to compare learning results and continue improving their design and implementation. Another possible approach would be to develop a cooperative EER, as the one in this proposal is developed to be carried out individually.

After all, the potential variants of this EER would offer a more satisfying, enriching and motivating learning experience, as well as allowing teachers and researchers to escape from the traditional classroom. Wouldn't you like to escape the routine in the classroom?

CONCLUSION

This chapter contains a proposal for the practical application of an educational escape room in a consumer behavior subject in an online higher education institution. The aim was to design this proposal for future implementation, as well as to serve as a reference for other practitioners. Moreover, the success obtained in the students' learning after the application of the EER can be considered as an evaluation indicator of the performance of the person who has implemented this methodology in the subject.

It is proposed that learning assessment be carried out at two points in time: during the course by means of questionnaires, and after completion of the syllabus by means of the EER. In addition, emphasis is placed on the need to analyze sociodemographic variables, experience and enjoyment with escape games, and the perceived difficulty of the subject, in case they could influence learning outcomes and motivation towards the EER. Finally, specific data analysis of these measures is proposed, as well as a series of aspects to be taken into consideration in their implementation.

It is clear that game-based learning is here to stay. Students need new methods of acquiring knowledge in the classroom and the traditional teaching model has become obsolete.

REFERENCES

Aguiar-Castillo, L., Clavijo-Rodríguez, A., Hernández-López, L., De Saa-Pérez, P., & Pérez-Jiménez, R. (2021). Gamification and deep learning approaches in higher education. *Journal of Hospitality, Leisure, Sport and Tourism Education, 29*, 100290. doi:10.1016/j.jhlste.2020.100290

Barber, C. S. (2018). Book Review: 3D Game Lab: Rezzly Heroic Learning. *Academy of Management Learning & Education, 17*(1), 114–117. doi:10.5465/amle.2017.0419

Boctor, L. (2013). Active-learning strategies: The use of a game to reinforce learning in nursing education. A case study. *Nurse Education in Practice, 13*(2), 96–100. doi:10.1016/j.nepr.2012.07.010 PMID:22910398

Chi, M. T. H., & Wylie, R. (2014). The ICAP framework: Linking cognitive engagement to active learning outcomes. *Educational Psychologist, 49*(4), 219–243. doi:10.1080/00461520.2014.965823

Clark, D. B., Tanner-Smith, E. E., & Killingsworth, S. S. (2016). Digital games, design, and learning: A systematic review and meta-analysis. *Review of Educational Research, 86*(1), 79–122. doi:10.3102/0034654315582065 PMID:26937054

Csikszentmihalyi, M. (1990). *Flow: The psychology of optimal experience*. HarperPerennial.

De la Flor, D., Calles, J. A., Espada, J. J., & Rodríguez, R. (2020). Application of escape lab-room to heat transfer evaluation for chemical engineers. *Education for Chemical Engineers, 33*, 9–16. doi:10.1016/j.ece.2020.06.002

Del Castillo, Á. (2022). Caso didáctico. Gamificación en educación superior: Dándole la vuelta a la formación en estudios presenciales y online [Didactic case. Gamification in higher education: turning around training in face-to-face and online studies]. *Journal of Management and Business Education, 5*(3), 282–296. doi:10.35564/jmbe.2022.0017

Deterning, S., Dixon, D., Khaled, R., & Nacke, L. (2011). From game design elements to gamefulness: defining "gamification". *Proceedings of the 15th international academic MindTrek conference: Envisioning future media environments*, 9-15.

Eukel, H. N., Frenzel, J. E., & Cernusca, D. (2017). Educational gaming for pharmacy students–design and evaluation of a diabetes-themed escape room. *American Journal of Pharmaceutical Education, 81*(7), 6265. Advance online publication. doi:10.5688/ajpe8176265 PMID:29109566

Ferrer-Sargues, F. J., Baixauli, P. E. K., Carmenate-Fernández, M., Rodríguez-Salvador, G., Domínguez, J. Á. G., Martínez-Olmos, F. J., & Valtueña-Gimeno, N. (2021). Escape-cardio: Gamification in cardiovascular physiotherapy. An observational study. *Nurse Education Today, 106*, 105062. Advance online publication. doi:10.1016/j.nedt.2021.105062 PMID:34304100

Fotaris, P., & Mastoras, T. (2019). Escape rooms for learning: A systematic review. *Proceedings of the European Conference on Games-Based Learning*, 235–243. 10.34190/GBL.19.179

Fotaris, P., Mastoras, T., Leinfellner, R., & Rosunally, Y. (2016). Climbing up the leaderboard: An empirical study of applying gamification techniques to a computer programming class. *Electronic Journal of E-Learning, 14*(2), 94-110.

Fuentes-Cabrera, A., Parra-González, M. E., López-Belmonte, J., & Segura-Robles, A. (2020). Learning mathematics with emerging methodologies-The escape room as a case study. *Mathematics*, *8*(9), 1–14. doi:10.3390/math8091586

González-Norniella, J., Cano Rodríguez, J. M., Alonso Orcajo, G. A., Pedrayes González, J. F., García Melero, M. E., Fernández Cabanas, M., & Rojas García, C. H. (2018). *Gamificación en el aula: "Escape Room" en tutorías grupales* [Gamification in the classroom: "Escape Room" in group tutorials]. Paper presented at the XXVI Congreso Universitario de Innovación Educativa en las enseñanzas técnicas. Escuela Politécnica de Ingeniería de Gijón.

Hamari, J., Shernoff, D. J., Rowe, E., Coller, B., Asbell-Clarke, J., & Edwards, T. (2016). Challenging games help students learn: An empirical study on engagement, flow and immersion in game-based learning. *Computers in Human Behavior*, *54*, 170–179. doi:10.1016/j.chb.2015.07.045

Lister, M. (2015). Gamification: The effect on student motivation and performance at the post-secondary level. *Issues and Trends in Educational Technology*, *3*(2), 1–22. doi:10.2458/azu_itet_v3i2_lister

López-Pernas, S., Gordillo, A., Barra, E., & Quemada, J. (2019). Analyzing Learning Effectiveness and Students' Perceptions of an Educational Escape Room in a Programming Course in Higher Education. *IEEE Access: Practical Innovations, Open Solutions*, *7*, 184221–184234. doi:10.1109/ACCESS.2019.2960312

Magadán-díaz, M., & Rivas-garcía, J. I. (2022). Classroom gamification in online higher education: The use of Kahoot. *Campus Virtuales*, *11*(1), 137–152. doi:10.54988/cv.2022.1.978

Naik, N. (2017). The use of GBL to teach mathematics in higher education. *Innovations in Education and Teaching International*, *54*(3), 238–246. doi:10.1080/14703297.2015.1108857

Navarro-Mateos, C., & Pérez-López, I. J. (2021). El escape room como estrategia didáctica en el Máster de Profesorado [Escape room as a didactical strategy in the Master's degree in Teacher Learning]. *Retos*, *44*, 221–231. doi:10.47197/retos.v44i0.91035

Nicholson, S. (2015). *Peeking Behind the Locked Door: A Survey of Escape Room Facilities*. https://scottnicholson.com/pubs/erfacwhite.pdf

Phelps, A., & Vlachopoulos, D. (2019). Successful transition to synchronous learning environments in distance education: A research on entry-level synchronous facilitator competencies. *Education and Information Technologies*, *25*(3), 1511–1527. doi:10.100710639-019-09989-x

Putz, L. M., Hofbauer, F., & Treiblmaier, H. (2020). Can gamification help to improve education? Findings from a longitudinal study. *Computers in Human Behavior*, *110*, 106392. doi:10.1016/j.chb.2020.106392

Santamaría, A., & Alcalde, E. (2019). Escaping from the English classroom. Who will get out first? *Aloma*, *37*(2), 83–92. doi:10.51698/aloma.2019.37.2.83-92

Veldkamp, A., van de Grint, L., Knippels, M. C. P. J., & van Joolingen, W. R. (2020). Escape education: A systematic review on escape rooms in education. *Educational Research Review*, *31*(January), 100364. doi:10.1016/j.edurev.2020.100364

Warmelink, H., Mayer, I., Weber, J., Heijligers, B., Haggis, M., Peters, E., & Louwerse, M. (2017). AMELIO: Evaluating the Team-building Potential of a Mixed Reality Escape Room Game. *Extended Abstracts Publication of the Annual Symposium on Computer-Human Interaction in Play - CHI PLAY '17 Extended Abstracts*, 111–123. 10.1145/3130859.3131436

Werbach, K., & Hunter, D. (2020). *For the Win, Revised and Updated Edition: The Power of Gamification and Game Thinking in Business, Education, Government, and Social Impact*. University of Pennsylvania Press. doi:10.2307/j.ctv2hdrfsm

Wiemker, M., Elumir, E., & Clare, A. (2015). Escape Room Games: Can you transform an unpleasant situation into a pleasant one? *Game Based Learning*, *55*, 55–68.

World of Escapes. (2022). *All escape rooms in the world on the map*. https://worldofescapes.com/countries

Zarzycka-Piskorz, E. (2016). Kahoot It or Not? Can Games Be Motivating in Learning Grammar? *Teaching English with Technology*, *16*(3), 17–36.

ADDITIONAL READING

Adams, V., Burger, S., Crawford, K., & Setter, R. (2018). Can you escape? Creating an escape room to facilitate active learning. *Journal for Nurses in Professional Development*, *34*(2), E1–E5. doi:10.1097/NND.0000000000000433 PMID:29481471

Aguiar-Castillo, L., Hernández-López, L., De Saá-Pérez, P., & Pérez-Jiménez, R. (2020). Gamification as a motivation strategy for higher education students in tourism face-to-face learning. *Journal of Hospitality, Leisure, Sport and Tourism Education*, *27*, 100267. Advance online publication. doi:10.1016/j.jhlste.2020.100267

Buckley, P., & Doyle, E. (2016). Gamification and student motivation. *Interactive Learning Environments*, *24*(6), 1162–1175. doi:10.1080/10494820.2014.964263

Groening, C., & Binnewies, C. (2019). "Achievement unlocked!" - The impact of digital achievements as a gamification element on motivation and performance. *Computers in Human Behavior*, *97*(March), 151–166. doi:10.1016/j.chb.2019.02.026

Kinio, A. E., Dufresne, L., Brandys, T., & Jetty, P. (2019). Break out of the classroom: The use of escape rooms as an alternative teaching strategy in surgical education. *Journal of Surgical Education*, *76*(1), 134–139. doi:10.1016/j.jsurg.2018.06.030 PMID:30126728

LaPaglia, J. A. (2020). Escape the evil professor! Escape room review activity. *Teaching of Psychology*, *47*(2), 141–146. doi:10.1177/0098628320901383

Miškov, J. (2022). The Place of Gamification in the Educational Context. In R. Ross, R. Hall, & S. L. Ross (Eds.), *Handbook of Research on the Influence and Effectiveness of Gamification in Education* (pp. 1–835). IGI Global. doi:10.4018/978-1-6684-4287-6.ch001

Novak, J., Lozos, J. C., & Spear, S. E. (2019). Development of an Interactive Escape Room Intervention to Educate College Students about Earthquake Preparedness. *Natural Hazards Review*, *20*(1), 06018001. Advance online publication. doi:10.1061/(ASCE)NH.1527-6996.0000322

Watermeier, D., & Salzameda, B. (2019). Escaping boredom in first semester general chemistry. *Journal of Chemical Education*, *96*(5), 961–964. doi:10.1021/acs.jchemed.8b00831

KEY TERMS AND DEFINITIONS

Consumer Behavior: The study of customers' actions in the marketplace and the underlying motives for those actions in selecting goods and services to satisfy their wants and needs. Furthermore, this topic is related to psychological knowledge about which brain areas are involved in consumer decision making.

Educational Escape Room: A game with an educational learning purpose in which you have to discover clues, solve puzzles and complete riddles in one or more rooms, in order to achieve an objective (usually escape from the room) in a limited time.

Game Master: The person who organizes and directs the game, gives clues, remembers the rules of the game, and mediates when necessary. It is usually the teacher of the subject.

Game-Based Learning: Type of game play with defined learning outcomes which uses gaming techniques to create a motivating and interactive e-learning environment.

Gamification: Use of game elements, such as reward systems, to motivate players to engage in a task they otherwise would not find appealing.

Motivation: An internal state of people that in some cases explains why a student begins, continues, and concludes any learning process.

Neuromarketing: The application of neuroscientific tools to the field of marketing and market research in order to understand the levels of attention and emotion that people show when faced with different stimuli.

Online Higher Education: Refers to higher level education provided telematically and encompassed in a university, such as undergraduate, graduate, and doctoral degrees, but also various professional schools.

Chapter 13
Escape Rooms for International Recruitment and International Business Management:
Developing Global Graduates With the United Nations Sustainable Development Goals

Lauren Amber Holly Crabb
Anglia Ruskin University, UK

Hanna Yakavenka
Coventry University London, UK

ABSTRACT

International education has been and continues to be a significant contributor to most developed economies despite COVID-19 preventing student mobility and severely impacting the way curricula were taught. Innovations in international recruitment and curricula were essential to ensure students had a legitimate taste of university life and to engage in internationalization activities. In this chapter, the authors present an escape room based on the United Nations Sustainable Development Goals, which were used for both academic sessions and as part of the business management undergraduate curriculum as an internationalization at home activity. The authors provide a guide of how to develop the escape room online and present tips for best practice.

INTRODUCTION

International education has been and continues to be a significant contributor to most developed economies despite Covid-19 preventing student mobility and severely impacting the way curricula were taught. For example, in 2019 international education was Australia's third largest export area (Chowdhury,

DOI: 10.4018/978-1-6684-6081-8.ch013

2022) and in the UK education exports are expected to reach £35 billion per year by 2023 (Department for Education and Department for International Trade, 2021). The travel restrictions associated with Covid-19 and increasing international competition has put pressure on Higher Education Institution (HEIs) international student recruitment targets, making it a strategic priority, further emphasised by increased student demands for outstanding learning experience. For international student recruitment and admission teams the process of recruitment and introduction into the University environment has also been affected as reliance on technology increased. In addition, due to the increasingly international scope and digital focus of the future business careers the ever so diverse international student body tend to demand more added value from taught curricula and their experience at overall. In addition to subject knowledge, university students expect to develop a range of transferable employment-focused skills such as international and cross-cultural awareness enhanced by advanced digital skills throughout their studies and extra-curricular activities.

The future-proof career enhancing skills are subject of an ongoing debate. The widely recognised skills of leadership, communication and subject knowledge are still necessary, however additional skills are required to navigate new, post Covid careers. Transferrable soft skills such as resilience, ability to cope with rapid and relentless change, digital and international communication are becoming more sought-after by the global labor market (Fakunle & Higson, 2021). This is in addition to the recent literature which has highlighted how there might be different skills needed to successfully manage one's career in different parts of the world. 'Employability in context' calls for a deeper understanding of the demands of the local labor market in different regions of the world and cultural context of companies operating there (Thi Tran et al., 2019).

Although Covid-19 prevented many forms of curriculum internationalisation and affected the traditional international recruitment drive, implemented technology innovations enabled students to gain some degree of international exposure and 'tasters' of university life whilst studying remotely. Escape Rooms are an example of such technology enabled tool which have been used throughout the Covid-19 pandemic to engage students in international learning or offer academic taster sessions to potential students. This book chapter builds on the authors' experiences of creating Escape Rooms for such purposes. It offers an example of a multi-purpose Escape Room used in student recruitment taster sessions and as an extra-curricular activity to enhance students' international exposure. The authors offer step-by-step guidance on how facilitators within the university setting can create an Escape Room for use as generic academic taster sessions or to enhance internationalization at home projects. The United Nations Sustainable Development Goals (SDGs) have been used as the subject for the Escape Room to provide added value to all curricula as these are embedded into sustainability agenda globally. The SDGs are also becoming increasingly important in Universities' sustainability outlook and being placed high on strategic plans of international organizations. Therefore, exposing learners to the application of SDGs in diverse contexts offers added value for those studying international business courses.

The chapter starts from the overview of the current literature on university student recruitment trends, intercultural exchange and its importance in developing transferable and employability skills in graduates and Escape Rooms as an education tool. The methodology section outlines the procedure alongside the approach to analysis of the findings from the qualitative interviews of Escape Room facilitators, which supported the development, enhancement, and implementation of the Escape Room. The authors offer detailed guidance on how to develop an International Business subject focused Escape Room using the Genially platform supported by facilitators' reflection and practical tips. Conclusions offer reflections on the practical use of Escape Rooms in Business Schools with the view of increasing internationalization of the curriculum and enhancing students' employability skills.

BACKGROUND

Global travel restrictions resulting from the Covid-19 pandemic affected the entire student journey, starting from the process of recruiting international students, onboarding into the university experience, the way the learning and assessment took place and all the way to graduation. Although there were existing processes of digitalizing many of the stages of the student journey, their use was expedited across all the segments of the Universities. The following section aims to shed light on current understanding of digital transformations and the opportunities available to education practitioners.

International Recruitment

The Covid-19 pandemic had a detrimental impact on the financial health of many HEIs, particularly due to losses in revenue from poor international student recruitment. In the UK for example, a 47% drop in international student numbers predicted to cost the Higher Education sector £1.5 billion (Qureshi & Khawaja, 2021). It would be untrue to justify this drop in recruitment numbers solely by the pandemic. Technology developments and innovation within Higher Education has enabled new types of courses and for curricula to be taught using different models, therefore reducing the actual number of international students on home campuses. For example, the rapid growth of Transnational Education delivery, distance learning, and development of overseas campuses, have all increased the number of students undertaking Higher Education degrees abroad but reduced student numbers on home campuses. In recent years there has also been a geopolitical shift in economic growth from the West to South-East Asian and South Asian countries. Whilst the competition from dominant markets such as Australia and USA remain, emerging new competitors from South-East Asia and the Middle East has toughened competition. Students wanting to study internationally now have many more options and opportunities compared to those at the turn of the millennium (Dennis, 2022).

Notwithstanding these factors, international student recruitment is still a strategic priority of most HEIs as typically international students pay a premium tuition fee (Qureshi & Khawaja, 2021). During the Covid-19 pandemic international student recruitment methods such as campus tours and in-person promotion fairs were replaced by online events (James, 2022). For some universities and individuals this meant catching up to those more proactive often larger institutions which were already engaging in digital technologies and social media recruitment drives before the pandemic (Hisel & Pinion, 2020). Smaller institutions have had varying levels of success as recruiters had to learn using new technologies to engage potential students and develop flexible and market-responsive recruitment strategies (James, 2022). These new strategies had at the same time to ensure that quality was not compromised whilst offering a genuine taste of university experience allowing potential students to prepare. This is especially important where new ways of learning, such as flipped and asynchronous strategies were implemented without sufficient trial testing of all the processes involved.

Albright and Schwanke (2021) found virtual campus tours, virtual school/college visits and online information sessions to be the most utilized forms of student recruitment throughout the Covid-19 travel restrictions. As online events removed physical barriers and borders, more applicants from non-strategic markets engaged and were potentially recruited to courses. Such move to online at promotion and recruitment stages has offered the long-term opportunities to engage with new markets without serious financial and human implications compared to in-person events at international destinations (James, 2022; Kanwar and Carr, 2020). It also highlighted the need for creativity and developing bespoke materials for on-line campaigns for different audiences as practice showed a universal approach was not effective (Reinartz and Saffert, 2013).

Internationalization at Home

Internationalization of the curriculum has been among the strategic objectives of most HEIs in recent decades. The labor market demands in the global economy have seen a rise in virtual, borderless, and cross-cultural working patterns. As a result, students demand exposure to international experiences at university in preparation for these increasingly global careers. Historically, students were socialized into the global economy through study exchanges, field trips, and semester/ year abroad programs (Mok et al., 2021). Beginning before the pandemic, but gaining traction throughout, widening participation agendas of HEIs meant these socialization methods were not achievable for all learners. HEIs had to reimage the essence and review the approach to internationalization of the curriculum and learning experience as a whole to offer a legitimate global experience to their students, including those unable to travel (Nghia et al., 2019). Some international experiences were moved online, bringing internationalization to one's home. Enabled by developments in technology, internationalization at home has grown within HEIs. Educators have started to introduce collaborative virtual learning opportunities to empower learners to engage with international peers, explore, evaluate, and create international knowledge.

With valuable lessons learnt, internationalization in Higher Education continues to grow (Galloway et al., 2020) in the post-pandemic environment, expediting pedagogic change in most disciplines with staff and students embracing new ways of learning (Neuwirth, 2021). Staff had to learn overnight new ways of engaging students in difficult circumstances, as Hisel and Pinion (2020) suggest, this might not have been their greatest hours teaching. In some cases, adapting to this change saw satisfaction rates drop with students perceiving online experiences as poor value for their investment in Higher Education (Neves and Hewitt, 2021). The significant financial investment needed by students mean they expect a high-quality learning environment (Tannock, 2018; Omorodion et al., 2021). At the same time, although students are often considered digital natives (Prensky, 2001), the move to online learning exposed gaps in their understanding of online pedagogy and willingness to engage. Nevertheless, the pressure to create innovative ways to engage learners in meaningful, new knowledge generating learning opportunities to enhance employability skills remained, affecting both the academic trainers and the students.

In the case of international business management education, the internationalization of the curriculum was to a great extent driven by skills sought after by global employers (Yakavenka, 2012; Ghani et al., 2021). These skills include leadership, innovation, the ability to work cross-culturally, critical thinking, problem solving and persuasive communication (Majid et al., 2012; Gyamera and Burke 2018). In a special issue introduction, Fakunle and Higson (2021) argue the Covid-19 pandemic has not only changed the way students learn, but also how they would work in the future. Employability skills would need to be reconceptualized to include the need to respond to future potential disruptions and global uncertainty. For example, graduates are now expected to live and work with technology, calling for technology being experienced in the university curriculum to go beyond an ordinary user level and most definitely not being perceived as a complementary pedagogic tool.

There is also a growing literature looking at understanding global employability patterns and 'employability in context' (Thi Tran et al., 2021) which appreciates employability complexities and relation to cultural contexts. Whereas employability in a Western Higher Education context is usually defined by skills such as leadership, enterprise and decision making, in South-East Asia, different attributes such as hardworking, loyalty, and obedience among employees are expected (Gribble, 2014). Understanding individual career pathways and identifying skills needed for diverse cultural contexts might therefore be an important part of graduate employability of the future. The demand for personalized learning with respect to global employability and transferrable skills for employment is likely to increase as diverse students make differing demands to the universities they choose.

Escape Rooms as International Engagement Opportunities

The advancement of digital platforms has enabled virtual learning and communication to become a central part of the Business courses at universities. With the borderless nature of virtual communication, it offers an increased potential for wider and more diverse intercultural exchanges among geographically spread participants (de Jonge and Labrador, 2020). Popular platforms such as Moodle and Blackboard have been widely used to enhance mass participation (Lima et al., 2020); and group conference call software such as Zoom has been essential to learning during the pandemic. As digital platforms become ubiquitous in Business curricula, smaller platforms which offer activity specific learning have also been emerging. This offers not only the exposure to different software, but the opportunity to practice digital skills for graduates to use beyond university.

Employability of the future points to soft skills being equally as important as subject specific knowledge with the employees needing to be able to navigate uncertain terrain. Gained at University, soft skills are said to be easily transferrable into workplaces (Gay and Betts, 2020), they can serve as enablers in enhancing one's interpersonal interactions, performance, and career prospects (Talaue, 2022). Research has shown that soft skills of Undergraduate students should be further enhanced during their studies and should be seen as a priority by HEIs (Tseng and Yeh, 2019). Learning whilst playing and exploring, having an opportunity to create their own learning spaces has been found to generate more personal learning outcomes and stronger engagement (Franco and DeLuca, 2019; Bakkum et al., 2021). Therefore, creating further virtual collaborative, and international learning opportunities for students offers numerous benefits particularly whilst operating during post-pandemic conditions.

Developing soft skills in students can be accomplished in many ways. Working in small groups for a competitive outcome is one approach and is suggested to be able to promote interaction while reducing cognitive stress and anxiety (York et al., 2021). In addition, creating a space for student interaction away from facilitators or formal learning environment could make students feel more at ease and able to converse with peers (Chen et al., 2005). Escape Rooms have been gaining traction among educators as a tool enabling the development of subject knowledge, teamwork and leadership skills or more generic skills by participants through a fun immersive time-bound activity (Veldkamp et al., 2020). According to Nicholson (2015) Escape Rooms are time bound, team or individual activities underpinned by problem-solving to find an answer or respond to clues. Originating from STEM education, they are in the early implementation stages across business courses (Bowyer, 2021; Martina and Goksen, 2022; Olvera-Lobo et al., 2021). Escape Rooms can have complex elements or be relatively straightforward depending on the participants' skill level, be facilitated virtually or physically (Tercanli et al., 2021), designed as standalone activity or be integrated as part of wider learning context, be assessed formally if require preparation or reflection afterwards (Veldkamp et al., 2020) or treated as a curricula enhancement exercise.

Escape Rooms which are underpinned by clear game-based learning design principles (activity theory, discovery learning, scaffolding) enable the participants to experiment, seek feedback, and engage more meaningfully with the content (Gee, 2009; Wiemker et al, 2015). Cleary defined goals of the game activity, motivational and learning strategies (Gopin, 2014) enable the participants to understand how the experience is integrated into the wider learning experience.

The skills and preparedness of the instructors are crucial to the success of the activity for students at every step of the way, so as the focus and the content of the Escape Room being at the right level (Martina and Gorksen, 2022; Bowyer, 2021). Clarke et al., (2017) reinforced the benefits of tailored support when facilitators develop Escape Room resources including thinking the activity through, planning for different game scenarios and specifically technology facilitation to monitor the engagement. The number of participants and teams playing at the same time, clues and scenario outcomes, the diversity of puzzle paths determine the complexity, requirements for prior preparation, and the level of support required (Lopez-Pernas et al., 2019). However, it has been observed that with the instructors playing the facilitator role, being there when needed (particularly at a debrief stage), the participants develop a stronger sense of independence and ownership of decisions made (Nicholson, 2015). While few studies investigated improved learning after completing an activity in an Escape Room, the majority did find an enhanced engagement of learners as a result (Veldkamp et al., 2020) and moving away from didactic learning environments (Franco and DeLuca, 2019).

This chapter aims to provide guidance on how to develop a multi-purpose Escape Room resource which can be used by academics in Business Schools. This Escape Room resource can be utilized as an academic taster session to introduce potential students to university learning and as a Collaborative Online International Learning project for undergraduate students to experience legitimate international exposure.

MAIN FOCUS OF THE CHAPTER

Virtual Escape Rooms have multiple uses within Higher Education in terms of academic taster sessions and developing a range of transferable graduate skills. The virtual Escape Room utilised as an example here was created on the Genially platform. Genially is a Spanish digital platform which provides personalised interactive content for educators. There is a free and premium version, plus a community of content creators who contribute to the platform and engage with users. The Genially platform was selected as it offers a wide range of Escape Room templates which can be easily tailored to the task or group of learners. There can be multiple collaborators on each Escape Room and the finished game can be easily shared or embedded into curriculum and range of virtual learning environments. The ability to embed Genially was particularly important for these Escape Rooms as students tend to get confused when multiple platforms being used within learning environments.

In total the Escape Room has been used seven times, four times in recruitment activities and three in Collaborative Online International Learning projects. The number of learners in each iteration of the Escape Room were between 10 and 34, with all participating online. The project was delivered synchronously and as a group work activity. However, the Escape Room could be used as an asynchronous individual activity as a knowledge refresher or introduction to the topic. By continuously collecting and analyzing data, the authors were able to refine the Escape Room for each iteration. By the final iterations, agreements were made that the optimum number of learners in each breakout group was 5. These learners were assigned to groups to ensure a diverse group. The Escape Room activity should take 90 minutes to deliver completely. In the first iterations the timings were much less, but a reflective exercise was included in the delivery. The reflective exercise enabled time for the breakout groups to discuss their own positionality and understanding of sustainable development and their role within society. This exercise used question prompts into the chat and then a wider discussion between all learners was facilitated by the Escape Room facilitator at the end. Further guidance on this is available in Table 1.

The Escape Room uses the content of the United Nations Sustainable Development Goals. The SDGs were agreed by the United Nations in 2016 aiming to create a sustainable planet for all by 2030. They replaced the Millennium Development Goal targets, which were widely seen as a failure. The SDGs encompasses all countries, not just developing countries as the previous Millennium Development Goals did (Crabb, 2018). The SDGs are focused around 17 goals (Fig 1) based on four dimensions: environment, economic, social and cultural; five pillars of people, planet, partnership, peace and prosperity (UN, 2018) underpin these. As the SDG embed into the global economy, they are becoming of strategic importance for many industries, requiring future managers to know how to operationalize them. Zhou et al., (2020) and Kestin et al., (2017) suggest Higher Education Institutions play an important role in disseminating scientific information, but also fundamental in leading social transformation and socialising students into the transformation (Zhou et al., 2020). With particular focus on the SDGs Kestin et al. (2017) suggested four ways HEIs can be influential to the success of the SDGs: (i) providing the knowledge and solutions to underpin the implementation of the SDGs; (ii) creating current and future SDG implementers; (iii) embodying the principles of the SDGs through organisational governance, operations and culture, and (iv) providing cross-sectoral leadership in implementation. Research into the SDGs and HEI has focused on all four of these functions (Sáez de Cámara et al., 2021; Nhamo and Mjimba, 2020; Crawford and Cifuentes-Faura, 2022). In the current case the SDG Escape Room would contribute to the second factor, helping to introduce future business leaders to the SDGs and their application to global business.

To understand the practicalities of using the SDG Escape Room in educational settings, primary data was collected in the form of facilitator reflections through qualitative interviews. Interview findings were thematically analyzed to enhance the use of the Escape Room and identify the areas of best practice. The interviews also informed the continued development of the Escape Rooms itself and how it was presented to learners. In total, four Escape Room facilitators shared their reflections on the use of the Escape Room and explored it as part of student recruitment activities and as part of internationalization at home activities. This included reflections from the lead author who created the Escape Room and facilitated two of the iterations. For all facilitators this was their first experiences of using Escape Rooms in an education setting, one facilitator was an international recruitment specialist with no teaching experience, the other three facilitators were experienced academics and module leaders.

The interviews were facilitated by the authors and took a semi-structured approach. The themes of the interview were developed through engaging with the academic literature on Escape Rooms and the authors own experiences of delivering the SDG Escape Room. Themes included facilitator delivery skills (Clarke et al., 2017), learner soft skill development (Martina and Gorksen, 2022; Bowyer, 2021) and appropriateness of the Escape Room for delivery. All interviews were between 25 and 55 minutes long and recorded on Microsoft Teams using the automatic transcription software. All transcripts were anonymised and cleaned before analysis with verifications sought where needed from the facilitators. Ethics clearance for data collection was sought through the relevant channels and secured by the University Ethics Committee.

Data analysis took a constructionist approach based on a process of identifying and interpreting the common themes from all interviews and constant data comparison. This enabled the researchers to create and continuously develop codes and categories until substantive theory was created (Santos et al., 2018). Substantive theory means that theories developed from this research can only apply to the context in which that was researched. For formal theory to be developed, a wider, more holistic approach would be more relevant (Heath and Cowley, 2004). This is outside the confines of the current chapter. The continuous data collection and analysis also enabled the lead author and creator of the Escape Room to continually improve the activity and develop guidance for best practice when used by others within the institution. Findings and reflections have formed the foundations for lessons learnt and best practice.

SOLUTIONS AND RECOMMENDATIONS

The platform utilized for this project is Genial.ly as it offers an effective framework for interactive visual content including gamification, Escape Rooms, presentations and official documents. It also enables educators to personalize quizzes, games and presentations for use in the classroom (Genially, 2022). There is a large, active and free to access community who provide help and support in addition to developing new content.

The Escape Room was built on the backwards design principal, whereby the educator starts with the end desired results in mind and designs learning from the end point (Wiggins and McTighe, 1998). In this case, cross cultural teamwork, independent and group research skills, and digital skills formed the foundation of both Escape Room scenarios. The recruitment-focused Escape Room required more content, including a detailed introduction to the university environment, with both the recruitment and international business project Escape Room needed opportunities to network. By starting with the desired end result the content is solely focused on skill development (Wiggins and McTighe, 1998). This approach works well for an Escape Room as the principles of learning become the questions the students answer to build the responses and 'escape.' The facilitator builds in the content through links to external learning materials which students work through and check their understanding via the clarification questions throughout the Escape Room experience.

The knowledge and facilitating skills which are developed throughout the Escape Room are distinguished across three levels of knowledge which Wiggins and McTighe (2005) discuss as "worth being familiar with," "important to know and be able to do," and "big ideas and core tasks" (p. 71). The big ideas and core tasks are to be anchored to the course / module, or what students should remember after upon completion (Wiggins and McTighe, 1998). The three-stage backward design approach has been applied to the SDGs project, with the learning outcomes around the understanding of the concept of sustainable development, appreciating the SDGs, and exploring the business applications of the SDGs whilst developing key employability skills. For the international business project Escape Room this also had a direct link to the course learning outcomes which had elements of sustainability as a concept and ability to apply digital skills.

The Escape Room was created on the Genially platform and distributed in breakout rooms on Microsoft Teams, initially used as it is the preferred institutional software. However, interview data suggested learners continued to chat in the Team after the event. This was particularly apparent in the recruitment iteration where learners asked the facilitator specific questions around different courses. Best practice

Figure 1. Front page of Genially once logged in. The creator should click gamification
Source: (Personal Collection)

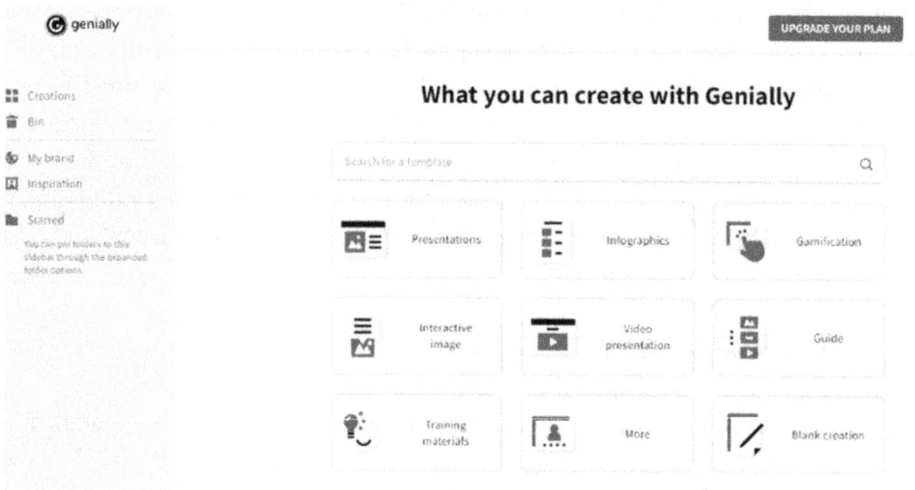

would be to ensure there is the opportunity for learners to continue to communicate with the facilitator and participants after the event.

In order to create the Escape Room, the facilitator needs to create an account on the Genially platform. The free version gives access to the Escape Room used in this chapter. Once signed in the user finds the creation page (Fig. 1) by clicking on the gamification link.

The different types of Escape Rooms can be found by scrolling through all options or selecting 'Escape Room' from the left-hand tool bar (Fig 2). In the free version of the platform, any premium content has a yellow star and will require the user to upgrade their account. The Breakout Adventure game was chosen as it fitted with the theme of the SDGs.

Once the game has been chosen the user can begin to personalise the Escape Room for their needs. The opening page (Fig 3) of the project is the interface the learner will first engage with. The Escape Room has hyperlinks already built in, so the facilitator only needs to personalise the content. They can scroll through the pages on the left-hand side tool bar. It is recommended to begin with an introduction which introduces the facilitator, explains the Escape Room and gives instructions for the participants. In current case the Escape Room had a different introductory video for each cohort which was recorded by the session facilitator. There was a more in-depth explanation for the recruitment taster session iteration as participants required further guidance. The mission section on page three of the framework is useful for explaining the task for all participants. This will be one of the first pages the participant will see. The task should be purposively vague, as this encourages participants to discuss the task in their groups while developing working relationships. It is recommended to change the wording 'characters' in the third section to the specific name 'The SDGs' in current case. By clicking on the text and the option to change the text becomes visible.

For the content of 'the SDGs', page 4 on the template, there needs to be some modifications. The characters and image need to be replaced with the SDG content (Fig. 4). For this page, SDGs 8, 9 and 10 were used alongside an introductory video. The text can be changed by clicking on the text and replacing

Figure 2. Screenshot of the different templates available on Genially. The author should choose 'escape room' from the list on the left. All premium resources are marked by a yellow star
Source: (Personal Collection)

with the appropriate title. To change the picture, select the image and then click on the replace icon. Images can be replaced with what is available on the computer or by searching from the Genially repository.

There is an interactive option on Genially which enables additional information or hyperlinks opening in new tabs. This feature was used so the participants could find out more information about the SDGs in the introduction and then about each SDG separately more in-depth.

Figure 3. Screenshot of the interface of the adventure escape room. The creators chose this template as it fitted with the theme of the UN SDGs
Source: (Personal Collection)

Figure 4. Screenshot of the first page the learners will see. The template has characters, they should be replaced with SDG labels, hyperlinks are already programmed into the template to take the learner to the correct page
Source: (Personal Collection)

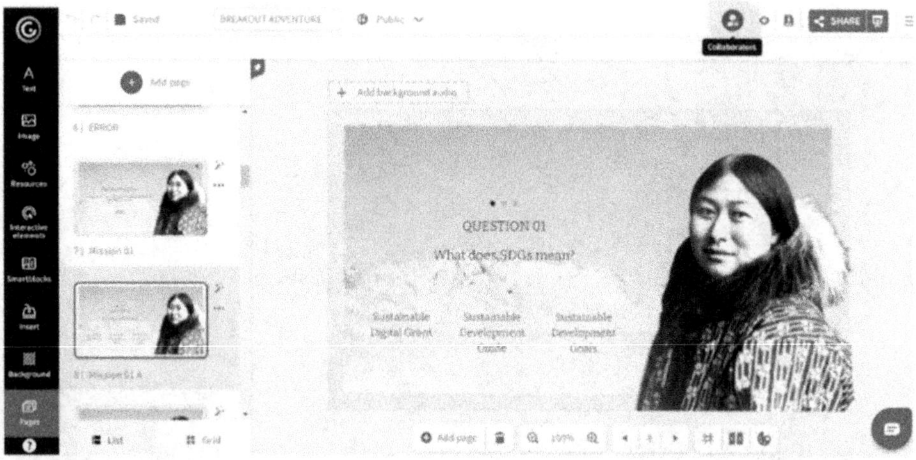

To create the interactivity, click on the image and then the blue finger icon. For the introduction, a video giving background to the SDGs is recommended. To input this, select the 'link' option on the toolbar (Fig. 5) and insert the relevant hyperlink. In current case the following video was recommended: https://www.youtube.com/watch?v=M-iJM02m_Hg

The individual SDG can be hyperlinked to an infographic created by the United Nations which are available at the following locations:

Figure 5. Screenshot of the input screen for the content. The labels need to connect to external videos. Hyperlinks are given within the text
Source: (Personal Collection)

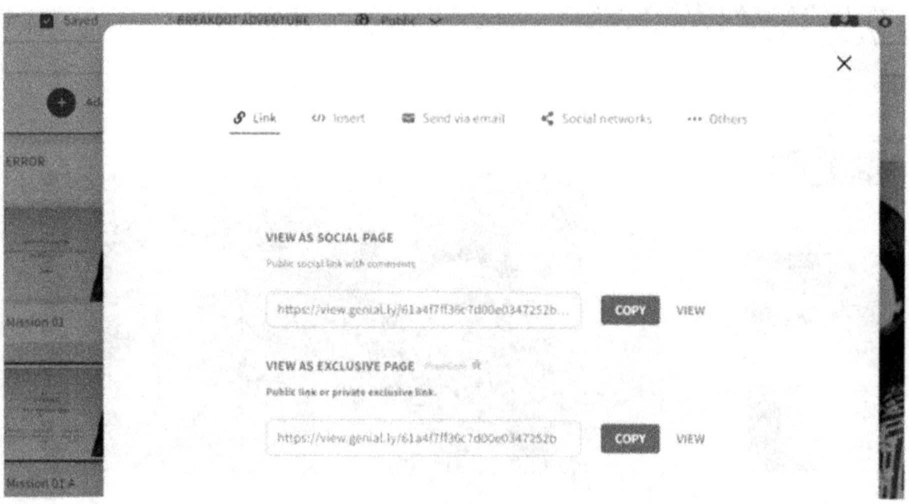

Figure 6. Screenshot of the journey of the escape room. The learners should work in their small groups to answer questions from all destinations and 'escape' the virtual room
Source: (Personal Collection)

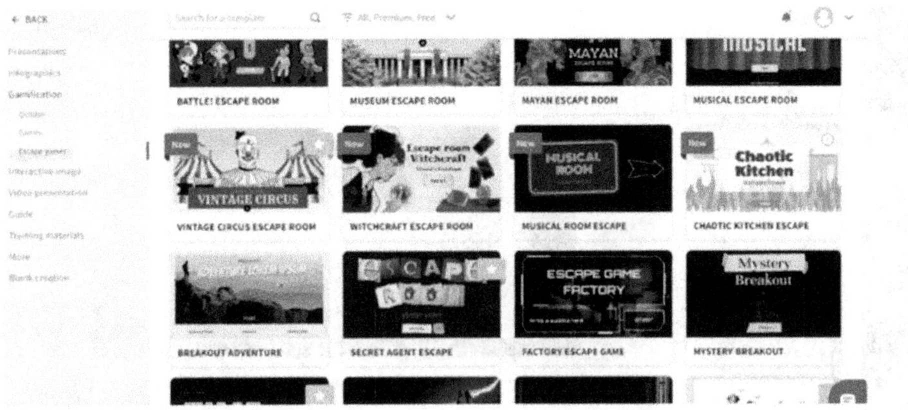

SDG 8: https://www.un.org/sustainabledevelopment/wp-content/uploads/2019/07/E_Infographic_08.pdf

SDG 9: https://www.un.org/sustainabledevelopment/wp-content/uploads/2019/07/E_Infographic_09.pdf

SDG 12: https://www.un.org/sustainabledevelopment/wp-content/uploads/2020/07/E_infographics_12.pdf

Once the students have engaged with the introduction video, the mission, and explored the SDGs through the external links to the UN website or appropriate YouTube videos, they are transferred onto the main game page (Fig 6). For each destination they are asked 5 questions on an SDG and its application to international business. At the end of each round of questions the participants receive a number (a code). On completion of all destinations, these numbers are used to unlock the safe and 'escape' from the room.

All questions in each section need to be designed by the facilitator. The hyperlinks are already written into the Escape Room framework, so the facilitator needs to only write the question and develop correct and incorrect answer options. The facilitator will be able to change the text by clicking on the appropriate text box and inputting the text. The template will indicate where to write the right and wrong answer (Fig. 7).

Once this has been inputted the participant will see the question and can select the answer, they think is correct (Fig 8). If the answer is correct, they will be taken to the next question.

At the end of the five correct answers in the section they will be given a number, each number from each section corresponds to a number on the safe which will allow the participants to 'escape' the room (Fig 9).

If any question is answered incorrectly, the participant will be sent to the incorrect answer screen, page six on the template (Fig 10), which then has an additional hyperlink to take them back to the question and try again.

At the end of the questions, once all sections have been answered, the participants can input the series of numbers collected from the different sections and escape the room (Fig 11).

Figure 7. Screenshot of one destination template. Each destination will have a pre-set hyperlinked questions. The creator needs to replace the text with their questions
Source: (Personal Collection)

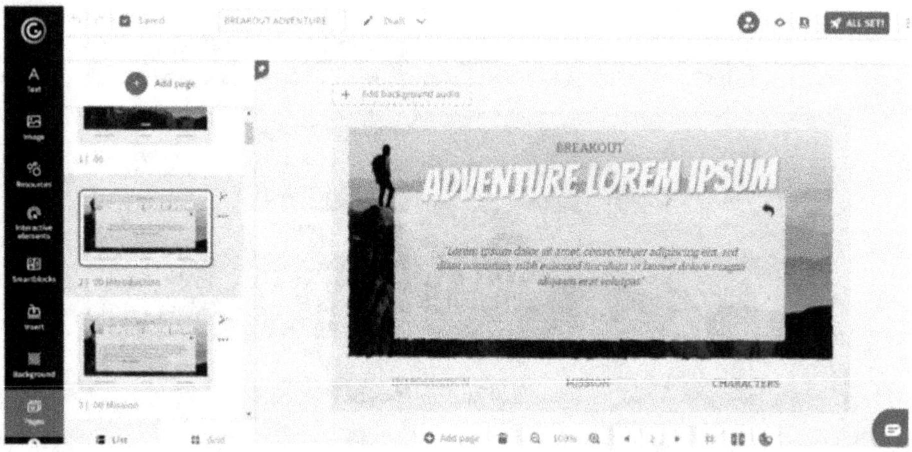

Genially will automatically save the changes and the facilitator will find their Escape Room creation in their personalised dashboard. The creation can also be shared with other Genially users by clicking on the share icon in the top right of the screen and entering the email address of the colleague (Fig 12).

Figure 8. Screenshot of a finished question. Once all questions are filled with the answers the hyperlinks will link to the next question
Source: (Personal Collection)

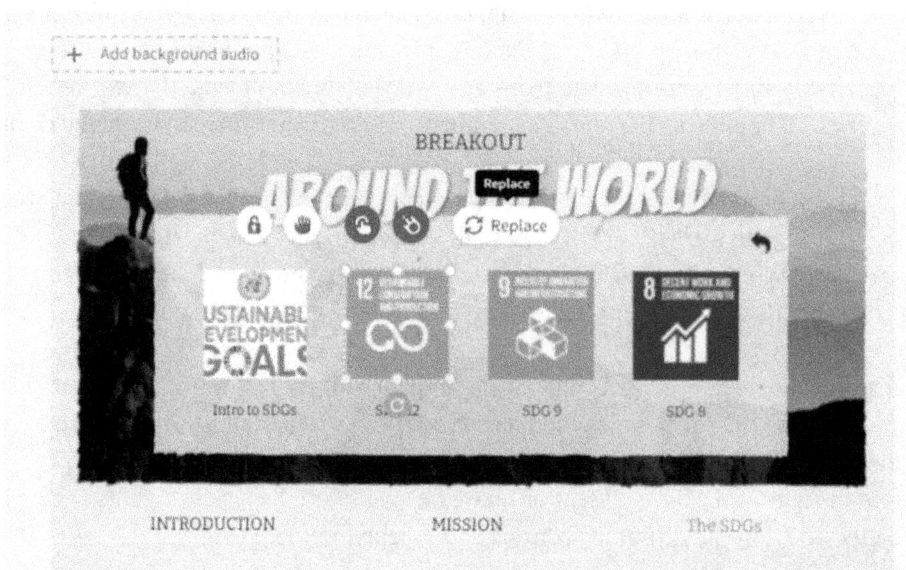

Figure 9. Screenshot of learners view when successfully completed a destination. When all answers are correctly given the participant received a number at each destination
Source: (Personal Collection)

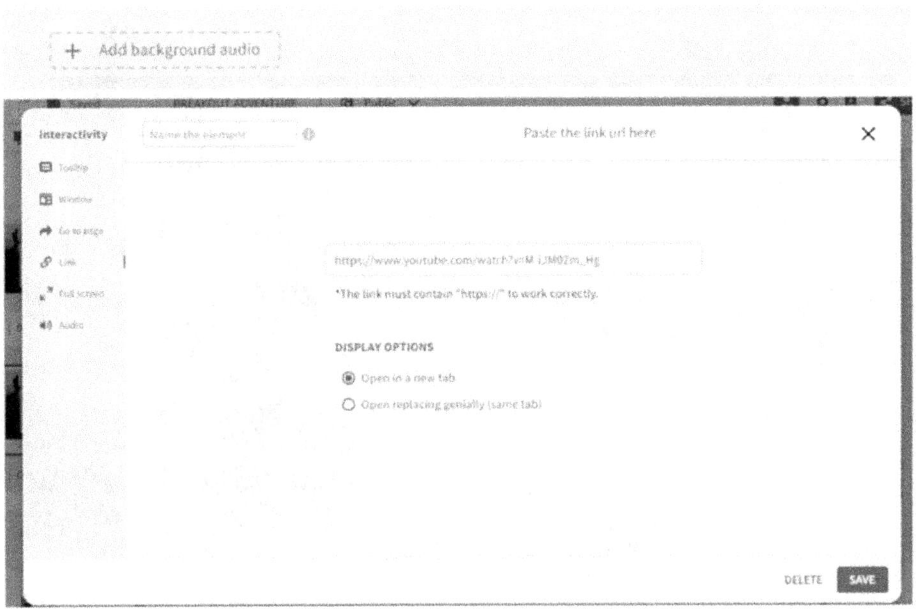

Once the Escape Room is created, it can be saved and shared with participants for use. Click on the 'share' button on the top right of the screen. The Escape Room can either be shared as a link or embedded into a VLE (Virtual Learning Environment) (Fig 13).

Figure 10. Screenshot of the screen when an incorrect answer is inputted by the learner. If an incorrect answer is given the participant can try again
Source: (Personal Collection)

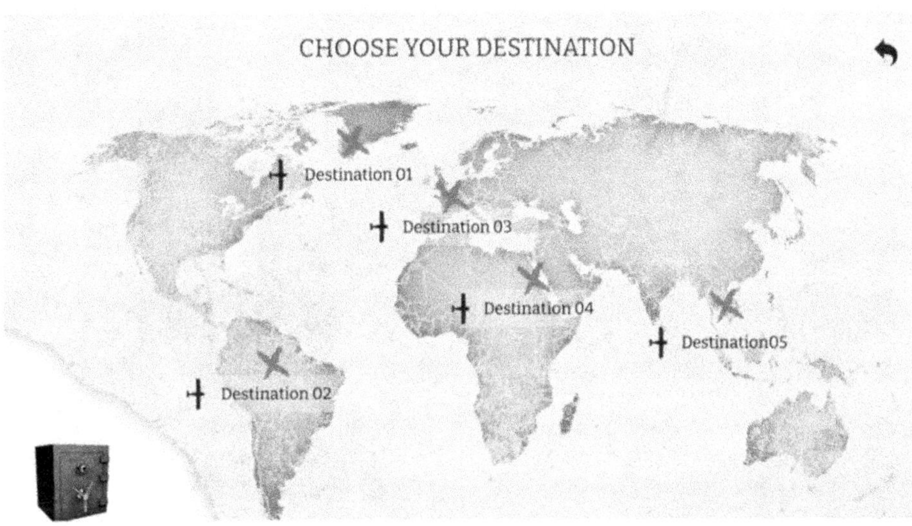

Figure 11. Screenshot of the page where the learners input their code. When all destinations are complete the participant can enter the code
Source: (Personal Collection)

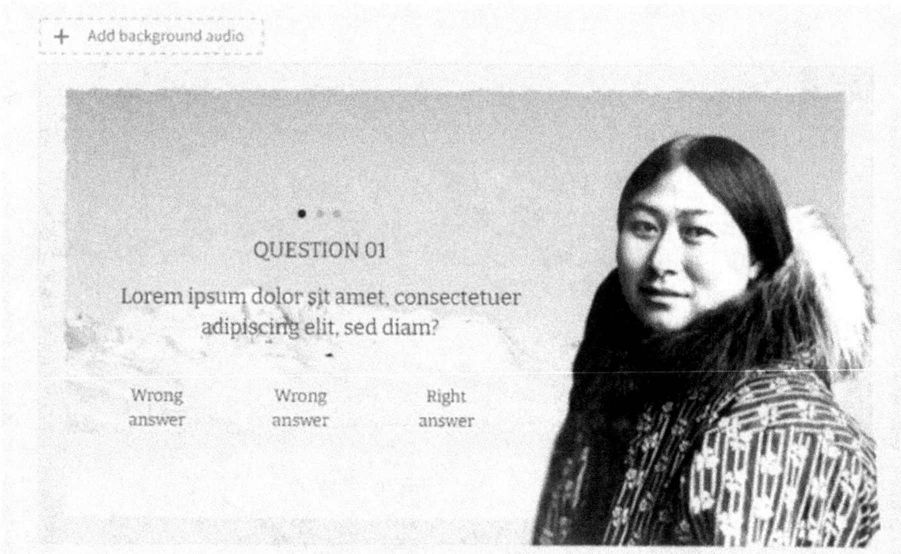

Once the Escape Room is created, it can be shared and re-used. It can also be duplicated by the creator and further modified for each use if necessary.

Figure 12. Screenshot of how to add collaborators to the escape room, creators can share with colleagues. Share the creation with colleagues by clicking 'collaborate' in the top right corner
Source: (Personal Collection)

Figure 13. Screenshot of the sharing options once the escape room is complete. The escape room can be linked or embedded into the creators VLE
Source: (Personal Collection)

Implementing the SDG Escape Room and Best Practice

The virtual Escape Room explored in this chapter has been utilised for two purposes, academic taster sessions for prospective students and as a COIL project for International Business Management Undergraduate students. The discussion below includes key learning points from the creation and application of the Escape Room in addition to the findings from the four qualitative interviews which directly informed this chapter.

The SDG Escape Room was created to contribute to an internationalization of the curriculum portfolio of activities. The Escape Room has specific learning outcomes, mostly around developing awareness of the SDGs, whilst it is expected to develop key employability skills within participant learners, the short duration of the project meant measuring the development of these skills was not appropriate. The Escape Room was designed on backwards design principles and the key employability skills of cross-cultural teamwork, independent and group research skills in addition to digital skills were targeted in this project.

The application of cross-cultural teamwork was reported as being difficult to foster by the facilitators. The platform did not allow inter-group communication; therefore, a second virtual platform was needed to host the Escape Room. This created an additional level of complexity as learners had to negotiate two platforms. However, facilitators reported an ease in how the Genially creation was embedded into VLE platform. Initial iterations also saw a facilitator share the Escape Room as a hyperlink. All the facilitators reported to use Microsoft Teams as the platform to create breakout rooms, where participants were split into smaller groups. Microsoft Teams is the institutional preference, although facilitators suggested other VLEs such as Zoom, BigBlueButton, Moodle or Blackboard to work equally as well with different communication functions.

Creating the opportunity for cross-cultural teamwork was embedded into the Escape Room design. Working in small groups the learners would have to investigate different aspects of the SGDs then answer questions to receive a code. For both the COIL project and the recruitment focused taster sessions, breakout rooms were used. During the first iteration of the virtual Escape Room, the facilitator reported the breakout rooms were created automatically via Microsoft Teams once all participants had entered the video call. The breakout rooms were essential to ensure group formation and cohesion (Chen et al, 2005). Each group had the space to interact and engage with discussion privately. It also enabled the facilitator to enter the breakout room to ensure participants understood the task, were focused on a task and answer any queries. The facilitator reported that the automatic breakout function made some groups homogenous and at times communication between team members was not fluid, opposing York et al., (2017) who seemed to suggest this would happen automatically. Despite efforts of the facilitator to encourage group communication, participants were reluctant to engage, especially when the facilitator entered the breakout room.

To ensure there was the diversity in the groups needed to be a legitimate cross-cultural activity, some facilitators reported to create the breakout rooms manually before the event. This was said to work well for the International Business projects iterations where the learners were known to the facilitator and has become an example of best practice. However, this was not possible for the academic taster sessions as not all registered participants attend the session, therefore, facilitators had to randomize the group forming as learners entered the Microsoft Teams space.

Results indicate that opposed to York et al., (2017) the communication between breakout room group members was not fluid. All facilitators on all iterations of the Escape Room, whether created manually or randomly, reported that communication between group members was slow. Facilitators in early iterations reported learners tended to complete a destination independently and come back with an answer, rather than working through the questions together as a team. By taking this approach to solving the Escape Room learners were not using the opportunity to develop cross-cultural teamwork and group research skills. Essential elements of the Escape Room design. In response to this, the creator of the Escape Room urged facilitators to give learners prompts for conversation and adequate time to introduce themselves in the breakout rooms. Prompts included initial knowledge of sustainable development, motivations for participating in the event and location from which they were attending the session. Two facilitators reported to use this approach and it was found to foster enthusiasm and increase the likelihood of legitimate teamwork.

In addition to the time given to learners in the breakout rooms, later iterations also included a stronger introduction to the event. A facilitator who used the Escape Room for academic taster session discussed how in their initial iterations, the Escape Room itself would last 10 to 15 minutes. With support from the development team, the facilitator was able to introduce the importance of the task, outlining the key employability soft skills and how the activity could be used as evidence on learner CVs. After the event, the facilitator reported learners were engaged in the breakout room chats, wanted more time to complete the activity and continued to communicate via the chat function on Microsoft Teams after the event. Due to the level of interaction on this particular taster session, the facilitator was able to respond to direct questions about specific courses with learners after the event. This best practice has been carried forward to encourage learners to engage directly with the international recruitment team.

The facilitators reported all participants, whether as part of the academic taster session or International Business COIL project bought into the activity once they were introduced to the importance of developing the key soft skills. The learning and sharing of best practice ensured there was a thorough introduction to the activity and time beforehand to enable the participants to introduce themselves in their breakout rooms. The early iterations which did not allow for this were not as successful as the later iterations in terms of inter-group communication and participation. The key employability skills of cross-cultural teamwork, group and individual research and digital skills (Majid et al., 2012; Gyamera and Burke 2018) were explained to all learners.

The Escape Room content itself is a relatively simple task for the learners to complete. It serves as an introduction to the SDGs; it is the developing of soft skills alongside learning the subject knowledge which is arguably of more importance. Facilitators in the initial iterations found the activity needed some reflection in order to help learners cement their skill development. Subsequent iterations were then given time at the end of the session to reflect on their skill development and knowledge of the SDGs. Facilitators suggested learners in the Business Management iterations initially struggled to see the benefits of the reflection task. The facilitator again needed to have a more prominent role in facilitating the discussion in the breakout room groups. Prompts given to learners to discuss included their positionality and experience of sustainable development, their understanding of intercultural skills and future personal development opportunities. The learner then was able to personalize the knowledge gained and created by communicating with peers. In turn, this allows students to develop a more meaningful experience. The learners from the academic taster sessions were not given the reflective element of the activity due to the time constraints of the session. However, this could be an additional element to begin students thinking reflectively and understand the importance of this skill in their future studies.

The development of the introduction and reflective activity for the Escape Room was developed over several iterations of the Escape Room. The facilitators reported this became easier as they grew in confidence and were able to facilitate more interactive sessions. As Martina and Gorksen (2022) and Bowyer (2021) suggest, ensuring the facilitators have the skills to run the activity was paramount. Constant communication between the development team and facilitators helped to grow institutional knowledge of virtual Escape Rooms and how best to deliver them to a diverse range of learners. They were also supported by the learning technologists in the institution. The learning technology team work to assist facilitators in developing technology use in the classroom. This additional support was essential for the facilitators; however, it is noted this might not be available to all practitioners through their institution.

Perhaps the most difficult challenge all facilitators experienced was the interactivity with participants. During the pandemic students were able hide online behind the computer screens by participating without cameras resulting in a lack of genuine participation. Encouraging them to introduce themselves, get to know others, and bringing their cultural knowledge into a wider community would bring them out of their shell for more meaningful communication. Challenging them and stretching the boundaries would enhance their ownership of knowledge. Encouraging students to turn on their cameras and engage fully with their colleagues was an issue for all facilitators. Future Escape Room practitioners could perhaps flip the learning experience and introduce more complex topics. This could be created where students have to bring their own knowledge to the Escape Room and co-create new knowledge with their peers. This may deviate from simply accepting information to personalizing the knowledge created. More complex problems could then be introduced to challenge participants.

The Escape Rooms detailed in this chapter have been implemented online. The Escape Room could be adopted to run on a face-to-face format with key elements of the activity such as group research being conducted online or in blended format. In a classroom setting the groups of questions could be posted on separate tables. Student groups would then move around the room from table to table until they have collected the release code. This would require individual students having access to the internet and ensuring the content is easily accessible on mobile devices. Whether delivered online or face-to-face, facilitator support is essential to ensure participants understand the task and are encouraged to actively engage. Facilitators also play a vital role in ensuring there is scope and space for networking after the event. The learning points and development of the multi-purpose Escape Rooms have been summarized below to enable future facilitators to utilize this knowledge (table 1).

Table 1. Best practice and learning points from the development of the multi-purpose escape room

Escape room implementation top-tips	Learning points
Create a VLE space where students can network	Networking is essential to create team ethic and further communities of practice
Enable reflection time	Reflection is essential for participants to personalize knowledge
Create diverse groups and explain importance of working in such teams	Participants were much more likely to actively participate when the rationale for the task was given
Encourage active learning by turning cameras on and flipping some content	This gives participants responsibility for the task and creates an environment of trust
Link content to curriculum although does not have to be explicitly linked through assessment	Will motivate students to continue learning outside taught curriculum
Ensure facilitators have necessary skills	Facilitation of activity including introduction and reflection is essential to ensure the success

FUTURE RESEARCH DIRECTIONS

The chapter was informed by qualitative interviews with facilitators and reflection from the development team. Future research could investigate the application of the Escape Room to other elements of university learning and explore the process of learning soft skills over a longer period.

CONCLUSION

The SDGs virtual Escape Room has been used as an academic taster session to facilitate recruitment and as a Collaborative Online International Learning project for undergraduate International Business Management students. The virtual Escape Room has gone through several iterations, from this, best practice has been developed and shared within this book chapter.

The SDGs are an essential aspect of the global sustainability agenda and are used increasingly across International business curricula. Future graduates are likely to work within the SDG framework and therefore will expect exposure to agenda during their studies (Moon et al., 2018). The Escape Room was used to facilitate this learning, form communities of practice and introduce students into the knowledge creation process (Yakavenka, 2012; De Back et al., 2021). Overall, the results indicated the Escape Room provided a novel and innovative way to engage students generating a successful outcome. All four facilitators would recommend the use of the Escape Room and will continue to use it in their practice.

In order for the SDG Escape Room to contribute to the creation of SDG leaders and implementers (Moon et al., 2018) participants need well designed space to reflect on their understanding and positionality on sustainable development. The space to discuss these stances with peers was also essential to enable personalized learning. The knowledge creation process was much wider than the actual task. The wrap around activities were just as essential to ensure students engaged with the task, personalized learning and developed soft skills (Yakavenka 2012; de Back et al 2021).

Escape Rooms have the potential to offer current and prospective students the opportunity to develop key soft skills essential in the global labor market. The ability to work cross-culturally is increasing in importance, alongside digital and leadership skills alongside known skills such as critical thinking, evidence informed decision making and persuasive communication (Majid et al., 2012; Gyamera and Burke 2018). The task itself would not be enough to prove evidence of development of these skills, but as part of an international curriculum, the Escape Room provides space and opportunity to enhance these skills. The implementation of the Escape Room in academic taster sessions for prospective students as well as COIL projects with international partners has enabled the participants to practice reflection and solve the challenges through continuous improvement of their understanding leading to knowledge gain. As Fakunle and Higson (2021) argue, the Covid-19 pandemic has changed the way students learn and will work in the future, it is the job of the educators to keep abreast of these changes and ensure their students are equipped for the global workplace. The online aspect of the Escape Room also adds another dimension. In addition to the SDG subject knowledge, this type of online engagement not only facilitates key soft skills, which are said to be easily transferrable into future careers (Gay and Betts, 2020).

This chapter provided facilitators with a guide on how to develop the Escape Room and shared best practice for how to implement the activity so it generates student engagement and enhances their soft transferrable skills.

This research received no specific grant from any funding agency in the public, commercial, or not-for-profit sectors.

REFERENCES

Albright, E. R., & Schwanke, E. A. (2021). University Admissions Leaders Rethink Recruitment Strategies in the Wake of COVID-19. *The Journal of Advancing Education Practice*, *2*(1), 4.

Bakkum, M. J., Richir, M. C., Sultan, R., Lambooij, A. C., van Agtmael, M. A., & Tichelaar, J. (2021). Can students create their own educational escape room? Lessons learned from the opioid crisis escape room. *Medical Science Educator*, *31*(6), 1739–1745. doi:10.100740670-021-01425-5 PMID:34950526

Bowyer, S. (2021) Learn, Play, Design: Using the Escape Room Concept to Teach Creativity and Innovation in a Business Course. *Business Education Innovation Journal, 13*(59).

Chen, S. J., Hsu, C., & Caropreso, E. (2005, October). Cross-cultural collaborative online learning: When the west meets the east. In *E-Learn: World Conference on E-Learning in Corporate, Government, Healthcare, and Higher Education* (pp. 1931-1941). Association for the Advancement of Computing in Education (AACE).

Chowdhury, M. B. (2022). Internationalisation of education and its effect on economic growth and development. *World Economy*, *45*(1), 200–219. doi:10.1111/twec.13174

Clarke, S., Peel, D. J., Arnab, S., Morini, L., Keegan, H., & Wood, O. (2017). EscapED: A framework for creating educational escape rooms and interactive games for higher/further education. *International Journal of Serious Games*, *4*(3), 73–86. doi:10.17083/ijsg.v4i3.180

Crabb, L. A. (2018). Debating the success of carbon-offsetting projects at sports mega-events. A case from the 2014 FIFA World Cup. *Journal of Sustainable Forestry*, *37*(2), 178–196. doi:10.1080/10549811.2017.1364652

Crawford, J., & Cifuentes-Faura, J. (2022). Sustainability in higher education during the COVID-19 pandemic: A systematic review. *Sustainability*, *14*(3), 1879. doi:10.3390u14031879

De Back, T. T., Tinga, A. M., & Louwerse, M. M. (2021). Learning in immersed collaborative virtual environments: Design and implementation. *Interactive Learning Environments*, 1–19. doi:10.1080/10494820.2021.2006238

de Jonge, J. S., & Labrador, B. (2020, November). Fostering critical thinking and motivation through digital escape rooms: preliminary observations. In Virtual exchange and 21st century teacher education: short papers from the 2019 EVALUATE conference (p. 157). Research-publishing. net.

Dennis, M. J. (2020). COVID-19 will accelerate the decline in international student enrollment. *Recruiting & Retaining Adult Learners*, *22*(12), 1–7. doi:10.1002/nsr.30639

Department for Education and Department for International Trade. (2021). *International Education Strategy: 2021 update. Supporting recovery, driving growth*. Available at: https://assets.publishing.service.gov.uk/government/uploads/system/uploads/attachment_data/file/958990/International-Education-Strategy-_2021-Update.pdf

Fakunle, O., & Higson, H. (2021). Interrogating theoretical and empirical approaches to employability in different global regions. *Higher Education Quarterly*, *75*(4), 525–534. doi:10.1111/hequ.12345

Franco, P. F., & DeLuca, D. A. (2019). Learning through action: Creating and implementing a strategy game to foster innovative thinking in higher education. *Simulation & Gaming*, *50*(1), 23–43. doi:10.1177/1046878118820892

Galloway, N., Numajiri, T., & Rees, N. (2020). The 'internationalisation', or 'Englishisation', of higher education in East Asia. *Higher Education*, *80*(3), 395–414. doi:10.100710734-019-00486-1

Gay, G. H., & Betts, K. (2020). From Discussion Forums to eMeetings: Integrating High Touch Strategies to Increase Student Engagement, Academic Performance, and Retention in Large Online Courses. *Online Learning*, *24*(1), 92–117. doi:10.24059/olj.v24i1.1984

Gee, J. P. (2009). Deep learning properties of good digital games: How far can they go? In U. Ritterfeld, M. Cody, & P. Vorderer (Eds.), *Serious games: Mechanisms and effects* (pp. 65–80). Routledge.

Ghani, A. N. A., Teo, P. C., & Mahadi, N. (2021). Sustainability In Business Education Through Internationalisation: Challenges and the Roles. *Journal of Contemporary Issues in Business and Government*, *27*(3), 398.

Gopin, E. (2014). Finding and Evaluating Great Educational Games. In Z. Yang, H. H. Yang, D. Wu, & S. Liu (Eds.), *Transforming K-12 Classrooms with Digital Technology* (pp. 83–97). IGI Global. doi:10.4018/978-1-4666-4538-7.ch005

Gribble, C. (2014). *Exploring 'employability' in different cultural contexts.* Final Report: Scoping Study. Society for Research into higher Education (SRHE). Deakin University.

Gyamera, G. O., & Burke, P. J. (2018). Neoliberalism and curriculum in higher education: A post-colonial analysis. *Teaching in Higher Education, 23*(4), 450–467. doi:10.1080/13562517.2017.1414782

Heath, H., & Cowley, S. (2004). Developing a grounded theory approach: A comparison of Glaser and Strauss. *International Journal of Nursing Studies, 41*(2), 141–150. doi:10.1016/S0020-7489(03)00113-5 PMID:14725778

Hisel, J. D., & Pinion, C. Jr. (2020). Student recruitment and engagement in the COVID-19 era. *Journal of Environmental Health, 83*(2), 36–38.

James, M. (2022). International student recruitment during the pandemic: The unique perspective of recruiters from small to medium-sized higher education institutions. *Higher Education Policy*, 1–19. doi:10.105741307-022-00271-3 PMID:35465058

Kanwar, A., & Carr, A. (2020). The impact of covid-19 on international higher education: New models for the new normal. *Journal of Learning for Development, 7*(3), 326–333. doi:10.56059/jl4d.v7i3.467

Kestin, T., van den Belt, M., Denby, L., Ross, K., Thwaites, J., & Hawkes, M. (2017). *Getting started with the SDGs in universities: A guide for universities, higher education institutions, and the academic sector*. Academic Press.

Lima, C. D., Bastos, R. C., & Varvakis, G. (2020). Digital learning platforms: An integrative review to support internationalization of higher education. *Educação em Revista, 36*, 36. doi:10.1590/0102-4698232826

López-Pernas, S., Gordillo, A., Barra, E., & Quemada, J. (2019). Examining the use of an educational escape room for teaching programming in a higher education setting. *IEEE Access: Practical Innovations, Open Solutions, 7*, 31723–31737. doi:10.1109/ACCESS.2019.2902976

Majid, S., Liming, Z., Tong, S., & Raihana, S. (2012). Importance of soft skills for education and career success. *International Journal for Cross-Disciplinary Subjects in Education, 2*(2), 1037–1042. doi:10.20533/ijcdse.2042.6364.2012.0147

Martina, R. A., & Göksen, S. (2022). Developing educational escape rooms for experiential entrepreneurship education. *Entrepreneurship Education and Pedagogy, 5*(3), 449–471. doi:10.1177/2515127420969957

Mok, K. H., Xiong, W., Ke, G., & Cheung, J. O. W. (2021). Impact of COVID-19 pandemic on international higher education and student mobility: Student perspectives from mainland China and Hong Kong. *International Journal of Educational Research, 105*, 101718. doi:10.1016/j.ijer.2020.101718 PMID:35719275

Moon, C. J., Walmsley, A., & Apostolopoulos, N. (2018). Governance implications of the UN higher education sustainability initiative. *Corporate Governance: The International Journal of Business in Society.*

Neuwirth, L. S., Jović, S., & Mukherji, B. R. (2021). Reimagining higher education during and post-COVID-19: Challenges and opportunities. *Journal of Adult and Continuing Education, 27*(2), 141–156. doi:10.1177/1477971420947738

Neves, J., & Hewitt, R. (2021). *Students highlight the challenges of their 2021 academic experience.* Advance HE. Available at: https://www.advance-he.ac.uk/news-and-views/students-highlight-challenges-their-2021-academic-experience

Nghia, T. L. H., Giang, H. T., & Quyen, V. P. (2019). At-home international education in Vietnamese universities: Impact on graduates' employability and career prospects. *Higher Education, 78*(5), 817–834. doi:10.100710734-019-00372-w

Nhamo, G., & Mjimba, V. (2020). The context: SDGs and institutions of higher education. In *Sustainable development goals and institutions of higher education* (pp. 1–13). Springer. doi:10.1007/978-3-030-26157-3_1

Nicholson, S. (2018). Creating Engaging Escape Rooms for the Classroom. *Childhood Education, 94*(1), 44–49. https://doi.or g/ doi:10.1080/00094056.2018.1420363

Omorodion, F., Coltman, L., Babajide, O., & Etowa, E. (2021). Learning Experiences and Challenges facing Black International Students at the University of Windsor. *Teaching Culturally and Linguistically Diverse International Students in Open and/or Online Learning Environments: A Research Symposium Learning Experiences and Challenges facing Black Int.*

Prensky, M. (2001). Digital natives, digital immigrants, part 2: Do they really think differently? *On the Horizon, 9*(6), 1–6. doi:10.1108/10748120110424843

Qureshi, F. H., & Khawaja, S. (2021). Is Covid-19 Transitioning Cash Cows International Students into Cats? *European Journal of Education Studies, 8*(7). Advance online publication. doi:10.46827/ejes.v8i7.3816

Reinartz, W., & Saffert, P. (2013). Creativity in advertising: When it works and when it doesn't. *Harvard Business Review, 91*(6), 106–111.

Sáez de Cámara, E., Fernández, I., & Castillo-Eguskitza, N. (2021). A holistic approach to integrate and evaluate sustainable development in higher education. The case study of the University of the Basque Country. *Sustainability, 13*(1), 392. doi:10.3390u13010392

Santos, J. L. G. D., Cunha, K. S. D., Adamy, E. K., Backes, M. T. S., Leite, J. L., & Sousa, F. G. M. D. (2018). Data analysis: Comparison between the different methodological perspectives of the Grounded Theory. *Revista da Escola de Enfermagem da U S P.*, 52. PMID:29668789

Talaue, G. M. (2022). Career Adaptability of Jubail University College Students: An Assessment for Employability Potentials. *International Journal of Project Management and Productivity Assessment, 10*(1), 1–19. doi:10.4018/IJPMPA.297087

Tannock, S. (2018). *Educational equality and international students: Justice across orders?* Palgrave Macmillan. doi:10.1007/978-3-319-76381-1

Tercanli, H., Martina, R., Ferreira Dias, M., Reuter, J., Amorim, M., Madaleno, M., Magueta, D., Vieira, E., Veloso C., Figueiredo, C., Vitória, A., Wakkee, I., Gomes, I., Meireles, G., Daubariene, A., Daunoriene, A., Mortensen, A., Zinovyeva, A., Rivera-Trigueros, I., López Alcarria, A., Rodríguez-Díaz, Olvera-Lobo, P. M.D., RuizPadillo, D.P., & Gutiérrez-Pérez, J. (2021). Educational escape rooms in practice: Research, experiences and recommendations. UA Editora. doi:10.34624/rpxk-hc6

Tseng, H., Yi, X., & Yeh, H. T. (2019). Learning-related soft skills among online business students in higher education: Grade level and managerial role differences in self-regulation, motivation, and social skill. *Computers in Human Behavior*, *95*, 179–186. doi:10.1016/j.chb.2018.11.035

Veldkamp, A., van de Grint, L., Knippels, M. C. P., & van Joolingen, W. R. (2020). Escape education: A systematic review on escape rooms in education. *Educational Research Review*, *31*, 100364. doi:10.1016/j.edurev.2020.100364

Wiemker, M., Elumir, E., & Clare, A. (2015). Escape Room Games: Can you transform an unpleasant situation into a pleasant one? *Game Based Learning*, *55*, 55–68.

Wiggins, G., & McTighe, J. (2005). *Understanding by design* (2nd ed.). Prentice Hall.

Yakavenka, H. (2012) Developing professional competencies through international peer learning communities. In Virtual Professional Development and Informal Learning via Social Networks. Premier Reference Source. IGI Global. doi:10.4018/978-1-4666-1815-2.ch008

York, J., Poole, F. J., & DeHaan, J. W. (2021). Playing a new game—An argument for a teacher-focused field around games and play in language education. *Foreign Language Annals*, *54*(4), 1164–1188. doi:10.1111/flan.12585

Zhou, L., Rudhumbu, N., Shumba, J., & Olumide, A. (2020). Role of higher education institutions in the implementation of sustainable development goals. In *Sustainable Development Goals and institutions of higher education* (pp. 87–96). Springer. doi:10.1007/978-3-030-26157-3_7

KEY TERMS AND DEFINITIONS

Employability in Context: A concept which acknowledges that different regions of the world may have different expectations of the transferrable skills needed in graduates. This is particularly important for institutions which have a large overseas student population.

Enhancement of International Business Curriculum: A process to continuously improve the international exposure opportunities for learners on Business related degree courses.

Escape Room as an Extra-Curricular Activity: An interactive activity which enables the participants to develop soft transferrable skills through participation. Participants have to problem-solve to answer questions and escape the room.

Facilitator: The UN SDG Escape Room should be largely led by learners. The facilitator is there for support and signposting but should not actively engage in knowledge sharing, creation, or transfer.

Global Labor Market: The labor market which graduates will enter. It is expected the skills required from employees would have changed due to the impact of COVID-19.

International Peer Community Building: An opportunity for students to meet and interact with peers through a topic which is relevant to the studied subject.

Internationalization at Home: Projects which offer international exposure to learners without travelling overseas. These became prominent during travel restrictions associated with COVID-19.

Transferable Skills: Soft skills that the global labor market expects from graduates.

United Nations Sustainable Development Goals: A set of principles driven by the concept of sustainable development which provides a framework for achieving a just and prosperous society for all.

Chapter 14
Escape Rooms in English for Specific Academic Purposes:
A Learning Design for Transnational STEM Education

Peter Bannister
University of Dundee, UK

ABSTRACT

This chapter explores the theoretical underpinnings, advantages, and potential limitations of employing a game-informed educational escape room in an online learning environment. Drawing on the wealth of literature published thus far on the virtues of such active methodologies for second language learning pedagogical contexts, the author explores its viability for a transnational education context. A Sino-British transnational education partnership was chosen as the didactic setting in which the proposal is grounded with a specific focus on a preparatory ESAP pre-sessional course prior to the commencement of the cohort's final and postgraduate year at the partner institution. The details of the learning design have been provided together with a final critical discussion that aims to inspire like-minded teaching practitioners to adapt and reflect on what has been written and experiment in their own classrooms.

INTRODUCTION

The promotion of learner autonomy on an intensive pre-sessional course in Higher Education is not only a ubiquitous component of EAP teaching practice, as established in the BALEAP Teacher Competency Framework for Teachers of English for Academic Purposes (BALEAP, 2016), but is also a key requirement for the future academic context of aspiring post-graduate Biomedical Sciences students as per the Subject Benchmark Statement penned by the Quality Assurance Agency for Higher Education, or QAA, (2015). Nevertheless, the high-stakes and logistically complex nature of such courses (Bruce, 2011), acerbated by the 'quick-fix attitude' held by some quarters together with arduous in-class time constraints (Ding & Campion, 2016, p. 556), oftentimes problematically implies that students are required

DOI: 10.4018/978-1-6684-6081-8.ch014

to develop autonomous learning skills in isolation with little motivation and limited success (Borg & Alshumaimeri, 2017). To address this issue of clear concern, a technologically enhanced and L2 game-informed pedagogical learning design (Reinhardt & Sykes, 2014) has been crafted, the particulars of which, in conjunction with a probative outline of the underpinning methodological and L2 pedagogical theories and a final critical reflection, are broached in the following lines.

BACKGROUND

Gamification and Language Learning

The use of the term digital natives has become synonymous with the learners who populate our face-to-face or virtual classrooms today (Prensky, 2001). The use of technological devices in their day-to-day lives has led to the use of learning designed empowered through technological affordances making the step from mere novelty to expectation for key stakeholders in many didactic contexts. Gamification as a methodology lends itself particularly well to this occurrence, although it ought to be noted that in fact the two are not co-dependent, but rather merry pedagogical bedfellows which can constitute a powerful tool for second language learning (Bicen & Kocakoyun, 2018).

The use of interactive and collaborative technology in teaching and learning has cemented itself as a popular staple in the language learning classroom. Learners now have access to a variety of online resources, and according to Ybarra and Green (2003), technology gives pupils an invaluable didactic opportunity to put into practice their language skills. To this end, the use of technology instruments has arguably made it simple for students to learn new languages. In addition to the online content that is accessible, platforms including blogs, web-based communities, social networking sites, and authentic and non-authentic audio-visual assets are now available for use by language learners (Hariadi et al., 2021).

Modern, engaging teaching methodologies and media are required by today's tech-savvy students to replace what they perceive to be as outdated, coursebook-focused education and unattractive learning environments (Tan & Liu, 2016; Batsila & Tsihouridis, 2018). Therefore, teaching practitioners are required to strive to make pedagogical offerings more interactive and come up with new, inventive ways to incorporate various digital technologies into classroom instruction in order for these digital resources to serve as a vital link between the traditional learning environment and the idea of student-centeredness in order to allay these worries (Nawahdah, 2018; Viberg & Grönlund, 2013). Games can be used into the classroom to do this while also enhancing student enthusiasm, classroom interaction, and being more akin to adapting themselves to higher and lower order thinking skills as required (Batsila & Tsihouridis, 2018; Dehghanzadeh et al., 2019).

It cannot be dismissed that games per se have always been a key component of the language learning process, leading some critics of the methodology to dismiss it out of hand and to question the premise of gamification as methodological innovation. However, this comprehensive methodological approach constitutes much more than child's play, although there are key elements found in games which can be applied to good pedagogical effect. According to Al-Azawi et al. (2016), the characteristics of games include being entertaining, making players experience multiple realities, being time independent, and being unpredictable, which piques their curiosity. The games created and used for instructional purposes are what are referred to in scholarship as educational games. In other words, in order to increase learners' academic motivation and active engagement in learning, educational games combine elements of enjoyment and instructional topics. The evidence-informed stance is maintained that game-based instruction improves learning environments and academic motivation, which aids students in developing their problem-solving abilities (Al-Azawi et al., 2016). The practice of encouraging students through game-based learning has given rise to the word "gamification." According to Michos (2017), gamification refers to the use of game characteristics in non-game contexts and non-game applications to foster and enhance motivation, focus, and other good aspects of games. This is therefore in juxtaposition to the former criticism given that it differs from the concept of an instructional game. While the concept of "gamification" focuses just on using game features, the latter also uses games to accomplish goals that are not just for fun (Dicheva et al., 2015).

Badges, leader boards, points and levels, and progress monitoring are the basic components of gamification. These elements can be used as indicators of accomplishment, competence, quality, or interest and can be acquired in a variety of learning situations (Tahir et al., 2022). Positive findings from numerous studies on the impact of badges on student engagement and motivation have been reported. For instance, Filsecker and Hickey (2014) come to the conclusion that while external rewards do not harm learners' motivation to study academically or their participation in the learning process, they do serve to advance learning. According to the researchers, when numerous elements including learner profiles, learning objectives, and the tool's purpose are taken into account, badges become successful tools (Filsecker & Hickey, 2014).

Many games and gaming platforms frequently employ leaderboards to boost player engagement (Jia et al., 2017). They are one of the key components of games and enable players to view their successes (O'Donovan, 2012). Points are frequently used in gamified settings. According to Zichermann and Cunningham (2011), points are a necessary component of any gamified environment, while Carr-Chellman (2015) emphasizes that include game elements like points in a learning environment encourages learners to participate actively. Finally, each gamified lesson has a progress tracking component. Since teachers and students may monitor the progress of every learner and the entire class, it can be utilized as a feedback tool in educational settings. Typically, progress monitoring is shown through graphics and character enhancements.

As gamification offers several advantages for learners, multiple studies have recently focused on the effects of gamification in various language environments, at various educational levels, and with variable language competence levels (Buckley & Doyle, 2016). According to Michos (2017), gamification enables the teacher to alter the climate in the language classroom. Additionally, it raises the students' overall happiness level. Additionally, gamification aids the teacher in boosting student enthusiasm and attention. Gamification increases students' involvement in classroom activities. In order for students to actively engage in the lesson, it also establishes a goal-oriented atmosphere within the classroom. Last but not least, it makes learning enjoyable for both the teacher and the students. The ability of gamified education to affect intrinsic motivation is highlighted by Zarzycka-Piskorz (2016), who claims that playing a game together in class goes beyond the norm and directly boosts motivation to learn a language.

In order to determine if language games can encourage adult learners to acquire grammar or not, Ali et al. (2020) conducted an invesitgative study of note. At a university in Pakistan, they used a sample of 31 male and 19 female first-year undergraduates to teach English grammar using language games as a motivating technique. The participants' ages ranged from 19 to 22, they were not majoring in English, and English was not their first language. The instructors—the researchers themselves—asked the students to complete a 25-item survey after one semester of grammar instruction to get their opinions on the usage of games. The survey asked about pre- and post-treatment grammar learning experiences as well as interest, satisfaction, effort, tension, choice, usefulness, and competition. The authors concluded that the use of gamification was effective with the chosen cohort and also came to the conclusion that teachers need instruction on how to incorporate games into the classroom.

In a 2015 study carried out by Bolliger et al. in Japan, the researchers looked into how college students felt about playing digital games in English classes. The results show that many participants thought employing video games was a good idea. Ebrahimzadeh and Alavi (2017) examined the motivational effects of digital video games on high school students. It was discovered that using online video games would boost students' interest for learning languages. Another study with second-year high school students in Norway demonstrated the value of including gamification components into language instruction (Cruaud, 2016). The study by Rachels and Rockinson-szapkiw (2017) also found that teaching Spanish to primary school kids using a mobile phone application was very effective.

For both students and teachers, gamification offers a variety of opportunities. It is possible to hypothesize that gamification and gamified activities for students encourage learning, boost learner accomplishment, encourage active involvement, create a calm environment where learners feel confident and eager to study, and spark social and communicative abilities (Yürük, 2019). From the viewpoint of the teachers, gamified activities assist teachers in achieving their objectives by establishing a suitable learning environment that acts as the foundation for learning. As a result, teachers should consider a number of elements when creating games or gamified activities, including student needs, interests, age, language competency level, personality, and the need to keep the activity enjoyable. When all of these factors are taken into account, the pedagogical significance of games and gamification cannot be understated, according to Yürük (2019).

Gamification and Augmented Reality

Augmented reality technologies have a long history in a multitude of often non-complimentary sectors; however, it is only of late that particular attention to their potential virtues has come to the forefront of the HE sphere. The evident potential to enhance teaching and learning experiences on a number of counts has led to a sharpened research and practical interest out of which the present chapter is borne. For this learning design proposal set in the didactic context of an undergraduate ESP STEM course it, this immersive gamification didactic approach was selected for its potential to motivate and enhance the development of key academic skills (Turner, 2012).

AR has been defined as an interactive 3D technology which improves a student's sensorial perception by superposing a contextual layer of digital information on the real-world environment (Arici et al., 2019). In this regard, it can be argued that both physical and digital elements coexist in the eyes of the student, which differentiates this technology from that of the closely related virtual reality, in which the entire real-world environment is replaced by that of a digital substitute (Elmqaddem, 2019). Furthermore, as Garzón et al. (2020) point out, it is in fact that physical and digital elements are combined and aligned together, which means that a student can become immersed in the reality which is created and thus, there may be real-time interaction between the student and the augmented reality itself (Yu et al., 2022).

Within the field, there are different levels of augmented reality which may be employed in the classroom, in accordance with Rambach and Stricker (2022) namely:

- Level 0- Physical World Connection: This can be through the use of QR codes or other objects which hold hyperlinks that students may interact with. In other words, these are gateways to other 2D learning contents and do not incorporate 3D elements.
- Level 1- Markers: This level incorporates the use of usually black and white square 2D markers with distinct patterns that are recognized which then trigger certain 3D augmented reality features.
- Level 2- Marker-free AR: Applications replace the use of markers with GPS and compass functionalities of mobile devices to determine the user's location and orientation and superimpose points of interest on real-world images. At this level there is also surface recognition, where the device is able to detect, in real time, a surface in the environment by means of the images obtained by the camera and position the digital content anchored to that surface.
- Level 3- Augmented vision: This level would be represented by devices such as Google Glass, HoloLens, high-tech contact lenses or others that, in the future, will be able to offer a fully contextualized, immersive and personalized experience.

Advantages of AR for HE Pedagogical Contexts

Many readers of the chapter will have been able to infer some of the key advantages for their own didactic contexts merely from the conceptual description thus far. Be that as it may, as part of the elaboration of the learning design, many of the potential benefits were pondered for the given pedagogical setting, for instance, as Basogain et al. (2007) point out, the user never loses contact and reference with the real world at hand and at the same time can interact with the overlaid virtual information. The use of such technology paves the way for experiential learning and has the potential to foment L2 interactions in or outside of the classroom environment.

For cohorts who find themselves in STEM disciplines the possibility to the interact with complex 3D structures provides an unprecedented degree of immersion which from an ESP perspective is arguably a power stimulus that lifts contents up off the page and facilitates motivation to engage and interact. Students are no longer just seeing 2D depictions of concepts of note, but rather are able to experience them, interact with them, manipulate them through sensory immersion. In settings in which resources are limited, AR can offer an important cost-effective opportunity for students to have 3D models at their fingertips, which can stimulate and support the development of ESP activities which rely on a razor-sharp focus on discipline specific contents as the axis for learning development.

The need to integrate discipline-specific signature pedagogies in the curriculum design and delivery of English for Specific Academic Purposes in-sessional support programmes is at the very core of the preparatory academic foundations of enabling students to become adept in the knowledge and skills pertaining to their future professional practice (Shulman, 2005). Numerous scholars (e.g. El Sayary et al., 2015; Jabarullah & Hussain, 2019; Astuti et al., 2021) make the persuasive case for the use of a problem-based learning approach as one such signature pedagogy in STEM education, which, as Lien et al. (2019) accentuate, is inherent in the pedagogical DNA of, and instrumental to, the prosperous implementation of an educational escape room in the specific context of a transnational STEM programme for undergraduate Biomedical Engineers in both online and face-to-face learning environments.

Through the integration of augmented reality technology (Ibáñez & Delgado-Kloos, 2018) together with the tenets of problem-based learning, learners are immersed in a realistic environment of an abandoned research lab and are required to design a medical device to help assuage the symptoms of a new threatening condition based on a host of academic sources that they must engage with in order to make informed design choices which will guarantee their escape. Working cooperatively in this multimodal experience is essential, in addition to using a range of complex skills to critically engage with the information available (Chernikova, et al., 2020) to successfully navigate each challenge, as not all the data and clues the students are provided with can be relied upon. The key to escaping can only be obtained when the students work together using skills from the relational and extended abstract stages of the SOLO Taxonomy (Biggs & Tang, 2011) as would be expected as part of their future professional practice.

PEDAGOGICAL CONTEXTUALIZATION

As part of a Sino-British Transnational Education Partnership, postgraduate students are required to complete a bespoke pre-sessional course as condition of entry onto a taught postgraduate program delivered entirely in English. Although the ultimate intention is for the cohort to receive tuition in a face-to-face setting, this particular course is delivered entirely online with a ratio of one student to one device.

At the heart of the curriculum design of this English for Specific Academic Purposes (ESAP) course is that of furnishing the students with the necessary academic skillset that they will be required to employ for study success for their duration of their postgraduate studies. The cohort itself comprises over 100 students, although tutors engage with class of no more than 15 students per class group over a 12-week period prior to their late September start date. Students have a total of 20 hours synchronous and asynchronous tuition per week and each lesson lasts for a period of 90 minutes.

Typically, many students enter with an IELTS score of 5.5 overall and are required to obtain an overall score of 6.0 in order to be admitted on to their program of study. Prior to embarking the course, students complete an online entry test in which trends of poor performance in academic writing have been noted.

LEARNING DESIGN

The present lesson proposal has an approximate duration of 90 minutes, although there is potential to reduce or expand on this considering differing student needs and contextual requirements.

Plot

The students take on the role of Biomedical Scientists who have been trapped in their laboratory by their corporate paymasters.

After months of worsening professional conditions and no respite, the scientists have had their worst fears confirmed- there is now no escape from the confines of the squalid working environment. They have been told by their supervisor that unless they work together to produce a written report on the top-secret device they have been developing, he will raise the entire complex to the ground.

The clock is ticking and the only option before the students is to work together and comply with the demands in order to guarantee their passage to safety. But first, four testing challenges await.

Challenges

Challenge 1

Each group of four to five students is presented with different QR codes which hold information of vital importance for the report that they will be asked to compose. Each QR code includes different extracts from a recommendation report, however, the information has been corrupted and students will need to put the information in the correct order to obtain a four-digit code, using the numbers at the beginning of the sentences.

The groups will be working against the clock. Each group will be awarded a digital badge for successfully completing the task. The fastest team to return to the main session from their breakout room with the correct solution will earn themselves a spot at the top of the leader board.

The extracts are as follows:

Extract 1

1. Of the many perspective computers, only several brands have been selected for this comparison and those that have been selected are Pentagon computers that boast the new MMX technology.
2. The first two features add to the speed of the machine and the last to the travelling lifetime.
3. MMX technology lends itself to portable computers because of the added internal processor cache, graphics acceleration, and lower power usage.
4. The purpose of this comparison is to help prospective quantum laptop purchasers in their decision and in today's mobile climate, the average person can make good use of a reliable portable computer; this report is designed to help in that search.

Extract 2

1. These computers all have Pentium 166 processors with a variety of other features that will be discussed in the following.
2. These computers are equipped with MMX processors and stood out among other MMX computers for their performance as well as their value.
3. Of the many quantum laptops available, some equipped with MMX, only four specific computers were chosen.
4. Those chosen for this comparison are the Compat Presario 1080, the Delx Latitude LM M166ST, the Gateway 2000 Solo 2200 166MMX, and the Micron Transport XPE P166.

Extract 3

1. Whether it be the processor, battery, or even the pre-installed applications, it became apparent that the Miron laptop is not able to hold its own.
2. Based on these comparisons, this report recommends the Gateway quantum computer.
3. With money in mind, the enhanced features it offers represent a pocket-friendly option which will do the job well.
4. It outperforms its competitors on a number of different counts after close examination.

Challenge 2

In the next challenge, the scientists will be asked to visit the following website in their teams of 4 or 5 students: https://www.phrasebank.manchester.ac.uk/signalling-transitio n/ ¡

Using the information that they decode from the site; they will then be asked to analyze and review the following paragraph from a report:

The process of how kidneys filter blood to remove waste comprises five primary stages involving the heart, kidneys, ureters, bladder and finally the urethra. The filtration process occurs in the kidneys using filtering units called nephrons.

Blood enters the kidneys through an artery from the heart. Once the blood is in the kidneys, it is filtered using nephrons. The nephrons remove waste from the blood whilst ensuring essential nutrients remain.

After the blood has been filtered, the newly cleaned blood is returned to the bloodstream. At the same time, the separated waste materials pass through the ureter and are then stored in the bladder as urine. When the bladder becomes full, urine passes out of the body through the urethra.

On completion each team will share their new and improved paragraphs with another and they will be asked to highlight and label the function of the signaling and transition language the other team has added.

The successful completion of this challenge will bring each team one step closer to winning another digital badge that will allow them to escape. The leader board will be updated in accordance with each team's performance.

Challenge 3

After watching the short video on paragraph structure here: https://www.youtube.com/watch?v=I0SMvLu2D1Y

Students will then work together in pairs to answers the following questions on Quizziz: https://quizizz.com/admin/quiz/63600c77aaa50b001ef14e3a?sour ce=quiz_share

Challenge 4

The fourth and final challenge requires each team to scan one of the QR codes included below. They will be given access to a specific biomedical device or process and will be asked to write a short well-structured paragraph to describe the process they see in order to be able to win their final badge and finally escape from the lab.

Each team will create a Microsoft Word online document and share progress with their tutor.

The QR codes can be created using https://es.qr-code-generator.com/ and the following 3D models are suggested:

https://www.visiblebody.com/learn/digestive/digestive-10-fac
ts

https://www.visiblebody.com/learn/nervous/brain

https://www.visiblebody.com/learn/circulatory/circulatory-th
e-heart

On completion of this challenge, the winning team can be announced and an optional prize may be awarded.

SOLUTIONS

Challenge 1

Extract 1

The purpose of this comparison is to help prospective quantum laptop purchasers in their decision and in today's mobile climate, the average person can make good use of a reliable portable computer; this report is designed to help in that search. 1. Of the many perspective computers, only several brands have been selected for this comparison and those that have been selected are Pentagon computers that boast the new MMX technology. 3. MMX technology lends itself to portable computers because of the added internal processor cache, graphics acceleration, and lower power usage. 2. The first two features add to the speed of the machine and the last to the travelling lifetime.

Extract 2

Of the many quantum laptops available, some equipped with MMX, only four specific computers were chosen. 2. These computers are equipped with MMX processors and stood out among other MMX computers for their performance as well as their value. 4. Those chosen for this comparison are the Compat Presario 1080, the Delx Latitude LM M166ST, the Gateway 2000 Solo 2200 166MMX, and the Micron Transport XPE P166. 1. These computers all have Pentium 166 processors with a variety of other features that will be discussed in the following.

Extract 3

Based on these comparisons, this report recommends the Gateway quantum computer. 4. It outperforms its competitors on a number of different counts after close examination. 1. Whether it be the processor, battery, or even the pre-installed applications, it became apparent that the Miron laptop is not able to hold its own. 3. With money in mind, the enhanced features it offers represent a pocket-friendly option which will do the job well.

Curriculum Fit

The thematic focus chosen for the materials is body paragraph structure, which is not only a staple constituent of a standard pre-sessional syllabus (Alexander et al., 2019), but also represents a particular challenge for learners to assimilate and apply over the duration of such intensive courses (Gardner, 2016). Learners are expected to engage independently and asynchronously, having previously addressed the topic in class, and may do so by accessing the materials through the institution's virtual learning environment- in this instance Moodle- using their own devices of choice (Pegrum, 2019). They are tasked with engaging both individually and collaboratively with a variety of multimodal activities over four distinct levels of increasing difficulty which have been designed in concordance with the five levels of understanding stipulated in the SOLO Taxonomy of Learning (Biggs & Tang, 2009). The successful completion of each interlocking level constitutes the awarding of points which students can accrue in exchange for badges, the quantity of which, in turn, is computed and, this figure constitutes each student's ranking on the whole-cohort leader board (Benini & Thomas, 2021). The additional prosperous completion of bonus challenges, which are integrated into several of the levels, affords learners the opportunity to collect trophies which add further points that may be exchanged to obtain further badges (Cornillie, 2017).

Discussion

The use of a game-informed L2 pedagogical approach in the design of the materials which frame the independent learning of body paragraph structure within the specific focus of the short essay question provides an important meaningful and contextualized dimension to the learning experience (Reinhardt, 2019), which signifies that these game-informed materials are not only highly relevant in the short term for the assessment requirements of the pre-sessional course but also in consonance with the genre-based requirements of the students' future program of post-graduate study. In support of this, Ellis (2015) highlights the importance of appropriately linguistically and situationally contextualizing teaching and learning for learners to engage in the style shifting required of this particular genre of writing. Furthermore, as the students had previously covered the topic of body paragraph structure in class, in accordance with Ausubel's Theory of Meaningful Learning, students can forge connections between the new knowledge encountered in the materials with what they already know (Sexton, 2020). Thus, learners are able to use language in a meaningful way in a specific context that builds on their previous knowledge and the use of these materials would therefore seemingly positively contribute towards the development of their academic writing skills.

In contrast to the evident pressures of an assessment on the course or arguably even the classroom environment, the game-informed L2 pedagogical approach taken in the materials design offers a low-stakes learning opportunity in which students may revisit contents as many times as they wish in juxtaposition to a synchronous in-class alternative which may not offer the same affordances. Moreover, this 'sheltered space for practice' (Reinhardt, 2019, p. 176) allows learners to engage in a scaffolded learning environment in which mistakes can be made and formative feedback can be offered privately (Reinhardt & Thorne, 2016). This, in the absence of their peers, would subsequently save face (Case & Xu, 2021) and plausibly, over time, increase student confidence to the detriment of the much-documented phenomena of the affective filter heightened by language anxiety (Krashen, 1982; Young, 1992; Gkonou et al., 2017) which in the case of academic writing skills development on a high-stakes context of an intensive pre-sessional course, as Cancan et al. (2022) remind, is even more acute. The aforementioned discreet nature of the learning design together with the increased level of confidence (Bandura, 2001) and lowering of the affective filter would also go some way to facilitating self-regulated learning and improving student motivation (Dörnyei & Ushioda, 2021), which as Ortega (2009) underlines, are also key tenets of second language acquisition.

Further contributions to self-regulated learning and student motivation may be attributed to the goal-orientated nature of the materials, akin to that found in a Task-Based Learning approach (Sailer & Homner, 2020), in that the intended learning outcomes are explicit in all levels and students are able to revisit these when necessary (Reinhardt, 2019). This accessibility promotes student motivation through function of value and expectancy- key in Keller's (1987) ARCS Model of Instruction Design, in that students may express their preference for given outcomes on the one hand, and formulate their own subjective valuation of success probability, on the other. In addition, learners are also afforded a certain degree of agency (Xiao, 2014), for instance, in the final two levels they are asked to make suggestions for improvement and write their own paragraphs respectively, - albeit within a structured and scaffolded framework- which further contributes to reducing language anxiety (Yang et al., 2022). Undoubtedly, the active role which needs to be taken by the learners throughout is in accordance with Vygotsky's social constructivist stance on the pro-active learner involvement in the learning process (Adams, 2006). This characteristic would furthermore seemingly be agreeable to the conceptualization of the diverse role of the learner in second language acquisition, also taking into account individual learner differences (Zafar & Meenakshi, 2012). That is to say, throughout the game-informed materials the cognitive demands made of the cohort (Sweller, 2010) have been designed to reflect a balance between individual learner differences and intended learning outcomes in terms of both the integration of receptive and productive skills in different tasks and the level of scaffolding provided throughout (Bahari & Salimi, 2021).

In addition, careful thought has been paid to integrating several collaborative tasks in the materials in an attempt to address and transcend the potential limitations of working on an individual basis (Jacobs & McCafferty, 2006), for instance, in the first activity of level three students are required to work in pairs with a class partner in order to compare and contrast two exemplar paragraphs and make suggestions for improvement in light of their developing understanding of body paragraph structure. This materials design choice would once again key into the theoretical underpinnings of social constructivist theories of learning and, in particular, to the salience of peer-to-peer interaction and discussion within the scope of reduce groupings (Palincsar, 1998; Schreiber & Valle, 2013) as is the case here. Moreover, the use of technology for the purposes of both individual and cooperative work afforded by the game-informed design not only offers the opportunity for personalized learning experience (Chen et al., 2021), but also arguably holds a certain degree of authenticity (Pegrum, 2016), which is evidently key to facilitating second language acquisition (Lightbown & Spada, 2013) and a hallmark which lies at the very heart of EAP pre-sessional curriculum design (de Chazal, 2014).

The process of materials development is both continuous and cyclical in nature and inherently entails critical reflection as a means to assure and further enhance the pedagogical quality and suitability for the given teaching and learning context (Mashura, et al., 2017). A practical entry point in this stage has been for me to reflect on the intended learning outcomes included in the lesson design, which were established, in accordance with the principles of constructive alignment, that is to say, as the central thread in the construction of 'learning activities appropriate to achieving the desired learning outcomes' with a specific focus on 'declarative and functioning knowledge' (Biggs, 2003, p.2).

The matter of student feedback in learning materials is not only instrumental in accordance with second language acquisition theories (Nassaji & Kartchava, 2021), but also plays a vital role in the enhancement of student motivation (Murphy & Roca de Larios, 2010) and development of autonomous learning skills in the field of EAP (Jamil, 2010). To that end, integrated three types of feedback into the learning design have been integrated, namely social ranking feedback through the means of the leaderboard (Mazarakis, 2015), peer feedback executed via asynchronous structured discussion fora (Salter & Conneely, 2015), and teacher-led individual evaluative written feedback (Kostka & Maliborska, 2016). Whilst all three have been chosen on their merits, on reflection, two of the feedback mechanisms in particular are not without certain shortcomings, for instance, the use of the leader board with cohort-wide visibility may somewhat go against the grain by permitting a certain level of public exposure and scrutiny which some learners may find demotivating (Jia, et al., 2017). To remedy this, it could put forward that a certain degree of anonymity could be afforded by incorporating an optional alias for students to use on the leader board. Furthermore, I fear that the use of structured discussion fora may be a somewhat limiting factor on student agency and creativity, given that, in its current guise learners are required to adhere to a set model which they are presented with beforehand. This issue might be addressed by implementing an unstructured forum setup and to use the salient features of the current rigid model as a checklist (Nathenson & Henderson, 2019), thus allowing students greater agency and creativity whilst still offering some scaffolding for those who require it.

In a recent systematic review composed by Krath et al. (2021) on the theoretical underpinnings of gamification, it is most interesting to note that of the theories identified from the studies reviewed an elevated quantity of these may be framed as stemming from a behaviorist approach to learning, which would seemingly be in concert with the affirmation asserted by Watters (2020) that 'Behaviorism won' when it comes to gamed-informed pedagogical platforms. Whilst in years gone by behaviorist approaches to learning contributed to the development of the field, over seventy years hence arguably very few EAP teaching practitioners, amongst whom I do not belong, would be keen to subscribe to this theoretical stance. Nonetheless, students are rewarded points for engaging appropriately, or executing the desired conduct, in accordance with Goal-setting Theory (Lee & Bong, 2019), throughout the four levels of the learning design. Despite the author's enthusiasm and passion for the L2 game-informed materials, this does not sit easily and this is found to be most challenging to contend with. Be that as it may, some solace may be found on this matter in burgeoning scholarly works which aim to reconceptualize our understanding of the matter (e.g., Khaleghi et al., 2021).

In future iterations of the materials, the aim would be to revisit the materials and identify specific areas in which elements which solely rely on behavioristic approaches to learning may be reduced and reimagined in favor of more pedagogically apt alternatives forged from social constructivist and cognitive approaches to learning. However, it would be also interesting to welcome other practitioners' perspectives to this to amplify how the pedagogical premises outlined can be adapted to differing learner pedagogical needs in distinct learning and teaching settings.

FUTURE RESEARCH DIRECTIONS

The prevailing nature of online instruction in the ever more abundant panorama of transnational education partnerships indicates that moreover than the practical implementation of the theoretical learning design proposed here, there is great scope to explore a wide range of diverse didactic alternatives to enrich the learning experience. Furthermore, investigation could be undertaken into tutor and student attitudes and perceptions of such pedagogical approaches to further inform and enhance tuition.

CONCLUSION

In sum, to address the limited success and low levels of motivation in the cultivation of autonomous learning skills on an intensive pre-sessional course for post-graduate aspirants of a University Biomedical Sciences course, a technologically enhanced and L2 game-informed pedagogical learning design (Reinhardt & Sykes, 2014) was crafted. Henceforth, the particulars of the materials, in conjunction with a probative outline of the underpinning methodological and L2 pedagogical theories and a final critical reflection have been discussed. The critical reflection of the instrument's validity to overcome the challenges identified has extoled a series of merits and has also yielded certain limitations together with suggestions for improvement to further fortify the quality of the learning design in the following cycles of materials development. It is only by engaging in this continuous and cyclical process that teaching practitioners and materials developers can truly ensure that the technologically enhanced materials are not only fit for purpose but in fact act as a true pedagogical catalyst for student learning.

REFERENCES

Adams, P. (2006). Exploring Social Constructivism: Theories and Practicalities. *Education, 34*(3), 243–257. doi:10.1080/03004270600898893

Al-Azawi, R., Al-Faliti, F., & Al-Blushi, M. (2016). Educational gamification vs. game-based learning: Comparative study. *International Journal of Innovation, Management and Technology*, *7*(4), 132–136. doi:10.18178/ijimt.2016.7.4.659

Ali, S. S., Ali, M. W., & Amin, T. (2020). Enhancing adult learners' motivation for learning English grammar through language games. *Research Journal of Social Sciences & Economics Review*, *1*(3), 143–150. doi:10.36902/rjsser-vol1-iss3-2020(143-150)

Argent, O., Argent, S., & Spencer, J. (2019). *EAP Essentials: A Teacher's Guide to Principles and Practice* (2nd ed.). Garnet Education.

Arici, F., Yilidirim, P., Caliklar, S., & Yilmaz, R. M. (2019). Research Trends in the Use of Augmented Reality in Science Education: Content and Bibliometric Mapping Analysis. *Computers & Education, 142*, 1–23. doi:10.1016/j.compedu.2019.103647

Astuti, N. H., Rusilowati, A., & Subali, B. (2021). STEM-Based Learning Analysis to Improve Students' Problem-Solving Abilities in Science Subject: A Literature Review. *Journal of Innovative Science Education*, *10*(1), 79–86. doi:10.15294/jise.v9i2.38505

Bahari, A. & Salimi, M. (2021). Challenges and Affordances of Developing Receptive and Productive Skills via Technology-Based Instruction. *Computer-Assisted Language Learning Electronic Journal, 22*(1), 25-55.

BALEAP. (2016). *BALEAP Teacher Competency Framework for Teachers of English for Academic Purposes*. https://www.baleap.org/wp-content/uploads/2016/04/teap-competency-framework.pdf

Bandura, A. (2001). Social Cognitive Theory: An Agentic Perspective. *Annual Review of Psychology*, *52*(1), 1–26. doi:10.1146/annurev.psych.52.1.1 PMID:11148297

Basogain, X., Olabe, M., Espinosa, K., Rouèche, C., & Olabe, J. C. (2007). Realidad Aumentada en la Educación: una tecnología emergente [Augmented Reality in Education: an emerging technology]. Online Educa Madrid'2007 Proceedings, 24-29.

Batsila, M., & Tsihouridis, C. (2018). Let's go Kahooting. Teachers' views on C.R.S. for teaching purposes. In M. E. Auer, D. Guralnick, & I. Slmonks (Eds.), Teaching and *learning in a digital world. The 20th international conference on interactive collaborative learning 2017* (pp. 563–571). Springer International Publishing.

Benini, S., & Thomas, M. (2021). A Critical Review of Research on Gamification and Second Language Acquisition. In M. Peterson, M. Thomas, & K. Yamazaki (Eds.), *Digital Games and Language Learning: Theory, Development and Implementation* (pp. 9–46). Bloomsbury Academic. doi:10.5040/9781350133037.ch-002

Bicen, H., & Kocakoyun, S. (2017). Determination of university students' most preferred mobile application for gamification. *World Journal on Educational Technology: Current Issues.*, *9*(1), 18–23. doi:10.18844/wjet.v9i1.641

Biggs, J. (2003). *Aligning Teaching for Constructing Learning*. The Higher Education Authority. https://www.advance-he.ac.uk/knowledge-hub/aligning-teaching-constructing-learning

Biggs, J., & Tang, C. (2011). *Teaching for Quality Learning at University*. Open University Press.

Bolliger, D. U., Mills, D., White, J., & Kohyama, M. (2015). Japanese students' perceptions of digital game use for English-language learning in higher education. *Journal of Educational Computing Research*, *53*(3), 384–408. doi:10.1177/0735633115600806

Borg, S., & Alshumaimeri, Y. (2017). Language Learner Autonomy in a Tertiary Context: Teacher Beliefs and Practices. *Language Teaching Research*, *23*(1), 9–38. doi:10.1177/1362168817725759

Bruce, I. (2011). *Theories and Concepts of English for Academic Purposes*. Palgrave Macmillan.

Buckley, P., & Doyle, E. (2016). Gamification and student motivation. *Interactive Learning Environments*, *24*(6), 1162–1175. doi:10.1080/10494820.2014.964263

Cancan, Z., Ye, T., & Shuanglin, G. (2022). Academic Writing Anxiety among Chinese International Postgraduates. *Linguistics and Culture Review*, *6*(S2), 52–68. doi:10.21744/lingcure.v6nS2.1909

Carr-Chellman, A. A. (2015). Games in Elementary and Middle School Settings. In J. M. Spector (Ed.), *The SAGE Encyclopedia of Educational Technology* (pp. 309–310). SAGE.

Case, R. E., & Xu, W. (2021). The Influence of Language Learning Environment on Negative Transfer and its Connection to Status and Face-Saving Refusal Strategies. *International Journal of Applied Linguistics and English Literature*, *10*(2), 33–42. doi:10.7575/aiac.ijalel.v.10n.2p.33

Chen, X., Zou, D., Xie, H., & Cheng, G. (2021). Twenty Years of Personalized Language Learning: Topic Modeling and Knowledge Mapping. *Journal of Educational Technology & Society*, *24*(1), 205–222.

Chernikova, O., Heitzmann, N., Stadler, M., Holzberger, D., Seidel, T., & Fischer, F. (2020). Simulation-Based Learning in Higher Education: A Meta-Analysis. *Review of Educational Research*, *90*(4), 499–541. doi:10.3102/0034654320933544

Cornillie, F. (2017). Educationally Designed Game Environments and Feedback. In S. Thorne & S. May (Eds.), *Language, Education and Technology* (pp. 1–14). Springer International Publishing. doi:10.1007/978-3-319-02237-6_28

Cruaud, C. (2016). The playful frame: Gamification in a French-as-a foreign-language class. *Innovation in Language Learning and Teaching*, *12*(4), 330–343. doi:10.1080/17501229.2016.1213268

de Chazal, E. (2014). *English for Academic Purposes*. Oxford University Press.

Dehghanzadeh, H., Fardanesh, H., Hatami, J., Talaee, E., & Noroozi, O. (2019). Using gamification to support learning English as a second language: A systematic review. *Computer Assisted Language Learning*, *34*(7), 1–24. doi:10.1080/09588221.2019.1648298

Dicheva, D., Dichev, C., Agre, G., & Angelova, G. (2015). Gamification in education: A systematic mapping study. *Journal of Educational Technology & Society*, *18*(3), 75–88.

Ding, A., & Campion, G. (2016). EAP Teacher Development. In K. Hyland & P. Shaw (Eds.), *The Routledge Handbook of English for Academic Purposes* (pp. 547–559). Routledge.

Dörnyei, Z., & Ushioda, E. (2021). *Teaching and Researching Motivation* (3rd ed.). Routledge. doi:10.4324/9781351006743

Ebrahimzadeh, M., & Alavi, S. (2017). The effect of digital video games on EFL students' language learning motivation. *Teaching English with Technology*, *17*(2), 87–112.

El Sayary, A., Forawi, S., & Mansour, N. (2015). STEM Education and Problem-Based Learning. In The Routledge International Handbook of Research on Teaching Thinking (pp. 357-365). Routledge.

Ellis, R. (2015). *Understanding Second Language Acquisition* (2nd ed.). Oxford University Press.

Elmqaddem, N. (2019). Augmented Reality and Virtual Reality. Myth or Reality? *International Journal of Emerging Technologies in Learning*, *14*(3), 234–242. doi:10.3991/ijet.v14i03.9289

Filsecker, M., & Hickey, D. T. (2014). A multilevel analysis of the effects of external rewards on elementary students' motivation, engagement and learning in an educational game. *Computers & Education*, *75*, 136–148. doi:10.1016/j.compedu.2014.02.008

Gardner, S. (2016). A Genre-Instantiation Approach to Teaching for Specific Academic Purposes: Student Writing in Business, Economics and Engineering. *Writing & Pedagogy*, *8*(1), 1–25. doi:10.1558/wap.v8i1.27934

Garzón, J., Kinshuk, A., Baldris, S., Gutiérrez, J., & Pavón, J. (2020). How do pedagogical approaches affect the impact of augmented reality on education? A meta-analysis and research synthesis. *Educational Research Review*, *31*, 1–19. doi:10.1016/j.edurev.2020.100334

Gkonou, C., Daubney, M., & Dewaele, J. (2017). *New Insights into Language Anxiety: Theory, Research and Educational Implications*. Multilingual Matters. doi:10.21832/9781783097722

Hariadi, M. F., Kuswandi, D., & Wedi, A. (2021). Development of Game-Based Supplementary Listening Materials to Improve Students' Higher Order Thinking Skills. In N.L.S. Nuraini, P.S. Cholifah, T.A. Rini, D. Prestiadi, C. Kurniawan, & K.M. Rahjaro (Eds.), *Proceedings of the International Conference on Information Technology and Education (ICITE 2021)* (pp. 128-133). 10.2991/assehr.k.211210.021

Ibañez, M. B., & Delgado-Kloss, D. (2018). Augmented Reality for STEM Learning: A Systematic Review. *Computers & Education, 123*, 109–123. doi:10.1016/j.compedu.2018.05.002

Jabarullah, N. H., & Hussain, H. I. (2019). The Effectiveness of Problem-Based Learning in Technical and Vocational Education in Malaysia. *Education + Training*, *61*(5), 552–567. doi:10.1108/ET-06-2018-0129

Jacobs, G. M., & McCafferty, S. G. (2006). Connections between Cooperative Learning and Second Language Learning and Teaching. In S. G. McCafferty, G. M. Jacobs, & A. C. DaSilva Iddings (Eds.), *Cooperative Learning and Second Language Teaching* (pp. 18–29). Cambridge University Press.

Jamil, M. D. G. (2010). Promoting Learner Autonomy on a University Course of English for Academic Purposes. *BRAC University Journal*, *7*(1-2), 45–52.

Jia, Y., Liu, Y., Xing, Y., & Voida, S. (2017). Designing Leaderboards for Gamification: Perceived Differences Based on User Ranking, Application Domain, and Personality Traits. In G. Mark, & S. Fussell (Eds.), *Proceedings of the 2017 CHI Conference on Human Factors in Computing Systems* (pp. 1949-1960). 10.1145/3025453.3025826

Keller, J. M. (1987). Development and Use of the ARCS Model of Instrumental Design. *Journal of Instructional Development*, *10*(3), 2–10. doi:10.1007/BF02905780

Khaleghi, A., Aghaei, Z., & Mahdavi, M. A. (2021). A Gamification Framework for Cognitive Assessment and Cognitive Training: Qualitative Study. *JMIR Serious Games*, *9*(2), 1–17. doi:10.2196/21900 PMID:33819164

Kostka, I., & Maliborska, V. (2016). Using Turnitin to Provide Feedback on L2 Writers' Texts. *TESL-EJ*, *20*(2), 1–22.

Krashen, S. (1982). *Principles and Practice in Second Language Acquisition*. Elsevier.

Krath, J., Schürmann, L., & von Korflesch, H. F. O. (2021). Revealing the Theoretical Basis of Gamification: A Systematic Review and Analysis of Theory in Research on Gamification, Serious Games and Game-Based Learning. *Computers in Human Behavior*, *125*, 1–33. doi:10.1016/j.chb.2021.106963

Lee, M., & Bong, M. (2019). Relevance of Goal Theories to Language Learning Research. *System*, *86*(2), 102–122. doi:10.1016/j.system.2019.102122

Lien, Y. H., Wang, C. P., Wang, S. M., Li, C. T., & Hou, H. T. (2019). Designing an Escape Room Educational Game and a Game-Based Learning Activity for Science Learning: An Analysis of Learning Achievement and Flow State. In *8th International Congress on Advanced Applied Informatics (IIAI-AAI)* (pp. 1049-1050). IEEE. https://doi.ieeecomputersociety.org/10.1109/IIAI-AAI.2019.00221

Lightbown, P. M., & Spada, N. (2013). *How Languages Are Learned* (4th ed.). Oxford University Press.

Mashuhara, H., Mishan, F., & Tomlinson, B. (2017). *Practice and Theory for Materials Development*. Cambridge Scholars Publishing.

Mazarakis, A. (2015). Using Gamification for Technologically Enhanced Learning: The Case of Feedback Mechanisms. *Bulletin of the IEEE Technical Committee on Learning Technology*, *17*(4), 6–9.

Mercer, S. (2012). The Complexity of Learner Agency. *Journal of Applied Language Studies*, *6*(2), 41–59.

Michos, V. M. (2017). Gamification in foreign language teaching. In M. Stanišić (Ed.), *Sinteza 2017-International Scientific Conference on Information Technology and Data Related Research Proceedings* (pp. 511-516). Singidunum University.

Murphy, L., & Roca de Larios, J. (2010). Feedback in Second Language Writing: An Introduction. *International Journal of English Studies*, *10*(2), i–xv.

Nassaji, H., & Kartchava, E. (2021). *The Cambridge Handbook of Corrective Feedback in Second Language Learning and Teaching*. Cambridge University Press. doi:10.1017/9781108589789

Nathenson, M. B., & Henderson, E. S. (2019). *Using Student Feedback to Improve Learning Materials*. Routledge.

Nawahdah, M. I. (2018). Gamifying the teaching and learning process in an advanced computer programming course. In H. Egi, T. Yuizono, N. Baloian, T. Yoshino, & S. Ichimura (Eds.), *10th International Conference on CollabTech 2018: Collaboration Technologies and Social Computing* (Vol. 1, pp. 89–95). Springer International Publishing. 10.1007/978-3-319-98743-9_7

O'Donovan, S. (2012). *Gamification of the games course*. The University of Cape Town.

Ortega, L. (2009). *Understanding Second Language Acquisition*. Routledge.

Palincsar, A. S. (1998). Social Constructivist Perspectives on Teaching and Learning. *Annual Review of Psychology*, *49*(1), 345–375. doi:10.1146/annurev.psych.49.1.345 PMID:15012472

Pegrum, M. (2016). Languages and Literacies for Digital Lives. In E. Martín-Monje, I. Elorza, & B. García Riaza (Eds.), *Technology-Enhanced Language Learning for Specialized Domains* (pp. 9–22). Routledge.

Pegrum, M. (2019). *Mobile Lenses on Learning: Language and Literacies on the Move*. Springer. doi:10.1007/978-981-15-1240-7

Prensky, M. (2001). Digital native and digital immigrant part 1. *On the Horizon*, *9*(5), 1–6. doi:10.1108/10748120110424816

QAA. (2022). *Subject Benchmark Statement: Biomedical Science and Biomedical Sciences*. https://www.qaa.ac.uk/docs/qaa/quality-code/sbs-biomedical-science-consultation-22.pdf?sfvrsn=cb8a581_4

Rachels, J. R., & Rockinson-szapkiw, A. J. (2017). The effects of a mobile gamification app on elementary students' Spanish achievement and self-efficacy. *Computer Assisted Language Learning*, *31*(1-2), 72–89. doi:10.1080/09588221.2017.1382536

Rambach, J., & Stricker, D. (2022). Advanced Sensory Perception. *Journal of Imaging*, *8*(10). Advance online publication. doi:10.3390/jimaging8100287 PMID:36286381

Reinhardt, J. (2019). *Gameful Second and Foreign Language Teaching and Learning: Theory, Research, and Practice*. Palgrave Macmillan. doi:10.1007/978-3-030-04729-0

Reinhardt, J., & Sykes, J. M. (2014). Digital Game and Play Activity in L2 Teaching and Learning. *Language Teaching & Technology*, *18*(2), 2–8.

Reinhardt, J., & Thorne, S. (2016). Metaphors for Digital Games and Language Learning. In F. Farr & L. Murray (Eds.), *The Routledge Handbook of Language Learning and Technology* (pp. 415–430). Routledge.

Sailer, M., & Homner, L. (2020). The Gamification of Learning: A Meta-Analysis. *Educational Psychology Review*, *32*(1), 77–112. doi:10.100710648-019-09498-w

Salter, N. P., & Conneely, M. R. (2015). Structured and Unstructured Discussion Forums as Tools for Student Engagement. *Computers in Human Behavior*, *46*, 18–25. doi:10.1016/j.chb.2014.12.037

Schreiber, L. M., & Valle, B. E. (2013). Social Constructivist Teaching Strategies in the Small Group Classroom. *Small Group Research*, *44*(4), 395–411. doi:10.1177/1046496413488422

Sexton, S. (2020). Meaningful Learning. In B. Akpan & T. J. Kennedy (Eds.), *Education in Theory and Practice* (pp. 163–175). Springer. doi:10.1007/978-3-030-43620-9_12

Shulman, L. S. (2005). Signature Pedagogies in the Professions. *Daedalus*, *134*(3), 52–58. doi:10.1162/0011526054622015

Sweller, K. (2010). Cognitive Load Theory: Recent Theoretical Advances. In J. L. Plass, R. Moreno, & R. Brüken (Eds.), *Cognitive Load Theory* (pp. 29–47). Cambridge University Press. doi:10.1017/CBO9780511844744.004

Tahir, F., Mitrovic, A., & Sotardi, V. (2022). Investigating the causal relationship between badges and learning outcomes in SQL-Tutor. *Research and Practice in Technology Enhanced Learning*, *17*(1), 1–23. doi:10.118641039-022-00180-4

Tan, C., & Liu, M. (2016). Using ICT in teaching the Chinese language: Practices and reflections from Singapore. In K. Soh (Ed.), *Teaching Chinese Language in Singapore: Retrospect and Challenges* (pp. 45–65). Springer. doi:10.1007/978-981-10-0123-9_4

Turner, R. (2012). *The Gamification of EAP*. 12th BUSEL International Conference on Language Teaching Issues: EAP in University Settings, Ankara, Turkey.

Viberg, O., & Grönlund, Å. (2013). Cross-cultural analysis of users" attitudes toward the use of mobile devices in second and foreign language learning in higher education: A case from Sweden and China. *Computers & Education*, *69*, 169–180. doi:10.1016/j.compedu.2013.07.014

Watters, A. (2020, October 8). *Behaviorisim won*. Hack Education. http://hackeducation.com/2020/10/08/behaviorism

Xiao, J. (2014). Learner Agency in Language Learning: A Story of a Distance Learner in China. *Distance Education, 35*(1), 4–17. doi:10.1080/01587919.2014.891429

Yang, Y., Hsieh, W., Wong, W., Hong, Y., & Lai, S. (2022). Reducing Students' Foreign Language Anxiety to Improve English Vocabulary Learning in an Online Simulation Game. *Computer Assisted Language Learning*, 1–23. Advance online publication. doi:10.1080/09588221.2022.2039203

Ybarra, R. & Green, T. (2003). Using Technology to Help ESL/EFL Students Develop Language Skills. *The Internet TESL Journal, 9*(3).

Young, D. J. (1992). Language Anxiety from the Foreign Language Specialist's Perspective: Interviews with Krashen, Omaggio Hadley, Terrell and Rardin. *Foreign Language Annals, 25*(2), 157–172. doi:10.1111/j.1944-9720.1992.tb00524.x

Yu, J., Denham, A. R., & Searight, E. (2022). A systematic review of augmented reality game-based learning in STEM education. *Educational Technology Research and Development, 70*(4), 1169–1194. doi:10.100711423-022-10122-y

Yürük, N. (2019). Edutainment. *Journal of Educational Technology & Online Learning, 2*(2), 89–101. doi:10.31681/jetol.557518

Zafar, S., & Meenakshi, K. (2012). Individual Learner Differences and Second Language Acquisition: A Review. *Journal of Language Teaching and Research, 3*(4), 639–646. doi:10.4304/jltr.3.4.639-646

Zarzycka-Piskorz, E. (2016). Can games be motivating in learning grammar? *Teaching English with Technology, 16*(3), 17–36.

Zichermann, G., & Cunningham, C. (2011). *Gamification by design: Implementing game mechanics in web and mobile apps*. O'Reilly Media.

ADDITIONAL READING

Boller, S., & Kapp, K. (2017). *Play to Learn: Everything you Need to Know about Designing Effective Learning Games*. Association for Talent Development.

Chou, Y. (2015). *Actionable Gamification: Beyond Points, Badges and Leaderboards* (2nd ed.). Octalysis Media.

Geroimenko, V. (2019). *Augmented Reality Games II*. Springer. doi:10.1007/978-3-030-15620-6

Pegrum, M. (2019). *Mobile Lenses on Learning: Language and Literacies on the Move*. Springer. doi:10.1007/978-981-15-1240-7

Peterson, M., Yamasaki, K., & Thomas, M. (2021). *Digital Games and Language Learning: Theory, Development and Implementation*. Bloomsbury Academic. doi:10.5040/9781350133037

Reinhardt, J. (2019). *Gameful Second and Foreign Language Teaching and Learning: Theory, Research, and Practice*. Palgrave Macmillan. doi:10.1007/978-3-030-04729-0

Schell, J. (2019). *The Art of Game Design: A Book of Lenses* (3rd ed.). CRC Press.

Vaz de Carvalho, C. & Coehlo, A. (2022). *Game-Based Learning, Gamification in Education and Serious Games*. Mdpi AG.

KEY TERMS AND DEFINITIONS

Augmented Reality: Use of technology to superpose computer-generated layers of reality on current surroundings.

Edutainment: Cross-section between education and entertainment, used pejoratively in literature at times.

English for Specific Academic Purposes: Discipline that furnishes students with the academic and linguistic skillset needed for study success with a focus on their chosen field of study.

Escape Room: A socially constructed virtual or physical space in which puzzles must be solved to leave.

Game-Informed Pedagogy: The application of game theory to pedagogical praxis.

Gamification: The application of certain ludic components to another field such as education.

Transnational Education: Tuition takes place from within a country which differs from that of the awarding institution.

Compilation of References

Abt, C. C. (1987). *Serious Games*. University Press of America.

Adams, P. (2006). Exploring Social Constructivism: Theories and Practicalities. *Education, 34*(3), 243–257. doi:10.1080/03004270600898893

Adams, V., Burger, S., Crawford, K., & Setter, R. (2018). Can you escape? Creating an escape room to facilitate active learning. *Journal for Nurses in Professional Development, 34*(2), 1–5. doi:10.1097/NND.0000000000000433 PMID:29481471

Adell, J., Castañeda, L., & Esteve, F. (2018). ¿Hacia la Ubersidad? Conflictos y contradicciones de la universidad digital [Towards Ubersity? Conflicts and contradictions of the digital university]. *RIED-Revista Iberoamericana De Educación a Distancia, 21*(2), 51–68. doi:10.5944/ried.21.2.20669

Afdal, H. W., & Spernes, K. (2018). Designing and redesigning research-based teacher education. *Teaching and Teacher Education, 74*, 215–228. doi:10.1016/j.tate.2018.05.011

Agreda, M., Ortiz, A. M., Tallón, S., & López, J. (2019). Escape rooms: actividades gamificadas para la formación de profesionales educativos [Escape rooms: gamified activities for the training of educational professionals]. In E. Sánchez-Rivas, J. Ruiz-Palmero, & E. Sánchez-Vega (Coords.), *Innovación y tecnología en contextos educativos* (pp. 399-409). UMA editorial.

Aguiar-Castillo, L., Clavijo-Rodríguez, A., Hernández-López, L., De Saa-Pérez, P., & Pérez-Jiménez, R. (2021). Gamification and deep learning approaches in higher education. *Journal of Hospitality, Leisure, Sport and Tourism Education, 29*, 100290. doi:10.1016/j.jhlste.2020.100290

Aguilera, A., Fúquene, C. A., & Ríos, W. F. (2014). Aprende jugando: El uso de técnicas de gamificación en entornos de aprendizaje. *IM-Pertinente, 2*(1), 125–143.

Al-Azawi, R., Al-Faliti, F., & Al-Blushi, M. (2016). Educational gamification vs. game-based learning: Comparative study. *International Journal of Innovation, Management and Technology, 7*(4), 132–136. doi:10.18178/ijimt.2016.7.4.659

Albright, E. R., & Schwanke, E. A. (2021). University Admissions Leaders Rethink Recruitment Strategies in the Wake of COVID-19. *The Journal of Advancing Education Practice, 2*(1), 4.

Ali, S. S., Ali, M. W., & Amin, T. (2020). Enhancing adult learners' motivation for learning English grammar through language games. *Research Journal of Social Sciences & Economics Review, 1*(3), 143–150. doi:10.36902/rjsser-vol1-iss3-2020(143-150)

Allen, D., & Tanner, K. (2003). Approaches to cell biology teaching: Learning content in context—problem-based learning. *Cell Biology Education, 2*(2), 73–81. doi:10.1187/cbe.03-04-0019 PMID:12888838

Alonso, G., & Schroeder, K. T. (2020). Applying active learning in a virtual classroom such as a molecular biology escape room. *Biochemistry and Molecular Biology Education, 48*(5), 514–515. doi:10.1002/bmb.21429 PMID:32812701

Álvarez, E., Bellezza, A., & Caggiano, V. (2016). Realidad aumentada: innovación en educación [Augmented reality: innovation in education]. *Didasc@alia: Didáctica y educación, 7*(1), 195–212. https://dialnet.unirioja.es/descarga/articulo/6568046.pdf

American Psychiatric Association. (2013). *Diagnostic and statistical manual of mental disorders* (5th ed.). APA.

Anderson, L. W., & Krathwohl, D. R. (2001). *A taxonomy for learning, teaching, and assessing: A revision of Bloom's taxonomy of educational objectives*. Longman.

Anderson, M., Lioce, L., & Robertson, J., Lopreiato, J., & Díaz, D. (2021). Toward defining healthcare simulation escape rooms. *Simulation & Gaming, 52*(1), 7–17. doi:10.1177/1046878120958745

Ang, J. W. J., Ng, Y. N. A., & Liew, R. S. (2020). Physical and digital educational escape room for teaching chemical bonding. *Journal of Chemical Education, 97*(9), 2849–2856. doi:10.1021/acs.jchemed.0c00612

Area Moreira, M. (2008). La innovación pedagógica con TIC y el desarrollo de las competencias informacionales y digitales [Pedagogical innovation with ICT and the development of informational and digital competencies]. *Revista de Investigación en la Escuela, 64*, 5–17.

Area, M. (2010). ¿Por qué formar en competencias informacionales y digitales en la educación superior? En Competencias informacionales y digitales en educación superior [Why train in informational and digital skills in higher education? In Informational and digital competences in higher education]. Revista de Universidad y Sociedad del Conocimiento, 7(2).

Area, M. (2015). La alfabetización digital y la formación de la ciudadanía del siglo XXI [Digital literacy and the formation of citizenship of the XXI century]. *Revista Integra Educativa, 7*(3), 21-33. http://www.scielo.org.bo/scielo.php?script=sci_arttext&pid=S1997-40432014000300002

Arechavala Vargas, R., & Sánchez Cervantes, C. F. (2017). Las universidades públicas mexicanas: Los retos de las transformaciones institucionales hacia la investigación y la transferencia de conocimiento [Mexican public universities: the challenges of institutional transformations towards research and knowledge transfer]. *Revista de la Educación Superior, 46*(184), 21–37. doi:10.1016/j.resu.2017.09.001

Argent, O., Argent, S., & Spencer, J. (2019). *EAP Essentials: A Teacher's Guide to Principles and Practice* (2nd ed.). Garnet Education.

Arici, F., Yilidirim, P., Caliklar, S., & Yilmaz, R. M. (2019). Research Trends in the Use of Augmented Reality in Science Education: Content and Bibliometric Mapping Analysis. *Computers & Education, 142*, 1–23. doi:10.1016/j.compedu.2019.103647

Arockiyasamy, G., Surendheran, K., & Bullard, S. K. (2016). The influence of playing video games on academic performance among graduates of Karunya University. *Journal of Advances in Humanities and Social Sciences, 2*(3), 119–132.

Arthur Lakes Library. (n.d.). *Open Educational Resources*. Colorado School of Mines. https://libguides.mines.edu/oer/simulationslabs

Asamblea General de las Naciones Unidas. (2015). *Resolución Aprobada por la Asamblea General el 25 de septiembre de 2015* [Resolution Adopted by the General Assembly on September 25, 2015]. https://www.senado.gob.mx/comisiones/fomento_economico/eventos/docs/resolucion_080916.pdf

Astuti, N. H., Rusilowati, A., & Subali, B. (2021). STEM-Based Learning Analysis to Improve Students' Problem-Solving Abilities in Science Subject: A Literature Review. *Journal of Innovative Science Education, 10*(1), 79–86. doi:10.15294/jise.v9i2.38505

Aubeux, D., Blanchflower, N., Bray, E., Clouet, R., Remaud, M., Badran, Z., Prud'homme, T., & Gaudin, A. (2020). Educational gaming for dental students: Design and assessment of a pilot endodontic-themed escape game. *European Journal of Dental Education, 24*(3), 449–457. doi:10.1111/eje.12521 PMID:32142189

Avargil, S., Shwartz, G., & Zemel, Y. (2021). Educational escape room: Break Dalton's code and escape. *Journal of Chemical Education, 98*(7), 2313–2322. doi:10.1021/acs.jchemed.1c00110

Bahari, A. & Salimi, M. (2021). Challenges and Affordances of Developing Receptive and Productive Skills via Technology-Based Instruction. *Computer-Assisted Language Learning Electronic Journal, 22*(1), 25-55.

Bai, S., Hew, K. F., & Huang, B. (2020). Does gamification improve student learning outcome? Evidence from a meta-analysis and synthesis of qualitative data in educational contexts. *Educational Research Review, 30*, 100322. doi:10.1016/j.edurev.2020.100322

Baker, C. M., Crabtree, G., & Anderson, K. (2020). Student pharmacist perceptions of learning after strengths-based leadership skills lab and escape room in pharmacy practice skills laboratory. *Currents in Pharmacy Teaching and Learning, 12,* 724-727.

Baker, C., Crabtree, G., & Anderson, K. (2020). Student pharmacist perceptions of learning after strengths-based leadership skills lab and escape room in pharmacy practice skills laboratory. *Currents in Pharmacy Teaching & Learning, 12*(6), 724–727. doi:10.1016/j.cptl.2020.01.021 PMID:32482276

Bakkum, M. J., Richir, M. C., Sultan, R., de la Court, J. R., Lambooij, A. C., van Agtmael, M. A., & Tichelaar, J. (2021). Can students create their own educational escape room?: Lessons learned from the opioid crisis escape room. *Medical Science Educator, 31*(6), 1739–1745. doi:10.100740670-021-01425-5 PMID:34950526

Balamuralithara, B., & Woods, P. C. (2009). Virtual laboratories in engineering education: The simulation lab and remote lab. *Computer Applications in Engineering Education, 17*(1), 108–118. doi:10.1002/cae.20186

BALEAP. (2016). *BALEAP Teacher Competency Framework for Teachers of English for Academic Purposes.* https://www.baleap.org/wp-content/uploads/2016/04/teap-competency-framework.pdf

Balloo, K. (2019). Students' difficulties during research methods training acting as potential barriers to their development of scientific thinking. In M. Murtonen & K. Balloo (Eds.), *Redefining scientific thinking for higher education* (pp. 107–137). Palgrave Macmillan. doi:10.1007/978-3-030-24215-2_5

Bandura, A. (2001). Social Cognitive Theory: An Agentic Perspective. *Annual Review of Psychology, 52*(1), 1–26. doi:10.1146/annurev.psych.52.1.1 PMID:11148297

Barab, S. A., Thomas, K., & Merrill, H. (2001). Online learning: From information dissemination to fostering collaboration. *Journal of Interactive Learning Research, 12*(1), 105–143.

Barak, M., & Ziv, S. (2013). Wandering: A Web-based platform for the creation of location-based interactive learning objects. *Computers & Education, 62*, 159–170. doi:10.1016/j.compedu.2012.10.015

Barari, N., RezaeiZadeh, M., Khorasani, A., & Alami, F. (2022, October 3). Designing and validating educational standards for E-teaching in virtual learning environments (VLEs), based on revised bloom's taxonomy. *Interactive Learning Environments, 30*(9), 1640–1652. Advance online publication. doi:10.1080/10494820.2020.1739078

Barber, C. S. (2018). Book Review: 3D Game Lab: Rezzly Heroic Learning. *Academy of Management Learning & Education, 17*(1), 114–117. doi:10.5465/amle.2017.0419

Barragán, R., Buzón, O., & García Pérez, R. (2007). Diagnóstico y evaluación de aprendizajes universitarios con e-portafolios: regulación de aprendizajes Blended-Learning y nuevos roles del alumnado [Diagnosis and evaluation of university learning with e-portfolios: regulation of Blended-Learning learning and new student roles]. In F. Etxeberría, L. Sarasola, J. F. Lukas, J. Etxeberría, & A. Martxueta (Coords.), *Actas del XIII Congreso Nacional de Modelos de Investigación Educativa, AIDIPE.* San Sebastián.

Basak, S. K., Wotto, M., & Belanger, P. (2018). E-learning, M-learning and D-learning: Conceptual definition and comparative analysis. *E-Learning and Digital Media, 15*(4), 191–216. doi:10.1177/2042753018785180

Basogain, X., Olabe, M., Espinosa, K., Rouèche, C., & Olabe, J. C. (2007). Realidad Aumentada en la Educación: una tecnología emergente [Augmented Reality in Education: an emerging technology]. Online Educa Madrid'2007 Proceedings, 24-29.

Batsila, M., & Tsihouridis, C. (2018). Let's go Kahooting. Teachers' views on C.R.S. for teaching purposes. In M. E. Auer, D. Guralnick, & I. Slmonks (Eds.), Teaching and *learning in a digital world. The 20th international conference on interactive collaborative learning 2017* (pp. 563–571). Springer International Publishing.

Becker, K., & Parker, J. (2014). An Overview of Game Design Techniques. In K. Schrier (Ed.), *Learning, education and games. Volume one: Curricular and design considerations* (pp. 179–198). Carnegie Mellon University.

Béguin, E., Besnard, S., Cros, A., Joannes, B., Leclerc-Istria, O., Noel, A., Roels, N., Taleb, F., Thongphan, J., Alata, E., & Nicomette, V. (2019). Computer-security-oriented escape room. *IEEE Security and Privacy, 17*(4), 78–83. doi:10.1109/MSEC.2019.2912700

Bellotti, F., Kapralos, B., Lee, K., Moreno-Ger, P., & Berta, R. (2013). Assessment in and of serious games: An overview. *Advances in Human-Computer Interaction, 2013*, 2013. doi:10.1155/2013/136864

Benini, S., & Thomas, M. (2021). A Critical Review of Research on Gamification and Second Language Acquisition. In M. Peterson, M. Thomas, & K. Yamazaki (Eds.), *Digital Games and Language Learning: Theory, Development and Implementation* (pp. 9–46). Bloomsbury Academic. doi:10.5040/9781350133037.ch-002

Bergwerf, H. (2015). *MolView*. https://molview.org/

Bernstein, H. J. (n.d.). *RasMol and OpenRasMol.* Molecular Graphics Visualisation Tool. http://www.openrasmol.org/

Berrios, G. E. (2012). Descriptive psychopathology: Historical and conceptual aspects. *Revista Latinoamericana de Psicopatologia Fundamental, 15*, 171–196. doi:10.1590/S1415-47142012000100012

Berthod, F., Bouchoud, L., Grossrieder, F., Falaschi, L., Senhaji, S., & Bonnabry, P. (2020). Learning good manufacturing practices in an escape room: Validation of a new pedagogical tool. *Journal of Oncology Pharmacy Practice, 26*(4), 853–860. doi:10.1177/1078155219875504 PMID:31566110

Bezard, L., Debacq, M., & Rosso, A. (2020). The carnivorous yoghurts: A "serious" escape game for stirring labs. *Education for Chemical Engineers, 33*, 1–8. doi:10.1016/j.ece.2020.06.001

Bhute, V. J., Inguva, P., Shah, U., & Brechtelsbauer, C. (2021). Transforming traditional teaching laboratories for effective remote delivery—A review. *Education for Chemical Engineers, 35*, 96–104. doi:10.1016/j.ece.2021.01.008

Bicen, H., & Kocakoyun, S. (2017). Determination of university students' most preferred mobile application for gamification. *World Journal on Educational Technology: Current Issues., 9*(1), 18–23. doi:10.18844/wjet.v9i1.641

Biggs, J. (2003). *Aligning Teaching for Constructing Learning*. The Higher Education Authority. https://www.advance-he.ac.uk/knowledge-hub/aligning-teaching-constructing-learning

Biggs, J., & Tang, C. (2011). *Teaching for Quality Learning at University*. Open University Press.

Bilbao, N., Romero, A., Portillo, J., & López, A. (2022). Escape room digital para el desarrollo del aprendizaje cooperativo en educación superior [Digital escape room for the development of cooperative learning in higher education]. *Education in the Knowledge Society, 23*. Advance online publication. doi:10.14201/eks27126

Blanco, M. (2020). La pedagogía en el aula en la era Nétflix: Explicar contenidos a través de la cartelera de las plataformas digitales [Pedagogy in the classroom in the Nétflix era: Explaining content through the billboard of digital platforms]. In Innovación Docente e Investigación en Educación y Ciencias Sociales. Avanzando en el proceso de enseñanza-aprendizaje. Academic Press.

Bloom, B. S. (1956). *Taxonomy of Educational Objectives: The Classification of Educational Goals* (1st ed.). Longman Group.

Bloom, B. S. (1956). *Taxonomy of educational objectives: The classification of educational goals. Book 1. Cognitive domain*. Longman.

Boal, K. B., & Schultz, P. L. (2007). Storytelling, time, and evolution: The role of strategic leadership in complex adaptive systems. *The Leadership Quarterly, 18*(4), 411–428. doi:10.1016/j.leaqua.2007.04.008

Bober, M. (2010). *Games-based experiences for learning*. Manchester Metropolitan University.

Boctor, L. (2013). Active-learning strategies: The use of a game to reinforce learning in nursing education. A case study. *Nurse Education in Practice, 13*(2), 96–100. doi:10.1016/j.nepr.2012.07.010 PMID:22910398

Bodnar, C. A., Anastasio, D., Enszer, J. A., & Burkey, D. D. (2016). Ingenieros en juego: Juegos como herramientas de enseñanza para estudiantes de ingeniería [Engineers at play: games as teaching tools for engineering students]. *Revista de Educación en Ingeniería, 105*(1), 147–200.

Bolliger, D. U., Mills, D., White, J., & Kohyama, M. (2015). Japanese students' perceptions of digital game use for English-language learning in higher education. *Journal of Educational Computing Research, 53*(3), 384–408. doi:10.1177/0735633115600806

Borg, S., & Alshumaimeri, Y. (2017). Language Learner Autonomy in a Tertiary Context: Teacher Beliefs and Practices. *Language Teaching Research, 23*(1), 9–38. doi:10.1177/1362168817725759

Borrás, O. (2015). *Fundamentos de la Gamificación* [Fundamentals of Gamification]. Gabinete de Tele-Educación. Universidad Politécnica de Madrid.

Borrego, C., Fernández, C., Blanes, I., & Robles, S. (2017). Room escape at class: Escape games activities to facilitate the motivation and learning in computer science. *Journal of Technology and Science Education, 7*(2), 162–171. doi:10.3926/jotse.247

Borrego, C., Fernández, C., Robles, S., & Blanes, I. (2016). Room escape en las aulas: Actividades de juegos de escape para facilitar la motivación y el aprendizaje de las ciencias de la computación [Room escape in the classroom: escape game activities to facilitate motivation and learning in computer science]. *Revista del Congrés Internacional de Docència Universitària i Innovació, 3*, 1–7.

Böttcher, F., & Thiel, F. (2018). Evaluating research-oriented teaching: A new instrument to assess university students' research competences. *Higher Education, 75*(1), 91–110. doi:10.100710734-017-0128-y

Botturi, L., & Babazadeh, M. (2020). Designing educational escape rooms: Validating the Star Model. *International Journal of Serious Games*, *7*(3), 41–57. doi:10.17083/ijsg.v7i3.367

Botturi, L., & Babazadeh, M. (2021). Fighting viruses though escape room design with students. *Proceedings of the European Conference on Games Based Learning*, 108-116. 10.34190/GBL.21.037

Bowyer, S. (2021) Learn, Play, Design: Using the Escape Room Concept to Teach Creativity and Innovation in a Business Course. *Business Education Innovation Journal, 13*(59).

Boyle, E. A., Hainey, T., Connolly, T. M., Gray, G., Earp, J., Ott, M., Lim, T., Ninaus, M., Ribeiro, C., & Pereira, J. (2016). An update to the systematic literature review of empirical evidence of the impacts and outcomes of computer games and serious games. *Computers & Education*, *94*, 178–192. doi:10.1016/j.compedu.2015.11.003

Boysen-Osborn, M., Paradise, S., & Suchard, J. (2018). The toxiscape hunt: An escape room-scavenger hunt for toxicology education. *Journal of Education and Teaching in Emergency Medicine*, *3*(1), 9–19. doi:10.5070/M531037616

Brady, S. C., & Andersen, E. C. (2021). An escape-room inspired game for genetics review. *Journal of Biological Education*, *55*(4), 406–417. doi:10.1080/00219266.2019.1703784

Brew, A., & Saunders, C. (2020). Making sense of research-based learning in teacher education. *Teaching and Teacher Education*, *87*, 102935. doi:10.1016/j.tate.2019.102935

Brígido, M., & Borrachero, A. B. (2011). Relación entre autoconcepto, autoeficacia y autorregulación en ciencias de futuros maestros de primaria [Relationship between self-concept, self-efficacy and self-regulation in science of future primary school teachers]. *INFAD Revista de Psicología*, *1*(2), 107–113.

Brown, N., Darby, W., & Coronel, H. (2019). An escape room as a simulation teaching strategy. *Clinical Simulation in Nursing*, *30*, 1–6. doi:10.1016/j.ecns.2019.02.002

Bruce, I. (2011). *Theories and Concepts of English for Academic Purposes*. Palgrave Macmillan.

Buchner, J., Rüter, M., & Kerres, M. (2022). Learning with a digital escape room game: Before or after instruction? *Research and Practice in Technology Enhanced Learning*, *17*(1), 1–16. doi:10.118641039-022-00187-x PMID:35310067

Buckley, P., & Doyle, E. (2016). Gamification and student motivation. *Interactive Learning Environments*, *24*(6), 1162–1175. doi:10.1080/10494820.2014.964263

Budgen, D. (2003). *Software design* (2nd ed.). Addison-Wesley.

Burke, B. (2012). *Gamification 2020: What is the future of gamification?* Gartnet.

Cadieux, M., Campos-Zamora, M., Zagury-Orly, I., & Dzara, K. (2020). Journal Club Using Virtual Breakout Rooms: Interactive Continuing Education with No Learner Preparation During COVID-19. *The Journal of Continuing Education in the Health Professions*, *40*(4), 217–219. doi:10.1097/CEH.0000000000000321

Cain, J. (2019). Exploratory implementation of a blended format escape room in a large enrollment pharmacy management class. *Currents in Pharmacy Teaching & Learning*, *11*(1), 44–50. doi:10.1016/j.cptl.2018.09.010 PMID:30527875

Cai, S. (2022). Harry Potter themed digital escape room for addressing misconceptions in stoichiometry. *Journal of Chemical Education*, *99*(7), 2747–2753. doi:10.1021/acs.jchemed.2c00178

Caldas, L., Eukel, H., Matulewicz, A., Fernández, E., & Donohoe, K. (2019). Applying educational gaming success to a nonsterile compounding escape room. *Currents in Pharmacy Teaching & Learning*, *11*(10), 1049–1054. doi:10.1016/j.cptl.2019.06.012 PMID:31685175

Calderón, M.E. (2020). SVOD: El nuevo campo de batalla por las audiencias [SVOD: The new battleground for audiences]. *Ctrl: Control & Strategias, 676*, 65-67.

Cancan, Z., Ye, T., & Shuanglin, G. (2022). Academic Writing Anxiety among Chinese International Postgraduates. *Linguistics and Culture Review*, *6*(S2), 52–68. doi:10.21744/lingcure.v6nS2.1909

Cano-Muñoz, M. Á., & Gómez-Núñez, M. I. (2020). Aprendizaje basado en el juego en la educación superior: análisis de una experiencia de escape room [Play-based learning in higher education: analysis of an escape room experience]. In E. López-Meneses, D. Cobos-Sanchiz, L. Molina-García, A. Jaén-Martínez, & A. H. Martín-Padilla (Eds.), *Claves para la innovación pedagógica ante lo nuevos retos. Respuestas en la vanguardia de la práctica educativa* (pp. 2731–2739). Octaedro.

Carr-Chellman, A. A. (2015). Games in Elementary and Middle School Settings. In J. M. Spector (Ed.), *The SAGE Encyclopedia of Educational Technology* (pp. 309–310). SAGE.

Case, R. E., & Xu, W. (2021). The Influence of Language Learning Environment on Negative Transfer and its Connection to Status and Face-Saving Refusal Strategies. *International Journal of Applied Linguistics and English Literature*, *10*(2), 33–42. doi:10.7575/aiac.ijalel.v.10n.2p.33

Casler, K. (2022). Escape Passive Learning: 10 steps to Building an Escape Room. *The Journal for Nurse Practitioners*, *18*(5), 569–574. doi:10.1016/j.nurpra.2022.01.020

Castañeda-Vázquez, C., Espejo-Garcés, T., Zurita-Ortega, F., & Fernández-Revelles, A. (2019). La formación de los futuros docentes a través de la gamificación, tic y evaluación continua [The training of future teachers through gamification, ICT and continuous evaluation]. *SPORT TK-Revista EuroAmericana de Ciencias del Deporte*, *8*(2), 55–63. doi:10.6018portk.391751

Castillo, H., Herrero, D., Checa, M., & Monjelat, N. (2015). Desarrollo de competencias a través de los videojuegos deportivos: alfabetización digital e identidad [Skills development through sports video games: digital literacy and identity]. *Revista de Educación a Distancia*, (33). https://revistas.um.es/red/article/view/233111

Castro, P., Gómez Guzmán, P., & Carranza, S. (2022). Investigación e Innovación en la Consolidación de una Disciplina Educativa [Research and Innovation in the Consolidation of an Educational Discipline]. *REICE. Revista Electrónica Iberoamericana sobre Calidad, Eficacia y Cambio en Educación*, *20*(1), 5–20. doi:10.15366/reice2022.20.1.001

CDC. (n.d.). *Data*. https://data.cdc.gov/browse

CERN. (n.d.). *OpenDataCERN*. http://opendata.cern.ch/

Chen, S. J., Hsu, C., & Caropreso, E. (2005, October). Cross-cultural collaborative online learning: When the west meets the east. In *E-Learn: World Conference on E-Learning in Corporate, Government, Healthcare, and Higher Education* (pp. 1931-1941). Association for the Advancement of Computing in Education (AACE).

Chen, X., Zou, D., Xie, H., & Cheng, G. (2021). Twenty Years of Personalized Language Learning: Topic Modeling and Knowledge Mapping. *Journal of Educational Technology & Society*, *24*(1), 205–222.

Chernikova, O., Heitzmann, N., Stadler, M., Holzberger, D., Seidel, T., & Fischer, F. (2020). Simulation-Based Learning in Higher Education: A Meta-Analysis. *Review of Educational Research*, *90*(4), 499–541. doi:10.3102/0034654320933544

Cheveldave, A. (Ed.). (2020). *Virtual Lab and Science Resource Directory*. BCcampus. https://opentextbc.ca/virtualscienceresources/

Chi, M. T. H., & Wylie, R. (2014). The ICAP framework: Linking cognitive engagement to active learning outcomes. *Educational Psychologist*, *49*(4), 219–243. doi:10.1080/00461520.2014.965823

Choudhury, S., & Pattnaik, S. (2019). Emerging themes in e-learning: A review from the stakeholder's perspective. *Computers & Education, 144*, 103657. doi:10.1016/j.compedu.2019.103657

Chowdhury, M. B. (2022). Internationalisation of education and its effect on economic growth and development. *World Economy, 45*(1), 200–219. doi:10.1111/twec.13174

Clapson, M. L., Gilbert, B., Mozol, V. J., Schechtel, S., Tran, J., & White, S. (2019). ChemEscape: Educational battle box puzzle activities for engaging outreach and active learning in general chemistry. *Journal of Chemical Education, 97*(1), 125–131. doi:10.1021/acs.jchemed.9b00612

Clark, D. B., Tanner-Smith, E. E., & Killingsworth, S. S. (2016). Digital games, design, and learning: A systematic review and meta-analysis. *Review of Educational Research, 86*(1), 79–122. doi:10.3102/0034654315582065 PMID:26937054

Clarke, S. A. S., Keegan, H., Morini, L., & Wood, O. (2016). EscapED: Adapting Live-Action, Interactive Games to Support Higher Education Teaching and Learning Practices. In Games and Learning Alliance. GALA 2016. Lecture Notes in Computer Science (Vol. 10056). Springer. doi:10.1007/978-3-319-50182-6_13

Clarke, S. J., Peel, D. J., Arnab, S., Morini, L., Keegan, H., & Wood, O. (2017). EscapED: A Framework for Creating Educational Escape Rooms and Interactive Games for Higher/Further Education. *Int. J. Serious Games, 4*(3), 73–86. doi:10.17083/ijsg.v4i3.180

Clauson, A., Hahn, L., Frame, T., Hagan, A., Bynum, L. A., Thompson, M., & Kiningham, K. (2019). An innovative escape room activity to assess student readiness for advanced pharmacy practice experiences (APPEs). *Currents in Pharmacy Teaching & Learning, 11*(7), 723–728. doi:10.1016/j.cptl.2019.03.011 PMID:31227096

Connelly, L., Burbach, B., Kennedy, C., & Walters, L. (2018). Escape room recruitment event: Description and lessons learned. *The Journal of Nursing Education, 57*(3), 184–187. doi:10.3928/01484834-20180221-12 PMID:29505080

Cornillie, F. (2017). Educationally Designed Game Environments and Feedback. In S. Thorne & S. May (Eds.), *Language, Education and Technology* (pp. 1–14). Springer International Publishing. doi:10.1007/978-3-319-02237-6_28

Cortizo Pérez, J. C. C., Carrero García, F., Monsalve Piqueras, B., Velasco Collado, A., Díaz Del Dedo, L., & Pérez Martín, J. (2011). Gamificación y Docencia: Lo que la Universidad tiene que aprender de los Videojuegos [Gamification and Teaching: What the University has to learn from Video Games]. In Retos y oportunidades del desarrollo de los nuevos títulos en educación superior. VIII Jornadas Internacionales de Innovación Universitaria.

CourseSource. (n.d.). Evidence-based Teaching Resources for Undergraduate Biology and Physics. Qubes. https://qubeshub.org/community/groups/coursesource

Cózar-Gutiérrez, R., & Sáez-López, J. M. (2016). Game-based learning and gamification in initial teacher training in the social sciences: An experiment with MinecraftEdu. *International Journal of Educational Technology in Higher Education, 13*(1), 1–11. doi:10.118641239-016-0003-4

Crabb, L. A. (2018). Debating the success of carbon-offsetting projects at sports mega-events. A case from the 2014 FIFA World Cup. *Journal of Sustainable Forestry, 37*(2), 178–196. doi:10.1080/10549811.2017.1364652

Craig, C., Ngondo, P., Devling, M., & Scharlach, J. (2019). Escaping the routine: Unlocking group intervention. *Communication Teacher, 34*(1), 14–18. doi:10.1080/17404622.2019.1593475

Crawford, J., & Cifuentes-Faura, J. (2022). Sustainability in higher education during the COVID-19 pandemic: A systematic review. *Sustainability, 14*(3), 1879. doi:10.3390u14031879

Cruaud, C. (2016). The playful frame: Gamification in a French-as-a foreign-language class. *Innovation in Language Learning and Teaching, 12*(4), 330–343. doi:10.1080/17501229.2016.1213268

Cruz, R. & López, G. (2007). Una visión general del m-learning y su proceso de adopción en el esquema educativo [An overview of m-learning and its adoption process in the educational scheme]. *2º Coloquio Internacional: Tendencias Actuales de Cómputo e Informática en México.*

Csikszentmihalyi, M. (1975). *Beyond boredom and anxiety*. Jossey-Bass.

Csikszentmihalyi, M. (1990). *Flow: The psychology of optimal experience*. HarperPerennial.

Csikszentmihalyi, M. (2011). *Flow*. Ed. Kairós.

Csíkszentmihályi, M. (2020). *Finding flow: The psychology of engagement with everyday life*. Hachette.

Dabbagh, N. (2005). Scaffolding: An important teacher competency in online learning. *TechTrends*, *47*(2), 39–44. doi:10.1007/BF02763424

Daltro, M. R., & Bueno, G. (2010). Ludicidade e narrativa: Estratégias de humanização na graduação médica [Ludicity and narrative: humanization strategies in medical graduation]. *Revista Brasileira de Educação Médica*, *34*(4), 497–505. doi:10.1590/S0100-55022010000400004

Darbyshire, D., & Baker, P. (2012). A systematic review and thematic analysis of cinema in medical education. *Medical Humanities*, *38*(1), 28–33. doi:10.1136/medhum-2011-010026 PMID:22282424

Davis, D., & Lee, J. G. (2019, June). Building escape rooms to increase student engagement in first-year engineering classes. *2019 ASEE Annual Conference & Exposition*. 10.18260/1-2--32486

Davis, K., Lo, H.-y., Lichliter, R., Wallin, K., Elegores, G., Jacobson, S., & Doughty, C. (2022). Twelve tips for creating an escape room activity for medical education. *Medical Teacher*, *44*(4), 366–371. doi:10.1080/0142159X.2021.1909715 PMID:33872114

De Back, T. T., Tinga, A. M., & Louwerse, M. M. (2021). Learning in immersed collaborative virtual environments: Design and implementation. *Interactive Learning Environments*, 1–19. doi:10.1080/10494820.2021.2006238

de Chazal, E. (2014). *English for Academic Purposes*. Oxford University Press.

de Jonge, J. S., & Labrador, B. (2020, November). Fostering critical thinking and motivation through digital escape rooms: preliminary observations. In Virtual exchange and 21st century teacher education: short papers from the 2019 EVALUATE conference (p. 157). Research-publishing. net.

de la Flor, D., Calles, J. A., Espada, J. J., & Rodríguez, R. (2020). Application of escape lab-room to heat transfer evaluation for chemical engineers. *Education for Chemical Engineers*, *33*, 9–16. doi:10.1016/j.ece.2020.06.002

De Miguel, M. (Coord.). (2006). Metodologías de enseñanza y aprendizaje para el desarrollo de competencias [Teaching and learning methodologies for the development of competences]. Alianza Ediorial.

De Soto García, I. S. (2018). Herramientas de gamificación para el aprendizaje de ciencias de la tierra [Gamification tools for earth science learning]. *Edutec-e Revista Electrónica de Tecnología Educativa*, *65*(65), 29–39. doi:10.21556/edutec.2018.65.1143

De Sousa Borges, S., Durelli, V. H., Reis, H. M., & Isotani, S. (2014). A systematic mapping on gamification applied to education. *Proceedings of the 29th annual ACM symposium on applied computing*, 216-222. 10.1145/2554850.2554956

de Souza, R. T. M. P., & Kasseboehmer, A. C. (2021). The thalidomide mystery: A digital escape room using Genially and WhatsApp for high school students. *Journal of Chemical Education*, *99*(2), 1132–1139. doi:10.1021/acs.jchemed.1c00955

Dehghanzadeh, H., Fardanesh, H., Hatami, J., Talaee, E., & Noroozi, O. (2019). Using gamification to support learning English as a second language: A systematic review. *Computer Assisted Language Learning, 34*(7), 1–24. doi:10.1080/09588221.2019.1648298

Del Castillo, Á. (2022). Caso didáctico. Gamificación en educación superior: Dándole la vuelta a la formación en estudios presenciales y online [Didactic case. Gamification in higher education: turning around training in face-to-face and online studies]. *Journal of Management and Business Education, 5*(3), 282–296. doi:10.35564/jmbe.2022.0017

Del Moral, M. E., Guzmán Duque, A. P., & Fernández García, L. C. (2018). Game-Based Learning: Increasing the Logical-Mathematical, Naturalistic, and Linguistic Learning Levels of Primary School Students. *Journal of New Approaches in Educational Research, 7*(1), 31–39. doi:10.7821/naer.2018.1.248

Delgado, A. M., & Oliver, R. (2006). La evaluación continua en un nuevo escenario docente. *Revista de Universidad Y Sociedad Del Conocimiento, 3*(1), 1–13.

Dennis, M. J. (2020). COVID-19 will accelerate the decline in international student enrollment. *Recruiting & Retaining Adult Learners, 22*(12), 1–7. doi:10.1002/nsr.30639

Department for Education and Department for International Trade. (2021). *International Education Strategy: 2021 update. Supporting recovery, driving growth.* Available at: https://assets.publishing.service.gov.uk/government/uploads/system/uploads/attachment_data/file/958990/International-Education-Strategy-_2021-Update.pdf

Deterding, S., Dixon, D., Khaled, R., & Nacke, L. (2011). Gamification: Towards a definition. *Proceedings of the 2011 Annual Conference Extended Abstracts on Human Factors in Computing Systems.* http://gamification-research.org/wp-content/uploads/2011/04/02-Deterding-Khaled-Nacke-Dixon.pdf

Deterding, S. (2011). Situated motivational affordances of game elements: a conceptual model. In *Gamification: Using Game Design Elements in Non-GamingContexts, a Workshop at CHI* (pp. 1–4). ACM.

Deterding, S., Khaled, R., Nacke, L., & Dixon, D. (2011). *Gamification: Toward a definition. In 29th Annual CHI Conference on Human Factors in Computing Systems.* ACM Press. https://bityl.co/3ify

Deterning, S., Dixon, D., Khaled, R., & Nacke, L. (2011). From game design elements to gamefulness: defining "gamification". *Proceedings of the 15th international academic MindTrek conference: Envisioning future media environments*, 9-15.

Dicheva, D., Dichev, C., Agre, G., & Angelova, G. (2015). Gamification in education: A systematic mapping study. *Journal of Educational Technology & Society, 18*(3), 75–88.

Dichev, C., & Dicheva, D. (2017). Gamifying education: What is known, what is believed and what remains uncertain: A critical review. *International Journal of Educational Technology in Higher Education, 14*(1), 9. doi:10.118641239-017-0042-5

Dietrich, N. (2018). Escape classroom: The Leblanc process - An educational "escape game". *Journal of Chemical Education, 95*(6), 996–999. doi:10.1021/acs.jchemed.7b00690

Ding, A., & Campion, G. (2016). EAP Teacher Development. In K. Hyland & P. Shaw (Eds.), *The Routledge Handbook of English for Academic Purposes* (pp. 547–559). Routledge.

Dittman, J. M., Amendola, M. F., Ramraj, R., Haynes, S., & Lange, P. (2022). The COMET framework: A novel approach to design an escape room workshop for interprofessional objectives. *Journal of Interprofessional Care, 36*(1), 161–164. doi:10.1080/13561820.2020.1870442 PMID:33588677

Dittman, J. M., Maiden, K., Matulewicz, A. T., Beaird, G., Lockeman, K., & Dow, A. (2021). A flexible customizable virtual escape room approach for interprofessional learners. *Journal of Interprofessional Education & Practice*, *24*, 100455. doi:10.1016/j.xjep.2021.100455

Dörnyei, Z., & Ushioda, E. (2021). *Teaching and Researching Motivation* (3rd ed.). Routledge. doi:10.4324/9781351006743

Dreimane, S. (2019). Gamification for education: Review of current publications. In L. Daniela (Ed.), *Didactics of smart pedagogy* (pp. 453–464). Springer. doi:10.1007/978-3-030-01551-0_23

Dzyubenko, S. V., Sergeyeva, M. G., & Samokhin, I. S. (2021). Improvement of Research Competencies of School Teachers in Context of Modernization of National Education. *Nauchnyi Dialog*, (2), 303–321. doi:10.24224/2227-1295-2018-2-303-321

Earle, A. J. (2022). A How to Guide and Template for Designing a Puzzle Based Escape Room Game. *CourseSource*, *9*. doi:10.24918/cs.2022.8

Ebrahimzadeh, M., & Alavi, S. (2017). The effect of digital video games on EFL students' language learning motivation. *Teaching English with Technology*, *17*(2), 87–112.

Educause. (2011). *7 things you should know about gamification*. Retrieved from http://www.educause.edu/library/resources/7-things-you-should-know-about-gamification

El Sayary, A., Forawi, S., & Mansour, N. (2015). STEM Education and Problem-Based Learning. In The Routledge International Handbook of Research on Teaching Thinking (pp. 357-365). Routledge.

Elford, D., Lancaster, S. J., & Jones, G. A. (2021). Stereoisomers, not stereo enigmas: A stereochemistry escape activity incorporating augmented and immersive virtual reality. *Journal of Chemical Education*, *98*(5), 1691–1704. doi:10.1021/acs.jchemed.0c01283

Ellis, R. (2015). *Understanding Second Language Acquisition* (2nd ed.). Oxford University Press.

Ellsworth-Lyman, P. (2021). *The Do-It-Yourself Escape Room Book*. Skyhorse Publishing.

Elmqaddem, N. (2019). Augmented Reality and Virtual Reality. Myth or Reality? *International Journal of Emerging Technologies in Learning*, *14*(3), 234–242. doi:10.3991/ijet.v14i03.9289

EMBL-EBI. (n.d.). *EMBL-EBI Services*. https://www.ebi.ac.uk/Tools

Eppmann, R., Bekk, M., & Klein, K. (2018). Gameful experience in gamification: Construction and validation of a gameful experience scale. *Journal of Interactive Marketing, Elsevier*, *43*, 98–115. doi:10.1016/j.intmar.2018.03.002

Esteve, F., Adell, J., & Gisbert, M. (2014). Diseño de un entorno 3D para el desarrollo de la competencia digital docente en estudiantes universitarios: usabilidad, adecuación y percepción de utilidad [Design of a 3D environment for the development of digital teaching competence in university students: usability, adequacy and perception of utility]. *Revista Latinoameericana de Tecnología Educativa*, *13*(2), 35–47.

Estriegana, R., Medina-Merodio, J. A., & Barchino, R. (2019). Analysis of competence acquisition in a flipped classroom approach. *Computer Applications in Engineering Education*, *27*(1), 49–64. doi:10.1002/cae.22056

Estudante, A., & Dietrich, N. (2020). Using augmented reality to stimulate students and diffuse escape game activities to larger audiences. *Journal of Chemical Education*, *97*(5), 1368–1374. doi:10.1021/acs.jchemed.9b00933

Etxeandia-Pradera, J. I., Martinez-Uribe, D., Bellver-Pradas, F., Gonzalez-Piqueras, J. C., Nacher, J., & Aguilar, E. J. (2021). Training Psychiatry Residents in Descriptive Psychopathology: A Systematic Review. *Psychopathology*, *54*(1), 1–17. doi:10.1159/000512791 PMID:33611314

Etxeberria, F. (2008). Videojuegos consumo y educación [Video games, consumption and education]. In Videojuegos: una herramienta educativa del "homo digitalis." Universidad de Salamanca.

Eukel, H. N., Frenzel, J. E., & Cernusca, D. (2017). Educational Gaming for Pharmacy Students Design and Evaluation of a Diabetes hemed Escape room. *American Journal of Pharmaceutical Education*, *81*(7), 62–65.

Eukel, H. N., Frenzel, J. E., & Cernusca, D. (2017). Educational Gaming for Pharmacy Students-Design and Evaluation of a Diabetes-themed Escape Room. *American Journal of Pharmaceutical Education*, *81*(7), 6265. doi:10.5688/ajpe8176265 PMID:29109566

Eukel, H., & Morrell, B. (2021). Ensuring educational escape-room success: The process of designing, piloting, evaluating, redesigning, and re-evaluating educational escape rooms. *Simulation & Gaming*, *52*(1), 18–23. doi:10.1177/1046878120953453

EZ EdTech! (2020). *Everything You Need to Know to Make a DIGITAL ESCAPE THE ROOM! Step by Step Tutorial.* YouTube. https://youtu.be/RT7sSLKvtxs

Fakunle, O., & Higson, H. (2021). Interrogating theoretical and empirical approaches to employability in different global regions. *Higher Education Quarterly*, *75*(4), 525–534. doi:10.1111/hequ.12345

Fernández, A. (2009). *Metodologías activas para la formación en competencias* [Active methodologies for competency training]. Universidad Politécnica de Valencia.

Fernández, M. R., & Valverde, J. (2014). A Community of Practice: An Intervention Model based on Computer Supported Collaborative Learning. *Comunicar: Media Education Research Journal*, *21*(42), 97–105. doi:10.3916/C42-2014-09

Fernández, M., Pascual, H. M., & Romero, M. A. (2018). Características del alumnado de los grados de Magisterio en las nuevas metodologías del EEES [Characteristics of the students of the degrees of Teaching in the new methodologies of the EHEA]. In C. Monge & P. Gómez (Eds.), *Innovando la docencia desde la formación del profesorado* (pp. 87–107). Editorial Síntesis.

Ferreiro-González, M., Amores-Arrocha, A., Espada-Bellido, E., Aliaño-González, M. J., Vázquez-Espinosa, M., González-de-Peredo, A. V., Sancho-Galán, P., Álvarez-Saura, J. Á., Barbero, G. F., & Cejudo-Bastante, C. (2019). Escape Classroom: Can you solve a crime using the analytical process? *Journal of Chemical Education*, *96*(2), 267–273. doi:10.1021/acs.jchemed.8b00601

Ferrer-Sargues, F. J., Baixauli, P. E. K., Carmenate-Fernández, M., Rodríguez-Salvador, G., Domínguez, J. Á. G., Martínez-Olmos, F. J., & Valtueña-Gimeno, N. (2021). Escape-cardio: Gamification in cardiovascular physiotherapy. An observational study. *Nurse Education Today*, *106*, 105062. Advance online publication. doi:10.1016/j.nedt.2021.105062 PMID:34304100

Filsecker, M., & Hickey, D. T. (2014). A multilevel analysis of the effects of external rewards on elementary students' motivation, engagement and learning in an educational game. *Computers & Education*, *75*, 136–148. doi:10.1016/j.compedu.2014.02.008

First, M. B., Erlich, M. D., Adler, D. A., Leong, S., Dixon, L. B., Oslin, D. W., Goldman, B., Koh, S., Levine, B., Berlant, J. L., & Siris, S. G. (2019). How the DSM is used in clinical practice. *The Journal of Nervous and Mental Disease*, *207*(3), 157–161. doi:10.1097/NMD.0000000000000953 PMID:30768542

Flanagan, S. (2015). How does storytelling within higher education contribute to the learning experience of early years students? *Journal of Practice Teaching & Learning*, *13*(2-3), 146–168. doi:10.1921/jpts.v13i2-3.822

Flecha, R., & Molina, S. (2015). Actuaciones educativas de éxito como base de una política educativa basada en evidencias [Successful educational actions as the basis of an evidence-based educational policy]. *Avances en Supervisión Educativa*, *32*, 1–18. doi:10.23824/ase.v0i23.23

Fletcher, G. (2019). Ingress Rooms: Sustainable and Scalable Games for Learning. *Proceedings of the European Conference on Games Based Learning*, 227-234. 10.34190/GBL.19.166

Fluyau, D. (2018). Integrating DSM/ICD, research domain criteria, and descriptive psychopathology in teaching and practice of psychiatry. *Frontiers in Psychiatry*, *9*, 484. doi:10.3389/fpsyt.2018.00484 PMID:30344498

Forkosh Baruch, A., & Meishar Tal, H. (2019). Strategies for Developing Mobile Location-Based Learning Activities by Teachers. In Mobile Technologies in Educational Organizations (pp. 85-95). IGI Global. doi:10.4018/978-1-5225-8106-2.ch005

Fotaris, P., & Mastoras, T. (2019, October). Escape rooms for learning: A systematic review. In *Proceedings of the European Conference on Games Based Learning* (pp. 235-243). Academic Press.

Fotaris, P., Mastoras, T., Leinfellner, R., & Rosunally, Y. (2016). Climbing up the leaderboard: An empirical study of applying gamification techniques to a computer programming class. *Electronic Journal of E-Learning, 14*(2), 94-110.

Fotaris, P., & Mastoras, T. (2019). *Escape rooms for learning: A systematic review. In Proceedings of the 13th European Conference on Games Based Learning, Dinamarca.* Universidad de Dinamarca del Sur. https://bit.ly/3c4q09v

Fotaris, P., & Mastoras, T. (2019). Escape rooms for learning: a systematic review. *Proceedings of the 13th European Conference on Games Based Learning ECGBL 2019*, 9.

Fotaris, P., & Mastoras, T. (2019). Escape rooms for learning: A systematic review. *Proceedings of the European Conference on Games-Based Learning,* 235–243. 10.34190/GBL.19.179

Fotaris, P., & Mastoras, T. (2019, October). Escape rooms for learning: A systematic review. In *Proceedings of the European Conference on Games Based Learning* (pp. 235-243).

Foulds, J. L., & Forbes, K. L. (2021). Escaping the Routine Journal Club, Virtually. *Medical Education*, *55*(5), 635–635. doi:10.1111/medu.14482

Franco, P., & DeLuca, D. (2019). Learning through action: Creating and implementing a strategy game to foster innovative thinking in higher education. *Simulation & Gaming*, *50*(1), 23–43. doi:10.1177/1046878118820892

Freixa, M. (2017). *Professorat novell: Copetències docents a l'inici de l'exercici professional* [Novice teaching staff: Teaching skills at the beginning of the professional practice]. Agencia per la Qualitat del Sistema Universitari de Catalunya.

Frenk, J., Chen, L., Bhutta, Z. A., Cohen, J., Crisp, N., Evans, T., Fineberg, H., Garcia, P., Ke, Y., Kelley, P., Kistnasamy, B., Meleis, A., Naylor, D., Pablos-Mendez, A., Reddy, S., Scrimshaw, S., Sepulveda, J., Serwadda, D., & Zurayk, H. (2010). Health professionals for a new century: Transforming education to strengthen health systems in an interdependent world. *Lancet*, *376*(9756), 1923–1958. doi:10.1016/S0140-6736(10)61854-5 PMID:21112623

Friedman, D., & Sunder, S. (1994). *Experimental methods. Cambridge Books.* Cambridge Books. doi:10.1017/CBO9781139174176

Friedrich, C., Teaford, H., Taubenheim, A., & Sick, B. (2020). Interprofessional health care escape room for advanced learners. *The Journal of Nursing Education*, *59*(1), 46–50. doi:10.3928/01484834-20191223-11 PMID:31945176

Fuentes, A., Parra, M. E., López, J., & Segura, A. (2020). Learning mathematics with emerging methodologies—The escape room as a case study. *Mathematics, 8*(9), 1586. doi:10.3390/math8091586

Fullerton, T. (2008). *Game design workshop: A playcentric approach to creating innovative games*. Morgan Kaufman. doi:10.1201/b13172

Fu, Q. K., & Hwang, G. J. (2018). Trends in mobile technology-supported collaborative learning: A systematic review of journal publications from 2007 to 2016. *Computers & Education, 119*, 129–143. doi:10.1016/j.compedu.2018.01.004

Galloway, N., Numajiri, T., & Rees, N. (2020). The 'internationalisation', or 'Englishisation', of higher education in East Asia. *Higher Education, 80*(3), 395–414. doi:10.100710734-019-00486-1

García Lazaro, I. (2019). Escape room como propuesta de gamificación en educación [Escape room as a gamification proposal in education]. *Revista Educativa Hekademos, 27*, 71–79.

García, I. (2019). Escape room como propuesta de gamificación en educación [Escape room as a proposal for gamification in education]. *Revista Educativa Hekademos, 27*, 71–79. https://hekademos.com/index.php/hekademos/article/view/17

García-Lázaro, I. (2019). Escape room como propuesta de gamificación en educación [Escape room as a gamification proposal in education]. *Revista Educativa Hekademos*, (27), 71-79. https://hekademos.com/index.php/hekademos/article/view/17/7

García, P. A., González, V., & Serrano, J. L. (2020). La habitación de escape como estrategia en la resolución de problemas [The escape room as a problem solving strategy]. *REDU. Revista de Docencia Universitaria, 18*(2), 97–114. doi:10.4995/redu.2020.13573

García-Tudela, P. A., Solano-Fernández, I. M., & Sánchez-Vera, M. M. (2020). Análisis de una Escape Room Educativa en clase de matemáticas en educación primaria [Analysis of an Educational Escape Room in mathematics class in primary education]. *REDIMAT – Journal for Research in Mathematics Education, 9*(3), 273–297. doi:10.17583/redimat.2020.4437

Gardner, S. (2016). A Genre-Instantiation Approach to Teaching for Specific Academic Purposes: Student Writing in Business, Economics and Engineering. *Writing & Pedagogy, 8*(1), 1–25. doi:10.1558/wap.v8i1.27934

Garmen, P., Rodríguez, C., García, T., García, P., & Suárez, N. (2018). El potencial de los videojuegos para intervenir con dificultades de aprendizaje [The potential of video games to intervene with learning difficulties]. *Novatica*. https://www.novatica.es/el-potencial-de-los-videojuegos-para-intervenir-con-dificultades-de-aprendizaje

Garritz, A., & Ortega-Villar, N. A. (2013). El aspecto afectivo en la enseñanza universitaria. Cómo cinco profesores enseñan el enlace químico en la materia condensada [The affective aspect in university education. How five professors teach chemical bonding in condensed matter]. In V. Mellado, L. J. Blanco, A. B. Borrachero, & J. A. Cárdenas (Eds.), *Las emociones en la enseñanza y el aprendizaje de las ciencias y las matemáticas* (Vol. 2, pp. 277–304). UEX-DEPROFE.

Garwood, J. (2020). Escape to learn! An innovative approach to engage students in learning. *The Journal of Nursing Education, 59*(5), 278–282. doi:10.3928/01484834-20200422-08 PMID:32352543

Garzón, J., Kinshuk, A., Baldris, S., Gutiérrez, J., & Pavón, J. (2020). How do pedagogical approaches affect the impact of augmented reality on education? A meta-analysis and research synthesis. *Educational Research Review, 31*, 1–19. doi:10.1016/j.edurev.2020.100334

Gay, G. H., & Betts, K. (2020). From Discussion Forums to eMeetings: Integrating High Touch Strategies to Increase Student Engagement, Academic Performance, and Retention in Large Online Courses. *Online Learning, 24*(1), 92–117. doi:10.24059/olj.v24i1.1984

Gee, J. P. (2009). Deep learning properties of good digital games: How far can they go? In U. Ritterfeld, M. Cody, & P. Vorderer (Eds.), *Serious games: Mechanisms and effects* (pp. 65–80). Routledge.

Genially. (2022). https://genial.ly/es/

George, D., & Mallery, P. (2003). *SPSS for Windows step by step: A simple guide and reference. 11.0 update* (4th ed.). Allyn & Bacon.

Ghani, A. N. A., Teo, P. C., & Mahadi, N. (2021). Sustainability In Business Education Through Internationalisation: Challenges and the Roles. *Journal of Contemporary Issues in Business and Government, 27*(3), 398.

Giannetto, D., Chao, J., & Fontana, A. (2013). Gamification in a social learning environment. *Issues in Informing Science and Information Technology, 10*, 195–207. doi:10.28945/1806

Gilbert, B. C. T., Clapson, M. L., & Musgrove, A. (2020). ChemEscape, Polymer Chemistry: Solving Interactive Puzzles Featuring Scaffolded Learning to Promote Student Understanding of Polymers and Structure–Property Relationships. *Journal of Chemical Education, 97*(11), 4055–4062. doi:10.1021/acs.jchemed.0c00863

Gkonou, C., Daubney, M., & Dewaele, J. (2017). *New Insights into Language Anxiety: Theory, Research and Educational Implications*. Multilingual Matters. doi:10.21832/9781783097722

Glavas, A., & Stascik, A. (2017). Enhancing positive attitude towards mathematics through introducing Escape Room games. In *Mathematics Education as a Science and a Profession* (pp. 281–294). Element.

Göbel, S., Hardy, S., & Wendel, V. (2010). Serious Games for Health – Personalized Exergames. In *18th ACM International Conference on Multimedia* (pp. 1663–1666). 10.1145/1873951.1874316

Gómez López, M, Manzano Sánchez, D, Sánchez, B.J., & Valero, A. (2022). The War of the Atlethes: una propuesta de gamificación aplicada a la docencia universitaria para favorecer los valores educativos y la responsabilidad. *Espiral. Cuadernos del profesorado, 15*(30), 38-50.

Gómez, J. L., Gómez, J., Albedín, L., Correa, M., González, E., & Cañadas, G. A. (2019). The impact on nursing students'opinons and motivation of using a "Nursing Escape Room" as a teaching game: A descriptive study. *Nurse Education Today, 72*, 73–76. doi:10.1016/j.nedt.2018.10.018 PMID:30453202

Gómez, M. (2020). A COVID-19 intervention: Using digital escape rooms to provide professional development to alternative certification educators. *Journal of Technology and Teacher Education, 28*(2), 425–432.

Gómez-Núñez, M. I., & Cano-Muñoz, M. Á. (2020). El desarrollo de la competencia investigadora: Experiencia online en orientación educativa [The development of research competence: Online experience in educational guidance]. *Revista Educativa Hekademos*, (29), 32-42. https://hekademos.com/index.php/hekademos/article/view/23

Gómez-Núñez, M. I., Cano-Muñoz, M. Á., & Torregrosa, M. S. (2020). *Manual para investigar en educación. Guía para orientadores y docentes indagadores* [Manual for research in education. Guide for counselors and teachers inquirers]. Narcea.

Gómez-Trigueros, I. (2019). Methodologies Gamified as Didactic Resources for Social Sciences. *International Journal of Emerging Technologies in Learning, 14*(23), 193–207. doi:10.3991/ijet.v14i23.10794

González, M., Rodríguez, A., & Padilla, M. T. (2021). La gamificación como estrategia metodológica en la Universidad. El caso de BugaMAP: percepciones y valoraciones de los estudiantes [Gamification as a methodological strategy in the University. The BugaMAP case: students' perceptions and assessments]. *Pixel-Bit. Revista De Medios Y Educación, 63*, 293–324. doi:10.12795/pixelbit.90394

González-Norniella, J., Cano Rodríguez, J. M., Alonso Orcajo, G. A., Pedrayes González, J. F., García Melero, M. E., Fernández Cabanas, M., & Rojas García, C. H. (2018). *Gamificación en el aula: "Escape Room" en tutorías grupales* [Gamification in the classroom: "Escape Room" in group tutorials]. Paper presented at the XXVI Congreso Universitario de Innovación Educativa en las enseñanzas técnicas. Escuela Politécnica de Ingeniería de Gijón.

Google Forms. (2022). https://docs.google.com/forms

Gopin, E. (2014). Finding and Evaluating Great Educational Games. In Z. Yang, H. H. Yang, D. Wu, & S. Liu (Eds.), *Transforming K-12 Classrooms with Digital Technology* (pp. 83–97). IGI Global. doi:10.4018/978-1-4666-4538-7.ch005

Gordillo, A., López-Fernández, D., López-Pernas, S., & Quemada, J. (2020). Evaluating an educational escape room conducted remotely for teaching software engineering. *IEEE Access: Practical Innovations, Open Solutions, 8*, 225032–225051. doi:10.1109/ACCESS.2020.3044380

Gracey, L. (2021). *Taking Among Us! to School.* Retrieved August 3, 2022, from https://blog.tcea.org/taking-among-us-to-school/

Granados, J., López, R., Avello, R., Luna, D., Luna, E., & Luna, W. (2014). Las tecnologías de la información y las comunicaciones, las del aprendizaje y del conocimiento y las tecnologías para el empoderamiento y la participación como instrumentos de apoyo al docente de la universidad del siglo XXI [Information and communication technologies, learning and knowledge technologies and technologies for empowerment and participation as instruments to support the teacher of the university of the XXI century]. *Medisur, 12*, 289-294. https://medisur.sld.cu/index.php/medisur/article/view/2751

Grande-de-Prado, M. (2019). Escape room: mapeo sistemático de literatura científica educativa en español [Manual for research in education. Guide for counselors and teachers inquirers]. In S. Alonso, J. M. Romero, C. Rodríguez-Jiménez, & J. M. Sola (Eds.), *Investigación, Innovación docente y TIC. Nuevos horizontes educativos* (pp. 117–128). Dykinson.

Grande-de-Prado, M., García-Martín, S., Baelo, R., & Abella-García, V. (2020). Edu-Escape Rooms. *Encyclopedia, 1*(1), 12–19. doi:10.3390/encyclopedia1010004

Gribble, C. (2014). *Exploring 'employability' in different cultural contexts.* Final Report: Scoping Study. Society for Research into higher Education (SRHE). Deakin University.

Gros, B. (2008). *Videojuegos y aprendizaje* [Video games and learning]. Graó.

Gros, B. (2009). Certezas e interrogantes acerca del uso de los videojuegos para el aprendizaje. *Comunicación (Cartago), 7*(1), 251–264. https://idus.us.es/handle/11441/58304

Gruber, M. J., Ritchey, M., Wang, S. F., Doss, M. K., & Ranganath, C. (2016). Post-learning Hippocampal Dynamics Promote Preferential Retention of Rewarding Events. *Neuron, 89*(5), 1110–1120. doi:10.1016/j.neuron.2016.01.017 PMID:26875624

Grupel, D., Wennstroem, E., & Moran-Gilad, J. (2022). Escape room—The next generation of problem-based learning? *Clinical Microbiology and Infection, 28*(6), 768–770. doi:10.1016/j.cmi.2022.03.017 PMID:35339676

Guerrero, M. (2016). *Historias más allá de lo filmado fan fiction y narrativa transmedia en series de televisión* [Stories beyond the filmed fan fiction and transmedia narrative in television series]. Universidad Popeu Fabra.

Guigon, G., Humeau, J., & Vermeulen, M. (2018, March). A model to design learning escape games: SEGAM. In 10th International Conference on Computer Supported Education (pp. 191-197). SCITEPRESS-Science and Technology Publications.

Guillén, J. C. (2017). *Neuroeducación en el aula: de la teoría a la práctica* [Neuroeducation in the classroom: from theory to practice]. CreateSpace.

Guimarães, L., & Lima, R. da S. (2021). Active learning application in engineering education: Effect on student performance using repeated measures experimental design. *European Journal of Engineering Education, 46*(5), 1–23. doi:10.1080/03043797.2021.1934406

Gutiérrez, L., Márquez, V., Román, P., Rodriguez, M., Ropero, C., & Molina, G. (2020). Escape rooms as a clinical evaluation method for nursing students. *Clinical Simulation in Nursing, 40*, 73–80. doi:10.1016/j.ecns.2020.05.010

Gyamera, G. O., & Burke, P. J. (2018). Neoliberalism and curriculum in higher education: A post-colonial analysis. *Teaching in Higher Education, 23*(4), 450–467. doi:10.1080/13562517.2017.1414782

Haake, S. (2019). Stealing the exams: using a narrative technique in designing an escape game in university context. In C. Busch (Ed.), *Proceedings of the European Conference on Games-Based Learening* (pp. 1004-1007). Academic Press.

Haake, S. (2019, October). Stealing the Exams: Using Narrative Techniques in Designing an Escape Game in University Context. In European Conference on Games Based Learning (pp. 1004-1007). Academic Conferences International Limited.

Hamari, J., Shernoff, D. J., Rowe, E., Coller, B., Asbell-Clarke, J., & Edwards, T. (2016). Challenging games help students learn: An empirical study on engagement, flow and immersion in game-based learning. *Computers in Human Behavior, 54*, 170–179. doi:10.1016/j.chb.2015.07.045

Hanus, M. D., & Fox, J. (2015). Assessing the effects of gamification in the classroom: A longitudinal study on intrinsic motivation, social comparison, satisfaction, effort, and academic performance. *Computers & Education, 80*, 152–161. doi:10.1016/j.compedu.2014.08.019

Hariadi, M. F., Kuswandi, D., & Wedi, A. (2021). Development of Game-Based Supplementary Listening Materials to Improve Students' Higher Order Thinking Skills. In N.L.S. Nuraini, P.S. Cholifah, T.A. Rini, D. Prestiadi, C. Kurniawan, & K.M. Rahjaro (Eds.), *Proceedings of the International Conference on Information Technology and Education (ICITE 2021)* (pp. 128-133). 10.2991/assehr.k.211210.021

Hawkins, J., Wiles, L., Tremblay, B., & Thompson, B. (2020). Behind the scenes of an educational escape room. *The American Journal of Nursing, 120*(10), 50–56. doi:10.1097/01.NAJ.0000718636.68938.bb PMID:32976152

Heath, H., & Cowley, S. (2004). Developing a grounded theory approach: A comparison of Glaser and Strauss. *International Journal of Nursing Studies, 41*(2), 141–150. doi:10.1016/S0020-7489(03)00113-5 PMID:14725778

Heckelman, L. N., & Bucholz, E. K. (2020). Designing a MATLAB-based escape room. *2020 ASEE Virtual Annual Conference Content Access*. https://peer.asee.org/34402 doi: 10.18260/1-2--34402.

Heckelman, L. N., & Bucholz, E. K. (2020, June). Designing a MATLAB-based Escape Room. *2020 ASEE Virtual Annual Conference Content Access*. 10.18260/1-2--34402

Heim, A. B., Duke, J., & Holt, E. A. (2022). Design, discover, and decipher: Student-developed escape rooms in the virtual ecology classroom. *Journal of Microbiology & Biology Education, 23*(1), 15–22. Advance online publication. doi:10.1128/jmbe.00015-22

Herreid, C. F. (2007). *Start with a Story: The Case Study Method of Teaching College Science*. NSTA press.

Hevia Artime, I., & Fueyo Gutiérrez, A. (2018). Aprendizaje situado en el diseño de entornos virtuales de aprendizaje: Una experiencia de aprendizaje entre pares en una comunidad de pràctica [Learning situated in the design of virtual learning environments: a peer-to-peer learning experience in a community of practice]. *Revista Aula Abierta, 47*(3), 347–354. doi:10.17811/rifie.47.3.2018.347-354

HHMI. (n.d.). *BioInteractive*. https://www.biointeractive.org/

Hirumi, A., Appelman, B., Rieber, L., & Eck, R. V. (2010). Preparing Instructional Designers for Game-Based Learning: Part 1. *TechTrends, 54*(3).

Hisel, J. D., & Pinion, C. Jr. (2020). Student recruitment and engagement in the COVID-19 era. *Journal of Environmental Health, 83*(2), 36–38.

Holmes, C. L., Harris, I. B., Schwartz, A. J., & Regehr, G. (2015). Harnessing the hidden curriculum: A four-step approach to developing and reinforcing reflective competencies in medical clinical clerkship. *Advances in Health Sciences Education: Theory and Practice, 20*(5), 1355–1370. doi:10.100710459-014-9558-9 PMID:25319835

Holzweiss, P. (2021). *How To Create a Virtual Escape Room.* YouTube. https://youtu.be/NXvLgLLzXCE

Huang, B., & Hew, K. F. (2018). Implementing a theory-driven gamification model in higher education flipped courses: Effects on out-of-class activity completion and quality of artifacts. *Computers & Education, 125*, 254–272. doi:10.1016/j.compedu.2018.06.018

Huang, B., Hew, K. F., & Lo, C. K. (2018). Investigating the efects of gamiication-enhanced lipped learning on undergraduate students' behavioral and cognitive engagement. *Interactive Learning Environments, 10*, 1–21.

Huang, R., Ritzhaupt, A. D., Sommer, M., Zhu, J., Stephen, A., Valle, N., Hampton, J., & Li, J. (2020). The impact of gamification in educational settings on student learning outcomes: A meta-analysis. *Educational Technology Research and Development, 68*(4), 1875–1901. doi:10.100711423-020-09807-z

Huotari, K., & Hamari, J. (2012, October). Defining gamification: a service marketing perspective. In *Proceeding of the 16th international academic MindTrek conference* (pp. 17-22). 10.1145/2393132.2393137

Hutchison, J. (2007). Giving birth to someone else's children? A case of disputed maternity. *Journal of College Science Teaching, 37*(1), 25–29.

Ibañez, M. B., & Delgado-Kloss, D. (2018). Augmented Reality for STEM Learning: A Systematic Review. *Computers & Education, 123*, 109–123. doi:10.1016/j.compedu.2018.05.002

Institute of Play. (2014). *Q Design pack, Games and Learning*. http://www.instituteofplay.org/work/projects/q-design-packs/q-games-and-learning-design-pack/

Iuppa, N., & Borst, T. (2010). *End-to-end Game Development: Creating Independent Serious Games and simulations from start to finish.* Elsevier, Focal Press.

Jabarullah, N. H., & Hussain, H. I. (2019). The Effectiveness of Problem-Based Learning in Technical and Vocational Education in Malaysia. *Education + Training, 61*(5), 552–567. doi:10.1108/ET-06-2018-0129

Jabbar, A. I., & Felicia, P. (2015). Gameplay Engagement and Learning in Game-Based LearningA Systematic Review. *Review of Educational Research, 85*(4), 740–779. doi:10.3102/0034654315577210

Jackson, C., & Drake, P. (2019). *101 Puzzles for Low Cost Escape Rooms*. Moosehead Publishing.

Jacobs, G. M., & McCafferty, S. G. (2006). Connections between Cooperative Learning and Second Language Learning and Teaching. In S. G. McCafferty, G. M. Jacobs, & A. C. DaSilva Iddings (Eds.), *Cooperative Learning and Second Language Teaching* (pp. 18–29). Cambridge University Press.

Jambhekar, K., Pahls, R., & Deloney, L. (2019). Benefits of an escape room as a novel educational activity for radiology residents. *Academic Radiology, 27*(2), 276–283. doi:10.1016/j.acra.2019.04.021 PMID:31160173

James, M. (2022). International student recruitment during the pandemic: The unique perspective of recruiters from small to medium-sized higher education institutions. *Higher Education Policy*, 1–19. doi:10.105741307-022-00271-3 PMID:35465058

Jamil, M. D. G. (2010). Promoting Learner Autonomy on a University Course of English for Academic Purposes. *BRAC University Journal*, *7*(1-2), 45–52.

Jenaro, C., Flores, N. E., Poy, R., González, F., & Martínez, E. (2013). Metodologías docentes en la educación superior. Percepciones del profesorado sobre su importancia y uso [Teaching methodologies in higher education. Faculty perceptions of their importance and use]. *Revista de Enseñanza Universitaria*, *39*, 1–16.

Jenkins, H., Purushotma, R., Clinton, K., Weigel, M., & Robinson, A. (2006). *Confronting the challenges of participatory culture: Media education for the 2º Century*. The MacArthur Foundation.

Jeong, J. S., González-Gómez, D., Gallego-Picó, A., & Bravo, J. C. (2019). Effects of active learning methodologies on the students' emotions, self-efficacy beliefs and learning outcomes in a science distance learning course. *JOTSE: Journal of Technology and Science Education*, *9*(2), 217–227. doi:10.3926/jotse.530

Jia, Y., Liu, Y., Xing, Y., & Voida, S. (2017). Designing Leaderboards for Gamification: Perceived Differences Based on User Ranking, Application Domain, and Personality Traits. In G. Mark, & S. Fussell (Eds.), *Proceedings of the 2017 CHI Conference on Human Factors in Computing Systems* (pp. 1949-1960). 10.1145/3025453.3025826

Jibson, M. D., & Seyfried, L. S. (2017). DSM-5 Teaching Materials: A Critical Review. *Academic Psychiatry*, *41*(1), 138–144. doi:10.100740596-016-0614-z PMID:27752943

Jiménez, C., Arís, N., Magreñán Ruiz, A. A., & Orcos, L. (2020). Digital escape room, using Genial.Ly and a breakout to learn Algebra at Secondary Education Level in Spain. *Education in Science*, *10*(10), 271. doi:10.3390/educsci10100271

Jiménez, L. (2017). *El poder y la ciencia de la motivación* [The power and science of motivation]. Autoedición.

Kagel, J., & Roth, A. (2020). *The handbook of experimental economics* (Vol. 2). Princeton University Press.

Kalogiannakis, M., Papadakis, S., & Zourmpakis, A. I. (2021). Gamification in science education. A systematic review of the literature. *Education Sciences*, *11*(1), 22. doi:10.3390/educsci11010022

Kanwar, A., & Carr, A. (2020). The impact of covid-19 on international higher education: New models for the new normal. *Journal of Learning for Development*, *7*(3), 326–333. doi:10.56059/jl4d.v7i3.467

Kapp, K. (2012). *The gamification of learning and instruction*. Pfeiffer.

Kapp, K. (2012). *The gamification of learning and instruction: Game-based methods and strategies for training and education*. John Wiley & Sons.

Kapp, K. (2012). *The Gamification of Learning and Instruction: Game-Based Methods and Strategies for Training and Education*. John Wiley and Sons.

Kapp, K. M. (2012). *The gamification of learning and instruction: game-based methods and strategies for training and education*. John Wiley & Sons.

Kapp, K. M. (2012). *The Gamification of Learning and Instruction: Game-based Methods and Strategies for Training and Education*. John Wiley & Sons.

Ke, F. (2014). An implementation of design-based learning through creating educational computer games: A case study on mathematics learning during design and computing. *Computers & Education*, *73*, 26–39. doi:10.1016/j.compedu.2013.12.010

Keller, J. M. (1987). Development and Use of the ARCS Model of Instrumental Design. *Journal of Instructional Development, 10*(3), 2–10. doi:10.1007/BF02905780

Kestin, T., van den Belt, M., Denby, L., Ross, K., Thwaites, J., & Hawkes, M. (2017). *Getting started with the SDGs in universities: A guide for universities, higher education institutions, and the academic sector*. Academic Press.

Khaleghi, A., Aghaei, Z., & Mahdavi, M. A. (2021). A Gamification Framework for Cognitive Assessment and Cognitive Training: Qualitative Study. *JMIR Serious Games, 9*(2), 1–17. doi:10.2196/21900 PMID:33819164

Kirschner, P. A., & Erkens, G. (2013). Toward a framework for CSCL research. *Educational Psychologist, 48*(1), 1–8. doi:10.1080/00461520.2012.750227

Klisch, Y., Miller, L. M., Wang, S., & Epstein, J. (2012). The impact of a science education game on students' learning and perception of inhalants as body pollutants. *Journal of Science Education and Technology, 21*(2), 295–303. doi:10.100710956-011-9319-y PMID:23926416

Knoll, M., & Brickmann, M. (2018). Concept for a generic serious Escape Game for virtual and physical teams. In Edulearn 18. 10th International Conference on Education and New Learning Technology:(Palma, 2nd-4th of July, 2018). Conference proceedings (pp. 10022-10026). IATED Academy.

Konopka, C., Adaime, M. B., & Mosele, P. H. (2015). Active Teaching and Learning Methodologies: Some Considerations. *Creative Education, 6*(14), 1536–1545. doi:10.4236/ce.2015.614154

Koster, R. (2005). *A Theory of Fun for Game Design*. Paraglyph Press.

Kostka, I., & Maliborska, V. (2016). Using Turnitin to Provide Feedback on L2 Writers' Texts. *TESL-EJ, 20*(2), 1–22.

Krashen, S. (1982). *Principles and Practice in Second Language Acquisition*. Elsevier.

Krath, J., Schürmann, L., & von Korflesch, H. F. O. (2021). Revealing the Theoretical Basis of Gamification: A Systematic Review and Analysis of Theory in Research on Gamification, Serious Games and Game-Based Learning. *Computers in Human Behavior, 125*, 1–33. doi:10.1016/j.chb.2021.106963

Kroski, E. (2020). What Is a Digital Breakout Game? *Library Technology Reports, 56*, 5–7.

Kupfer, D. (2014). DSM-5: New opportunities and challenges for teaching and training. *Academic Psychiatry, 38*(1), 58–60. doi:10.100740596-013-0002-x PMID:24488597

Kusainov, A., Yessenova, K., Kassymova, R., Moldassan, K., & Sembayeva, A. (2021). Comparative analysis of the process of training education managers in educational institutions. *International Journal for Research in Vocational Education and Training, 8*(2), 186–207. doi:10.13152/IJRVET.8.2.3

Kutzin, J. M. (2019). Escape the room: Innovative approaches to interprofessional education. *The Journal of Nursing Education, 58*(8), 474–480.

Labrador, E. (2020). *Gamificación, juegos serios y ABJ* [Gamification, serious games and BPA]. Retrieved April 10, 2022, from http://emil-lab.eu/gamificacion-serious-games-y-abj

Laerke Weitze, C. (2014). Developing Goals and Objectives for Gameplay and Learning. In K. Schrier (Ed.), *Learning, education and games. Volume one: Curricular and design considerations*. Carnegie Mellon University.

Landers, R. N., & Callan, R. C. (2011). Casual social games as serious games: The psychology of gamification in undergraduate education and employee training. In M. Ma & A. Oikonomou (Eds.), Serious games and edutainment applications (pp. 399-423). Springer.

Landers, R. N. (2014). Developing a theory of gamified learning: Linking serious games and gamification of learning. *Simulation & Gaming*, *45*(6), 752–768. doi:10.1177/1046878114563660

Landers, R. N., Armstrong, M. B., & Collmus, A. B. (2017). How to use game elements to enhance learning: Applications of the theory of gamified learning. In *Serious games and edutainment applications* (pp. 457–483). Springer. doi:10.1007/978-3-319-51645-5_21

LaPaglia, J. A. (2020). Escape the evil professor! Escape room review activity. *Teaching of Psychology*, *47*(2), 141–146. doi:10.1177/0098628320901383

Lathwesen, C., & Belova, N. (2021). Escape rooms in STEM teaching and learning—Prospective field or declining trend? A Literature Review. *Education Sciences*, *11*(6), 308–308. doi:10.3390/educsci11060308

Lázaro, I. G. (2019). Escape Room como propuesta de gamificación en educación. *Revista Educativa Hekademos*, *27*, 71–79.

Lee, J., & Hammer, J. (2011). Gamification in Education: What, How, Why Brother? *Academic Exchange Quarterly*, *15*(2), 1–5.

Lee, M., & Bong, M. (2019). Relevance of Goal Theories to Language Learning Research. *System*, *86*(2), 102–122. doi:10.1016/j.system.2019.102122

Levchyk, I., Chaikovska, H., Yankovych, O., Kuzma, I., & Rozhko-Pavlyshyn, T. (2021). Formation of sustainable development competencies in primary school children. *Journal of Education Culture and Society*, *12*(2), 341–360. doi:10.15503/jecs2021.2.341.360

Ley Orgánica 2/2006, de 3 de mayo (BOE del 4 de mayo), de educación (LOE).

Licorish, S. A., Owen, H. E., Daniel, B., & George, J. L. (2018). Students' perception of Kahoot!'s influence on teaching and learning. *Research and Practice in Technology Enhanced Learning*, *13*(9), 1–23. doi:10.118641039-018-0078-8

Lien, Y.H., Wang, C.P., Wang, S.M., Li, C.T., & Hou, H.T. (2019). Designing an Escape Room Educational Game and a Game-Based Learning Activity for Science Learning: An Analysis of Learning Achievement and Flow State. In *8th International Congress on Advanced Applied Informatics (IIAI-AAI)* (pp. 1049-1050). IEEE. https://doi.ieeecomputersociety.org/10.1109/IIAI-AAI.2019.00221

Lightbown, P. M., & Spada, N. (2013). *How Languages Are Learned* (4th ed.). Oxford University Press.

Lima, C. D., Bastos, R. C., & Varvakis, G. (2020). Digital learning platforms: An integrative review to support internationalization of higher education. *Educação em Revista*, *36*, 36. doi:10.1590/0102-4698232826

Lister, M. (2015). Gamification: The effect on student motivation and performance at the post-secondary level. *Issues and Trends in Educational Technology*, *3*(2), 1–22. doi:10.2458/azu_itet_v3i2_lister

Liu, C., Patel, R., Ogunjinmi, B., Briffa, C., Allain-Chapman, M., Coffey, J., … Shelmerdine, S. C. (2020). Feasibility of paediatric radiology escape room for undergraduate education. *Insights Imagine,* 11.

Llorens-Largo, F., Gallego-Durán, F. J., Villagrá-Arnedo, C. J., Compañ-Rosique, P., Satorre-Cuerda, R., & Molina-Carmona, R. (2016). Gamificación del Proceso de Aprendizaje: Lecciones Aprendidas [Manual for research in education. Guide for counselors and teachers inquirers]. *VAEP-RITA*, *4*(1), 25–32.

Löffler, E., Schneider, B., Zanwar, T., & Asprion, P. M. (2021). Cysecescape 2.0—A virtual escape room to raise cybersecurity awareness. *International Journal of Serious Games*, *8*(1), 59–70. doi:10.17083/ijsg.v8i1.413

López Martín, R. (2019). La Innovación docente en la formación del profesorado. Principios y directrices de futuro [Teaching innovation in teacher training. Principles and guidelines for the future]. *Crónica, Revista científico profesional de la pedagogía y psicopedagogia, 4,* 83-94.

López-Noguero, F. (2008). Hacia un espacio europeo de aprendizaje para toda la vida. Evolución y desarrollo de la Educación Permanente en la Unión Europea [Towards a European area of lifelong learning. Evolution and development of lifelong learning in the European Union]. *Pedagogía social. Revista interuniversitaria, 15,* 123-135.

López-Pernas, S., Gordillo, A., Barra, E., & Quemada, J. (2019). Analyzing learning effectiveness and students' perception of an educational escape room in a Programming Course in Higher Education. *IEEE Access: Practical Innovations, Open Solutions*, *7*, 184221–184234. doi:10.1109/ACCESS.2019.2960312

López, S., Gordillo, A., Barra, E., & Quemada, J. (2019). Examining the use of an educational escape room for teaching programming in a higher education setting. *IEEE Access: Practical Innovations, Open Solutions*, *7*, 31723–31737. doi:10.1109/ACCESS.2019.2902976

López-Secanell, I., & Ortega-Torres, E. (2020). Escape room educativa: Concepción de los futuros maestros de Educación Secundaria en especialidad de Educación Física y Tecnología sobre la experiencia de diseñar y participar en una escape room educativa [Educational escape room: conception of future teachers of Secondary Education in specialty of Physical Education and Technology on the experience of designing and participating in an educational escape room]. *Didacticae*, (8), 1–17. doi:10.1344/did.2020.8.176-192

Lozada, C., & Betancur, S. (2016). La gamificación en la educación superior: Una revisión sistemática [Gamification in higher education: a systematic review]. *Revista Ingenierías Universidad de Medellín*, *16*(31), 97–124. doi:10.22395/rium.v16n31a5

Lozano-López, C. M., & Lázaro, M. N. (2019). Escape FolRoom: Propuesta de juego integrada en clase de Formación y Orientación Laboral [Escape FolRoom: Proposal of integrated game in class of Training and Career Orientation]. *International Journal of Nursing Education*, (4), 91–105. doi:10.24310/IJNE2.2.2019.7453

Lozano, R. (2011). De las TIC a las TAC: Tecnologías del aprendizaje y del conocimiento [From ICT to TAC: learning and knowledge technologies]. *Anuario ThinkEPI*, *5*, 44–47.

Ludwing-Hardman, S., & Dunlap, J. C. (2003). Learner support services for online students: Scaffolding for success. *International Review of Research in Open and Distance Learning*, *4*(1), 1–8.

Macías-Guillén, A., Díez, R. M., Serrano-Luján, L., & Borrás-Gené, O. (2021). Educational Hall Escape: Increasing Motivation and Raising Emotions in Higher Education Students. *Education Sciences*, *11*(9), 527. doi:10.3390/educsci11090527

Magadán, M., & Rivas, J. (2021). El empleo de los recursos audiovisuales como herramienta de aprendizaje [The use of audiovisual resources as a learning tool]. *Techno Review. International Technology. Science and Society Review*, *10*(2), 185–198. doi:10.37467/gkarevtechno.v10.3118

Magadán, M., & Rivas, J. I. (2022a). Gamificación del aula en la enseñanza superior online: El uso de Kahoot [Classroom gamification in online higher education: The use of Kahoot]. *Campus Virtuales*, *11*(1), 137–152. doi:10.54988/cv.2022.1.978

Magadán, M., & Rivas, J. I. (2022b). Percepções dos alunos de pós-graduação em face da gamificação em sala de aula com Quizizz [Percepções dos alunos de pós-graduação em face da gamificação em sala de aula com Quizizz]. *Texto Livre*, *15*, e36941. doi:10.35699/1983-3652.2022.36941

Majid, S., Liming, Z., Tong, S., & Raihana, S. (2012). Importance of soft skills for education and career success. *International Journal for Cross-Disciplinary Subjects in Education*, *2*(2), 1037–1042. doi:10.20533/ijcdse.2042.6364.2012.0147

Majuri, J., Koivisto, J., & Hamari, J. (2018). Gamification of education and learning: A review of empirical literature. In *Proceedings of the 2nd international GamiFIN conference, GamiFIN 2018*. CEUR-WS.

Majuri, J., Koivisto, J., & Hamari, J. (2018). Gamification of education and learning: A review of empirical literature. *Proceedings of the 2nd international GamiFIN Conference, CEUR-WS.*

Makri, A., Vlachopoulos, D., & Martina, R. (2021). Digital escape rooms as innovative pedagogical tools in education: A systematic literature review. *Sustainability, 13*(8), 4587. doi:10.3390u13084587

Manzano León, A., Aguilar Parra, J. M., Fernández, J. M., Trigueros Ramos, R., Martínez Martínez, A. M., & Rodríguez Ferrer, J. M. (2022). Play and learn: Influence of gamification and game-based learning in the reading processes of secondary school students. *Revista de Psicodidáctica, 27*(1), 38–46.

Manzano, A., Camacho, P., Guerrero, M. Á., Guerrero, L., Aguilar, J. M., Trigueros, R., & Alias, A. (2021). Between level up and game over: A systematic literature review of gamification in education. *Sustainability, 13*(4), 2247. doi:10.3390u13042247

Marczewki, A. (2013). *Game Mechanics in Gamification.* Gamified UK. https://www.gamified.uk/2013/01/14/game-mechanics-in-gamification

Marczewski, A. (2012). *Gamification: A Simple Introduction.* Lulu.

Marczewski, A. (2018). *Gamification. Even ninja monkeys like to play.* Unicorn Edition.

Marín, V., & Ramírez, A. (2012). Posibilidades educativas de los videojuegos y juegos digitales en educación inclusiva [Educational possibilities of video games and digital games in inclusive education]. In V. Marín (Coord.), Los videojuegos y los juegos digitales como materiales educativos (pp. 165-191). Síntesis.

Marín, V., Morales, M., & Reche, E. (2020). Aprendizaje con videojuegos con realidad aumentada en educación primaria [Learning with video games with augmented reality in primary education]. *Revista de Ciencias Sociales, 26*(2), 94-112.

Marne, J., Wisdom, B., Kim-Bang, H., & Labat, J-M. (2012). *The six facets of serious game design: a methodology enhanced by our design pattern library.* Paper presented in 21st Century Learning for 21st Century Skills, Saarbrücken, Germany.

Martina, R., & Göksen, S. (2020). Developing educational escape rooms for experiential entrepreneurship education. *Entrepreneurship Education and Pedagogy, 16*, 495–527. doi:10.1177/2515127420969957

Martín-Gómez, P., García Rodríguez, M. L., & Mena Marcos, J. J. (2022). El prácticum en el grado de maestro/a de educación infantil: Análisis de diarios docentes [The practicum in the degree of teacher of early childhood education: Analysis of teaching diaries]. *Revista Complutense De Educación, 33*(1), 131–140. doi:10.5209/rced.73838

Martín-González, E., Godoy-Giménez, M., Fernández-Martín, P., León, J., González-Rodríguez, A., Mora, S., Sánchez-Kuhn, A., Carmona, I., García-Pérez, Á., Flores Cubos, P., Estévez, A. F., & Moreno, M. (2021). Escape room as a tool to improve the motivation and commitment of students. *Actas 15th International Technology, Education and Development Conference INTED2021*, 5868-5873. 10.21125/inted.2021.1180

Mashuhara, H., Mishan, F., & Tomlinson, B. (2017). *Practice and Theory for Materials Development.* Cambridge Scholars Publishing.

Mateu, G. (2021). Innovative education management: An empirical study. *TEC Empresarial, 15*(3), 2–17. doi:10.18845/te.v15i3.5760

Mayoral Marín, S. (2021). *Desarrollo e investigación de aplicaciones software formativas en enseñanza superior con el motor gráfico Unreal Engine*. Academic Press.

Mazarakis, A. (2015). Using Gamification for Technologically Enhanced Learning: The Case of Feedback Mechanisms. *Bulletin of the IEEE Technical Committee on Learning Technology*, *17*(4), 6–9.

McGrath, N., & Bayerlein, L. (2013). Engaging online students through the gamification of learning materials: The present and the future. In *ASCILITE-Australian Society for Computers in Learning in Tertiary Education Annual Conference* (pp. 573–577). ASCILITE.

Medina, V. L., & Martín, H. V. (2022). Analysis of the validity of a psychopathology escape room in high education. In *16th International Technology, Education and Development Conference Proceedings* (pp. 6536-6536). IATED.

Mellado, V., Borrachero, A. B., Brígido, M., Melo, L. V., Dávila, M. A., Cañada, F., Conde, M. C., Costillo, E., Esteban, R., Martínez, G., Ruiz, C., Sánchez, J., Garritz, A., Mellado, L., Vázquez, B., Jiménez, R., & Bermejo, M. L. (2014). Las emociones en la enseñanza de las ciencias [Emotions in science teaching]. *Enseñanza de las Ciencias*, *32*(3), 11–36. doi:10.5565/rev/ensciencias.1478

Menon, D., & Romero, M. (2020). Game mechanics supporting a learning and playful experience in educational escape games. In *Global perspectives on gameful and playful teaching and learning* (pp. 143–162). IGI Global. doi:10.4018/978-1-7998-2015-4.ch007

Mercer, S. (2012). The Complexity of Learner Agency. *Journal of Applied Language Studies*, *6*(2), 41–59.

MERLOT. (n.d.). https://merlot.org

Merrian, S. B. (1988). *Case study research in education*. San Francisco, CA: Jossey Bass.Murtonen, M., & Salmento, H. (2019). Broadening the Theory of Scientific Thinking for Higher Education. In M. Murtonen & K. Balloo (Eds.), *Redefining scientific thinking for higher education* (pp. 3–29). Palgrave Macmillan.

Michos, V. M. (2017). Gamification in foreign language teaching. In M. Stanišić (Ed.), *Sinteza 2017- International Scientific Conference on Information Technology and Data Related Research Proceedings* (pp. 511-516). Singidunum University.

Millán, M. (2017). La gamificación en la evaluación continua de los procesos de enseñanza-aprendizaje en la educación superior. Una aportación basada en la evidencia en el ámbito de las Ciencias Sociales [Gamification in the continuous evaluation of teaching-learning processes in higher education. An evidence-based contribution in the field of Social Sciences]. In J. Ruiz-Palmero, J. Sánchez-Rodríguez, & E. Sánchez-Rivas (Eds.), *Innovación docente y uso de las TIC en educación* (p. 114). UMA Editorial.

Miller, S. (2015). *The art of the escape room*. Retrieved from https://www.newsweek.com/2015/05/01/art-escape-room-323150.html

Miller, K., Sonnert, G., & Sadler, P. (2018). The influence of students' participation in STEM competitions on their interest in STEM careers. *International Journal of Science Education*, *8*(2), 95–114. doi:10.1080/21548455.2017.1397298

Mok, K. H., Xiong, W., Ke, G., & Cheung, J. O. W. (2021). Impact of COVID-19 pandemic on international higher education and student mobility: Student perspectives from mainland China and Hong Kong. *International Journal of Educational Research*, *105*, 101718. doi:10.1016/j.ijer.2020.101718 PMID:35719275

Molins, L. L., & Vidiella, M. C. P. (2018). La competencia de aprender a aprender en el marco de la educación superior [The competence to learn to learn within the framework of higher education]. *Revista Iberoamericana de Educación*, *78*(2), 59–76. doi:10.35362/rie7823183

Monnot, M., Laborie, S., Hébrard, G., & Dietrich, N. (2020). New approaches to adapt escape game activities to large audience in chemical engineering: Numeric supports and students' participation. *Education for Chemical Engineers, 32*, 50–58. doi:10.1016/j.ece.2020.05.007

Monteiro, B. M. M., Ono, B. H. V. S., Silva, E. D. S. M., & Souza, J. C. (2020). Acrostics and Crosswords as Advance Organizers to Meaningful Learning in Medical Education. *Creative Education, 11*(8), 1213–1222. doi:10.4236/ce.2020.118090

Moon, C. J., Walmsley, A., & Apostolopoulos, N. (2018). Governance implications of the UN higher education sustainability initiative. *Corporate Governance: The International Journal of Business in Society.*

Moore, L., & Campbell, N. (2020). Effectiveness of an escape room for interprofessional learning. *Medical Education, 54*(11), 1047–1048. doi:10.1111/medu.14327 PMID:32885479

Moore, L., & Campbell, N. (2021). Effectiveness of an escape room for undergraduate interprofessional learning: A mixed methods single group pre-post evaluation. *BMC Medical Education, 21*(1), 1–8. doi:10.118612909-021-02666-z PMID:33879150

Moral Pérez, M., Fernández García, L. C., & Guzmán Duque, A. P. (2016). Proyecto Game to Learn: aprendizaje basado en juegos para potenciar las inteligencias lógico-matemática, naturalista y lingüística en primaria [Game to Learn Project: game-based learning to enhance logical-mathematical, naturalistic and linguistic intelligences in primary school]. *Píxel-Bit. Revista de Medios y Educación, 49*, 177–193.

Morell, B., Eukel, H., & Santurri, L. (2020). Soft skills and implications for future professional practice: Qualitative findings of a nursing education escape room. *Nurse Education Today, 93*, 104462. doi:10.1016/j.nedt.2020.104462 PMID:32791421

Moreno Fuentes, E., Perales Molada, R., & Hidalgo Navarrete, J. (2019). Estudio cualitativo sobre el uso de la gamificación en la Educación Superior para promover la motivación del alumnado [Qualitative study on the use of gamification in Higher Education to promote student motivation]. *Aula de Encuentro, 21*(2), 5–26. doi:10.17561/ae.v21.n2.1

Moreno, E. (2019). El "Breakout EDU" como herramienta clave para la gamificación en la formación inicial de maestros/as [The "Breakout EDU" as a key tool for gamification in the initial training of teachers]. *EDUTEC. Revista electrónica de tecnología educativa*, (67), 66-79.

Moreno-Fuentes, E. (2019). El "Breakout EDU" como herramienta clave para la gamificación en la formación inicial de maestros/as [The "Breakout EDU" as a key tool for gamification in initial teacher training]. *Revista electrónica de tecnología educativa, 67*, 66-79.

Moreno-Martínez, N., Leiva, J. J., & Matas, A. (2016). Mobile learning, Gamificación y Realidad Aumentada para la enseñanza-aprendizaje de idiomas [Mobile learning, Gamification and Augmented Reality for language teaching-learning]. *International Journal of Educational Research and Innovation, 6*, 16–34.

Morris, J. (2020). *Escape Rooms in Education: A Practical Guide*. Amazon Publication.

Murphree, C., & Vafa, S. S. (2020). Use of escape rooms in education. In *Society for Information Technology & Teacher Education International Conference*. Association for the Advancement of Computing in Education (AACE).

Murphy, L., & Roca de Larios, J. (2010). Feedback in Second Language Writing: An Introduction. *International Journal of English Studies, 10*(2), i–xv.

Musgrove, H. B., Ward, W. M., & Hiatt, L. A. (2021). Escape from Quant Lab: Using Lab Skill Progression and a Final Project to Engage Students. *Journal of Chemical Education, 98*(7), 2307–2312. doi:10.1021/acs.jchemed.1c00026

Mystakidis, S., Cachafeiro, E., & Hatzilygeroudis, I. (2019, July). Enter the serious E-scape room: A cost-effective serious game model for deep and meaningful E-learning. In 2019 10th International Conference on Information, Intelligence, Systems and Applications (IISA) (pp. 1-6). IEEE.

Naik, N. (2017). The use of GBL to teach mathematics in higher education. *Innovations in Education and Teaching International, 54*(3), 238–246. doi:10.1080/14703297.2015.1108857

Nakamura, J., & Csikszentmihalyi, M. (2002). The concept of flow. In C. R. Snyder & S. J. Lopez (Eds.), *Handbook of Positive Psychology* (pp. 89–105). Oxford University Press.

NASA. (n.d.). *EarthData: Open Access for Open Science.* https://www.earthdata.nasa.gov/learn/find-data

Nassaji, H., & Kartchava, E. (2021). *The Cambridge Handbook of Corrective Feedback in Second Language Learning and Teaching.* Cambridge University Press. doi:10.1017/9781108589789

Nathenson, M. B., & Henderson, E. S. (2019). *Using Student Feedback to Improve Learning Materials.* Routledge.

National Science Teaching Association. (n.d.). *NCCSTS Case Collection.* https://www.nsta.org/case-studies

Navarro, C., & Pérez, I. J. (2022). El escape room como estrategia didáctica en el Máster de Profesorado [The escape room as a didactic strategy in the Master's Degree in Teachers]. *Retos, 44*, 221–231. https://dialnet.unirioja.es/servlet/articulo?codigo=8127983

Navarro-Mateos, C., & Pérez-López, I. J. (2021). El escape room como estrategia didáctica en el Máster de Profesorado [Escape room as a didactical strategy in the Master's degree in Teacher Learning]. *Retos, 44*, 221–231. doi:10.47197/retos.v44i0.91035

Nawahdah, M. I. (2018). Gamifying the teaching and learning process in an advanced computer programming course. In H. Egi, T. Yuizono, N. Baloian, T. Yoshino, & S. Ichimura (Eds.), *10th International Conference on CollabTech 2018: Collaboration Technologies and Social Computing* (Vol. 1, pp. 89–95). Springer International Publishing. 10.1007/978-3-319-98743-9_7

NCBI. (n.d.). *All Resources - Tools.* https://www.ncbi.nlm.nih.gov/guide/all/

Negre i Walczak, C. (2017). 'BreakoutEdu', microgamificación y aprendizaje significativo ['BreakoutEdu', micro-gamification and meaningful learning]. *Educaweb.* https://www.educaweb.com/noticia/2017/07/26/breakoutedu-microgamificacion-aprendizaje-significativo-15068/

Negre, C., & Carrion, S. (2020). *Desafío en el aula: Manual práctico para llevar los juegos de escape educativos al aula* [Classroom Challenge: A practical manual for bringing educational escape games into the classroom]. Paidós Eduación.

Neira, E., Clares, J., & Sánchez, J. (2021). New audience dimensions in streaming platforms the second life of Money Heist on Netflix as a case study. *El Profesional de la Información, 30*(1), e300113. doi:10.3145/epi.2021.ene.13

Nephew, S., & Sunasee, R. (2021). An Engaging and Fun Breakout Activity for Educators and Students about Laboratory Safety. *Journal of Chemical Education, 98*(1), 186–190. doi:10.1021/acs.jchemed.0c01109

Neumann, K. L., Alvarado-Albertorio, F., & Ramírez-Salgado, A. (2020). Online approaches for implementing a digital escape room with preservice teachers. *Journal of Technology and Teacher Education, 28*(2), 415–424.

Neuwirth, L. S., Jović, S., & Mukherji, B. R. (2021). Reimagining higher education during and post-COVID-19: Challenges and opportunities. *Journal of Adult and Continuing Education, 27*(2), 141–156. doi:10.1177/1477971420947738

Neves, J., & Hewitt, R. (2021). *Students highlight the challenges of their 2021 academic experience*. Advance HE. Available at: https://www.advance-he.ac.uk/news-and-views/students-highlight-challenges-their-2021-academic-experience

New Media Consortium. (2018). *NMC Horizon Report - 2017 Higher Education Edition*. Retrieved from: http://cdn.nmc.org/media/2017-nmc-horizon-report-he-EN.pdf

Nghia, T. L. H., Giang, H. T., & Quyen, V. P. (2019). At-home international education in Vietnamese universities: Impact on graduates' employability and career prospects. *Higher Education, 78*(5), 817–834. doi:10.100710734-019-00372-w

Nhamo, G., & Mjimba, V. (2020). The context: SDGs and institutions of higher education. In *Sustainable development goals and institutions of higher education* (pp. 1–13). Springer. doi:10.1007/978-3-030-26157-3_1

Nicholson, S. (2015). *Peeking behind the locked door: A survey of Escape room facilities*. https://goo.gl/1eaC7G

Nicholson, S. (2015). *Peeking Behind the Locked Door: A Survey of Escape Room Facilities*. https://scottnicholson.com/pubs/erfacwhite.pdf

Nicholson, S. (2015). *Peeking Behind the Locked Door: A Survey of Escape Room Facilities*. White Paper. Available at Http://Scottnicholson.Com/Pubs/Erfacwhite.Pdf

Nicholson, S. (2015b). *Peeking behind the locked door: A survey of escape room facilities*. https://scottnicholson.com/pubs/erfacwhite.pdf

Nicholson, S. (2016). *The State of Escape: Escape Room Design and Facilities Meaningful Play*. https://scottnicholson.com/pubs/stateofescape.pdf

Nicholson, S. (n.d.). *Scott Nicholson Website*. https://scottnicholson.com/

Nicholson, S. (2012, March). Completing the experience: Debriefing in experiential educational games. In *Proceedings of the 3rd international conference on society and information technologies* (pp. 117-121).

Nicholson, S. (2015a). A RECIPE for Meaningful Gamification. In T. Reiners & L. C. Wood (Eds.), *Gamification in Education and Business* (pp. 1–20). Springer International Publishing. doi:10.1007/978-3-319-10208-5_1

Nicholson, S. (2018). Creating engaging escape rooms for the classroom. *Childhood Education, 94*(1), 44–49. doi:10.1080/00094056.2018.1420363

Nicholson, S., & Cable, L. (2020). Unlocking the potential of puzzle-based learning: Designing escape rooms and games for the classroom. *Sage (Atlanta, Ga.)*.

NOAA. (n.d.). *National Centers for Environmental Information*. https://www.ncei.noaa.gov/

Novak, J., Lozos, J. C., & Spear, S. E. (2019). Development of an interactive escape room intervention to educate college students about earthquake preparedness. *Nature Hazards Review, 20*(1).

Nybo, S. E., Sahr, M., Young, M., Axford, K., Sohn, M., Lyons, M., & Klepser, M. (2020). Design of a large-scale escape room for first-year pharmacy student orientation. *Currents in Pharmacy Teaching & Learning, 12*(11), 1340–1347. doi:10.1016/j.cptl.2020.06.002 PMID:32867932

O'Brien, K., & Pitera, J. (2019). Gamifying instruction and engaging students with Breakout EDU. *Journal of Educational Technology Systems, 48*(2), 192–212. doi:10.1177/0047239519877165

O'Donovan, S. (2012). *Gamification of the games course*. The University of Cape Town.

O'Donovan, S., Gain, J., & Marais, P. (2013). A case study in the gamification of a university-level games development course. *Proceedings of the South African Institute for Computer Scientists and Information Technologists Conference*, 242-251. 10.1145/2513456.2513469

Oestreich, J. H., Hunt, B., & Cain, J. (2021). Grant deadline: An escape room to simulate grant submissions. *Currents in Pharmacy Teaching & Learning*, *13*(7), 848–854. doi:10.1016/j.cptl.2021.03.013 PMID:34074517

Oliva, H.A. (2016). La gamificación como estrategia metodológica en el contexto educativo universitario [Gamification as a methodological strategy in the university educational context]. *Realidad y reflexión, 44*, 30-47.

Omorodion, F., Coltman, L., Babajide, O., & Etowa, E. (2021). Learning Experiences and Challenges facing Black International Students at the University of Windsor. *Teaching Culturally and Linguistically Diverse International Students in Open and/or Online Learning Environments: A Research Symposium Learning Experiences and Challenges facing Black Int.*

Onecha, B., Sanz, J., & López, D. (2019). Los límites de la ludificación en la enseñanza de la arquitectura. La técnica del Escape Room [The limits of gamification in architecture education. The Escape Room technique]. *Journal of Interdisciplinary Studies in Architecture and Urbansim, 12*(12), 122–133. doi:10.26754/ojs_zarch/zarch.2019123549

Onecha-Pérez, B., Sanz-Prat, J., & López-Valdés, D. (2019). Los límites de la ludificación en la enseñanza de la arquitectura. La técnica del Escape Room [The limits of gamification in the teaching of architecture. The Escape Room technique]. *ZARCH: Journal of Interdisciplinary Studies in Architecture and Urbanism*, (12), 122-133.

Ortega-Ruipérez, B. (2018). Directrices pedagógicas para la docencia de innovación y TIC en la formación de futuros docentes [Pedagogical guidelines for teaching innovation and ICT in the training of future teachers]. In R. Roig-Vila (Ed.), *El compromiso académico y social a través de la investigación e innovación educativas en la Enseñanza Superior* (pp. 345–355). Octaedro.

Ortiz-Colón, A. M., Jordán, J., & Ágreda, M. (2018). Gamificación en educación: Una panorámica sobre el estado de la cuestión [Gamification in education: an overview of the state of the art]. *Educação e Pesquisa*, *44*(1). Advance online publication. doi:10.15901678-4634201844173773

Otemaier, K. R., Zanese, P. G., Grein, E. E., & Bosso, N. S. (2020). Educational escape room for teaching Mathematical Logic in computer courses. *SBC—Proceedings of the SBGames,* 7-10.

Ouariachi, T., & Van Dam, M. (2022). Educational innovation to address climate change issues: The emerging trend of (online) escape rooms. In *Handbook of Research on Using Disruptive Methodologies and Game-Based Learning to Foster Transversal Skills* (pp. 263–278). IGI Global. doi:10.4018/978-1-7998-8645-7.ch013

Ouariachi, T., & Wim, E. (2020). Escape rooms as tools for climate change education: An exploration of initiatives. *Environmental Education Research*, *26*(8), 1193–1206. doi:10.1080/13504622.2020.1753659

Pacheco, M., & Causado, R. (2018). El aprendizaje basado en videojuegos y la gamificación como Estrategias para construir y vivir la convivencia escolar [Classroom Challenge: A practical manual for bringing educational escape games into the classroom]. *Revista CEDOTIC, 3*(1), 59-80. http://investigaciones.uniatlantico.edu.co/revistas/index.php/CEDOTIC/article/view/1971

Pakhalov, A., & Rozhkova, N. (2020). Escape rooms as tourist attractions: Enhancing visitors' experience through new technologies. *Journal of Tourism, Heritage & Services Marketing, 6*(2), 55–60. https://papers.ssrn.com/sol3/papers.cfm?abstract_id=3748091

Palincsar, A. S. (1998). Social Constructivist Perspectives on Teaching and Learning. *Annual Review of Psychology, 49*(1), 345–375. doi:10.1146/annurev.psych.49.1.345 PMID:15012472

Paniagua, A., & Istance, D. (2018). *Teachers as designers of learning environments. In Educational Research and Innovation.* OECD. doi:10.1787/9789264085374-en

Parra, M. E., Segura, A., Morales, M., & López, E. (2020). Relación de los factores asociados en el desarrollo de experiencias gamificadas [List of factors associated with the development of gamified experiences]. *Campus Virtuales, 9*(1), 113–123. http://www.uajournals.com/ojs/index.php/campusvirtuales/article/view/641

Parra-González, M. E., & Segura-Robles, A. (2019). Traducción y validación de la escala de evaluación de experiencias gamificadas (GAMEX) [Translation and validation of the gamified experiences evaluation scale (GAMEX)]. *Bordón. Revista de Pedagogía, 71*(4), 87–89. doi:10.13042/Bordon.2019.70783

Pedrinaci, E., Caamaño, A., Cañal, P., & de Pro, A. (2012). *11 ideas clave: El desarrollo de la competencia científica* [11 key ideas: The development of scientific competence]. Grao.

Pegrum, M. (2016). Languages and Literacies for Digital Lives. In E. Martín-Monje, I. Elorza, & B. García Riaza (Eds.), *Technology-Enhanced Language Learning for Specialized Domains* (pp. 9–22). Routledge.

Pegrum, M. (2019). *Mobile Lenses on Learning: Language and Literacies on the Move.* Springer. doi:10.1007/978-981-15-1240-7

Pekrun, R. (2005). Progress and open problems in educational emotion research. *Learning and Instruction, 15*(5), 497–506. doi:10.1016/j.learninstruc.2005.07.014

Peleg, R., Yayon, M., Katchevich, D., Moria-Shipony, M., & Blonder, R. (2019). A lab-based chemical escape room: Educational, mobile, and fun! *Journal of Chemical Education, 96*(5), 955–960. doi:10.1021/acs.jchemed.8b00406

Peñalver, E. A., & Urbieta, A. S. (2020). Enhancing medical translation skills through a gamified experience. Failure or success? *Panace, 21*(51), 4–12.

Pérez Vázquez, E., Gilabert Cerdá, A., & Lledó Carreres, A. (2019). Gamificación en la educación universitaria: El uso del *escape room* como estrategia de aprendizaje [Gamification in university education: The use of the *escape room* as a learning strategy]. In R. Roig-Vila (Ed.), *Investigación e innovación en la educación superior. Nuevos contextos, nuevas ideas* (pp. 660–668). Octaedro.

Pérez, E., Gilabert, A., & Lledó, A. (2019). Gamificación en la educación universitaria: El uso del escape room como estrategia de aprendizaje [Gamification in university education: The use of the escape room as a learning strategy]. In R. Roig-Vila (Ed.), *Investigación e innovación en la Enseñanza Superior. Nuevos contextos, nuevas ideas* (pp. 660–668). Octaedro.

Pérez-López, I. J. (2020). *De las 7 Bolas de Dragón a los 7 reinos de Poniente: viajando por la ficción para transformar la realidad* [From the 7 Dragon Balls to the 7 kingdoms of Westeros: traveling through fiction to transform reality]. CopiDeporte.

Pérez-López, I. J., Rivera, C., & Trigueros, C. (2017). The Prophecy of the Chosen Ones": An Example of Gamification Applied to University Teaching. *Revista Internacional de Medicina y Ciencias de la Actividad Física y del Deporte, 17*(66), 243–260.

Pérez-López, I., & García Rivera, E. (2017). Formar docentes, formar personas: Análisis de los aprendizajes logrados por estudiantes universitarios desde una experiencia de [Train teachers, train people: analysis of the learning achieved by university students from an experience of]. *Signo y Pensamiento, 70*(36), 112–129. doi:10.11144/Javeriana.syp36-70.fdfp

Pérez-Manzano, A., & Almela-Baeza, J. (2018). Gamificación transmedia para la divulgación científica y el fomento de vocaciones procientíficas en adolescentes [Transmedia gamification for the popularization of science and the promotion of pro-science vocations in adolescents]. *Comunicar, 26*(55), 93–103.

Pérez-Manzano, A., & Almela-Baeza, J. (2018). Gamification and Transmedia for Scientific Promotion and for Encouraging Scientific Careers in Adolescents. *Comunicar: Media Education Research Journal, 26*(55), 93–103. doi:10.3916/C55-2018-09

Pfeifer, M., Völker, B., Böttcher, S., Köhler, S., & Scholl, P. M. (2021, March). Teaching Embedded Systems by Constructing an Escape Room. In *Proceedings of the 52nd ACM Technical Symposium on Computer Science Education* (pp. 1103-1109).

Phelps, A., & Vlachopoulos, D. (2019). Successful transition to synchronous learning environments in distance education: A research on entry-level synchronous facilitator competencies. *Education and Information Technologies, 25*(3), 1511–1527. doi:10.100710639-019-09989-x

Pico, S. (2013). Formación TIC del profesorado para garantizar el éxito en la integración de la tecnología [ICT teacher training to ensure success in technology integration]. *Ítaca:Revista de Filologia, 4*(4), 65–80. doi:10.14198/ITACA2013.4.03

Piñero Charlo, J.C. (2019). Análisis sistemático del uso de salas de escape educativas: estado del arte y perspectivas de futuro [Gamification in education: an overview of the state of the art]. *Espacios, 40*(44).

Piñero, J. C. (2020). Educational escape rooms as a tool for horizontal mathematization: Learning process evidence. *Education Sciences, 10*(9), 213. doi:10.3390/educsci10090213

Pisabarro, A. M., & Vivaracho, C. E. (2018). Gamificación en el aula: Gincana de programación [Gamification in the classroom: programming gymkhana]. *ReVisión, 11*(1), 85–93.

Pisabarro, A. M., & Vivaracho, C. E. (2018). Gamificación en el aula: Gincana de programación [Gamification in the classroom: programming gymkhana]. *ReVisión: Revista de Investigación en Docencia Universitaria de la Informática, 11*(1), 85–93.

PLOS. (n.d.). *Open Data*. https://plos.org/open-science/open-data/

Prat, Q., Camerino, O., & Coiduras, J. L. (2013). Introducción de las TIC en educación física. Estudio descriptivo sobre la situación actual [Introduction of ICT in physical education. Descriptive study on the current situation]. *Apunts. Educación Física y Deportes, 113*, 37-44. .(2013/3).113.03 doi:10.5672/apunts.20140983.es

Prensky, M. (2001). *Digital game-based learning*. McGraw-Hill.

Prensky, M. (2001). Digital native and digital immigrant part 1. *On the Horizon, 9*(5), 1–6. doi:10.1108/10748120110424816

Prensky, M. (2001). Digital natives, digital immigrants, part 2: Do they really think differently? *On the Horizon, 9*(6), 1–6. doi:10.1108/10748120110424843

Prieto, A., Díaz, D., Monserrat, J., & Reyes, E. (2014a). Experiencias de aplicación de estrategias de gamificación a entornos de aprendizaje universitario [Experiences in the application of gamification strategies to university learning environments]. *Revisión, 7*(2), 76–92.

Putz, L. M., Hofbauer, F., & Treiblmaier, H. (2020). Can gamification help to improve education? Findings from a longitudinal study. *Computers in Human Behavior, 110*, 106392. doi:10.1016/j.chb.2020.106392

QAA. (2022). *Subject Benchmark Statement: Biomedical Science and Biomedical Sciences.* https://www.qaa.ac.uk/docs/qaa/quality-code/sbs-biomedical-science-consultation-22.pdf?sfvrsn=cb8a581_4

Quintero, L. E. (2021). *EXPANDEF. La Educación Fïsica y las tecnologías de la información y la comunicación (TIC)* [EXPANDEF. Physical education and information and communication technologies (ICT)]. Autopublicación en Amazon Fullfilment.

Quizizz. (2022). https://quizizz.com/

Qureshi, F. H., & Khawaja, S. (2021). Is Covid-19 Transitioning Cash Cows International Students into Cats? *European Journal of Education Studies*, *8*(7). Advance online publication. doi:10.46827/ejes.v8i7.3816

Rachels, J. R., & Rockinson-szapkiw, A. J. (2017). The effects of a mobile gamification app on elementary students' Spanish achievement and self-efficacy. *Computer Assisted Language Learning*, *31*(1-2), 72–89. doi:10.1080/09588221.2017.1382536

Rahim, A. S. A. (2022). Mirror mirror on the wall: Escape a remote virtual stereochemistry lab together. *Journal of Chemical Education*, *99*(5), 2160–2167. doi:10.1021/acs.jchemed.2c00050

Raitskaya, L., & Tikhonova, E. (2019). Habilidades y competencias en la educación superior y más allá. *Revista de Lengua y Educación*, *5*(4), 4–8.

Rambach, J., & Stricker, D. (2022). Advanced Sensory Perception. *Journal of Imaging*, *8*(10). Advance online publication. doi:10.3390/jimaging8100287 PMID:36286381

Ramos-Villagrasa, P. J., Fernández-Campo, A., Oliván, B., Fernández del Río, E., Berges, A., Hernández, S., Huarte, S., & Martín-Peña, J. (2019). Storytelling: Una metodología de aprendizaje activo para la enseñanza de la psicología social en la educación superior [Storytelling: An active learning methodology for teaching social psychology in higher education]. *Suma Psicologica*, *16*(1), 11–19. doi:10.18774/0719-448x.2019.16.349

Rayón Rumayor, L., de las Heras Cuenca, A. M., & Muñoz Martínez, Y. (2011). La creación y gestión del conocimiento en la enseñanza superior: La autonomía, autorregulación y cooperación en el aprendizaje [Train teachers, train people: analysis of the learning achieved by university students from an experience of]. *Revista Iberoamericana de Educación Superior*, *2*(4), 103–122.

RCSB Protein Data Bank. (n.d.). *Mol* 3D Viewer*. https://www.rcsb.org/3d-view

Rebollo Catalán, M. Á., García Pérez, R., Barragán Sánchez, R., Buzón García, O., & Vega Caro, L. (2008). Las emociones en el aprendizaje online [Emotions in online learning]. *RELIEVE-Revista Electrónica de Investigación y Evaluación Educativa, 14*(1). https://www.uv.es/RELIEVE/v14n1/RELIEVEv14n1_2.htm

Recommendation of the European Parliament and of the Council of 18 December 2006 on Key Competences for Lifelong Learning (2006/962/EC). Retrieved from https://eur-lex.europa.eu/eli/reco/2006/962/oj

Reinartz, W., & Saffert, P. (2013). Creativity in advertising: When it works and when it doesn't. *Harvard Business Review*, *91*(6), 106–111.

Reinhardt, J. (2019). *Gameful Second and Foreign Language Teaching and Learning: Theory, Research, and Practice*. Palgrave Macmillan. doi:10.1007/978-3-030-04729-0

Reinhardt, J., & Sykes, J. M. (2014). Digital Game and Play Activity in L2 Teaching and Learning. *Language Teaching & Technology*, *18*(2), 2–8.

Reinhardt, J., & Thorne, S. (2016). Metaphors for Digital Games and Language Learning. In F. Farr & L. Murray (Eds.), *The Routledge Handbook of Language Learning and Technology* (pp. 415–430). Routledge.

Revuelta, F. I. (2015). *Gamification to learning motivation.* Ponencia presentada en Conference Asia-Paciic Economic Cooperation - Observatory of Best Practices with ICT, Lima, Perú.

Richter, G., Raban, D. R., & Rafaeli, S. (2015). Studying gamification: The effect of rewards and incentives on motivation. In T. Reiners & L. C. Wood (Eds.), *Gamification in education and business* (pp. 21–46). Springer International Publishing. doi:10.1007/978-3-319-10208-5_2

Ricoy, M.C. & Fernandez-Rodriguez, J. (2013). La percepcion que tienen los estudiantes universitarios sobre la evaluacion: un estudio de caso [College students' perception of assessment: a case study]. *Educación XX1, 16*(2), 321-342.

Rivera-Trigueros, I., López-Alcarria, A., Ruiz-Padillo, D.-P., Olvera-Lobo, M. D., & Gutiérrez-Pérez, J. (2022b). A Digital Escape Rooms for Learning General Physics in HEIs: Building the Universe in Five Rooms. In Handbook of Research on Using Disruptive Methodologies and Game-Based Learning to Foster Transversal Skills (pp. 376-396). IGI Global. doi:10.4018/978-1-7998-8645-7.ch019

Rivera-Trigueros, I., López-Alcarria, A., Ruiz-Padillo, D.-P., Olvera-Lobo, M. D., & Gutiérrez-Pérez, J. (2022a). Design and Implementation of an Escape Room About the Discovery of the Periodic Table. In *Handbook of Research on Using Disruptive Methodologies and Game-Based Learning to Foster Transversal Skills* (pp. 397–422). IGI Global. doi:10.4018/978-1-7998-8645-7

Robson, K., Plangger, K., Kietzmann, J. H., McCarthy, I., & Pitt, L. (2015). Is it all a game? Understanding the principles of gamification. *Business Horizons, 58*(4), 411–420.

Rodríguez, F., & Santiago, R. (2015). *Cómo motivar a tu alumnado y mejorar el clima en el aula* [How to motivate your students and improve classroom climate]. Texto-Digital.

Rodríguez-Ferrer, J. M., Manzano-León, A., Cangas, A. J., Aguilar-Parra, J. M., Fernández-Jiménez, C., Fernández-Campoy, J. M., Luque de la Rosa, A., & Martínez-Martínez, A. M. (2022). Acquisition of Learning and Empathy Towards Patients in Nursing Students Through Online Escape Room: An Exploratory Qualitative Study. *Psychology Research and Behavior Management, 15*, 103–110. doi:10.2147/PRBM.S344815 PMID:35046736

Rodríguez, G., Gil, J., & García, E. (1999). *Metodología de la investigación cualitativa* [Qualitative research methodology]. Aljibe.

Rodzuan, A. R., Ahmad, A., Ali, N. M., & Nordin, A. I. (2018). Understanding Emotional Engagement Amongst Primary School Children for Designing Gamification in Learning. *Advanced Science Letters, 24*(3), 1599–1602. doi:10.1166/asl.2018.11117

Rogers, J., & Revesz, A. (2020). *Experimental and quasi-experimental designs*. Routledge.

Romero, A., López, A., Tejada, E., & Bilbao, N. (2019). Calidad tecnopedagógica del escape room en educación superior [Techno-pedagogical quality of the escape room in higher education]. In E. Sánchez-Rivas, J. Ruiz-Palmero, & E. Sánchez-Vega (Coords.), *Innovación y tecnología en contextos educativos* (pp. 389-398). UMA editorial.

Romiszowski, A. (2003). The future of E-learning as an educational innovation: Factors influencing project success and failure. *Revista Brasileira de Aprendizagem Aberta e a Distância, 2*(1), 1–14.

Ross, R., & de Souza-Daw, A. (2021, April). Educational Escape Rooms as an Active Learning Tool for Teaching Telecommunications Engineering. In Telecom (Vol. 2, No. 2, pp. 155-166). MDPI. doi:10.3390/telecom2020010

Ross, J. M., Wright, L., & Arikawa, A. Y. (2021). Adapting a classroom simulation experience to an online escape room in nutrition education. *Online Learning, 25*(1), 238–244. doi:10.24059/olj.v25i1.2469

Ross, R., & Bell, C. (2019, August). Turning the classroom into an escape room with decoder hardware to increase student engagement. In *2019 IEEE Conference on Games (CoG)* (pp. 1-4). IEEE. 10.1109/CIG.2019.8848020

Ross, R., & Bennett, S. (2020). *Increasing engagement with engineering escape rooms.* IEEE Transactions on Games.

Ross, R., Hall, R., & Ross, S. L. (2022). Converting Course Material to Educational Escape Room Formats. In O. Bernardes, V. Amorim, & A. Carrizo (Eds.), *Handbook of Research on the Influence and Effectiveness of Gamification in Education* (pp. 164–188). IGI Global. doi:10.4018/978-1-6684-4287-6.ch009

Ross, S., & Morrison, G. (2013). Experimental research methods. In *Handbook of research on educational communications and technology* (pp. 1007–1029). Routledge.

Rouse, W. (2017). Lessons learned while escaping from a zombie: Designing a Breakout EDU game. *The History Teacher, 50*(4), 553–564.

Ruiz, R., & Tesouro, M. (2013). Beneficios e inconvenientes de las nuevas tecnologías en el aprendizaje del alumno. Propuestas formativas para alumnos, profesores y padres [How do we learn? A scientific approach to learning and teaching]. *Revista Educación y futuro digital, 5,* 17-25. https://redined.mecd.gob.es/xmlui/bitstream/handle/11162/118963/EYFD_72.pdf

Ruíz-Martín, H. (2020). *¿Cómo aprendemos? Una aproximación científica al aprendizaje y la enseñanza* [How do we learn? A scientific approach to learning and teaching]. Graó editorial.

Ryan, R. M., & Deci, E. L. (2000). Self-determination theory and the facilitation of intrinsic motivation, social development, and well-being. *The American Psychologist, 55*(1), 68–78. doi:10.1037/0003-066X.55.1.68 PMID:11392867

Sabariego, M., Cano, A. B., Gross, B., & Piqué, B. (2020). Competencia investigadora e investigación formativa en la formación inicial del docente [Research competence and formative research in initial teacher training]. *Contextos Educativos. Review of Education*, (26), 239–259. doi:10.18172/con.4326

Sabitzer, B., Groher, I., Hörmann, C., & Hofer, A. (2021). Toward the implementation of escape room games in an educational context. *Proceedings of the European Conference on Games Based Learning*, 925-928. 10.34190/GBL.21.125

Sáez de Cámara, E., Fernández, I., & Castillo-Eguskitza, N. (2021). A holistic approach to integrate and evaluate sustainable development in higher education. The case study of the University of the Basque Country. *Sustainability, 13*(1), 392. doi:10.3390u13010392

Sailer, M., Hense, J. U., Mayr, S. K., & Mandl, H. (2017). How gamification motivates: An experimental study of the effects of specific game design elements on psychological need satisfaction. *Computers in Human Behavior, 69*, 371–380. doi:10.1016/j.chb.2016.12.033

Sailer, M., & Homner, L. (2020). The Gamification of Learning: A Meta-Analysis. *Educational Psychology Review, 32*(1), 77–112. doi:10.100710648-019-09498-w

Sainz, B., de la Torre, I., López, M., Aguiar, J., & de Castro, C. (2019). Aplicación plural de herramientas para gamificar. Análisis y comparativa [Plural application of tools to gamify. Analysis and comparison]. *V Congreso de Innovación Educativa y de Docencia en Red*, 991. http://ocs.editorial.upv.es/index.php/INRED/INRED2019/paper/viewFile/10467/4798

Saleem, A., Noori, N., & Ozdamli, F. (2021). Gamification applications in E-learning: A literature review. *Technology, Knowledge and Learning*, 1–21. doi:10.1007/s10758-020-09487-x

Salen, K., & Zimmerman, E. (2004). *Rules of play: Game design fundamentals.* MIT Press.

Salinas, J. (2004). Innovación docente y uso de las TIC en la enseñanza universitaria [College students' perception of assessment: a case study]. *Revista Universidad y Sociedad Del Conocimiento, 1*(1), 1–16.

Salinas, M. I. (2011). *Entornos virtuales de aprendizaje en la escuela: tipos, modelo didáctico y rol del docente* [Virtual learning environments at school: types, didactic model and role of the teacher]. Universidad Católica de Argentina.

Salmento, H., Murtonen, M., & Kiley, M. (2021). Understanding Teacher Education Students' Research Competence Through Their Conceptions of Theory. *Frontiers in Education, 6*, 763803. doi:10.3389/feduc.2021.763803

Salter, N. P., & Conneely, M. R. (2015). Structured and Unstructured Discussion Forums as Tools for Student Engagement. *Computers in Human Behavior, 46*, 18–25. doi:10.1016/j.chb.2014.12.037

Salvador-Gómez, A., Escrig-Tena, A. B., Beltrán-Martín, I., & García-Juan, B. (2022). El escape room virtual: herramienta docente universitaria para el desarrollo de competencias transversales y para la retención del conocimiento [The virtual escape room: university teaching tool for the development of transversal competences and for the retention of knowledge]. *Tecnología. Ciência & Educação (Bauru), 21*, 7–48. doi:10.51302/tce.2022.664

San Martin, L., Walsh, H., Santerre, M., Fortkiewicz, J., & Nicholson, L. (2021). Creation of a "Patient" hospital escape room experience to reduce harm and improve quality of care. *Journal of Nursing Care Quality, 36*(1), 38–42. doi:10.1097/NCQ.0000000000000485 PMID:32282503

Sánchez Martin, J., Zamora Polo, F., Corrales Serrano, M., & Luque Sendra, A. (2017). Exit for success. Gamifying science and engineering university-level classes using escape-room pedagogy. *Heliyon.*

Sanchez, E., & Plumettaz-Sieber, M. (2018). Teaching and learning with escape games from debriefing to institutionalization of knowledge. In *International conference on games and learning alliance*. Springer.

Sánchez-Caballé, A., Gisbert Cervera, M., & Esteve-Mon, F. M. (2020). The digital competence of university students: A systematic literature review. *Revista de Psicologia. Ciències de l'Educació i de l'Esport, 38*(1), 63–74.

Sánchez, D. R., Langer, M., & Kaur, R. (2020). Gamification in the classroom: Examining the impact of gamified quizzes on student learning. *Computers & Education, 144*, 103666. doi:10.1016/j.compedu.2019.103666

Sánchez-Martín, J., Corrales-Serrano, M., Luque-Sendra, A., & Zamora-Polo, F. (2020). Exit for success. Gamifying science and technology for university students using escape-room. A preliminary approach. *Heliyon, 6*(7), e04340. doi:10.1016/j.heliyon.2020.e04340 PMID:32671257

Sánchez-Rodríguez, J., Ruiz Palmero, J., Sánchez Rivas, E., & Sánchez Vega, E. (2019). *Escape room y breakout. Aproximación bliométrica en bases de datos* [Escape room and breakout. Bibliometric approach in databases]. Universidad de Málaga. https://riuma.uma.es/xmlui/bitstream/handle/10630/19157/EscapeRoom_BreakOut.pdf?sequence=1&isAllowed=y

Sánchez, T., Barbeito, S., Becerra-García, J. A., & Calvo, A. (2017). Progress of Health Psychology regulation: A comparison between countries. *Acta Medica International, 4*(1), 46–50. doi:10.5530/ami.2017.4.9

Santamaría Urbieta, A. & Alcalde Peñalver, E. (2019). Escaping from the English classroom. Who will get out first? *Aloma: Revista de psicologia, ciències de l'educació i de l'esport Blanquerna, 37*(2), 83-92.

Santamaría Urbieta, A., & Alcalde Peñalver, E. (2021). Multimodal Discourse in Digital Storytelling: An Assessment Tool Proposal. *Computer Assisted Language Learning Electronic Journal, 22*(2), 14-25. http://callej.org/journal/22-2/Urbieta-Penalver2021.pdf

Santamaría Urbieta, A., & Alcalde Peñalver, E. (2020). Una experiencia universitaria de gamificación en línea o en el aula presencial: ¿es este recurso de aprendizaje posible en ambos entornos? [A gamification university experience online or in the face-to-face classroom: is this learning resource possible in both environments?]. *Revista Brasileira de Lingüística Aplicada, 20*(4).

Santamaría, A. & Alcalde, E. (2019). Escaping from the English classroom. Who will get out first? *Aloma: revista de psicologia, ciències de l'educació i de l'esport Blanquerna, 37*(2), 83-92.

Santamaría, A. & Alcalde, E. (2019). Escaping from the English classroom. Who will get out first? *Revista de psicologia, ciències de l'educació i de l'esport, 37*(2), 83-92.

Santamaría, A., & Alcalde, E. (2019). Escaping from the English classroom. Who will get out first? *Aloma: Revista de Psicologia. Ciències de l'Educació i de l'Esport Blanquerna, 37*(2), 88–92. doi:10.51698/aloma.2019.37.2.83-92

Santos, M. J. Miguel, M. Queiruga-Dios, A., & Encinas, A. H. (2020). Looking for the antidote for contaminated water: learning through and escape game. *Advances in Intelligent System and Computing, 951*, 217-226.

Santos, J. L. G. D., Cunha, K. S. D., Adamy, E. K., Backes, M. T. S., Leite, J. L., & Sousa, F. G. M. D. (2018). Data analysis: Comparison between the different methodological perspectives of the Grounded Theory. *Revista da Escola de Enfermagem da U S P.*, 52. PMID:29668789

Sawyer, T., Eppich, W., Brett-Fleegler, M., Grant, V., & Cheng, A. (2016). More than one way to debrief: A critical review of healthcare simulation debriefing methods. *Journal of the Society for Medical Simulation, 11*(3), 209–217. doi:10.1097/SIH.0000000000000148 PMID:27254527

Scavarda, A., Dias, A., Reis, A., Silveira, H., & Santos, I. (2021). A covid-19 pandemic sustainable educational innovation management proposal framework. *Sustainability, 13*(11), 6391. doi:10.3390u13116391

Schreiber, L. M., & Valle, B. E. (2013). Social Constructivist Teaching Strategies in the Small Group Classroom. *Small Group Research, 44*(4), 395–411. doi:10.1177/1046496413488422

Seebauer, S., Jahn, S., & Mottok, J. (2020, April). Learning from escape rooms? A study design concept measuring the effect of a cryptography educational escape room. In *2020 IEEE Global Engineering Education Conference (EDUCON)* (pp. 1684-1685). IEEE. 10.1109/EDUCON45650.2020.9125333

Selinker, M., & Snyder, T. (2018). *Puzzlecraft: How to Make Every Kind of Puzzle* (F. Heany, Ed.). Lone Shark Games.

Selznick, B., & McCarthy, S. (2020). Toward a theory of social innovation for higher education. In A. J. Fulford (Ed.), Philosophy and Theory in Higher Education (pp. 49–69). Peter Lang. doi:10.3726/PTIHE032020.0004

Selznick, B. S., Dahl, L. S., Youngerman, E., & Mayhew, M. J. (2022). Equitably Linking Integrative Learning and Students' Innovation Capacities. *Innovative Higher Education, 47*(1), 1–21. doi:10.100710755-021-09570-w PMID:34334931

Serra-olivares, J., Garcia-rubio, J., Madrona, P. G., Cejudo, C., & Gonzalez, S. (2018). Estilos de aprendizaje y evaluacion formativa: Estudio con universitarios de Educacion Fisica chilenos [Learning styles and formative assessment: Study with Chilean Physical Education university students]. *SPORT TK-Revista EuroAmericana de Ciencias Del Deporte, 7*(1), 129–137. doi:10.6018/321991

Sexton, S. (2020). Meaningful Learning. In B. Akpan & T. J. Kennedy (Eds.), *Education in Theory and Practice* (pp. 163–175). Springer. doi:10.1007/978-3-030-43620-9_12

Shakeri, H., Singhal, S., Pan, R., Neustaedter, C., & Tang, A. (2017). Escaping together: the design and evaluation of a distributed real-life escape room. In *Proceedings of the Annual Symposium on Computer-Human Interaction in Play*. ACM. 10.1145/3116595.3116601

Sharp, J. G., Hemmings, B., Kay, R., Murphy, B., & Elliott, S. (2016). Academic boredom among students in higher education: A mixed-methods exploration of characteristics, contributors and consequences. *Journal of Further and Higher Education, 41*(5), 657–677. doi:10.1080/0309877X.2016.1159292

Shulman, L. S. (2005). Signature Pedagogies in the Professions. *Daedalus, 134*(3), 52–58. doi:10.1162/0011526054622015

Sierra Daza, M. C., & Fernández-Sánchez, M. R. (2019). Gamificando el aula universitaria. Análisis de una experiencia de Escape Room en educación superior [Train teachers, train people: analysis of the learning achieved by university students from an experience of]. *Revista de estudios y experiencias en educación, 18*(36), 105-115.

Sierra, M. C., & Fernández-Sánchez, M. R. (2019). Gamificando el aula universitaria. Análisis de una experiencia de Escape Room en educación superior [Gamifying the university classroom. Analysis of an Escape Room experience in higher education]. *Revista de Estudios y Experiencias en Educación, 18*(36), 105–115. doi:10.21703/rexe.20191836sierra15

Simões, J., Redondo, R. D., & Vilas, A. F. (2013). A social gamification framework for a k-6 learning platform. *Computers in Human Behavior, 29*(2), 345–353. doi:10.1016/j.chb.2012.06.007

Skeptical Educator. (2020). *Digital Escape Room Playlist.* YouTube. https://www.youtube.com/c/TheSkepticalEducator

Slussareff, M., Braad, E., Wilkinson, P., & Strååt, B. (2016). Games for learning. In R. Dörner, S. Göbel, M. Kickmeier-Rust, M. Masuch, & K. Zweig (Eds.), *Entertainment computing and serious games.* (pp. 189-211). Springer. http://link.springer.com/chapter/10.1007%2F978-3-319-46152-6_9

Smash with GSuite. (n.d.). *BreakoutEDU.* https://sites.google.com/genoaschools.com/breakoutedu/play-here

Sotoca, P. (2020). Rally Edukar: Una propuesta de gamificación que promueve el empoderamiento de la mujer en el deporte [Edukar Rally: A gamification proposal that promotes the empowerment of women in sport]. *EmasF. Revista digital de Educación Física, 65*, 16-31.

Sotoca, P. [@PabloSotoca]. (2019, Apr. 30). *Capítulo 1. Terminó la espera. Arranca la nueva temporada de #LaEFvaEnSerie* [Chapter 1. The wait is over. The new season of #LaEFvaEnSerie begins] [Tweet]. Twitter. https://twitter.com/PabloSotoca/status/1123285948551389186?s=20&t=oQ-TuHlhN9-lhMFYLYmR5Q

Sotoca, P., & Pérez-López, I. (2019). Gamificación educativa: kit de montaje basico [Educational gamification: basic assembly kit]. In Didáctica de la Educación Física en Educación Infantil y Primaria (pp. 393-406). Universidad Internacional de la Rioja.

Strachan, R., & Liyanage, L. (2015). Active student engagement: The heart of effective learning. In Global Innovation of Teaching and Learning in Higher Education (pp. 255-274). Springer.

Summers, R. F., & Kreider, T. R. (2014). DSM-5: A teachable moment. *Academic Psychiatry, 38*(1), 55–57. doi:10.100740596-013-0009-3 PMID:24419821

Sweller, K. (2010). Cognitive Load Theory: Recent Theoretical Advances. In J. L. Plass, R. Moreno, & R. Brüken (Eds.), *Cognitive Load Theory* (pp. 29–47). Cambridge University Press. doi:10.1017/CBO9780511844744.004

Swiss Institute of Bioinformatics. (n.d.). *Expasy: Swiss BioInformatics Resource Portal.* https://www.expasy.org/

Syzdykbayeva, A. D., Bainazarova, T. B., & Aitzhanova, E. N. (2015). Formation of research competence of the future elementary school teachers-in the process of professional training. *International Education Studies, 8*(4), 200–209. doi:10.5539/ies.v8n4p200

Tahir, F., Mitrovic, A., & Sotardi, V. (2022). Investigating the causal relationship between badges and learning outcomes in SQL-Tutor. *Research and Practice in Technology Enhanced Learning*, *17*(1), 1–23. doi:10.118641039-022-00180-4

Talaue, G. M. (2022). Career Adaptability of Jubail University College Students: An Assessment for Employability Potentials. *International Journal of Project Management and Productivity Assessment*, *10*(1), 1–19. doi:10.4018/IJPMPA.297087

Tan, C., & Liu, M. (2016). Using ICT in teaching the Chinese language: Practices and reflections from Singapore. In K. Soh (Ed.), *Teaching Chinese Language in Singapore: Retrospect and Challenges* (pp. 45–65). Springer. doi:10.1007/978-981-10-0123-9_4

Tannock, S. (2018). *Educational equality and international students: Justice across orders?* Palgrave Macmillan. doi:10.1007/978-3-319-76381-1

Taraldsen, L. H., Haara, F. O., Lysne, M. S., Jensen, P. R., & Jenssen, E. S. (2020). A review on use of escape rooms in education – touching the void. *Education Inquiry*, *13*(2), 169–184. doi:10.1080/20004508.2020.1860284

Teding van Berkhout, E., & Malouff, J. M. (2016). The efficacy of empathy training: A meta-analysis of randomized controlled trials. *Journal of Counseling Psychology*, *63*(1), 32–41. doi:10.1037/cou0000093 PMID:26191979

Teixes, F. (2015). *Gamificación: Fundamentos y aplicaciones* [Gamification: Fundamentals and applications]. UOC.

Tejado, I., Pérez, E., Traver, J. E., Nuevo-Gallardo, C., Rodríguez, P., & Vinagre, B. M. (2021). Design of an Escape Room to Support Learning of Industrial Process Control in Engineering Degrees. In *INTED2021 Proceedings* (pp. 2171-2180). IATED. 10.21125/inted.2021.0471

Tejedor, E. (2021). El impacto de las tecnologías en el mundo de la enseñanza [The impact of technologies on the world of education]. *Revista de Investigación e Innovación Educativa*, *49*, 33–49.

Tercanli, H., Martina, R., Ferreira Dias, M., Reuter, J., Amorim, M., Madaleno, M., Magueta, D., Vieira, E., Veloso C., Figueiredo, C., Vitória, A., Wakkee, I., Gomes, I., Meireles, G., Daubariene, A., Daunoriene, A., Mortensen, A., Zinovyeva, A., Rivera-Trigueros, I., López Alcarria, A., Rodríguez-Díaz, Olvera-Lobo, P. M.D., RuizPadillo, D.P., & Gutiérrez-Pérez, J. (2021). Educational escape rooms in practice: Research, experiences and recommendations. UA Editora. doi:10.34624/rpxk-hc6

The King's University. (n.d.). *Centre for Visualization in Science*. https://www.kcvs.ca/

Tobias, S., Fletcher, J. D., Bediou, B., Wind, A. P., & Chen, F. (2014). Aprendizaje multimedia con juegos de ordenador. In R.E. Mayer (Ed.), The Cambridge handbook of multimedia learning (pp.762–784). Cambridge University Press.

Tobias, S., Fletcher, J. D., & Wind, A. P. (2014). Game-Based Learning. In J. M. Spector, M. D. Merril, J. Elen, & M. J. Bishop (Eds.), *Handbook of Research on Educational Communications and Technology* (pp. 485–503). Springer. doi:10.1007/978-1-4614-3185-5_38

Tokuhama, T. (2010). *The new science of teaching and learning: using the best of mind, and education science in the classroom*. Columbia University Teachers College Press.

Torres Martín, C., Acal, C., El Homrani, M., & Mingorance Estrada, Á. C. (2021). Impact on the virtual learning environment due to COVID-19. *Sustainability*, *13*(2), 582. doi:10.3390u13020582

Tseng, H., Yi, X., & Yeh, H. T. (2019). Learning-related soft skills among online business students in higher education: Grade level and managerial role differences in self-regulation, motivation, and social skill. *Computers in Human Behavior*, *95*, 179–186. doi:10.1016/j.chb.2018.11.035

Turner, R. (2012). *The Gamification of EAP*. 12th BUSEL International Conference on Language Teaching Issues: EAP in University Settings, Ankara, Turkey.

Ulloa, R., & Barrantes, E. G. (2008). *Construyendo un escenario para la simulación de ataques en sistemas de agentes* [Building a scenario for the simulation of attacks on agent systems]. Jornadas Chilenas de Computación.

Universidad Internacional de la Rioja. (2021-2022). *Innovación docente e Iniciación a la Investigación Educativa* [Teaching Innovation and Initiation to Educational Research] [Course program]. Author.

University of Colorado Boulder. (n.d.). *Simulation by PhET Interactive Simulations*. https://phet.colorado.edu/

USGS. (n.d.). *Science Data Catalog*. https://data.usgs.gov/datacatalog/

UW Center for Game Science and Institute for Protein Design. (2017). *Foldit Beta. Solve Puzzles for Science*. https://fold.it/

Valero Cerdá, J. I. (2019). *Escape Room for Robotics Academy* [Doctoral dissertation]. Universitat Politècnica de València.

Van Aalderen-Smeets, S. I., & van der Molen, J. H. W. (2015). Improving primary teacher attitudes toward science by attitude-focused professional development. *Journal of Research in Science Teaching, 52*(5), 710–734. doi:10.1002/tea.21218

Van den Beemt, A., Groothuijsen, S., Ozkan, L., & Hendrix, W. (2022). Remote labs in higher engineering education: Engaging students with active learning pedagogy. *Journal of Computing in Higher Education*. Advance online publication. doi:10.100712528-022-09331-4 PMID:35974997

Varys, L. [@RedPajaritos]. (2019, Apr. 30). *Continuamos con el segundo capítulo de esta apasionante temporada... Espero que sigáis con este mismo entusiasmo e ilusión #LaEFvaEnSerie* [We continue with the second chapter of this exciting season... I hope you continue with this same enthusiasm and enthusiasm #LaEFvaEnSerie] [Tweet]. Twitter. https://twitter.com/RedPajaritos/status/1123297647094267905?s=20&t=oQ-TuHlhN9-lhMFYLYmR5Q

Vázquez, A., & Manassero, M. A. (2007). En defensa de las actitudes y emociones en la educación científica (I): Evidencias y argumentos generales [In defense of attitudes and emotions in science education (I): Evidence and general arguments]. *Revista Eureka sobre Enseñanza y Divulgación de las Ciencias, 4*(2), 247-271. http://hdl.handle.net/10498/16108

Veach, C. C. (2019). Breaking out to break through: Re-imagining first-year orientations. *RSR. Reference Services Review, 47*(4), 556–569. doi:10.1108/RSR-06-2019-0039

Veldkamp, A., Daemen, J., Teekens, S., Koelewijn, S., Knippels, M. C. P., & Van Joolingen, W. R. (2020). Escape boxes: Bringing escape room experience into the classroom. *British Journal of Educational Technology, 51*(4), 1220–1239. doi:10.1111/bjet.12935

Veldkamp, A., van de Grint, L., Knippels, M. C. P., & van Joolingen, W. R. (2020). Escape education: A systematic review on escape rooms in education. *Educational Research Review, 31*, 100364. doi:10.1016/j.edurev.2020.100364

Vergne, M. J., Simmons, J. D., & Bowen, R. S. (2019). Escape the Lab: An Interactive Escape-Room Game as a Laboratory Experiment. *Journal of Chemical Education, 96*(5), 985–991. doi:10.1021/acs.jchemed.8b01023

Vergne, M. J., Smith, J. D., & Bowen, R. S. (2020). Escape the (remote) classroom: An online escape room for remote learning. *Journal of Chemical Education, 97*(9), 2845–2848. doi:10.1021/acs.jchemed.0c00449

Viberg, O., & Grönlund, Å. (2013). Cross-cultural analysis of users" attitudes toward the use of mobile devices in second and foreign language learning in higher education: A case from Sweden and China. *Computers & Education, 69*, 169–180. doi:10.1016/j.compedu.2013.07.014

Vicari, C. (2020). Escape the Planet: Empowering Student Designers to Create a Science-Based Escape Room with Augmented Reality. *International Journal of Designs for Learning, 11*(2), 80–95. doi:10.14434/ijdl.v11i2.24110

Vidal-Esteve, M. I., Vega-Navarro, A., & López-Gómez, S. (2019). Uso de materiales didácticos digitales en las aulas de Primaria [Use of digital teaching materials in Primary classrooms]. *Campus Virtuales, 8*(2), 103-119. http://www.uajournals.com/campusvirtuales/journal/15/8.pdf

Villagrasa, S., & Duran, J. (2013). Gamification for learning 3D computer graphics arts. *Proceedings of the First International Conference on technological ecosystem for enhancing multiculturality*, 429-433. 10.1145/2536536.2536602

Villalustre, L., & del Moral, M. E. (2015). Gamificación: estrategia para optimizar el proceso de aprendizaje y la adquisición de competencias en contextos universitarios [Gamification: strategy to optimize the learning process and the acquisition of skills in university contexts]. *Digital Education Review, 27,* 13-31. https://revistes.ub.edu/index.php/der/article/view/11591

Vörös, A. I. V., & Sárközi, Z. (2017, December). Physics escape room as an educational tool. In AIP Conference Proceedings (Vol. 1916, No. 1, p. 050002). AIP Publishing LLC. doi:10.1063/1.5017455

Vygotsky, L. S. (1978). *Mind in society: The development of higher psychological processes.* Harvard University Press.

Walsh, B., & Spence, M. (2018). Leveraging escape room popularity to provide first-year students with an introduction to engineering information. *Proceedings of the Canadian Engineering Education Association (CEEA).* 10.24908/pceea.v0i0.13054

Wang, V., Hitch, L., & Torrisi-Steele, G. (2022). Active learning online: Necessity, faculty role, and a concept model for course design. *International Journal of Online Pedagogy and Course Design, 12*(1), 1–13. doi:10.4018/IJOPCD.2022010105

Warmelink, H., Mayer, I., Weber, J., Heijligers, B., Haggis, M., Peters, E., & Louwerse, M. (2017). AMELIO: Evaluating the Team-building Potential of a Mixed Reality Escape Room Game. *Extended Abstracts Publication of the Annual Symposium on Computer-Human Interaction in Play - CHI PLAY '17 Extended Abstracts*, 111–123. 10.1145/3130859.3131436

Watermeier, D., & Salzameda, B. (2019). Escaping boredom in first semester general chemistry. *Journal of Chemical Education, 96*(5), 961–964. doi:10.1021/acs.jchemed.8b00831

Watters, A. (2020, October 8). *Behaviorisim won.* Hack Education. http://hackeducation.com/2020/10/08/behaviorism

Wedding, D., Boyd, M. A., & Niemiec, R. M. (2014). *Movies and mental illness: Using films to understand psychopathology.* Hogrefe Publishing.

Welcome to Zooniverse. (n.d.). https://www.zooniverse.org/

Werbach, K., & Hunter, D. (2012). *For the win: How game thin-king can revolutionize your business.* Wharton Digital Press.

Werbach, K., & Hunter, D. (2020). *For the win, revised and updated edition: The power of gamification and game thinking in business, education, government, and social impact.* Wharton School Press. doi:10.2307/j.ctv2hdrfsm

WHO. (n.d.). *Global Health Observatory Data Repository.* https://apps.who.int/gho/data/node.home

Wiemker, M., Elumir, E., & Clare, A. (2015). Escape room Games. "Can you transform an unpleasant situation into a pleasant one?" *Game Based Learning, 55.*

Wiemker, M., Elumir, E., & Clare, A. (2015). Escape room games. *Game Based Learning, 55*, 55-75.

Wiemker, M., Elumir, E., & Clare, A. (2015). Escape room games, "Can you transform an unpleasant situation into a pleasant one? *Game Based Learning, 1*, 55–68.

Wiemker, M., Elumir, E., & Clare, A. (2015). Escape room games. *Game Based Learning, 55*, 55–75.

Wiemker, M., Elumir, E., & Clare, A. (2015). Escape Room Games: Can you transform an unpleasant situation into a pleasant one? *Game Based Learning, 55*, 55–68.

Wiggins, G., & McTighe, J. (2005). *Understanding by design* (2nd ed.). Prentice Hall.

Wilkinson, C., & Little, H. (2021). "We had to be very clear that they weren't going to try to break into any of the cases": What potential do 'escape rooms' offer as a science communication technique? *Journal of Science Communication, 20*(1), C07. doi:10.22323/2.20010307

Willegems, V., Consuegra, E., Struyven, K., & Engels, N. (2017). Teachers and preservice teachers as partners in collaborative teacher research: A systematic literature review. *Teaching and Teacher Education, 64*, 230-245. doi:10.1016/j.tate.2017.02.014

Wimpfheimer, T. (2020). A physical chemistry escape room laboratory: Is Schrödinger's Cat dead and/or alive? *Journal of Laboratory Chemical Education, 8*(1), 1–5. doi:10.5923/j.jlce.20200801.01

Wise, H., Lowe, J., Hill, A., Barnett, L., & Barton, C. (2018). Escape the welcome cliché: Designing educational escape rooms to enhance students' learning experience. *Journal of Information Literacy, 12*(1), 86–96. doi:10.11645/12.1.2394

Wiswall, M., Stiefel, L., Schwartz, A. E., & Boccardo, J. (2014). Does attending a STEM high school improve student performance? Evidence from New York City. *Economics of Education Review, 40*, 93–105. doi:10.1016/j.econedurev.2014.01.005

World Health Organization. (2020). *Physical activity. Key facts.* Retrieved April 16, 2022, from https://www.who.int/en/news-room/fact-sheets/detail/physical-activity

World of Escapes. (2022). *All escape rooms in the world on the map.* https://worldofescapes.com/countries

Xiao, J. (2014). Learner Agency in Language Learning: A Story of a Distance Learner in China. *Distance Education, 35*(1), 4–17. doi:10.1080/01587919.2014.891429

Yakavenka, H. (2012) Developing professional competencies through international peer learning communities. In Virtual Professional Development and Informal Learning via Social Networks. Premier Reference Source. IGI Global. doi:10.4018/978-1-4666-1815-2.ch008

Yañez-Florez, S. M., Hernández-Cueto, J. L., Salinas-Aguirre, M., & Moncada-Rodriguez, G. R. (2022). The university perception of the teaching learning process: Online education vs fase-to-face education. *Journal of Teaching and Educational Research, 8*(21), 12–19. doi:10.35429/JTER.2022.21.8.12.19

Yang, Y., Hsieh, W., Wong, W., Hong, Y., & Lai, S. (2022). Reducing Students' Foreign Language Anxiety to Improve English Vocabulary Learning in an Online Simulation Game. *Computer Assisted Language Learning*, 1–23. Advance online publication. doi:10.1080/09588221.2022.2039203

Yayon, M., Rap, S., Adler, V., Haimovich, I., Levy, H., & Blonder, R. (2019). Do-it-yourself: Creating and implementing a periodic table of the elements chemical escape room. *Journal of Chemical Education, 97*(1), 132–136. doi:10.1021/acs.jchemed.9b00660

Ybarra, R. & Green, T. (2003). Using Technology to Help ESL/EFL Students Develop Language Skills. *The Internet TESL Journal, 9*(3).

Yllana-Prieto, F., Jeong, J., & González-Gómez, D. (2021). Analysis of Pre-Service Teachers' emotions during a STEM online Escape Room. *Proceedings of SOCIOINT 2021 8th International Conference on Education and Education of Social Sciences.* 10.46529ocioint.202155

York, J., Poole, F. J., & DeHaan, J. W. (2021). Playing a new game—An argument for a teacher-focused field around games and play in language education. *Foreign Language Annals*, *54*(4), 1164–1188. doi:10.1111/flan.12585

Young, D. J. (1992). Language Anxiety from the Foreign Language Specialist's Perspective: Interviews with Krashen, Omaggio Hadley, Terrell and Rardin. *Foreign Language Annals*, *25*(2), 157–172. doi:10.1111/j.1944-9720.1992.tb00524.x

Youngerman, E., & Culver, K. C. (2019). Problem-based learning (pbl): Real-world applications to foster (inter)disciplinary learning and integration. In T. Trolian & E. Jach (Eds.), *New Directions for Higher Education* (pp. 23–32). Wiley. doi:10.1002/he.20342

Yu, J., Denham, A. R., & Searight, E. (2022). A systematic review of augmented reality game-based learning in STEM education. *Educational Technology Research and Development*, *70*(4), 1169–1194. doi:10.100711423-022-10122-y

Yürük, N. (2019). Edutainment. *Journal of Educational Technology & Online Learning*, *2*(2), 89–101. doi:10.31681/jetol.557518

Zabalza, M. Á. (2012). Las competencias en la formación del profesorado: De la teoría a las propuestas prácticas [Competences in teacher training: From theory to practical proposals]. *Tendencias Pedagógicas*, (20), 5-32. https://dialnet.unirioja.es/servlet/articulo?codigo=4105027

Zabalza, M. Á. (2016). Ser profesor universitario hoy [Being a university professor today]. *La Cuestión Universitaria*, (5), 68-80. http://polired.upm.es/index.php/lacuestionuniversitaria/article/view/3338/3403

Zafar, S., & Meenakshi, K. (2012). Individual Learner Differences and Second Language Acquisition: A Review. *Journal of Language Teaching and Research*, *3*(4), 639–646. doi:10.4304/jltr.3.4.639-646

Zamora, F., Luque, A., Sánchez, J., & Aguayo, F. (2019). Conceptual frameworkfor the use of building information modeling in engineering education. *International Journal of Engineering Education*, *35*(3), 744–755.

Zarzycka-Piskorz, E. (2016). Can games be motivating in learning grammar? *Teaching English with Technology*, *16*(3), 17–36.

Zarzycka-Piskorz, E. (2016). Kahoot It or Not? Can Games Be Motivating in Learning Grammar? *Teaching English with Technology*, *16*(3), 17–36.

Zhang, F., Doroudian, A., Kaufman, D., Hausknecht, S., Jeremic, J., & Owens, H. (2017). Employing a user-centered design process to create a multiplayer online escape game for older adults. *Proceedings of the Annual Symposium on Computer-Human Interaction in Play*, 296–307. 10.1007/978-3-319-58536-9_24

Zhang, X. C., Diemer, G., Lee, H., Jaffe, R., & Papanagnou, D. (2019). Finding the 'QR' to patient safety: Applying gamification to incorporate patient safety priorities through a simulated 'escape room' experience. *Cureus*, *11*(2), e4014. doi:10.7759/cureus.4014 PMID:31007972

Zhang, X. C., Hyunjoo, L., Rodriguez, C., Rudner, J., Chan, T., & Papagnou, D. (2018). Trapped as a group, escape as a team: Applying Gamification to incorporate team-building skills through an "Escape Room" experience. *Cureus Journal of Medical Science*, *10*(3), 50–62. doi:10.7759/cureus.2256 PMID:29725559

Zhou, L., Rudhumbu, N., Shumba, J., & Olumide, A. (2020). Role of higher education institutions in the implementation of sustainable development goals. In *Sustainable Development Goals and institutions of higher education* (pp. 87–96). Springer. doi:10.1007/978-3-030-26157-3_7

Zichermann, G., & Cunningham, C. (2011). *Gamification by design: Implementing game mechanics in web and mobile apps*. O'Reilly Media, Inc.

Zotti, G., Hoffmann, S. M., Wolf, A., Chéreau, F., & Chéreau, G. (2021). The simulated sky: Stellarium for cultural astronomy research. *Journal of Skyscape Archaeology*, *6*(2), 221–258. doi:10.1558/jsa.17822

About the Contributors

Alexandra Santamaría Urbieta holds a PhD on Tourist Translation from the University of Las Palmas de Gran Canaria and currently works as a teacher and researcher at the Universidad Internacional de La Rioja (Spain). She has a degree in Translation and Interpreting by the University of the Basque Country and her facet as a translator has led her to teach specialized translations subjects in several national and international universities. Likewise, she has made public the results of the investigations carried out in the field of translation in several congresses.

Elena Alcalde Peñalver is an Assistant Professor at the Department of Modern Philology at the University of Alcalá. She has authored and co-authored several papers on different aspects of translation. She has experience teaching translation and English and Spanish as a foreign language. She also works as a professional translator and interpreter in the legal and financial field.

* * *

Irene Aliagas Ocaña holds a Ph.D. in Psychology from the Complutense University of Madrid. She is currently a professor at the International University of La Rioja (Spain). Her thesis on Consumer Psychology won the Junior Research Award 2022 of the Insights Analytics Association. Her lines of research are oriented towards psychology, consumer behavior, consumer neuroscience, neuromarketing, gaming environments and active methodologies.

Marta Arévalo holds a PhD in Education Sciences and is a lecturer and researcher at the Universidad de Alcalá. She teaches in the academic disciplines of body expression, creative dance, physical education and digital environments. Although her main work is related to the university environment, for research, training and connections she rather to discover and being related with what is going on outside the academic world than inside. Her educational innovation projects and some of her research are based on the connections between body expression, art, creativity, critical thinking, play and technology.

Peter Bannister graduated from the University of St Andrew's with a Master in Teaching English as a Second Language with a Specialism in Assessment. His master's dissertation on the assessment of L2 critical listening competency was awarded distinction and has been nominated for several awards. Prior to this, he studied Primary Education at the Universidad Internacional de La Rioja, Spain. He has worked in numerous pedagogical contexts over the last decade which include language academies, schools and national and international universities. In his current role at the University of Dundee, Scotland, as the Deputy Head of English for International Students, he has carried out a number of research projects related to English for Specific Academic Purposes and online pedagogical innovation in the English for General Academic Purposes Classroom. Furthermore, he has also worked as a Speaking Examiner and Team Leader for Cambridge English Assessment for numerous years.

Ana Calvo is Full Professor at Department Of Personality, Assesment and Clinical Psychology. School Of Psychology. Universidad Complutense de Madrid, Spain.

María Ángeles Cano-Muñoz is a PhD in Pedagogy. Accreditation of Contracted Doctor and Professor of Private University by ANECA. Her teaching work is carried out at the International University of La Rioja, focusing her research activity on education methods, TIC, innovation in university teaching and family-school relationships.

Lauren Crabb is the Director of Internationalisation, Partner Colleges and Apprenticeships in the Faculty of Health, Education, Medicine and Social Care at Anglia Ruskin University. She is experienced in developing and operationalising international academic partnerships and creating Collaborative Online International Learning Projects. Lauren's research interest in critical environmental management and mega sports-events has seen her conduct research in Brazil and the Philippines and present her findings at conferences in New York, Berlin and Cambridge. She is also a Senior Fellow of the HEA.

Patricia de Paz-Lugo is a PhD in Biological Sciences and Professor of Didactics of Mathematics and Experimental Sciences at Universidad Internacional de La Rioja (UNIR). Member of UNIR research group "Active Methodologies and Mastery Learning". Her research activity focuses on science didactics and the evaluation of active methodologies in the learning process.

Juan Antonio Gómez-Núñez is Graduate in Primary Education with a speciality of Physical Education from the University of Castilla-La Mancha. He also has a Higher Degree in Administration and Finance. His work career focuses on the stages of Early Childhood, Primary and Secondary Education, performing his teaching role in schools, specialized academies and centers with difficult performance in education of children with specific educational support needs and their families.

María Isabel Gómez-Núñez is a PhD in Educational Research. Accreditation of Contracted Doctor and Professor of Private University by ANECA. Her teaching work is carried out at the International University of La Rioja, focusing her research activity on school anxiety and school refusal, aggressive behavior, research competence, innovation in university teaching and music education.

Àngela Hidalgo is a PhD in Education from Universitat Autònoma de Barcelona (Spain). She is currently a professor in the Teaching Innovation area of the Master's Degree in Secondary Teacher Training at the Universidad Internacional de la Rioja (Spain). She is a member of the research group GAPEF-GIPE (Analysis of Educational Training Policies) at Universitat Autònoma de Barcelona and Coordinator of the JIPS (Young Researchers in Social Pedagogy) of the SIPS (Ibero-American Society of Social Pedagogy). Her lines of research are Comparative Social Pedagogy and Educational Innovation.

Beatriz Lopez-Bermudez is a Ph.D. in Economic Analysis and Business Strategy from the University of A Coruña (UDC) with publications in the economy of education and competencies learning.

Lara Mata, Ph.D. in Chemistry, is currently a professor at the Faculty of Business and Communication Sciences of Universidad Internacional de La Rioja (Spain). She is interested in online teaching and learning.

Jessica Ortega Barón, PhD, is an assistant professor of the Faculty of Education and researcher in the Cyberpsychology group at Universidad Internacional de la Rioja (UNIR), Spain. Her research interest is mainly focused on the teaching innovation in higher education and the analysis and prevention of Internet risks among adolescents.

Eleni Petkari is an Associate Professor, specialized in mental health and illness. Has worked in several universities across the globe (Spain, UAE, Cyprus, the UK) and has plenty of experience with undergraduate and postgraduate students of Psychology.

Annie Prud'homme-Généreux has been designing curriculum and teaching science at the university level for over twenty-five years. She is recognized with numerous awards, notably the National Association of Biology Teachers' University Teaching Innovation Award, which highlighted her achievements among 5,000 of her peers. She has also worked outside of academia, leading one of Canada's largest science museums, where she led the development of multi-million-dollar galleries and escape rooms. Now back in academia, she combines her love of play and learning in science education. She has a PhD in Biochemistry, a Master of Science Journalism, and she is currently completing a Master of Open, Digital, and Distance Education.

Marta Retamosa Ferreiro () is lecturer in Marketing Department at Castilla La Mancha University. Marta has gained PhD with thesis about University Branding. Her fields of investigation are brand management, consumer behavior and neuromarketing.

Jesús I. Rivas-García is a Senior Lecturer in Applied Economics at the International University of La Rioja (UNIR).

Elisa Rojas received her PhD in Information and Communication Technologies engineering from Universidad de Alcalá, Spain, in 2013. As a postdoc, she worked in IMDEA Networks and, later on, as CTO of Telcaria Ideas S.L., an SME dedicated to both research and development of virtualized network services. She currently works as an Assistant Professor in the University of Alcala where her current research interests encompass SDN, NFV, high performance and scalable Ethernet, IoT and data center networks. She is also involved in diverse groups for innovation in teaching, as well as in Erasmus+ projects, such as e-CLOSE for enhancing online teaching environments.

Carmen Romero-García is a PhD in Biological Sciences and Coordinator of the Didactics of Mathematics and Experimental Sciences Department at the International University of La Rioja (UNIR). Her main lines of work focus on E-Learning, active methodologies and evaluation of educational processes in virtual environments and emerging technologies. Principal investigator of the research group "Development and Innovation of Educational Models" of the University of Seville and the group "Active Methodologies and Mastery Learning" of UNIR. Editor of the Journal of Technology and Education Sciences (JOTSE).

Natalia Serrano My original academic background is PhD in Biological Sciences, by the Universidad Autónoma de Madrid, in 2010, researching the development of the hematopoietic system in the fetal liver. In 2012 I started my teaching career, specializing in the didactics of natural sciences and specifically, in the promotion of creativity in this area. I currently teach at the International University of La Rioja (UNIR).

Pablo Sotoca Orgaz has a degree in Physical Activity and Sports Sciences and a degree in Teaching Primary Education. Since 2013 he works as a Physical Education teacher in a High School. Currently, he also works in the Department of Educational Sciences at the University of Alcalá as an Associate Professor. He investigates the use of active methodologies in the classroom through board games, serious games or gamification in initial university education. Ph.D. candidate.

Hanna Yakavenka is the Associate Dean of Internationalisation and Business Development at Coventry University London, UK. She has extensive experience in setting up and growing Higher Education partnerships internationally. Hanna's previous role as a Principal Lecturer and Senior Link Tutor at the University of Greenwich in 2006 - 2017 followed the completion of her PhD in International Knowledge Transfer at the Manchester Metropolitan University. Her research interests lie in the field of knowledge management and cross-cultural communications, where she particularly has been focusing on peer learning and professional capacity building, internationalisation of the university curricula, and programme design. She holds CMI Coaching Qualification and is a Senior Fellow of the HEA.

Index

F

G

H

I

K

L

M

T

U

V

CPSIA information can be obtained
at www.ICGtesting.com
Printed in the USA
LVHW051459260123
737979LV00006B/239

9 781668 460818